Maurice Blanchot

Maurice Blanchot

A Critical Biography

Christophe Bident

Translated by John McKeane

FORDHAM UNIVERSITY PRESS
New York 2019

Copyright © 2019 Fordham University Press

All rights reserved. No part of this publication may be reproduced, stored in a retrieval system, or transmitted in any form or by any means—electronic, mechanical, photocopy, recording, or any other—except for brief quotations in printed reviews, without the prior permission of the publisher.

This book was originally published in French as Christophe Bident, *Maurice Blanchot: Partenaire invisible; Essai biographique,* Copyright © 1998, Éditions Champ Vallon.

Cet ouvrage, publié dans le cadre du programme d'aide à la publication, bénéficie du soutien du Ministère des Affaires Etrangères et du Service Culturel de l'Ambassade de France représenté aux États-Unis.

This work received support from the French Ministry of Foreign Affairs and the Cultural Services of the French Embassy in the United States through their publishing assistance program.

Fordham University Press gratefully acknowledges financial assistance and support provided for the publication of this book by the University of Reading and by the Centre de recherches en Arts et Esthétique, Université de Picardie Jules Verne.

Fordham University Press has no responsibility for the persistence or accuracy of URLs for external or third-party Internet websites referred to in this publication and does not guarantee that any content on such websites is, or will remain, accurate or appropriate.

Fordham University Press also publishes its books in a variety of electronic formats. Some content that appears in print may not be available in electronic books.

Visit us online at www.fordhampress.com.

Library of Congress Cataloging-in-Publication Data

Names: Bident, Christophe, 1962– author.
Title: Maurice Blanchot : a critical biography / Christophe Bident ; translated by John McKeane.
Other titles: Maurice Blanchot. English
Description: New York, NY : Fordham University Press, 2019. | Includes bibliographical references and index.
Identifiers: LCCN 2018011232 | ISBN 9780823281763 (cloth : alk. paper) | ISBN 9780823281756 (pbk. : alk. paper)
Subjects: LCSH: Blanchot, Maurice. | Authors, French—20th century—Biography.
Classification: LCC PQ2603.L3343 Z55 2019 | DDC 843/.912 [B] —dc23
LC record available at https://lccn.loc.gov/2018011232

Printed in the United States of America

21 20 19   5 4 3 2 1

First edition

CONTENTS

Translator's Note ix
Preface xi

Part I 1907–1923

1. Blanchot of Quain: Genealogy, Birth, Childhood (1907–1918) 3
2. Music and Family Memory: Marguerite Blanchot in Chalon (1920s) 10
3. The Fedora of Death: Illness (1922–1923) 13

Part II 1920s–1940

4. The Walking Stick with the Silver Pommel: The University of Strasbourg (1920s) 21
5. A Flash in the Darkness: Meeting Emmanuel Levinas (1925–1930) 24
6. There Is: Philosophical Apprenticeship (1927–1930) 29
7. Aligning One's Convictions: Paris and Far-Right Circles (1930s) 34
8. "Mahatma Gandhi": A First Text by Blanchot (1931) 41
9. Refusal, I. The Revolution of Spirit: *La Revue Française*, *Réaction*, and *La Revue du Siècle* (1931–1934) 44
10. Journalist, Opponent of Hitler, National-Revolutionary: *Le Journal des Débats*, *Le Rempart*, *Aux Écoutes*, and *La Revue du Vingtième Siècle* (1931–1935) 51
11. The Escalation of Rhetoric: The Launch of *Combat* (1936) 62
12. Terrorism as a Method of Public Safety: *Combat* (July–December 1936) 67
13. Patriotism's Breaking Point: *L'Insurgé* (1937) 71

14. These Events Happened to Me in 1937:
    Death Sentences (1937–1938) — 82
15. On the Transformation of Convictions:
    A Journalist of the Far Right (1930s) — 88
16. From Revolution to Literature:
    Literary Criticism (1930s) — 91
17. Murderous Omens of Times to Come—Writing the
    Récits: "The Last Word" and "The Idyll" (1935–1936) — 101
18. Night Freely Recircled, Which Plays Us:
    Thomas the Obscure (1932–1940) — 111

Part III 1940–1949

19. The Universe Is to Be Found in Night:
    Resistance (1940–1944) — 121
20. Using Vichy against Vichy: Jeune France (1941–1942) — 127
21. Admiration and Agreement: Meeting Georges
    Bataille (1940–1943) — 135
22. In the Name of the Other: Literary Chronicles
    at the *Journal des Débats* (1941–1944) — 145
23. A True Writer Has Appeared: The Publication
    and Reception of *Thomas the Obscure* (1941–1942) — 160
24. Lift This Fog Which Is Already of the Dawn:
    The Publication of *Aminadab* (1942) — 163
25. Writers Who Have Given Too Much to the Present:
    NRF Circles (1941–1942) — 170
26. From Anguish to Language: The Publication
    of *Faux pas* (1943) — 178
27. The Prisoner of the Eyes That Capture Him:
    Quain (Summer 1944) — 182
28. The Disenchantment of the Community:
    Editorial Activity after Liberation (1944–1946) — 187
29. The Year of Criticism: *L'Arche*, *Les Temps Modernes*,
    and *Critique* (1946) — 192
30. Respecting Scandal: Literary Criticism (1945–1948) — 195
31. The Black Stain: Writing *The Most High* (1946–1947) — 208
32. The Passion of Silence: Denise Rollin (1940s) — 219
33. The Mediterranean Sojourn: The Writing
    of the Night (1947) — 225

34.	Something Inflexible: *The Madness of the Day*, a New Status for Speech (1947–1949)	229
35.	The Turn of the Screw: The Second Version of *Thomas the Obscure* (1947–1948)	232
36.	The Authority of Friendship: The Completion of *Death Sentence* (1947–1948)	235
37.	Quarrels in the Literary World: Publication and Reception (1948–1949)	239

Part IV   1949–1959

38.	Invisible Partner: Èze, Withdrawal (1949–1957)	245
39.	The Essential Solitude: Writing the *Récits* (1949–1953)	248
40.	The Radiance of a Blind Power: *When the Time Comes* (1949–1951)	254
41.	Are You Writing, Are You Writing Even Now? *The One Who Was Standing Apart from Me* (1951–1953)	261
42.	The Critical Detour: A Few Articles of Literary Criticism (1950–1951)	266
43.	The Author in Reverse: The Birth of *The Space of Literature* (1951–1953)	271
44.	Always Already (The Poetic and Political Interruption of Thought): Toward *The Book to Come* (1953–1958)	280
45.	Of an Amazing Lightness: *The Last Man* (1953–1957)	290
46.	Grace, Strength, Gentleness: Meeting Robert Antelme (1958)	297
47.	In the Gaze of Fascination: The Return to Paris (1957–1958)	301
48.	Refusal, II. In the Name of the Anonymous: The *14 Juillet* Project (1958–1959)	303

Part V   1960–1968

49.	Note That I Say "Right" and Not "Duty": The Declaration on the Right to Insubordination in the Algerian War (1960)	315
50.	Invisible Partners: The Project for the *International Review* (1960–1965)	324
51.	Characters in Thought: How Is Friendship Possible? (1958–1971)	336
52.	Act in Such a Way That I Can Speak to You: *Awaiting Oblivion* (1957–1962)	342

53. The Thought of the Neuter: Literary and Philosophical
Criticism—the *Entretien* and the Fragment (1959–1969)   349
54. A First Homage: The Special Issue of *Critique* (1966)   362
55. Between Two Forms of the Unavowable:
The Beaufret Affair (1967–1968)   370
56. The Far Side of Fear: Political Disillusionment
(May 1968)   375

Part VI   1969–1997

57. Life Outside: *The Step Not Beyond*, a Journal Written
in the Neuter (1969–1973)   389
58. Friendship in Disaster: Distance, Disappearance
(1974–1978)   403
59. The Last Book: *The Writing of the Disaster* (1974–1980)   406
60. Forming the Myth: Readings and Nonreadings
(1969–1979)   416
61. Making the Secret Uncomfortable: Blanchot's
Readability and Visibility (1979–1997)   424
62. With This Break in History Stuck in One's Throat:
The Unavowable Community (1982–1983)   435
63. Even a Few Steps Take Time: Literature
and Witnessing (1983–1997)   445

Amor: Blanchot since 2003   465
John McKeane

Acknowledgments   479
Notes   481
Bibliography   599
Index   605

TRANSLATOR'S NOTE

Christophe Bident's book, published in French as *Maurice Blanchot, partenaire invisible: Essai biographique* (Seyssel: Champ Vallon, 1998), has been translated but not substantially updated. References have been modified to reflect the volumes of Blanchot's work published since then in French (now listed in the bibliography) and translations of them into English. In general, quotations given by Bident have been taken from Blanchot's translated works, although they have often been modified. My afterword relates some of the major developments since 1998 concerning Blanchot's work and life.

My very warmest thanks are due, for their expert help with the typescript in various ways, to Christophe Bident, Holly Langstaff, Pierre de Boissieu, Philip Armstrong, Mike Holland, Leslie Hill, and Lucy Burns. I am also grateful for the support provided by the University of Warwick and the University of Reading, and to Tom Lay, the anonymous readers, and the late Helen Tartar at Fordham.

PREFACE

Ignorance, whether of his life or of his work, was the twentieth century's favored response to Maurice Blanchot, born in 1907. Yet he incessantly recounted his life to that century, just as he incessantly made his work accessible to it. Baseless and persistent mythologies paint Blanchot as the conspicuous absentee, the invisible ghost, the unreadable author of utterly abstract work, a man literarily terrifying and politically impure. None more than he, however, interrogated the presence, visibility, readability, vitality, culpability, and *possibility* of the writer. He worked incessantly on these notions, contesting them, placing them in a dialectic, pushing them to their limits, where paradox carries them far from the false simplicity of the political language that masquerades as our common language. This permanent struggle—the struggle of the body, of writing, of thought— fascinated and inspired, in an often reciprocated exchange, the greatest contemporary creators of forms and thoughts (and forms of thought), starting with Blanchot's two most intimate friends, Emmanuel Levinas and Georges Bataille.

This book in turn will interrogate the presence, visibility, readability, vitality, culpability, and possibility of *the biographical*, in a life and a work, in a life-made-work, a life sustained through the most extreme confrontations with death. For this life-become-work addresses being, as Bataille wrote, "in an unbearable surpassing of being," in an unbearable surpassing of the work. This life is bequeathed infinitely through *narrative writing*, which bears witness with untiring patience, inflexible courage, and excessive pain to the worst visions of death, to the worst wounds caused by it. This life is infinitely conducted via a prose whose sustained intensity and almost drunken attentiveness tears through novels and *récits*, essays and fragments.[1] It addresses our modes of knowledge: What can we make of it *together*—and where can we take this? In what friendship, in what community of real thought can we discover its obverse and reverse sides, its errors, its lapses and its insights? This life also asks questions of our responsibility: What form of attentiveness and judgment does it demand, what infinite sensitivity, bordering on almost impossible witnessing, does it impose? Within it a political element and a flesh-and-blood existence jostle in uncertain and shifting ways, coming together and moving apart. With respect and care for this man who is still alive, we shall only include in this work knowledge about Blanchot's life that helps the understanding of its public element, its share of community (of being-together).[2] But given the need to bring matters out of the shadows, we shall also include everything that allows this element to be understood.

Beyond Blanchot, what is at issue is the capacity to uphold and maintain a thinking of the most inexplicable reversals in history's most terrifying century. Here, "beyond" means that whether thought or unthought, but always *given to thought* on our part, this life puts at our disposition (or indisposition) the elements that allow us to understand what Shestov called "the transformation of one's convictions." And it is precisely because such elements are present in this life that attempts have been made to silence them, to cast suspicion on them, to protect, idolize, degrade, ridicule, deform, dramatize, refuse them. Absolute denials and partial cover-ups all stem from the same weakness or negligence (simply justified in different ways): the refusal to see death at work, in the end, facing us. Strategies of literary revisionism, avant-gardist reversals, defensive forms of divisiveness, the will to dominate the intellectual horizon, aesthetic moralism—all of these proceed from the same refusal to read what is at stake here. To read? Reading here means acknowledging what has been said about the inscription of bodies (opened, unlimited, sovereign) in the spaces of memory, what has been said about the shared legibility of these spaces, about the community's production of this memory; such a reading is the critical goal of the only real capital we hold.

Blanchot's constant task will have been to write his life as the "last man," that of a "man like any other existing in a century of unparalleled conflagrations"—whether they were ethical, ideological, or esthetic, he knew them all intimately. He wrote his life in line with the most stubborn demand (that of friendship), the maddest responsibility (that of memory), the most intense promise (that of childhood, as Nietzsche would have said). Writing this incessant back-and-forth between writing and life, between life and writing, is the task of every biography, and is the task that none can fulfill. To write it without recourse to the imaginary, from the position of a third party, with attention focused constantly on the name of the other—and adhering to the movement that, by way of literature and inspired by the friendship of Robert Antelme, allows responsibility to become aware of itself and requires that it be endlessly acknowledged—that is what this biography will at least essay.

The pensive smile of an unenvisageable visage; this much—
sky and earth having disappeared, night and day having
become one another—is left to he who looks on no longer,
and who, destined to return, shall never depart.

—Maurice Blanchot, *The Writing of the Disaster*

PART I

1907–1923

Neither synchrony nor diachrony, an anachrony of every instant. *Demourance* (old French had such a word) as anachrony. There is no single time, and since there is no single time, since no instant shares a measure with any other—thanks to death, thanks to death coming between, thanks to interruption by cause of death intervening, if you will, by cause of passing-away—well, there is no chronology or chronometry. Even when the sense of the real has been regained, time cannot be measured. And thus the question returns, how many times: how much time? How much time? How much time?

JACQUES DERRIDA, *Demeure: Fiction and Testimony*

CHAPTER I

Blanchot of Quain
Genealogy, Birth, Childhood (1907–1918)

On Sunday, September 22, 1907, at 2:00 a.m., in the depths of the night that would become for him the time of exile and of writing, Maurice Blanchot was born in Quain, a hamlet of Devrouze, near Saint-Germain-du-Bois in the Saône-et-Loire. It was the feast day assigned to Saint Maurice. The family was Catholic and baptized its last child in accordance with the calendar of saints' days. A day or two on either side, and the newborn might have been known as Janvier, Eustache, Mathieu, Andoche, or Lin.

This place mattered to this well-off and distinguished family, which, through the maternal line, owned farmland and also, for over a century, had owned a fine large dwelling that in *The Instant of My Death* the writer would later name, exaggerating somewhat, the "Château."[1] Maurice Blanchot's mother, Marie Eugénie Alexandrine Mercey, had been born there on December 9, 1874, at 9:00 a.m. A legitimate child and the family's youngest daughter, the future inheritor of the property, she had been given as her first Christian name that of her mother, Marie Moreau (thirty-eight years old), as her third a feminized version of her father's, Alexandre Mercey (thirty-nine years old), and as her second that of the Empress, the wife of Napoleon III who had surrendered to Prussia four years earlier. Eugénie's

3

rigid Catholicism and political machinations must have had some influence over the choice made by the Mercey family, which was the dominant lineage in the hamlet of Quain, a family that even if not gentry still kept up relations with the only aristocratic family in the *commune*, that of the Baron du Marais, which owned a real *château* known as Ronfand. The Mercey family took pride in its roots in Quain. Still today in the church cemetery, a tomb is adorned with the words "BLANCHOT-MERCEY FAMILY OF QUAIN," creating a noble and sober effect. Inside the nave, a commemorative plaque hails Élise Mercey, Marie Eugénie Alexandrine's elder sister, "FOR 57 YEARS OF UNTIRING COMMITMENT TO THIS PARISH."

At the time of Maurice Blanchot's birth, Devrouze (a name from the Gaulish *dubron*, meaning a stretch of water or small river) had 796 inhabitants, which has declined to around 300 today. It is a small village in the Bresse region of Burgundy, less than nineteen miles (30 km) east of Chalon. It is farming country, with forests here and there, slightly rolling but for the most part desperately flat, quite capable of evoking the distress caused by the numerous wars that have been fought across it. Blanchot himself would speak of the "climate of despair" in this countryside. In addition to four large ponds, including one at Quain, one finds the marshy environs of the cemetery where, according to early twentieth-century tales, wills-o'-the-wisp can be seen. Round about, most dwellings are grouped together, but Devrouze is spread out, with the hamlet of Quain being about 1.2 miles (2 km) from the center, at a crossroads. One of the roads leads east, toward Saint-Germain-du-Bois, a market town known for fairs; the other comes from the north, from Navilly on the River Doubs, the hometown of Blanchot's father.

Joseph Isidore Léon Blanchot was born there at midnight on April 30, 1859.[2] He was the oldest son of Léon Blanchot, a landowner and farmer (twenty-three years old) and Marie Jacquin (twenty-two years old). He was baptized a few days later, on May 5: his godmother was Louise Jacquin, his aunt; the godfather was Joseph Blanchot, his grandfather, whose name he used only for official purposes. He would instead go by another of his first names, Isidore, in social and family circles, a practice that was common at the time. Born on July 24, 1861, his younger brother François Joseph Léon, more commonly known as Edmond (a name that eventually replaced Léon on the birth certificate), would take the cloth. He worked as the parish priest in the church at Devrouze for several decades, baptizing all Joseph-Isidore's children. Born into an agricultural (*paysanne*) family that does not seem to have been without financial means, the two brothers would gain other forms of social recognition, a clericalism that was literal for one and symbolic for the other. Joseph Isidore Blanchot became a teacher of literature, a tutor for children of well-off families.

On Wednesday, September 5, 1894, at 11:00 a.m., Edmond married Joseph and Marie in the church at Devrouze. Joseph was thirty-five, Marie nineteen. It was no longer necessary to follow the model of a year's difference in age, as between the parents on each side. The biblical analogy of a meeting between Joseph and Mary was not evident in everyday practice: Joseph was known as Isidore and Marie as Alexandrine, and these were the names they used to sign the parish register. Isidore's mother had died in 1879, at only forty-two years old, and Alexandrine's mother two years earlier. Isidore's father became an accountant and lived in Chalon. Alexandrine's mother single-handedly managed a property that henceforth would be run by women alone: by her daughters and then her granddaughter. The Merceys' sedentary lifestyle contrasted with the Blanchots' nomadic existence. At the time they were married, Isidore Blanchot was pursuing his role as a tutor at Aillières, in the distant *département* of Sarthe, where the young married couple would first live together. Henceforth, until the war, the couple would live independently and move house often, living far from their region, from Normandy to Paris, as dictated by Isidore's tutoring work (Marie-Alexandrine never took on a profession). However, in a concession to tradition, all four of their children were born at the house of their maternal grandmother, their births recorded at Devrouze, and their baptisms performed a few days later by their uncle Edmond.

A year after the wedding, on October 2, 1895, the first child was born: George [*sic*] Antoine Marie Joseph. Naturally, the two surviving grandparents were chosen as godmother and godfather. Less than two years later, on May 15, 1897, a daughter appeared: Marguerite Élise Marie Geneviève. This time, in accordance with a rigorous logic but inverting it, the baptism would be witnessed by the paternal uncle and the maternal aunt (who were thereby thanked for their charitable work). Edmond, who baptized Marguerite, would also be her godfather, and the child took her second Christian name from Élise, the pious and charitable godmother.[3] At the turn of the century, the parents and children left Sarthe for Paris. They would dwell for nearly seven years in the Rue de Montessuy, in the shadow of the Eiffel Tower, not far from the Trocadéro. Their arrival in the capital was marked by that of another child: 1901 was the year René Ferdinand Marie Antoine was born.

Two years separated George and Marguerite, four Marguerite and René, six René and Maurice. When on September 22, 1907, Maurice Léon Alexandre was born and was given the names of a saint and his two grandfathers, he had a forty-eight-year-old father, a thirty-two-year-old mother, two brothers of twelve and six, and a sister of ten. He was the family's last child. Eight days later, George would be named as his godfather, and Anne-Marie Thevenot, a cousin from Chalon, as his godmother.[4] Born and baptized in Quain, Maurice was brought back to the family house at 10 Rue des Hayes, Elbeuf. A precocious talent on the piano, Marguerite recounted: "At 11 years old [it was therefore 1908], I sometimes played the great organ in the church at Elbeuf when the usual player, who was blind, was not available."[5] This was how, still a young child, she was recognized by Marcel Dupré, who was born in Rouen and was then only twenty-two years old.[6] She would later be a brilliant student at the Conservatoire in Paris. According to their father's demands, the four children received a solid classical education. He is said to have been very erudite, speaking Latin and forcing his children to speak it at table. Marguerite would become an organist, George a well-qualified (*agrégé*) teacher of German, and René an architect.[7] Maurice Blanchot passed his baccalaureate at the age of fifteen.

Around the beginning of the war, the family returned to Burgundy and set themselves up in Chalon. Isidore Blanchot gave many private lessons. At 1916, at the age of nineteen, Marguerite was asked to begin playing the great organ at Saint-Vincent cathedral; the incumbent organist, Mr. Moine, had been called to the trenches. Quain was not far away. We can imagine that the family regularly spent a few days or weeks there. As an adult, Maurice Blanchot would return there often, usually in summer. The "upper room" would be kept for him, and he must have written there. He would always remain attached to the house where he was born and, at the end of the Second World War, nearly died. The house and the grounds, which today can be seen from the road, cannot have changed much. They are not without charm or tranquility. On the facade of this large dwelling (*demeure*) a date is written in iron numbers: 1809. Set slightly back from the road, the building is surrounded by trees, outbuildings, a well, and two discreet tombstones lying flat, known as cenotaphs. The grounds are planted with oaks, lime trees, hazels, chestnuts, and other fruit trees. The trees form a small copse in the part of the grounds bordering the road to Saint-Germain.

In *The Instant of My Death*, Blanchot speaks of a young man who goes away from the "dwelling" "until he found himself in a distant forest, named 'the heathland,' where he remained sheltered by trees he knew well."[8] It is only the trees of one's childhood that one knows well. They are as if always-already inscribed in the time-without-time of writing. Blanchot would evoke them much later, in what could be the "primal scene," presented as autobiographical, of the child-writer. We can imagine him in Quain, at the beginning of the war, in 1914 or 1915:

> (A Primal Scene?) You who live later, close to a heart that beats no more, suppose, suppose this: the child—is he seven years old, or eight perhaps?—standing by the window, drawing the curtain and, through the pane, looking. What he sees: the garden, the wintry trees, the wall of a house. Though he sees, no doubt in a child's way, his play space, he grows weary and slowly looks up toward the ordinary sky, with clouds, grey light—pallid daylight without depth.
>
> What happens then: the sky, the same sky, suddenly open, absolutely black and absolutely empty, revealing (as though the pane had been broken) such an absence that all has since always and forevermore been lost therein—so lost that therein is affirmed and dissolved the vertiginous knowledge that nothing is what there is, and first of all nothing beyond. The unexpected aspect of this primal scene (its interminable feature) is the feeling of happiness that straightaway submerges the child, the ravaging joy to which he can bear witness only by tears, an endless flood of tears. He is thought to be suffering from a childish sorrow; attempts are made to console him. He says nothing. He will live henceforth in the secret. He will weep no more.[9]

Despite the discretion of the parentheses, despite the precaution of the question mark and the indefinite article, the event (at once psychological, metaphysical, and mystic) still presents an *irremediable* character, opening onto the entire atheological reach of Blanchot's work. This event is a promise of solitude, solitude as children experience it, which Rilke uses as the model of the only "great inner solitude," "with the grown-ups going to and fro around us," indifferent to the profundities of childhood, separated from any link to life's density.[10] It is an event that "[carves] out in the darkened body of memory," puts to the test, via a "figure of chance," a child who would continue to confide his entire inner experience, his entire abyssal feeling of being shaken (*émoi*), to the profundity and the fragmentation of the outside. It would do so "at the greatest distance from mere questions," with the creative authority of childhood, a childhood outside mere representation or discussion precisely because it would remain (*demeurera*) as the impersonal subject of vision and fascination.[11] And this event opens onto the time of the absence of the heavens, the absence of the gods who have "already disappeared and not yet appeared," the Hölderlinian time of distress.¹² It eclipses the daylight and condemns one, in a Pascalian night, to the mystical joy of an experience without transcendence, which is to say without object. It tears open a distressing gulf that eludes our conceptual grasp and gaze, but nonetheless takes hold of our bodies as if from a distance, interminably giving rise to a spinning of vision. We bore down into what is no longer a discovery but a fall into an avid drunkenness "as liberating as that of the great swarms of stars," and we do so in complicity with the obscene movement of death, its unfeeling and violent presence.¹³ In undergoing this event, we are confronted with the brilliant nudity of what is *wholly other*, with the devastating emptiness of the *there is* (not: there is nothing, but: there is nothing other than this *there is*). The entire friendship of thought is already there, saturating the scene, binding it together, inflexible, with its anachronistic reference and its inevitable worklessness, with no other origin than this first experience of the *supplement*. This event without date, an irresponsible lightness, traces out the responsibility of all the *récits* to come, that of all common knowledge and all nonknowledge, beginning with the nonknowledge of death, so inevitably encountered, "as if the death outside of him could henceforth only collide with the death in him."¹⁴ An event like the silent reservoir from which proceed all these haphazard clashes (*heurts*)—whether in happiness (*l'heur*) or misfortune (*le malheur*). And in the figure of chance.

Many years later, Maurice Blanchot would happen to discover another of these unexpected scenes that the voice of authority, frustrated by an irrepressible desire, reluctantly names "primal." On September 23, 1912, in his *Diary*, Kafka described the exceptionally sleepless night he had just had. He recounts writing in one sitting, with a sensation of shame and of vertigo, the entirety of *The Judgment*; he remembers bidding farewell to real time because he looked at his watch for a final time at 2:00 a.m. (the time at which, five years and one day earlier, Blanchot had been born). The latter felt compelled to comment on his discovery of this coincidence, and his writing twice mentions this knowing wink on the part of fate, this ambiguous date of September 22.¹⁵ Is there any better sign than this near-coincidence according to which, give or take a night, Kafka discovered his vocation as a writer on Blanchot's birthday? Could he remain indifferent to this grace in the far-off encounter that chose Kafka, of all possible (and impossible) writers? Indifferent to this encounter with Kafka, in whom he would recognize the century's greatest writer, Kafka to whom he would know and declare himself to be so close, via a dizzying movement of speech, body, illness, life, love and its ruptures, friendship, writing? Last, could he set aside the family legend according to which Joseph-Isidore declared 2:00 a.m. as the time of birth when in reality it had been midnight? Here the Mallarmean hour and Kafkaean night combine their effects, inevitably becoming the sign under which Blanchot was born, a sign relating to numbers, to the zodiac and to the seasons, and that would be evoked with discreet humor at several points in his work.

CHAPTER 2

Music and Family Memory
Marguerite Blanchot in Chalon (1920s)

For the children, the period following the war was devoted to university study. Marguerite Blanchot was perfecting her musical skills at the Paris Conservatoire. And in 1922, Maurice Blanchot earned his baccalaureate before leaving for the University of Strasbourg. George married Marie Marguerite Canque in Montmerle, in the Ain *département*.[1] In 1925, Uncle Edmond died at the age of sixty-four. He was buried on August 1 in his Devrouze parish.

The same year, Marguerite returned to Chalon, and the father of the family retired, buying the house on the Avenue Boucicaut that became for a long while the urban base for the Blanchot family. The land at Quain would henceforth be managed from here. Marguerite spent almost all the rest of her life there. Little by little, she would come to represent the memory of their origins. Never having married, due to religious devotion it was sometimes said, she lived first with her parents, later with her Aunt Élise, and then finally alone, following the death of all her predecessors. Handed down by a father who died there, situated a short walk from the cemetery where he was buried, the never-changing house would outlast time, would be a new site of *demourance*, of residence. Following Alexandrine's death, Marguerite would leave one of its rooms almost intact, a room she continued to call "my mother's room." A journalist who visited her in 1979 evoked the residence with an almost Blanchotian formulation: "situated close to the center of Chalon," it was nonetheless "of another place and time." Philippe Merley recounted that "time there seems to stand still, and Marguerite Blanchot receives visitors in a sitting-room which could easily have been described by Proust." After an interview lasting two hours, "I find myself in the street... somewhat lost. I am returning from another age, from a world that no longer exists."[2]

The interviewer was no doubt interested in the fact that in the meantime Marguerite Blanchot had become a figure in public life in Chalon. Her return from Paris brought with it the airs of life in the capital. The person who came to be known in Chalon via the English expression "Miss Blanchot" took on a certain profile around town, with her unmistakable originality and the charm as well as authority of her pale and lively eyes.[3] She gave individual piano lessons at home, almost adopting her father's role, but in a musical capacity. Her lessons quickly became the most sought-after in Chalon. She gave lessons on three upright pianos, one grand piano, and an organ, and is widely remembered as having lived for her music and her pupils. On the retirement of Mr. Moine, at the end of the 1920s, she took over the cathedral's organs as a volunteer and held the post for more than fifty years. Her discreet, slightly precious authority, known across town, was bolstered by a pride that could turn to anger if silence was not respected in what she considered her domain. She had a tendency, in her tacit but never-ending conflict with the religious authorities, to see the mass as her own recital. The priest followed the organ rather than the organ following the priest. One Sunday when this conflict was more pronounced than usual, she refused to stop playing Handel, drowning out the voice of a priest who was desperately attempting to continue mass and to sing the liturgy. Perhaps this was her own form of celebration and prayer. There was certainly no doubt about her devotion. Each year she would go to the monastery at Pradines near Roanne to visit a cousin who had taken the cloth. There she would give organ lessons to the nuns. In every part of her life she seemed to bring together a concern for distinction and the duty of self-effacement.

Her erudition relied on a perfect knowledge of the history of the organ and of music in general. She received Marcel Dupré in Chalon in 1965, gave lectures, wrote articles. With this specialized knowledge, as well as her own funds, she contributed to the restoration of the organ in Saint-Vincent Cathedral, after first drawing attention to this necessity and exerting a real influence on the relevant authorities at the end of the 1960s. The unceremonious manner in which, at over eighty years of age, she was relieved of her functions at the beginning of the 1980s would leave her with a bitter taste.

If the house in Chalon remained a site of memory throughout these years, this is also due to the music with which it was filled. Like her father, Marguerite Blanchot showed little interest in contemporary music, preferring classical or romantic pieces. While more open, a lover for instance of Schoenberg and Boulez, Maurice Blanchot nonetheless preferred a composer like Schumann. Music, which he named the "art par excellence," was paramount in the family's tastes, just as it was in those of his friends Louis-René des Forêts and Roger Laporte, who would often refer to their preference for music over literature, despite being writers themselves.[4] Maurice Blanchot's extreme discretion with respect to music in his critical writing reveals, paradoxically, his admiringly silent relationship with it. For his part, he had studied music theory and was an outstanding piano player.

Marguerite Blanchot venerated her brother Maurice. She was very proud of him and complained of not seeing him often enough. She placed great store in his political ideas, despite maintaining rather conservative views herself. She read a lot, often late into the evening, in the heart of the "other night" when her brother would be writing. They would speak on the telephone and exchange letters. They shared, from a distance, the same natural authority, the same concern for discretion.

Maurice Blanchot would also remain very close to his brother René, who would often protect him, welcoming him in difficult moments, making his homes available. George seems to have led his life in a more distant way. But among the three brothers and their sister there would remain, despite the distance in their lives and their convictions, a sense of solidarity and great respect for their parental link, for the past. Not to mention for its hauteur.

CHAPTER 3

The Fedora of Death
Illness (1922–1923)

In 1922, at the time of his baccalaureate exams and just before his sixteenth birthday, Maurice Blanchot had surgery on his duodenum. A medical error affecting his blood would cause aftereffects for the rest of his life. The first of these was that he had to wait for nearly a year to recover and leave for Strasbourg, where he began university study.

This medical mishap is discreetly referred to on several occasions in his work. He would write of Henry James:

> It is tempting to think that that is his way of constantly alluding to the accident of which he was a victim when he was about ten, and about which he has spoken only rarely and obscurely: as if something had happened to him that brought him as close as possible to a mysterious and exalting impossibility.[1]

In fact, the few descriptions of this fateful mistake, for instance in *Death Sentence* or *The Madness of the Day*, count less than the proximity to death that such an inner experience causes, when one lives through such an internal and organic repetition of the "primal scene." Illness would remain for Blanchot a fact of the body, a facet of the world, and he would share its pain and its ecstasy with his friend Georges Bataille. It is not irrelevant that he should evoke this in an article on *Madame Edwarda*:

> The efforts we make to theoretically isolate the point where scandal touches us (calling, for instance, on what we know of the sacred, object of desire and horror), are like the work of blood cells to restore the wounded part. The body returns to normal, but the experience of the wound remains. The wound is healed, but the essence of the wound cannot be healed.[2]

The essence of the blood remains at work in the perception of the body and in the work of memory. The unending metamorphoses of the first version of *Thomas the Obscure* will speak to this, as will the hospital-based world of various *récits*, or at least some sections of them.

Illness would affect Maurice Blanchot for his entire life. He would rarely be spared the attentions of recurrent asthma, chronic influenza, pleurisy, tuberculosis, vertigo, constricted breathing, and nervous conditions. He generally ate very little.[3] His fatigue was extreme, his sense of exhaustion almost permanent, his insomnia—this "nocturnal wandering," this way to "make the night present"—exceedingly tenacious.[4] The death sentence was to be confronted regularly. *Demourance* places it as if outside of time. Each of Blanchot's correspondences would be undertaken in a spirit of friendship, as "a prelude to the silence from which calm issues."

It is striking, as if paradox were written into this man's very flesh and bones, and as if it condemned him to endlessly confront dying, that someone living with this permanent fragility should have lived so remarkably long. A large factor was hereditary (Maurice Blanchot's father died at seventy-six, his mother at nearly eighty-three, his aunt Élise at ninety-five, his brothers at seventy-seven and ninety-one, his sister at ninety-five).[5] Of sickly appearance despite his height, Blanchot would rarely show his suffering; although he often discussed his illnesses, it was to reflect as if in a mirror those of others, of his friends, with a disabused rather than elegiac fatalism. This real concern passed beyond mere charitable pity, moving into true attentiveness, a gentle attitude sometimes showing lightheartedness and even humor. While friendship might have suggested that he should relay news of his health, he was not able to do so for the simple reason that there was never, as it were, any *news*; illness would have condemned him to repeat the same unending avowals, to trouble his friends, to continually worry them and make them feel obligated. However, friendship was precisely the place where he was able to soften the avowals he did make, and to downplay any drama, as a way to inhabit a culpability marked by tragedy. In the moments of exhaustion when illness isolated him, as if on the far side of time, friendship made possible this particular mode of presence that is "absence etched by writing."[6]

He would often let it be known, from the 1930s or 1940s on, that he was writing the final book or the final letter of his life. "We used to wonder how, with all his pills and always in ill health, he managed to pull through and get better," declared Emmanuel Levinas.[7] Xavier de Lignac confided that "he always seemed to me to have survived something," and Michel Butor stated that he "had been surviving since his childhood, which seemed to me to retreat into a mythical period before the war, but one didn't know which war; he seemed ageless and unable to age."[8] A fighting spirit was allied with family longevity—adversity stimulated him. Suffering, out of breath, and walking with difficulty, he nonetheless took part in all the protests in 1968, including clashes with the police. At nearly ninety, almost totally isolated from the world and extremely weak, he was given a dose of vigor by the Bruno Roy affair and intervened publicly (denouncing by letter the publisher who had allowed a book by Alain de Benoist to appear); this vigor improved his health for a time. Between despondency and ardor, the man knew his limits.[9] "To ask for more would be to ask too much," he once wrote from Germany to Dionys Mascolo.[10] He would have to face long years of silence, crisscrossed with periods of intense activity. During these periods, when he was able to work at the same time for numerous newspapers or journals and to continue writing his books by night, he expended a kind of reckless energy. The rhythm of writing, of producing writing and prose, was partly reliant on the rhythms of the body. Gilles Deleuze would make this point, bringing Blanchot together in a community of thought with Samuel Beckett and Henri Michaux:

> Literature therefore appears as an enterprise of health: not that the writer would necessarily be in good health (there would be the same ambiguity here as with athleticism), but he possesses an irresistible and delicate health that stems from what he has seen and heard of things too big for him, while nonetheless giving him the becomings that a dominant and substantial health would render impossible.[11]

It is as if the ill were chosen in order to allow the limit-experience to pass, in an uncertain and risky way, into thought's dispossessed relationship with the body, or of the body's with thought. It is as if their sacred quality lent authority to a cryptic ordeal, to atheological thinking, to fragmentary writing: "illness is divine—but in these conditions divinity is not 'sufficient,' which is to say that no 'completion' is conceivable starting from the anguish to which incompletion exposes us."[12] It is as if life, illness, and the diabolical chance of writing were one and the same, Blanchot would one day say to Mascolo, remembering their conversation with Robert Antelme.[13]

All those who knew Maurice Blanchot recall this mixture of fragility and authority, of austerity and gentleness, of attentiveness and effacement. Maurice Nadeau, remembering Blanchot on the judges' panel for the Prix des Critiques, wrote, "I can still see his tall, thin silhouette, his light coloring, his pale eyes, I hear the words that come from his mouth in a slow and uneven rhythm—one feels that he is forcing himself in order to make them audible—and I hear the authority that they represented for everyone."[14]

Madeleine Chapsal, who interviewed him at the shrillest moment of the controversy around the Manifesto of the 121, recalls meeting "the gentlest of men." Louis-René des Forêts remembers their first meeting: "What struck me about him was an upright quality, the gentleness of his smile, but most of all the authority inherent in his presence, even when silent, for he spoke rarely."[15] Pierre Prévost indicates with a firm, raised set of his chin: "Blanchot was impressive." In the 1920s Emmanuel Levinas met, according to Marie-Anne Lescourret's formulation, "the precious, mysterious, aristocratic Maurice Blanchot," who was "almost twice as tall as him." Blanchot was nineteen: "Very tall, very thin, very pale, heavy-lidded and with brown-blond hair, sickly looking, he cried whenever he laughed, but was always impeccably turned out. . . . He seems to have fascinated his classmates."[16] In the 1930s, his acquaintances of the far right described him in similar terms: "translucent," according to Pierre Monnier, "he hides, in a fragile casing, a tough and polemic personality. He expresses himself in a clear voice, with a sharp intelligence and a biting wit." He intimidated everyone around him.[17] The wife of Jean-Pierre Maxence confirms this:

> Blond, pale, of already fragile health, for a long time afflicted by tuberculosis, his attitude was always somewhat stiff, but he had an extraordinary, dry sense of humor. [Jean-Pierre] much admired his intelligence. . . . He wouldn't mystify matters, and types like Maulnier and most of all Brasillach seemed somewhat ill at ease in his presence. What's more, there was something mysterious concerning his childhood, his past.[18]

Dominique Aury met him at *L'Insurgé*. She discovered "a tall thin lad, who walked slowly, and who sat in his office with a blanket over his knees."[19] Claude Roy, during the same period, saw him as "shriveled, bent, sensitive, fragile." "He was a diaphanous apparition: with light-colored hair, pale coloring, light horn-rimmed glasses, pale eyes, and a clear, blank voice, Maurice Blanchot . . . wore a tartan blanket hiding his shoulders, like Mallarmé in the old photos."[20] Xavier de Lignac, who met him three years later, when Blanchot was thirty-three, confides that "the way he held himself, the beauty of his smile, as well as his sense of irony, all made me think of a particular high-ranking priest I had known in my youth." On a poetic note, he added: "Blanchot was an Ibsen character. A pastor from the North Pole living very comfortably in the Parisian world. Everything about him was white: his face, his skin tone, and also his speech. But he was dressed in black." Blanchot would often carry an umbrella, and a hat, that Georges Bataille would describe secretly in a poem:

Blanchot,
the fedora
of death,

a stanza that became, in the published version,

Fedora
hat
of death.[21]

Sobriety of tone would become the spirit of the age. In 1968, according to Jacques Derrida, Blanchot most often wore a black roll-neck pullover. Another sign of discreet authority. His "gentle smile" opened and prolonged his "silent attentiveness." Roger Laporte, who in 1959 met a man who was already nearly entirely bald, with a little very pale blond hair, also speaks of an extremely gentle smile, "of a great attentiveness, a great kindness," which revealed "a genius of the heart at least the equal of the genius of the mind."[22] For all of them, Blanchot most often represented an astonishing mixture of mystery and simplicity, of fascination and openness, of distance and presence. "I did not find it displeasing that he remained a little mysterious. Nothing bothered me about this everyday stranger," declares Xavier de Lignac, smiling. Even-tempered, rarely melancholy and never taciturn, not lacking a sense of humor, extremely courteous, he was also able to be surprising, changing the tempo of an encounter with a dynamic, creative, insistent remark, exerting considerable pressure on others' ideas—or doing so via the impact of a look or a short remark, for instance on death or on madness. "For Blanchot, for example, that's how it is," Marguerite Duras would say. "He has a madness that tracks him. Madness is also death."[23] Respect must pass by way of this scandal. Pain must pass by way of this refusal.

These portraits, which are coherent and complementary even in their contradictions, expose again and again Maurice Blanchot's illness as one of the defining characteristics of his appearance. Bataille's stanzas express nicely how far the question at hand was that of effacing the persona even as one described it, masking the face, poetically muffling a name and a presence bearing the aura of a funereal silence.[24] In this text, Blanchot even rhymes with *sanglot*—a "sob" in English—but the full phrase is "*sanglot/gai*," or a happy sob, and the poem goes on, as if an entire *demourance* of wisdom appeared in it, as if in a tempo without regularity, resources or reference-points, to describe the following:

> the absence
> of death
> is smiling.

PART II

1920s–1940

Writing as the question of writing, a question that bears writing that bears the question, no longer allows you this relation to being—understood first as tradition, order, certainty, truth, all forms of rootedness—which one day you received from worlds past, a domain that you were called to administer the better to strengthen your "Ego" [*Moi*], even though it had as it were cracked open, the day the sky opened onto its emptiness.

MAURICE BLANCHOT, *The Step Not Beyond*

CHAPTER 4

The Walking Stick with the Silver Pommel
The University of Strasbourg (1920s)

Maurice Blanchot arrived in Strasbourg in 1923 or 1924, aged sixteen or seventeen.[1] He began university studies in German and philosophy. According to Roger Laporte, Blanchot and his family chose this town due to its Faculty of Protestant Theology, the only such public institution in France. But a simpler economic and family motivation existed: René was studying architecture in Strasbourg and could share an apartment with his brother. Two further reasons also had an influence: the proximity of Germany and the university's reputation. In 1919, Kaiser-Wilhelm University was reintegrated into French higher education, soon becoming one of its leading lights. Strategic development and political assimilation were at stake. For four decades, Strasbourg had been the figurehead of German culture; now it would play that role for French culture. The buildings themselves, in all their prestige, offered a sumptuous setting for solemn starts to the academic year, marked by political and diplomatic implications. The library was the best endowed in France after the national library. The professors held doctorates from the École Normale Supérieure, along with the national teaching qualification, the *agrégation*. Every Saturday afternoon, they would gather for a session of historical synthesis, engaging a broad spectrum of disciplines.

We must picture for ourselves the universities of the period, with their formal mode of address (*vouvoiement*) between students, their codes of honor, their rigorously controlled dress. Ties, jackets, and hats were sometimes accompanied by a walking stick, one bearing a silver pommel if one had nationalist sympathies or even belonged to Action Française. In this provincial town with its ever-present nationalism, Blanchot was one of the students who carried a walking stick with a silver pommel. In doing so, he intensified the values he already held: cultural prestige, social ambition, moral honor. Although deep down he was probably a supporter of Barrès, he nonetheless rejected being earmarked for a career in education. From the outset he preferred journalism or writing to a career as a professor, and we can wonder whether he ever even considered it. A brilliant student, both proud and solemn, he was also academically restive, and although he could inspire tears of admiration in certain professors, he abandoned his studies relatively early, before the stage of thesis writing. A music lover and a constant reader, he impressed his fellow students; one described him as a "sort of *grand Meaulnes* opening the door of Parisian life for his Strasbourg cousins."[2] In 1929, the 773 students of the Faculty of Letters elected him as a reserve member of the student association committee.

Blanchot must have had a number of well-known professors, such as—in "general philosophy"—Maurice Pradines, a critical inheritor of the Enlightenment and a philosopher who worked on sensation; Henri Carteron, a specialist on Aristotle and Thomas Aquinas, a Catholic, and a Maurrassian, to whom Levinas would dedicate his first book;[3] Maurice Halbwachs, a sociologist; and Charles Blondel, an anti-Freudian psychologist. Indeed, Blanchot stated as much: "So many great teachers made it impossible for us to think of philosophy as something mediocre."[4] Between 1927 and 1929, he completed sufficient classes to be awarded a Certificate of Higher Education: a module in German, taking the classic literary studies option (July 27, 1927); a module in psychology (March 10, 1928); and two modules in philosophy, one in sociology and moral philosophy (July 25, 1928), and one in general history and general philosophy (July 24, 1929).

In this period, however, the new glory of Strasbourg was already in decline. Lacking any outlet beyond the university, intellectual activity withered away and the professors began to try to return to Paris. Pfister, the dean of faculty, remarked resignedly that "we have the glory of being the waiting room for the Sorbonne." By the late 1920s, both the established figures and the upstarts of the philosophical scene were in the capital. That is where Bergson and Brunschvicg were teaching their theories of "creative evolution" and of "the progress of consciousness." With a mixture of lectures, cliques, and reviews, Groethuysen, Berdjaev, Shestov, Gurvitch, Wahl, and Marcel were beginning to break away from the dominant rationalist and spiritualist traditions. Almost unknown until now, Hegel and Kierkegaard were beginning to be read, translated, and commented on; people were beginning to talk about Husserl, who was at the Sorbonne in 1929, and about Heidegger. In Strasbourg, although it was close to Freiburg, the professors rarely mentioned German phenomenology. Blanchot came across these thinkers by chance or due to his own interest, being able to read the texts in the German original (thankfully, given that the first translation of Heidegger only appeared in 1938). His attentiveness to margins and borders brought him closer to philosophical modernity, if not initially in terms of Marxism and psychoanalysis (which he would soon encounter, however), then at least regarding phenomenology.

Jacques Derrida declared himself "impressed," stating that Blanchot, despite not being a specialist, professor, or historian, had a "philosophical learning [*culture*] without equal in the French university system." For him, Blanchot carried out a "double gesture": a questioning carried out from within literary thought or writing, a place inaccessible to philosophy itself; and an absolute affirmation, a rallying cry for the necessity of philosophy, in a context in which it was threatened institutionally and epistemologically.[5] This knowledge and the way it was articulated began in Strasbourg, and they were transformed by meeting Emmanuel Levinas.

CHAPTER 5

A Flash in the Darkness
Meeting Emmanuel Levinas (1925–1930)

Jacques Derrida puts it thus: "The *friendship* between Maurice Blanchot and Emmanuel Levinas was an instance of grace, a gift; it remains a blessing on our time."[1]

A student in philosophy, Emmanuel Levinas arrived in Strasbourg in 1923. Born in Lithuania in January 1906 and Blanchot's senior by slightly less than two years, he came from a wealthy family that experienced difficulties due to the war, the Soviet revolution, and exile. He was extremely cultivated, having received a broad Western, Russian, and Lithuanian-Jewish education. He came to Strasbourg for the "prestige of French," the town itself being chosen only for its proximity, however relative.

Levinas dates his meeting with Blanchot to 1925 or 1926. He recounts it in these terms:

> Straight away I got the feeling of an extreme intelligence, of a thinking setting itself up as an aristocracy; in political terms, he was very far away from me during that period, he was a monarchist, but very soon we had access to one another.

> He sometimes mentions me in his books and elevates me greatly, in all senses of the term. I mean that I find myself highly elevated when in his interventions he comes close to me. On many points our thinking is in agreement. He has undergone a completely internal evolution in which there has never been the slightest concession, even in relation to himself. My impression is of a man without opportunism. . . . He would always choose the most unexpected and the noblest, the hardest path. This moral elevation, this deep-rooted aristocracy of thought is what counts most, it is what elevates. . . .
>
> Very early on, he introduced me to Proust and Valéry: we did not, if I remember rightly, discuss surrealism much. Our conversations also revolved around his very early interest in these phenomenological things . . . where, in these very abstract notions, he saw unexpected lines of enquiry and where with him things took on new destinies. . . .
>
> For me, it was as if he were the expression of French excellence: not so much due to ideas, but due to a certain possibility of saying things, very difficult to imitate and appearing as a lofty strength. Yes, it is still in terms of loftiness that I speak to you about him.[2]

It is clear that in speaking of their meeting and its immediacy, Levinas is careful to place the main forces that animated it within a certain perspective. We can read this as an aestheticizing, obliging way of downplaying the political violence of a friend who later would show such interest in Judaism and Jewishness. And we can also reread here, in parallel, the interest in integration, in elevating oneself socially and in being recognized culturally, of a Lithuanian Jew whose political moderation and Republican nationalism are well known. But to leave it at that would be to remain blind to the immediate desire for friendship, in spite of and *in place of* political opinions (which is to say: the positions adopted regarding cultural belonging and the space it required, the community it made possible). Everything about Blanchot was seductive, as soon as you met him, in spite of and *in place of* the silver pommel. Levinas demands that "the transformation of convictions" be thought of without any reference to compromise. Friendship alone can justify this absolute, can force us to glimpse the permanency that lies beyond change. Levinas sets up a paradoxical portrait of a Blanchot who was already wholly self-present in 1926, while also being completely still to come. Everything was indeed there already: the aristocracy, the loftiness, the gaze, the demand, the excess and the excellence, the ability to surprise (via little-trod paths, surprises, paradoxes). Levinas describes a Blanchot ignorant of himself, learning about himself, who would learn to recognize his aristocracy in forms different from the—imaginary—ones he inherited. The Blanchot of 1926 was a Blanchot without an oeuvre, but able to impress, elevate, agitate, be insubordinate: everything was already there, everything would find its way, but slowly, with difficulty, erratically. This slowness would respond to the demand not to judge, not to judge immediately, to know how not to be satisfied with immediate judgment, and to know how to move beyond one's everyday life, one's automatic opinion, one's agitated blindness, to move beyond these by way of an unending quest which, confronting the real (thanks to the demand of friendship and the hard work of writing), would also eventually come into being. This quest allows one to approach being by way of thought, by way of a harsh apprenticeship in the most sovereign worldviews and their endless assimilations. When this apprenticeship is complete, when these worldviews have been fully absorbed and invested with a decisive experience, they can finally be critiqued and filtered by a now indefatigable personal approach, strengthened by this long *faux pas*, more assured due to its past mistakes and in tune with the events of current History. This approach is able to instantly interpret these events in absolute terms, in the radical way they appear or as mere insignificant blunders; it is able to question itself regarding the only point on which it is uncertain or undecided, namely interactions between this collective destiny and singular experiences of interiority (intersections which will be staged by *récits* such as *Death Sentence*). This approach would only find a niche for itself in the inimitability of the "French excellence" already mentioned: style, the precise rhythms of style, a capacity that Levinas recognized as belonging to the language in which he would write or inscribe his thought.

For his part, Blanchot would describe the meeting as follows: "I would like to say, quite simply, that meeting Emmanuel Levinas when I was a student at the University of Strasbourg was the happy encounter that illuminates what is darkest in a life."[3] Blanchot later used carefully chosen terms to reiterate how rare this illumination was in a letter to Pierre Prévost, evoking in Georges Bataille "he who, alongside Emmanuel Levinas, has been my closest friend."[4] He signaled it in the final lines of *For Friendship*: "Emmanuel Levinas, the only friend—ah, distant friend— whom I call *tu* and who calls me *tu*; that happened not because we were young but out of a deliberate decision, a pact that I hope never to breach."[5] And in a letter to Salomon Malka, made public by *L'Arche*, he refers to Levinas as my oldest friend, the only one with whom I feel authorized to use the familiar address [*le tutoiement*]. . . . Did this meeting happen by chance? One could say so. But the friendship was not random or fortuitous. Something profound carried us toward one another. I won't say that it was already Judaism that brought us together, but I would say that, besides his gaiety, it was his indefinably serious and beautiful way of envisaging life, a way of deeply examining it without the slightest pedantry.[6]

And yet, it was indeed Judaism that brought them together: even if Blanchot does not dare say so overtly, it was already in play. At least, a certain way of approaching Judaism was in play, a certain way that Blanchot would theorize, fragment, spread far and wide. In other words, this was already a certain relation to the other guided by the informal address [*le tutoiement*] (that of God to his creature), the freedom to act, the necessity of distancing, and a priority given to ethical thought above all others. Such are the stakes of what passed between Levinas and Blanchot even as early as their Strasbourg years, and while they must have felt it immediately, as they felt the glorious, silent reserve of their friendship (a glorious silence, no doubt, for it could only strengthen their friendship, make it exceptional, marvelous, and astonishing), they probably did not think it to be such until much later.

And even if Blanchot had only been a moderate nationalist in Strasbourg (we have no more exact information concerning his views or his persona), we would still have to consider that he was already the man who would soon call for violence against Léon Blum.[7] Blanchot's precise political positions in the 1930s will be detailed later. Let us suppose however that in Strasbourg they were the worst imaginable, if only in order to underline how friendship remained possible all the same, including all its variations from gaiety to seriousness, and to beauty as well. We must then turn to Levinas and recall his pacifist, pro-Briand views;[8] his closely held convictions against violence; his familiarity, since childhood, with national and racial suffering (war, exile, revolution, ostracism, oppression, scorn); his feeling of freedom and release at living in France; his desire for integration, sometimes practiced with deferent attentiveness, always experienced as an institutional form of moral gratitude; his prudent silence over Heidegger's commitment to the Nazis, of which he became aware very early, "perhaps even before 1933";[9] and above all his innate ideas (purity, nobility, moral grandeur, elitism, authority, severity), as he saw them incarnated in the

France of the Revolution and the Enlightenment, the bourgeois France of the Third Republic, even in the Resistance and in the power of General De Gaulle, whom he would admire until the end. Finally we recall Levinas's critical perception of ontology, a "philosophy of power" that "does not question the Same" and therefore is a "philosophy of injustice," as in Hegel or Heidegger, which "subordinates the relation with Others to the relation with Being in general." "Placing *being* before *beings*, ontology before metaphysics—is to place freedom (even that of theory) before justice. It is a movement within the Same before any obligation with regard to the Other." This philosophy "inevitably leads" to tyranny based in "rootedness in the earth, in the adoration that men in slavery devote to their masters."[10] However it may have shifted in later years, this judgment recalls that ethical finality is what matters most to Levinas, and that it is what always mattered to him, even and especially when facing political decisions, which in fact must proceed from this ethical finality, no matter how insignificant it might seem in relation to other forms of community links. That Blanchot should have had, that he should *already* have had this initial concern for the Other is what made friendship possible, cheerful, and thinkable; he and Levinas named this concern dialogue, infinite conversation, and, as they regarded one another in gratitude, "without the slightest pedantry," Judaism.

CHAPTER 6

There Is

Philosophical Apprenticeship (1927–1930)

Having gained a first degree in 1927, Levinas began preparing his doctoral thesis, *The Theory of Intuition in the Phenomenology of Husserl*. Over the next two years, he spent time in Freiburg and was received by the patriarch, Husserl, whose courses he followed. On the recommendation of another professor, Martin Heidegger, who had just published *Being and Time* and who was not yet forty, he was also selected by Strasbourg to participate in the second Franco-German meetings at Davos, from March 17 to April 6, 1929. There he was present at the famous and decisive disagreement over Kant between Cassirer and Heidegger; the latter was moving toward the deconstruction of metaphysics that he had begun two years earlier. In the debate between the two German philosophers, Levinas had chosen his side. All those who knew him at the time describe his enthusiasm for a phenomenology that, he would later say, was reawakening the verbality and the event-quality of Being.[1] During the stay in Davos, his first article on Husserl appeared, in the *Revue Philosophique de la France et de l'Étranger*. On May 4, 1929, back in Strasbourg, the young philosopher was invited with his friends Blanchot, Rontchewski, Madeleine Guéry, and Suzanne Pentillas to the house of Professor Blondel (several photographs, today well known, remain of the students' departure by car on this occasion).

While Blanchot introduced his friend to the work of Proust and Valéry, and to a certain French mindset (*esprit*), Levinas gave him access to Russian literature (Dostoevsky, whom he preferred), as well as to German phenomenology. Blanchot wrote:

> Thanks to Emmanuel Levinas, without whom I could not have begun to understand *Being and Time* as early as 1927 or 1928, reading that book provoked a true intellectual shock within me. An event of primary importance had just occurred: impossible to attenuate it, even today, even in my memory.[2]

And:

> As soon as I met Emmanuel Levinas, more than fifty years ago—a happy meeting, in the strongest sense—it was through a sort of manifest obviousness that I persuaded myself that philosophy was life itself, youth itself, in its unbound passion, yet reasonable nonetheless, renewing itself continually and suddenly by the brilliance of entirely new, enigmatic thoughts.[3]

This presence of life in philosophy, and of philosophy in life, first experienced in the enthusiasm of an apprenticeship with the professors of Strasbourg, now became manifest in the radicality of phenomenological discovery. Levinas recounts how, reading first of all Husserl in 1927, he felt that he had

> not come up with another unknown speculative construction, but with new possibilities for thought, with a new possibility of passing from one idea to another, of bypassing deduction, induction, and dialectics: the feeling of having come up with a new way of unfolding "concepts," above and beyond Bergson's appeal for inspiration in "intuition."

He directed his eagerness and devotion to this feeling of giving life to the object by making it visible through the intentionality of consciousness. Here was the capacity to unfurl a new *gaze* over things, to make an event *visible*, to remove all power of fascination from the distribution of things in the world: Blanchot's eye, as one can imagine, was receptive to this sharp approach. The rarity of his approach was thus inscribed in an impossible, critical admixture of rationalism, idealism, and phenomenology. Through "this new attentiveness to the secrets or the blind spots of consciousness which, beyond the psychological or the objective, reveals the sense of objectivity or of Being," his novelistic aesthetic emerges.[4]

This is not to say that Levinas's entire philosophy and Blanchot's entire literature were already decided, or fundamentally oriented in one direction, during this student era in Strasbourg. The two men's critical training merely opened a pathway for them. The composition of *Thomas the Obscure* began three years after Davos. Reelaborated, discussed, tested, the notions that owe much to this debate, such as those of origin, solitude, work, neuter, as well as the questioning on death, truth and errancy, revelation and dissimulation, would direct the aesthetic reflections of *The Work of Fire* and *The Space of Literature*. In Blanchot's text, "the accent with which the word Being is proffered is Heideggerian," Levinas would write.[5] Blanchot, too, would discover existence with Husserl and Heidegger. His critical work cannot be conceived outside "the radical idea of intentionality," an idea that is nonetheless "removed from the logic of objectification."[6] The presence of consciousness in all its manifestations, be they paradoxical ones such as sleep, dream, or the passivity of insomnia, is as radical in Husserl's reasoning as it is in Blanchot's narration, even if it is less certain in the latter that this proximity of consciousness to the world remains a proximity to itself (Freud and Bataille's contributions consisted perhaps in introducing a split at the heart of this certainty, while that of Nietzsche was to make this newness or initialness of the event take on the disconcerting status of a return). However, the notion that the phenomenological reduction should also be an astonishment before the world, or that the vivacity of presence should be irreducible to knowledge's maneuvering, opens a breach that would stimulate Levinas and Blanchot, like a point of obscure but possible radiance, a breach into which they would plunge, always with and through their language.[7]

The dialogue between the two friends is woven together by the fact that, in place of the assurance of Heidegger's *es gibt* Levinas places the ubiquity of the *there is* and Blanchot hears the presence of the neuter. They would quote each other often on this point, this "density of the void," this "murmur of silence"; "something resembling what one hears when one puts an empty shell close to one's ear, as if the emptiness were full, as if the silence were a noise."[8] As early as 1947, in *From Existence to Existents*, Levinas refers his readers to the first pages of *Thomas the Obscure* and their pure description of the *there is*: "the presence of absence, the night, the dissolution of the subject in the night, the horror of being, the return of being to the heart of every negative movement, the reality of unreality are admirably expressed there."[9] Levinas would always situate this notion on the boundaries of literature and philosophy, seeing it as both more abstract than the concept of *Being*, in which it provokes a crisis (to this extent following, in its own way, Heidegger's initial interrogations in *Being and Time*), and as more concrete, infinitely stimulating the senses, drawing on a dynamic passivity which pushes back the limits of perception and places that perception contrariwise to all possible philosophies and phenomenologies, at once guarantee and threat, resource and perdition. A paradoxical edge to discourse, this proto-deconstructive notion was inscribed in a long tradition featuring—each in its own way but each time as the margin of the sensory or the perceptible—Parmenides's non-Being, Heraclitus's becoming, Hegel's sacred, or Bataille's impossible. It is at this limit of ontology that Levinas would like to hypostatize the concepts authorizing the primacy of ethics. Blanchot would attempt to write a new, poetic prose responding to this uneasy strength, thus discovering a hitherto unarticulated sensory space. Without there being any possibility of chronologically or genetically analyzing the intimate discussions that took place between the two men, we understand that the *there is* imposes itself on their madness like a shared discovery. It imposes itself on the madness of their belief, dramatizing it: "Rather than to a God, the notion of the *there is* leads us to the absence of God, the absence of any being." It imposes itself on the madness of their childhood, that of the "primal scenes" from which it appears: "the *there is* . . . goes back to one of those strange obsessions that we retain from childhood and which reappear in insomnia when silence is resonating and the void is filled," Levinas confides, before adding: "my reflection on this subject starts with childhood memories. One sleeps alone, the adults continue life; the child feels the silence of his bedroom as 'rumbling.'"[10] Sharing in this way must have been one more reason to seal their friendship, a friendship based in experience and based in literature (Levinas refers to Shakespeare and Rimbaud), a community of language (their titles and their notions echo one another, they quote one another anonymously, they pay public homage to one another).

This community of language still remains to be thought. Most commentaries proceed in the same direction: they start from Levinas's philosophy and lead to Blanchot's critical or narrative experience, as if the relation between the two consisted entirely in one fulfilling an apprenticeship in the other's thought, as if thought somehow had to take precedence over its own gestation in experience. Is it really possible to state so categorically that "Blanchot thinks beginning from the space of literature" and "Levinas thinks beginning from the space of philosophy"?[11] It seems that the Strasbourg experience served as a crucible, an origin, one that would always be at work in the two friends' creative endeavors, and that would make their modes of thinking responsive ones, alive to sensation, interlaced with one another by a fascination with what escapes them, drawing on experiences that were at once singular and stripped bare, and leading to commentaries that were at once untiring and impatient. The engagement of these responsive modes of thinking with extreme literature on the one hand, and with the Bible or the Talmud on the other, does not stem from any opposition of literature to philosophy, but simply from a diverging of paths.

A year after Davos, on April 4, 1930, having definitively returned from Freiburg, Levinas defended his doctoral thesis with Maurice Pradines as examiner. The thesis was published almost immediately. Armed with his doctorate, he then left for Paris where he took a post as a modest supervisor at the Alliance Israélite Universelle, where he would spend thirty-three years of his life. In 1931, he was naturalized as a French citizen, and his translation of Husserl's *Cartesian Meditations* appeared, which had been produced in collaboration with Gabrielle Peiffer, a thinker discovered by Alexandre Koyré and Henri Gouhier. Levinas's exceptionally friendly relations with Blanchot would remain of a rare quality, but the two would meet less and less, the frequent and even daily rhythm of earlier years having been definitively broken. The distinct ways in which their thinking developed had both the grace of imminence and the necessity of separation, taking place as this did under the gaze of the other. These gazes were so lacking in glib benevolence or negation that they recall a complicit freedom continually brought back into play, without demands or priorities, but with excessive gentleness, and which the tolerance of that excess would reshape.

CHAPTER 7

Aligning One's Convictions
Paris and Far-Right Circles (1930s)

Maurice Blanchot probably went to Paris in 1929, at more or less the same time as Emmanuel Levinas. In June 1930, he sat for a further degree, the Diplôme d'Études Supérieures, at the Sorbonne with a dissertation entitled "The Skeptics' Conception of Dogmatism."[1] The following year, 1931, marked his first collaborations on newspapers and journals of the far right.

He also undertook studies in medicine at Sainte-Anne Hospital, specializing in neurology and psychiatry, without ever defending a doctoral thesis, and perhaps without ever beginning his training as an intern. He might have crossed paths there with Jacques Lacan. Throughout his life, he would remain readily conversant with medical interpretations, which he would use to help his friends, not to mention himself.

He can be imagined to have had a relatively comfortable life in Paris. His position writing editorials for the *Journal des Débats*, the ultraconservative daily of the "two hundred families," would soon grant him a regular salary, which would often be augmented by other income related to other roles in the press, which he held at the same time.[2] Friends reported seeing him in a splendid, very expensive car. According to other reports, however,

Blanchot did not have a car, at least not in 1937, since his "habit of taking taxis all over Paris" was strikingly unusual.[3]

These years of comfort, perhaps of luxury, were also the years when a global crisis was setting in, the world was drifting into fascism and marching inexorably toward war. At the beginning of the decade, France was still relatively prosperous and still had the best army in the world. Briand's foreign policy was reassuring, just like Poincaré's economic and fiscal policies. The pacifist dream, born of the First World War, still seemed possible. But from 1932 onward the country was unable to escape the depression. Dragged down by the fall in foreign trade, the decline of diplomacy on the international stage, posturing among government departments, the Stavisky affair, and antiparliamentarian feeling, the victory and then failure of the popular front, and the Munich crisis, France would experience upheavals continuously until the war.

Our aim here will not be to reconstruct an epoch, in a few pages, with the distortions that are unavoidable in any quick, summary representation.[4] We need only recall the great divergence in accounts of the period, for instance in the novels of Céline, the scandals of Bernanos, the notebooks of Sartre, the articles of Bataille or the confessions of Leiris, cubist and surrealist paintings, the films of Renoir or the photography of Kertész. Between the obsession with breakdown and pleasure (whether gentle or violent), between personal and public life, between destinies shared and friendships undone, it is impossible to argue that this was a stable period. This period will not escape the responsibility of having ultimately consented—on a massive scale, and blindly, without being able, knowing how, or wanting to think it through—to what led to the unthinkable. Today we must at least attempt to think this period's insufficiency, its disorder, its ignorance, we must attempt to explain its hybrid legacies and tortuous dissidences, and to recognize how it normalized violence to a shocking extent.

Blanchot arrived in Paris brilliantly cultivated; his rightist elegance and his rural origins were such that for several years he would still prefer the "true traditions of *la France profonde*."[5] The Parisian Blanchot of the early 1930s could only direct himself, among the bewildering range of possible encounters, toward circles of the far right; these circles brought together, hierarchically, ladies and men, intellectuals and students. *L'Étudiant Français* would unite Philippe Ariès, Pierre Boutang, Robert Brasillach and Claude Roy (Nizan too, briefly). The figures this movement looked up to were Barrès, Drumont, Péguy, La Tour du Pin. A spiritual leader since the Dreyfus affair, Charles Maurras was editor of *Action Française*; Jacques

Bainville and Léon Daudet assisted him. An influential political player, which was strongly represented in parliament, the League also had an eponymous daily of its own. Beyond this, it financed *La Revue Universelle*, an austere bimonthly publication created in 1920, which was edited by Bainville and Massis, and carried articles by the neo-Thomist philosopher Jacques Maritain, the novelist André Maurois, and the critic André Rousseaux. Friendships and acquaintances were common in the daily, philosophical, or literary press: from *Temps* to the *Journal des Débats*, from *Esprit* to *Je Suis Partout*, from the *Revue des Deux Mondes* to *Nouvelles Littéraires* and the *Nouvelle Revue Française* (*NRF*). Anger, resentment, and a reactionary spirit that sometimes saw itself as revolutionary brought political leaders and students together. Slogans whipped things up; the aristocratic mindset ennobled one, gave one authority, legitimacy. This easy combination proved attractive to the secretly held nihilism and the impatience for glory of young Romantics who did not know their own minds and would not discover that they were Romantics until some later date. While little by little the 1930s would heighten differences and consciousnesses, the legacy of the 1920s was instead one of possible consensus between extremes, the search for agreement or for unnatural solutions to put an end to the crisis. Friendships were free and easy, ideologies were diffuse: Malraux wrote a preface for Maurras and corresponded tempestuously but at length with Maulnier, whom Paulhan approached in view of a collaboration at the *NRF*, which in turn ran articles by Arland and Thibaudet that viewed favorably the anti-Semitic pamphlets of Céline or Bernanos. The aspiring reactionary-revolutionaries put together the sort of cocktails that justified all kinds of mixtures. Claude Roy's memory of what they read is as follows:

> I set up for myself, all alone in the provinces and then in the Latin Quarter, a bizarre concoction of half-baked and self-taught philosophy, a dinner for a young, rabid dog [*bouillie pour jeune chat enragé*]: I took the critique of *democracy* from Baudelaire, Georges Sorel, and Maurras, the "cult of energy" from Nietzsche, Barrès, and Stendhal, the revolt against the sedentary from Rimbaud and Vallès, the vague and violent idea of socialism from Proudhon and Malraux, and the permissibility of pleasure from Gide's *Fruits of the Earth*.[6]

The occasional name excepted, this is the reading that we can imagine Blanchot to have been doing at this time, he who fifty years later would recall in *Intellectuals under Scrutiny* his intimate and subtle knowledge of Barrès's work.[7] This was a period that allowed both ill-tempered splits and the compatibility of opposites, both heated invectives and compromising personal allegiances. Nothing held, nothing hung together. A lack of reflection could lead one to support publically someone who had been sidelined on a personal level. It was possible to shout anti-Semitic slogans before going to dinner with Jewish acquaintances who were perhaps themselves members of the League, as certain naturalized foreigners were. Barrès was given a state funeral in 1923, and Blum recognized his anti-Semitic friend Jaurès as a "guide" and a "teacher." Like many others, Blanchot found himself in this situation. He was close to Levinas and close to Maulnier. These were the contradictions of the times, borne lightly and irresponsibly: no one knew quite *where* to position themselves, no one placed real emphasis on doing so. This did not prevent a lofty and strong identity being proclaimed all the more violently.

Action Française, which always united over refusals (of the Jew, of the Republic, of the defeat), albeit amid great heterogeneity and effervescence, still presented itself in an unclear image, at once conservative, reactionary, and revolutionary (this confusion would explain a number of calls for "dissidence," which would influence Blanchot—the word after all would come from him). The movement still enjoyed a certain intellectual prestige. Its literary beauty and its darkness were still attractive features. But it had found itself being disowned by the two institutions that its dogma sought to serve, the Church and the monarchy, having been condemned by the former in 1926 (a fact that removed the official support of French clergymen and led to the loss of a number of the faithful, of members and readers, beginning with Maritain, who devoted himself to justifying the Pope's condemnation), and having also been discredited by the latter at the beginning of the 1930s (the count of Paris, then exiled in Brussels, took on independent advisors and spokesmen). Moreover, from 1928 on and above all in 1930, the very heart of the movement was threatened; while Maurras remained seductive, young "dissidents" reproached him, more or less openly, for preaching an activism without actions, limited to the untiring repetition of archaic slogans and a few exploratory disturbances in the Latin Quarter.[8] "A huge song and dance built around a fictitious system," would later be Rebatet's judgment.[9] The dissidence itself, which created a greater stir on the media and political scene, would nonetheless only lead to verbal inflation, being unable to formulate a new political thinking, and while it would call for revolution, terrorism, or fascism, it would be happy to do no more than call for them.

Thierry Maulnier, a phlegmatic, sporty, and brilliant graduate of the École Normale Supérieure, with a stylistics indebted to Nietzsche's energy and Racine's purity, would leave his mark on Action Française as the leader and strategist of this youthful dissidence. Born in 1909, two years after Blanchot, he became the figurehead of a new militant, contestatory generation. His newspaper articles paid homage to Pascal and Gide in a way that Maurras could not have endorsed. Even in taking on the lead role in the main dissident journals, Maulnier would always manage to maintain a link to the leader. He did not hesitate in borrowing from Proudhon, Marx, or Sorel as much as he did from Maurras, Barrès, or Fustel de Coulanges. He pleaded the shared cause of nationalist and proletarian violence; his attention to the workers linked up with that of Henri Lagrange, whom Action Française had judged twenty years earlier a heretic. According to Henri de Montety, Maurras "passed all his whims" to his young disciple:[10] he would entertain a possible rapprochement with the nascent early-1930s movements *Esprit* or *Ordre Nouveau*, as well as that of editing extremist periodicals like *Combat* or *L'Insurgé* and, at the beginning of the war, working for *Le Figaro*. During all these years Maulnier would cultivate a mixture of monarchism, classicism, rationalism, nationalism, ethnocentrism (based on Europeans, and especially the French), of Germanophobia (at once political, military, literary, and ideological), and antiparliamentarianism that would take him, like the entire right-wing Action Française—but him more than others due to his populist and anticapitalist spirit—to a practical dead end. Imprisoned by Vichy and disliked by the newspapers that supported Pétain, he would be linked to networks close both to collaborators and to the Resistance.

Maulnier lambasted Surrealism, the roaring twenties (*années folles*), Morand and Cocteau, since "man needs to rediscover essential, virile, total reasons to live and to die."[11] But he read Marxism closely, refusing its rationalizing totalitarianism, the primacy it gives to economics, its functional pragmatism, its class dialectics, while approving of its theoretical coherence (not shared by any contemporary worldview, he stated), its denunciation of bourgeois capitalism, its analysis of workers' alienation. In July 1936 he even argued for an extension of the social advantages that had recently been introduced after the popular front had come to power. Hitler's rise to power in turn frightened and inspired him, and he denounced the cowardly, corrupt powerlessness of the democratic countries' reaction to it. In his eyes, and for different reasons, communism, fascism, and Nazism shared the same ideology of the masses, of collectivity, a simplified or nonexistent version of the mythical demand, which repressed the spiritualist tendencies of the individual, his one and only real treasure. He took up the notion of the proletariat in order to show that it lacked money, capital, ownership of the means of production, but most of all culture, a national culture. However, Maulnier would never arrive at any true philosophical or political synthesis, beyond arguing for a "path for organic overcoming," for mystical reunion with a national cultural consciousness and, while waiting for this "revolution," for "minimum fascism" (the restoration of the state's political independence, national reconciliation, economic recovery, and cultural freedom). This gives a meaning to the formulation recalling that of Maurras, from whom Maulnier takes up the theory of "reasonable anti-Semitism": which is to say, an anti-Semitism whose anticapitalist rationale cannot be associated with any form of "vulgar anti-Semitism."

We should not attempt to downplay the frequency in the press of violent writing and of anti-Semitic opinion, nor to neglect how those media-oriented and ideological ways of thinking influenced one another, nor should we remain blind to how they contributed to making the unjustifiable palatable, nor—last—should we attempt to state that these ways of thinking or the League prevented the worst from happening.[12] Nonetheless, a distinction must be drawn between the positions of Action Française's dissidents and the overt and unchanging demand for fascism by ideologues who were close to it, such as Drieu, who from 1934 onward was calling for all and any syntheses: nationalism, trade unionism, socialism, but also fascism, Nazism, Stalinism (in 1936 he joined Doriot's French Popular Party); or such as Brasillach and Rebatet, dissidents among dissidents who, at *Je Suis Partout*, declared themselves supporters of Mussolini, willingly backed Hitler, delighted in anti-Semitism, and expressed disdain for the French people as "scum."

This was the uncertain, diffuse, and most often violently irresponsible ideological backdrop into which Maurice Blanchot arrived, finding a place, finding a voice and finding strength. Little by little he entered the journals, created friendships, was given positions of responsibility, often as the right-hand man or lieutenant for Maxence or Maulnier. Whereas the young extremists would meet in the bars of Montparnasse or the Latin Quarter, at the Coupole or at Lipp's, Blanchot adopted a singular profile and took part only sparingly in their festivities.

Each of the different groups, movements, or journals to which Blanchot belonged had its tone or tones, its own forms of engagement, its epoch, its ideologies, its particular strategies. Each had a different approach to the *demonstration* that taking part in public debate represented. Individual articles cannot be read independently of this precise context, to which they belong, on which they depend, which they influence, and which it is our task to reconstitute. Even if it means spending more time on certain rare, isolated, or unknown texts, we must consider all the possible affiliations, inflections, and orientations of the diverse statements that reveal the certainties and wanderings of a brilliant young 1930s journalist, who was not yet—or not completely—a writer. We must follow the *movements of conviction*, the way they were displaced and transformed, the real substance of intellectual experience. Blanchot's political thought was nonexistent at this time; it would only come to exist through the slow, patient, long, and still-latent thought that stems from an intimate experience of death, of writing, which at this time accompanied him like a shadow.

CHAPTER 8

"Mahatma Gandhi"
A First Text by Blanchot (1931)

"Mahatma Gandhi" is not the first publication by Blanchot that we know of, but the fiction that it might be is an attractive one. After all, it contains the substance of most of the beliefs and leanings that Blanchot would go on to explore for nearly ten years.[1]

The article was published in 1931 in the last edition of a journal that changed its name according to the year. Founded and initially run by Jean-Pierre Maxence in 1928, and edited by his brother, Robert Francis, the names it would adopt—whether as title or subtitle—were *Cahiers de Littérature et de Philosophie*, *Cahiers d'Art, de Littérature et de Philosophie*, and then *Les Cahiers Mensuels*. As the 1928 manifesto stated violently, it was a Catholic student journal. Here one could read that,

> we wish to kill the modern world through the spiritual violence of sacrifice. We wish to be the anarchists of love. . . . When poetry becomes Word and Blood: it is called Christ. Let us say then that it is redeemed in him along with all things.

The following is also found:

What must be broken are the chains of universal negation! . . . Charity is the key to the forthcoming feast. It supposes knowledge while also surpassing it with all the power of the Spirit [*l'Esprit*]. From the Word to us, charity is a bridge thrown across to silence.

And the final paragraph stated: "Our message is the freedom of the SONS OF GOD—who are constrained by nothing but the immensity of the HOLY CATHOLIC CHURCH the mother of martyrs and the learned!" Those behind this journal called themselves "Catholic revolutionaries." The editorials bore the signature of Jean-Pierre Maxence, a former seminary pupil with a passion for Maurras. Faithful to Maritain's theology, the new journal was political and most of all, literary, like those for which Blanchot would write in the 1930s. It published texts, some of them providing interesting openings, by Maritain, Massis, Bernanos, Bardèche, Vincent, Fabrègues, Gabriel Marcel, Daniel-Rops, Chesterton, T. S. Eliot, Max Jacob, Supervielle, and Reverdy. In February 1930, it devoted an entire issue to Charles Péguy. It was generally opposed to postwar literature, to the "rarefied surrealism" of a writer such as Drieu, affirming instead that there was only one surrealism: that of the supernatural.

"He has been compared to Saint Francis of Assisi, to Moses guiding his people; Romain Rolland calls him the Indian Christ": thus opened Blanchot's article on Gandhi, who was sixty-two at the time and whose *Memoirs* had recently been translated into French.[2] The article initially critiqued a cultural *métissage* that was said to be foreign to the true vocation of all "great souls" (this being the meaning of *Mahatma*). "Let us bow before this life which has lacked neither sufferings nor mortifications, but martyrdom alone cannot excuse the errors of thought or render them harmless."[3]

Of course, Blanchot would recognize in Gandhi a sense of freedom that was strangely shared by them both: "He does not demand the independence that he dreams for India in the name of any abstract right, he does not demand its freedom on the basis of a principle, but he arouses it, he appeals for it from the very heart of the race, by seeking to awaken its essential traditions, those of religion, language and cottage economy."[4] In this world of nations and races, the freedom of a people was ordering him to follow his deepest traditions. Thus it was said that Gandhi "wants to re-educate the youth of India in the rhythm and cadence of the ancient ages. . . . Gandhi gives all its meaning to such advice: . . . it is the spirit that must be liberated, the first concern should be toward it: all revolution is spiritual."[5] *All revolutions are spiritual revolutions*: this is exactly what Blanchot would assert endlessly in the coming years.

And yet Gandhi's behavior seemed impure to him, his revolutionary agitations clumsy, his traditionalism phony, his spiritualism hypocritical, his intellectualism unaccounted for. Gandhi's spiritual certainties were thought by Blanchot to have been discovered in Europe, from Ruskin and Tolstoy. "Carlyle revealed Mohammed to him, and he had to read Edwin Arnold's book *The Light of Asia* to be touched by the Buddha's smile. That is strangely suspect."[6] Also suspect, but most of all unbearable for Blanchot, was the idea of *Ahimsa*, nonviolence, which "asked each being to disappear," stripping the individual of any real spiritual experience. God for Gandhi was nothing but a "sort of emblem of moral conscience whose every element is psychological: it does not introduce him into another universe, it does not oblige him to undergo experiences other than those of a life that attempts to pursue fasting and mortifications as far as possible."[7]

Opening on to another universe was what Blanchot expected from a revolution of the mind, at least since the opening provided by his own "primal scene." That another world should open up in the bosom of this world, illuminating, enlarging, effacing, and erasing it; that was what a true religious experience ought to do. But such mysticism was lacking in Christianity, concluded Blanchot, recalling as Massis had done the words of G. K. Chesterton, a recent convert to Catholicism: "There has been a return of mysticism, but without Christianity. Mysticism alone has returned and it has brought with it seven devils stronger than it."[8]

Catholicism's task was to reappropriate this mysticism. This was one of the main goals of the "spiritual revolution." And there was no need of a foreign model for that: "Is that [Gandhi's false spiritualism] really how we shall rediscover our soul? And are we so deprived that we must surrender our salvation to foreign hands[?] . . . We do not suffer from a lack of faith; we suffer because so many impure elements, so many false values have appeared at the very heart of our faith."[9]

It was now clear: The spiritual revolution would involve a national purification.

CHAPTER 9

Refusal, I: The Revolution of Spirit
La Revue Française, Réaction,
and *La Revue du Siècle* (1931–1934)

In January 1931, Blanchot gave his first text, a book review, to *La Revue Universelle*. He would provide two more, and this slim collection would represent his only contribution to a journal closely associated with Action Française. In fact, very quickly he would enter the dissident movement and publish in several of its journals. He took the chance to develop his political opinions by writing several articles published in 1932 and 1933. Founded in July 1905, *La Revue Française Politique et Littéraire* for a long time reflected the two major concerns of Action Française: "politics first," the famous motto of Maurras, and the equally predominant interest in literature. From 1930 to 1933, the journal's final three years would be turbulent ones.

First and foremost, this was a review comprising a mixture of literary, popular, and satirical elements, aimed at the provincial Catholic bourgeoisie (one column offered its readers "gossip from all over"). It included adverts and illustrations, not least on the cover page, which was often given over to festivals in the religious calendar or to the seasons of the year. February 1931 saw the appearance of the title: "Beware of negroes [*nègres*]." At the beginning of June, the journal ran a special issue on Joan of Arc, three weeks before announcing the start of summer with an *image d'Épinal*, a simplified folk-themed woodcut, beneath which Blanchot's name featured for the first time (a sign of his standing, since not all authors in that edition figured there); his contribution was an article on François Mauriac.

In November 1930, the journal's readership was gradually falling away and a relaunch was attempted (although it still had six or seven thousand readers). The editorship was given to Jean-Pierre Maxence, who took things in a new direction, aiming to be more intellectual, heroic, and impertinent. He brought with him his collaborators from the *Cahiers* and welcomed the young dissidents of the Maurrassian movement, whom he had recently met: Maulnier, Bardèche, Brasillach. In 1931, the paper changed from weekly to fortnightly publication. The cover picture was abolished, replaced by the table of contents, presented in a very austere—even ugly and forbidding—way. Maxence and his faction worked alongside the old team until June 1932, not without disagreements; the journal then became a monthly, taking up 160 pages, and claimed the patronage of Maurice Barrès's "superior journalism." The layout changed once again, as did the way the journal was organized. After an editorial by the manager and editor, Antoine Rédier, the box at the top of the front page heralded texts by Brasillach, Fabrègues and Maulnier . . . but also cameos by Emily Brontë and Rainer Maria Rilke. Further articles were provided by Maxence, Francis, Bardèche, Pelorson, René Clair. Little by little, with the onset of the economic and political crisis in France, the unrestrained attacks and the positions adopted became harsher. They were revolutionary, antiparliamentarian, anticapitalist, a forewarning of the days of unrest ahead: "in a year, riots," Francis wrote prophetically in February 1933. In April, an issue appeared on French youth featuring members of the new team and directors of *Ordre Nouveau* (Aron, Dandieu, Daniel-Rops). In August, the journal disappeared for financial reasons.

Of the four articles published by Blanchot, the latter two, which showed a certain political breadth, appeared under the aegis of the new team. They were subject to more demanding intellectual scrutiny, which chimed well with their author's austerity and with the strategy of confrontation with the *Ordre Nouveau* team. Blanchot was chosen by Maulnier and Maxence to reply to Aron and Dandieu, which was a vote of confidence in him. In the special issue of April 1933, his "Marxism against the Revolution" followed the article by the two leading figures in *Ordre Nouveau*, "Marxism and Revolution"; and he reviewed *Le monde sans âme* by Daniel-Rops with an objective, critical strength lacking from the mocking piece on the same author in *La Revue Universelle*.

Blanchot's intransigent diagnosis of spiritual decadence was shared by Daniel-Rops's book, and he recognized the strength of the author's thought and the dignity of his writing, which best marked the resistance of spirit in a disordered universe. This recognition was couched in an elegant, reserved *hauteur*, which with its measured paradoxes was already an identifying characteristic. "This luxury that we retain, when what is essential is under threat, is a fine mark of culture, and what an homage given to true honor!"[1] The syntax is neatly ordered, the adjectives balanced, exophora and anaphora are present in classically accepted proportion, while lyrical culmination is also retained in a perfectly anapaestic alexandrine ("*quel hommage rendu à l'honneur véritable!*"). This austere purity of style was the first quality that Maxence and Maulnier recognized in Blanchot. The order of thought as it protested against the disorder of matter, the tranquility of spirit as it prevailed over the errors of history—this was the first political and literary necessity that the young dissident leaders approved of in Blanchot and that he himself faithfully affirmed in Daniel-Rops. Blanchot insisted that it was necessary to safeguard the cultural grandeur of spirit, which he saw as uniting Massis, Bloch, Aron, and Maxence, against the spiritual degradation of a "soulless world," against the *materialization* of spirit; it will be noted that at the very moment that Bataille was criticizing the idealism of all materialism, Blanchot was criticizing the materialism of all idealism: this speaks volumes about how much separated them at the time.[2] He reserved special praise for Thierry Maulnier, for both intellectual and strategic reasons: his ideas on Marxist materialism, which "destroys the Revolution on which it draws," because it is an imitation, perversion, and recasting of the capitalist model, closely followed those of Maulnier.[3] This interest in Soviet Russia ("it alone provides the perfect expression and explanation of our times, and it alone could justify them, if it did not condemn them in the most terrible way") allowed him to extend the purview of Maurrassian dissidence as well as to adopt a position opposing Daniel-Rops, who did not accept that this dissidence was important.[4]

During all these years, for Blanchot Marxism would remain a despiritualizing and dehumanizing enterprise, and therefore a betrayal of the idea of revolution.[5] He barely referred to the French Revolution, not only because he was loyal to the monarchist tradition but also because he believed that no true revolution had yet taken place. He needed to show that true revolution would not simply add disorder to disorder, would not simply limit itself to being a "prophecy without power."[6] *Refusing* the world as it is allowed for no objections or renunciations, it condemned one to restlessness. The revolution had to impose itself as the "sudden passage from the impossible to the necessary," breaking its way through and imposing its "inalienable and incoercible presence," even and especially if the revolution always appeared to be anything but possible and necessary, and was therefore much more likely to be necessarily alienable and coercible.[7]

Stalinism falsified the essence of revolution by falsifying that of refusal, since refusal only led to "the most unforgiving slavery in a society where refusal is totally inconceivable," and since it led to an impasse between "historical materialism that reduces [revolution] to the endpoint of a necessary process and economic materialism that changes it into slavery."[8] This thought is not without interest and, with a little more Hegelianism, could have led Blanchot at this early stage to think the end of History. However, idealism, which was dialectical up to a point, reduced revolution to refusal, a refusal that was at once sovereign ("subordinate to no condition, except to the condition of not refusing oneself"), violent ("the way to refuse such a way of organizing the world is not to hold it in disdain, but to strike it down"), ecstatic ("throwing [man] into a true death and completely outside himself"), without any allegiance to anarchism or nihilism ("refusal is absolutely foreign to all true negation, to all absence, to all *nothingness*"), but also purely verbal and without any practical articulation.[9] For Blanchot, refusal had no essence beyond its spiritual property ("the rebellious spirit searches stubbornly, amidst these defeats and these deaths, for something proper to it, that gives it expression"—something like terrorist purity).[10] Unable to define it in any other way, he closed the debate on a note of pure intellectual strategy, choosing in this properness of spirit an advanced form of *personalism* ("refusal ... shows [the rebellious spirit] to be a *personal* existence whose accomplishment is the ultimate object and the guarantee of refusal itself").[11] This was a friendly act of conciliation with the members of Ordre Nouveau and beyond them, with Mounier and Esprit, whose thinking was based on this concept.

Condemning the abandonment of revolution as a clear utopia, condemning Marxism for providing a counterimage of revolution, in this article Blanchot formulated what was nothing more than a statement of principles: revolution is the sustained refusal, in all its demands and excesses, of any form of spiritual disorder. This text did not set out to prove that this spiritual disorder called for antiparliamentarianism or anticapitalism. But the absence of any critical or programmatic elements allowing the "sudden move from the impossible to the necessary" allowed refusal to be caught in the trap of its own condemnations. While refusal would remain Blanchot's determining political attitude (in 1958, he would even place his return to politics under this sign), this was not—as some have stated—due to sheer persistence in his thought, but due to the desire to orientate or articulate it differently, to *affirm* it by taking it beyond the dead end into which spiritualist thought had led it.

This same critique of Marxism led Blanchot to contribute to the final issues of *Réaction*, a journal that existed in an extremely chaotic and ultimately ephemeral way (1930–32), edited by Jean de Fabrègues, Maurras's former secretary and someone close to Maritain. This journal allowed great freedom of expression, at times being very far removed from Maurrassian orthodoxy. Of all the dissident journals of the time, it was perhaps the one that most allowed this freedom of expression. It set itself apart from the literary judgments of the "master" and from his anti-Semitism. It aimed to explore other approaches to economic disorder and to place Christian politics in the foreground.

Although he did not endorse the manifesto published in the first issue, in April 1930, Blanchot's position ultimately suggested a solidarity with it. The dominant idea was simple: order was "the law of Being." Indeed "order has crushed [men] when they have tried to ignore it." Thus the "crisis of the modern world" had placed man "under the yolk of the democratic, despotic and tentacular State. Man is nothing but a standardized cog in an enormous mechanism that is chewing him up." Like Christ, invoked after Maurras at the close of the peroration, we must chase "the moneylenders from the Temple." Haphazardly, and with sometimes Pascalian overtones, the manifesto nonetheless affirmed its values: for the fatherland and the nation, against democratic decadence; for "the free human person in its natural social settings," against individualism, statism, and the class struggle; for Thomist rationalism, monarchy, and Christian order.[12] To rediscover the lost order would constitute a reaction. "There is an avenue for reality; it is the past. . . . Let us return to the sources of life in order to heal ourselves." "Intelligence is reactionary."

For its final issues, in 1932, the journal would welcome contributors from *Ordre Nouveau*. At this time Blanchot also figured as a contributor, notably stating his position on the technological revolution. Being opposed to any argument for perfectibility as well as to most of the critics of mechanical alienation, he rejected both "ancients" and "moderns," given that both sought "material causes" for this development without ever making humankind "the master of his failure or of his triumph."[13] Blanchot criticized this predominance of materialist analysis, exceeding as it did the boundaries of Marxism, in the name of a classical thinking of moral conscience and of Christian guilt. It was necessary, he stated, to confront humankind "with his true faults, those that touch his soul" and that make him "lose even the privilege of his death." Blanchot was calling for the restoration of an order of thought, which, over and above all "directionless pretentions to saintliness" and other mindless (*sans conscience*) demonizations, would align action with consciousness, consciousness with intention, and intention with submission to a moral authority.

The role of *Réaction* was taken up by *La Revue du Siècle*, edited by Jean de Fabrègues and launched in April 1933. It was a monthly title with greater financial resources, which produced two or three thousand copies and reforged links with Maurrassian orthodoxy. Gérard de Catalogne, the director who had had the idea for the journal, added to the group from *Réaction* that of *Latinité*, whose members were of a slightly different generation, with differing objectives. This meant that the tone became more academic and the concerns more those of Parisian society. At the end of 1933, a banquet was given in honor of François Mauriac's election to the Académie Française, thus echoing the gesture of that summer's special issue containing contributions from Daniel-Rops, Drieu, Halévy, Maurois, Rousseaux, but also Cocteau, Morand, Martin du Gard, and Montherlant. Exchanges of views continued with *Esprit* and *Ordre Nouveau*, notably with a dossier in February 1934 where Fabrègues had the final word, discussing what united them: "this whole generation is rising up against the egotism of the bourgeois-liberal world, against materialism, both economic and spiritual, against the impotence of a politics without spirit and without soul." These were recognizably also Blanchot's positions at the time.

In June 1933, the journal published a text by Benito Mussolini, "Fundamental Ideas of Fascism." A note presented the text as follows:

> The *Revue du Siècle* is happy to be able to provide its readers with a first taste of the writings by the *Duce* that will soon be appearing. They open the volume on *Fascism* that will shortly be published by Denoël and Steele, authored by Benito Mussolini. Whatever reservations about fascist doctrine the team at the *Revue du siècle* might have, a document such as this is essential. We thank Denoël for entrusting us with it.

The least that can be said is that the journal made little effort to reprove or criticize Mussolini's text. Two months earlier, it had presented itself to its readers as "the mouthpiece of the new generation," concerned with "defending what matters in the natural order: family, profession, nation." With only the slightest of changes, the slogan would go far.[14]

Nonetheless, Blanchot came out implacably against Nazism in the May 1933 second issue of the *Revue du Siècle*.[15] His uncompromising firmness against Germany drew on nationalist arguments: "Germany occupies a strange place in Europe that no other country shares: it is not aware of where its borders lie, it does not conceive of itself as a complete form, with the latter's contours and precise beauty." This meant that "the national mysticism of national land, as conceived by Barrès, could not exist in Germany," as Sieburg had put it.[16] Paradoxically, in the perspective of a worst-case scenario, Blanchot called for a Europe of Nations, an idea that he hated, as a way to fight against the unhealthy nationalism of pan-Germanism. "As things currently stand, there is no balancing point, no possibility of order and stability, outside the treaty of Versailles. This is demonstrated by Germany's violent rejection of the treaty, by its furious resistance to its destiny."[17] Blanchot raged against the League of Nations, which was not enforcing even this badly conceived treaty. Representing "the free reign of hypocritical lies and of hot air," the League of Nations was said to have been created in the image of democracy: "it gives a face to the abuses of a policy that has been unthinkingly confused with morality."[18] The League provided comfort for the dominant political imaginary, the myth of democracy, which "each day is laying us open to events as if to a blind destiny."[19]

CHAPTER 10

Journalist, Opponent of Hitler, National-Revolutionary

Le Journal des Débats, Le Rempart, Aux Écoutes,
and *La Revue du Vingtième Siècle* (1931–1935)

If in the final analysis Blanchot's participation in the world of journals was limited, it was because he had a daily responsibility: writing the foreign policy column for the *Journal des Débats Politiques et Littéraires*, a daily paper founded in 1789, whose glory days were those of Benjamin Constant and Chateaubriand, and which more recently had come to be presented as "the newspaper of the élite"—the employers and the intellectual élite of the far right.[1] Having probably joined the paper in the summer of 1931, at the latest in March 1932, he was soon named its leader-writer and editor-in-chief, and for almost ten years he would spend most of his time in these roles.[2] Thus he became one of the successors of André Chaumeix, who had been in charge of editing at the beginning of the century and who retained a strong but contested influence on editorial policy.[3] The work, which he enjoyed, involved both writing editorials and acting as editor: formatting, modifications, corrections. Blanchot would have this role until 1940; then, after a hiatus of several months, he would write a literary column throughout the war years, which would only come to an end a few days before the final closure of a paper that had existed for 150 years.

The *Journal des Débats*, with its archaic format and makeup, its ever-smaller distribution (perhaps 25,000 copies in 1939, or 10,000 according to other estimates), and its readership mostly comprising subscribers, nonetheless remained a landmark in the journalistic landscape, thanks to the content of its political and cultural columns (it was seen more as a source of commentary than as a dispenser of information). The quality of its links with the political, diplomatic, and commercial world also contributed to its status. Owing to successive flotations on the stock market in the 1920s and the early 1930s, the majority of its shares were held by François de Wendel, a steel magnate, president of the Comité des Forges (a heavy-industry body), a director of the Banque de France, and a senator. He shaped editorial policy via the intermediary of Étienne de Nalèche, whom he had installed as editor. From this period on, links would form between the far right and the conservative editorial policy of a newspaper, which, in the early days of the Third Republic, had been linked to the center-left, and which had therefore been clearly radicalized, notably in terms of domestic policy.

The paper consisted of six pages, each of which had six columns, with no large headline on page one. On the first page began the main articles of each section. The second, in addition to serialized novels, was dedicated to international current affairs; the third, to domestic matters, to *faits divers* and to reviews of the press; the fourth page dealt with cultural events and sport; the fifth with the stock exchange; the last page was given over to advertisements and to breaking news. Occasionally a literary column would be provided by André Bellessort, a Maurrassian critic, a teacher in the *hypokhâgne* program (an elite university preparatory program) at the famous Parisian *lycée* Louis-le-Grand (a few years earlier he had taught Maulnier, Bardèche, Brasillach, Beaufret; following in Chaumeix's footsteps, he would enter the Académie Française a few years later).

Blanchot the anticapitalist wrote on a daily basis for the "two hundred families," without always diluting his position.[4] These articles, and especially the editorials, were most often anonymous. Here we shall concentrate on signed texts, signed that is either with his name or with the initials Bl. or M. B. (even if the latter can lead to some confusion, given that a journalist by the name of Marcel Bastier also contributed to the newspaper at the time). The twelve signed articles, of 1931–33, all appeared on page one.

Blanchot's anticommunism and Germanophobia in this period ingratiated him with a readership that fully shared these sentiments. They would provide the dominant tone for the *Journal des Débats*. This can be seen in his piece of September 17, 1933, reporting on a speech by Von Neurath, six months after Hitler had seized power in Germany and a month before Nazi Germany's first major decision on foreign policy (the withdrawal from the League of Nations). Blanchot saw the full danger of the latter and made an appeal to national vigilance:

> The puerile daydreams of Geneva are, in September 1933, in the era of Hitler's Germany, incredibly absurd.... Europe today is unable to control Hitler and the Nazis.... Germany is completing the rebuilding of its army and is preparing to overwhelm Europe.... As soon as it has an instrument for its strength, it will use it to get its way through diplomacy, if that is enough, or if necessary through violence.... Mr. Von Neurath has declared that Germany wants peace. But he meant pan-Germanic peace, the peace that today Germany is trying to impose on Austria and the Saarland, before turning to other countries.[5]

Blanchot called for an end to all policies of disarmament, and events soon showed his judgment to have been correct, as on October 14, five days before leaving the League of Nations, Germany left the negotiations on disarmament. The article did not say whether re-armament was required for prevention, intimidation, or war. But its author called for, and for several years would continue to call for, a realist policy in a fragmenting Europe. Blanchot foresaw lucidly what would happen, but not without a fear that would continue to make itself felt for some time.[6]

Communist opportunism was just as unbearable for him, with its willingness to benefit from anti-Hitler feeling.[7] He thought it wholly illegitimate to "appeal to the most violent and unjust regime to protest against the violence and injustice of the new Germany." Materialists were said to have no knowledge of humankind's spiritual needs, as well as to have atrociously persecuted intellectuals in Russia; "Communists and Marxists have lost any right to speak in the name of free thought and true culture." This violent discrediting would influence Blanchot's anticommunism at least until the period of *L'Insurgé*, when it would influence his position on the Spanish Civil War.

It was precisely because the Communists had no right to set themselves up as the "guardians of culture" that Blanchot called for intellectuals to commit themselves to "public affairs" (*la chose publique*).[8] He also took an interest in teaching, which he thought should not become too liberal, judging it unfortunate to "give up on a cultural ideal whose benefits we have felt for centuries"; he criticized the internationalist vision of history, brushed clean of jingoistic sentiment, that was contained in French school textbooks, quoting the view of a Belgian historian: "reading your history books, one would think they had been written by the enemies of France."[9] The articles often concentrated on cultural issues, attempting to look at the national, traditional, and spiritual dimensions whose absence explained the contemporary crisis, even including its economic aspects; for "all men have their part in the same spiritual nature."[10]

In 1932, Blanchot began drafting *Thomas the Obscure*. Due to the pressure of events and of his journalistic duties, he had to interrupt it the following year, when he joined the newspaper *Le Rempart* (*The Rampart*), publishing an article—sometimes two—almost every day, on domestic or most often on international policy.[11] He seems to have written almost every night: while the *Journal des Débats* was an evening paper, *Le Rempart* appeared in the morning, and Blanchot's pieces were often found on the page named "Tonight's Latest News." We must picture him during the day reporting on a protest by striking workers, and then in the evening, working with the excitement of a looming deadline.[12] At this early stage, journalistic writing was thus also that of the night, of a night whipped up by the day's passions, unrelated to the dispossession of "the other night," whose density came later for Blanchot, leading toward "the space of literature."[13]

Launched on April 22, 1933, *Le Rempart* appeared seven times weekly. It was a journal providing general information, most often eight pages long, containing columns on politics, economics, finance, sport, fashion, and the arts. It also included a review of the national press, written by Jean-Pierre Maxence, and the rarer feature of a rich review of the international press, which often occupied a whole page. A caricature on page 1 was followed by others throughout the paper. The underlying idea (*esprit*) of the paper was clear from its title, but also from the formulation that appeared below it: "Independent from power and from all powers: this is the motto of this free newspaper." It could also be seen from the banners that on both sides blared such often-changing statements as "Our only aim . . . to tell the truth. Our only method . . . our readers' confidence and support," or, "If you are aware of a wrongdoing, and if elsewhere you are turned away, come to us: you will see that we do not use the word 'independence' in vain." Responding to a reader's question regarding the meaning of its title, the newspaper defined itself as "a citadel in which the rights of France will be defended without mercy and without respite. A fortress in which we will fight the enemies of the Fatherland, whatever garb they adopt."[14] *Le Rempart* started out by seeking a large cohort of writers, featuring on the first page texts by figures such as Bernus, Bourget, Giono,

Halévy, Massis, Maurois, and Montherlant. The aim was to have 50,000 subscribers and 150,000 readers.

Le Rempart was founded and managed by Paul Lévy, a rich and intriguing man, an important figure in the press who was often embroiled in libel cases. This associate of the nationalist deputy Georges Mandel, who had been close to Clemenceau, drew together a group of about fifteen permanent staff, "of different ages and opinions," to whom he gave "total, complete freedom."[15] With Blanchot, Maxence, and Maulnier in key posts, the "young right" nonetheless had an important role. The newspaper's sympathies were clearly patriotic, antidemocratic, antiparliamentarian, anticapitalist, anti-internationalist, anti-Hitler and, as the latter's seizure of power unfolded, more and more anticommunist and national-revolutionary.

Condemning the ravages of Hitler's policies, and notably anti-Semitic persecution, would be one of the major concerns of *Le Rempart*, which would often dedicate its front page to this end, in order to "inform the few Frenchmen who still retain any illusions regarding Hitler, who take this madman for a defender of social order." As early as that spring, some headlines condemned "Hitler's anti-Semitism," which led to "the boycotting of men of science and of letters," or the "show of strength" by which "Hitler is having the leaders of socialist trades unions arrested and is laying his hands on workers' banks." The "Freudian side of Hitler" was evoked sarcastically, given the desire to "free Germany from its inferiority complex," but sarcasm is not able to hide the article's unease: "10,000 youngsters marched bearing torches in Odin's valley and, gathered around the bonfires of Walpurgis night, celebrated spring and the reawakening of the fatherland." Another day saw the publication of a photograph of the Jewish cemetery of Tubnitz, which had been desecrated by the Nazis (swastikas painted on tombs); a caricature condemned the burning of books. An article on the swastika provided information about its origins and showed how it reversed the symbolism of the Hindu swastika, becoming a "fetish of destruction and death." In June and July, Paul Lévy signed a series of editorials entitled "the Hitler plague." When Goering set up martial law in July, "Terror in Hitlerland" was the headline for the front page.

Blanchot himself condemned the first persecutions of the Jews, the first work camps, the setting up of the Terror. A false mysticism and a false materialism came together to serve pan-Germanism, according to his analysis.

> All Hitler's actions have been inspired by obvious demagogy. The barbarous persecutions of the Jews only express the desire to provide

pan-Germanism with some sort of testimony, with a sign of its essential status, of its incomparable origin. They never had any particular political goal. They helped satisfy the powers of instinct, the frenzy of passions unleashed by revolution. (134)

By the acts of violence, by the overspilling of the powers of instinct, he moved a whole people and caused it to rise up for a grandiose undertaking. By persecuting the Jews and struggling stubbornly against Marxist internationalism, he tried to give back to that people a feeling of its unique origins and, in truth, the religion of Germany. (148–149)

This government, "which is trying to base itself on mysticism" (134), gave a theatrical setting to the May Day celebrations that, while appearing to celebrate the strength of the proletariat, "gives expression to the revenge of collective forces, to unreserved devotion to an ideal of grandeur and domination" (135). What was truly barbaric about Hitler was not so much the recourse to violence as the betrayal of the social and national revolution through cultural mystification. Hitler's pan-Germanism was perverting nationalism with the idea of racial imperialism. German youth "has been brought up to worship the military civilization at the heart of the Prussian spirit" (143). The work camps became a method for mobilization, "which used new constraints to link each individual to the State" (142). The Third Reich was thus said to be preparing "the onset of a civilization in which, in a socialized society, the individual person and the spirit will be stripped of their essential freedoms" (143). A few months later, this was in no further doubt: The government of the Reich "has claimed the power to decide on life and death" for Germans (290).

"Germany has already armed itself. It has reformed its military forces. It has reformed the warrior spirit of a people that now awaits its destiny in battle" (148). Blanchot therefore called for a firm and aggressive foreign policy: "As *Le Rempart* demanded yesterday, as it will not tire of demanding, because at stake is the destiny of an entire youth and an entire civilization, and the only way of ensuring peace is to stay one step ahead of the threat, and to disarm it: Mayence must be reoccupied" (150).

Blanchot would repeat this call on two or three occasions, but not to the point of becoming an out-and-out hawk. He demanded that Daladier not meet Hitler, since "if we find it natural to work with Germany and with Hitler . . . then we will only have . . . to wait for the moment when we will be forced to choose between slavery and war" (201–202).

However, we know that the policy of neither Paris nor Geneva (where the League of Nations was based) would respond to these demands or principles, and this would only reinforce Blanchot's antidemocratic and anti-internationalist feeling. France was no longer France: it was entirely given over to Geneva.

> For ten years, the Quai d'Orsay [the French foreign ministry] has been one of the places in France where France itself has been most poorly served and where the least French thought has taken place.... France, silenced by a government that is not worthy of it and that is betraying it, continues not to show what it is capable of, namely of rising up and facing up to events. It only seems able to submit and to capitulate. (116–118)

The demand for national strength overrode even the idea of democratic equity. Versailles was a bad treaty, only viable if one brought it to life (Blanchot quoted Clemenceau's statement that the treaty could be whatever governments made of it), because it was based on the mistakes of "Rousseauist and Wilsonian ideology." "Without reason, it mixed morality and politics. It founded an entire balance of power on the debatable values of law and justice" (237). After all, "one of democracy's main mistakes is to have slandered strength." Thus Blanchot was able to paradoxically condemn "the criminal conceptions of disarmament, the absurd pacifist philosophy" (162). When three or four years later he would come to accept these ideas that he had originally judged to be absurd, it would not be due to any change of deep-seated convictions, but due to a sense of resignation and the necessity of adapting to the new situation, which saw Hitler in a position of power and demanded that the army be given time to revise its strategies. The pacifism of 1936–1937 would be a coherent development from the antipacifism of 1933, because the strategic reasons for pacifism were quite different (even if the room for maneuver would seem very small), as were the military implications (even if fatalists would still be arguing for capitulation).

Therefore, the contingent nature of these judgments was not hiding any element of Blanchot's profound political beliefs. His critique of democracy was not linked to more than what he saw as an epoch of decadence and corruption. His attack focused on the very conception of the Republican regime (this would never be clearer than in the era of *Le Rempart*). "Disorder lies not only in the immorality of the men who lead us and who are betraying us, but in the madness of institutions" (172–173). Blanchot preferred order to "Republican freedoms, which we disdain" (224). He condemned "the inhuman Declaration of the Rights of man," which defined the freedom of the citizen as being "freed of historical antecedents, liberated from his natural bonds." With Maurras, he sniped at "the veritable anarchy of all liberal thought" (151). He was passionate about the taxpayers' strike, supported business owners, disdained bureaucrats. He fostered hatred for almost all varieties of right-wing politics and saw the left everywhere, in the army, in education, in power. He condemned "the slavery of the government of cartels": "a minister supported by the socialists only has the freedom to act against himself and against the public interest that he represents" (136). He tended to make communism into the essence of democracy, its predictable outcome.

The "necessary revolution" (218) against the dominance of capital and the socialist state takeover of both France's material and spiritual heritage would thus be a national revolution. "The spiritual revolution, the national revolution is no longer an image or a symbol. The events of each day bring it closer, make it more necessary. And little by little, they are showing us what it will be like: tough, bloody, unjust, and our last chance at safety" (*salut*, 220).[16]

Blanchot stated that he could feel a revolutionary ferment among the people. On several occasions he called for insurrection against the state. He called—already here, as he would do later in a very different way—for insubordination.

> When the State has become incapable of working in favor of the State and in favor of the nation, the public good can only be defended by resisting the public authorities. The general interest can be saved by private initiative. Every man has the power to condemn unjust laws and to remove himself from their jurisdiction. Thus do revolutions begin.
>
> We are in a revolution (211).

This was a revolution in favor of order, one that was to take place via revolutionary disorder. Blanchot would confirm this a few years later: "The return to virtue . . . is simply the product of the impurities of violence."[17] The revolution's lack of method, of strategy, of practical thinking nonetheless revealed the weakness of such appeals, and thereby allowed the most dangerous of fatalisms to gain ground. "In this regard, the adventures of Italy and Germany are full of promise. While they do not show us the kind of revolution that we should hope and prepare for, they do show us that we can hope for a revolution that will save us" (267).

The distinction here is clear, all the more so given that other articles, and the general spirit of the newspaper, avoided any confusion; however, the absence of any manifesto demonstrated a lack of responsibility that already condemned this discourse to a dangerous drifting, condemned its language to aporia, and condemned the face it put on to a kind of dismay.

The adventure of *Le Rempart* ended in late 1933. Blanchot did not abandon Paul Lévy, being reunited with him at *Aux Écoutes*, a weekly paper whose "backbone" he would come to represent, according to its director.[18] Probably as early as 1934, and at the latest in 1937, he became its editor-in-chief.[19] This role was in addition to the editing of the *Journal des Débats*: Blanchot was still projecting the image of a journalist with competing priorities, using up time and energy that he could have devoted to writing. After the war, he would never hold an alienating day job, with its rhythms and pressures, for so long.

Founded in 1918, *Aux Écoutes* was a satirical, even scandalous journal (its cover each week being entirely covered by a caricature), but also included a finance section aimed at those who dabbled on the stock market. It contained numerous advertising banners. Its circulation, of perhaps more than 100,000 copies, and its distribution were without comparison to those of the *Journal des Débats*. Blanchot probably earned a lot more money there.

Its articles, which were short critical or satirical paragraphs interspersed with advertisements or illustrations, were rarely signed. Here and there a few book reviews bore the initials "Bl," and these can be attributed without any doubt to Blanchot due to their tone, style, and choice of subjects, which were similar to those in the other journals he was writing for at the time. An entire page of criticism on Sartre's *Nausea*, published in 1938, is a precious exception to this rule of anonymity.

It is difficult to know precisely how Blanchot reacted to the events that must have moved him at this time, and whose intensity, pressure, and dangerous quality caused numerous dissidents to abandon their doctrinal beliefs. The "demonstrations" of February 6, 1934, certainly marked him, so much so that for him they represented the only significant domestic event of the 1930s, at least before the election of the popular front. Two years later he would call them "magnificent in their ardor, their devotion and their sublime actions," stating that "their strength and generosity are incalculable."[20] We can imagine his disgust on learning that Action Française had decided not to act, fearful of carnage, of deaths and injuries. This could only have pushed him closer to Maulnier, Maxence, and Francis who, caught up in the enthusiasm, had drafted in a few weeks *Demain la France*, in which they took February 6 as "the first manifestation of the nation's energy" and called for insurrection. It must also have brought him closer to Paul Lévy, who on February 8 declared, "The national Revolution is under way: nothing can stop it now, France wishes to become French again, France wishes to be governed by men who are deserving of the task, it wishes to retain its status as a power of the very first rank."[21]

Nonetheless, Blanchot continued to be most exercised by Hitler's rise to power. In November 1933, he learnt from the press that the Führer had been to visit Elisabeth Förster-Nietzsche.[22] A year later, Levinas published in *Esprit* his text "Some Reflections on the Philosophy of Hitlerism."[23] He gave a philosophical approach to the analyses published the previous year by Blanchot in *Le Rempart*. This is to say that he radicalized what had been purely journalistic positions, without recourse to any strategic or diplomatic reading. He raised the level of debate on the topic of an organic conception of society, "on the basis of shared blood," or on that of a biological conception of mankind in which "the essence of the spirit consists entirely in its situatedness within the body." Refusing any social ideology that plunged into "the mysterious voices of the blood, the appeals made by inheritance and the past," Levinas brought to bear the order of an ethical thinking. In short, he was dissatisfied with any reflection that was limited to political contingency: "It is not this or that dogma, whether democracy, parliamentarianism, dictatorial regime or politics of religion, that is at stake. It is the very humanity of mankind."

In this same month of November 1934, the *Revue du Vingtième Siècle* officially took up where the *Revue du Siècle* had left off eight months earlier. Still edited by Jean de Fabrègues, with Maxence and Maulnier as his right-hand men, the journal in fact presented itself as the successor to *Réaction*: it took the latter's contributors and its program, albeit abridged and articulated in a few words in the first issue with three guiding principles: against democratism, against capitalist materialism, for returning his spiritual (which was to say Christian) destiny to humankind. It remained close to the Count of Paris.

It was to be a short-lived affair. The sixth issue, of May–June 1935, warned of the journal's financial difficulties; it would also be the last issue.

In February and May 1935, Blanchot contributed to the journal with two pieces on foreign policy. His aggressive positioning on the approach to be taken toward Germany had not changed. Indeed, it could only harden, after Hitler's decision of March 16 to abandon the treaty of Versailles and to reestablish compulsory military service, taking the number of divisions in the German army to thirty-six. Blanchot attacked the "malfunctioning of French diplomacy," condemning the latter's constant contradictions, its apparent firmness and its underlying negligence of responsibility, the desire, based in fear, not to confront pan-German imperialism, and the refuge taken in an international system whose lack of means condemned it to ineffectiveness and ridicule.[24]

CHAPTER 11

The Escalation of Rhetoric
The Launch of *Combat* (1936)

At the end of 1935, Fabrègues and Maulnier joined forces to create *Combat*, which they would edit together for four years. The new monthly publication was launched on January 10, 1936, and appeared regularly until the war, in the form of ten issues of either sixteen or thirty-two pages per year. The editors targeted their readers carefully. The first three issues were sent to former subscribers to the *Revue du Vingtième Siècle*. By October 1936 there were nine hundred subscribers, by December more than a thousand. The journal would go on to command the loyalty of between two and three thousand readers. Despite this small circulation, it would enjoy a certain prestige and would never attempt to enlarge its readership; growing used to this elitism, it would instead make use of *L'Insurgé*, a weekly launched in 1937, to spread its ideas more widely.

Combat seems to have come into existence thanks to a convergence of interests and aims on the part of its two editors. Maulnier, who was then becoming increasingly well known, was trying to escape the constraints of Action Française in order to sketch his ideas more freely, putting forward uncompromising solutions. Fabrègues, whose only outlet this now represented, suggested to Maulnier in October 1935 that the two of them react to the League of Nations' condemnation of Italy, an episode that pushed fascism into an agreement with Nazism. One of the features of *Combat* was that while it brought together the monarchist tradition with revolutionary violence, in the direct lineage of "dissidence" (whose extreme nature it would underline), it also resisted fascism and "vulgar anti-Semitism," stating that it stuck to "a reasonable anti-Semitism" that drew on anticapitalism.[1] This explains why it would be attacked by Maurrassian loyalists and by the extremists of *Je Suis Partout*. The journal refused the war that was approaching, welcomed the Munich agreement and, when it was clear that disaster was imminent, declared that it was preparing for the war without enthusiasm or determination.[2]

Bearing the collective signature "Combat," the manifesto that opened its first issue gave the intellectual movement the task of "reestablishing a new realism." This movement had to address historical reality (it was against the idealism limited to "games of pure intelligence"), even as it refrained from rallying to any partisan cause (it was also against any materialism limited to "games of conscripted intelligence"). The era seemed to be condemning thought to powerlessness or submissiveness. Although Marxism had been right to bring intelligent thinking back to reality, it also "increases every day the danger of intelligence soon being subjugated." This meant that "intelligence should not be placed in the service of the masses, but ought to inform and guide them; it must not follow but rather create the evolution of history."

We can have our doubts as to whether this was really a question of intelligence; but the insubordinate tone is clear, and it would be the consistent mindset of *Combat*. For example, the third issue contained a prominent letter, written by Brasillach, to the "cuckolds of the right."[3] The collective and anonymous editorial for April 1936 was entitled "A France That Disgusts Us"; in November of that year, Maulnier could be found asking whether "we shall ever emerge from the abject condition of France." Fabrègues thought that "Hitlerian democracy" was "a materialist mysticism" (January 1937). Ambitions were far-reaching, even megalomaniac, in texts such as "Reconquering Our Universe," again written by Maulnier (June 1936).

Each issue contained a variety of short, dense texts, and comprised two columns: "Facts" and "Inventory," a review of the satirical press. A further column, "Texts to Reread," was introduced in issue five and presented extracts from Maurras, then from Sorel, Proudhon, and Drumont. Another, "Conversations," in February 1937 put out a call for pieces by writers "whose works express ideas dear to *Combat*." Gabriel Marcel was the first to participate; Ramon Fernandez, Gaxotte, Drieu, Jouvenel followed. A celebratory fifty-year overview of Maurras's writing was given, and an article by Vincent saluted "Bernanos the Visionary." Sartre was heavily criticized (although this came after Blanchot had written a dense and overall favorable piece on him in *Aux Écoutes*); a column signed "Marchenoir pour les ennemis" was created; the short, violent texts of "the Massacre Game" fulminated against Georges Duhamel or "Céline the Jew."[4] Other bylines that the journal managed to include were those of Pierre Andreu, whose roots were in Sorelian trade unionism, Jean-Pierre Maxence, Claude Roy, and for the culture columns, Dominique Aury and Kléber Haedens.

After the two main editors and René Vincent, a further editor, Blanchot was one of the main figures involved in running the journal but, always and already, he did so discreetly: while *Combat* frequently held public meetings featuring some of its writers, Blanchot's name only figured once. This was in January 1938, for a "large private meeting . . . in the great hall of the Learned Societies" in the Rue Danton, on the theme of "How to Free the Nation of Money, Free Socialism of Democracy, and Defend Culture against Totalitarian Orthodoxies." It also featured Maulnier, Fabrègues, and Georges Blond. This appearance of Blanchot's name is the last in the review, for which he ultimately wrote only eight texts, six between February and December 1936, and two in November and December 1937. Of course, his articles were important, two of them being placed first in the list of contents, and the interruption during 1937 can be explained very precisely by his time at *L'Insurgé* (which lasted ten months, from January to October). But from January 1938 to July 1939, none of the seventeen final issues of *Combat* carried a text by Blanchot.

"The Stavisky scandal is over, the Sarraut administration is beginning. This is completely logical." After a government that lasted from one February (1934) to another (1936), Blanchot began his contribution to *Combat* with an article taking note of "the end of February 6" while also, paradoxically, issuing a rallying cry based on that date.[5] He took note of it insofar as he denounced what ultimately appeared as Republican "logic" (363): the establishment of invariably transitory and corrupt governments (the Sarraut administration was acting in a caretaker capacity, until the elections in May), containing "the desired number of crazy men, of compromised characters, of traitors and of moderates" (363), under the leadership of a "derisory character," "whose insignificance condemns him to obscurity," "slightly tired, slightly discredited, entirely forgotten" (363), and who was precisely what was required in order to put public opinion to sleep and to allow the ruling classes to "hide everything, obscure everything, smother everything" (366). He issued a rallying cry because he believed that these silent maneuvers of power were paradoxically supported by the fuss surrounding the regular memorials for February 6. We can therefore understand that for Blanchot, *nothing* had happened during the preceding two years. In his eyes, Sarraut took over the premiership not from Laval, but from Daladier, whose time as prime minister had been ended by the riots in February 1934. He denounced the contradictory actions of a "destructive, catastrophic parliament," which for two years had brought down government after government, and at the same time had "become resigned to being innocent and to approving measures on public safety" (*mesures de salut*, 364; in 1935, Laval governed via hundreds of laws summarily issued by the cabinet, bypassing parliament altogether). Thus the logic of the Republic was said "to work against its nature and against its own laws" (364). Blanchot was criticizing the contrasting mixture of capitalism and democracy, this incoherent logic of an unstable regime. And he was doing so with self-confident, cunning, and rhythmic phrasing that was sometimes long and sometimes short, that always drew on anaphora and cadence, and whose syntax brought any contradictions to light—this phrasing was capable of tactical hyperbole, of malicious irony, of the well-chosen insult.

This ability to carve out sentences allowed Blanchot to dismiss not only the two years of 1934–36, but fifteen, in an article the following month looking back at the Franco-Soviet pact for mutual assistance that had been signed in May 1935. Having denounced the internal contradictions in the diplomatic policies of the left- and right-wing parties, Blanchot claimed that these "false thoughts show that the unreason and the uncertainties of these last fifteen years still live on" (369). Once again, his accusations were aimed at an "absurd diplomacy" that, having privileged international commitments since Versailles, was returning to a bilateral agreement between two states that had no "interests in common" (369). Blanchot was not wrong to state that the USSR had more interests in common with Germany than with France, that between the former two "secret negotiations are ongoing" (370) and that the Franco-Soviet pact therefore "exposes us to war [with Germany] for no reason," without giving "any insurance against war" (with the USSR); initially at least, history would show him to have been right (371).

As he was finishing that text, events reinforced both his most lucid and most dubious convictions. On March 7, Germany invaded the Rhineland with thirty thousand soldiers, breaking the treaty of Versailles and the Locarno Treaties. France's initial reaction was a muscular speech by Sarraut that, thanks to a statement by the military that recommended general mobilization before any armed conflict, almost immediately fell flat. The fear was of contradicting the wishes of pacifist public opinion in the middle of an electoral campaign, as well as of disagreeing with Great Britain and being left without international support. Blanchot wrote about this reaction in his next article, which again tried to show via a series of short, powerful paradoxes, worthy of a campaign speech, how inconsistent it was to have a diplomatic policy that "demands what is impossible and neglects what is necessary" (372).[6] It was no longer two or even "fifteen senseless years" (*années folles*, 375) that had to be forgotten, but twenty-five, because the same system of government had been humiliating the country since before the war. From one article to another, this escalation of rhetoric can be explained by his being exasperatedly aware of an ever more serious threat to national identity. Blanchot thus took issue, in a piece of suicidal logic, not with the external enemy, but first and foremost with the enemy within, "with out-of-control revolutionaries and Jews, whose ideological fury seems to demand the immediate imposition of every sanction on Hitler" (373). With a sentiment of general xenophobia, he condemned what he saw as an unthinking, perverse strategy ("propaganda for national honor put forward by suspicious foreigners," 374) and denounced, even more than Hitler's expansionism, the supposed "delirium of verbal energy" (374) of this Jewish-Marxist "clan" (372). He went on to attack "the sentimental reveries of Geneva," which, aided and abetted by "British Puritanism" (374), had always imposed on France a weak attitude, a nonattitude, nonexistence. What he was also refusing here was idealism and verbalism. What he wanted to say, and what Sarraut would not say, was that "the League of Nations no longer exists" (376). What he declared, by way of a conclusion, was that only two ways out remained: "the regime will continue to move between provocation and capitulation, until it invites war through weakness or until a national revolt puts an end to its abuses" (376). We can guess which solution he preferred; we know which came to pass.

Five days after the "German show of strength," Maurice Blanchot's father died. Isidore Blanchot passed away at nearly seventy-seven years of age on March 23, 1936, at 6 a.m., in his house on the avenue Boucicaut in Chalon. He is buried a short walk from there, in the Western cemetery, a little further down the same avenue.

CHAPTER 12

Terrorism as a Method of Public Safety
Combat (July–December 1936)

Often cited, starting from immediately after its publication in July 1936, for its revolutionary violence, Blanchot's fourth article for *Combat* was also the first that he published after the Blum government was formed. Positions were becoming more deeply entrenched.

How can "the beneficial effects of terrorism" be given a basis in law?[1] And how can they be given an *immediate* basis? How can urgent appeals be made? Blanchot was inviting his readers to enter into the persistence and the insistency of a certain type of reasoning.

This is because since his first articles in *Combat*, in foreign as in domestic policy, it was the same Republican logic that he had been analyzing, bringing to light, and denouncing. This was the unproductive logic of cowardice, of timidity, which consisted in surrendering to one's enemies, in flattering them, in seeing their point of view rather than fighting against them. France signed a treaty with the USSR in order to be prepared against Germany (but this did not provide any protection). Parliament chose a weak prime minister in an attempt to keep its corruption from being revealed (it would be anyway, and a scandal would break out). Britain saw no "threat of hostility" in Hitler's moves (those were Anthony Eden's words on March 9); Sarraut kept quiet, in order to avoid war (although it would come soon enough). The logic of compromise was that of compromising oneself. Blum had dialogue with the radicals and on his return "took his best propagandists from the classes he claims to be threatening" (377). Once again, there was nothing, nothing but emptiness, nothing happening—nothing was happening except collusion between "pale imitations of reformists and pale imitations of conservatives" (377).

> It seems that they are linked together in order to do nothing, destined to neutralize one another by reciprocal concessions; in reality they keep one another afloat in order to do the types of wrong in which each respectively is competent.... This is the source of strength of this nothing government that the Blum government is (377).

This government was said to be betraying its social program and forcing its partners, via an "exchange of deceptions" (377), to betray their national program. Blanchot's logic bases itself here on "reasonable anti Semitism": "A fine union, a holy alliance," he declared to no one in particular, "is what this conglomeration of Soviet, Jewish, capitalist interests represents" (378). Here everything that he hated seemed to join forces against everything he held dear. Once more, and for the same reasons that had pushed parliament to choose Sarraut, "legal, traditional opposition" was powerless, it was "henceforth annulled" (378). Nothing was happening: Nothing could happen. Blanchot drew on this desperately nihilist appraisal, at which he had been hammering away since February, in his attempts to restore the purity of "fine French blood" (379) and the thought of a true revolution. Given that the world of legality had been neutralized, he thought it necessary to smash the law by actions that would be brisk and "if necessary, frenzied" (378) summary, nothing less than a "bloody upheaval" (380) to bring back reason, order, and justice. Morals were above the law. Blanchot was calling for an elitist and, most of all, wholly idealistic terrorism, "the work of a few men and a few groups, which needs neither mass support nor allies, but strong and just ideas, and great feeling" (378). He savored his words, hating as he did a regime that he demanded be "removed," "brought down" (380). He placed the Sadean purity of his language above the impurity of all forms of decline.

"This is not at all comfortable, but precisely, there must be no taking comfort. This is why at the present time terrorism appears to us as a method of public safety" (*le terrorisme nous apparaît actuellement comme une méthode de salut public*, 380).

For "when the majority of the representatives of the people are corrupt, gangrenous, we cannot expect any help from them regarding the safety of the nation"; these "enemies within are allied with the enemies without," and the moderates are in their pay, "always hurrying to caress current public opinion, and no less careful never to throw light upon it, most of all never to confront it." These few phrases were uttered not by Blanchot but by Robespierre, the leading member of the Committee for Public Safety, the main vehicle, alongside the Committee for General Security and the Revolutionary Tribunal, of the Terror.[2] Blanchot's rhetoric sometimes matched that of Robespierre, celebrating, through the endless back-and-forth of its well-balanced phrasing, "the virtue without which terror is harmful, the terror without which virtue is powerless."

Blanchot's sarcasm reached a high point a few months later when he attacked "moderates" for their position regarding the Spanish Civil War.[3] He ridiculed their progress in now being capable of "great passion," they who previously could have been found "disappearing like rats into the holes of total neutrality." "That was the period when moderates still dared to appear as moderates." "What is the new titillation?" "As soon as they find an autocrat, they throw themselves madly at his feet" (385–386). The trickery, however, was not only theirs but that of Hitler, Mussolini, and Franco; it was not certain that this trickery was allied with reason. Thus Blanchot drew on whatever resources he could: against these moderates "glowing with pride, as if they had uttered a few spicy obscenities" (386), against the dictators but only because they allowed themselves to be "admired beatifically," finally against the "gang of degenerates and traitors" (387) that was governing the country (this was a variation on the mention of the Jewish-Marxist "clan" that, located at the end of the piece, slips in a dose of decidedly more "vulgar" anti-Semitism).

Blanchot played impressively with antiphrasis, informal digressions, hints of caricature, cutting adjectives, ludicrous metaphors or hyperboles, comic-heroic crescendos, dry oxymorons, carefully selected insults and, as always, grating paradoxes. These varieties of sarcastic phrasing were the vehicles for value judgments that were intolerable and all the more pernicious for being stated coldly. A worker "who puts in overtime constructing machine guns" (385) was said to be more worthy than his fellow worker who attends communist rallies and emits "the most senseless cries, and the most deadening to reason, that have ever rent the air" and who does so in a "gutter drunkenness" (384). Elsewhere in the piece, the reader is told that among the excesses of war, "barbarians who rape" are no more or less to be condemned than "arsonists" or "those who uproot fruit trees" (383).

Blanchot's rhetorical thunder served the ends of his implacable argumentation. The latter denounced the "dazzling logic" of the Soviets, who wanted France to take the side of the "reds in Spain"; it also criticized the mystifying logic of the French communists, who tried to pass on this message, as well as the cowardly logic of the "moderates," who beneath a cloak of neutrality were waiting to see which way the wind would turn before giving in to the strongest party (384). This was a worst-case logic that Blanchot would return to in his December article. He stigmatized the moderates' hard-bitten anticommunism and their timidity in the face of closer enemies (Mussolini, Hitler), with whom they were trying to ingratiate themselves in a cowardly fashion: This was a shameful "caravanserai" strategy, an "utterly empty policy," which represented a death penalty for national identity (390).

According to Blanchot, it was necessary to put together a true front based on refusal, struggle, and Terror, which would be anticapitalist, antimoderate, antigovernment. It would be necessary to settle accounts "with a few bullets" (390) directed at the leaders of these "limited, weak, puny" beings, of these "subservient imbeciles" (389). This was a call for murder in the direct lineage of Maurassian rhetoric, a call to purify the "caravanserai," the nation that had become "French abjection" (391).

CHAPTER 13

Patriotism's Breaking Point

L'Insurgé (1937)

Alongside *Le Rempart, Aux Écoutes,* and *Le Journal des Débats, L'Insurgé* was one of the journals to which Blanchot contributed most continuously. We must see things in this light: during these years, Blanchot was above all a man of the press, of the newspapers rather than journals, let alone books.

L'Insurgé Politique et Social was launched on January 13, 1937. It was a weekly publication of eight large-format pages, financed by Maulnier, Maxence, and Blanchot—who seem to have been the stockholders—as well as by Jacques Lemaigre-Dubreuil, scion of a rich industrial family. The first issue was placed under the sign of Vallès and Drumont, who were quoted on the front page in a column named "Portraits of the Insurgent"— which would last only two weeks—alongside extracts from Proudhon and Bakunin. Thierry Maulnier provided the first editorial: "France must be reconquered," a watchword that was explained by the central article, "The Coming-Together of the Corrupt," with its elegant subtitle: "The radicals, the moderates, and the corporations are preparing a new administration. All those who are corrupt will feature in it: Mandel, Reynaud, Flandin, Chautemps, Boncour." The inner pages bore two articles by Blanchot: one,

"Indictment against France," continued the line of the editorial; the other, "From Revolution to Literature," launched a column headed "Readings of the Insurgent."[1] Maurras, who was in prison at the time, immediately expressed to Maulnier his discomfort at this anti-French cursing. To no avail: The tone had been set and would remain; it would remain as the extreme point reached in journalism by this group of "dissidents," who were mostly xenophobic, anti-Semitic, antidemocratic, unionized, and corporatist. The frequent publication of *L'Insurgé*, its rhythms, its irony, its violence, would make it the attack dog of *Combat*, the public face intended to spread its national-syndicalist ideas among the masses. The contributors were often the same, but the weekly paper, being closer to events, was able to give space to the muscular vivacity of a commentary that was passionate, immediate, off the cuff. The links between *L'Insurgé* and La Cagoule, a terrorist organization run by Eugène Deloncle, were weak but nevertheless real. Lemaigre-Dubreuil belonged to both, and the paper's editorial team occupied the former offices of the revolutionary group in the Rue Caumartin.[2]

Not a week passed without the editors attacking the policies of Blum, that "social-traitor" and soon enough "social-executioner," the servant of capital, purveyor of liquidity to the middle classes, robber of the people, and assassin. Caricatures by Ralph Soupault underlined the journalists' violent language. For instance, Blum was depicted sitting on a pile of coffins, a seven-branched candelabra in his hand, commemorating February 6, 1934, "the day the Popular Front was born." After the events at Clichy on March 16, 1937, when the police killed five workers who were protesting against a meeting of the Croix-de-Feu League, Soupault drew Blum, stiff, evil-looking, nightmarish, his hands dripping with blood (there was also a pool at his feet), his cruel gaze interrogating the reader, and the caption reading: "Who said I don't have any French blood?" "Vulgar anti-Semitism" was playing on the whiff of accusations leveled at an allegedly deicidal people.

The violence of *L'Insurgé* would remain purely verbal. Even so, on several occasions this violence got the publication into hot water with the law. On March 3, a front-page article by Michel Lombard attacked Blum and Thorez, "these two government crooks who have assassins in their charge." The journalists' hatred focused on "the Israelite" and "the Soviets' man," to whom they preferred French fascists and members of the League. The article was preceded by an editorial, which accused "Maurice Thorez's men" of the assassinations of Manuel Marchon, a member of Doriot's Parti Populaire Français, and Maurice Creton, a member of La Rocque's Parti

Social Français. These insults and accusations were accompanied by a threat: "Blum and Thorez will have to pay for the blood that they have caused to be spilled," and also by a call for summary, illegal vengeance: "It will soon be necessary . . . that the French themselves serve justice, given that the government is incapable of doing so."[3] The reaction to this was not long in coming. The next morning, the police searched the paper's premises and seized the remaining copies. The managing editor, Guy Richelet, a young student in Action Française, was charged with being responsible. The main editors, Maulnier, Maxence, Blanchot, Haedens, and Soupault, decided that they would "take responsibility for the article in question in order to accompany [their] colleague in court." This sacrifice was made joyfully; *L'Insurgé* of March 10 bore the headline, "Blum charges us as guilty/Thank you! . . ." with the subtitle reading, "Prison is less ignominious than the Légion d'honneur." The charge for "incitement to violence and murder," which was the cause of such pride for the editors, was dated March 13. Maulnier chose as his attorney a famous jurist, who would also represent Céline: Maître Tixier-Vignancourt. On March 24, the undersecretary of state to the prime minister, Marx Dormoy, had another issue of the paper seized, the one containing the bloody caricature of Blum, but also an article that led to a second charge. However, the affair was slow moving. The government made threats without following them up. The editors grew indignant and renewed their provocations. The six men charged demanded to appear before a magistrate. On June 16, an article by Henri Fallier attacked Vincent Auriol, the finance minister. On June 18, the paper was seized once again and Henri Fallier was charged with "demeaning the nation's reputation." But in actual fact, Henri Fallier was a collective pseudonym, and this time nineteen journalists claimed to have collaborated on the article. For the six main figures, this was the third time they had been charged. Ultimately the affair would lead to nothing except Richelet's appearance in court on September 18, a process in which Dormoy, who by then had become minister of the interior, took only an indirect interest.

Despite becoming relatively disaffected by the time the journal folded, in summer and autumn 1937 Blanchot wrote two articles, one on foreign policy and another on literature, in almost each issue of *L'Insurgé*. The twenty-eight political texts always appeared in the same very prominent place, at the top of the page, divided into two columns and in a separate box, underneath the title "Liberate France." In this collective enterprise of calling for a national revolution, Blanchot was clearly a lieutenant relative to the leaders in charge of the front page, Maxence and Maulnier.[4]

The "Readings of the Insurgent" column, in which thirty-seven articles appeared, was his own. This underlines well enough how strong his position at the paper was. And this strength was matched on the page by strong phrasings and incisive rhetoric able to paint the smallest incident or event in the light of his thinking and its "national-dissident" worldview. These texts formed something like a serialized thriller, in which the narrative logic grows stronger week after week, the same characters coming back to fill out their own roles in a series of adventures. There were few surprises, however: the only things to change were that these characters became more starkly depicted, which led to a certain monotony, despite the esthetic, violent depictions. Blanchot's diplomatic thriller constructed no story, instead repeating for almost six months the same analysis no matter what events took place. This allows us to see that over this relatively short period, his reasoning became both more coherent and more emphatic and, in becoming more emphatic, also became more self-satisfied.

Its first principle was that the carelessness of the democratic era leads to an identity crisis, to lamenting one's own downfall. "For eighteen years France has been debasing itself" (393); "For fifteen years we have done everything possible to try to lose our status as a world power capable of victories" (400); "Fifteen years of ideological foolishness during which a growing number of treaties have cluttered the streets of Geneva like dead leaves" (409); "Is it not the last straw for a great people to be weakened, divided, separated from its destiny?" (408). The weakness, cowardice, and fear present in democracy had split apart the nation's power. They allowed it to agree to everything, to be proud of nothing, to accept even death (Clichy); they allowed for egotistical and short-sighted compromise, immense complacency, hypocritical silence, lack of self-respect, the sickness of keeping up appearances, all that can be called the complex of the moderates (following on from *Combat*, Blanchot was still attacking them). The perversion of democracy lay in its principle of representation. Whatever the precise circumstances of the elections, little by little the government elected superimposed its own image over that of the nation, while each day its weakness progressively sapped the citizen's self-image, alienating the image of a national subject contained within him. How was it still possible to be French, if to be French was to be Republican, if to be French was to be Blum? Blanchot tried to show "the reader the mirror of his shame" (435). Self-hatred became a principle of how dissident ideas should be communicated, however reprehensible it was for Maurras. Blanchot's very first article for *L'Insurgé* argued that the Frenchman's self-image of satisfaction, pride, and everyday victories was in fact an image of vanity, cowardice, and weakness: it provided "an excuse for their passivity and an alibi for their nothingness" (411). The desire for individual well-being (*salut*) was premised on this false construct of the imagination, on this "tragic misunderstanding" (399), thanks to a race to the bottom ("When a nation falls apart, there comes a moment when the national instinct which usually helps it be preserved in fact helps to destroy it," 396). And the desire for individual well-being, or simply the need for it, led those who were lacking any will to power to call on the Other in order to escape from this narcissistic flight from ideals. This Other, representing the worst for Blanchot at the time, appeared in the guise of the foreigner (the Jew, who was said to appropriate capital) and of the communist (who worked for a system which appropriated and denatured revolution). Such were the bases of his redoubled violence, his persistence against Blum, in whom the two figures of the Jew and the communist were united, and who was said to have appropriated the economy, the national revolution, democratic practices. Blanchot argued that Blum was insinuating himself into the heart of the image of French identity, imposing himself as a new ideal of the French self ("France is Blum. Everything that Blum says and does is our responsibility, the dishonor of it weighs upon us," 395). In Blanchot's logic, which had reached this degree of blindness, a purification was necessary, over and against these false identities. Vilifying Blum allowed a reappropriation to take place: an authentification, a disalienation, even an exorcism. "In each of us there is an accomplice of Blum's treason, and horrible though this might be, a second Blum and a second Viénot" (397).⁵

The anti-Semitism attributed to Blanchot is one element among several within this logic of purification. Unlike a number of his close associates, he would never make it the direct object of his reflections. It is a theme that arises only at certain points, as a rhetorical tool allowing for eloquent oratory and for various insidious touches, and so a rhetorical tool that had in that sense come to appear common or banal (and this in itself is a terrifying fact). In terms of clear-cut statements, the instances of anti-Semitism that can be imputed to Blanchot in *L'Insurgé* come to a total of two: "[Blum] represents exactly what is most deserving of scorn for the nation he is addressing, a backward ideology, an old man's mentality, a foreign race" (399–400); Blum is labeled a *métèque*, a suspect foreigner, with his main characteristics being "cosmopolitan instincts, an unvirile temperament, a taste for flimsy rhetoric" (435).⁶ Anti-Semitism featured in this discourse only as an exhibit in the cause of supposed eloquence. It was an easy way of attacking Blum, a conscious and controlled slip, one that was rarely used, and it could not conceal the confusion and embarrassment that this friend of Emmanuel Levinas, Paul Lévy, and Georges Mandel had to confront when faced with his own internal contradictions, in this far-right milieu from which he was soon to dissociate himself.

Much more than the Jew, the figure of the Russian was the object of all Blanchot's obsessions. Most of the texts in *L'Insurgé*, like those of his previous journals and newspapers, attack "Soviet rottenness" (457). Communism was said to be governing France, now a "Bolshevized nation" (439). The government was obeying Moscow's orders, pushing the country toward war, "a war that would not be our own" (396). The treaty subjugated both France and the League of Nations to communism: "it is in Geneva that pacifism and internationalism best serve Soviet designs" (452). At this time, anticommunism blinded Blanchot so much that it took precedence over his refusal of fascism and Nazism, which was expressed much less radically than four years previously for *Le Rempart*.

While Blanchot believed that "for our country, Germanism represents the greatest danger and Bolshevism only increases this peril," he immediately added that "these distinctions, which proceed from a just political reason, would not have meaning or reach if they did not clash profoundly with the nature of the regime." Indeed, "the regime is such that it cannot do anything against Germany without giving the impression of being influenced by Moscow's agents" (463–464). Blanchot strove to show that Hitler was right in all regards (on the League of Nations, on Bolshevism, on "the right for his people to live"), but for the wrong reasons ("his plans for domination"). The more he represented reason, the less likely France would be to believe him and the more dangerous he would become ("it is because today Germanism has won out against France that France has never been more threatened by Germanism"). Being vigilant regarding Hitler demanded a sane national reaction. "France can still save itself, not by superficially moving closer to Germany, but by profoundly moving closer to itself" (401–404). The military and diplomatic strategy that Blanchot drew from this was nonetheless a shocking one. The Spanish civil war was in full flow, and he believed that there had to be no hesitation in opposing the Spanish rebels, in order not to "get drawn in to Hitler and Franco's game" (398). It was necessary to refuse all "blackmailing of opposition to Hitler" (454). And this led Blanchot to underplay Germany's attacks. In truth, he always saw communism as the worst enemy. Instead of using the necessity of opposing Hitler as a way of blackmailing people into supporting the Spanish Republicans, Blanchot attempted blackmail based on an anticommunism that was not afraid to pull at the heartstrings in its speechifying: "Therefore let the French be warned: against their security, against the security of their children, and against peace, the most formidable and the most criminal of plots is being planned" (454). The disaster, the tragic situation, seemed close to him: signing a treaty with the Soviets had led France into a "dead end," that of submission to one or the other version of state totalitarianism.

Blanchot's impossible diplomacy gave at once provisional and strategic expression to his paradoxical patriotism, which accepted that it was necessary to recognize the present decline.

> It is certainly hard to suddenly lose pride in being French and to build patriotism not on the awareness of a glorious past and the feeling of contemporary grandeur, but on the feeling of shame and debasement. But it would be harder still to give oneself, via a dishonest admiration of oneself and amidst universal derision, supreme reasons to have disdain for oneself when the moment of final disaster comes. (394)

> In a time when patriots are named Thorez and Blum, we are proud to be anti-patriots ready to recognize our country only when they have made it once more worthy of its past, equal to its glory, and, so many years after the armistice, victorious at last. (429)

While Maurras would accuse Blanchot of antipatriotism, it was in fact a paradoxical antipatriotism, a superpatriotism, patriotism pushed to its breaking point, which explains the maniacal intransigence of his proposals on diplomacy (as well as their rapid collapse into utter silence). "In order to fight Germany, we must support Franco" (465). The logic of paradox was pushed to its absurd breaking point. He wrote of "intervening with as much strength as possible in Franco's favor, supporting him all the more given that he is also supported by Germany, fighting Germany not by fighting Franco, but by fighting for France and by making his victory not the victory of Germany, but the victory of France" (466). Trying to play Hitler's high-stakes game was not the best solution at such a time.

Here Blanchot was addressing "true French revolutionaries." He called for a national-revolutionary diplomacy that was still undefined and was powerless to adopt a position in relation to any particular ideology, whether this be democracy or communism, both of which had broken apart "France as it was, as it no longer is," or whether it be fascism or antifascism, "meaningless entities."[7] He believed that national-revolutionary diplomacy had to intervene in the space between this disaffected glorious identity and this lack of meaning. And there was nothing more to it. This strategically dubious engagement quickly led his aggressive, repeated laments over spiritual and national disintegration into a dead-end.

July 14, 1937, was the first time that the column "Liberate France" did not bear Blanchot's signature.[8] He would not write it again. In October, he would also suspend his literary column. Only one exception—albeit a major one—would be made to this detachment: on October 27, he returned on the final page of the final issue with an article, in its own separate box, arguing for a "revolutionary diplomacy."

This final issue, which had only six pages, was concerned with justifying the decision to stop publishing, "as part of an effort to refine and broaden our actions." Yet precisely the opposite came about. The editors only put forward political and strategic beliefs in order to mask the real reasons for the closure, which were financial and personal. The newspaper was in good health, with two thousand subscribers and twenty thousand loyal readers, but Lemaigre-Dubreuil had withdrawn his funding, finding the paper too anticapitalist. The collective of *L'Insurgé*, writing a front-page article, declared its intention to return to the original ideological line: that of an anti-Marxist, pacifist, and above all antidemocratic and anticapitalist nationalism, perhaps as a final defiance of its funder. It would therefore entertain no affiliation with any political party, whether closely or at a distance; nonetheless, since August its regular attacks on La Rocque had easily allowed its position to be understood. In a context of the breakup of both parties and leagues, of activists feeling let down (both by how the country was changing and by the decisions of their leaders), it was necessary to work toward broadening one's actions. This was to be done "in relation to the tasks that our actions must fulfill"; but we must instead underline how demotivated Blanchot, perhaps Fabrègues, and certainly Maulnier were. The latter had never had more than a limited interest in *L'Insurgé*, given that his salary was paid by Action Française and his ambition was dedicated to *Combat* and to his books. In July, Maulnier had written to Maurras: "I have decided to leave [*L'Insurgé*] fairly shortly."[9]

In fact, *L'Insurgé* had always operated contrariwise to its apparent strategy, something it had in common with most of the mouthpieces of Maurrassian dissidence. When questioned by readers at the end of January, Maulnier and Fabrègues had refused to recognize any interdependence between the journal and the new newspaper, even clarifying "that *Combat*, a polemical, documentary, and doctrinal journal, stands to one side of all political activism, and is independent of all groups and all other publications, due to both the wishes of its founders, and the way it is run." This was a clear assertion of their elitism, and of thought's dominance over action in their eyes. In this light, how are we to interpret *L'Insurgé*'s declaration that it was changing direction, if not as the weak version of a rebellious agitprop trying to place itself beyond the reach of its own terror? This is what the most extremist members of the two editorial teams had understood, having already departed for more hard-line publications such as *Je suis partout*. Nothing would come to anything, to any concrete action; paralysis reigned.

The German occupation and the Vichy regime would force these dissidents to abandon this paralysis, and this, which needed time, would lead to further faux pas, to doubt, aimlessness, and complacency—for some, it would lead to periods of silence. Thierry Maulnier's letter of July 1937 to Maurras, already quoted, stated, "I intend to abandon fairly shortly my contributions to *L'Insurgé* and at the same time, all political activities, because those that correspond to my thinking are running into difficulties that I had not properly gauged." We cannot make judgments about disappointment, weariness, or resignation, but we can at least state something that Maulnier did not perceive but that Blanchot would come to know for himself: these "difficulties" did not signal simply a failure [*défaut*] of strategy, but the failing of thought itself.

Did he recognize this at the end of 1937? The suspension of *L'Insurgé* preceded the end of Blanchot's contributions to *Combat* by only two months (he would supply only two more articles, in November and December). He continued working for the *Journal des Débats* and for *Aux Écoutes*, but his clearly defined engagement in the most virulent circles of the far right stopped definitively at this point. The sworn enemy of Brasillach at the heart of these dissident groups, he also distanced himself from Maxence and Maulnier, thus putting an end to any risk of his own positions being conflated with those of fascism, Nazism, or anti-Semitism.[10] This breaking point proved suffocating, much more than it allowed for any breakthroughs. Blanchot's journalistic activities continued, but his thinking would henceforth develop through literature. The few articles of 1938 to 1940 bearing his name looked at Sartre, Nerval, or Lautréamont, and there seem to be good reasons to think that these years were more intensively dedicated to writing *Thomas the Obscure*.

Even at this dead end, even on the cusp of withdrawal, he felt that he owed loyalty to lost fraternity, and the rhetoric of a spirited defense made the task easier. "France, Nation to Come," Blanchot's November 1937 contribution to *Combat*, which opened the issue, took its themes from his final piece for *L'Insurgé*, of October 27, on France as a "nation to be built." They were written concurrently and featured the same arguments, though in different terms. The editors of *Combat* placed Blanchot's piece prominently, thus suggesting that it was the culmination of a mode of thinking, even as this thinking was preparing to plunge into silence.

Blanchot's last text for *Combat*, however, can be read as a farewell.[11] Such a reading clearly draws on the fiction of biography, but it also indicates how much such fictions can tell us about reality, for instance Blanchot's political evolution after the war. The article discusses dissidence, a weapon in the service of purity, but a double-edged sword. This form of "extreme thought," of awareness and reflection in this "reactions factory that parties represent," was also a "momentary good fortune for a revolution in ferment." This revolution was a mode of opportunism, an aborting of action, a paradoxical mode of belonging, a catastrophic postponing of any break from ideological submission. How can a call such as that of the article's title be made, then, namely the call for dissidents to exist? We must recognize dissidence as "the demand that can lead one to oppose all parties." This attitude recalls to some extent 1933's demand for refusal, which would return in 1958—against De Gaulle who, precisely, was attempting to adopt a position above party politics. But for Blanchot "to oppose all parties" was neither to "declare oneself above all parties" nor "to take up once more the vulgar watchword: neither left nor right." This clearly signifies his resistance to French fascism (the watchword was that of Valois in 1926). Instead, to do so was a utopian demand, and most of all a demand for thought that Blanchot would make his own for the rest of his life, whether at this stage, by ceasing his activities at *Combat* (although we can have serious doubts about this) or a few years later (fulfilling, perhaps without realizing it, the rule that he set out in the final lines of this call for dissidence: "the true form of dissidence is one that abandons a position without ceasing to retain the same hostility for the opposing position, or even abandons its position in order to accentuate this hostility"). Perhaps Blanchot was a dissident among dissidents, retaining for a while his various aversions to democracy, parliamentarianism, capitalism, and communism. Perhaps he was already abandoning nationalism, having criticized the nation too much, and thus illustrating the law of dissidence that he had just formulated: "The true dissident nationalist is someone who foregoes the traditional formulae of nationalism, not in order to move toward internationalism, but in order to combat internationalism in all its forms, among which feature economics and the nation itself." The latter two entities would later become the frequent object of his critiques. The anti-internationalist and antinationalist nationalist, the anticapitalist and anticommunist communist: Such were the types of dissident to whom Blanchot was appealing in December 1937. The factors that would establish the revolutionary demand for movement and for friendship in the 1960s could serve, at this stage, only as a way of thinking clearly about a personal dead end. This inertia was also the beginning of withdrawal, the crisis that would set his thinking to work.

CHAPTER 14

These Events Happened to Me in 1937
Death Sentences (1937–1938)

On June 26, 1937, Maurice Blanchot, editor-in-chief of *Aux Écoutes*, paid tribute to the journal's secretary, Claude Séverac, who had just passed away.[1] The previous week, Paul Lévy had also paid his respects.

A text in *Aux Écoutes* bearing Blanchot's name is sufficiently rare to slip under the radar. The article in question was exceptionally warm. It began in friendly terms, declaring that he would miss the late woman's attentiveness, charm, and simplicity. "In Claude Séverac there was a mysterious sensibility that was in intimate and violent agreement with every human thing, and even more in agreement with the secret life of the world, a rare proof of extreme generosity." The portrait resembled, to a surprising degree, Blanchot's later descriptions of characters. Of fragile health, like them, Claude Séverac had demonstrated courage, dignity, and great strength of character in her struggle against the fatal illness that struck her down.

> Sometimes, when her condition—which she struggled against with astonishing willpower—allowed her a premonition of her unjust fate, she would become regretful for the oeuvre she could have accomplished and which she sacrificed to the tasks of her day job. But these

regrets only lasted an instant. These tasks, due to the value imbued by her devotion, ultimately seemed to her to be most deserving of her efforts.

A year later, on June 11, 1938, Blanchot would once again pay homage to his late friend, in the form of two short texts, one written as editor-in-chief and on behalf of all contributors to the journal, and the other more personal.

The first, which consisted in around thirty lines bearing the signature M.B., gave a foretaste of his future thinking on community:

> [Claude Séverac] is present not only in what she did, but in what they are doing. She was on the margins of the venture and part of that venture too. She introduced into the loud noise of our common efforts a large degree of silence. . . . She who was anxiety itself established a higher zone of certainty and calm.

Blanchot finished with these words: "This year spent without her has been a year of work in which she has shared and which she has led." The community of work and of friendship thus appeared first as part of the editor's role at *Aux Écoutes*.

The few lines of the personal homage did not appear in isolation; several other contributors also provided texts. Yet Blanchot's tone was much more intimate, and he spoke of the novelistic mystery of this character:

> It is impossible to know whether those with whom she shared every working hour have not irreparably misunderstood this hidden person. And this uncertainty, for some of those who knew her, but do not know whether they knew her, adds to her absence, which is a deeper absence and the very image of regret.

This public expression of mourning bore witness to a developed sensibility, one of infinite concern, whose authority would be clear when thirty years later it led to a book (and almost a genre): *Friendship*. Nothing allows us to see Claude Séverac's death as wholly irreparable for Blanchot. However, the regretful tone and the insistency of his homages, in addition to several troubling coincidences between his biography and his novels, give us cause to wonder about several real traces. These traces shine a little more brightly than others among all the tales of encounters with death that would mark, even in his flesh, the person who was no longer entirely a journalist and not yet entirely an author. The death of Claude Séverac, in summer 1937, coincided with Blanchot's first withdrawal from politics.

Her dignity would be shared by the dying woman J., in *Death Sentence*, and by Claudia in the three-person drama of *When the Time Comes*.

We shall largely avoid inferring from Blanchot's fictions precise events that enhance the narrative of his life. *Death Sentence*, however, repeatedly grabs our attention. A short, retrospective narrative published in 1948, it has all the features of an autobiography, except that it does not allow us to collapse the distinction between the narrator and the author. An astonishing amount of narrative information is present, at times making it almost a realist novel: The narrator, like Blanchot, is a Parisian foreign-affairs journalist with considerable responsibilities who later becomes a novelist in fragile health who confronts the experiences of death in the most extreme ways. These tempting parallels, however, do not usually allow the reader to progress, given that the author's whole life remains concealed. There is an intensity to his ordeals with women and with death, coming and going and always in a state of violence and fright; there are obsessions that return again and again, whether as central scenes or marginal episodes, in other *récits*; there is a way of relating events that foreshadows the allusive, stripped-down quality of *The Madness of the Day* (the first narrative published after *Death Sentence*, only a year later, in a journal that was more confidential, less exposed, and allowed discretion to be maintained). All of this represents a cunning way of muddying the waters even while also referring to facts, of recounting things precisely and concisely, even while sheltering behind the fictional status and the theory of authorial effacement, the latter distancing the reader from the idea that such a writer could be speaking about himself. Today, everything suggests that the *récit* revolves around the author as a person, though nothing allows it to be proven, with the narrative incessantly wandering between autobiographical suggestion, more or less in novel form, more or less close to autofiction, and an autonomous and sovereign construction of the imagination.

When in 1994 Blanchot would publish *The Instant of My Death*, its title's mention of the first person and our previous knowledge of some of the events recounted allow us to identify the narrator and to authenticate the *récit*, thus producing a broad consensus that it is autobiographical. However—as we shall see—the way in which certain facts and dates are altered demands greater vigilance. Blanchot's *récits* are never more cunning than when they openly draw near to the author's life. In a similar but inverse way, the first lines of *Death Sentence* provoke the reader to a large extent. "These events happened to me in 1938": Such a beginning raises all sorts of temptations. It suggests doubt even as it creates a semblance of certainty, but if our mistrust is valid, it is not for the reasons we imagine. Nothing is less certain than these events having taken place in 1938. When Blanchot has the narrator add: "I will write freely, since I am sure that this story concerns only myself," this freedom concerns first of all the dating of the *récit* and therefore makes an even greater intervention in the question of autobiography. Simply checking the calendar allows us to realize that Wednesday, October 13, the date the narrator presents as the only certain one, did not occur in 1938 but ... in 1937.[2]

It is of some interest to hypothesize that Blanchot really experienced in September and October 1937 the events related in the first part of *Death Sentence*. It is a fruitful hypothesis. Indeed, it will be remembered that after Claude Séverac's death, Blanchot suspended his political column in *L'Insurgé* in July, gave up his literary column at the end of September, and would only start writing articles for *Combat* again in November. We also know that around the end of the 1930s, tuberculosis forced him to take a long sojourn in the southwest of France, in the sanatorium at Cambo-les-Bains near the Spanish border, around 9.3 miles (15 km) from Bayonne. Was Blanchot there in the summer of 1937, and more precisely in September, so that in the fiction Arcachon would stand in for Cambo? Or was he really convalescing in Arcachon in September, as the *récit* states? The number of coincidences is troubling enough for us to be able to imagine things as follows: It is there that he receives word that his friend is dying. He does not return to Paris immediately, in order "not to interrupt [her] repose." But the sense of guilt created by his absence becomes unbearable: "Today I am trying in vain to understand why I stayed away from Paris then, when everything was calling me back." He returns on "a Monday evening" (this would have been October 11). J. is pronounced dead that night. After the miraculous event that brings her back to life, she dies on Wednesday, October 13.

However unjustified the hypothetical narrative we have just outlined, it nonetheless allows us to understand, like a myth might do, some of Blanchot's profound changes—even if they were spread out over a longer period—at the end of the 1930s.

1. First of all, there is the withdrawal from politics. After the final three articles for *L'Insurgé* and *Combat* (which can almost be considered as two articles, as we have seen), Blanchot did not put his name to any political text among the circles of the far right. Although he continued to write for the *Journal des Débats* and for *Aux Écoutes*, he henceforth refused to take intellectual or personal responsibility for signed articles on the country's foreign policy. Such a gesture of withdrawal is depicted in *Death Sentence*, when the narrator twice refuses, the same day, to respond to urgent demands

from his newspaper. This is the reason why there is no stance taken by Blanchot on the *Anschluss*, the Sudetenland, or on the general atmosphere of growing danger. We can debate over which factor was ultimately decisive: the proximity of the Spanish border to Cambo, the ever-shrinking margin for diplomatic maneuver, the profascist and anti-Semitic radicalization of certain journalist colleagues, or the personal upheaval provoked by his recent experiences. But over and above all of this, it remains the case that Blanchot would henceforth constrain himself to withdrawal. Events "were becoming more serious: living and thinking no longer went hand in hand."[3]

2. Then there is the plunge into personal matters. At this time, Blanchot's life was sufficiently marked by illness for him to be tempted to transfer this experience into writing (let us also recall the literature he loved: Kafka, Mann, Proust). Tuberculosis would discreetly invade his *récits*.[4] In *Death Sentence*, J. herself suffers from choking and coughing; and in the same way that Thomas sometimes becomes Anne, can J. not also become *Je*, the author, the subject? This hypothesis is made less impossible by another secret avowal by Blanchot contained in the *récit*: that he had almost met his own death, almost received his own *death sentence*. The event experienced as he was taking his baccalaureate—the mistaken diagnosis, the surgery, the damage to his blood—is thus related here. "My blood became 'atomic' *avant la lettre*, which meant that it became as unstable as if it had been exposed to radiation. I rapidly lost three-quarters of my white blood cells and became frighteningly ill." After "two days of a peculiar struggle" against imminent death, the narrator-author is saved; but he still has "enigmatic blood, so unstable that it confounds all analyses."[5]

3. There is also the decisive withdrawal into writing. It was probably at this time that the author, being both detached from political narratives and plunged into an abyss of personal matters, found a form for *Thomas the Obscure*, in which novelistic notions (*le romanesque*) play the role adopted by myth in the first two narratives, written two or three years earlier, *The Idyll* and *The Last Word*. We can understand how Blanchot began writing narratives of aimlessness and metamorphosis, in which the figures of incredulity and resurrection are important, in which there are multiple scenes depicting death throes, especially for the strangely similar female characters, in which death rattles—that intimate external expression of death—provide the form of a being-for-others (*pour-autrui*) that cannot be assimilated, a terrifying version of the *there is*. Blanchot would say it again in *The Madness of the Day*, placing these deaths before the war chronologically: "I have loved people, I have lost them. I went mad when that blow struck me,

because it is hell. But there was no witness to my madness, my frenzy was not evident; only my innermost being was mad."[6] Writing, narrative split between autobiography and fiction, would be this impossible witness of terminal illness, of death, and of mourning; in it autobiography would be the nighttime of fiction, in the very image of its author. (Blanchot indeed continued: "People said to me, 'Why are you so calm?' And yet, I was burning from head to foot; at night I would run through the streets and howl; during the day I would work calmly.")

4. The final change concerns the historicity of lived experience. Once again, Blanchot would give a historical dimension to his personal narrative. Mixing the individual narrative of 1937 and the historical narrative of 1938 allowed personal and collective history to be brought together (a similar transaction would take place, as we shall see, in *The Instant of My Death*). Death personally experienced would be inscribed as if sacrificially in the death of History (the Munich Agreement). A narrative such as *Death Sentence* attempts to explore unhappy consciousness, unhappy owing to the impossibility of dying to which such a civilization condemns one; it thus uncovers or discovers death as never before. Retrospectively and symbolically, the complex late 1930s mixed together for Blanchot political renunciation and personal depression, setting in around his thirtieth birthday. If the events of the narrative are reconstructed chronologically, September 22 is the date on which J. signs the form indemnifying the doctor in case of an accident. She signs her own death sentence; it was also the date of a historical collapse (the meeting of Chamberlain and Hitler in Godesberg on September 22 made the Munich agreement of September 29 inevitable).

For further reasons still, to mix Munich together with Cambo and Paris was to make public some trace of a private narrative. For Germany had married into the family, something that cannot have been without its tensions. On February 22, 1938, René Blanchot married Anna Emilie Elisabeth Wolf at the prestigious town hall of the fifth *arrondissement* in Paris. From a very rich family, Anna Wolf had fled Nazi Germany several years previously. Until her death she would remain very close to Maurice Blanchot.

CHAPTER 15

On the Transformation of Convictions
A Journalist of the Far Right (1930s)

As a lead editor of the *Journal des Débats* and *Aux Écoutes*, a writer of editorials specializing in foreign policy, someone with nationalist ideals, a staunch spiritualist, in the 1930s Maurice Blanchot seems to have had a single goal: restoring the glory of French culture, which in his eyes had grown corrupt, had perhaps even disappeared. He joined the young dissident milieus of the Maurrassian far right, becoming one of its most prominent and influential members. Having initially been motivated by Catholic, traditionalist reasons directly related to his family upbringing, he adopted positions that were more and more radical, privileging antidemocratic, antiparliamentary, and anticapitalist rhetoric, occasionally of limitless violence, under the tutelage and influence of Thierry Maulnier. But he was also the friend of Emmanuel Levinas, and he lived in close relation to nationalist Jews like Paul Lévy. He shared their struggle against the resistible rise of Hitler, denouncing at a very early stage the first work camps, state totalitarianism, anti-intellectualism, warlike morality, and the mythology of organic community, all of which were prevailing across the Rhine. He quickly grasped Hitler's threat to the Europe of nations, but his fervent anticommunism forced him to adopt strategically dubious and even—as he would later recognize—irresponsible positions in diplomatic and military terms. He sought out all ways of preserving peace and deplored the successive climb-downs by international organizations and national governments, inviting a humanity "always driven by the candid and boastful nobility of a better future" not to forget "the laws governing its difficult condition."[1] Over the years, the increasing speed and pressure of events exploded the fragile cohesion of activism on the far right. This made Blanchot choose between the two groups that he frequented. He refused to spend further time in the company of certain anti-Semitic, fascist, radicalized, and protocollaborationist circles, such as those of Brasillach and Rebatet, and even distanced himself from Maxence and Maulnier.[2]

The recent history of pan-Germanism had led to the emergence of Germanophobia, but Blanchot did not hate French identity, even in its fragmented state, enough to go over to the enemy; admiration for the nobility of thought, and the inner exile of writing in its confrontation with death, remained the object of his deepest desires. The volatility of his journalism perhaps stemmed from the fact that unity was impossible, something he might have become aware of at the end of the 1930s, at a time when personally dramatic events came to represent something like a way of experiencing the irreparable march of history. The abandonment of false alliances, which had become so common in a decade excelling in blindness, bore a paradoxical mark: He stopped producing signed articles. These would have committed Blanchot's name too far—except in one case when it was necessary to protect the all too easily decipherable name of a friend, who would otherwise have been threatened with death (in 1940, with the onset of German occupation, Blanchot managed Paul Lévy's newspaper).

Striving for recognition, occasionally deluded by its own contradictions, separating its ideas the better to relate them to the precise place and time in which they were expressed, the narrative in which he was engaged forbid itself any theoretical evolution. A rhetoric of imitation held sway, as he first adopted then rejected borrowed ideologies, all in the absence of a published book—an absence that further confirmed the vanity of the past. Blanchot would not attribute the value of real thought to the ideas he expressed journalistically during the 1930s. He did not gather them, reflect upon them, or prolong them in a book. Unlike his father figures (Barrès, Massis, Maurras) or brother figures (Fabrègues, Maxence, Maulnier—who from 1932 to 1939 published ten works), he therefore did not lay claim to any theoretical authority in this period. This does not remove the slightest degree of responsibility, but it does make possible the emergence of a wholly other, conflicting movement of thought.[3]

This failing of thought (*défaut de pensée*) led him close to "the capital error," anti-Semitism, the memory of which would later cause Blanchot to declare that imperative weighing on all thought was to "think and act in such a way that Auschwitz may never be repeated."[4] This is our invitation to consider what made possible such a "transformation of convictions," such an evolution for this man, such a future for this body of work.[5] It is an invitation to question what his early writings drew on: inherited convictions, ideological parasitism, or stubborn strategy? We must also question the status of this speech, between the usual overemphasis of the press and publishing prewar, the pamphlet tradition and the common themes of far-right rhetoric, and the singular eloquence of a never-failing rhythm and confidence.[6] Caught up with all these considerations are one man's ethical and political choices, the responsibility for his public interventions, for his commitments and "unreasoned attractions," as well as the conditions that made it possible for him to flee from this original moment, thus marking the beginning of his *thought*.[7] The way in which writing—let us already say: the space of literature—would *set aside* such a subject tells us a great deal about the very different depth and kinds of companionship it imposes (a companionship bound to the private and historical workings of death). Little by little, this thinking of writing will become the subject's true site of recognition. Of course, this took place over and against the contradictory, past and passing, adherence to a community that subjugated all ideals to purity of blood, to the rules of order, to the great work of death—*and of fear*. But above all it was under the sign of infinite responsibility for the other (the wholly other) that "the acts of the day" and the "the pure (nocturnal) product of doing nothing" would henceforth, via "the twists and turns of a very long journey," become manifest.[8]

CHAPTER 16

From Revolution to Literature
Literary Criticism (1930s)

Blanchot's criticism in the 1930s is a criticism of ideas, books of ideas, and above all books of ideas from his milieu. It is also a criticism of literary works, for the most part novels (there is not a single article on poetry or theater). It rarely moves beyond these forms—as if literature or the written word counted above all.

Within Maurras's sphere of influence, or for those dissenting from him, the main critics of the time were Bellessort, Rousseaux, Brasillach, Maulnier, Vincent, Haedens, and Claude Roy. For a certain period Arland's signature appeared alongside theirs, for *Réaction*. Blanchot was far from the most prominent among them. His critical texts are few; most often, they are reading notes that remain largely undeveloped. However, in 1937 Maulnier asked him to write the *Readings of the Insurgent* column, something that demonstrates his intense respect for Blanchot.[1] This was perhaps a decisive experience: being constrained to producing criticism at a quick, coherent, weekly rhythm, with each article Blanchot develops his penetrating and insistent analyses, taking as his pretexts varying publications in order to develop his exacting research. The *Insurgé* column comes to reflect the creative preoccupations of the secret novelist. As the months went by, the texts become more profound, the choices more decisive. Several theoretical notions are sketched out: the abolition of the author, the function of myth, the work's relation to time. Perhaps we ought to see this search for critical thinking as a turning point. For literature seems to become Blanchot's main concern from 1938 onward. That is when the literary pages of *Aux Écoutes* became longer, more diverse, and over a period of two years, the editor-in-chief arranged to have contributions from Arland, Haedens, Jaloux, Maulnier, Maxence, and Pelorson. It was probably Blanchot himself who, in an unsigned article of November 12, 1938, penned a vibrant homage to Henri Mondor, whose biography of Mallarmé he would analyze a few years later, and with whom he would establish contact.

This critical discourse, however, gained recognition only in the spheres Blanchot moved in. It is unlikely that many bought *L'Insurgé* for its literary column alone, unlike the *Journal des Débats* in the 1940s or the *Nouvelle Revue Française* in the 1950s and 1960s. Much later, Claude Roy stated, "Maurice Blanchot used to write enigmatic, fascinating, and suggestive texts on Maurras and Kafka, as well as obscure, elaborate narratives" (this memory is debatable, because Blanchot had written no text on Kafka at that point; and the two writers do not seem to have been so friendly that Blanchot would have shown Roy any prepublication texts).[2] Pierre Monnier seems to be more credible in conceding that "his 42 installments of literary criticism were a stimulant for me, a drug." "Between January and October 1937 he weighed up, dissected and judged everything in a way that seemed original and invigorating, with a mixture of seriousness and ease that left me breathless with admiration."[3]

Where would Blanchot therefore fit in on the critical scene of the far right? Where would his judgments, tastes, and preferences take him? Maurras's authoritarian intransigence was well known, having led him to censure Baudelaire, Rimbaud, Gide, Proust (authors nonetheless respected by Daudet), to admire the classics and detest the romantics. He preferred starchy, pompous writers to those of the avant-garde, and he even avoided discussing foreign works. Brasillach, who wrote the "literary chat" column for *L'Action Française* from 1931 to 1939, broadly followed these trends. He was lethal in his views of Gide and Flaubert, censured Céline's *Death on the Installment Plan* but praised *Bagatelles for a Massacre*. He took a reserved view of Morand, a slightly more critical one of Chardonne, and was violently opposed to Drieu. He liked Aymé, Claudel, Colette, Alain-Fournier, Giraudoux, and Pirandello. He was less favorable toward those he was supposed to favor: Barrès, Péguy, Bourget and, closer to home, Bainville,

Maurras, Daudet. He admired the fascist writer in Corneille, and the "great dramatic poet" in Mussolini. He thought *The Magic Mountain* was full of "endless chatter." Claude Roy, at *Je Suis Partout*, was interested in Nerval, Kipling, Supervielle, Giraudoux, Anouilh, La Tour du Pin, and Margaret Mitchell. Overall, there was criticism of the tendencies for psychologism, misplaced introspection, pronounced individualism, the perverse demonstration of mental or sexual intimacy, the affirmation of pleasure, the search for vivid description, for the exotic or the monstrous, and surreal delirium (surrealism was an antimaterialism, a critique of decadence that had gone astray). It was underlined that the only surreality deserving of any attention or grandeur was that of spirituality.

We do not need to point out that these judgments rely on blind spots, prejudices, constraints, and prohibitions; this is often the case with their form, which alternates between scholarly and irreverent. We do not need to dwell at length on the conception of literature and of literary criticism that they presuppose. They merely show the limitations Maurice Blanchot's criticism had to overcome and the milieu it was initially confronted with.

It seems highly probable that Blanchot, whose university education had been primarily in philosophy, should initially have adopted the literary references of his milieu. He would confirm this: "I remember (it is only a memory and perhaps false) that I was astonishingly cut off from the literature of the time and knew about nothing except so-called classical literature, with nevertheless some inkling of Valéry, Goethe, and Jean-Paul."[4] A false memory? We have our doubts about this. The classical literature would probably have been down to his symbolic father, Maurras, and his inflexible tradition. Goethe and Jean-Paul would have been due to his study of German literature at Strasbourg. Valéry and Goethe would be quoted in the columns for *L'Insurgé*. We can add Barrès to their number: this was the era when it was only really the Surrealists who did not admire him. When he would think back to the authors of his youth, in "After the Fact" or "Intellectuals under Scrutiny," Blanchot would often mention Barrès and Valéry, the first in terms of lucid intransigence, the second of sympathetic disagreement.[5]

Blanchot's criticism, in the 1930s, is a criticism of judgment. It can take the form of warm, affective homages, or of coldly disparaging sarcasm (but still less so in *L'Insurgé*, even if the first installment of the column closed by formulating the desire to "judge").[6] We also see Blanchot celebrating "Maurras's genius" and the Platonic power of his dialectic,[7] the "exemplary style" of Daudet, "which glides easily and with unparalleled variety and movement";[8] he placed similar store by the works of Massis, Maxence, and even Drieu, with whom he had begun corresponding.[9] A third of the articles in *L'Insurgé* are dedicated to writers clearly situated on the right, and half of the total take on a political bent if we add the often devastating—as if on principle—critiques of communist authors. The references to Francis, Brasillach, and Haedens are full of praise. Blanchot is not without admiration for Arland and even Alain, whose soul he declares superior to his thought;[10] there is also admiration for Mauriac, Jouhandeau, and Maeterlinck ("a marvelous music that proceeds, beyond grace, to Being," "a demanding philosophy that takes us to the outer edges of the mind").[11] There is nothing, not a single text on the classical culture so dear to Maurras or Maulnier—except, for almost political reasons, for a vigorous defense of "French culture," taking issue with the views "of a German" (Curtius).[12] The present day is what preoccupies him, to the point of paying great attention to texts that we might view as insignificant.[13]

He agrees with André Rousseaux who sees in Cocteau an "intelligence which usurps the role of the mind."[14] Gide is said to have "perverse aesthetics";[15] for him, as for Rilke or Dostoevsky, "anxiety alone gives our lives a meaning," something that Blanchot underlines with irony. Anxiety and "the dissociation of the self" were the "commonplaces of 'young' literature," falling under the malign influence of Freudian psychology:

> Despite its claim to be renewing the study of the human soul, this psychology is still only scraping the surface. Is giving oneself over to literary variations on the topics of schizophrenia or mythomania really the way to look for the underlying meaning, the true movement of the lost soul that is excluded from the real and from itself? In order to address the principles of personality, one needs to have principles—and rational principles—; and in order to understand its profundity, the science of the mystics is indispensable.[16]

Despite the limits of such a judgment and the blindness that is necessarily part of it, despite the dated and starchy terminology, some preoccupations do appear that would remain those of Blanchot's literature, starting with *Thomas the Obscure*, which was being written in this period.

Whether it is due to writing, or experience, or writing as an experience, Blanchot's critical discourse changes palpably over the decade, notably with the columns for *L'Insurgé*. While there is undeniably a real consistency, and while some positions even become more radical in 1937 (for example the condemnation of "the dangerous confusion spread by the acrobat-thinkers of the journal *Esprit*" or the panning of a book by Daniel-

Rops that is said to be "inhabited by doppelgangers of the truth that we recognize and which we are extremely unwilling to accept," a final twist regarding this "unflustered short-term borrower of truth"), a change nonetheless seems to set in, to be at work beneath the surface and to show itself most clearly in the very final columns.[17] The articles are sprinkled with kind or praising references to authors not usually appreciated in his milieu, some of whom had been criticized by Blanchot himself several years previously; the names of Lermontov, Dostoevsky, Poe, Joyce, Nerval, and most of all Mallarmé, thus draw our attention.[18] Rilke was said to be shaking up "some of the most important problems in thought"; "*Joseph and His Brothers* will later count among the most important and significant works of contemporary literature"; "Virginia Woolf's works will one day appear as some of the rarest creations of our time."[19] Blanchot places these clear signals in the first lines of each article, to grab the attention of readers who would probably have been suspicious. Apart from the April text on Thomas Mann's novel and several others on Francophone (Belgian or Swiss) authors, for a long time the columns in *L'Insurgé* only address French writers. Yet four of the final five articles look at foreign writers, albeit often from an aristocratic background or existence (some were already well-known or even universally recognized, for instance Rilke or Huxley); this was not without intellectual and aesthetic risks for the author of the articles, whose stubbornness provided one more reason for conflict or at least tension with the newspaper's editors. It remains significant, symbolically at least, that Blanchot's column should close with a series of articles addressing foreign works, having moved so far from the spirit of the "Mahatma Gandhi" piece with which it began.

A few elements or words filter through from the still-secret novel writer, from the critic to come. The thinking of effacement begins with Roger Martin du Gard, who is celebrated for "an indifference to the solicitations of publicity, an aptitude for ceding only to the injunctions of the art of writing." The final two volumes of the Thibault series had been in circulation for eight years before Blanchot wrote of their author: "His silence has been his best chance to express himself."[20] On the other hand, he denounces the "fairly deep confusion" of Mauriac, the "strange equivocality" that consists in "understanding the destiny of the artist as inseparable from the destiny of the man," in "claiming to see as a single being the man who created the work of art and the man who can be inferred from this work." The distinction is already clearly set out: "Between the creator whose adventures are played out in the depths of his mind and the man who is devoured by anecdotes, there lies an abyss that cannot be crossed. The author becomes tenaciously irreducible to the man." Racine's way of "radically expelling himself from his work" sets up the critical terminology of *Faux pas*. Blanchot even hijacks an expression of Mauriac's to let it be known that between author and work there is something like an . . . "*arrêt de mort*" (death sentence/stopping of death).[21] With reference to Mallarmé, he already discusses the "abolition," "annulation," or "annihilation" of the author.[22]

Above all Blanchot appeals for cultural and historical responsibility, even for militant activism on the part of writers: "In an era when spiritual values are under threat, at the same time as what we value more concretely, the interest in politics demonstrated by intellectuals is an interest in their fate and a reminder that stability and order are basic conditions, without which the finest works of the mind are in vain."[23]

His approach to what, when commentating on a book by Denis de Rougement, he calls the writer's "commitment," is spiritual, cultural, national, and revolutionary.[24] For Blanchot, literature *is* political, from the start. This does not mean that it depends on a party mindset or that it attempts to respond to new internal or external criteria. Literature is political because "in an era when revolution is desirable" its task is to demonstrate an exemplary, magisterial power of refusal. The title of the inaugural piece in *L'Insurgé* underlines the links between revolution and literature (just as the exigency that passes "from anguish to language" would be recalled at the beginning of *Faux pas*). "How can the destiny of art intersect with and perhaps assist the destiny of the man who refuses"—that is the question.

> What is more important is the oppositional strength expressed in the work and which is measured by its power to suppress other works or even to abolish part of ordinary reality, as well as by its power to call for the existence of new works, just as strong or stronger than it, or to affect a higher reality. There is also value in the strength of the resistance with which the author has opposed his work through the freedoms he has refused it, the instincts he has dominated, the rigor with which he has subjugated himself.[25]

Blanchot's articles of the 1930s track these possibilities, these liberties, these conventions—those of the "atmosphere novel," of the realist or allegorical novel, and above all those of the psychological novel—doing so more and more systematically with the *L'Insurgé* columns.[26] This aesthetic vision, which was a constant for right-wing criticism, becomes a demand, a dominant leitmotif, the shrill proof of a thought penetrating only its own depths. Blanchot sets in opposition, on the one hand, reductive character analysis, which he sees as falsely realist (and realism itself is a falsehood), objectively moralizing (objectivity itself being a moralistic idea), always superficial and ultimately sterile; and on the other hand, the necessity of grasping the "depths" of our "obscurity," of "our true abysses." Psychological discourse seems facile to him; it prevents us from "ruining ourselves dangerously within our depths" in this "obscure, incoherent life inhabited by monsters and lethal powers."[27] This language of the abyss and the obscure, not lacking in Baudelairean romanticism, is threaded through the critical texts in *L'Insurgé*. It sketches out the search for a novelistic world that Blanchot calls in turn unreal or imaginary, mythical, or symbolic: loose and outdated notions that he does not really attempt to think through again. This is a world that novelists had approached without ever really entering into. It is a world belonging more to the Blanchot of *Thomas the Obscure* than to the authors studied. Each author therefore serves imperfectly to develop this hesitant, public research, which allows another type, creative and secret, to advance. This leads to the necessarily paradoxical turn taken by many of the pieces in *L'Insurgé*, a turn that sees Blanchot judging works that are able only to approach the obscure, but that succeed by way of their ultimate failures.

Faced with this demand, which he forces himself to recognize more and more often, Blanchot finds its paradoxes at work in the novels of Thomas Mann and Virginia Woolf.[28] He praises *The Waves* as "a fiction from which all psychology is excluded" and whose "sole character," the "absolute character," is Time "in its metaphysical nudity," in its foundational essence ("the time that founds all consciousness," "the time within which history is made"). The dissemination of the characters, their various modes of relating to time, their final, joyous, saving failure in relation to this supreme character who is ultimately death itself, all of this contributes to the loftiness of their existence: "For Mrs. Virginia Woolf, it is a question of expressing not what a person has thought in actuality, but what they must think in order to really exist," in order to "produce a sentiment of authentic existence." Thus "rarely has a work so foreign to the ordinary novel form so closely touched the essence of the novel." In *Joseph and His Brothers* he sees "the novel of Time," "the very novel of Myths," "the festival of Narration," "the novel of the novel." It is also said to be "an investigation into duration" that refuses to see time simply as an "inexhaustible improvisation of events." To question myths in this way is to uncover how beliefs arise, to consent both to the pure and the impure, and to give shape to "what remains most formidable in the most authentic saintliness and what is saintly above all saintliness." All in all, this is "the good fortune of a great personal thinking." This critical discovery also makes up part of the matrix from which *Thomas the Obscure* emerges, as do the encounter with Bataille and the reading of Sade and Lautréamont. The time of myth also announces the time of "the other time." With these influences acting upon him, Blanchot chooses "the novel of the novel": the absolute vigilance of language as a way to approach "the obscure."

The demand of the obscure imperceptibly becomes the revolutionary demand, which refuses to be subjugated to psychology or realism, and sets in chain the characters' forceful journeys to their own limits. Escaping history, the better to return to it; exiting time in order to irrupt into mythic time: the novel can be revolutionary, for instance in regarding and rethinking itself, in thinking about how it is constructed, in becoming "the novel of the novel." It is not a question of technique (Woolf's interior monologue is not the same as that of Settanni), but of sovereignty.[29] In Bernanos Blanchot likes the refusal of servile sentiments (such as those of a Mauriac) and of "horrific abstractions" (those of a Jouhandeau), as well as the fact that these are literary or antiliterary tours de force. His writing is designed to bring literature, via a "sovereign constraint," to expose what Blanchot cites as "the faceless beings without origin to whom all attempts at a *cosmos* relate, and on whom they depend."[30] It is necessary to push toward the extreme, to carry ideas "to their point of extreme tension," not to "fear being carried further than one would like."[31] It is necessary, over and against works whose attempts remain insufficient, to allow there to be "another chance against death," and to "seek out [this chance] through the demand of indefatigable spirit."[32] The mask of spiritualism continues to cover the face of death itself. "The inexpressible" often remains linked to "the question of God."[33] Blanchot is unable to name this "obscure" element except by using the usual terms, those belonging to the spiritual or philosophical language he had inherited: the soul, Being, the profundity of Being. And yet, occasionally he also calls it . . . "the impossible"; for the rule of rules, the golden rule of the refusal most often set up in opposition to realism, psychology, and moralism, is that one must avoid "overdoing the possible."[34]

In 1938, in the only literary-critical text he signed in *Aux Écoutes*, Blanchot praised Sartre's *La nausée* without any political reservations.[35] The language is similar to that employed in the articles on Thomas Mann and Virginia Woolf: wanting to form a myth "with the very source of myths," Sartre "has shown an interest in the fundamental drama"; "he has placed himself close to Being itself." "He takes the novel to a place where there are no more episodes, no more plots, no more individual characters, to this place where the mind survives only by relying on philosophical notions, such as existence and Being." "Nausea is the overwhelming experience that reveals to him what it is to exist without being; this is the pathos-laden illumination which, in the midst of existing things, puts him in contact not with things, but with their existence." Blanchot expresses no reservations, except to say that this attempt is "incomplete" because it retains realist and psychological elements and because it is reticent about the use of symbols; otherwise he praises this "undertaking, which is so rare, so important, so necessary." The demand of literature seems to definitively impose its primacy in the shadow of the *there is* and in underlining the importance of Heidegger (who had recently been translated into French for the first time and on whom the article closes); this thinker who "offers art a new viewpoint from which to contemplate its necessity."

It is a happily troubling fact that we do not have to wait until 1937 or 1938 and the texts on Mann, Woolf or Sartre to find this "new viewpoint," this search for the "true movement of the lost soul which is outside the real and outside itself," in which the sentiment of the disaster and the outside can already be seen at work. Indeed, it appears as early as 1931 in an article by Blanchot on François Mauriac's final novel, *Ce qui était perdu*.[36] Beyond all the obvious reasons, what attracts Blanchot to Mauriac at this time is the sadistic, violent, unwell nighttime into which the characters "with hearts full of mud" are thrown. How can we not find foreshadowings in this commentary of what Blanchot would later call the neuter, of Levinas's *there is*, of what Bataille and Blanchot would impose as the authority of an unnamable "inner experience"?

> Everyone, among these shadows, is confronted with a presence that is obscure, hidden, but sensed *avant la lettre*, against which everyone comes up short. Not everyone will recognize its ineffable power, not everyone is able to name it, but we can hear its terrible crashing against all these mediocre or monstrous souls.

How could we not also glimpse here an obsessive and tormenting biographical echo? Irene's "injured soul," "utterly within night," struggling against death and giving into it when "it can uncover nothing more for us, nor bear witness to this final encounter which carries her, victorious, beyond the shadows"—this is already, in a spiritual, confessional form, Anne's combat in darkness in *Thomas the Obscure*. "Such a community is established despite bodily hatred, despite divergences of sentiment, and it introduces us into regions of the soul that ordinary psychology does not touch": Blanchot always holds psychological discourse, that of his studies, at arm's length, preferring instead an experimental, more literary and philosophical "non-knowledge." Of course, experience is not yet naked enough or, as Bataille would say, sufficiently "free of ties, even that of an origin, to any confession whatsoever."[37] Nonetheless, Blanchot does not hesitate in bearing witness to its intimacy, concluding that these characters "do not remain strange to us, because we are engaged in the same debate, and because they are wholly human, made of the poverty of flesh, with troubled heart in their defeats and their new beginnings, they are fraternal to us *like those who seek through their groans*."

CHAPTER 17

Murderous Omens of Times to Come
Writing the *Récits*: "The Last Word" and "The Idyll" (1935–1936)

The author's opening note in the second version of *Thomas the Obscure* indicates that the book was written between the summer of 1932 and May 1940, whereupon it was sent to Gallimard, probably addressed to Jean Paulhan. Perhaps it is no accident that this period coincides with the tumultuous decade that ran from the economic crisis in France to the debacle of defeat by Germany. Several hypotheses are possible: that in May 1940 Blanchot wanted to save his manuscript, to have it at least recognized, having already written (and perhaps destroyed) a lot without publishing it;[1] that he wanted to save what he would indeed be unable to preserve at the end of the war, when soldiers from the German army took away several manuscripts, having searched the house at Quain; that urgency stemming from the atmosphere of fear led him to move more quickly to hand over the manuscript; or that inversely the impending war actually provided the cover if not of anonymity, then at least of discretion, and thus led to the first appearance of a new countenance—these hypotheses are all likely in their own way. And we can add one more to the list: that following his father's death in 1936, after betrayals by successive governments and the ever-weakening power of diplomacy, after the step forward represented by the publication of his critical research in *L'Insurgé*, after the illness and perhaps the mourning of 1937–38, after a significant reduction in journalistic activity, his work on the novel must have become more intensive and moved toward its conclusion. What's more, Blanchot had spoken of his novel in the preceding years and perhaps allowed sections of it to be read by writers and journalists in his political milieu.[2]

In 1932, Blanchot was twenty-five years old. Whether it was a rational decision, a mystical illumination, or a stepping-up of some unknown previous writing practice, all hypotheses about how he started to write are possible, because none is discussed by him, apart from the mention of the long period over which the novel was prepared. Eight years of apprenticeship and research, marked as we can imagine by doubts and fruitless searches, by joys and disappointments, abandonments and new beginnings, all of which led to the lack of satisfaction that one can imagine by recalling that once the second, drastically shortened, rewritten version was published, he never allowed the first to be reprinted. These eight years also saw Blanchot engaged in a writer's life, which he would not abandon—the only one of his various lives, perhaps, to have that status. These years saw writing engaged in a subterranean task, extending his fidelity to Levinas, to readings that remained secret, the happily accursed share of a journalist still engaged in the name of perfidy, with the absence of shadow, the absence of thought. "*Thomas the Obscure* was never-ending," Blanchot would write in 1983, and "in the search for annihilation (absence) it encountered the impossibility of escaping being (presence)."[3] These were therefore eight years during which he attempted to think—through writing—a fidelity to the unknown, the account that needs to be given of the inexpressible, and ultimately the certainty of having grasped the only demand on being, the real vocation, that which responds to the "primal" call: that of the opening of the sky, that which already and forever takes place *in the name of the other*. They were eight years in which a strange narrative was created, surreal without being surrealist, mythical without edifying myth, poetic without fetishizing words or the spaces between them, loyal to the community of the *there is* without making it the dwelling of concern. There is nothing equivocal here, but there is a desire to listen to what is indistinct and to find an equivalent in words that would respect its silent indifference. Annihilation within words becomes an image of suffocation. The vertigo or collapse whereby the author, character, and plot are effaced are the prose narrative of an ephemeral fate. It took eight years for Blanchot to annihilate himself little by little, annihilating the face that was being presented to the world, maintained in public. It took eight years to give "death another chance."

To rid oneself slightly naïvely of one's youth, which was still naïve (even more so), as Valéry said of his own:

> Youth is a time when conventions are, and must be, ill understood; either blindly rejected or blindly obeyed. It is impossible to conceive, at the beginnings of the reflective life, that only arbitrary decisions enable man to *found* anything at all: languages, societies, knowledge, works of art. As for me, I could so little conceive it, that I made it a rule secretly to see as null or contemptible all opinions and habits of mind that grow out of life in common, out of our external relations with other men, and which disappear in voluntary solitude.[4]

But for Blanchot these eight years are the ones during which he eventually distances himself from this romantic naivety (for which he would long reproach Valéry, tenderly and yet harshly, in that he also aimed this reproach at himself). They are the years during which, insubordinate to himself, he would refuse to turn his mistakes into his destiny (to create a Monsieur Teste), during which he would set himself the task of thinking through conviction and its limitations, its inner shadow, and the annihilation that constantly threatens and accompanies it (as it does the character of Thomas). We can imagine Blanchot thinking he might sink into its abyss. We can also imagine how important readings such as those of Rilke or Kafka were, even if Blanchot as yet remained totally silent regarding the latter. It is difficult to prevent ourselves thinking that all these influences must also have touched Sartre, who also set himself the task, at the same time, of a long journey toward narrative, having begun *Nausea* in 1931 and only completing it in 1938. Theirs were different voices and they had greatly divergent politics, but their concerns for fiction converged. Each writer would comment on the early work of the other, with a mixture of reticence and respect, of fascinating proximity and clear differences.

We also know that the rhythm of these eight years of work was interrupted by the production of two *récits*, "The Last Word" (1935) and "The Idyll" (1936). Perhaps we ought to see these interruptions as a necessary crisis and one that benefitted the work on the novel. Blanchot states as much: "The *récit* ["The Last Word"] was an attempt to short-circuit the other book in progress, in order to overcome the interminable." "It was not a text intended for publication."[5] We shall probably never know anything of the initial form of these two *récits*, which Blanchot would only publish ten years later, in spring 1947, in two different journals and at two months' distance from one another, and which in 1951 he would place together in a book, *Vicious Circles*, and then again in 1983, this time with an additional afterword, "After the Fact," in which he commented on the conditions in which they were created. The only extra piece of information is provided by *La Licorne*, Caillois's journal: the month "The Idyll" was written, July 1936. This information invites us to think that the crisis in the writing of *Thomas the Obscure* was not the only factor explaining why the *récits* were written, and that there was in fact a double motivation at work, a historical and family one. In July 1936, four months after the death of Blanchot's father, his *récit* depicts a wandering character without any family, constantly confronted with authority figures (a hospice director, an old man, an executioner). These are so many figures of substitution: in offering him his daughter in marriage, the old man offers to be the protagonist's new father; according to the protocol for the ceremony that has been arranged, the director will be "like his father"; but ultimately it is the executioner who officiates, since the wedding is replaced by the character's execution. The biographical roots of the *récit* go even deeper than this, however. The old man, the tenderest of substitute fathers, recounts his origins: "I was born in the neighboring *département*, in Samard."[6] Blanchot's father had come to Quain from the neighboring *canton*, specifically from the parish of Devrouze, whose priest for a long time had been the uncle on his father's side, and which was situated a few kilometers from that of *Simard*, to which it was attached. Another link can be found in the name of the character: Alexandre Akim evokes the first name most often used for Blanchot's mother, Alexandrine. His maternal aunt is also present through her first name Elise, who is the Alexandre's fiancée in the *récit*. Last, the difference in age between the director and his wife recalls that between Blanchot's parents; it is even addressed in one of the director's first statements to Akim, evoking both conjugal joy and conflict.[7]

July 1936 was also the date when Blanchot interrupted his contributions to *Combat* for several months, after having written "Terrorism as a Method of Public Safety." This date reminds us of the potential historical and political justifications for the *récits*, not because they receive their legitimacy from politics and history, but because they attempt to frame, align, and sublimate a strategic demand and a supposed political thinking. In so doing they allow us to think about how the certainty of convictions and the search for what was less certain might be related: this too is their *origin*. These *récits* are most often seen as omens: the camps described by "The Idyll," including the incredible detail of the shower rooms into which new detainees are rushed ("we're very concerned about hygiene here," states the director's wife),[8] and the disappearance of the library and the apocalyptic ruin of "The Last Word" today seem charged with premonition.[9] Blanchot was the first to have been at once struck and sickened by this. He would write of "The Idyll" that it was "also prophetic, but for me (today) in a less easily explainable way, since I can only interpret it via events that came afterward and were not known until much later, meaning that this later knowledge does not illuminate the *récit*, but withdraws comprehension from it."[10]

However, nothing is withdrawn, least of all from the historical comprehension of the *récit*, if we recall that in 1933 Blanchot and his fellow contributors were among the first to denounce tirelessly Hitler's regime, the concealment of the work camps, and the violent acts against Jews. What Blanchot denounced in the press, namely the growth of the state and the deprivation of liberty, provided the major themes for the dialogues and narrative conception of "The Idyll."[11] What he could not bear, namely the aura of mystery around collective ceremonies and mass events, gave rise to the descriptions of "The Last Word." He also made allusions to the Soviet camps via the Russian aspect of the names chosen (the first names of the characters of "The Idyll" are those of the Russian tsars: Pierre, Alexandre, and Nicolas Pavlon, whose two names recall the "Iron Tsar" Nicholas Pavlovich, who annexed Poland and suppressed the Hungarian revolution)—this is no surprise when we recall Blanchot's anticommunist positions of 1936. Although these realist considerations never win the day, because they clash with all the aesthetic notions that the articles in *L'Insurgé* would soon set out, they nonetheless act as so many points at which the *récits* touch history, mixing Germanic and Russian references, gathering together the two hated regimes of Nazism and Communism in the same critique of a totalitarian figure. Thus they give cultural signs and national resonances a referential function that, thanks to its extreme clarity, sets in chain the movement of a narrative prose that until then had been lost in the obscure abyss of the secret novel. This public presence (albeit in two *récits* destined to remain private, for the time being) bears witness to this role and to this way of managing novelistic writing, which was still not based on any substantial or consistent thinking. While after the fact Blanchot seemed to suggest that he had foreseen the extermination camps, he did not for one second imagine any systematic link to Jewishness. Jews are addressed only marginally in these texts, not being the objects of any omens or any thinking of the time, whereas Blanchot in his links to the community in question seemed convinced that passive defense was the best strategy. Although among those deported in "The Idyll" figures a certain Isaïe Sirotk, who brings together Judaism (first name) and Trotskyism (an anagram of the surname) and thus reproduces the associations that Blanchot occasionally made in the press, he is more an unpleasant character than a victim. Twice he "attacks," impulsively and violently, a fellow prisoner (first Akim then the strangely Kafkaesque Grégoire), on both occasions accusing the other of spying (we find here the clichés of anti-Semitism, the anti-Jewish judgment of a people of sacrifice and, having almost neurotically become its own opposite, the national-capitalist judgment of a "Jewish plot").

That the *récits* play a role as the still unfulfilled but henceforth possible underside of journalistic rhetoric, as the literary shadow that would end up (almost) totally obscuring this polemicist's frenetic engagements; and that they should momentarily take over in 1935 and 1936—both from the novel that was not managing to give ethical force to obscurity, and from journalism, which was continuing to lose its way through ill-considered eloquence (and all the more so because its views on diplomacy and on revolution were so desperate)—all of this speaks volumes about Blanchot's lack of personal tranquility and about the necessity of a literature allowing him to enter into a different relationship with history—beginning with his own history.[12] The literary imposes itself here, as it distances itself definitively from realism, as a way of giving shape to the political imaginary and to the process of making judgment less blind. Whatever the faults of these first two *récits* (the structural accumulation of mythical episodes in "The Last Word," which limits the text to an enigmatic allegory; and in "The Idyll" the system of symbolic totalization, which overlays it with a kind of dictatorship of meaning), these very faults carry within them the grandeur of the demand being responded to. For example, the mythical structure of "The Last Word," emptied of any divine presence, provides an echo chamber to Kafka's narratives by the imposition of striking theatrical or choreographic figures. They stem from an original perception of the possibilities of writing, and from deadening habits being mercilessly discarded, which leads to all behavior appearing as immediately reversible, spaces being altered in surprising ways, new doors constantly being opened onto what is possible, death being announced in brutally banal ways, or even the appearance of formless, abject, or monstrous presences.

His narrative manner was finding its way. However different they might be from the novels and notably from the *récits* that would follow, "The Idyll" and "The Last Word" lay the groundwork for the later physical apprehension, corporeal breathing, stretches filled with light, and perception of space. Their light without shadow infinitely underlines how violent totalitarian space is. Sun and heat assail the penal workshops in "The Idyll." In "The Last Word," it is invariably the case that "the sun bathes [the esplanade] in a true light," the esplanade where children who have gathered to play on the sand throw stones at a passer-by, "squawking hideously."[13] When the narrator dreams of dying from blindness, "the worst" remains still to come, with the return in inverse form of the childhood "primal scene": "At the back of my sightless eyes the sky that saw everything opened up anew, and the vertigo of steam and tears which obscured them rose to infinity, where it dissipated among light and glory" (52). Space has been obscured to an extreme degree, or illuminated without end, has in either case violently opened out, leaving no space that is not immediately expelled, not shown to be impossible to occupy. The death of this "primal scene" lies as if at the origin of this measureless violence encountered in all public domains, which appears as early as childhood. This violence appears whenever a space is constructed for struggle and power, for illumination and glory. Such illumination is lethal. It kills twice in "The Last Word," with the narrator's body ending up fallen, downfallen, "face to the floor," "face in the dirt." While his work is so often read as being inaccessible to childhood, we can wonder whether Blanchot's narrator will always remain a child, both refusing and not knowing how to refuse what in "After the Fact" he would name the "contentment of the masters" (67). This is already the Sadean question of an idyll that is also an idyll of death, a consenting to loss, a permanent threat of intimate violence, hysterical unleashings and paranoid fear always being present. The attackers can become the attacked, torture can lead to soft pleasure, the powerful can be isolated and smothered, having become the pitiful, humiliated victims of state centralization, the violated cogs of an infernally cruel machine. The violence between the masters (the director of the hospice-camp-prison and his wife) is what is intriguing about "The Idyll," even more than the violence exercised on the detained tramps.

How can space be explored, how can one still move and breathe within it ("breathing something foreign," 16), how can one still remain attentive to equivocal despair and to the unhealthy joys of the other? Answers to these questions are attempted by the "theory," the procession, the advances, the prose of the narrator, of the character Akim, whose viewpoint we adopt. How can one retain one's bearings when the configuration of buildings and streets is constantly changing? How can borders be pushed back when the only maps are town maps, when the only unchanging spaces are the cemetery at the centre and the hospice in the margins (these imperious, devouring margins)? Where can one go when space itself is empty, when there are no more books on the "empty shelves" of the library, when one is the last reader in a library that will disappear when one leaves it? In this public space abolished in favor of an agonizing neutrality, which leaves no exit, Blanchot gives shape to political dead ends, to the absolute closure represented by conviction. The experience of the political, historical world, the experience of the world such as he had forged it for himself, such as he had acquiesced to it—even in refusing it—this experience was one of suffocation. "I have no air, I am choking," says Akim (21). "The smell was becoming suffocating" (23). The pestilential indoor smell invades the outdoors; the hospice invades nature, which is definitively corrupted by this action. "At night, a kind of poison came out of the earth, heavier and more loaded with stench than that of the big swamps" (28). In "The Last Word," an old woman takes the narrator to his house: "When we arrived in front of my house, she opened the door for me, forcing me to follow a long corridor which went down into the earth. Walking into this cellar, I became short of breath and I begged her to take me back outside" (43–44).

Limits are erased in this putrid indistinction of inside and outside, in which no space with breathable air remains. Nothing aligns with anything else: "In my own house, I'm no more than an intruder" (44), a formulation which has its counterpart in the condemnation to exile in "The Idyll," pronounced by Akim when he addresses the new detainees: "You will learn in this house that it is hard to be foreign. You will also learn that it is not easy to cease being so" (25–26). The state is a machine that produces exile (suffocation); the hospice holds on to you if you do not make a good impression, "but if you manage to come to terms with your new surroundings, you will be sent back to your home where, differently disoriented, you will begin a new exile" (26).

Against this threat of suffocation, one can only draw on relation and on language. Over and against the fear of "dying of suffocation," there are the possibilities of "exchanging words," "speaking to someone," "moving beyond one's thoughts" (20). How can communication take place in a world where the tower of Babel has collapsed, and where the meaning of relation and the relation of meaning have been lost? How can one communicate this impossibility itself? "'O city,' I prayed . . . 'soon I will not be able to communicate with you through my language'" (44). How can one communicate in a world where the words *until such time as* and *not* take precedence over the *there is*? Blanchot imagines a world of slogans where totalitarianism ruins even language.

> I walked with [the old woman] from street to street amidst the debris of a celebration signaled by torches in the middle of the day. A tremendous din of shouting, obeying some subterranean order, suddenly seized the crowd, now in the east, now in the west. At certain junctions, the earth trembled and it seemed that the populace was march-

ing over the void, crossing it via a bridge made from its cries of rage. The great consecration of the *until such time as* took place around noon. The chanting of a saying that could transpire through any uproar was suggested through the debris of words, as if the only thing to survive were the shapes of a long sentence that had been trodden underfoot by the crowd. This saying was *until such time as*. (43)

Totalitarianism effaces language. Once she has been seized by the crowd, the old lady speaks "without having to say a word." "Her cries came from a very deep place, they went through my body, and surfaced again at my mouth. I spoke without having to say a word" (44). Totalitarianism leaves one's mouth gaping open, being a form of connective scansion (*scansion qui abouche*), cries that are surprising, arresting, suffocating.

Blanchot wrote "The Last Word" in 1935, a year before Levinas published *On Escape*. And "the last word" is *there is*.[14] Even though it is contaminated by the ravages of the *until such time as*, "the word *there is* was still able to reveal things in this faraway area" (45), at the philosophical hour of dusk. Put differently, the last word is not a word, or is only a word because it draws on reserves of silence.

How can one move toward a greater lightness, such as the one that Thomas discovers? This question can only be asked for the moment, but Thomas does already appear in "The Last Word," as if the book being written were a nod to the completed *récit*. He does so in a "fable" that the narrator, who has momentarily become a teacher, tells to his schoolchildren (47). Thomas is a marginal character who is not included in the roll call and who can be compared to someone under siege who escapes into thin air without knowing what has happened to him; "he can only express what has happened to him by saying: nothing happened" (47). This is therefore the last word. The commentary offered by the teacher could be that of "The Idyll": "no sooner did the inhabitant set foot on free ground than he discovered the walls of his enormous prison all around him" (47).

Thus the dominant figure of Blanchot's fictions is already present in his first two *récits*, albeit marginally, inversely, contrariwise. He is present as a double of the narrator and Akim, an eternal and eternally vulnerable double, who is vulnerable and guilty precisely because he is eternal: "I am vulnerable, because no one can condemn me" (46). Here he is a transparent character, neither a teacher nor God, neither the "All-Powerful" (the master of the Tower) nor the Most High.

"Fear is your only master. If you believe that you no longer fear anything, reading is useless. But it is the lump of fear in your throat that will teach you how to speak," we are taught by the narrator of "The Last Word" (46). Perhaps it is in order to infinitely confront and dispel fear that Blanchot begins writing. Perhaps it is fear that gives him, once again, a way into narrative, and respect for the last word, for reestablishing relation. The dignity that Blanchot assigns to the literary would always find its ultimate source of strength here, even in times of exhaustion or of distress. He would later confirm that for him fear was fear of the city, of communal life, *political* fear with all that it stood for: the oblivion of insomnia, the sleep of refusal, the inattentiveness of the *there is*. The first fragment of several on fear in *The Step Not Beyond* reads thus: "*When he was crossing it, the city constantly whispered within him: I am afraid, be the witness to fear.*"[15] The engagement that the *récits* represent can be seen to mean a witnessing of fear, political fear. This is a fear that the writer carries but does not appropriate, a fear for the inexorable death to come, "the fear for *someone* who does not let anyone approach them and whom death already turns away from our assistance, which they nonetheless request and await."[16] When it takes on this familiar countenance, when it confronts this "death sentence," when it demands a mode of companionship that is without any relationship to the law, that is when fear becomes a weight: we become afraid of fear and it places itself beyond language. The intensity of such a noncathartic fear, experienced at night, is at work in Blanchot's writing as early as *Thomas the Obscure* (as when Thomas accompanies the death of Anne), then relayed without intermediaries, or via intermediaries who are ever more effaced, to a confrontation with narrative that is ever more anonymous and bare.

CHAPTER 18

Night Freely Recircled, Which Plays Us
Thomas the Obscure (1932–1940)

However much we explore the influences on or the imperfections of the first version of *Thomas*, they will not convey the striking quality of this first novel, already so charged and so "Blanchotian." Critics have often pointed out, with more or less justification, the influences of Giraudoux (metaphors that are hyperbolic, twisted, antithetical, contrasting), Kafka (concrete spaces from which all certainty is removed), Thomas Mann (more spaces, in which the ill keep each other company, and the same solitary quest, casting one into the unlikely, the limitless, the mysterious), Proust (a certain conception of set pieces, the sometimes fluctuating, alternating, swaying, always precise rhythm of the phrasing), Bernanos (characters who are clearly divine or satanic, the dissolution of subjectivity, normalization of the unlikely, the nocturnal, abyssal, diabolical experience of doubleness), Bloy, Barbey D'Aurevilly... or even Dostoevsky, Lautréamont (the excessiveness of metamorphosis), and Sade (a certain form of nakedness and of scandal, a certain refined syntax). To these could be added the influences of Nietzsche (a period of great mourning, an exposure to collapse), Malraux (the Self's obsessive, adventurous and fearful gaze over natural abjection, animalistic devouring, monstrous squirming), surrealism, for example Leiris (syntactical drought with occasional oases, description through images and adjectives, the unlikely certainty of a magic or marvelous world). The writing in the novel contains unnecessary repetitions (of adjectives, adverbs, syntax), an abundance of adjectives, deliberate attempts to be superlative, a certain wallowing in metaphors, oxymorons, and even allegories. These characteristics are often referred to as "stylistic defects," as baroque exaggerations contrary to the French "temperament." They are present in abundance in Blanchot's novel, demonstrating that he has been seduced. These indulgences will be removed in the "new version" and excluded from his future narratives.[1]

No one has described the style of *Thomas the Obscure* better than Blanchot himself: As he would often do, he analyzes his own writing by commenting on someone else's (the main role of the critical texts thus seems to be that of an aesthetic autobiography). Published in April 1940, the article in question, on Lautréamont, gives him the opportunity to list a series of "qualities singularly lacking from the novelistic literature of today, at least in France" (except in Giraudoux, he adds).[2] *Thomas the Obscure*, sent to Gallimard a month later, clearly attempts to fill the necessary gaps: "a deeply felt horror that steadily distances itself from the natural course of things"; "the refusal of psychology, the cancer of the French novel"; "the artificial quality of human emotions"; "an effort to conceive and create time in a way like no other"; "the time of a superior action in which creation takes place under conditions of efficiency and promptitude for which no human equivalent can be found"; an action with unpredictable consequences, "more because it can annihilate itself than because it can create anything"; evil, "that irremediable deterioration of all things, of which animal metamorphoses are the powerful image," associated with a creative force "that is like an excess of the real"; and all of the above taking place within "the seeming discontinuity of the text" and "the extremely interlinked quality of the prose . . . that syntax directs by arranging the way it moves, thus creating a progression which meaning never forgets to follow, but only from a distance and with an ironic delay." This is to say that the reader's unease cannot tear him or her away from the work: "To tear oneself away from it is to tear oneself away from necessity itself. To follow one's path within it is to continue within the impossible" (something that Blanchot would also say of Sade, and something that he would soon evoke with Bataille).

Aesthetic (novelistic) choices are also life choices. Long before the critical language comes to bear, they become *the* life choice for Blanchot. This is a way of prolonging his nocturnal interrogations, of offering identity another chance, of bearing the possibility of his own identity. A way of effacing oneself even while narrating oneself. And of giving form to the experience of being suffocated by the loss, mourning, illness, and deaths that gave rise to it all. It is not a question of recounting anecdotes or events, even extreme ones, nor of recounting the consequent suffering; but rather of opening up to the space of writing, to the time of fiction: like a joyous *askesis*, a voice is proffered which is sometimes hesitant, sometimes full-throated. It sketches out various gestures, it tolerates weight, breathing becomes a daily possibility once more. A long time would be necessary before the right form for this *unsuffocation* could be found. A long time will always be necessary. And perhaps it never will be found: This is a writing constantly undergoing metamorphoses.

The first book, the first text in which Blanchot agrees to give himself over, to give himself permission, *Thomas the Obscure* marks the first absolute engagement of the self by fiction, in fiction, in the confrontation on the title page between a surname—that of the author—and a first name—that of Thomas—a surname and first name that would remain associated in several later novels. The two are fused together from the outset: The first letters of Thomas are similar to the last of Blanchot, and Thomas ends as Maurice begins; indeed the book's title almost forms an anagram of Maurice Blanchot. This Thomas who dwells in a sanatorium is also Thomas Mann—whose surname has the same assonance as the novel's female character, Anne, and also means "mankind," therefore representing a sort of "first Adam." This character with the biblical first name is also Thomas Jude the apostle, or perhaps *Jude the Obscure*;[3] this christic Thomas (Hegel's second son was called Thomas Emmanuel Christian) is the dialectical confrontation of nonbelief and Christianity, "the fusion of the extremes by friendship and by philosophy"; and finally, this hero of the obscure is Heraclitus the obscure, the paradoxical philosopher of matter.[4]

What questions do these names raise? The capacity for an individual to live through the loss of love; the capacity for a body to represent all others, to give space to their movements in the air, to their gestures in space, even as it brings them back to itself; the capacity for a name to leave space for its shadow, its dark or sacred side, to recognize and almost to prepare its own abyss. For Blanchot, *Thomas the Obscure* will be if not an entry into the silence of poetry, then at least the marker of a predominant nocturnal demand, over and against "the madness of the day," that of the world, and not least his own. It will be the creation of a creature that comprehends its creator, which is to say includes him and turns him inside out, giving him an identity. Blanchot is Thomas, not that the text is strictly autobiographical, or that it sketches out his fate or cycles through changes in the manner of Madame Bovary. Blanchot is Thomas in the sense that Thomas is no one, or is everyone at some point in his metamorphoses, providing a figure for the body's permanent encounter with death; this novel of the fantastic, which is nonetheless extremely intimate, cannot be reduced to any physical or psychical figuration, or to any anecdote. The events of the narrative are as impossible as the author's life-as-mysticism had become, and they try to extend, via the creation of a novelistic world or what we could name an *exobiography*, an externalized, dismembered, exploded biography, one which exposes its own ruins as part of the megalomaniac adventures of an impossible, divine destiny. These adventures are tirelessly adumbrated by a narrator who still believes in them and is alone in doing so, for we read this illusory construction with the greatest skepticism, even as it is extended, unfolded, and extrapolated. This is an exobiography that is an endobiography on a large scale, giving form to the author's intimacy by enlarging its dramatic changes of course, its sanguine itinerary, the breadth of its gestures; and exposing the inside to the outside, somewhere between psychology and cosmogony (without either ever being understood as pure or self-contained), between humanization and pantheist divinization.

Daniel Wilhem quite rightly says that Blanchotian narration "is the denial that any space is forbidden." We must take this to also apply to the interdiction of biography (though still without approaching the narrative "in the pregnancy of an avowal"). For here there is no "rarity of the event," of narrative or of saying, "mapping out the same space"; on the contrary, there is total mobility and constant movement pushing the body of the unsayable ever further back. As Wilhem also suggests, the endless rehearsal (*ressassement*) of mistakes means that repentance takes on a spatial dimension, which does not find any affirmation or redemption in temporality.[5] In this sense, and linking perfectly with the mobility of Thomas, the gluttony of novelistic space constantly carries the memory of error, which is at once unbearable and impossible to convey, except by constantly dying *in the name of the other*, in the duality of the work. Derrida also invokes the infinite nature of this task: "The narrative is interminable because the force that opposes it, just like attempts to set it at a distance, in fact produces that against which it is acting; it does so without any hope of arriving at a moment of conclusion, a negation of negation, or a denial [*dénégation*]."[6]

This is to say that the narrative does not produce any avowal because *it is writing itself that is avowal* (its "differences of step/of not" [*différences de pas*], its "step/not of death" [*pas de mort*]). In this sense, the first line of *Thomas the Obscure*, "Thomas sat down and looked at the sea," strongly embodies the desire of what would eventually become a work. It is truly the first *line* of his entire work. Blanchot returned to it at the beginning of *The Step Not Beyond* in order to underline how these few words, "words in themselves without future or claim: '*he—the sea*,'" signify the "power to rip away, to destroy or to change" that sets the oeuvre in motion.[7] These words inscribe "the possibility of a radical transformation, if only for a single person, namely his suppression as a personal existence," as well as the impossibility of unifying existence "through writing that disunifies." Blanchot also clarifies that these first words were written "facing the sky," namely facing the openness, *the division* of the sky; writing begins with the "primal scene," seeming to repeat it indefinitely, to disseminate its destiny. This image of death to come is disorientating, linked as it is to the infinitely rehearsed image of death inverted.

What actually happens in *Thomas the Obscure*? The opening sentence, a measured, calm line, "Thomas sat down and looked at the sea," is simple enough (even though such banality concretizes the mobile space of the narrative as well as—already—the site of its completion). Hereafter the narrative moves toward a highly unrealistic fate, comprising bodies and spaces in constant metamorphosis and in which Thomas, the main character, who is by turns human and monstrous, dead and alive, meets two young women.[8] Anne and Irene enter into strange, impossible, metapsychic, and often unspeakable relationships with him before choosing their death and dying, Irene struck in the throat by a sharp object, Anne from simple exhaustion. At this point Thomas imposes a new gaze on a world created anew and sends men into the sea. It remains unclear what motivates all of this behavior, but whatever it might be, it traverses the characters with the clarity of certainty; categories such as willpower, determination, or freedom remain wholly foreign to this immediately aesthetized world, which is absolute without ever being absolved, perfect because it has so many imperfections. Everything takes place under the tutelage of a law according to which things are anything but solid and one comes upon spaces in which a just reciprocity can be established with the other (even in cruelty). Nonetheless, this does not mean that the narrative simply describes a range of behavior, nor that it brings to light spectacular or fantastic events, providing one anecdote of the impossible after another. The narrative exists in order to counter at once the "invisible leprosy" of feelings (43) and "the illusion of light" (301).[9] Without the reference points provided by categories, it makes use of concepts habitually tolerated in our readings of the world, but only to deny their capacity for adequate understanding and interpretation. When comparisons open up a distance, they are immediately closed down again ("her movement was not that of a sleepwalker," 136). It is a question of drowning and then resuscitating the figures used, in an infinite, infinitely open movement, opening up bodies, forms, and gazes.

This refusal to name the particular opens intimacy to the outside, the singular to the universal. Likewise, it is not through identifiable reference points but rather faint traces that Thomas provides an echo to Blanchot's life. Something is inscribed by this unspeakable intimacy, is set in motion and seeks to be said, to be protected, to be torn away and to be breathed. A 150-year-old lime tree provides a glimpse of the solitude of a faraway, collapsed childhood, one confronted with nothingness. Thomas's main bodily preoccupation is his stomach, perhaps "the dominant agony in his life" (42), and his illness, this weakness that can reach even the summits of vigor, sometimes takes refuge in sanatoria. Although it is impossible for many, death is reached by tolerating the smile, a terrifying one, of a dying man. These are some of the broken, disseminated elements providing the backdrop for the narrative: so many obscure lines, waves of joy and exhaustion, moments of bodily suffering and of the opening of the gazes, all of which mark life in the porous universe of fear and fascination.[10]

Fear precedes the appearance of any face, as a condition of the ethical stage. It is a fear of the inside of things, an inside that is always unhealthy, exhausted, masked, disfigured as soon as it is unfolded, liquefied, corrupt, muddily black. It is fear of time accelerating and distending, of light blanching, of space becoming unbound. Over and against the constant threat of suffocation, it hopes to find a way of breathing, the only guarantee that faces might be put back together, a tense ordeal that demands that one bear "breathing in asphyxia" (79).

Space is in short supply and from the outset, from the endless struggle of Thomas's swimming, must be created. The body also seems to be missing, both space and the body being detached and as if floating, despite being heavy and coarse; the sensation is one of a projection being given in a very localized form. The body's absence charges it with a senseless density: the more it is hollowed out by emptiness, the fuller it is of an invisible presence. This struggle with an angel produces the suffocating sensation of the site of an anguishing, monstrous, excessive, incoercible *occupation* of the body as a site. Thomas's strength is not to give in or efface himself, but eventually to come to take the place of the other body, assimilating it, taking the place of other bodies everywhere, becoming multiple and therefore dividing himself into so many small abysses with which men will be confronted. He is death in them, the possibility of them replacing their own bodies, of twinning themselves with their abyss. This is christic experience, an experience of friendship, one able to bear the enormous demands on patience, listening, and fatigue; "in death itself, deprived of death" (78). The fluidity of the writing makes this mysterious attentiveness into the blessing and the clarity of consciousness, as well as the clarity of a bodily state. Anaphoras delve into—and paradoxes exhaust—the possible; but the thinking of this leveling-down shows itself to be a happy one, the maintenance of belief (as well as of fear, of paranoia, of strength) as and through the movements of the phrasing.

Thomas reveals Anne to herself. She is "the first dead woman to be there" (290). Their first meeting violently reveals Thomas's power. Anne is the site where this force that reaches her from behind a partition is explored, where it doubles itself in her, annihilates her. She has encountered her invisible partner, the other body that subdues her.

> Her body received from the invisible body wounds which shattered her; a shadow crushed her. At that moment she heard distinctly a powerful heart beating behind the partition, arteries closing and opening in accordance with the pressure from an irritated, hurrying life. She heard a terrible noise: a flash of blood illuminated her; a flood of humors, of broken veins, of tissues hit by lightning struck her. She saw the partition fold before her; she felt the beatings of a monstrous life, she felt ready to die. And she ran away, blind and deaf, until by falling she was restored to liberty. (54)

There are some moments, Blanchot would write in an article for the *Journal des Débats*, when "night reveals itself as being composed of organs and filled with a physical expectancy."[11] This is Thomas's night, the night of bodies that are invisible, absent, inhuman, lightweight, consisting of luminosity, divided, ripped away from themselves, *neutral* (164); the night of constant metamorphoses, of imperceptible but repeated passages from life to death. This night is not without divinity. In turn described as the "first man," as a creator, destroyer (there are many references to both *Genesis* and *Revelations*), Thomas stubbornly strikes into the thickness of matter, as if he had always forgotten what he had created. He strikes into the darkness in order to break down all immanence with the object, clothed by a light that "does not have any fundamental strangeness," and in order to better rediscover solitude, the alterity of things, the division of *jouissance* and of sobbing.[12] Thomas's night is this "wound to thought," this "thought taken ironically as an object by something other than thought." "It [is] night itself" (33). It is the other night, the other night of essential solitude, the other night of Orpheus. Thomas's experience here is indeed that of Blanchot, that of the writer caught up in the Hölderlinian world full of divine presences. Who is playing us? Who is playing Thomas, Orpheus, the author? Who returns them to their own nights: the untouchable Christ, the invisible Eurydice, the unreadable work? In this madness of night, which is constantly troubled, carried away, returned, the dice are cast, the *space of literature* is decided upon.

> Just as there are several different nights in space, there are several gods on the shores of day. But they are so spread out that between breath and springing, a life has gone by.
>
> The gods do not decline nor do they die, but with an imperious and cyclical movement, like the ocean, they withdraw. You approach them only among the waterholes, buried.
>
> Best child of the old solar disk, and as near as possible to its celestial slowness. This substantial longing came again, came again, then its spot vanished.
>
> Night freely recircled, which plays *us*?[13]

PART III

1940–1949

I will tell you what I will do and what I will not do. I will not serve that in which I no longer believe, whether it calls itself my home, my fatherland, or my church: and I will try to express myself in some mode of life or art as freely as I can and as wholly as I can, using for my defense the only arms I allow myself to use— silence, exile, and cunning.

JAMES JOYCE, *A Portrait of the Artist as a Young Man*

CHAPTER 19

The Universe Is to Be Found in Night

Resistance (1940–1944)

In April 1940, Thierry Maulnier, still a contributor to *L'Action Française* and *La Revue Universelle*, together with Kléber Haedens and Marie-Thérèse Barrelet (the friend of the publisher Edmond Buchet), launched the *Revue Française des Idées et des Oeuvres*.[1] The first issue, which would be the only issue, contained texts by Drieu, Fraigneau, Giraudoux, and a column by Maurice Blanchot.[2]

The collective positions of the journal were aligned with nationalist and Germanophobic traditionalism compatible with Blanchot's ideas of the time.[3] An anonymous editorial denounced the German cult of "brute force": "the return to brutal origins, the appeal to blood and soil," as well as the disdain for cultural refinement that was so opposed to French culture: "the very existence of France is a centuries-long form of protest against the senseless theories which necessarily make force brutal and civilization a naturally dissolute phenomenon." The editorial concluded that "France is the daughter less of blood and soil than of order and style."

Nonetheless, the ideas invariably espoused by the editorial collective must be understood in relation to external events: the radicalization of the extremes, the expectation of real conflict with Germany. Drieu fulminated against "Thierry's journal," predicting that it would fail "because it will not take a clear position." The relatively nuanced line adopted by Maulnier, which was the helpless reflection of the dead ends into which he had run, indeed tolerated literary viewpoints that were slightly more open in their modernity, and would cause Drieu to state that "Kléber Haedens and Blanchot are infected with surrealism."[4] Although Blanchot's article began with a devastating denunciation of the Surrealist critique of the *Chants de Maldoror*, it still addressed Lautréamont, and indeed did so in very laudatory terms ("this hidden attempt at a sort of pure book"), in a way that could only irritate Drieu, and be seen by him as a provocation. Choosing a writer born in Uruguay and venerated by the surrealists, the author of an apparently immoral and disordered book, albeit one with perfect syntactical poise (like Sade's), an aesthetic that he compared to those of Giraudoux and Jean-Paul, Blanchot speaks to the national value defined by the editorial's conclusion, and finds an outlet for it in this breezy, cunning, knowingly left-field viewpoint.

On May 10, 1940, the German invasion began. The editorial of the *Journal des Débats* vigorously demanded that the government reject the offer of an armistice. Several of these texts were censored. On May 19, Reynaud called Pétain into the government. On June 3, Paris was bombed (Blanchot would allude to this in *Death Sentence*). On June 8, the front page of issue 1150 of *Aux écoutes* carried a caricature of a bull with Hitler's head and a body covered in tattoos of swastikas about to leap on to an impassive bullfighter dressed as a French soldier; the caption compared "the onrushing Beast" to "French calm." But on June 10, the government was moved to Tours, and on June 13, at the Château de Cangé, Pétain addressed its ministers: "In my eyes, armistice is the condition on which the continuity of eternal France rests." For him, only an armistice could allow the government to remain in the country to protect the French from the occupier and from the communist putsch that was still feared. Blanchot was despairing: on June 15 the Germans, who were making progress across the country, were at Chalon-sur-Saône, and on June 16, as Reynaud was resigning and Pétain was forming a government in Bordeaux and immediately requesting an armistice, Levinas was taken prisoner in Rennes. On June 18, Blanchot was in Bordeaux, where he heard General de Gaulle make his appeal. On June 22, the armistice with Germany was signed at Rethondes. A dividing line separated France into two zones. On July 10, the Senate and the National Assembly, which had come together in Vichy, voted with an overwhelming majority to confer full powers on Pétain, who was to draw up a new constitution. The two chambers were dissolved. It was the suicide of the Third Republic. Blanchot was watching from the gallery: he felt that he had reached the end. This event shocked him, more than February 6 and more than Munich. It left him stupefied, not knowing what to do.[5] Such a betrayal of the nation, and of the idea of culture that it represented, would definitively—if there were still any doubt—set him against any moderation in political matters. It became clear to him that all moderation was compromise, and that all right-wing extremism walked the path toward collaboration. It was also by a process of elimination that Blanchot would move closer to the far left as the only tenable solution, even for the idea of the nation.

He tried, unsuccessfully, to convince those in charge of the *Journal des Débats* to suspend all publication. But since June 15 the newspaper had withdrawn to Clermont-Ferrand and had been receiving financial support from the government, on condition of its unwavering support and the submission of copy to the censor. On July 7, after an interruption of eighteen days due to the Germans' entry into Clermont, the newspaper reappeared bearing a column named "After the Disaster," probably thought up and written by Blanchot. Its author was against constitutional reform, but the death of the Third Republic on July 10 put an end to the column. The tone of the editorials, which in the spring had constantly been calling for a "war government," in summer became more and more reactionary and, from November 1940 on, concerned with the triumphs of Marshal Pétain. At this point Blanchot gave up on any political responsibility at the *Journal des Débats*.[6] Without his editorialist's job, he was soon without financial resources. For while he had taken on the editorship of *Aux écoutes*, which in mid-June had also withdrawn to Clermont (indeed to the same street) and reappeared on July 13, Paul Lévy's weekly was banned by Laval on August 17.

If in Blanchot's "transformation of convictions" there was one political rupture that was more decisive than any other, it is perhaps that of summer 1940. It was perhaps experienced as an additional death, less passionate but just as depressing as the previous one(s), at a stroke erasing the apprenticeships, certainties, and sometimes violent engagements of many years, even a lifetime. Blanchot was thirty-three years old. This death carried off what once passed as friendship but that would often seem to have been nothing but acquaintance. It created a commitment to future, headless communities without father figures, a commitment to an infinite gift (which would be that of life, of the texts, of the *récits*, the very possibility of the *récits* as the possibility of staying alive). A true kernel of effacement, this death created a commitment not to return to the same place, but to return only in ghostly form. Friendship would be born from this spectral reserve. Dedicating a copy of *Thomas the Obscure* to Xavier de Lignac in September 1941, Blanchot would quote Gérard de Nerval: "Voices said: the Universe is to be found in night."[7]

Nonetheless, Blanchot would retain some links with Maulnier, who continued to contribute to *L'Action Française*, proposed a programmatic doctrine for the national revolution in the *Revue Universelle*, prowled the lobbies in Vichy, and wrote anonymous articles for *Candide*. From April 1941 until the last days of the war, Blanchot would provide a regular literary column to the *Journal des Débats*, a paper that was ever more in favor of the Vichy government and especially Pétain. On June 5, 1941, he even put his name to an article attacking the state's abandonment of the new, middle-class poor and therefore calling for the reinstatement of private assistance, invoking the difficulties of the war, the aftereffects of the winter, the undernourishment of children and adolescents, the exhausted devotion of the volunteers, the difficulties of maintaining their dignity for those who had fallen into poverty.[8] At no point during the war would he publish in any of the clandestine journals. In 1941 *Thomas the Obscure* would appear with Gallimard. With *Aminadab* in 1942 and *Faux pas* in 1943, he published three books in occupied France with a regularity mirroring that of his columns, and without ever having any trouble with the German censors. The question of the political morality of these publications cannot be avoided. But neither can one omit to add that in the same era and in the same place, publications appeared by Bataille, Sartre, Leiris, and Camus.

There was no radicalism on Blanchot's part at this stage. Was there any for anyone? We have to try to imagine the fear of the occupier, the collapse in ideals, the strategies of deception; we have to imagine some who increasingly failed to understand and others who saw a duty to speak out, all of whom fell into their own traps. Mauriac, Valéry, Gide, Giraudoux, and Montherlant adopted positions that were no closer to being "commendable." The Maurrassians, their "dissidents," those close to them from *Esprit* and *Ordre Nouveau*, mostly rallied to Pétain. But there were numerous divisions. *Je Suis Partout* expressed contempt for Thierry Maulnier. Blanchot became a target for the extreme right-wing press.

Blanchot's silence henceforth bore the clear weight of responsibility, a concern for decency, an awareness of the impropriety of public statements and of the despair of the epoch. Lacking any external mark of heroism, this silence could not conceal the collapse of the aristocratic ideal. Dedicating *Aminadab* in September 1942, once again to Xavier de Lignac, Blanchot now quoted Nietzsche: "It is difficult to live among men, because it is difficult to keep silent."

This silence also bore the trace of effective discretion, of solitary courage, of a dignity rediscovered through devotion. In November 1940, Blanchot and his sister saved Paul Lévy, warning him that he was about to be arrested.[9] When the decrees of October 18, 1940, and of April 26, 1941, appeared, which barred Jews from all public professions, Blanchot—at the *Journal des Débats* and then at Jeune France—must have been aware of them. Perhaps he saw them as history's way of spurring him into action. The climate had become so unsavory that Jewish families were beginning to fear for their children. After Levinas's arrest, his daughter Simone was sent to the Normandy countryside to stay with friends of Blanchot and his father.[10] However, these friends, perturbed by the strange looks that the young girl was attracting, brought her back to Paris. One day in 1941, Blanchot offered to lend his apartment for a few weeks to Levinas's wife Raïssa and her daughter. He then found them a hiding place near to Orléans, in the Saint-Vincent-de-Paul convent, which also assisted in the Resistance, to which would go first the daughter (probably in 1941, at the latest in early 1942) and then the mother (in August 1943). A professional journalist who was always in the loop, Blanchot had discreet links to the Resistance. Denise Rollin and Claude Roy confirm this engagement.[11] He met René Char as early as 1940. Any real opposition to the occupying forces would only begin two or three years later. In the region of Quain, Blanchot would drive cars in order to help clandestine figures cross the border.[12]

Speaking much later of the Resistance, in a distinctly personal tone, Blanchot would see it as an apprenticeship for intellectuals in the "dark struggles that make war and revolution resemble each other"; they also learned how hard it was to "sustain a just moral correlation between means and ends."[13] This was an all the more personal reading given that these were questions that he had been asking himself for years, without finding any resolution except first through rhetoric, then through silence. The "national-revolutionary" utopia found the Resistance to be a way of balancing, in the struggle for refusal, between the nationalism he was shortly to abandon and the communism he was moving toward.

If "there can be absolute hostility only *for* a brother," perhaps Blanchot experienced some difficulty in entering a fratricidal rivalry, in confirming that the clan had split apart.[14] We can understand his subsequent refusal of all legacies and his reluctance to overly politicize refusal. Clear abstention from the political led to a paradoxical neutrality, an active effacement, standing above a breach created by an engaged withdrawal. Henceforth friendship had no site.

CHAPTER 20

Using Vichy against Vichy
Jeune France (1941–1942)

Jeune France was an association under the control of the Vichy government, created by Pierre Schaeffer in order to assist unemployed artists, though it would never really fulfill that role.[1] It took up the baton from a national radio program, "Radio-Jeunesse," also directed by Schaeffer and also answering to Vichy, which was named for a group of prewar musicians including both Daniel Lesur and Olivier Messiaen. Jeune France was formed officially on November 25, 1940. Its aims were to "renew the great tradition of French quality in artistic and cultural matters," to "bring together groupings of young artists," and, with a young audience in mind, to create study and resource centers. It also envisaged training organizers in cultural *"maîtrises,"* where apprentices were led by a *maître*, establishing centers for artistic creation, journals based on information and propaganda, touring exhibitions and theatrical productions, as well as drama festivals and celebrations. Beyond its own resources (subscriptions, shows, sales, and so forth), its financing came from the state (the General Secretariat for Youth, the Commission for the Struggle against Unemployment, the office of Marshal Pétain), as well as from the *départements* and towns that hosted the tours. Nonetheless, the association's finances were always in the red. The headquarters was in Lyon, with Pierre Schaeffer as its head. Paul Flamand in Paris was in charge of its activities in the occupied zone. But the difficulties in communicating between the two zones made any concerted organization impossible. Those in each zone would always be at odds with one another over differences in how they conceived the undertaking; in the north, they privileged artistic creation and the formation of professional groups, whereas in the south they dedicated themselves to dissemination, to educating groups of young people, and to assisting preexisting groups and movements. Last, Roger Leenhardt was tasked with exploring ways to expand the association's activities to North Africa.

Preparing the activities was a long and difficult task. Encountering difficulties with the German occupiers in the north, Jeune France initially established itself in a minuscule apartment behind the Place Saint-Michel, then in 1941 in Rue Jean-Mermoz, near the Champs Elysées roundabout, although the old premises were still retained. In the south, it was divided between Vichy and Lyon. The five main services were the research service, the implementation service (in charge of publications, events, organizing tours, workshops, construction, and notably the "*maîtrises*"), the administrative and financial service, the general service (for propaganda and market research), and the centers in the provinces. In total the association employed 126 people, who came from different backgrounds (far-right dissidence, Esprit, Ordre Nouveau, the scout movement). The figurehead role of the presidency was given—it seems without his knowledge (he was a prisoner of war at the time)—to Patrice de La Tour du Pin.

The most important personalities were in charge of the research service: Xavier de Lignac (general management, Paris); Jean Vilar (assisted by Romain Petitot, theater, Paris); Maurice Jacquemont (theater, Lyon); Maurice Blanchot (literature, Paris); Albert Ollivier, with Roy, Barjavel, Fabrègues (literature, Lyon); Jean Bazaine (plastic arts, Paris); and Daniel Lesur (music), Claude Roy (radio) and Leenhardt (cinema), all in Lyon. Louis Ollivier managed the administrative and financial services in Paris, in addition to the general services, whose documentation section was looked after by Yette Jeandet, a bookseller who seems to have remained in touch with Blanchot for a long time. Romain Petitot was in charge of the implementation of services in Paris, where Blanchot dealt with publications. Schaeffer was always head of the propaganda service for shows and for the radio, and Albert Ollivier was editor of Radio-Jeunesse. The implementation of each service was all the more piecemeal given that not all those involved arrived at Jeune France at the same time.

Georges Pelorson, a friend of Maulnier since their *préparation* and the École Normale Supérieure, introduced Blanchot to Jeune France as his successor, having just been given a role at the Vichy ministry of Education and Youth. A friend of Pelorson and a former Ordre Nouveau activist, Pierre Prévost introduced Blanchot to Ollivier, Petitot, and Lignac, who became his closest friends at Jeune France. They worked alongside each other in their unheated offices, in nearby cafés, and in the restaurants where they would lunch together at least once a week. Blanchot seemed to them to be utterly discreet and dedicated. His past on the far right, although it was recent and known to his friends, was never mentioned. Nothing in his magisterially indifferent attitude, discourse, or behavior gave it away. Indeed, nothing would give anyone cause to believe that he was subject to any major political influence. Subsequently, Lignac would always ask himself why Blanchot came to Jeune France. Perhaps he needed a safe haven: an official role that gave him lots of free time, without requiring compromises (this is the only way Lignac can explain it). As an unemployed journalist, Blanchot also needed money.

Those who contributed to Jeune France indeed seem to have been very well paid. Jean Bazaine recalls the figure of three thousand francs per month for section leaders such as himself and Blanchot. He states that he remembers this all the more exactly because this sum had come as a surprise. An item from the association's 1942 draft budget confirms this figure, proposing 3,000 to 4,500 francs for the leaders of the artistic sections and administrative services.

Each artistic section was charged with establishing guiding principles for its policies, discovering works-in-progress, scrutinizing projects, and organizing roundtables, colloquia, and lectures. The literary section was asked to put together a committee in order to solicit works from young authors and to direct them toward publishing houses. It was also envisaged that a monthly journal of art and literature (both texts and critical studies) would be created. There was an ambition to launch multiple book series with the publisher Albin Michel: Works (anthologies providing a theoretical, genre-based way of approaching French works, including the most recent), Exchanges (aimed at publishing foreign authors), and Critical Essays (one of the two works envisioned was a collection named *Tradition and Creation*, which—as Blanchot wrote in a report—would "attempt to go deeper into the thought that fidelity to tradition is fidelity to a creative spirit"). It seems, however, that Blanchot did not carry through these projects during the many months he spent at Jeune France. In fact, it seems that he did nothing at all, that he went there precisely in order to do nothing. In the north, only one work appeared, that by Albert-Marie Schmidt on *La Jeune Poésie* (Young Poetry). It is true that the regime of censorship was particularly strong in the literary domain. If Jeune France did not have the infrastructure necessary for a real, working publishing house, it is doubtful whether Blanchot ever really tried to give it the means it would have needed to that end.

Demonstrating a similar indifference to government directives, the plastic arts section in the occupied zone appealed to tradition the better to encourage creation. It was rather active. In May 1941, Jean Bazaine organized an exhibition at the Braun gallery, "Twenty Painters from the French Tradition." The painters included Manessier and Tal Coat. This was a daring exhibition at a time when Nazi sculpture was benefitting from enormous propaganda. The violent reactions it provoked, however, came less from the Germans than from the French editors and readers of *Je suis partout*.

Being close to Bazaine and Manessier at this time, Blanchot liked this type of painting, although without being intensely interested in it.[2] He frequently visited Bazaine in his studio, where the two of them would discuss mainly literature. He went to the cinema and to the opera performances with which the Germans were trying to dazzle Parisian audiences at the time. He was close to Bernard Milleret, his office companion and an artist who regularly drew portraits in pencil, and who must have drawn Blanchot more than once.

Despite the presence of a considerable number of intellectuals, the actions of Jeune France remained largely empirical and were dictated by the artistic desires and political attitude of the individuals in question. According to Lignac, in Paris there was never a single "active member of the Resistance or dedicated *Pétainiste*": "there were those who consented." As an independent association, Jeune France did not depend on Vichy administratively, even though the latter provided 100 percent of its funding. While the government only oversaw the projects intermittently, the general idea remained that of reorganizing the cultural life of a half-occupied country and of renewing French inspiration, by way of a reconciliation between artists and the people. Some pieces of writing would push allegiance to the "national revolution" and with Maurice Bardèche there would even be a fascistic program of films; certain open-air theater celebrations would border on being epic personality cults; but overall, the members of Jeune France, especially in the north, would refrain from producing anything that too closely resembled propaganda.

The pressures on the association increased with time. The public powers demanded to be better represented on the management and administrative committees. The financial generosity of the state can be measured against the demands it made, which hardened from August 1941 onward, when Paul Marion and Pierre Pucheu joined the government, the former at the Ministry of Information and Propaganda, the latter at the Ministry of the Interior. Mounier, who rebelled against the fascization of the regime, was immediately stripped of his journal (*Esprit* was banned in August 1941) and shortly afterward removed from Jeune France.

In the fall of 1941, Lignac's friends were still holding the line: that of remaining insubordinate to Vichy. However, inaction was no longer a possibility. Blanchot's September 1941 dedication on the cover page of a copy of *Thomas the Obscure* announced the struggle that was around the corner: "To Paul Flamand, this book destined to estrange all readers." It reflected the elitist challenge that was being set in opposition to the sometimes outlandish populism of the leadership.

Examining Xavier de Lignac's archives leads us to contradict, at least in part, the accounts of the breakup of Jeune France given by Véronique Chabrol and Pierre Schaeffer, who in a few words (and making a few mistakes) brush over the association's final months, which were in fact extremely tempestuous. Was Lignac's attempt to regain control, assisted by Blanchot and Petitot, really an attempt at autonomy in the face of a government that was becoming more hardline? We can indeed think so, but not without underlining both the demanding nature and the naivety of such an undertaking. It is as if Lignac and Blanchot, in 1942, still believed in the possibility of working with Vichy money even while retaining independence in their creative choices.[3] Or on the contrary, it could have been that amidst the general collapse, there was a move to voluntarily scuttle Jeune France in the name of a brief statement of dignity; this would have been a case of double or nothing, an extremely risky gamble but perhaps also the only possible, tenable one.

In October 1941, the appearance of a leaflet on Jeune France, which was the idea of the management, brought latent hostilities into the open. A weighty exchange of correspondence between Schaeffer or Flamand, on one side, and Lignac on the other, bore witness to this.

On October 27, Lignac sent two notes to Schaeffer. In a "note to the managing director of Jeune France" consisting of three typed sheets, he denounced the concessions made, the dithering, the lack of seriousness, the equivocation and the "most dangerous vulgarity" of the leaflet published. He introduced a second note containing "practical conditions" which were "the only ones on which Blanchot, Petitot and [myself] could still envisage contributing to Jeune France," and without which they would resign publicly, causing as much noise as possible. "The values which we would have liked to work toward safeguarding are too insidiously compromised." Lignac also denounced the leaders' authoritarianism and betrayal.

> When those who started Jeune France came to ask me to work with them on founding and leading a new branch of the association in Paris, I thought that for them and for me it was essentially a question of working, as fully as possible, toward the conditions necessary for a free culture to survive even when threatened from all sides, from both within and without the new French regime. It seemed a matter of agreement between us that while the association envisaged playing some official role, taking on certain tasks of dissemination—without giving in to the requests or injunctions of propaganda—this was justified by the wider concrete support it received from the public purse. This timely concession represented the opportunity to use all the more freely the financial powers thus obtained in order to act in total independence and with the forethought and rigor that are necessary if we are to safeguard our spiritual values.

The following day, October 28, a meeting between Schaeffer and Lignac broke down; in Schaeffer's words, it took place "in a regrettable atmosphere of mistrust."

On October 29, Schaeffer responded in writing to Lignac's two notes and to their meeting, stating that creative freedom was not incompatible with the task of dissemination. Not without reason, he denounced the inactivity of "your colleague Blanchot": "a year on, no written work has been produced by Jeune France." As he was summing up his letter, he received the resignations—written the day before—of Lignac, Blanchot, and Petitot, who no longer had "any illusions over the role that the association is destined to play." Schaeffer added a few further sentences: he accepted the resignations, kept open the possibility of the three contributing as individuals, but warned against any further attempts to destabilize Jeune France.

On November 1, Lignac responded to Schaeffer's demand with a further letter outlining the reasons behind his resignation. "The general activities of the association can only discredit the exemplary role" of the work of a number of free artists who had happened to believe in the association. A draft of this letter is corrected in Blanchot's hand, confirming that he participated in drawing it up and was broadly in agreement. Lignac would even confirm later that he hardly ever did or wrote anything for Jeune France without gaining Blanchot's approval. The latter was said to be "the real instigator" of this attempt at an "intellectual putsch," and to have had no intention either of washing his hands of it or of profiting from it. This is not impossible: such a position of active withdrawal, of sovereign discretion, would also be that taken by Blanchot, the editor in the shadows, in the 1960s.

In reality, Lignac was preparing a counterattack. He checked that he had the support of Commissioner Hillairet, the second-in-command to Commissioner Perrin, whom the government asked to lead an inquiry into Jeune France.

On January 31, 1942, Commissioner Perrin sent a note to Mr. Jardel, general secretary to the government. He requested that Jeune France be dissolved and proposed that Lignac be named as the head of a new, free organization, and asked that the various activities be shared out in a coherent way. The new association would be in charge of artistic creation, without intervention by the state, with the latter overseeing "the organization of large events" and the management of *maîtrises*. "The state fulfills its functions by conserving, dedicating, supporting that which has proved itself; it cannot itself intervene regarding that which is seeking its form or still proposing it."

On February 10, Lignac wrote a note echoing, sometimes word for word, that of the commissioner. He declared himself ready to dissolve Jeune France and to set up a new association. Annex 1 clearly defined the objective: "responding to the legitimate demands of those who wish, through works without concession, to reach the true sources of culture." This required the stimulation of "private initiatives in favor of literature and the arts, while allowing them to remain independent," as well as the staging of investigations and projects, editions, reissues, spectacles, concerts, exhibitions, "excluding any desire for simple dissemination, for propaganda or for entertainment." On March 12, the minister who was secretary of state for national education and youth, Carcopino, officially conferred upon Lignac the task of forming "a new association destined to replace Jeune France." The same day, he informed Schaeffer that Jeune France was being dissolved (the decree appeared in the *Journal officiel* on July 11). Dismissed on March 15, Flamand for a while refused to leave the premises or relinquish his role.

On April 2, Lignac sent to Carcopino a dossier of more than thirty pages on the creation of the new "Association for the Defense and Illustration of

Artistic Values." It established the need for a steering committee led by Giraudoux; a management team comprising Lignac as general secretary and Petitot as his assistant; an associate board with Bazaine, Dumay, Schmidt, and Blanchot, "literary critic at the *Journal des Débats*, resident in Paris." On April 4, the minister replied favorably.

The success of Lignac, Petitot, and Blanchot would lead to nothing. Between the two letters just mentioned, on April 3 Pétain consulted Goering over the opportunity to call Laval back to power. In less than two weeks, Laval replaced Darlan in government and was given exceptional constitutional powers. Vichy overtly entered into collaboration. Any margin for autonomy for the new association became unthinkable: it was liquidated before it came into being.

Remaining totally inactive until fall 1941, reduced to powerlessness at the very moment they had placed themselves in a position to intervene, Lignac and Blanchot would never be able to "use Vichy against Vichy." So much so that today Lignac states, "in a sense Jeune France never existed."

CHAPTER 21

Admiration and Agreement
Meeting Georges Bataille (1940–1943)

The meeting of Bataille and Blanchot would go on to be widely recognized, whether by friends, readers, those close to them, or their opponents, as the necessary encounter of two shared modes of thinking, of two lives put at stake through thought (and writing), of two experiences that engaged with all facets of being, including its uncertainties, its conversions, its unlimited openings. We can imagine that from the time they first saw and listened to one another, there was an immediate, almost instinctive sensation of recognition, with a slow-burning but intense effect; we can imagine how each paid attention to the quiet voice of the other, to the other's fascinating, imposing, and mysterious presence, to his slow and precise way of speaking which was always searching for something, to the constant risks and the ability to grip any audience ready to share these risks, even if doing so meant moving toward death. It is no surprise that Blanchot puts it best when he writes of Bataille: "Here is the first gift that this true speech gave us: speaking is our fortune, our chance, and to speak is to go in search of chance, the chance of a relation 'immediately' without measure." And regarding the two of them, he spoke of a silent appeal to attentiveness so as to confront the risk of a speech spoken in common, also an accord with this reserve that alone allows one to say everything, and, finally, an allusion to a movement toward the unknown to which, almost immediately, two persons together who are bound by something essential are as though obliged to bear witness.[1]

Bataille would suggest the same thing regarding Blanchot: "he never failed to live up to the feeling of discretion that means that when I am with him I thirst for silence."[2] They would always refer to this complicit reserve, only shedding light on their friendship with great caution. While they would often see each other (almost daily, at the beginning), while they would write to each other a lot, while they would always pay great attention to the other's health and life, this would remain hidden, withdrawn from the gaze of others. This pact—private, cherished, as if eternally cherished—is suggested by many expressions but notably by the following, written by Blanchot to Bataille (who was clearly exhausted): "Be sure that my thoughts are close to your own, in the common awaiting that it seems to me we have always shared, since we have known each other."[3]

Each one embodied what was latent in the other, doing so as a secret, silent, and veiled tendency. Blanchot was something like Bataille's passivity (his peaceable, withdrawn, reserved side), and Bataille something like Blanchot's passion (his inner violence, his mental disorder). These asymmetrical crossings or bodily inversions (these bodies of the converted, likewise said to be "superior" or priestly, which were intimidating and absent in turn, these torn-apart bodies, these paradoxical bodies) were overlaid by certain mutable passions—for example, that for Denise Rollin—as in a Dostoevsky novel.

It was the end of 1940, "precisely at the end of that sinister year."[4] Pierre Prévost, who had been close to Bataille since 1937, introduced him to Maurice Blanchot.[5]

At the time Bataille was known, much discussed and argued over, but had not yet written many books. He was living through a particularly difficult period. He had lost Colette Peignot (Laure) in 1938, had undergone the violent breakup of the Collège de Sociologie and then the start of the war; all of this had provoked a frenetic aversion to satisfaction, causing him to write—a notable exception in his lifetime—a journal that was shockingly denuded ("a brothel is my true church, the only one unquenching enough," he wrote on September 8, 1939).[6] More than ever, eroticism imposed itself on him like a crucifixion. Whether this eroticism was "the edge of the abyss," whether this edge was "the breaking point, where everything is let go, where death is anticipated," or whether this abyss was "the ground of the possible," this ecstasy-inducing wound had to convey its ardor to Blanchot's own wound.[7] These two strong yet sickly bodies were getting to know one another, two bodies able to draw immense energy from their weakness, able to exhaust themselves on the brink of asphyxia.[8] Bataille recounted that, on October 16, 1939, a few months before they met,

> I had to stop writing. I went over, as I often do, to sit in front of an open window. As soon as I sat down I fell into a sort of ecstasy. This time I no longer doubted . . . that such a state was more intense than erotic pleasure. I see nothing: *that* is neither visible nor palpable. *That* makes you sad and heavy-hearted at not dying. . . . *What is there* is wholly fitting to the experience of fright.[9]

Facing the sky, experienced *in the neuter*, this abyssal and solitary experience replays Blanchot's "primal scene," Thomas's infinite metamorphosis. A few weeks previously, Bataille had written:

> With sharpened serenity, before the black starry sky, before the hillside and the black trees, I have found what makes my heart into embers covered with ash, but burning within: the feeling of a presence that was irreducible to any and all notionality, this sort of thundering silence to which ecstasy leads us. I become an immense flight from myself, as if my life were running like slow rivers across the ink of the sky. At this moment I am no longer myself, but what has issued from me reaches and encloses in its embrace a limitless presence, itself similar to the loss of myself: what is no longer either me or the other, but a profound kiss in which the lips' edges melt away, becomes linked to this ecstasy which is just as dark and just as non-foreign to the universe as the course of the earth across the sky's abyss.[10]

The infinite improbability of birth gives way to the vertigo of atheological mysticism. Together, Bataille and Blanchot will enrich their critical readings of Christianity, mysticism, and also phenomenology, to which they had been introduced in different ways. One of the main axes of *Le coupable* sets the utilitarian God of Christian eschatology in opposition to Pascal's or Kierkegaard's God, in whom Bataille sooner sees an absence. In this point of NOTHING, of "the fear of NOTHING" resonating in an empty world, of "the fear reached only by the limitlessness of thought," the two writers converge.[11] They communicate thanks to a relation with death that reduces being to a horrifying Nothing. Bataille's belief that communication between beings passes over an annihilating abyss, that the other is this very abyss, that in Christian terms this communication takes on the figure of sin or, in inverse form, that of the sacred, and that the subject's experience (whether the lack at the heart of plenty or the evil lurking within laughter) is able to open out infinitely within this communication; all these are things that can only be attractive to Blanchot, he who is a reader of Heidegger, is close to Levinas, is the author of *Thomas the Obscure*. The opening onto Nothing—onto the figuration of the *there is* provided by this communication—secretly and almost innocently binds the two friends together via the intermediary of a third party, in a new form of grace. It must be said, we must go this far: for Blanchot, Bataille will be the other great friendship of his life ("he who was, with Emmanuel Levinas, my closest friend")—and it is remarkable that this friendship should appear at the very moment when Levinas had just disappeared, having been taken prisoner by the German army, in whose captivity he would remain for the rest of the war.[12] Things were similar for Bataille for whom Blanchot, together with, but differently to, Leiris or Masson, would be "the one who will accompany him beyond/life, himself without life, capable of free/friendship, detached from all ties."[13]

While the experience of death knits together communitarian ecstasy,[14] it seals the friendship of Bataille and Blanchot in a "piece of eternity too large for the eyes of men."[15] Both had lived through extreme experiences in relation to death: their own deaths, "primal scenes" so close to them, and the deaths of those close to them, which were also—albeit in a different way—their own. Living up to these deaths, placing or displacing in them the sovereignty of writing would be what was at stake in *Death Sentence*, and in Bataille's recognition of it as one of the extreme works of literature.

We must also understand everything that had separated them up to that point, from the parts of the country they came from to their fathers and families, from their temperaments to their studies, from their more or less well-ordered, well-conceived, well-explored vocations to their political, aesthetic, or literary convictions. While they might have read some of the same authors (one thinks of Dostoevsky, Lautréamont, or Pascal, as well as of their mistrust of Surrealism), their approaches were divergent (for instance over Nietzsche or German philosophy in general). To use shorthand, the authors from Gide to Maurras that were important in the youth of one did not always have a major influence on that of the other. Although their desires for recognition were expressed, abandoned, challenged, and displaced in different ways, what was really at odds were the ways in which they participated in shared or collective enterprises—from the journalist to the activist, from the newspaper editor to the director of a luxury journal, from a withdrawal into solitude to the mysteries of a secret society. They even had different ways of being elegant. The possibility of this encounter and of "admiration and agreement" therefore forces us to ask what at this time Blanchot thought of eroticism and the sacred, two issues at the heart of Bataille's thinking and life. Eroticism certainly did not have the charge or the frequency for Blanchot that it did for his friend, but its discreet presence could have its striking moments. As for the hypermoral and atheological positions adopted by Bataille (the opening of God to evil, to obscenity, to absence), at the end of 1940 Blanchot was ready to entertain them. By fall 1941 he was ready to read *Madame Edwarda*, to be "shocked into silence" by it, and to "suggest [to Bataille] that such an encounter was ample for [his] life, just as having written it must have been sufficient for [Bataille's]."[16] Perhaps it was even Blanchot who pushed furthest this divinization of eroticism according to his logic of absence, effacing all excesses of figuration from his fiction in order to comment on its incommunicability and its distance. Blanchot therefore presented at least this point of difference: Eroticism cannot have provided for him any momentary appeasement of solitude, of the pain inflicted by a knowledge of one's limitations.

The differences between them were important, and often counted in Bataille's favor: He was the more experienced, more diverse thinker who had already produced publications, he was politically lucid and inflexible and had become familiar with public confrontations through polemical exchanges with Breton, by editing journals and running the Collège de Sociologie. But the withdrawal, the uncertainty, the feeling of failure, the *absolute lack* that were Blanchot's, exacting themselves in the extreme courtesy and infinite attentiveness to the other that they shared, also meant that Bataille shared in the joyous feeling that a book, a summa, an *authority* was necessary (and all the more necessary when lucidly critiqued). Once they had met, Bataille and Blanchot began to publish their works generously and regularly, and they knew the same *absence of self*, the same *absence of books*, the same destitution, the same lack of satisfaction. Bataille, too lacking in hope and too sovereign to act as a brother (even if he was the same age as Blanchot's sister), but without being old enough or dominant enough to act as a father, offered Blanchot—at thirty-three years of age—a new model of friendship and community, outside the Judaic *tutoiement*, and outside the body of the nation. What forty years later Jean-Luc Nancy would name "the inoperative community" might have been born at this moment, in the absolute despair of that historical present, in the necessity of thinking a form of community beyond all finitude, beyond what can be communicated, beyond nothingness.[17]

With them, what came into being was perhaps a new chapter of history, of life, of the thinking of friendship. Of course, this was a friendship reserved for two people and kept at a distance even from others close to them; but it was not a friendship founded on any mourning to come, or any celebration, because in a sense these two living beings were already dead, dead to death, dead to one another. If "it is even through the possibility of loving the dead that a certain *loving* [*aimance*] comes to be decided," then this incommensurability was the condition necessary in order to exist: the loved one was, or had to be, "soulless."[18] Blanchot would write that "in truth, it is as if man had at his disposal a capacity to die that far surpasses what is necessary for him to enter into death." This difference in capacity and energy, which draws on dying as a process, was made available to and *expended* for the friend. There could therefore be no completion of mourning, no funeral oration. The postmortem homage (which it would fall to Blanchot to give) would be anything but a living invocation of the dead man; instead it would attest to the presence near death of the still-living partner. In other words, this was the presence of a person dead and alive, alive and dead—in speech, at the edges of speech, on the cusp of silence. Friendship was no longer the path to wisdom, but the site of nonknowledge.

Friendship? "Friendship begins *prior to* friendship," Derrida would write.[19] We must try to deconstruct this movement in light of the supposed first encounter between Bataille and Blanchot, when each was able to love the other for the share of death within him, the share, in the gaze or beyond the gaze, of someone who had seen death (Laure, the death sentence), who had discovered what an inalienable gift it presents, who had known "the disaster . . . without which there is no friendship, the disaster at the heart of friendship."[20] Both knew Aristotle's phrase "O my friends, there is no friend," both knew that there are no friends because death, the impossible, prevents it. But they also knew that all possible friendship, at the limit of the possible, transcends friendship, just as all possible literature is beyond literature. "*Friendship: friendship for the unknown without friends,*" Blanchot would say.[21] This was an immediate friendship for what was unknown in the other, for the part of the other that is invisible to all, visible to no other friend, but known by this new friend, this friend beyond friends. This was a friendship for the other's dying, for the other's writing, and it provided the ability to replace the other, to give oneself to the other; it is the salvation, relief, accompaniment of thought. This marginal friendship also gave rise to a political affirmation. Over and against those who think of death as a founding event in the community, the death of each person created within each person the community of those who have no community, a community beyond all community.

This was a community in search of itself: it put itself to work, and to the test, with one or two groups of Bataille and Blanchot's friends.

Bataille, Prévost, and the contestatory group from Jeune France (Blanchot, Lignac, Petitot, sometimes Ollivier) met regularly at first in a small restaurant in the Rue de Ponthieu, or in the offices on the Rue Jean-Mermoz. Then, from fall 1941 to March 1943, the meetings took place in the apartment of Bataille's partner Denise Rollin at 3 Rue de Lille, once or twice a month (except for an interruption of several months in 1942). A second group also formed, containing Queneau, Leiris, Fardoulis-Lagrange, and perhaps also Limbour. Bataille and Blanchot were the only two to be part of both groups . . . except for Denise Rollin, whom Blanchot met at this time and who was a silent figure, even more silent than he was.[22] "This woman, of enigmatic appearance, did not speak, barely responded to being greeted, disliked people smiling at her child, and listened mutely to our long conversations," Prévost would write.[23] Blanchot's silence weighed on the debates, a "silence that in theory meant his perception was enhanced, but which in reality was sometimes interrupted to allow him to support Bataille's choices," Fardoulis-Lagrange would say.[24] However, Bataille and Blanchot were almost the only ones who spoke, without any hierarchy between them, even if beyond the frequent coincidences in their thinking Blanchot had several "ways of withdrawing" (in Louis Ollivier's words) when he thought that Bataille was overdramatizing.

Bataille would read aloud and provide commentary on *Inner Experience*, which he was writing at the time. These meetings were important for him, especially so due to Blanchot's involvement. He would leave traces of this in his work, both in the book published in 1943 and elsewhere too. The heart of "inner experience" is attributed to a phrase uttered by Blanchot: Bataille attributes to it nothing less than "the Galilean significance of a reversal in the exercise of thought," capable of "replacing at once the Church tradition and philosophy." This historic phrase is only a few words long: "inner experience itself is authority (but all authority is expiated)." Bataille receives these words as a shock: They neutralize the anguish into which he has been plunged by "inner experience" lived as a "voyage to the end of the possible," without the security of an external authority, be it religious, mystical, philosophical, or literary. "This response immediately calmed me, barely leaving me (like a scar slowly closing over a wound) any residue of anguish." It allows all knowledge to be refused and contested ("the principle of contestation is one that Blanchot insists on, as if on a foundation"). Bataille thus places under Blanchot's authority the experience that he has felt for such a long time: that of the impossible lying beyond authorities in history, mysticism (Eckhart, Angelo di Foligno), philosophy (Descartes, Hegel, Nietzsche), or literature (Proust). *Thomas the Obscure*, which he quotes twice, seems to him to be the only other book "where the questions of the new theology, even if they remain hidden within it, are truly insistent."[25]

We can only be struck by the way what is most proper to Bataille is constantly, exclusively and glorifyingly attributed to Blanchot. Perhaps he sees him first of all as a literary authority (he would often quote *Thomas the Obscure* and *Aminadab*); perhaps also as an authority of experience (of the encounter with death, in which Blanchot had advanced "more nakedly," "to the ends of the possible"); or perhaps it is even a case of stating that this excess can only be recognized together, in a community founded on the element of friendship that cannot be experienced, namely the effacement and explosion of the individual as he sinks into the difficulty of dying.[26] This brings with it a complicit and almost anonymous dramatization; Blanchot will later admit to Dionys Mascolo that "I have always thought that it was 'dramatic' for *Inner Experience* to evoke in this unprepared and unjustified way these unwritten thoughts, suddenly transcribing them, thoughts that despite the name given remain incognito."[27]

After all, the "revelation" of these principles had already been put forth in Bataille's texts.[28] The instant calm that he felt can also be read as an obscure feeling of triumph (the unconscious return and confirmation of a previous finding) and of recognition (in which a community of thought was acknowledged). Throughout all the years to come, it will often seem that not a single lexical choice, not a single movement of thought by one of these two figures would take place without the vigilance and friendship of the other. It goes far beyond any simple influence. And perhaps even beyond any real presence, too. Blanchot's presence is clear in Bataille's statements on the impersonal (language as if borrowed), on death (as if a natural leaning), in the intensified paradoxes (even for key statements), in the sparseness of his articles (especially on literature), in the impossible tendency toward systematization (even if this was a systematization attempted via fragmentary jolts).²⁹ Bataille's presence can be seen in the sparseness of Blanchot's *récits* (we know how struck Blanchot was by *Madame Edwarda*, "only a few pages," a "unique work, beyond all literature," a "sort of absolute"), in the growing insistency of the fragmentary (even and especially after Bataille's death), in the radicalized encounter with the excess (the nudity) of experience, in the formulation of dialectical thinking (from the "dialectic of forms" in *Documents*, which was so strongly linked to the obscure powers of seduction, and from Kojevian negativity, to Blanchot's discourses on art, on "literature and the right to death," or on poetry as an "image of language").³⁰ These presences do not prevent the thinking of each man from retaining its singular nature, and indeed probably allow them to become more pronounced and dramaturgical (in their excess, in their paradoxes), but which, between the two oeuvres, set obstacles in the way of any possible speech. Bataille and Blanchot would each write several articles on the other; but Blanchot would not contribute to the 1958 issue of *La Ciguë* that paid homage to Bataille, and Bataille abandoned the project of a book on Blanchot that he had often imagined.³¹ Their writing would only truly meet up in death: the ultimate, ecstatic desire of the dying man to "be present at the death of thought" extends an invitation that would be taken up by *The Step Not Beyond*, the first fragmentary book and one produced as if from beyond the grave: "Death, thought, so close to one another that thinking, we die, even if in dying we excuse ourselves from thinking; every thought would be mortal; every thought, the last thought."³²

Just as Levinas's presence marks the oeuvre from the outset and as it is written continues to insist and bear upon it with the demands of the other, of infinite *tutoiement*, and of a first, strangely inassimilable man named Thomas (a memory of unavowable mistakes); so that of Bataille will demarcate the itinerary followed, providing its access to nakedness, opening out its language, hobbling its stride, being as it is the permanent presence of the end, of the last man. We must note that once Bataille had died, Blanchot never published another *récit* (at least no *récit* in the exacerbated form of a language infinitely extended).

Toward the end of 1942, probably on his return from Panilleuse in the Eure *départment* in Normandy where he had written *Le Mort*, Bataille drew up the project for a 'Socratic college.' This was a way of formalizing the meetings that had already been taking place "for some months now." Torn between the awareness of incommunicability and the desire to communicate, Bataille was attempting to truly lay bare the life of the mind. He did so without thinking of any publication or propaganda, even as he planned a series of presentations aimed at making speech less flighty and less open to chance.

> I suggest that we draw up a body of scholastic data concerning inner experience. . . . Only thoughts reduced to a clear format—the one most bare of poetic artifice—can truly engage with consciousness and link experiences that would previously have been called mystical to the unveiling of their inner workings. These thoughts cannot be the work of a single person but must result from a joint effort linked to the sharing of profound experience, and at the same time to its stimulation.[33]

Bataille left Paris for Vézelay at the end of March 1943. The Collège Socratique had not come to fruition. "The last gasp of a communitarian experience incapable of being realized," it "could only fail," Blanchot would write (he seems to have taken his leave several times himself).[34] However, we must point out what the encounter between Bataille and Blanchot would lead to in the community of thinkers and writers of the second half of the twentieth century. Their excessive advances into the experience of the impossible, into the thinking of the unthinkable; the question of whether it can be transmitted via the radical contestation of language; the power of literature, a literature "beyond all literature" to "name the ineffable—and the unspeakable—and, in naming them, to reach what is most out of reach": "this spectral swarming that is proper to it, which is its life in *hell* or rather the life of *death* within it";[35] all of these hitherto unexplored avenues would open up possibilities for thinkers such as Foucault and Deleuze and would be heard echoing through the poetry of Char and Michaux.

CHAPTER 22

In the Name of the Other
Literary Chronicles at the *Journal des Débats* (1941–1944)

On April 16, 1941, Blanchot began his "Chronicles of Intellectual Life," which were essentially literary, at the *Journal des Débats*.[1] They would continue uninterrupted until August 1944, totaling 171 articles, to which should be added two texts he published on the newspaper's front page. Slightly less than a third (54) were reprinted in *Faux pas*, Blanchot's first wide-ranging collection, which appeared at the end of 1943.

This newspaper, which overtly supported Pétain, had only begun to appear regularly again in March 1941. Of course, it was still just as little read, just as pompous and boring, just as incapable of satisfying readers on the far right. Blanchot's elegant, arrogantly indifferent articles were printed alongside intolerable propaganda, whether in the form of articles or advertisements. This was a strange object, a conciliatory invective, which seemed to lack any feeling for history: how was this column possible? How was it tolerated by the editors and by those in power? How did Blanchot experience its publication? Did he think at this time that authors were not judged by the platforms they wrote for? Did he badly need the money, as he would later say to Roger Laporte? That at least is not entirely true: he was receiving a salary from Jeune France. But it is true that he was expecting this salary to soon stop being paid, and the precaution of undertaking this column at the *Journal des Débats* would quickly show how financially useful it was.[2]

Although they are of extremely varying quality, these chronicles contain the first high points of Blanchot's critical work. While this might have represented—as Bataille put it—a "wholly accidental origin," Blanchot would transform this accident into a calling and follow through the logic of even the most sovereign critic, as well as the author in question, expiating or atoning for his authority.[3]

The title "Chronicles of Intellectual Life" recalls to some extent "Les lectures de *L'Insurgé*" ("The Readings of the Insurgent") owing to its weekly publication, its length, its position at the foot of the page, sometimes its choices of authors, and finally (and above all) the way its subjects are given renewal: Even classic authors are presented in the light of reissues, critical editions, secondary works, putting them in a contemporary setting . . . *inciting* one to write. Blanchot imposes his authority, his style, his erudition, his quality of judgment. The varied roll call of authors addressed is a curious one, mixing together those admired and those hated by the far right. It gives rise to papers on general theory; to texts on classic authors, most commonly from the seventeenth century (Racine, Molière, Madame de La Fayette); an increasing number of articles on nineteenth-century authors (Lamartine, Balzac, Stendhal, Baudelaire, Rimbaud, Mallarmé, Huysmans, Maupassant), great foreign literature (Dante, Machiavelli, Goethe, Blake, Melville, Joyce, Rilke), contemporaries who were already well known (Claudel, Valéry, Gide), were becoming so (Sartre, Camus), or would become so (Des Forêts, Bataille, Michaux). There are also a few texts on literary criticism or philosophy (Thibaudet, Paulhan, Parain, Alain, Dumézil, Kierkegaard, Bergson); even articles on his far-right friends (Maulnier, Haedens) or on authors of the right, including some associated with collaboration (Benoist-Méchin, Montherlant, Chardonne, Jouhandeau, Drieu); regularly, his texts look jointly at several novels or collections of poetry as a way of giving an updated view of the genre (interests for Duras or Leiris, Fardoulis-Lagrange, Claude Roy, or Henri Thomas also begin to be apparent). There is something surprising about the often considerable inconsistency of tone between one article and the next; one will address an important work inventively, loftily, demandingly, then another will look at a completely worthless novel in a superficial, accommodating, complacent way (as if the critic were giving in easily to indifference).[4] This inconsistency can be explained by the genre of the press article, which is often closer to a review than to commentary, even if sometimes Blanchot moves close to a true essay. Such inconsistency does not change over the four years. Overall, the authors most often addressed will be Valéry and Mallarmé (four articles each) and Montherlant (five articles). There are three articles on Michaux, to whom Blanchot would subsequently return too rarely, and three on Paulhan.

The judgments made had changed significantly since the articles of the 1930s. There is no better way of seeing this than by looking at the column of September 22, 1943 (Blanchot's thirty-sixth birthday) on Kléber Haedens's *History of French Literature*. Blanchot confides under the cover of the impersonal that Haedens "always displays a striking love for other authors that have come to be hated." He argues against the weight of traditionalist readers' conventionality: "One admires those whom one has got into the habit of admiring, one expresses violent disdain for those whom it has been agreed to disdain." In order to discover Blanchot's preferences, we can simply read the article against the grain. "For Kléber Haedens, the outstanding seventeenth-century novel was not *The Other World* by Cyrano de Bergerac, but *The Princess of Clèves*, and the strongest eighteenth-century writer was Laclos and not Sade." Blanchot does not waste time with Musset or Fénelon, expresses disdain for Voltaire, neglects Verlaine, rates highly Hugo, Stendhal, and Flaubert, and admires Mallarmé, Rimbaud, and Lautréamont. A year later he will discuss the areas of interest opened up to him by "these nonclassified minds that in France form the tradition of those beyond the tradition."[5] He rehabilitates Freud, praises the "edicts of French surrealism," quotes Breton as well as Gide several times, always gladly, and sometimes even in the knowledge that he is making good one of his most serious past errors.[6]

This means that Blanchot can now be found expressing scorn for Bernanos, Drieu, and even those he has previously been close to, such as Francis. Of these previous relationships, only the attachment to the critical gaze of Thierry Maulnier remains. Blanchot produces unfriendly judgments on Mauriac (in an article that would not be collected in *Faux pas*) and on Chardonne (this was in July 1941, just after the publication of what would be called "a small mystical, pro-Hitler essay in Drieu's *NRF*."[7]). He still finds psychologism as well as moralism as violently unbearable as ever. This leads him to condemn Montherlant for the latter's "poor quality" moral hyperinflation: "There is nothing more lowly or more guilty than the man who preaches in the name of silence and who makes the enigma of the summits into a commonplace."[8] At the empty heart of silence, at the noontide of the summit (even he would lose his way there), Blanchot henceforth is in the company of Bataille and Nietzsche.

Blanchot's literary culture is now in broad daylight, without anything being secret or reserved.[9] Here, "culture" means that Blanchot cites as real role models for his creative thought authors in whom he has been immersed for years. They secretly (begin to) act as reference points, the models in relation to which he begins to construct his own critical and novelistic oeuvre. Only those who have acted as architects for a palpable universe manage to survive among all those, almost exclusively on the Right, who make up "past culture": Péguy, Claudel, and above all Giraudoux, with the "furrow he ploughed so astonishingly," his "unbearable perfection," his "sense of what is unique." But even with these authors, Blanchot tones down such excesses of lyricism when reworking the articles for *Faux pas*.[10] The three authors who count, those who set in motion the movement of palpable intellectual creation that marks *Faux pas*, are Mallarmé, Lautréamont, and Valéry. Their names appear dozens of times, as do longer references to their texts or their theories.

In the wake of Lautréamont and Mallarmé there follow something like waves or flurries of names: Baudelaire, Rimbaud, Nerval, and the German romantics Novalis, Hölderlin, and Jean-Paul. For contemporaries, the preference is for Michaux, Ponge, Parain, Leiris, or Queneau. Beyond Thomas Mann or Virginia Woolf, in whom Blanchot had already taken an interest in *L'Insurgé*, the greatest novelists of the era are said to be "Sade, Melville, Dostoevsky, Proust, Kafka, Joyce, Malraux, Faulkner," a list that is already close to the names that will be chosen in the future; it is also knowingly constructed, featuring as it does authors impossible to address at greater length in the *Journal des Débats*.[11] Kafka, Sade, and Malraux are cited only once or twice in four years, and we can see why, when we recall what sort of newspaper the articles were being published in. In a significant gesture, Blanchot would dedicate one or two important texts to each after the Liberation.

It should be clear that Blanchot's concern is not to account for contemporary literature (this was simply his role as a journalist), but instead to put in position what is necessary for contemporary creation. His concern is to forge a path toward what he calls the "young novel," doing so via a criticism that is more anticipatory than explanatory—a new rhetoric setting up laws of construction and deconstruction.[12] Little by little, journalism serves the strategy of conquering not literature but fiction. This leads to a reorganization of critical discourse, which is also a different way of presenting a public persona politically and ideologically, a way of exposing the intimate that is both overt and obscure, palpable and neutral. It is still a question of returning to oneself, but now it takes place via a nascent *thinking* carried out *in the name of the other*.

His official role was clear: Blanchot was being asked to act as a young scribe (*clerc*) for the French state, no more and no less. The same impetus led to his literary responsibilities at Jeune France and at the *Journal des Débats*. In two articles with which the column began, two texts whose interdependence would be interesting to read in greater detail, Blanchot defines his responsibilities, accepting them while contesting and evading them at the same time.[13] Initially it was a question of the critic serving readers, to help them perceive "the true movement of minds"; for amidst the uncertainty of war, with the refusal of enemy values (Blanchot was careful not to say which ones) and "tacit consent to all the rest," the public that was so keen to read found it hard to identify frauds. Subsequently, it was a question of helping writers themselves define their place in public life: how, in an era "given up to disaster and to tempest," were they not to feel embarrassed by their masterpieces, not to "scorn themselves for simply being themselves?" How could they break the isolation that was necessary without forgetting "that audience which is made up of their entire nation, in whose service they are ready to sacrifice a great deal?" But at the same time Blanchot refuses to subscribe to any form of press-ganging: "save art by restoring to it a public," "save artists by turning them into educators of youth," "admit only works conceived in praise of the homeland, the earth, and traditional values," "[bid] the artist serve, enlist, compromise himself . . . by adhering to political ideas or principles which he is quite incapable of judging"; these are so many ways of distancing artists from their capacities for creation and for breaking with tradition. Thus Jeune France was speaking through Blanchot, but a Jeune France that was no longer itself: its contestatory approach, similar to that of Lignac or Bazaine, whom Blanchot cites in the article in question, cuts through any aesthetics of imitation and indirectly lays claim to "an art of seeking and absence."[14]

Blanchot would indirectly quote Bazaine again two months later, on the subject of the exhibition "Twenty Painters of the French Tradition": "They quite rightly made a point of appealing to tradition, while emphasizing that fidelity to tradition does not consist in being faithful to certain forms, but in searching for a genuine creativity without which nothing can be transmitted and nothing endures."

Blanchot criticizes the "strange fatigue of the mind" that had taken hold of those commentators unable to understand how tradition could be approached in this way.

> When one sees those critics who talk endlessly of a return to classicism reserving their praise for the most mediocre and insipid efforts, the product of unstudied imitation, one wonders what weakness of imagination, what banality of form is to be found, for them, in the works of the great creative periods, which were all periods of great rupture.

Thus can be seen Blanchot's margin of contestation within a traditionalist milieu: It consists in pushing traditional discourse to a paradoxical point where a claim to modernity is made in the name of classicism. The dominant arguments have to be turned against themselves; what is decadent is to passively accept tradition (or copies of tradition): such eras undergo "a spiritual decline that makes them unworthy of the models they have adopted."[15] In counterpoint, dignity demands the "risk" of "scandal" (that which Blanchot will demand be respected in Sade). This discourse would soon become impossible at Jeune France, although it would always retain some leeway in the Vichy press. A critical way of conceiving the world was being developed, at once undercover and riskily, in the public eye.

Blanchot will insist more and more openly on the independence of art, which is also that of his criticism. As early as November 1941, an era when he was still at Jeune France, he removes his mask and decides to stop speaking with borrowed words:

> It is therefore in our interests to repeat today that a writer worthy of the name need not, strictly speaking, take his audience into account, and that it is enough for him to be loyal to himself, this loyalty consisting in squeezing himself into his work, in being faithful to this necessary work. . . . People often speak about art and its audience, about how important it is for the creator to move closer to those for whom he is creating. It must be said that this signifies exactly nothing, if not that those who deal with these serious questions without knowing anything about them are extraordinarily mediocre. Absolutely nothing can be said about, or asked of, the creator. He moves in unknown ways.[16]

This appeal to "inner necessity," this divinization of the poet as creator, form the first axis of his critical thinking, which is concerned with locating the necessary conditions for the creation of the contemporary novel. The necessity of the work does not have to come from any naturalist or psychological exterior, nor from any rhetorical concern, but "from the work itself." Without this "law of inner necessity," a term and a way of thinking that would mark this period for Blanchot,[17] the novel becomes "more and more foreign to the essential demands of literature, which is to say to a certain creative power giving rise to a work, and to the recognition of a certain number of conventions and laws without which creation cannot take on the status of an order."[18] This is all the more so given that "the literary work is constructed according to its own laws, ordered according to its own conventions, asks its consistency of an indestructible form."[19]

The influence of Jean Paulhan can be recognized here, one of "those rarest of minds who cherish what is rare."[20] We know how important Blanchot took the author of *The Flowers of Tarbes, or Terror in Literature* to be, dedicating three articles from October to December 1941 to this book that significantly complemented Valéry in the area of theories of form. The three articles were collected in a short work published by Corti in 1942, *How Is Literature Possible?* It was Blanchot's first critical book. Only the second and third were published in *Faux pas*, bearing the same title (the first mostly provides a synthetic view of Paulhan's theory).

The way Paulhan attacks the Terror that had seen the doctrine of inspiration reign over literature for fifty years, denying the writer any rhetorical resources and any conformity to rules, can only prove attractive to Blanchot, who seeks the greatest risk available to literature, and the best way to communicate it. Paulhan shares with Valéry the fact of forcing one—to put it simply—to see all ground as form, and impure form. Thus he is able to turn the weapons of the writers of Terror against them by showing that their metaphysical and fantastical conventions . . . are just as formal as openly-declared rhetoric, while being less rigorous. He calls for the return of theoretical and rhetorical necessity, something Blanchot sees as the best guarantor in approaching the impossible: the only way of accounting for the most abyssal "inner experiences." Paulhan acts as a bridge between Valéry and Bataille, imposing another form of Terror that is rhetorical or post-rhetorical. To respond with excess to the naivety of Terror is to "make theatre *a bit more* theatrical, the novel violently novelistic, and literature in general more literary."[21]

Paulhan casts doubt over all criticism in a way that Blanchot would exploit and benefit from. He casts absolute doubt over the "extreme purity of the soul and the freshness of a communal innocence" which was proper to the romanticism of Terror.[22] He is infinitely attentive to the effect of words in language (Paulhan was anything but hostile to language), to their power, their erosion, their effacement, their lack of power, which could still turn out to be a kind of power. In all of this there is a belief in language, which had always raised more concerns for Bataille than for Blanchot.

The latter takes Paulhan's thinking and the ways it is formulated to their breaking point, even when it is highly paradoxical.[23] He takes up the extreme conclusions of this thinking, but always *in the name of the other*. This allows us to understand why Paulhan repeatedly states that Blanchot's articles reveal his own text to himself. Thus to call Terror into question is to call into question the entirety of literature, because it is not "just any aesthetic or critical concept whatever" but instead the very soul of literature and of every writer. This posits an extreme demand:

> In the heart of every writer there is a demon [a logical demon, the first two versions said] who urges him to strike dead all literary forms, to become aware of his dignity as a writer by breaking free from language and literature; in short, to put into question, inexpressibly, what he is and what he does.

Every writer? The Mallarmean demand is legitimized by such statements. This is a demand that can bring salvation. The new rhetorical tension consists in not allowing the writer any rest: he can neither blindly obey old rhetorical codes nor give vent to Terror's inspiration. "It is a question of revealing to the writer that he gives birth to art only through a vain and blind struggle against it"—a permanent struggle. Blanchot continues by arguing that the more the writer knows he is subordinate, the freer he is: This awareness that he is under the sway of commonplaces allows him to make them even more common and attempt to dominate them. In this case, for the writer the rules will no longer be received as "an artificial track showing the path to follow and the world to be discovered, but as the means of its discovery and the law of its progress through obscurity." Paulhan's work serves to justify and to found the theory of necessity. Blanchot's conclusion is that "the rigors of the laws found the absolute world of expression, outside of which chance is nothing but sleep"; this amends the first version from the *Journal des Débats*, which reads "outside of which there is nothing but chance and sleep." To restore chance to literature is the final throw of the dice for an article that brings things back to the Mallarmean demand—just as it brings them back to Georges Bataille.[24]

Armed with such confidence in language, on condition that it contest itself and relate playfully to itself, Blanchot extends the Mallarmean poetic demand to all literature, and notably to novels.[25] He also draws together Melville and Mallarmé and defines *Moby Dick* as a "total book," "the written equivalent of the universe." Literature is a *creative* experience, of a spatial, cosmic, divine order, as it is in Joyce, Nerval, Poe, Lautréamont. "This mode of writing attempts, in a vertiginous claim, to return to the word *creation* the meaning that it has in the expression 'the creation of the world.'"[26] Thus the idea of mythical power, which had already been developed in a few articles for *L'Insurgé*, can be found in *Faux pas*, consolidated this time by the Mallarmean theory of language (namely that poetic language is not everyday language; it is an "ensemble of sounds, cadences, numbers and, as such, through the linking of forces that it symbolizes, reveals itself to be the foundation of things and of human reality"[27]). The work is "the full-scale substitute for the universe," he writes of *A Throw of the Dice*, or, in reference to Rimbaud's poetry, the world's "sonorous equivalent."[28] We must believe that for Blanchot the world has become the double, and indeed the sacrificed double, of literary creation. He is attracted by the way the capacities of perception are extended, the way rhythms and distances are unexpectedly disrupted. He delights in the power of the metamorphoses taking place in Lautréamont and in Jean-Paul, "one of the first novelists to feel that metaphor could be an extraordinary instrument of transmutation," allowing prose to "recreate the world"; in this way the reader's gaze is led "from the visible to the invisible, from the known to the unknown, from the familiar to the clarity of enigma."[29]

"To move, with Mallarmé, toward the principles of language": Such is Blanchot's proposal for the new novelist. This is language as "the essence of the world," revealing mankind to itself, to the world, and to the existence of the world. It is to "suddenly shine forth from amidst cloud"; "to cause one to fall silent by exercising an intelligence caught up in infinite work and by the rigor of a mind constantly discovering chance." Of course, this novelist is Blanchot himself. Here he is speaking of his own creative anguish in an impersonal way. "The novelist who reflects on the work that he is to compose is immediately faced with such grave and exhausting problems that they must seem impossible. This impossibility must be the secret soul of his work." And Blanchot adds, perhaps in an attempt to ethically describe his first novels:

> The novelist has a destiny quite other than that of making himself understood, or rather he must make the reader grasp what cannot be heard in everyday, inauthentic language. He undertakes to bring into the absolutely continuous universe of events, images, and words the essential dialogue that constitutes him. Thus he heads, by the same path as any other artist, toward those strange shadows whose contact

gives him the feeling of waking up in the deepest sleep, toward this pure presence where all things appear so bare and so reduced that no image is possible; in a word, he heads toward this primordial spectacle in which he never wearies of contemplating what he can see only through a complete self-transformation.

Such is the Mallarmean, rather than Kafkaesque, ambition of Blanchot's first novels.[30]

The inner necessity of the work, accessed through language, allows one to reach the inner forces of being, the stakes of what can be perceived, between the pained and the exalted body, that of death and that of *jouissance*, that of oblivion and that of memory. *Faux pas* is crisscrossed with the adjectives "obscure," "invisible," "mysterious," "strange," "secret": they serve to translate the unspeakable and often inaccessible places that such a literature can reach ("an alliance with singular figures," Blanchot wrote of Michaux's poetry). For the erudite, delirious creation of a world leads to abysses of annihilation, to mythical struggles of solitude with gods (even invisible ones), to overwhelming exaltations, to the vertigo of the unfathomable. To create such a world is to provide a mythical equivalent for the debates around "inner experience," namely via the infinite extravagance of forms and via reminders of the almost mechanical rigor of time. To do so is to perceive incredibly shifting spaces, the sudden opening of regions that are emptier than emptiness itself (and nonetheless still full of organic or spiritual presences), the disruptions experienced by a body as if externally aware of its own gaze, a body empty-hearted from wandering and disgusted at its own steps. An infinite paradox is opened up by the disconnect between the profound immanence of experience and the fact that it is rarely visible, and is impossible to formulate. Literary language is able to introduce itself at this site—both concealed and open—of the gaze. Such is Blanchot's discovery, thanks to his research and his formulations. He never sets down the latter without a certain objective irony, which provides an implicit compensation for what he had previously been involved in, nor—above all—without drawing on his own memories (whether of his body, of death, of mourning, of the "primal scene"). The works of Mallarmé and Lautréamont, the language of Paulhan, the shared experience with Bataille prolongs Levinas's friendship and allows—even *grants*—him this access.

Some, including Blanchot himself, have attempted to see as mystical, fantastical, or magical this infinite attentiveness to oneself and to Being, in which the other is present as something like a fissure. This can only be done on condition that each of these adjectives be contested as soon as it is suggested, and on condition that they be played off against one another. It then becomes possible to evoke specific parallels between poetry and Hindu thought (the *ātman* of silence[31]), or between poetry and Christian mysticism (nonknowledge, St. John of the Cross). But poetry cannot "rely on a preestablished religious certainty": it is "an inexorable principle of movement, a creative speech that forms its object"; "it supposes that the one who receives it be a man capable, in exercising his gifts, of calling himself completely into question, of constantly considering himself a problem and, each time he touches port, of throwing himself back into the open sea."[32]

Such a calling-into-question stemming from "inner experience" would make Blanchot's journey at the *Journal des Débats* a decisive one. It became more intensive in fall 1942 (specifically, in November), even if we do not know why (there were no events that stood out, it would not change anything regarding the authority and the necessity of this step [*pas*], of this passage). One after the other, three articles on authors as varied as Meister Eckhart, Gide, and Camus make resolute statements in which the experience of the other and that of the self are fused together, intensified by the thought of "inner experience," intensified by everything that Blanchot's thinking would become.[33]

The rehabilitation of Gide is not uninteresting. This "impression of sensual presence superimposed on a perceptible absence" in the journal of *The Fruits of the Earth* catches Blanchot's eye—as if in a mirror. The attraction of the writer's journal extends the journalist's experience: they appear to have nothing in common, and yet there is a precious shared sense of fascination, of capture, an obsession with turning things over (*ressassement*), with the weight of time's demands, an infinite perception of the slightest gap in daily routine. The journal is like the still obscure place at the heart of a tree in which the sap rises slowly, secretly, imperceptibly. Daytime is subject to the same weight, the same thickness or stickiness as nighttime, its features become just as blurred. Blanchot reads Gide's journal like he will read Kafka's: as being as unjournalistic, as empty of events and even of sensations as possible, but also as charged with empty presence, with disorderly, folded, and cut-down spaces which serve to fix the author's imaginary in pure perception.

> *The Fruits* is not a journal, even a spiritual one, but an absence of any journal, the void of existence, the narrative—wiped clear of events—of a life that we know through commentaries that often apply to it only indirectly.

Blanchot's critical work is put together like such a journal, with its commentaries applying first and foremost to their author (to write about others would often mean to write about oneself), a "character lacking in substance" that we only know about indirectly, or more precisely: that we only know as indirectness. In this way, each "subject" becomes the critical, invisible partner of an author who only speaks of himself via the other, the others, *in the name of the others*.[34]

Whether it represents extreme pride or extreme modesty, the confrontation with the other always becomes, as the search for points of equivalence, the mirror of movement, of the body, of experience. The critic therefore also becomes the invisible partner of others' work. Sometimes, as if in an equivocal carelessness, his free indirect discourse is so uncontrolled that it disturbs the way in which the ideas mentioned are formulated, attributed, or even agreed grammatically. For it is not a question of appropriating the other, but of better disappropriating oneself through the other, and of disappropriating the other through oneself. The need for delicacy therefore leads to the figure of the other fading away gently and slowly (in the endless *writing* of the critical work), behind what is no longer his or her work, but without having become one's own: neither one nor the other, *ne-uter*, what Blanchot would name the neuter.

The critical work would therefore become something like the diary of the research being carried out, a fiction about fiction. There are countless passages in which Blanchot seems to comment on his own narratives, particularly from 1941 onwards (recognition by Bataille and Paulhan and the reception of *Thomas the Obscure* must have played a role in how aware he was of his fate as a novelist). The universe of *Thomas* or *Aminadab*—as well as that of the works still to come—is powerfully described, always appearing in the article in unexpected ways, sometimes revealing how unfaithful they are to the work being remarked on because it is deemed preferable to evoke the heights that work could have reached.[35] They thus define a more or less secret ideal for the novel. Only a few would be collected in *Faux pas*.

The biographical approach therefore remains as if necessary for Blanchot, albeit a biographical approach carefully controlled and carried out according to certain criteria. If he writes about Goethe or Vigny, it is in order to evoke their relations with Bettina von Arnem and Marie Dorval. Maupassant is addressed less in terms of his art than in those of his madness. With Baudelaire, he asks questions relating to the interest of his sources, and with *The Song of Roland*, moves straight to the history of the manuscripts. He is interested in Rilke in terms of Malte Laurids Brigge, and in La Fontaine "without the Fables." In a less anecdotal and frivolous form, this tendency will mark his entire critical work. Blanchot comments less on the work than the experience that precedes and accompanies it. His interest in biography is located at this intersection of life and creation. Is biography an acceptable form? Yes, if it is a biography of "genius" (understood in terms of the genesis or the creation of the work).

This was the approach with which Henri Mondor had succeeded regarding Mallarmé. Blanchot's admiration for this member of the Académie Française was real (and it would last: he would cite him fairly frequently and would send him some of his books, with dedications). The third piece for the *Journal des Débats* looks at this paradoxical biography,[36] which "knows the 'genius' and ignores the 'man,'" and from which Blanchot extracts criteria that it seems legitimate to demand of future biographies:

1. That the man in question be spared his "visibility," his common weakness;
2. That anecdotal tales should not appropriate the work: otherwise "the lines we read are nothing more than the reference points for a story";
3. Inversely, that biography should serve the work: thus "the most precious documents, the most unexpected testimonies, the rarest letters" make biography into "the reflection of a wonderful intellectual life" (Blanchot recognized that "certain texts, containing the first versions of poems or letters by Mallarmé, are of priceless importance");
4. That biography should show the mind's creation at work, that it should "know the 'genius' and ignore the 'man,'" because this work is what renders all subjects, all personae absent ("what he has accomplished, what resources he drew on in order to do it, to what inhuman conditions he condemned itself, with what torments he paid for the formation of a world detached from all mortal prestige," all of this simply leads to an "impenetrable and pure absence");
5. In sum, that biography efface itself before the work, and not vice versa; that it should remain purely fictitious, that it should disappear as soon as it has been read, that it should return us to the work even as it leaves us to "dream" of what it could have been; that it become the work's unavowable, impossible-to-circumscribe reverse-side, exposed to the reader.

Blanchot will formulate these demands for a biography in equivalent terms in his commentary on *Conversations with Eckermann*, which portray Goethe as a "hero of creation." Eckermann "knew how to be present in the artist's solitude, seeking to discover what the creator is when he is alone."[37] His interest in Brisson's book *Molière's Life in his Works*, had a similar feel: "It seeks to know Molière in the coming-together of character and creative power, in those tendencies in which it is less a matter of psychological particularities than of the movement of the mind trying to produce something other than itself."[38]

Thus Blanchot defends the rigor of certain biographical approaches and, not allowing himself any mythology of pure creation, even calls for them to exist. While the beginning of the Mondor article is "resigned" to authors' presence or life, still dreaming of them as pure creators who had not lived, "who were nothing outside of their art", "entirely consumed by their masterpieces," the Baudelaire article reverses the trend, not without irony, painting what formerly had been dreamt of as impossible:

> The hypothesis that definitively separates the man from the author and leaves whoever wants to enjoy a poem with only its bare text, however close it may be to the poetic truth—this hypothesis is also based on certain prejudices and makes creation an absolute that is prodigiously sheltered from chance and accident, against which no man, even divine, has ever been protected.[39]

The article on Mondor also evokes this "future biographer against whom [writers] defend themselves weakly." Biography can be revealed as the invisible thread of every body of work, albeit one indefinitely suspended.

Blanchot would always dream of such a biography for himself: a biography following the itinerary of creation, tracking the invisible, the nocturnal torments, the torsion of the work, the search for the impossible. For he will sketch out just such an invisible thread, such an *autobiography*—albeit disseminated, displaced, altered—throughout his critical work. He will do so through isolated pockets of presence, through holes or absences within the commentary on works and on their creation, in alignments or at times friendships knotted together, in which losing oneself in the other means perceiving distance as proximity. In this sense, the critical work is extremely playful (*jouissive*): its sentences serve to set up, like the bridge in "The Judgment," a "literally mad traffic" in which can be perceived, both in common and distinctly, the sufferings of the other, of oneself, and of, say, Mallarmé or Kafka, in their night which resembles a "mystical night."

> Mallarmé, through an extraordinary ascetic effort, opened an abyss in himself where his consciousness, instead of expiring, survives itself and grasps its solitude in a desperate clarity. Having detached himself utterly and unceasingly from all that appears, he is like the

hero of emptiness, and the night that he touches reduces him to an indefinite refusal to be anything at all—which is the very definition of the mind.[40]

There is no doubt that Blanchot dreamed of being this hero of emptiness, empty of all heroism, which he rejoins through the "infinite distance" to and from the other, his friend rather than his brother.

CHAPTER 23

A True Writer Has Appeared
The Publication and Reception of *Thomas the Obscure* (1941–1942)

In fall 1941, *Thomas the Obscure*, Blanchot's first book, was published. Although one critic called it "a work of Jewish decadence," it was not added to the list of works censored by the Nazi occupiers.¹ Paulhan recorded that it was badly received by the press in Paris: "here, newspapers are discussing it nastily. Bras[illach] is even saying that Blanchot has only ever worked for the Jews." Personally, he thought that the novel was "*true*"; in November he wrote to Claude Roy that "I think that this is how things happen, that the mind as well as the gaze has this blind spot."² A few weeks later, at Christmas, he presented this "very fine book" to Roger Caillois as the only real literary find since the series had been relaunched.³ Monique Saint-Hélier uncovered "rich gifts, slightly inebriated but with a controlled inebriation," she admired how fresh the landscapes were as well as "the sense of light in a book constructed from night." She evoked Lautréamont, Kafka, and notably Rilke and Kierkegaard in this book, which happily guarded its secrets, waited for words to play themselves out in "the time of other explications," "in which each signification will break apart like a cloud and then pour down like rain."⁴

Camus found the metaphysical aspect of the narrative attractive and believed that the key to it lay in the penultimate chapter: "One must then reread, and all becomes clear—but according to the light without sparkle which illuminates the asphodels of our mortal sojourn."[5] And in an elegant article in *L'Action Française*, Thierry Maulnier wrote that "a true writer has appeared."[6]

Thomas the Obscure attracted the literary world's attention, if not its respect and admiration. When it came out, the book perhaps was even more successful than the novels and *récits* to come would be. It was generally compared to Giraudoux, Lautréamont, Nerval, and the German romantics. But it also escaped these frameworks and gave its author, at the start of his literary career, a mysterious appearance. In his novels column at the *NRF*, Arland spoke of it as an "extremely strange book, despite the very pure line of its phrasing." "It sounds like the phrasing of a song in an airless world, or of a long quest in a dawn which is more than half in shadow."[7] In the journal *Confluences*, Auguste Rivet also called it "strange." It was said to have faults such as "sentences that get lost awkwardly among multiple subordinate clauses, a penchant for antithesis which makes some passages completely unintelligible" (and recalled Proust, a rather flattering fault), "a jargon that is sometimes scientific and sometimes philosophical," or "a misuse of extraordinary adjectives, an excessive vividness almost comparable to that of Léon Bloy." Nevertheless, the book had many qualities too: "its synthetic strength, its ability to evoke, the art of describing strange realities." Rivet encouraged the author to get rid of the "junk" affecting his novel. This judgment is perhaps not unrelated to the "uneasiness" that he admitted he felt: "[the reader] feels threatened by unknown but terrible forces." This stemmed from the mystical element within the book: Blanchot "has heard some imperious inner voice, and has obeyed the pressure of instinct."[8]

In the southern, "free" zone, the *Journal des Débats* carried an article that was bound to be laudatory, given that this was the first novel by its faithful contributor. Jean Mousset put his name to this piece, which replaced, for the only time in four years, Blanchot's "intellectual chronicle."[9] He began by stating "this is a great novel," and continued: "One of the greatest novels of contemporary literature since *In Search of Lost Time*. Which is to say that many men of today will find it unrewarding, irrelevant, *bizarre*." Such a work was damned to short-term failure, and to long-term success. Blanchot "prefigures the future twists and turns of thought." The article gave an insipid recap of the narrative before providing an ultimately insightful remark, rare at the time and still rare today: "Mr. Blanchot's novel is ultimately the most cutting and the most ironic refutation of the thesis according to which intellectualism detracts from sensibility."

CHAPTER 24

Lift This Fog Which Is Already of the Dawn
The Publication of *Aminadab* (1942)

A stranger (*étranger*), Thomas, arrives in a village and, on a woman's invitation, enters one of the houses. The reader knows nothing of his intentions, does not even know whether Thomas has been looking for this woman. A caretaker shows him, not entirely enthusiastically, into a room with paintings representing the rooms of the building. He asks him to choose one to rent. This is how the prose begins: It is the beginning of the endless visit in the building, which proceeds ever onward, with no point of return. Assigned to an inmate, Dom, Thomas meets servants, a *maître d'hôtel*, and a young woman, Mademoiselle Barbe (Miss Beard), who takes him to visit the upper floors, the game room, the former information office, and the sick bay, which is serving as a court of law. Thomas enters a long discussion with two new characters, Jérôme and his friend Joseph; loses Dom; loses Barbe, and then finds her again. Barbe explains to him that he has "walked the wrong way." At the end of the conversation, Thomas collapses on the ground; he will begin a long convalescence. Lucie, who has the neighboring room, takes him for a servant. Ultimately she embraces him and asks him to sign a form confirming that he entered the house willingly and that he has been well received there. Having returned, Dom explains to him in turn that he has gone the wrong way: To find true freedom, he ought to have gone below ground. Lucie begins to resemble the house. Night falls on the three characters. Thomas still has not "clarified" anything: These are the last words.

When was *Aminadab* written? In less than two years, after *Thomas the Obscure* had been given to Gallimard? In less than a year, after Blanchot had met Bataille? Was he reusing passages written in the 1930s (we can recall how close some are to "The Idyll" and "The Last Word")? If we are to believe Paulhan's letter to Drieu, the work was completed in December 1941 or February 1942, which is to say shortly after the publication of the first version of *Thomas*.

Aminadab came out the following fall. Printing was completed on September 24, only two days after Blanchot's thirty-fifth birthday. Paulhan called the book "a second *Thomas*." He was aware of it early on, at manuscript stage, and in January 1942 recommended that Drieu publish a chapter of it in the *NRF*. He added: "What [Blanchot] has written is almost unbearable over 400 pages but perfectly good over 10 pages. He seems to me the sort of writer who comes across best in a journal."[1] Was it really unbearable? Probably, but we can understand this differently to Paulhan. Namely, in the sense suggested by Bataille—another one of its first readers—of *Aminadab* bringing us "knowledge and manifestation of the destiny of man as a whole."[2]

The publication of *Aminadab* further developed Blanchot's reputation—whether good or bad—in literary circles. Numerous articles appeared, including some weighty ones: their authors were Bousquet, Sartre, and Maulnier. Bataille quoted the novel several times in *Inner Experience*, which he finished in summer 1942 and published in spring 1943. Although they remained silent at the time, a number of readers took note of it and were just as impressed, among them Roger Laporte and Louis-René des Forêts. Albert Camus already saw this second metaphysical novel as "a new form of the myth of Orpheus and Eurydice."[3]

Bataille, Camus, and Paulhan were not alone in comparing Blanchot's first two works of fiction—although the differences between them are considerable. *Aminadab* is the first *récit* published by Blanchot; its itinerary is linear, proceeding via tableaux that uncover the characters, keep up their hopes, increase their stupefaction. It has the language, framing, and aesthetic forms of the *récit*, with its unplaceable and almost fantastic world, its characters who come up against nonsense, and themselves perform unexplained acts. The reader is initiated into the obscure little by little, instead of it utterly overwhelming him or her. The novel provides a foretaste of

Blanchot's narrative rhetoric, being something like the concentrated version, the literal clarity, the embryonic law of that rhetoric. In its stripped-down quality we can see the influence of Bataille and Kafka.[4]

Aminadab also bears the memory of Emmanuel Levinas (its title being the first name of one of his younger brothers, who had recently been shot by the Nazis in Lithuania) and, beyond this, of the Jewish people (as a first name Aminadab means "my people are generous" or "wandering people").[5] But its main debt is to Georges Bataille. Whether failure, stupor, *jouissance*, or mortification, the experiences related allowed one to travel to the limits of Being (the *ipse*), and out the other side. The Thomas character obeys this logic, or rather this "nonlogical difference" of identity. Joë Bousquet's comment was: "a being is born: his task is to search for what kind of being he *is*, precisely. *He therefore has to learn painful lessons everywhere where what he is searching for is not.*"[6] In Bataille's terms, "agreement with oneself is perhaps a kind of death"; he was considerably touched by the ending of *Aminadab*.[7] This ending dares to remain, risks remaining suspended in nothingness. The entirety of human destiny is at stake through Thomas and his new epic of inner experience, "the human odyssey finishing with *Aminadab*." Is this a song of the sirens? *Aminadab* is already the *récit* of navigation, this pure *récit* or "movement toward song" that in *The Book to Come* Blanchot would set in opposition to the novel. It is the approach to the event: "the opening of this infinite movement which is the encounter itself," the encounter as "imaginary distance in which absence is realized and only at the end of which does the event begin to occur."[8] *Aminadab* is the *récit* of Bataille and Blanchot's experience, their chance, their encounter. "No one arrives at this point except those who are exhausted," Bataille would say. Ultimately, "there is nothing," "*there is the night*," "*there is nothing but night.*"

> Once history [*l'histoire*] is complete, mankind's existence would enter into animalistic night. Nothing is less certain. But does night demand this first condition: that one be unaware that it is night? The night that knew it was night would not be night, would only be the decline of day....

This forgetting, the world's forgetting to know that it carries mankind's destiny, is "the extreme lucidity" given "in the collapse of lucidity": "what falls is the night of *Aminadab*."

Blanchot's writing closes over, like this night, a world belonging to it alone, belonging to literature alone. It forces the simulacrum's unhappy consciousness to take written form (a simulacrum that, whether erotic or bookish, is always that of death). It also forces its sovereignty upon one. It permits meaning only after an effacement of the habitual world of signification, via a practice of *in-significance*. Language's referential capacities collapse. Its power to signify is neutralized. The house in *Aminadab* so little resembles a house that the reader asks himself or herself whether the word "house" still refers to the same concept. This is precisely Thomas's situation when he enters a room and thinks "that he [has] stepped into a café"; he has a language applicable to things, but this world neutralizes it.[9] The same word can change meaning several times; the sign advancing on the chessboard of narrative is impeded by this lack of self-identity. The narrative is full of logical operators ("similarly," "thus," "this is why" . . .), but this logical operation is never integrated into any reasoning.[10] Last, the first-person narration refuses the task of creating meaning. The narrative's frequent slippages into free indirect discourse bear witness to Thomas's interruptions, hypotheses, reasonings, and attempts to piece the facts together. "Was it true? Was it simply a word of encouragement? . . . Was it possible? There was certainly a misunderstanding" (50); "the plan itself must have been interrupted" (51); "he had certainly been very ill" (155), and so on.

Thomas is a neutral sign, without a past, a face, a family; beginning with his first description, he is stripped bare: "alone," alone in his perplexed questioning, in his solitude linked to "the anguish of his own destitution" (6). He has no choice except to go on, decisively, stubbornly, sometimes blindly, so much so that the quest takes him into narcissistic vexation, the ambition for power, and the desire for knowledge. Death constantly forces him to confront the anguish of the present, leading him to the dead-end of his illusory desire, that of "clarifying everything." He is faced with a coercive, explicitly authoritarian universe, or one most often silent, and whose silence is terrible, suffocating, full of negation ("nothing is happening, there is nothing" says a young man, 75); faced with a passive voice, an anonymous, unplaceable power that disallows freedom all the more through its claims to dispense it, Thomas—this Bartleby who moves forward—only continues to progress thanks to the desire to see what alienates him in the moments he is captured by images. However, faced with a world full of virile characters, who all seem to know more about it than he, a world in which the few women turn out to be instruments of power, Thomas fails to be initiated. He is ignorant, constantly threatened or locked up; he suffers or becomes depressed, is tossed around in the masculine universe only to end up facing an authoritarian woman; a laughing stock, loved by no one, "Thomas" incarnates the motifs of a guilt anxiety, a castration anxiety.

The narration invents a closed world devoid of external references, one that is not believable, not defined by tasks or by individuals, but is a world of play around a character who—unaware of the comic illusion and of its ability to be protective—becomes afraid, tries to understand but does not, and gives in to anguish. Baroque illusion takes the place of the world as a stage. Like Sade's château, the house in *Aminadab* does not belong to the world of production; only luxury and play make it possible. The Sadean world, where everyone is yoked to a task, produces only *jouissance*. The Blanchotian house, where everyone pretends to have a task, produces only anxiety, an endlessly risible anxiety.

There is something of René Char in the version of Blanchot given by Bousquet: "He has shattered the union of the soul and the body. By hiding from mankind the cardinal points of his habitual actions, he gives an inner centre to each fact, transforms life into a cloud and beyond thought, lifts this fog which is already of the dawn."[11]

Bousquet was a poet of the palpable who even in drawing our attention to insignificant elements related them "to emotions in which thought rediscovers its depth." Bousquet situates Blanchot in the position of a poet *out ahead of others*. His political reading of the narrative does not prevent him from admitting that Blanchot does not believe in "social solutions." He recognized *Aminadab* as the kind of work needed by literature and by a world at war. "*It is a question of making one's own life an instrument with which to explore collective life.*"[12]

More than ever, Thomas represents the fate of his author, ignorant as he is of the world in which he is evolving, blind to the games being played out at his expense, and unwavering in the hermeneutic illusion which removes all thought from him. The house is the site of hygienic, political, religious enclosure: There Thomas undergoes "a long imprisonment in these rooms that are insufficiently ventilated, overheated, and contaminated by the frequent presence of the sick" (184). He eventually discovers that "the earth ... is a place that fosters one, in which each body finds its subsistence, in which breathing too is a sort of food, and which offers unheard-of possibilities for growth and duration" (186). Heliotropic plants bud from the ends of his fingertips; his eyes grow larger and "their roots extend down the back of the neck to the top of the shoulders" (188). The solar violence of these images, which call to mind Lautréamont and Bataille and are set in opposition to any concrete form of nausea (roots) and any conventional thoughts (on trees), speaks to the sovereign madness of these "storms of visions."[13]

Whether they are unplaceable and deformed spaces or faceless subjects, reworkings of presupposed events or the shifting of the things one has invested in (touching both the aesthetics of representation and the functioning of the sign), syntactical alteration or the breaking of the logics of sameness and noncontradiction, narrative incoherence or ellipsis, the lack of dénouement, the main character occupying the focus of knowledge, or the anguish of nonsense . . . the signs of the narrative advance as in a dream sequence, with or without images, they are commented upon and comment upon themselves indefinitely. They advance in the obsessive ritual of isolated speech, bearing traces of the painful process of becoming a subject, and representing the remainders of an inner dialogue with the most remote elements of experience. The impossible does not rely on any conventions to justify itself. Improbable formulations rely on no thematization. The narrative sometimes functions like a dream or a hallucination, only then to immediately cease doing so. If it were presented as a dream, it would protect the reader and would not set free any anguish—or would only set free an anguish that remained make-believe. The narrative forms no "pact" with its reader, simply commentating, commentating freely: by so doing it places every subject in the position of the dreamer unable to comprehend that he is dreaming (an insomniac of the "outside"); or in that of the mourner who gives in to the hallucinatory psychosis of desire (and survives death itself); or in that of the guilty person who constantly sees the face of his misdeed (a victim of torture torn apart by himself). This mode of speech is talkative because it is alert, pays attention to detail, remains on the lookout for the smallest signal, is always keen to interpret, manically keen to explain (via parentheses, incisions, suppositions, alternatives, rectifications, overemphases . . .). It is infinitely polished and given form by a maniacal preciousness that offers a position of relative security ("I tried, by sheltering under this word, to advance further forward"). This mode of speech holds the subject under the sway of an agonizing but explainable exteriority, holding him there by means of a semiotic activity in which he locates the necessity of his existence (there is already something here of what Beckett's writings would be). This work within language allows us to appreciate how much the subject finds all discourse indifferent, and how much the narrative becomes an excessive simulacrum. "What cannot be, that alone satisfies [writing]."[14]

Yes, perhaps his political past was becoming something akin to a dream, a past that we can imagine was never experienced, like one of those experiences where one does not recognize oneself. Perhaps it was becoming a past in which language and rhetoric had floated close to an unformed, uncomfortable ideal that must be infinitely condemned, shown no mercy; perhaps in the past language and rhetoric had provided cover amid convictions that were tolerated, self-justified, self-accepted, and then unacceptable, unjustifiable, impossible—but still conceivable, thus imposing on this wandering man the duty of thinking.

> So where is the fault? For it does exist; we feel it with no less force than we feel our purity. It is in this world in which we had thought we were so happy. It suddenly fouls the air. We can no longer breathe. (103)

CHAPTER 25

Writers Who Have Given Too Much to the Present

NRF Circles (1941–1942)

The first letter that Blanchot received from Paulhan was dated May 10, 1942: "We will remember these days," he wrote.[1] The two men had had the chance to come across one another a few years previously, at the end of the 1930s, when Blanchot discovered *The Flowers of Tarbes: or, Terror in Literature*, which had appeared in article form in the *NRF*. Paulhan's leading role in the literary world was well known. He had been director of the *NRF* since 1925, even if the official role had only been his since 1935. Since 1936 he had published Artaud, Caillois, Leiris, Michaux, Ponge, Queneau, and Rilke in the "Metamorphoses" series. Thus both in terms of ideas and in terms of strategy, at first it was certainly Blanchot who was more interested in Paulhan than vice versa. We cannot rule out the possibility that the theory of literary language developed in *The Flowers of Tarbes* played a positive role at a moment of doubt and silence.

In June 1940 the *NRF* was taken over by the Germans. Paulhan withdrew, and Drieu was to succeed him. The former joined the Resistance that fall. After his arrest in May 1941, he was freed following Drieu's intervention on his behalf. He founded the underground publication *Lettres Françaises* with Jacques Decour, who would be tortured and executed in

May 1942. Described as a "shy patriot" by Claude Roy, he remained one of the leaders of French literary life, never abandoning his adventurous, paradoxical, destabilizing, calculating, ever-curious way of thinking.[2] "He saw things in just proportion, abandoning what is unnecessary in order to hold on to what is best. This means that he maintains certain friendships despite deep disagreements"—friendships with Drieu or with Jouhandeau, for example.[3] He attended social gatherings of German officers and intellectuals while belonging to one of the earliest Resistance networks. In this we come across a position shared by Blanchot for a time: "using Vichy against Vichy."

At the beginning of the war, Paulhan, for Blanchot as for others, was a gateway into literary life:

> At the time I was close to Jean Paulhan, who used to advise me. I recall that, during a trip in the metro, he came close to me and said in my ear: "Watch out for so and so, watch out for this other one." Nothing more; I did not need explanations, and I refrained from asking for any.[4]

In the fall of 1941, Blanchot dedicated a copy of *Thomas the Obscure* to Paulhan with the following words: "So long as his life lasts, each man carries within his secrecy the invisible lover that was given to Psyche—in recognition of immense gratitude and faithfulness."[5] This gesture suggests that they knew each other well. It intimates that Blanchot had a profound and secret relationship with the image of an *invisible partner*. It foreshadows the future work on the myth of Orpheus, of which it gives a reverse version: Whereas Orpheus cannot look on Eurydice in the darkness of hell, Psyche for her part is unable to see Cupid in daylight. Whether it is feminine or divine, the work will only ever shine forth thanks to its absence. It is the invisible partner of the person who creates it, who loves it and by loving it, continues creating it, but whom it always ends up eluding.

With Blanchot writing three articles on *The Flowers of Tarbes*, appearing in the *Journal des Débats* between October 21 and December 2, 1941 (Paulhan's book had come out in March), the relationship between the two men was bound to change. It would now be Paulhan's turn to be at once honored and impressed. He seems to have been aware of the articles at a sufficiently early stage to be able to write to Monique Saint-Hélier on November 22, when only the first had been published: "If you will believe it, yesterday I received an article (from *Débats*!) or rather three articles on the *Flowers*, about which I am enthusiastic and which understand my work better than I do, truly revealing its meaning to me."[6] This statement by Paulhan is revealing regarding Blanchot's commanding tone: The impression that he is able to reveal the meaning of works reveals only that he will often proceed by appropriating and expanding a work, by identifying its blind spots, its areas of unconscious activity, the assumptions it makes, and by linking the discoveries made to his own questioning and to his own inner conflict (here, notably, on the question of the existence and possibility of literature).

Nonetheless, Paulhan would also feign astonishment and pretend not to know the writer of commentaries on his work. His letter to Monique Saint-Hélier continues: "This Blanchot is the author; I didn't know that he had read the *Flowers*, nor that he might be interested in doing so." Also on November 22, when he had just received the articles, he asked Jean Prévost to send them to him.[7] On December 1, he asked Francis Ponge to send them to him, who duly did so from Roanne a few days later.[8] At the end of January, he told Ponge that he had recently met Blanchot.[9]

In fact, the three articles were soon gathered together into a short book edited by José Corti (who also distributed clandestine texts). There seems to be no doubt that this was on Paulhan's initiative. On January 10, 1942, he wrote to André Dhôtel to ask him to read "the proofs of a short book that will soon appear with Corti, by Blanchot."[10] *How Is Literature Possible?* was published in February (in 350 numbered copies, very handsomely printed).

A month after having read the three articles, Paulhan had another idea: he recommended Blanchot for the steering committee of the *NRF*. It was December 1941. Blanchot was linked to the Resistance; with Lignac, he had begun planning the attempt to shake things up at Jeune France.

According to Paulhan in his letter of December 22 to Monique Saint-Hélier, an agreement was reached: "I recommended Blanchot, who was accepted." This proposal was clearly part of a long-term strategy: "Blanchot is at once subtle and rigorous; I believe that he can bring to the review column a *justness* it has not always had. This will be of benefit later." Paulhan also suspected that Blanchot was less concerned than he with the Jewish question: "as for me," he added, "I cannot return to the *NRF* until Jews are also allowed to return."[11]

But Paulhan had moved too quickly. A letter of January 1942 to Drieu contradicts the account just given. It shows that Paulhan was assisting Drieu or rather advising him, in an unofficial role and with a fairly imperious tone. "Perhaps Blanchot could be asked to *organize* the reviews section," he now suggested amid much hedging, before adding in a parenthesis: "But would he want to? His books make me think he is intimidating."[12] It seems that in January 1942 Blanchot was still neither aware of this proposal concerning him nor, therefore, ready to agree to it. Five or six months later, the project was close to collapse. On May 18, Léautaud transcribed in his diary a telephone conversation with Drieu, who introduced him to "his secretary, one Mr. Blanchot, a very nice boy," and said that he had brought him into the journal to relieve his own fatigue; but in a letter to Drieu, Paulhan wrote: "Ultimately, I have no reason to believe that the time for reconciliation has come. Do you not think that the provisional arrangement we are trying to establish with Blanchot could in fact last?"[13] However the following day, June 10, everything seems to have reached a conclusion! It was necessary "to help Maurice Blanchot as much as we can to edit the apolitical journal that we have given to him," wrote Paulhan.[14] Finally, two weeks later, on June 25, Paulhan wrote to Monique Saint-Hélier: "Blanchot is leaving."[15] This endless back-and-forth, attested by a correspondence that began with strategic aims, in the end tells us only how intense the negotiations were, notably in April.

This is because Drieu himself did not seem to know what tactics to pursue — and for him Blanchot was only one piece in a wider game. Since the beginning of the year, he had been trying to reduce his role at the journal, even to withdraw from it altogether. He was not at all satisfied with the solutions proposed, but the journal ceasing to publish would have been a personal defeat in his eyes. Was it Drieu, was it Paulhan, or was it Blanchot who proposed an advisory committee composed of "weighty writers" (Claudel, Fargue, Gide, Valéry) alongside an editorial committee with writers who were well known but less senior (Arland, Giono, Jounandeau, Montherlant, Paulhan)? This is probably the only part of this affair that could have held Blanchot's attention for any time. Paulhan would take care of things with his contacts. But Gide left things to Valéry, Claudel refused to work with Montherlant (and asked "who is this unknown Blanchot?"). Paulhan suggested that Mauriac could replace Claudel, Drieu opposed this suggestion, Valéry demanded that the first issue be entirely edited by the four senior advisors, and in his turn ruled out Montherlant, whom Drieu once again insisted be included. After four months of negotiations, Drieu wrote a letter of resignation to Gallimard — which he did not send.

Some have said that Blanchot actually did help Drieu in the journal's offices, in April 1942.[16] In a letter to Jeffrey Mehlman of November 26, 1979, Blanchot confirmed that negotiations did take place, but vigorously denied any suggestion that he collaborated. Against all the evidence, he also maintained that he only spent "a few weeks" at Jeune France, and dated his resignation to before Paulhan's proposal that he meet Drieu. This meeting led to nothing. It would have taken place at the latest in April

1942. Blanchot and Drieu met a second time, probably at the end of the month or at the beginning of May, but possibly as late as the end of June. Blanchot let it be known that he would not be joining the journal. His letter to Mehlman suggests that from spring onward he had lost interest in being part of any complex strategy: "it was naïve and dangerous to try to use Vichy against Vichy." The way in which Laval's return to power put an end to the attempt to win control of Jeune France left no room for doubt: in April 1942, Blanchot could not make the same mistake with the *NRF*. Gallimard, who for his part was ready to abandon the journal in order to save his publishing house, ardently wanted the negotiations to continue, while Blanchot, together with Paulhan and knowing full well that Gallimard would not give in, accepted this waiting strategy for several months. On August 6, 1943, he would write to Prévost with relief: "Latest news: the *NRF* has finally folded."

The attempt to relaunch Jeune France, Paulhan's active and strategic gratitude to Blanchot, and the negotiations around the *NRF*, must all be seen in parallel to the clearly uneasy, dangerous, and troubling agitation surrounding the editorship of the *Journal des Débats* between November 1941 and January 1942.

In November 1941 Blanchot published a study on Montherlant's youth.[17] It had a direct strategic aim, which was to contribute to the attempt to take over *Jeune France*. In the same way that Blanchot had already praised Bazaine's initiatives in the *Journal des Débats*, in this period when he believed that action alongside Flamand and Schaeffer was possible, it was now a question of using Montherlant, and hence Vichy, against Vichy. Indeed, the French State supported the author who wrote that "a great writer serves his country through his work more, much much more, than through the action he may involve himself in." Blanchot quoted this passage and related it to one from Goethe (which gave it a tone at once universal and . . . Germanic): "Whoever wants to do something for the world should have nothing to do with it."[18] The article thus served to support the aesthetic policy, refusing any propagandistic aims, that Lignac, Petitot, and Blanchot were then trying to bring in at Jeune France.

Two months later, Blanchot addressed Montherlant in another article.[19] It looked at *Solstice de Juin*, whose collaborationist eloquence is well known. Its ambivalent tone and its inclusion in *Faux pas* (it forms the final chapter in the collection), where its decontextualization and depoliticization form a more surreptitious mode of support, indicate that this article is indulgent on several counts. Insolence is discussed in terms of the virtues of action and sacrifice, but also of vengeance, mystification, malice, individualism, and disdain. It thus could serve as a moral basis for the *insurgent* statements of a few years previously. Blanchot claimed, and repeated this claim at the end of 1943 with *Faux pas*, that "Montherlant has written some very fine lines" such as the following: "Here is the summit. The masses below survive as well as they can."[20]

However, the text closes with an unambiguous, trenchant condemnation: Montherlant has written a book on the present situation, says Blanchot, and when he thought that he was able in the haughtiness of his disdain to set aside the baseness of history, the latter in fact dragged him with it into its own breakdown. What Blanchot cites and writes in the final lines of *Faux pas* militates against Montherlant, whose remarks act against him, but also militates in favor of the sovereignty of literature and of its indifference to morals:

> It sometimes happens that the writer is taken by the abyss: he is no longer able to fly above it, he preaches, he draws conclusions, he moralizes, all signs that the event has fascinated him and carried him off. Or rather, he muddles through with a few thoughts whose haughty tone does not hide their insignificance, an ideology that seems barely superior to the habitual meditations of writers lost in politics, and so we think of his warning to them: "For the writers who for some months have given too much to the present, I predict that this part of their work will be utterly forgotten. When I open today's reviews and newspapers, I hear the indifference of the future washing over them, as the sound of the sea can be heard by placing certain seashells next to one's ear."[21]

And this also applied to Blanchot, for his past and his present, his article and his book—for the *faux pas* that the latter represented. The lines just quoted should be read as a renouncement that, beyond this localized and little-read article, the book was publicly imposing on all future readers. This gesture is sealed with an image, the final image in *Faux pas*: "the sound of the sea when one holds certain shells next to one's ear," one of Levinas's favored images in his descriptions of the *there is*.

Addressing the political articles and publicly compromised positions through the oblivion of the *there is*, under the pressure of the obsessions of night, was a way of expressing the shift at the end of the 1930s and the beginning of the 1940s, the search for "salvation" (*salut*) through a writing that had long been sought, and had finally been found. Thus the final traces of oblivion were borne by *Faux pas*, this writer's ultimate *faux pas*, in its role as the work that recognized and summed up previous *faux pas*, confiding them to the disseminated presence of a book in the world.

In its first version of January 1942, however, the article does not close on this image of the sound of a seashell. A few additional lines temper the criticism and self-criticism ("it would be ridiculous to make an author so ready to revise his works condemn himself"); they rehabilitate *in extremis* the author in his greatness. Eight months later, Blanchot would again attack Montherlant's moralism.[22] It is not impossible that he was asked to discuss certain subjects or certain authors, and that this was the price he had to pay for his other publications. But even the way in which he avoids praising this figure betrays a form of compromise, for Blanchot's criticisms of Montherlant's moralism and moderation are made in the name of values sufficiently ambiguous to be tolerated by the Vichy regime.

A week after the article on *Solstice de Juin*, a text largely favorable to Drieu appeared, referring to his latest work as "a sympathetic analysis of the most recent political and literary movements of the twentieth century."[23] *Notes pour Comprendre le Siècle*, an Aryanist and collaborationist work placed under the sign of Rimbaud ("to possess the truth in one soul and in one body"), presented an apologia for modern totalitarianisms (in ascending order: Stalinism, fascism, Nazism), based on their ability to restore the medieval ideal: the united strength of mind and body, reaching the entire people, the entire nation. Of course, Blanchot signals the fact that "Drieu La Rochelle's remarks will probably provoke endless objections and some stout opposition," but he does not sketch these out in any way.[24] It is as if he were indifferent to the content of Drieu's political and literary allegiances, on which he says very little; he mostly dedicates his attention to "what is truly interesting" in his analysis: "to perceive the ideal to which, through the medium of a historical myth, a writer in search of his own movement finds himself attracted."[25] This critical disengagement entirely contradicts Blanchot's theories of the time on such questions. Its total break from the previous year's columns indicates that the article as a whole is a gesture of pure compromise. For while he sees as unacceptable the "collaboration between symbolism considered as a restoration of the soul, and modern political forces considered as a restoration of the body," Blanchot nonetheless recognizes that "political athleticism" (he accepted this euphemism, taken from Drieu's book) had the merit of providing, "in its thirst for physical furor, the physical equivalent of a true adventure, which is the deepest need of a human being." Blanchot concludes that Drieu had attempted to marry symbolism and athleticism "as one studies a dream, with resolute serenity, calm logic, a burning desire for equilibrium, and all the optimistic qualities that are particularly necessary in writers who know they are attempting the impossible."[26] Even if it was in order to play Vichy against Vichy, with *Jeune France* and perhaps also the *NRF* in mind, such statements of froideur, such tranquil approval remain as signs of a rare cruelty, and of an exceptional self-censorship, in these war years.

Following on from the two articles on Drieu and on Montherlant, a further piece of January 20, 1942, praises a collection of Giraudoux's studies of French literature.[27] While lacking the studiedly serious character of the others, this article once more—but for the last time—takes precedence over the genesis of Blanchot's critical theory. Its nationalist reading of French literature would be attenuated on its publication in *Faux pas*. "The honor of French destiny" becomes simply "the honor of our destiny." Some glorifying epithets disappear: Giraudoux is no longer "a writer, and even a great writer," but simply "a writer"; Racine is no longer referred to as "France's premier writer."[28]

January 1942 was a strange month at the *Journal des Débats*. In less than a fortnight, Blanchot produced three articles, one after the other, which represented a radical change of direction from the 38 that preceded them and the 132 that would follow. Whether this was a willing strategy or a period of external pressure, it momentarily hindered the progress of an evolution that, while it could not be homogeneous, might have been better served by a less strenuous rhythm. The following year, Blanchot would denounce the positions that he had publicly defended. In April, in an article on Machiavelli, he took a stand against "the absurdity of all compromise," in the name of the "full scope of [the] demands" which could be made of "the spirit of practical achievement [*l'esprit réalisateur*]."[29] In June, he denounced the inanity of all nationalist and spiritual judgments on literature, thereby justifying the writer's right to silence on the question of the nation.[30] In July, he praised Orestes's freedom: "Each of his actions is a defiance of order."[31] The hero was now Nietzschean, a thinker Blanchot had read with Bataille, he who "tries to go beyond the possible," and "only ever wins one victory, that of his death, that mid stage between 'practice' and meditation, that point at which day and night meet."[32] Blanchot was now looking only at this point: such was his heroism, still one of literature and of arms, but now situated differently in relation to the real.

CHAPTER 26

From Anguish to Language
The Publication of *Faux pas* (1943)

In 1943, keeping away from anything that could compromise him, Blanchot again began hoping that the war would end.[1] Germany had capitulated at Stalingrad on February 2 and retreated massively from the Soviet Union, beginning that summer. In Algiers, the Committee for National Liberation was beginning to take shape.

In March, Bataille moved to Vézelay with Denise Rollin and her son Jean. Blanchot visited them several times, in spring and in summer; he was also thinking of leaving Neuilly, where he lived. But in October, Bataille separated from Denise Rollin, returned from Vézelay, and moved into Balthus's studio in the Cour de Rohan, in Paris. At the end of the year, according to Prévost, he proposed to Blanchot, Lignac, Ollivier, and Petitot that they write a manifesto for political action to be sent to Algiers. All declined the offer with "polite skepticism," and the idea was abandoned.[2]

In August, Gallimard founded a new literary prize, the Prix de la Pléiade.[3] The prize was 100,000 francs and it was open to young writers, with the winners being free to publish their manuscripts wherever they wanted. As a sign of the recognition he had gained thanks to his first two novels, and perhaps also of his strategic involvement in the *NRF* affair, Blanchot joined the panel of judges alongside Paulhan, Arland, Malraux, Queneau, Bousquet, Grenier, Camus, Sartre, and Éluard.

His presence at Gallimard allowed him to make a new acquaintance, which in other circumstances, fifteen years later, would grow into a friendship: that of Dionys Mascolo. At this time, the two men did little more than briefly acknowledge each other. Blanchot knew little of Mascolo's life, of his closeness to Robert Antelme and to Marguerite Duras, who were state employees and, from September of that year, the active forces behind a Resistance movement.

A friend of Michel Gallimard (Gaston's nephew), Mascolo had for several years been tasked with reading difficult manuscripts for the publishing house.[4] This is what had led him to read *Thomas the Obscure*. On January 1, 1942, he officially became part of the reading committee, and a year later, Mascolo passed on to Blanchot the news that Gaston Gallimard wished to collect and publish his column from the *Journal des Débats*; he himself was to be in charge of editing the collection. The proposal was a "shock" for Blanchot, who had clearly never thought of making the column into a book. Had he even truly decided to construct a critic's oeuvre? "*Faux pas* really was a *faux pas*" and, as he would state in a confused mixture of reproach and gratitude, "I owe it to Dionys Mascolo." Blanchot came to this view very soon. The wordplay of the title was far from being lost on him. He finally decided on that title in August 1943, thus changing the name of a work that had initially been known to the review committee as *Digressions*.[5]

The expression itself is used three times in the articles for the *Journal des Débats*, but, except for the title, it would not be used in the work itself. The reference is in part to the "faux pas" that is forbidden by Valéry's vigilant gaze on the world: "He scans its depths, and turns his analyses into an adventure where it is possible to get lost, but not to put a wrong foot forward (*faire un faux-pas*)."[6] Elsewhere, the absence of *faux pas* is said to describe the aesthetics of Jean Follain, as he moves "from the level of appearances . . . to [the] level of reality."[7] And the *faux pas* of a character in Georges Magnane plunges him into a ravine: a fatal fall.[8]

But the "step" (*pas*) is above all the notion Blanchot uses to refer to his own critical approach. His articles advance jerkily, through successive investigations, deepening lines of enquiry, turning paradoxes on their head: these are so many steps taken in approaching the work (we also read of taking "a final step" at the end of the chapter on Paulhan).[9] However, the criticism remains as distant from the work as the work does from experience: one is always the "unfaithful depository" of the other; singular experiences can only move toward one another by carrying out "illusory steps."[10] Each step (*pas*) by the critic is therefore also a "faux pas."

Playing on the ambiguity over whether the *faux pas* of the title is singular or plural, Blanchot allows it to be understood that each of the fifty-five chapters constitutes a "faux pas," a "flower of evil" of the critical approach. Not all of them are taken from the *Journal des Débats*. Blanchot also includes two articles on Settanni and Woolf which had appeared in *L'Insurgé*, one on Lautréamont from the *Revue Française des Idées et des Oeuvres*, both journals edited by Maulnier.

The book was published in December; Blanchot greatly altered the articles, which he himself had chosen. The opening text, "From Anguish to Language," which is steeped in Bataille's vocabulary and experience, was previously unpublished. It attempts to bring the ensemble together, profiling the way in which the other pieces are ordered. The chronological order of Blanchot's intellectual itinerary is reversed: questions on the renewal of the novel as a genre, creation, and myth are placed below those on the nudity of inner experience and its conflict with language. Even though they were recent (dating from March and May 1943), the texts on Rilke, Bataille, and Proust—which are decisive—head up the collection. "What anger constructs, is destroyed by anguish or fear," Blanchot writes apropos of Michaux in August 1944.[11] We could say as much about his critical itinerary in the 1940s, which was constructed in the anger provoked by the enslavement of young literature by a debased tradition, but then torn apart by the real anguish of inner experience, which now determined how the space of research was oriented within the confines of the book.

Solitude only has meaning in the name of the other. It carries within it an invisible partner.

> It is to the intelligent witness that the mute animal appears to be tormented by solitude. It is not he who is alone who experiences the feeling of being alone; this monster of desolation needs the presence of another for its desolation to have meaning.[12]

At such times solitude comes face to face with its own dying. As for writing, it comes face to face with the silence of such a situation.

> The writer finds himself in the increasingly comic condition of having nothing to write, of having no means with which to write it, and of being constrained by the utter necessity of always writing it. . . . It seems wretched and preposterous that anguish, which opens and closes the heavens, needs, in order to manifest itself, the activity of a man sat at his table tracing letters on a piece of paper. . . . The writer is

summoned by his anguish to a real sacrifice of himself. He must expend and consume the forces that make him a writer. . . . He must be destroyed in an act that really puts him in question. . . . Anguish does not allow the solitary person to be alone. It deprives him of the means of being in relation to an other, making him more estranged from his human reality than if he were suddenly changed into vermin; but, thus stripped bare, and ready to sink into his monstrous particularity, it casts him outside himself and, in a new torment that he experiences like a suffocating radiation, it confuses him with what he is not, making his solitude an expression of his communication and making this communication the meaning his solitude takes, and drawing from this synonymy a new reason to be anguish added to anguish.[13]

Part Pascalian wager, part Kafkaean destitution, part Batalliean expenditure, "From Anguish to Language" is one of Blanchot's finest autobiographical texts. Lived, physical anguish shines clearly through it. This anguish provides the authority behind the quality of this criticism, and gives it the force of a writer's criticism.[14]

CHAPTER 27

The Prisoner of the Eyes That Capture Him
Quain (Summer 1944)

Blanchot was still present in Paris on March 5, 1944, when the famous "Discussion on Sin" took place in Marcel Moré's luxurious apartment on the banks of the Seine, gathering around Bataille figures such as Adamov, Camus, Gandillac, Leiris, Marcel, Merleau-Ponty, Paulhan, Sartre, Simone de Beauvoir, various Jesuit fathers including the future cardinal Daniélou, and Klossowski—then a seminarist—in his cassock.[1]

Many were leaving Paris in this period: a very ill Bataille left in April for Samois, near Fontainebleau, and at the end of the month, Prévost was sent to Morocco (he recalls a final lunch with Blanchot and Lignac).[2] In May, Paulhan went underground, having been denounced by Élise Jouhandeau, and the same month, Blanchot left for Quain. He would spend a long summer there, only returning to Neuilly at the end of November, once France had been liberated.

For Quain and the surrounding region, it was a tragic summer. The German army intervened on several occasions; half the houses in Devrouze were burned down; ten men were shot dead. A memorial at a small crossroads in the hamlet, almost facing Blanchot's house, is a reminder of how intense the fighting was, notably in August, when half a dozen were killed in three weeks.

As we knew without really knowing it (Nadeau and Prévost had reported more or less laconic revelations, and *The Madness of the Day* alludes to it), as we have known (almost) openly since 1994, since he recounted the event himself, Blanchot was almost executed in Quain in June 1944.[3] Perhaps it happened on June 29, the date of the only fighting with the German army in June; perhaps it happened a few days earlier, for on June 29 the *Journal des Débats* published an astonishing article named "On the Different Ways of Dying."[4] "Death has the effect of changing us into pure objects. A man we are looking at is already partly abandoned by life. For a moment, he is the prisoner of the eyes that capture him." Death definitively hands us over to others, "we exist only through our relation to others," Blanchot writes in the wake of Sartre, whom he cites: "Death is the triumph over us of others' point of view: it transforms life into destiny."

We can reconstruct the narrative of what happened from a letter to Prévost of November 30, as well as from statements by Roger Laporte and Dionys Mascolo, to whom Blanchot told the story.[5]

One day in June, then, in the context of other reprisals, a German officer comes to the Château accompanied by at least a dozen soldiers.[6] He claims that Blanchot has been writing for underground newspapers, shoves him, puts him up against the wall, with the soldiers brandishing their machine guns at him, while he has the house searched. He is probably the person who seizes several manuscripts (perhaps a first version of *Death Sentence*). Down below, who exactly is lined up alongside Blanchot, facing the firing squad? There are two divergent versions of the tale. The published *récit* mentions his aunt, his mother, his sister, and his sister-in-law; the letter to Prévost states that one of his brothers was there (probably René). Meanwhile, due to a diversionary intervention by members of the Resistance, the officer is called to the front line, which is reasonably far away, outside the village. At this point the soldiers reveal their identity: They are Russian and belong to the Vlasov Division, which is fighting for the Reich. They are satisfied with their plunder of cash and valuable objects and, clearly happy and willing to be merciful, they spare the lives of Blanchot and his brother, who, according to the letter to Prévost, hurry into the woods they have known since childhood in order to avoid the returning German officer. Perhaps instead Blanchot simply takes his chance when the soldiers' attention is diverted, slipping away from the corner of the wall, discreetly escaping: "I made myself absent", he told Mascolo. All around, farms are burning; the Château is spared thanks to its noble appearance. Thus by chance, by pure improbability, Blanchot finds himself at liberty and escapes death. He will not be a target in August's actions. In the mean time, in July, Malraux will live through a similar episode.[7] We might well think that the author of *L'espoir* is quoted at the end of *The Instant of My Death* in the name of this shared relation to (mis)fortune.

The event sweeps over the author and his family like an explosion. It is not death's first appearance in Blanchot's life, nor probably its most spectacular one, nor the one that marked him the most. It is probably because this is "the encounter of death with death" that it matters.[8] For this is certainly death's most historical, surprising, accidental, instantaneous appearance. Is it this, is it this eternal return of death that Bataille comments on almost immediately, at the beginning of *Sur Nietzsche*? Nothing could be less certain.[9] We can however at least imagine how fascinated Bataille must have been by Blanchot undergoing such an episode, such anguish-inducing happenstance, revealing how precarious the subject is and granting it to lawless chance:

> *The return strips all motivation from the instant, frees life of any goal and in this way above all others, ruins it. The return is the dramatic mode and the mask of the entire man: it is the desert of a man for whom henceforth each instant is without motivation.*

Fifty years later, Blanchot would write that after the shouting, brutality, robbery, destruction, and death, "all that remains is the feeling of lightness that is death itself or, to put it more precisely, the instant of my death henceforth always in abeyance."[10]

A nomad wandering from *demourance* to *demourance*, Blanchot perhaps then discovers, violently and through writing, that it is impossible to die.[11] He says as much in *The Madness of the Day*: "At that point I stopped being insane."[12]

Commenting the following year on *The Hunter Gracchus*, the very person who had been chased into the forest, chased out of both life and death, would write the following: "We do not die, that is the truth, but it means that we do not live either; we are dead while we are alive, we are essentially survivors."[13] Writing remains: "writing in order to be able to die," writing to reach the level of one's own death and, as Kafka says, writing to "be able to die happy." Writing the second version of *Thomas the Obscure*, *The Most*

High, and *Death Sentence*, all in just three years, represented so many renewed engagements with death. In this way death is placed centrally once more, and stared in the face: literature is the right to death. This would also lead to *Lautréamont and Sade*, to Maldoror with his head beneath the blade of the guillotine three times, to "the definitive impossibility of having done with it." In 1949, as if he were relieved, Blanchot is able to write in *The Madness of the Day*: "That is saying too little: I am alive, and this life gives me the greatest pleasure. And what about death? When I die (perhaps any minute now), I will feel immense pleasure." Death can become levity. Life can become tranquil hedonism: "I am happy about what has been, I am pleased by what is, and what is to come suits me well enough."[14] As a subject all the happier for being rendered absent, he reaches "the stability—the positivity—of the world posited before all theses, a rest behind all agitation and all desire and which bears, encompasses, or comprehends all absurdity."[15] This incredible *reserve* is Blanchot's strength. It allows others to relate to themselves without him—or through him. It does not work like any divine force, though it does have the effect of grace. It allows for his uneasy friendship, which is endlessly careful, attentive, and so much in solidarity that it suffers on others' behalf. There is no "I" to be well, "I" exists alongside others and from that moment enters into the suffering of the world. Constantly forgotten *in the name of the other*, his being-himself never risks becoming contentment. Suffering for the other and with the other gives him a feeling of invulnerability. It seems to rise to the level of every avowal. Everything is ready for a face-to-face confrontation with the Law; everything is ready for another encounter to come about: that of Robert Antelme.

Everything is indeed ready, up to and including sheer historical fortune. Blanchot is saved by Soviet soldiers, having spent years denouncing their homeland as the main danger, albeit one hidden behind Germany. He is saved from the firing squad at the final moment, just as Dostoevsky—to whom he was so close—had been by the Emperor's mercy; he is perhaps saved thanks to his aristocratic bearing, similarly to the unjust favoritism given in Tolstoy to prince Andrew, who is treated before the other wounded men;[16] he is perhaps saved because of his writer's aristocracy (according to another version of the story, he was told to make himself scarce after being asked his profession); he, the future friend of Robert Antelme, *is already* the Russian who smokes the last cigarette of *The Human Race* in an act of calming companionship. All that remains for him to do, in the intensity of silent communication, is to invent the type of approach, the type of listening that are those of *friendship* and that consist, before speech or chatter, in this murmuring of language at the origin of writing, and that consists in *marrying the other in her language*. This is how the narrator of *Death Sentence* will put it, as he communicates with N., his Slavic friend, through inebriation, irresponsibility, and lightness regained.[17]

CHAPTER 28

The Disenchantment of the Community
Editorial Activity after Liberation (1944–1946)

Bataille and Blanchot returned to Paris in the fall of 1944. Blanchot spent a difficult winter in his Neuilly apartment. The temperature was freezing, and the Seine flooded the cellars in which the heating fuel was kept (Rue Soyer, where he lived, ended at the river, facing the Île de la Jatte). On returning from Morocco in September 1945, Pierre Prévost remembers going to this apartment where Blanchot lived alone, fairly modestly. In the years following the Liberation, he would sometimes be able to provide his friend with rare supplies (such as milk and coffee).

We can imagine Blanchot's increasing disappointment during the winter of 1944 and the spring of 1945. This was irreparable, anguish-inducing disappointment. He had narrowly avoided being killed, and he had lost several manuscripts. Levinas returned from Germany, but Bataille left in May and set up home in Vézelay for several years. The same month, Mascolo rescued Antelme from death, and the Allied victory revealed the unthinkable to the world: the unspeakable horror of the concentration and extermination camps. Blanchot would say that anti-Semitism revealed the intellectual to himself—thinking also, or perhaps most of all, of himself.

The revelation of the camps further embedded the feeling of responsibility, and definitively ruled out any political complacency.

> The categorical imperative, losing the ideal generality given to it by Kant, has become the one which Adorno formulated more or less thus: *Think and act in such a way that Auschwitz may never be repeated*; which implies that Auschwitz must not become a concept, and that an absolute was reached there, against which other rights and other duties must be judged.[1]

The climate of purification or *épuration* in literary circles cast Blanchot into a deep malaise. Maurras was sent to prison, while Brasillach was executed. The agents of justice were primarily attentive to journalists, and the moral *épuration* was carried out by the Comité National des Ecrivains, led by Aragon and *Lettres Françaises*: in September 1944 lists of undesirable writers were published. Blanchot attended the first public meeting of the CNE.[2] The seven members of the *épuration* commission featured writers alongside whom Blanchot had coexisted in various guises: Marcel, Queneau, and Rousseaux. The commission's list of targets also featured those he knew and had supported: Bernanos, Gide, Mauriac, Montherlant, Paulhan, and even Camus, Sartre, and Malraux. There were negotiations, compromises, accusations, slanders, desertions, moments of cowardice, small conspiracies; there was spin, the settling of scores, the rhetoric of hatred: this detestable climate reminded Blanchot of a past that he had definitively rejected. The new atmosphere did not prevent him from being intransigent, however (an ethical attitude on which he and Levinas could agree, an agreement on which he was able to base some authority); Blanchot went on to write an article in favor of Malraux in *Actualité* as well as taking up an invitation to write for *Carrefour*, a popular right-wing weekly that had been set up after the Liberation,[3] and publishing in Maulnier's journal, the *Cahiers de la Table Ronde*, which had been founded precisely to welcome authors rejected by the CNE.[4]

Although he would go on to align himself with communism, he could not stand the CNE's diktats. He only took sides in order to calm hearts and minds and to argue against one of his previous attitudes, which he now clearly thought to have been short-sighted: anticommunism.[5] His limited sharing of a conception of community, differing considerably from the one that some communists were putting into practice at the time, explains his greater or lesser proximity, over the coming years, to Camus, Breton, and Bataille, who were brought freely together by the same path of *refusal*.

The Disenchantment of the Community

At this time of disenchantment, nothing could have brought him back toward what he called "everyday politics." Nothing could have brought him back to what he referred to in a letter to Prévost as the 150 journals then being founded, none of which had any real aim. He turned down the editorship and the political column of an opinion-forming newspaper. He denigrated a political and intellectual life that, unable to renew itself, seemed to him to be stricken with nullity.[6] His growing anguish led to uneasy activity. Withdrawal was not simply a refuge: it was also the best way of thinking death, relation, communication—the possibility of community. "Some time has to pass," he would later write of this period; "the time in which we meet the death that awaits each of us and only barely misses us. I was living very far away. . . . I was silently absent."[7]

Thus his concern for politics remained, but was circumscribed by the disquiet that troubled both a measured presence and any sudden return. This concern remained, but had to find other forms than those of mediocrity, failure, and surrender. These other forms were being tested out. In the meantime, Blanchot would remain a public figure—something that he would never cease to be.[8] Without always sitting on the panel, he took part in new prize juries,[9] for a while produced a new column for a weekly newspaper, and occasionally gave texts to the new journals.[10] Some of these mattered to him, taking up as they did important positions.

At the end of 1944 he agreed to participate in Georges Bataille's journal project, *Actualité* which had advanced to a stage where these *Cahiers* would have a clearly political character. Blanchot shared the adjunct editorship of *Actualité* with Prévost.[11] However, only one issue of what had been planned as a journal would appear, addressing *L'Espagne libre* and published by Calmann-Lévy at the very start of 1946 (the registration of copyright dates to the last trimester of 1945), with violently democratic contributions from Camus and Cassou, texts by Bataille, Fouchet, Grenier, but also García Lorca, Hemingway, and Quero-Morales, a former member of the Republican government. Blanchot's presence as this issue was conceived and edited, even if his contribution was a literary text on Malraux and *L'Espoir*, clearly *inscribed* his political turn. The antirepublican of 1937 now coedited an undertaking that began with this preface by Camus: "Men of my generation have had Spain in their hearts for nine years now. For nine years they have carried it with them like a bad wound." This was also true for Blanchot, but in a very different sense. Introduced by Camus in the name of the universal struggle for liberty, the text on Malraux was overtly political. Demonstrating his new tolerance for both anarchism and communism,

Blanchot worked through theories of permanent revolution, internationalism, revolutionary discipline, class consciousness, all of which were made possible by a single, unconditional choice: the choice of freedom.[12]

In August 1945, he joined *L'Arche* for its first "Parisian" issue. He was entrusted with its literary column. Having been launched in February 1944 in Algiers (which at the time was a real literary capital), edited by Amrouche and Lassaigne, and placed under Gide's patronage, this journal enjoyed a remarkable reputation: it attracted French and foreign authors, and featured many international correspondents. Its publications were interrupted between March and July 1945, before beginning again from Paris on a monthly basis. It was compared to the defunct *NRF*; the texts by Camus and Blanchot were particularly remarked upon. In February 1946, it gained an editorial committee: Blanchot was part of it, alongside Camus and Lassaigne; Amrouche remained editor-in-chief and Gide the tutelary figure. Blanchot would remain at *L'Arche* until the end, contributing sixteen articles, his first long critical texts. Thirteen of them would be collected in *The Work of Fire*, for which they would provide the framework.

The collective, anonymous manifesto printed in the first issue, which had Du Bellay's famous verse as its epigraph: "France, mother of arts, of arms, and of laws," clearly placed the journal on the side of the government in Algiers, in a spirit of peace, generosity, and virtue, without any desire for vengeance or destruction. It presented an elegy to the republican and universal French nation ("the history of the past 150 years has been that of peoples being richly sowed with the universal principles of 1789").

> To help France reconquer its compromised freedoms, to once again become aware of itself and of its mission, to recover and reassemble its dispersed strength, to reanimate its energies and its hopes, and thus to allow international recognition of its face, its signification, the capital importance of its role: such is this journal's aim, its raison d'être.

We can imagine how satisfied Blanchot must have been to belong to the editorial committee of a review whose struggle was that of allowing each Frenchman "[to recognize] the pure face of his country and, stepping beyond the errors and the shames of our recent past, to dream of a new spring in France, of a French order given to its deepest being." To write such words was to immediately demonstrate the journal's growing notoriety on the side of a national, republican, and pacific Resistance movement.

As well as being a place in which Blanchot could regularly and fairly freely carry out his critical research, such aims made this journal what he expected of it: a way of restoring his own image, showing what he now was—a brilliant critic, and one of integrity. At the end of 1946, he would confide humorously to Prévost that he was pleased with the first issues of *Critique*, since he had never been able to bring himself to read a single line in *L'Arche*.

CHAPTER 29

The Year of Criticism
L'Arche, Les Temps Modernes, and *Critique* (1946)

Many plans would remain vague until the last and would always be marked by unforeseen developments. But in November 1945 it was Blanchot's turn to leave Paris, and he would not return to live there for many years. After one or two weeks in Chalon, with his family, he stayed in Grasse in a boardinghouse on the Boulevard Reine-Jeanne, in the upper part of town. At that time he was thinking of moving to somewhere near Monte Carlo for a period. Health reasons were not without influence on this choice.

The beginning of January indeed found him on the outskirts of the principality, at Villa Margot in Beausoleil, in a dwelling that seems to have disappeared today. This new arrangement was not definitive—none ever was. For the whole period up to 1957, during which he lived (*demeure*) in the south, Blanchot would come up to Paris frequently but very irregularly, sometimes for months at a time—without counting passing visits to Chalon and some solitary stays in Quain.[1]

He returned to Neuilly in spring 1946 but was back in Beausoleil by the summer. In November he referred to an imminent move to Èze, where he indeed set up home at the end of the year, with assistance from his brother, in a small house that was charming but still not entirely comfortable. For example, he remained without electricity for several weeks; it was wintertime, and the experience of Èze, where so many *récits* would be written, thus began in night.

The year 1946 was nonetheless one of intense participation in various journals. Critical activity weighed on Blanchot, but as well as being a contributor to *L'Arche*, he played a decisive role at *Critique*, wrote for *Saisons* and then *Les Cahiers de la Pléiade*, and even *Les Temps Modernes*. His position in these numerous journals was clearly due to more than simple respect.

The authors he discussed were less numerous and more carefully selected than during his periods writing for *L'Insurgé* or the *Journal des Débats*; these choices set the stage for his championing of aesthetic modernity. Blanchot's decisive turn was made clear by the presence of Sade, Nietzsche, and Kierkegaard, the three main figures referred to by *Acéphale*, Bataille's prewar journal. His interest for the writers he named "men of blackness" (Sade and Lautréamont, but also Restif and Cyrano), to whom he would dedicate numerous articles, was just as evident in *Saisons* as in *Les Temps Modernes*.

Saisons: Almanach des Lettres et des Arts was a luxury review, which appeared irregularly and ephemerally, and was edited by Marcel Arland for the Pavois publishing house. It reproduced the facsimiles of manuscripts, drawings or etchings, and secured high-quality literary and artistic contributions. It would lose this role to the *Cahiers de la Pléiade*, founded by Paulhan in April, to which Blanchot immediately gave an extract from *The Most High*, just as he had done for the *Cahiers de la Table Ronde*. The first issue of this new publication, typeset by Fautrier, featured the names of Gide, Dubuffet, Michaux, Char, and Caillois. Blanchot would give two further articles to these *Cahiers*, both of them prepublications: a preface for Restif's *Sara*, and a text on Kafka that appeared simultaneously in *The Work of Fire*. To some extent, he therefore played the game of reputation-building and literary publicity in this journal, which also published Bernanos, Chardonne, and Boutang.

The important questions, however, lay elsewhere. Blanchot published little in *Les Temps Modernes*, but when he did so, it always demanded attention, whether because his signature featured at the head of the article, or due to the length of the texts, or their placement in the journal (his text on Sade, in July 1947, headed up the issue). All this shows that he was able to elicit some appreciation or at least toleration both from Sartre—who had previously slated him—and from Gide, who had replied sharply to the first editorial of *Les Temps Modernes*.[2] Blanchot thus featured in the two reviews that claimed to be the successors of the *NRF*: *L'Arche*, whose benefits for him we have already looked at, and the *Les Temps Modernes*, which at the time was strongly linked to Sartre's theoretical manifesto on "committed literature" and to Jean Pouillon's article against the Indochina war, the first in the French press. He was even one of the rare writers able to straddle both journals. He commented on Sartre's novels in *L'Arche* the same month as the first issue of *Les Temps Modernes* appeared. Similarly, at a time when Bataille was far from forgiving toward existentialism, Blanchot (a member of the editorial committee at *Critique*) was the only writer apart from Leiris (a member of the editorial committee of *Les Temps Modernes*) who maintained some relationship between the two journals that were the new leading lights of the literary and intellectual field.

The first issue of *Critique* appeared in July 1946.[3] We know how important Blanchot was for Bataille in carrying out his project: "Without Blanchot, and without Éric Weil, I could not have founded the journal," he said in an interview with the *Figaro Littéraire* (17 July 1947). Blanchot's physical distance, however, did not make things easier. He did not even assist with preparing the first issue, in which he features only because he is named as part of the editorial committee, and he initially refused even this. It seems that his role was more advisory and hidden than active or day-to-day. As early as December 1945 when Bataille presented the project to Prévost and Girodias, the shape of the book reviews which formed the entire output of this multidisciplinary review was clear: "We will take as a model the studies by Maurice Blanchot (which are now being published in *L'Arche* and are collected in *Faux pas*)." Blanchot would give key articles to *Critique*, nine over two years, which would complement those from *L'Arche* and *Les Temps Modernes* in the collection *The Work of Fire*.

CHAPTER 30

Respecting Scandal
Literary Criticism (1945–1948)

The articles collected and published with some delay in 1949 in *The Work of Fire* and *Lautréamont and Sade* had mostly been written between summer 1945 and the end of 1947, that is, in less than two and a half years. Arguments had been whittled down, had lost their journalistic irregularity. *Research* was beginning. A singular mode of judgment was taking shape: an authority.

The places he was publishing, and the subjects on which he was publishing, can serve to indicate Blanchot's position in the field of criticism after the Liberation. For him as for Bataille, the success of existentialism (even in its theoretical bases) had an element of mythmaking about it, and betrayed true *existence*, which they felt was much better expressed by surrealism. Blanchot set out his approach to the stakes of surrealism in three pieces, each published a year after the next, and only one of which would be collected in *The Work of Fire*, which does not really convey how constant this strategic and speculative preoccupation was. "The deciding role [surrealism] has played in French literature is readily—even more readily than before the war—acknowledged": the impersonal nature of this phrase, one of the earliest in "Reflections on Surrealism," fools no one. While Blanchot holds on to the notion of what he names "the failure of surrealism," he now sees this as the most truthful of failures, one that asks real questions of the writer. "In every person who writes there is a surrealist calling that is admitted, that miscarries, seems sometimes usurped, but that, even if it is false, expresses a sincere effort and need."[1] The "greatest creative ambition" (301) has to be attributed to surrealism. What's more, the alterations made to the article written in 1945 by the time it was published in 1949 leave little room for doubt: They all attenuate or remove reservations initially expressed (for example the judgments that in surrealism there was a "naturalism" or a "naivety" disappear).[2] But Blanchot's admiration goes above all to a surrealism overspilling its boundaries: that of the poets who were more or less the movement's dissidents; that of Bataille or Artaud. While the article on the marvelous begins by citing Breton, it closes with a reference to *Acéphale*, "the sovereign exaltation of a severed head" (given that the marvelous is ultimately defined as a "freedom of the head"), and with a long citation of Artaud where the writer avows that he has disappeared, melted into his style, into the "bizarre truth" of his work, into a participation in the inexpressible.[3]

This rehabilitation of surrealism accompanies a theory of literature that in this period is being set out in ever more brilliant and developed ways, leading to the adoption of new and newly firm political, aesthetic, philosophical, and critical positions.

To speak of Blanchot's absence from the political at the end of the 1940s would be to admit that one's concept of the political is very weak and unimaginative. Writing articles in *Les Temps Modernes*, rehabilitating surrealism, praising René Char's poetry are all important indications of this. To define surrealism and above all Char's surrealism as an art of refusal is to recognize in it the workings of an infinite political demand.[4] Blanchot defends the surrealists' drawing of a parallel between political revolution and linguistic liberation. Breton's commitment as a communist is no "vagary" on his part: "the phase was neither fortuitous nor arbitrary, and it remains very significant as an example of the profound commitments that literature cannot prevent itself from forming as soon as it becomes aware of its greatest freedom" (91). Surrealism expects that communism would only prepare the way for a free society: "mankind, having nothing more to do, because everything has been done, discovers the meaning and value of this *nothing*, the proper object of poetry and freedom both" (96). The writer cannot be content with the Marxist notion of "total man," for, beyond any completion in classless society, he will always have to work with directionless negativity. Holding surrealism up as an example is not only a critical statement, but also a speculative one. When coupled with the feeling of independence that would be provided by any immediate and supposedly painless commitment, the fact of subordinating the political to the sovereignty of literature explains Blanchot's paradoxical, provisional withdrawal.

In this way, in parallel to the manifesto in *Les Temps Modernes* and more than two years before "Literature and the Right to Death," which is often read as an anti-Sartrean text, Blanchot was constructing his own kind of links between literature and politics. The "uncommitment" (*dégagement*) he speaks of is not directly in opposition to Sartrean commitment. Rather, it is its *Aufhebung*:

> the most uncommitted literature is at the same time the most committed, because it knows that to claim to be free in a society that is not free is to accept responsibility for the constraints of that society and especially to accept the mystifications of the word "freedom" by which society hides its intentions. (97)

"Uncommitment" is the mark of a sovereign commitment. "In sum, literature must have an efficacy and meaning that are extraliterary, that is, it must not renounce its literary means, and literature must be free, that is, committed" (97).[5]

The necessity of reading surrealism became clear to Blanchot both in political and personal terms. During this period he frequently cited this phrase from the *Surrealist Manifesto*: "what is admirable in the fantastic is that there is no longer anything fantastic: there is only the real." He was busy writing *The Most High*, and Breton's formulation reminded him of the movement of his novels, which consists in unfolding the fantastic until the law of uncertainty becomes the revelation of the real itself, until the law of extravagance becomes its truth (its interruption).[6] This formulation also defines literature's exceptionality and completes the rejection of naturalism elaborated as early as the articles in the *Journal des Débats*. "The proper nature of the fantastic ... is to pass for reality itself, is to be *everything* that is real." In what Blanchot interchangeably names the fantastic or the marvelous he sees "an appearance in fantasy and in play, in truth a man's most profound experience." He insists on this in terms recalling those of "inner experience": ones that are intimate, essential, agonizing, terrorizing. This is the fantastic of Kafka, Michaux, Lautréamont, and Leiris. It provides a model for inner experience, an experience lived, but lived by the *invisible partner* within us:

Michel Leiris's *récit* [*Aurora*], in showing how the author is expressed and given form within it, gives us an understanding of how Lautréamont is present in *Maldoror* and tells us what depths we must descend to if we wish to see this invisible face, tells us in what forever-sealed chamber remains (*demeure*), still alive and with his eyes fixed on us, the adolescent that we have never seen.[7]

Is literature capable of transmitting this experience? Is it "comical and destitute," an "unfaithful repository" or a "necessarily faithful translation"? In light of this question, which haunts *Faux Pas* and *The Work of Fire* just as it haunted Valéry, who reproached Pascal for "this distress which writes so well," Blanchot seems to have always been more ready than Bataille to reestablish literature's *equivocal sovereignty*.

Whether transitive or intransitive, manifest or latent, intended or reactive, meaningful or nonsensical, active or truthful, modest or ambitious, subjective or willfully realist, autonomous or sovereignly powerless, literary language can change meaning, be interested or disinterested, realize or unrealize (or unrealize the better to realize), make itself present or absent (or make itself absent as a way to make itself otherwise present). It is the site of endless reversals. In Blanchot's statement that literature can only be ambiguous, equivocal, and that this is its very essence, there is no residue of political or moral complacency, no desire to mask any compromised attitude past or present. While literature is indeed "the life that endures death and maintains itself in it," according to the Hegelian formulation repeated five times in "Literature and the Right to Death," it "refers us to the nothingness of death" (344) on which all meaning relies, but it always refers us to it in an unstable way. This is the "point of instability" (343) that literature aims at, the irruption into the heart of language of what Blanchot would later name "dying," the irruption of the being of language, therefore of being and no longer simply of experience. Literature becomes possible by making death impossible, by preserving it from the possible, by making it harmonize or disharmonize with dying.[8] The ambiguity of literature lies in the double hold of death as impossible and of dying (*le mourir*) as ineffable.

> If we try to restore literature to the movement that allows all its ambiguities to be grasped, that movement is here: literature, like ordinary speech, *begins* with the *end*, which is the only thing that allows us to understand. If we are to speak, we must see death, we must see it behind us. When we speak, we lean on a tomb, and the void of that tomb is what makes language true, but at the same time the void is reality and death becomes being. (336)

This is the heart of Blanchot's experience, the experience of his own writing, that of *Death Sentence*, which he was precisely just finishing when he published these lines.

A clear response, showing how far Hegel's and Heidegger's thinking had been taken on board, is given in "Literature and the Right to Death":

> What is written is neither well nor badly written . . . : it is the perfect act through which what was nothing when it was inside emerges into the monumental reality of the outside as something which is necessarily true, since what it translates only exists through it and in it. (305)

Blanchot makes it explicit (302) that he is drawing on Hegel's general phenomenology, rather than on his aesthetic philosophy.[9] For instance he sees the writer as nothing more than a product of his work, a being existing only thanks to or in relation to that work. As for Heidegger's thinking on art, which he had been aware of since the "Origin of the Work of Art" lecture in 1936, it had seduced him so greatly that it is not impossible to think that he attempted to become for René Char what Heidegger was attempting to become for Hölderlin. Blanchot cites Heidegger on multiple occasions, most frequently in his articles on the two poets. These citations are often indirect and very free. He writes about the image in René Char, "in which are united this undamageable nature of solid things and the stream of becoming, the thickness of presence and the scintillation of absence," carrying life, "and even more than life, that which in our life but unknown to it, *keeps courage and silence vigilant*: its truth" (109–110). In doing so he sticks close to Heidegger, for whom poetic language "alone brings what is, as something that is, into the Open for the first time. Where there is no language, as in the being of stone, plant, and animal, there is also no openness of what is," and for whom the work is "the fighting of the battle in which the unconcealedness of beings as a whole, or truth, is won."[10] Numerous pages in "Literature and the Right to Death" are steeped in Heideggerian aesthetics. Blanchot writes that:

> Yes, happily language is a thing: it is a written thing, a bit of bark, a sliver of rock, a fragment of clay in which the reality of the earth continues to exist. The word acts not as an ideal force but as an obscure power, as an incantation that coerces things, makes them *really* present outside of themselves. (327–328)

This passage can be compared with the following one in Heidegger:

> When a work is created, brought forth out of this or that work-material—stone, wood, metal, color, language, tone—we say also that

it is made, set forth out of it. . . . [This] setting-forth is needed. . . . The work sets itself back into the massiveness and heaviness of stone, into the firmness and pliancy of wood, into the hardness and luster of metal, into the lighting and darkening of color, into the clang of tone, and into the naming powers of the word. That into which the word sets itself back and which it causes to come forth in this setting back of itself we called the earth. . . . The work sets forth the earth. . . . *The work lets the earth be an earth.*[11]

Elsewhere, Blanchot writes: "the poetic image, in this very absence of thing, claims to restore the foundation of its presence to us, not its form (what one sees) but the underside (what one penetrates), its reality of earth, its 'matter-emotion'" (108).

The question of faithfulness disappears. Having recourse to Heidegger allows Blanchot to define the sovereignty of literature differently. All authority is henceforth given to the equivocal authenticity of a paradoxical language. Literary experience only has authority if it contests and tears apart its own language; it only has authority in the absence it presents, the death it puts to work, the void it excavates. This movement in which the unified *coherence* of language is contested attacks the reality of things as they stand, but also its own images, its own "matter-emotion," its own "rhetoric become matter" (89), its own "physical adherence to something completely strange" (170), its own "hammerlike density" (107). This material movement is based on the kind of resistant *hardness* that had been experienced by the surrealists, Lautréamont (Blanchot often speaks of Maldoror in terms of an uncracked block), Mallarmé ("calm block here fallen from obscure disaster"), and Rimbaud ("Rimbaud was thirsty for pebbles, rock, and charcoal, that is to say, for what is most drying in the world. And starting from this absolute hardness, he wanted the absolute porosity of sleep, the innocence of caterpillars, moles, limbs, the toad's idleness, infinite patience capable of an infinite forgetfulness," 160).[12] This hardness is what lends authority to literary language. In this double marriage to the reality of things and the reality of words, literature ultimately makes language into "shapeless matter, formless content, a force that is capricious and impersonal and says nothing, reveals nothing, simply announces—through its refusal to say anything—that it comes from night and will return to night" (330). The neuter can already be heard in this, and literature draws its authority from this movement toward the neuter, which also recalls the movement toward the *there is* (which Blanchot evokes on the following page, dedicating a note to Levinas's *Existence and Existents* which had just been published). Some readers would not be able to bear Blanchot's approach to this shadow of matter—nor that he should have seen shadow itself as material, shadow often being considered as mere transparency, imminent evanescence. The myth of Orpheus would later come into play around the boundaries of these two conceptions, and would have to bear the weakness of the first, which for its part often screens the danger of the second.

Blanchot thus sees literary language as more metonymic than metaphorical, as infinitely opening the image onto the unimaginable, without assigning it any equivalencies, whether insidious or surprising. After Mallarmé, he denounces

> the fault of simple metaphor . . . in its stability, its plastic solidity; it is as weighty and present as what it represents, it is as if placed immutably in front of us, with its meaning that nothing comes to change. (32)

On the contrary, to follow one silence with another is to never step beyond language; it is only ever to be led to "a new language that is never the last" (41), but one that always moves toward the last word, without embodying it.[13] This reading of movement, which only suggests images the better to deconstruct them, is the line pursued in *Lautréamont and Sade*.

It is in the attempt to exhaust this endless back-and-forth of literary language that critical language accedes to its own paradoxical essence.

Paradox becomes at once the form, method, and object of Blanchot's critical discourse, being at once the law of experience (of his entire reading experience), the "work of fire" itself, the "spark of fire," "flame," Ariadne's thread, the "passionate assurance" that allows one to guide oneself through the torments of the night. It often stands out right from the outset, forming part of the dramaturgy or the poetics of critical writing. The articles go on to throw light on the obscurity of this paradox, but never resolve the underlying contradiction. The initial paragraphs set it up, establish it by describing a series of light and almost unnecessary paradoxes, which are all the more surprising given that they are seemingly endless and are stated as if they were facts. Some sort of consistency then takes hold, the analysis centers itself around an essential paradox: this is explored, excavated, enriched, and led toward a paroxysm of complexity a few paragraphs before the conclusion. The latter brings no dénouement, instead confirming that none is possible before returning to silence. This rhetoric of critical writing, which would contribute to Blanchot's glory, is an improved version of his prose in the *Journal des Débats*, which develops by broadening out short anaphoric phrases, digging into paradox via chiasmus and oxymoron, but with less depth and speed. This dramatic and spectacular, reproducible and specular rhetoric is now present wherever thinking takes place, and its rigor proves seductive; the challenge it presents makes reading a pleasure (we know how Blanchot's articles are able to fascinate their readers, and their regular rhythm of publication only increased this pleasure by forcing readers to wait for them). The detachment of the long but lucid phrasing, often toward the start of an article following one or two short, lapidary sentences setting out some fact, enchants readers by setting forth the question, then developing it via various rhythms and enumerations that are always measured and symmetrical, harmonious and self-contained, while also being extended by oratorical redundancies that enclose the problem within the circularity of incompatible elements. Of course, the task of reasoning being pursued here consists in opening, prizing apart all of this, even though it seems impossible, and is made to seem impossible.[14]

This method of repetition, which is also a heightening, an accumulation, a vertiginous deepening, a plunge into the unpredictable, is a way of underlining the movement of criticism itself, the movement of criticism as Blanchot conceives it—that is, as causing a crisis for the text or giving it over to the crisis and movement within it, making the critical text itself that of crisis and movement. Such a method can be read as a mania for paradox, which proceeds via *jouissance* to experiment with all possible forms (hyperbole, irony, contradiction, paralipsis, denial), a paradox also found at work in phrases undermining their own logical predicates (such placing of qualifications prior to the predicate characterizes even Blanchot's narrative writing, they are presuppositions that undermine the permanent presence of the voice of utterance). But this is only meaningful if we read this mania as a way of setting aside the melancholy that might proceed from multiple encounters with the impossible. Each time, the exhausting writing of critical reason plays a role in tearing its author apart. But it is also a way for him to find new life, to seize the madness of the day during the wearying labor of the night. And it is a way of bringing himself back to life, if the work constructing the oeuvre of the other can also be said to be his own. Paradox is Blanchot's *flower of Tarbes*: he does not enter into any text without the decision, the incision of seeing in it—to the point of excess—the contradictory movements of his own mind and the metamorphoses of his own body.

He also tests the texts of the community that he *unworks* through the effacement of the self, which is his particular way of making assertions: unworking these texts, analyzing—more than the texts themselves—the process by which they had been constructed and which demonstrate that this very construction is impossible. The partner that the critic represents becomes less and less visible. This invisibility belongs to the insistent, tireless movement of his writing, which is becoming more and more the critical research of a writer.[15]

"The essential impulse of such a way of thinking is to contradict itself" (290), Blanchot writes of Nietzsche. He now tracks this movement of thought and writing in all the works he encounters. Critical thought requires a thinking of time. Even in its maddest moments, such as those when a relation to the divine provokes endless reversals, the movement of experience is what disrupts the feeling of duration.[16] The critical text is protected against dogmatism by constantly calling the results of analysis into question, submitting them to paradox. Later, Blanchot would describe this in a letter to Mascolo: "the declarative mode can carry the entire trembling of thought, its torment and its infinite search, not affirming anything but forcing us to take risks where no affirmation is possible: truly over the abyss."[17] Ultimately perhaps it is only possible to grasp paradox in a "time of distress," at an "end of History," where contradiction becomes exhausted, unable to relaunch itself while remaining full of energy: paradox governs how ideas are present for the "inoperative community." Enunciating paradoxes does not lead to any purification or any catharsis.[18]

This is what we are given to understand by the pages on Terror, which Blanchot's detractors have attempted to read as a direct resurgence of his political past. We must see the passages in question for what they are: less than five pages (317–322) of "Literature and the Right to Death," which, although intense and decisive in tone, are in no way conclusive. They carry out a simple task: at the close of the 1940s and at the dénouement of *The Work of Fire*, Blanchot reorients his research and his allegiances in criticism. The Terror discussed here now has nothing to do with Jean Paulhan's Terror; it is a way of removing Paulhan from these critical reflections (his use of political language no longer coinciding exactly with Blanchot's). Critical language becomes at once aesthetic, historical, and philosophical. As an excessive form of anguish, Terror seizes the writer through "experience." Taking place in "times of distress," at the "end of History," Terror is much more than a political equivalency: it is the coming-together of two freedoms experienced as absolute, of two sovereignties put at stake, made to face the void of existence and the alarming possibility of creating a world. Terror means that the writer cannot accept any compromise, either in the ethics of his work (his relation to language) or in the uncommitment he has allowed himself, which only takes on its full meaning in an absolutely free society (which also means that it will never take on its full meaning, and thus that Terror is inevitable). Blanchot here is introducing only the shadow of terrorism into literature, and this terrorism is the reverse of totalitarianism; he knows that power is nothing, that *everything* comes down to *nothing*. Revolutionary Terror is that of Sade: it claims even those who control it. Terror knows no power. What about Robespierre and Saint-Just? "The Terror they personify does not come from the death they inflict on others but from the death they inflict on themselves. . . . Their thinking is cold, it has the freedom of a decapitated head" (320). The terrorist of the fantastic is exposed to his own death and exposes the liberty of all to death—to what Blanchot names dying (*le mourir*). If literature is Terror, he continues,

> it is because it finds its justification in revolution, and if it has been called the Reign of Terror, this is because its ideal is indeed that moment in history, that moment when "life endures death and maintains itself in it" in order to gain from death the possibility of speaking and the truth of speech. (322)

But in order for life to maintain itself in death, death also has to maintain itself, and this death is dying.

"Any writer who is not induced by the very fact of writing to think, 'I am the revolution, only freedom allows me to write,' is not really writing" (321). The excessive vigor of his thinking makes much literature unreadable for Blanchot, perhaps because he had tolerated it too much previously. Ethical judgment takes place on no other issue than that of death, in order that he can lay claim to the "inoperative community" (a movement that gives literature "every right").[19] This vigor of his thinking proves magnetic, and almost makes the fate of this or that writer into a sacred destiny. And yet it is necessary to understand what this sacralization means: as Blanchot says of Hölderlin, the writer is only the witness, witnessing that it is impossible for the sacred to move into literary language.[20] Over and against all the readings attempting to make Sade into a breviary of immorality, Blanchot states on the opening page of *Lautréamont and Sade*, "Here we have the most scandalous book ever written. . . . Moreover, to all his present and future publishers and commentators, we cannot stop ourselves from discreetly uttering this avowal: Ah, in Sade, at least, respect the scandal."[21]

This Terror with its destructive capacity and divine atheism presents a real challenge to reason. In his fiction Blanchot analyzes the contradictory and "infinitely" expansive construction of this challenge. He draws a symbolic principle of energy from it: "nothing evil will ever happen to the man actively connected to evil."[22] Nothing stands up in Sade's theoretical construction: man is overcome by the name of God, God by the name of Nature, Nature by the energy of contestation. When it is taken on board even in the face of death, this principle of energy leads one to sovereignty. In this, things have gone very far beyond a Gospel of Evil: literature is the site of apathy. Sade can carry the principle of energy to this site, this ambiguous and equivocal energy, making it the principle of his work itself. This principle of his work is neither a moral nor an immoral principle. Blanchot is careful to make this explicit in concluding his essay on Sade:

> We are not saying that this thought is viable. But it does show that of the normal man who locks up the sadistic man in an impasse, and the sadistic man who turns this impasse into a means of escape, the latter is the one who is nearer to the truth, who understands the logic of his situation, and who has the deeper intelligence of it, so much so that he can help the normal man to understand himself by helping him change the conditions of all perception.[23]

Literature is this energy of comprehension, and is all the stronger for being contradictory, mobile, and unceasing, for endlessly producing contradictions. Blanchot would say this of Lautréamont too: "At no time was evil simply a theoretical idol for him," with the entire movement of the *Chants* consisting in bringing to light (and to the reader) "his awareness of this."[24]

Blanchot reproaches critics for not seeing this power of infinite contestation on the part of consciousness either in Sade or in Lautréamont; he reproaches them for not reading these authors, for *isolating* certain questions as if obsessed, obsessively preoccupied by their own thematics. Something very real becomes necessary:

> [analysis] only makes up for what is illegitimate in its method (which separates out what is together) through its excesses and by indefinitely prolonging its activity. . . . Only perpetual movement justifies analysis, for once it stops, all of its suspended conclusions, its provisional explanations take on definitive value and the work, violently separated from itself, breaks apart to make room for a rudimentary framework which is clumsily reconstructed from without.[25]

Energy has to become the very principle of criticism.

The opening of the essay on Lautréamont denounces the "mirage of sources" as having rendered most critics blind, as well as denouncing thematic commentary for fixing the work in a single position (the book's becoming "a homogeneous, unmoving expanse, like a thing that has always existed, its meaning—sought independently of the direction it moves in—

neglecting in particular the movement by which it has been made").[26] This failing is all the more apparent in the case of the *Chants* because this work *is* movement (something that justifies the exception Blanchot makes in dedicating this long and patient study to a single book). Here the analysis attempts not to separate the work from its movement, which is to say from itself. This explains the genetic point of view that is repeatedly adopted, for instance by comparing the first two publications of the first *Chant* (from Dazet to animals, from Ducasse to Lautréamont). Blanchot looks at the endless contradictions and reversals that give progression to the narrative; the "progressive experience" of metamorphosis, now as something awesome, a "paroxysm of frenzied violence," now as something heavily slithering, thick, patient, and menacing, "the power of an infinite passivity," which is always excessively organic.[27] He also turns to the permanent uncertainty created by dreams and insomnia, the instability of representation corroded by irony, "*the very experience of metamorphosis carried out at the heart of language*," an experience lived out at the heart of the work's structure (which changes in the sixth *Chant*) and of its writing (which changes again in the *Poems*).[28] Blanchot reads this endless movement, this prose and this genesis of writing, as the narrative of the author's birth, "the progressive birth of the *novelist*": "in this collaboration of patience and violence that is birth, Lautréamont, definitively pushing Ducasse aside, brought himself into the world."[29]

It was 1948 or 1949. This birth of a novelist, in which he draws on the power of a "night made of organs," is also that of Blanchot. Alongside *Death Sentence* and the second version of *Thomas the Obscure*, another oeuvre is being created, one that had already been present beneath the surface, in the metamorphoses of the former. It would become less ornate, more secret, while remaining just as mobile. Its traces, its innovations, its movements are commented on in advance in *Lautréamont and Sade*: "the possibility [for the character] of entering into situations and of escaping them, of living the present moment as if this present were perpetually behind him . . . of being simultaneously sick, dead, and healed"; "there is a continuous exchange of situation, of nature, and of power" with God; the unexpected fall of language "into the semi-darkness of insomnia; [words] get stuck, and their effort to track down obscurity only results in an endless pursuit, in the insubstantiality of a dream that is transformed as soon as one touches it in the fatality of a death that is always its own resurrection." To this can be added the apparent imperceptibility of experience, which is endlessly churned and sometimes suddenly torn apart by the monstrous, ungraspable, gripping movement of shadow, and the "indeterminate moment between life and death when the same disappears and the other approaches."[30]

The energy of metamorphosis requires infinite patience. *Lautréamont and Sade* is laden with the suffering and the weight of the past. The process of creating a novelist was a double one: before becoming the author of the *récits* of the 1950s, Blanchot had had to become that of *Thomas the Obscure*. Lautréamont's energy, similar to that of Sade, was also similar to the energy of the 1930s writer. Let us read this long passage on Lautréamont and think of what Blanchot could be saying about himself:

> At no time was evil simply a theoretical idol for him. It could be said that "evil" was in him and, quite nearly, *was* him. This evil not leaving him free, he put up an admirable fight, and since he found nothing in himself that was evil, except for his awareness of it—a sovereign power that he marvelously backed up—he was only able to combat evil with evil, making himself its accomplice and pushing it as far as possible, in the steadfast—but also spellbound—courage of his resolution and in the hope of a radical overthrow which might return him to himself, or cast him outside everything. If today he preaches reason and order, it cannot be said that he has disowned his former beliefs, for his tragic struggle was a struggle for daylight, and he always wanted to see clearly. In this sense, he remains perfectly faithful to himself and, as he says in a letter, "in short, it is always the Good that one sings." But it is also quite true that between yesterday and today the change risks being significant: the man who moves from keeping his eyes open when darkness reigns to easily taking pleasure in reasonable tranquil clarity is no longer the same man. And he changes all the more given that, thinking that he has changed more than he actually has and turning toward a past that he pushes away, he will now see this struggle from long ago as an unhealthy indulgence for night, this shadowy will as a weakness, a game or experience without sincerity or value.[31]

What remains then is only—to use the title of the section immediately following these words—"to write, to die."

CHAPTER 31

The Black Stain
Writing *The Most High* (1946–1947)

A thick novel—one that had been a work in progress for several years, and which can be read in political, theological, and psychological ways—was completed at the beginning of 1947. Through it we can glimpse Blanchot's striking thinking of nudity, the body, illness, and death, which little by little would push him toward the *récits* that would follow. *The Most High* is his most openly political, realist, and familial novel. The twenty-four-year-old narrator, Henri Sorge, relates to his mother and his sister Louise in a way that seems to dictate his behavior toward other women, such as Marie the photographer and Jeanne the nurse. Sorge's dedication to the law—his main topic of conversation—is dictated by his respect for his father, a "man of duty" who had died seventeen years previously, and by his hatred for his stepfather, an important and corrupt statesman. The novel plunges the reader into the unhealthy and hate-filled familial world that is ultimately foreign to the young man, before taking an interest in the parallel developments of an epidemic and an insurrection in the city (which, though unnamed, quite closely resembles Paris). The plague spreads and the security measures become more and more draconian and dictatorial: The police search passers-by, lock up the insubordinate, erect barriers, shoot into the crowd. Little by little, buildings are transformed into dispensaries. A group of insurgents led by Bouxx, the narrator's former neighbor, profits from the epidemic and takes control of the health centers, which become more and more numerous. A willing hostage to Bouxx, Sorge remains in his building, which has also become a dispensary. Through the partition he communicates with Dorte, a friend of Bouxx who is badly affected by the illness. The epidemic gets worse; at night, insane and ill people rush through the streets in gangs, attacking houses, stealing food. The chaos is at its worst, the epidemic spreads to other quarters, the insurrection seems about to be successful, when the nurse Jeanna Galgat takes Sorge—in whom she has recognized "the Most High"—away to a building for isolated treatment where he seems to undergo once again fits of epilepsy, this "great evil" that has already been discussed in a scene with Marie.[1]

Such at least is the fantastic plot of an impossible *récit* which is narrated by a person who is in turn reasoned, unwell, mystical, "idiotic," perhaps mad, and who is also confronted by other figures who are just as troubling, providing as they do multiple, contradictory versions of the events in their dialogues. Nothing in this novel, beyond the fantastic treatment of political subject matter, reminds one of the realist aesthetics and moralist ethics of *The Plague*, which was published as Blanchot was finishing his book. Any concern for reasoned commentary, whether universal or particular, small-scale or totalizing, is immediately limited, and often referred back to what gives the *récit* its force: its permanent ability to open new spaces of perception and dialogue, the speed with which the narration invents new forms of light, new boards to walk on, new steps to walk with, new objects, new debates, with infinitely minute attention to detail. Events happen as quickly as the fist that punches the narrator in the opening lines "with fascinating speed."[2] The progressive discovery of thoughts, characters, and places is led by the narrator's vision, and by a writing that

> [slows] down this flow of reflections passing through me with incredible speed: everything is going too fast, it is running, it is as if I always had to walk faster, and not only me but also other people, things, and even dust; everything is so clear; these are the thoughts that never get confused, thousands of infinitely small and distinct shocks. (77)

We have to be able to follow this flux of transformation of space and air, to abandon any desire for physical permanence and to follow the narrator's consciousness according to the metamorphoses it undergoes. The more the novel advances, the more bodies become able to multiply, until the final chapter where the various states of immanence become unthinkable, impossible, so much so that only a brazen, blistered, and irritated perception at the edge of the limitless, *granted* by illness or by disgust, seems to have been driving this ever-changing description.

Much rather than in the plot, it is in these divagations, these glances, these rhythms that traces and echoes of Blanchot's life can be found. For his only fiction that places its main protagonist in a family setting is also his least overtly biographical. There can be no direct transposition of Henri Sorge's relationship with his family onto Blanchot's. A certain number of differences rule this out (the father dying early, the mother remarrying, and so on); and despite some points of similarity (solitude, illness, writing, a certain "idiocy"—in the Dostoyevskian sense), the character is not a portrait of Blanchot.[3] We have to accept that *The Most High* is neither an autobiographical novel nor a family romance.

Nonetheless, we can note certain tendencies. Unlike the "man without qualities" who wanders alone in the strange world of *Aminadab*, "overcome by a feeling of solitude and by the anguish of his own destitution," the first line of *The Most High* states: "I was not alone," and it continues on the following page: "Having a family, I knew what that meant" (1, 2).[4] This novel, which is so little centered on the family, opens with a definition of it: "That was what family was. The recollection of the time before the law, a cry, primitive words from the past" (3). For the family indeed seems only to survive in Blanchot via a "recollection": the palpable political and intellectual distance established by adulthood allows the novel of childhood to resurface only in fragments, in certain scenes, in its happy lack of differentiation and its natural freedom. This is a love kept alive by what was obvious in the past, but that one or two scenes have been able to tear apart after a certain moment in childhood: the "primal scene" and the opening of the sky, perhaps also a forbidding of incest, which is a difficult and recurrent topic in *The Most High*, in which the figure of the sister plays a major role. The family is a reservoir of dark signs. The family in the novel, which is highly structured, ordered, run like a state due to the stepfather's profession, is in fact undermined by the brutality that governs the relationships within it: the "common speech" (*paroles brutes*) that signals correspondences between the events of childhood and their resurgence and transposition in adulthood. We cannot fail to be alert to the fact that Blanchot's only novel addressing family relationships, ancestors, and children, opens with such a view of the family. *The Most High* traces the contours of familial aridity.

The absence of father figures in *all* of Blanchot's fiction appears, in a way, to be made up for and explicated here with Sorge's father dying at an early stage in his life, and his mother then marrying a hated stepfather. Two of Henri Sorge's childhood memories converge: his mother's violence toward her daughter Louise ("a thin five-year-old ghost," "my mother with her fist in the air, the majesty of my mother reduced to this threat," 56–57); and the scene in which Louise is seduced, "kissed and caressed" by her stepfather (68). These scenes give Henri and his sister a predisposition for an Orestes complex, which is symbolically put into action by the solemn declaration that they will take vengeance, as well as by the fantasy of the axe, of injuring the stepfather, who by now has become ill (71, 68). The contrast with the dead father is clear, with him being idealized, referred to as "a true icon" and a "man of duty" who has been ousted by a man of hypocritical, blind power (52); this can only encourage brother and sister to come together. Incestuous love for the sister takes over from love for the mother, this "monumental person who could drag me into totally crazy things" (3). Louise will indeed be the one who is capable of provoking Henri into madness, as in the strongly erotic cemetery scene in which brother and sister come together in the father's empty tomb, and in which words of resentment and vengeance are spoken by a face that "reveres, horrified and cursing, only the dark side of death" (70), "foaming on her mouth . . . becoming sweat and water" (71), "letting off with the flowers "a scent of earth and stagnant water" (72).[5] The sister is the solitary, dirty, accursed, dominating being who carries out a burial. She hides in the darkness of the tomb like Madame Edwarda beneath a public arch, provoking desire in horror and fright (70–71), but while she eludes the sexual act, doing no more than miming it, she is not able to mime anguish: for she *is* anguish. Threatening her brother with scissors, she slaps him and makes his lip bleed, as a reminder of the time when they were children and she threw a brick at his temple. In this way she passes on her mother's violent heritage. She will only ever look at Henri with "extremely old eyes," intimidating him so much that he regularly sweats in her presence, this sweat that he perceives as "deathly water which had flowed and would flow from me, again and to the end" (51).

The incest is of course never consummated. But that is precisely its true state, according to Blanchot in an article on Musil: "Here appears the profound meaning of the incest that is fulfilled in the impossibility of its fulfillment."[6] Like death, incest signals "the definitive impossibility of having done with things" that condemns Henri Sorge to a series of transfer displacements and hallucinations as symptoms. The *eau de mort* associated with the sister proves an obsession for her brother. She is the seat of his gaze and of his desires. The black stain he sees, which grows larger and larger and is more hallucinated than real ("was it even visible? It did not exist under the wallpaper," 43), on the walls of the apartment and of the hospital room, recalls a similar stain on the walls of his parents' house; it is "water leakage," "oozing humor," "thick and invisible streaming" (43, 195). This fantastic growth is able to communicate the sick neighbor's sweating through the wall. As "black water, stagnant with filth and poverty," it starts to refer to the air being breathed, which becomes more and more unhealthy as the epidemic progresses (120). This "black tide against which authoritarian forces were now being established," or "blind, black tide in which rottenness, hardship, and humiliation rolled" also refers to the ill, turned mad by their illness, who go out at night to attack houses, this "rabble of ruined people," these "true beacons of death," "men and women beside themselves with their own insanity" (180, 187). For the narrator, it will only ever come from a single source, Louise:

> I watched her unremittingly, I stared at the fabric of her dress, a kind of black silk, shiny in some areas, dull in others; it was not a piece of clothing, but rather: a stain, something she had soaked up which was now seeping out, something that had neither form nor color, something that looked like that broad blot of mildew on the wall. And even thinking that it would go away gave me a feeling of wrongdoing, of guilt. (121)

Does it represent Louise's black eyes, "which seemed to have always examined me with this expectant, disapproving and commanding air" (51), which Henri hallucinates seeing in the stains on the wall, all the more frequently given that he no longer sees his sister? Or does it represent the black material of her dress, "a dirty and faded black" (15), the abjection of her hateful virginity, "black thing," "small, swarthy, ugly," whose ideal state is to "feel bad and look like a slob" (86–87)? Or then again, it might be the dirtiness of the tapestry in the room, "chaos in rags," a "bug nest," from which Henri suddenly sees emerging "the image of an enormous horse that reared up toward the sky," a vision whose meaning, overcome with hatred as he is, he locates in "something old, criminally old" (54). The black material itself will lead him to his neighbor, Marie Scadran, who wears clothing made from it when she gives herself to him. The erotic scene is described in a similar way to that in *Aminadab*, which insists on both the fusion and separation of bodies. "With a shattering suddenness this (shared) body broke in two, dissolved, and in its place a burning density formed, a moist and voracious strangeness that could see nothing and recognize nothing" (39). Ancestral eroticism therefore leads to black moistness via bodily smoothness and radical strangeness ("I swear, she became other," "I swear, I had become a stranger"). The stain that is the sign of sickly distance (the malady of death?) forever separates the beings in question at the moment of excess (eroticism, ecstatic vision, movement toward death). It gives shape to the body of separation, which becomes available to touch and smell ("No one will believe me, but, at that moment, we had been separated, we felt and breathed this separation, we gave it a body," 39).

At a late stage, Henri will state explicitly that Jeanne Galgat, the nurse, "resembled my sister" (242). In fact this comparison of the two is even greater and more shocking than it seems. The ensuing mad, erotic scene involving cries, phlegm, bodies hurled against the wall, is only an extension of the scene with Louise in the grave (238–240). This erotic body is a liquid body: "I felt her stuck against me, a foreign flesh, a dead, liquefying flesh" (239). The narrator has already seen this body half-naked: "that black and thick water was dripping down her body, water similar to what had once percolated through the walls" (225). This body, which it is impossible to feel, see, or breathe, this deathly body, is the one that obsesses Blanchot in *The Most High*, *Thomas the Obscure*, and *Death Sentence*.

But unlike in the latter two texts, the narrator of this novel is also a subject of the city. This aspect seems to be a little more overtly autobiographical. It recalls what the narrator of *The Madness of the Day* states:

> As I walked along the pavements, plunged into the bright lights of the metro, turned down beautiful avenues where the city glowed superbly, I became extremely dull, modest, and tired. Gathering an excessive share of anonymous dilapidation, I then attracted all the more attention because it was not meant for me and was making of me something rather vague and formless.[7]

But the Parisian city in *The Most High* only retains its luminosity—its overwhelming luminosity—at the beginning of the novel. It quickly becomes unhealthy, and the narrator will no longer be simply "extremely dull and tired," but concretely ill, worn out, exhausted (more, the architecture described will be an object of disdain: Blanchotian buildings are empty, as if they have been hollowed out). Sorge will only attract attention for a limited time, for he already bears this "care" inscribed in his surname, he is and shall remain the "Most High": He who "gather[s] an excessive proportion of anonymous dilapidation." Like Thomas, Sorge carries others' deaths on his shoulders, the guilt of the world. When his concerned face attracts attention, he is met with affront and insult. In a palpably

Christic episode at the start of the narrative, Sorge is punched by a man he has lightly bumped against. He remains peaceful and refuses to press charges when the two are taken to the police commissioner. He asks real ethical questions of his assailant and is taken to be "an oddball." Ultimately he is the one thrown out of the police station: his account is no more acceptable to the police than the one Christ gave to Pontius Pilate or than the one the narrator of *The Madness of the Day* gives to his doctors. From the outset, the novel is taken into a space that cannot be assimilated into the moral consensus of the social order, into the way the interrogations seek to press guilt upon those being questioned. The difference introduced by this punch opens an ethical space which places the novel incredibly close to Robert Antelme's contemporaneous (1947) reflections; for instance the recognition of similarity ("now you know that I am a man like you," 1), which prevents the attacker from continuing to hit him (in this sense, the novel's beginning prefigures its ending; as if Blanchot were saying: "No, no novels, never again").[8] It is only ever difference that is trampled and killed, Sorge continues. It is only ever this black stain, this vomiting, that makes the State's reprisals possible. This rotten punch casts a dark light over the beginning of the tale, placing itself between Sorge and the State.

The itinerary taken by the narrative consists entirely in separating the State and Sorge, even though initially he breathes it "through [his] every fiber" and feels "its existence in everything [he does]" (19). He is excessively conscientious in his work ("I have to do my job," 2; "work is the basis of existence," 23; "a real veneration of the authorities," 40); this "good citizen's" conscientiousness leads him to make unbending, extreme statements ("it is a duty to raise young people who are strong," the search for "good, clean fun," 16). He takes infinite pleasure from the feeling that the law, different from but ultimately similar to Hegelian reason, finds ingenious solutions; each man works in his own way but all work for the law, even and especially when they transgress it: "If everyone was equally faithful to the law—ah, that idea intoxicated me" (18). This senseless love for the law paints Sorge as an infinite reasoner, an exhausting chatterbox, a naïve, intrusive clown, all the more tiresome for being so courteous. His behavior gives rise to some joking (identification itself is not without humor). But whether it is due to illness, love, his farewell to his family, or the mysticism that gradually takes him over, his character changes over the course of the narrative: He vomits on simply seeing his identity card (114–115), drafts a letter of resignation (126), sympathizes with the insurgents even though he thinks that their agitations are in vain. "The State is everywhere" (176), and even if it is wounded, it will end up trapping you. Blanchot's bitterness and utter disillusionment for what he names here "political fatality" are palpable (179). There is no way of opposing the anonymous, impersonal power of the State, which in the end always swallows up figures such as Bouxx or the stepfather. When Sorge tells Bouxx, in a phrase used as the novel's epigraph, "everything that you get from me is, for you, only a lie, because I am the truth" (176), we should understand that this superior truth (that of the Most High) does not belong to the same sphere as political untruth. It is the only possible site for difference.

The episode of the mugging in the metro recalls the opening scene of the punch (as well as that of bread being stolen in Robert Antelme's work). "The man had stolen but was all the same still a man," ponders the narrator; guilt does not exist, difference is only "a kind of game to keep the law moving along" (28). Justice creates differences but reveals beneath it a vast space that renders all equal. The movement of the law is an *effacement* (65–66): "its even, transparent, and absolute light illuminating everyone and everything in an always different and yet identical way" (29), giving rise only to the inebriation of the dead. Initially, Sorge is unable to create any difference between women and the law: when with Marie, he reflects that difference is no more forthcoming from hands and flesh than it is from the law. The world of the restaurant bathes in the lack of all concern, in the impersonality of the *there is* (such is what Sorge says, talking about himself and his name: "nobody looked at me or seemed to have noticed my presence, just as if no one had been there, as if around us there had only been a noisy void," 29). Resemblances are everywhere: in illness, which is a great leveler ("What happens is strange . . . you no longer recognize people . . . everything is displayed in a peaceful and full light, the points of view of all people coincide, they have disappeared," 30–31); in the hundreds of photographs examined, which all seem to be the same, and which are anything but *identity* photographs ("All these photos looked alike. . . . They were the same, but the same in an infinite number," 37);[9] in the silence, where even minimal forms of hatred brood (the narrator relates an anecdote where he has asked for a new role due to a colleague he cannot stand; but he then learns that the colleague has also asked for a new role: "I was the same as him," 83). There are further resemblances with Bouxx ("You are like me," Sorge tells him (44)—Bouxx does not accept this); with things (the world begins to resemble Sorge: "All these things! They are like you! It is as if they are satisfied because you look at them, because you look only at them. Ugh! What a world!" says Jeanne in a sickened manner, 237); and with Marie ("our faces look alike, our thoughts are the same," he says to her; they look at their faces in a mirror: "Little by little the resemblance emerged in this world before us . . . with the serenity of an inaccessible presence," 100). Yet it is also with Marie, following this accumulation of semblances, that difference will appear (38–39). Women are what are missing from, and are able to elude, the world of the law. A long dream by Sorge recalls Thomas's itinerary in *Aminadab* and prefigures the passage in *The Madness of the Day* where the law finally submits to the guilty party: The judges "became my servants" (46); the law "declared herself perpetually on her knees before me. . . . She would say to me . . . 'here I am, your servant forever.' . . . In these surroundings, overpopulated by men, she was the only feminine element."[10] "I had been searching for days, with these judges, and what I could not find anywhere . . . was a woman. . . . There were none. Because of this the world of justice is oppressive" (46). Women cannot free one from guilt, but they can free one from semblances: They set difference free. Disentangling himself from all politics of brotherhood, sliding into a narrative space bordered by women (two women), the Blanchotian character will slowly return toward men, but this time they will be last men, friends, with friendship now opening up—differently—the space of the political.

The narrator was looking at Marie's hand, and the feeling of otherness will appear in a similar moment, in proximity to Louise's hand.

> "Listen," I said looking at the hand that she had rested on my arm, which I feebly brushed aside, "I have just had a strange feeling. Your hand, I had the impression that it belonged to another world, that it was something that I did not know, something completely other. Yes, it is strange." (118–119)

The other body, the deathly body, gives rise to strange perceptions. To perceive the deathly body in fact demands that one perceive the incredible, the impossible, the imperceptible, the indescribable, it demands a state in one's own body that is deferred (*différé*), permanently shifted, visionary, ecstatic—and yet also conscious and extremely lucid. Like a body in the theater, occupying the whole stage, this body no longer knows the limits of flesh: It is addressed by the stain and by what lies behind it. The narrator sees "behind him," over his shoulders, and always beyond the other. This is an exhausting ability. Perception spreads not transparent light, the light of day which illuminates objects, but "a penetrating and suspicious light that I also saw, which disclosed itself," for it illuminates itself 'at work' before it does objects (75). It could be said to be the light of darkness, that which allows us to see differently. That which beats down upon the skull, makes it numb from glimpsing another world in its weightiness, its thickness, its fugitive nature. Another character also has this ability:

> Dorte looked at me crazily, a look full of pleading and horror. Fixed on me, his eyes did not seem to see me where I was, but further away, on the other side of the wall, against the door, then further, beyond this room and this house; they found me everywhere and they kept going further to find me again. (187)

Thus he and Sorge are able to look at each other, over and against their faces, without actually looking at each other: a mystical, blind, enhanced perception. To do so is to reach the broadest serenity: "We kept looking at each other, and there was nothing calmer than the two of us, nothing more peaceful than the room and the house" (194). Space is pacified. Through this mystical force, this ability to penetrate matter, the exchange of gazes allows Dorte to pierce the wall, to shake the world and to impress her almost monstrous mark, the *black stain*: "coming from the bowels of the wall like an oozing humor, resembling neither a thing nor the shadow of a thing, flowing and extending, forming neither head nor hand nor thing, nothing but a thick and invisible streaming" (195). This stain is nonetheless seen, experienced, and perceived so strongly by the narrator that he suffocates, his eyes boggling. A senseless vision closes one of the final chapters, one that Sorge seems to be able to tolerate but that strikes Dorte like an arrow, a flame, a vision of a condemned man:

> he was on his feet in one terrible bound and, letting out a piercing scream, like the cry of a woman, he started howling, "I am not dead, I am not dead," and even when my hand covered his mouth, pressing against it and crushing it down to make him be quiet, my fingers kept on grasping the same cry, and nothing could silence it. (195)

If he is able to bear this death of the other to the point of suffocating, to the point where being able to see behind him is no longer of use, the narrator is indeed the Most High. Toward the end we read, "I was covered with an earthy, almost cold, slobber, which flowed in and out through my nose and mouth; it filled me and smothered me; I was already suffocating" (243). This "slobber" enters him and withdraws again on several occasions. Ultimately it is seen as

> an extremely slow panting, as if someone were there, breathing, stopping himself from breathing, hidden right next to me. I wanted to open my eyes and get away, but then, horrified, I realized that my eyes

were already open and were already looking at and touching and seeing what no gaze should ever have fallen upon, could ever have endured. I had to scream, I howled, I tore at myself with the feeling of howling in another world. (243)

Another world that adheres, *sticks* to one's gaze, to one's eyes, skin, suffocating one infinitely, contracts one, forces one to cry, spasm, scream. Such is the striking autobiographical perception of the novel.

This is the role of the *Most High*'s narrator:

And I too had a role. My role was to intervene in the story as a perpetually absent but always implied listener. I said nothing, but everything had to be said before me. Throughout the solemn chanting, as the memories of the days of anguish were repeated, as if present-day suffering were at stake, everyone was no doubt listening, but someone most high listened as well, someone who, through his attentiveness, gave these appalling ruminations a hopeful and beautiful character. (190–191)

This deportation into the externality of death, of women, of friendship, grasps the time of distress in which the novel masks its biographical side, and reveals how historical it is. As the narrator had said, all the events return, "everything is appearing, everything is being revealed clearly and truthfully" (88), this "extraordinary clarity, terrible clarity, without a single shadow," which is a call for responsibility and makes him believe he is suffocating ("it was as if all of history in every sense had passed through me," 107; "all the events of history are there around us, just like the dead," 88). This impossible return is given unto reading, unto suffocation (for how would one not be suffocated by the end of history, when one thinks of how one has contributed to it). It cannot be said in any other way: not in celebration, or in commemoration, or in recognition.

CHAPTER 32

The Passion of Silence
Denise Rollin (1940s)

Denise Lefroi, who on marriage took the name Rollin-Roth-Le Gentil, was born the same year as Maurice Blanchot. She met him at the end of 1941 through Georges Bataille, with whom she had been having a tumultuous affair for several years. She took part, in her strange, silent way, in the meetings on "inner experience" that saw Bataille's friends gather in his apartment. After an initial period spent in Vézelay, she and Bataille separated in fall 1943. She grew close to Michel Fardoulis-Lagrange, then to Blanchot.

Her relationship with Blanchot began around 1945 (at the earliest at the end of 1944, at the latest in spring 1946). It hardly had time to flourish: from the end of 1945, Blanchot most often remained in the south, and we have been told that Denise Rollin never went there.[1] She herself left Paris for the Alps in the 1950s for the health of her then-adolescent son Jean. We can wonder whether two beings with such solitary temperaments ever had a chance of living together some day. Writing was Blanchot's priority, and Jean occupied the entire attention of his mother, who was extremely possessive of him. Neither wished to live as a trio, but they may have discussed the possibility of marriage and children, despite everything. But probably this was even less likely than it was for Kafka (which also means that the discussions must have been even more lively). We can see what would concern Blanchot, notably in *The Space of Literature*, about the impossible link between passion and writing as it is suggested in Kafka's *Diaries* and correspondence.

They seem to have exchanged a considerable number of letters; both were often to be found writing, in any case. Denise Rollin's letters to Francine and Michel Fardoulis-Lagrange bear witness to their author's striking personality and to her passion for Maurice Blanchot. Their strong, hot-tempered style, their barely punctuated phrasing, their impulsive immediacy, all give a voice to the mixture of tenderness and violence which made up Denise Rollin's character, extremely tender in its attentiveness to the other, and extremely violent against everything that lay in the path of this responsibility.[2]

We can imagine their first meeting, how an invisible weight struck two such quiet creatures, who each reserved a similarly large and creative role in their lives for silence.[3] Like Fardoulis and like Bataille, perhaps even more than them, Blanchot was struck by the reserved nature of this melancholically and taciturnly beautiful woman. Like Fardoulis and like Bataille, and even more than them (such is the law of community), Denise Rollin appreciated everything that was unsaid when this man was speaking. We can imagine another, later meeting, more secret than the first, similar to certain scenes in *Death Sentence*, and thus perhaps also similar to the one Bataille had experienced a few years previously, which he describes as follows:

> Denise came into my room with the blind gentleness of destiny.
> One day, the woman whose existence touched me the most but whom I had no reason to meet was sitting in front of my table, forgetful of my presence as if we had been used to living with one another for a long time.
>
> A month ago she came into my room, and no other woman would have been so silent, so beautiful, so silently inviolable as to come in: at least not without me suffering like a shining mirror that wished to be dulled.

He had no choice but to love "this heavy purity of Denise who was more beautiful than I could have dreamed," "until I felt this malaise of the heart that gives one the chills of death."[4]

Bataille would eventually tire of this increasingly capricious sovereignty. Denise Rollin would end up despising his exhibitionist, talkative intellectualism. She detested conversations that moved away from the nakedness of experience. "I do not and do not wish to understand anything about literary discussions," she wrote in 1947, adding: "I find all 'ideas' unpleasant, only love counts." She would always place the falsity of literature in opposition to the authenticity of "written notes," which were "as beautiful as a storm." She read books as if they were letters. On this point, her contestation of language was even more radical than those of Bataille or Blanchot. She only valued the "written notes" of Proust, Sade, or Kierkegaard, as well as Dostoevsky, of course.

> It does not matter that Sade is known as an erotic writer, that Kierkegaard tried to find proof of God's existence, these are only words and definitions, only the sensation of truth is important and exists, and it is perfectly incomprehensible to me.

This uncompromising purity, which she maintained up to her death, was in Denise Rollin's eyes what Bataille would debase with betrayals of the body and of language. It is what Blanchot would represent, what he would align himself with.

> Passion can only be reached in the void; in this void; in the absence of all shapes, in this absence which is ultimately absolute presence, a gaze that is unique and blind to external things, this absence of language and shapes, where no images remain, where ultimately everything is overtaken, erased, the void as the presence of Being through which passion has found a way to reach itself.

These lines written by Denise Rollin recall Blanchot's article on Benjamin Constant for *L'Arche* of October 1946 (this was at the beginning of their relationship).⁵ It is rare to find in his critical work such lyrical pages on passion and on the paradox of a desire "which takes as its object its constitutive lack." Blanchot sets this way of experiencing desire, that of Constant, in opposition to that of Proust:

> Proust does not desire this absence as the motive of all communication, in the way that Constant does: he does not desire it at all, but it is absence that makes someone desirable to him, while making him suffer from not being able to attain it.⁶

We can imagine Blanchot to be closer to Constant here, in this radicality of the desire for absence. Let us at least imagine that a movement in him carries him toward this unbearable demand, which made absence, according to Denise Rollin, an "absolute presence," or according to Bataille, "a heavy purity." Blanchot writes:

> We communicate fully with someone only by possessing not what they are but what separates us from them, their absence rather than their presence and, even better, the infinite movement to surpass this absence and cause it to be reborn.[7]

This frightening *death sentence* which was projected onto every relation of desire fascinated them, both him and her, although perhaps less repetitively or obsessively than it did Bataille. "Everything that is not a question of life and death must be forgotten, I can only experience things that are absolute," Denise Rollin wrote in a letter. And this was a radical absolute: "my absolute is to be alone."

Thus we can understand the paradox of a relationship that could not find completion. "I have been saying no to Maurice Blanchot for 14 years now, and yet he is the being who was 'destined' for me," Denise Rollin wrote at the end of the 1950s. We must add that Blanchot just as much said no to her, and while there is no evidence that she was just as much destined for him, it is not unthinkable. In truth, this refusal was a singular way of affirming, creating, continuous creation. Blanchot would continue in this relationship during his Mediterranean sojourn and his creation of novels. The presence of Denise Rollin is palpable throughout *Death Sentence* and Blanchot would say that he wrote *When the Time Comes* for her. On her side, she too would live through letters and books, through books read as if they were letters, not under the illusions of hope or knowledge, but in the solitary passion of an inner gaze, of a way of overestimating "written notes," sometimes incorporating them and sometimes managing not to. "Sometimes reading is like living together looking at the Other's writing like looking at him, living with him having never left him, a fact beyond facts." This "community of lovers" was already impossible and unavowable.

Denise Rollin came to name the absence she loved in Maurice Blanchot *idiocy*. No character more resembled Blanchot, she said again and again in her letters, than Dostoevsky's Prince Myshkin.[8] Indeed, the moral and physical portrait painted of the prince brings to mind numerous remarkable similarities to Blanchot. Attentive to the demands of all, so much so that he uncovers their most secret desires and suffering, Myshkin imposes with gentle authority the grace of often silent lucidity, which loosens its tongue only out of generosity or when carried away. It has often been said of Blanchot that his reserve of personal knowledge, this innocence that could also be a mode of address, gave rise to a mode of friendship that was never totally private and never totally public. What's more, that Myshkin should have been initially conceived as a headstrong insurgent, a future Stavrogin, and that in the writing of the novel he should have become the opposite, is not without recalling part of Blanchot's development; thus the figure of the gift becomes ethically and esthetically necessary. Something like salvation comes about, and this grace was, as we have seen, the fruit of a long itinerary, as can only be confirmed by "the instant of my death." Indeed, Myshkin is precisely the one who brutally narrates the story of the man condemned to death who is pardoned at the final moment, which was also the story of Dostoevsky and of Blanchot. Ultimately, the single prince declares that he is unable to marry due to his illness: he spends several years in a sanatorium. But he likes women, asks the most beautiful ones in the novel to marry him, fails in each case and yet tries to love both of them, together, somehow already dreaming of a community of lovers. This anti-Catholic *ecce homo* presents its hero as a unique or first man, but fails in its attempts at salvation: such is the nobility of its "idiocy," in a world clearly living through a "time of distress." Such is the sovereign simplicity of generosity.

Denise Rollin wrote that "for me no 'grandeur' exists unless it is accompanied by great 'humility.'" "M.B. is the 'humblest' being I know, he strongly resembles the prince in Dostoevsky's *Idiot* (which is to say that he resembles what has been translated as the 'idiot') he is utterly unaware of what he is." She eroticized this lack of awareness, this absence to himself, which she perceived in his very presence, in his correspondence, and ultimately in the universe of his novels. This absence, this capacity for effacement or for being no one was what she found so fulfilling. She idealized this ability to "carry the suffering of the world within him," to be "the only being who helps you without asking for reciprocation, perhaps because he really has managed to become no one." The events of the end of the war had taken him to such a point, and brought him closer *avant la lettre* to Robert Antelme's infinite attentiveness to the other; Denise Rollin attributed this experience to that of a God, a God who has experienced death.[9] She idealized him because she wanted to move closer to him, and she sometimes stated as much with unthinking strength and beauty: "I can be as if I were no one"; "I can feel the life of another as if my own life were dead"; "putting oneself in the other's place does not mean seeing the other as an object, but *being* the other." "If I knew how to write I would say things with 'I' because in truth I think without 'I.' There is no 'I' because there is 'you.'" She idealized him because she would have liked to write him, to write without being aware of doing it, avowing that she did not know she was doing it, she continued to write *to him* as the *invisible partner* of her relationship. She idealized him, and she told him, she told them, she told everyone, moving from one ideal to another, that he was only a child, that his way of being absent was that of a child; this allowed her once more to displace this absence and to make it present. "For me a being's superiority is determined by what he retains of his childhood. . . . All Dostoevsky's characters are children, *their childhood is intact in them.*"

For Denise Rollin, Blanchot's absence was that of Prince Myshkin, that of strangeness and silence, from which he emerged in moments of grace that, without ever giving warning, illuminated and possessed one.[10]

> Come forward sun, toward me, who am most solitary of all. You have come. We have been friends since the beginning: we share sorrow, fright, and reason-unreason; we even share the sun. We do not speak to one another because we are too knowledgeable: we remain silent, we smile to one another, and thus knowledge is passed between us . . . The boundless, endless Yes is shared between us.

Blanchot translated these lines and sent them to Denise Rollin.[11]

CHAPTER 33

The Mediterranean Sojourn
The Writing of the Night (1947)

Having moved to Èze at the end of 1946, Blanchot remained there almost all the following year.

He would say that he needed time to get over the past, the war—death. But even as he looked the latter in the face that year, writing or finishing *Death Sentence*, his Mediterranean sojourn would nonetheless be one of *ease*: one of consolation, repair, the calming of nerves, happy tears, sun, blue sky. Later he would speak of this place in pacific, miraculous terms, offering the utopian site to Salman Rushdie and to Ayatollah Khomeini's successor, stating that it was the only place the *fatwa* could be overturned and a dialogue constructed.[1] And yet not everything was idyllic. In 1947, he would say that his situation reminded him of being confined in Neuilly and that the unexpected poor weather was bothering and upsetting him. Such weather would regularly interrupt a happy, relaxed period. This alternation would also give a rhythm to writing, between anguished fixity (interiors, night) and external freedom (the outside, sunlight). The walkway along the Mediterranean would be the site of isolation and respiration. The benefits of silence would define another way of being in the world, in the community. Blanchot would write humorously in a letter to Prévost:

Here, the political struggle is very important. It is between the people from down below, Èze-mer, who are separatists and would like their own *mairie*, and the rest of us, men of *hauteur*, who look down upon them with disdain from our 500 metres in height and 2,000 years of existence.[2]

In the village of Èze, Blanchot resided (*demeure*) in the Rue du Bour-Nou, an alleyway at the top of the promontory looking over the Mediterranean. He would later describe the interior of his room:

When I was living in Èze, in the little room (made bigger by two views, one opening onto Corsica, the other out past Cap Ferrat) where I most often stayed, there was (there still is), hanging on the wall, the likeness of the girl they called "The Unknown Girl from the Seine," an adolescent with her eyes closed, but alive with such a fine, blissful (veiled) smile, that one might have thought she had drowned in an instant of extreme happiness.[3]

Whether the "little room" in Èze or the "high-up room" in Quain, the writing room was always a site of elevation. Here it looked over the path that saw Nietzsche write part of *Zarathustra*. It was filled with imaginary presence, the feminine presence of the *récits*, the young woman and death.

Èze then stood for night, the writing of the night. "A writing in which the intensity of night is also the violence of silence."[4] Pierre Fedida speaks of it as follows:

I am evoking the night-time writing, I am evoking not simply a nocturnal rhythm of writing, but this intense entreaty to night, including its anguish and its discouragement, its fatigue; I am evoking this because I believe that the most controlled fragility comes at this moment. This writing which takes place at night is certainly . . . it comes instead of sleep, instead of dreams. We cannot say that it replaces dreams, it does not replace dreams, but it relates to the day in a similar way, and in that relation one touches the dead, to use Heraclitus's fine expression, as if the intensities that one might take for the intensities of life are certainly that, but are probably what they are because death is there.

Writing moves into heavy, weighty, intense night, that of 3:00 or 4:00 a.m., with its absence of forms, or their fantastical presence. The visions from Henry James, the windows and the staircases will feature in *The One Who Was Standing Apart from Me*. An imaginary and monstrous child, who is necessarily someone else's child, wanders around the house, charging it with its presence. The attentiveness to the child, as marked as ever, becomes something of a phantasm here. Blanchot wrote as much to Bataille: "I sometimes evoke the figure of Julie in a shadow in the corridor."

The move to the *récit*, in the heavy presence of the images of death, therefore took place in Èze, during the Èze night (still sometimes followed by that of Neuilly). His first *récits* were published this year: "The Last Word" heading up the May issue of the journal *Fontaine*, edited by Max-Pol Fouchet, and "The Idyll" in the ephemeral *Licorne*, also in the spring. Above all, it was the year when two new *récits* were completed. *Death Sentence* and the new version of *Thomas the Obscure* were written at precisely the same time, have similar aesthetics and perform a double, decisive, irreparable turn of the screw on Blanchot's writing. If we are to believe the *récit* itself, Blanchot began or rather began again *Death Sentence* on October 8 (not an unlikely date). He would therefore have been *rewriting* both *Death Sentence* and *Thomas the Obscure* at the same time—we know from a letter to Bataille that he finished fine-tuning the latter in Neuilly in early January 1948 (a few months after the publication of *Existence and Existents*, in which Levinas cites the book's first edition). However, the second version of *Thomas* would only appear two years later.

Rewriting is the path that the *writing* of the two new *récits* has to take. It is something more than simple churning-over (*ressassement*), instead imposing its necessity as a return, a strengthening, and a pure creation that expose the narrative event to a new status, to a new way of saying truth and of creating fiction. Blanchot wrote in the cover blurb for *Death Sentence* (which was presented there as a *récit*) that novels "are born at the moment when words have begun to withdraw from reality," and language was now pushed further, having no reason to fear. "I do not fear that I am revealing any secrets" he adds, accentuating the autobiographical impact of the *récit*, for the fear of exposure gives way to the anguish created by the force inherent in relating the event. In this way, all images of reality are masked, even as they are exposed. The *récit* conveys autobiography in the form of a photographic negative, like Blanchot's holy shroud on which the author's face can be glimpsed. This unstable superimposition between autobiography and fiction, the undecipherable exposure of this border, makes up the event, the experience of the reader.[5]

He needed time and a place to gather his thoughts and once again to feel, but now so differently, invulnerable. This was now the period of a confrontation with the Law. Blanchot kept silent because it said to him: "now you are a special case; no one can do anything to you. You can talk, nothing commits you."[6] He refused to do so, and spoke without implicating anything except the way language is attributed to a subject, in doing so taking the *decision for literature*. In less than a year, there was a new version of *Thomas the Obscure*, *The Most High* completed the cycle of novels, and a condensed version of it began that of the *récits*. This at least was how Blanchot presented things, in the *prière d'insérer* of the first edition of *Death Sentence*:

> Doubtless there is nothing in common between these two works, *The Most High* and *Death Sentence*, which are being published at the same time. But, as the person who wrote them, I believe that one is as it were present behind the other, not in the manner of two interconnected texts, but like two irreconcilable and yet always concordant versions of one reality, which is equally lacking from both.

Composed of a short, brief, naked *récit* followed by a second part which shatters it and scatters the pieces, the structure of this death sentence poses the question of who language is attributed to, and that of a biographical reserve; like *The Madness of the Day*, which appeared in a journal, it already sketches out the last of all *récits*, in light of which all others would be unwritten.

CHAPTER 34

Something Inflexible
The Madness of the Day, a New Status for Speech (1947–1949)

This *récit* was not yet called *The Madness of the Day*, but simply *Un récit* or, with a question mark, *Un récit?* It appeared in the journal *Empédocle* in May 1949 under this title, with or without question mark (with it on the cover and the running heads, without it in the table of contents and at the start of the narrative).

It takes place in the first person and is presented, whether playfully or awkwardly, as a mixture of fictitious self-portrait and autobiographical fragmentation, sometimes humorous and sometimes obscure, as if such obliqueness were necessary when talking about oneself. The importance, seriousness, and decisive character of the events related give it its weight. It interrupts itself in order to directly address the reader (or strictly speaking, the person being narrated to), insisting that the events are real, however unlikely they might appear: "All that was real, take note."[1] There are clear references to the war; the allusions to Blanchot's private life are plausible (some of them have since been confirmed). Any reader can recognize echoes of the previous *récits*. However, nothing guarantees that making such connections will lead anywhere. The first sentence is an early warning: "I am not learned; I am not ignorant" (5), and the narrative voice retains the right to deny anything it might put forward. It shatters any possible spatial continuity, any continuity of the sign. The "I" present at the beginning is not the "I" that, in a long dreamlike, mystical or fabulous passage, dialogues with the Law, and that seems to have divine powers ("To see you was worth one's life. To love you meant death," 16). The denouement does not lead to any final event, but to narrative speech itself, which is suddenly brought back to its semblance of a beginning, because the first sentences ("I am not learned; I am not ignorant," etc.) are repeated in a dialogue with two doctors. This means that the *récit* seems not to begin or finish anywhere, except in distance, the gaze toward the end, as if the latter were the only thing that makes up the *récit* presented to the reader, an impossibility of *récits*, a *récit* which immediately cancels itself out, stops (*s'arrête*), signs its own death sentence, its definitive effacement: "A story [*récit*]? No. No stories, never again" (18). Blanchot circumvents all academic, medical, psychiatric, and psychoanalytical demands and expectations regarding the stories we tell. "To wring out the story like an unavowable secret" is what biographical speech risks doing, i.e. ignoring the (neutral) "narrative voice" and replacing it with a "narrating [*narratrice*] voice" (which can be thematized, attributed, identified).[2] The first autobiographical revelation is that the *récit* is *disfigured* even as it is constructed, that it is *unwritten* at the same time as it is written. Here Blanchot brings to an end the period of his previous novels (even *Death Sentence* is an inverse version of a drama or spectacle). *The Madness of the Day* reaches a level of extreme visibility that condemns the *récit*.[3] Self-inscription will henceforth only be possible through self-effacement.

We can recognize this effacement not as an underhand desire to deprive one of what is private, to secrete what is secret, but instead as the least shameful point toward which the exposure of intimacy can lead, following the discovery of the Nazi concentration and extermination camps. Adhering to silence, to gentleness, to restrained tones are all gestures that align Blanchot with Robert Antelme. They represent an attempt to take upon himself (which is to say, upon the *récit*) the impossibility of still simply telling stories, an impossibility that constitutes the aesthetic fate imposed by Auschwitz. This was the only format in which Blanchot bore witness at this stage; he probably considered it the only one of any dignity. "The unknown in other people" (9) was growing "tired of being the stone that beats men alone to death." In *The Madness of the Day*, Blanchot evokes a large part of his own political, psychological, medical, and amorous past. And he does so in an *oblique*, intensely *literary* way, as if literature had the task of dealing with what no public avowal, even that of the novel, can either compensate for or produce. Literature *levels out* the differing orders of events within the singularity of an itinerary and a destiny, a singularity both vindicated and taken on as one's own. This neutrality asks questions of us: It asks questions about the impurity of our avid expectation of an avowal, about our propensity to condemn impatiently and indiscriminately, about our blind faith in our ability to safely categorize the intolerable. It asks questions about our expectations of literature itself, of autobiography, justice, and the secret. Literature is the site where what is public becomes private without being made unavailable, where what is private becomes public without being revealed. It is the site where the relation between "the immensity of others" and the "solid" self decide on the health of the body.[4] It is the site where public and private cancel each other out in a mutual bearing (where what is tolerable and what is unthinkable are distinguished), and where, finally, the future of ideas, of engagements, of writings, of passions is decided. Blanchot finds no other site to occupy than this. Literature is the site of insubordination to the Law, beyond all wounds, which he evokes in the final pages of *The Madness of the Day*.[5] Literature smashes all ideals, spins their reasoning around, leaving it close by and always available if necessary, but retains something inflexible, provides another way of looking, often a feminine one, that of death. It magnifies things and loosens one's grip, and is as scrupulous as the demand to which the death sentence has condemned language.

Literature allows no moment of rest: critical glory has its dignity to maintain, has to appropriate these restless torments, all the more so given that repose, the room's opening onto Corsica and the headland, is close by, coiled up, only a gaze away. It is as unshifting as the horizon, it tears space apart and allows only disorienting phenomena to appear in its field of activity. Trying to be as inflexible as death, it knows how to recall its ability to tear bodies apart, and accepts nothing from the author if his gaze at the time is not blind ("a wound"), his head "a hole" (a pineal hole?), his body "a disemboweled bull" (17). This was the only sense in which one can talk of the pacification of literature.

CHAPTER 35

The Turn of the Screw
The Second Version of *Thomas the Obscure* (1947–1948)

Published in early spring 1950, the "new version" of *Thomas the Obscure* opens the way to the *récits* that would follow. It shows that a tightening of narrative is under way, as a note to the reader makes clear:

> The present version adds nothing to the pages entitled *Thomas the Obscure* begun in 1932, delivered to the publisher in May of 1940 and published in 1941, but as it subtracts a good deal from them, it may be said to be a different, and even an entirely new version, but identical at the same time, if one is right in making no distinction between the figure and that which is, or believes itself to be, its center, whenever the complete figure itself expresses no more than the search for an imaginary center.[1]

Perhaps the first, heavy, novel version was already on the path toward this central episode, even if it is a shifted, displaced center, just as the pages on the gaze of Orpheus would form the decentered center of *The Space of Literature*. Anne's death here becomes the "imaginary center" of the *récit*, which itself is the "imaginary center" of the novel. Blanchot's concern, paradoxically, is to insist that the two works are as one, underlining only the perspectival difference between them, even as he feels it necessary to point out that the difference in the writing is such that the second version now replaces the first, annulling it and establishing it as a secret, thereby creating a death scene. (Indeed, the latter stopped being reprinted, comparison between the two versions therefore becoming the reserve of the original readers, curious admirers, and university researchers.) The whole withdraws behind its center, becoming that center.[2]

Anne's death now took up twenty pages across two chapters of the 130 in the book (instead of twenty pages in a single chapter of 230 pages in the first version). There was considerable reduction of the book overall (a hundred pages fewer, but that does not tell the whole story: The format of the first book was much larger and its type smaller). Among the elements removed are Irène and the keeper of the village hotel; the precise references to a vividly colored universe, to profuse nature, and to a metropolis. There are fewer scenes of social life. Anne is now Thomas's only companion, is closer to him, takes over some of Irène's lines and never now leaves the hotel; she becomes much more untimely as a character. The chapter on Thomas's mourning for Anne takes up more room proportionally. The beginning (the sea, the wood, the hotel, the room) and the ending (the march through the countryside) are retained. The *récit* is tightened around Thomas's journey of initiation. The passage on his childhood is removed. As in *Death Sentence*, the *récit* seizes (somewhat brutally) our attention and directs it to the nakedness of his solitude, his anguish, mourning and death. Around Anne's bedside, as around J.'s bedside, ignorant people busy themselves, a hurried mother overladen with pathos grows tired, all of them infinitely less close to the dying woman than the narrator or Thomas are, who however do not know them or refuse to do so, while deeply experiencing in the final moments intense death rattles and death appearing via the bodies of the dead. This wholly precarious narration relates an extreme confrontation with inner experience. For instance, Blanchot formulates this recurring preoccupation: "What, then, calls me into question most radically? Not my relation to myself as finite or as the consciousness of being-to-death or being-for-death, but my presence-for-another who makes himself absent by dying." He imagines that the dying person's caregiver might reply:

> You not only distance yourself, you are also still present, for here you grant me that dying as the granting that surpasses all suffering, and here I tremble softly in what rips things apart, losing speech as you do,

dying with you without you, letting myself die in your place, receiving that gift beyond you and me.[3]

But the anguish derives as much from the impossibility of dying as it does from the imminence of death.

Anne's final throes are oblique, unspectacular, lacking in events or images, forgetful of the ecstatic and metamorphic landscape that had previously gripped her visions. The *récit* is therefore only able to provide a commentary on the impossible journey toward what it is to be present at death. It follows the movement whereby Anne withdraws from the world without conveying how she comes to see things. Her dreams are pure dreams of dreams, without content, without a home, "no palace, no constructions of any sort; rather a vast sea, though the waters were invisible and the shore had disappeared." Her consciousness has lost its humanity, and it only remains for it "to *be*, to marvelously *be*." Anne is given over to a death without false image or pretence, including that of saintliness. While a few monsters still inhabit this pure horizon, "there is no way to express what they are, because, for us, in the midst of the day something can appear which is not the day," something like a primordial dawn? The *récit* denies all novelistic development, all possibility of action and even of imagery, such is now its law. It offers "a world stripped of artifice and perfidy."[4]

As he who is always a neighbor, Thomas belongs at once to "two shores" consisting of a "real body" and a "negation of the body," his gaze stemming from one lucid eye and one blind one, and representing both "living Thomas" and "nothingness Thomas," "obscure Thomas," he alone is able to move close to Anne, and beyond her, to the death within her, "the eternal man taking the place of the moribund," he who "dies alone in place of all."[5] The author's twin, he brings to completion what Blanchot had only ever been able to sense when confronted with the deaths of those close to him, of loved ones. His Christic name is now effaced behind other figures, atheist ones, of generosity. They would be called *the last man*, or *the friend*.

CHAPTER 36

The Authority of Friendship
The Completion of *Death Sentence* (1947–1948)

Perhaps friendship was already what authorized *Death Sentence*.

The strange similarity has often been noted between the death of J., in the first part of *Death Sentence*, and the death of Laure as witnesses have passed it on to us, not least among them the pages removed from Bataille's *Guilty*. "A death tore him apart in 1938," wrote Bataille for an autobiographical note: Blanchot, at the time, did not know him.[1] But while the first sentence of *Death Sentence*: "These events happened to me in 1938" is misleading regarding the year in which Blanchot himself began his mourning, perhaps it also served to bring him closer to a different truth, that of similar events experienced by Bataille.

If it is true that the first part of *Death Sentence* is among other things the *récit* of Laure's death, then the alteration and the fictionalization of such an extreme event give considerable value to friendship; such staunch tenacity can be seen to work in the name of a twin suffering, of a concern for a shared discretion, and of an agreement over aesthetic convictions. When friendship becomes clear with the strength, the suddenness, and the good fortune that marked the meeting of Bataille and Blanchot, when it shows itself to be a fascinated and brutal coincidence, friendship receives the grace of memory and the *hauteur* of gratitude by erasing any difference between two names, by delegating and authorizing fictional *récits*, written or cited *in the name of the other*. One friend takes on the other's mourning, and it is by friendship alone that this *pass*, this *veronica*, this wiping of the Other's Holy Face, takes place; even if—in Blanchot's version—its absence remains present on the cloth. Via this superimposition, introducing "only the shadow of a bull's horn" in the *récit*, friendship offers to literature the sovereign authority of effacement, of the neuter, of the universal. Bataille does not sign this *récit* with a pseudonym, as he often does with his own, but with a heteronym, the name of a friend, "Blanchot," the "Blanchot" of *Death Sentence*, who is cited in the foreword to *Blue of Noon* as one of the very rare authors who *forced* him to write, to write an "intolerable, impossible ordeal."[2] Without Bataille, Blanchot would perhaps have been unable to undergo such a *forcing* of the *récit*; we should remember that he would cease writing *récits* after the death of his friend.[3]

In an article on Kafka written less than a year after *Death Sentence* was published, Blanchot states:

> he writes narratives about beings whose story belongs only to them, but at the same time about Kafka and his own story which belongs only to him. It is as if the further he moved away from himself, the more present he became. The fictional narrative puts a distance, a gap (itself fictive), within him who writes, without which he could not express himself.[4]

Blanchot embodies then erases in his friend this distance, this absence, this fictitious interval.[5] With this superb, reserved point of coincidence, he becomes the *invisible partner* of Georges Bataille.

With this text, which proves troubling for readers, transgressing the normal limits of individual lives and works, it is ultimately of little importance to discover what precise level of condensation of or transference between two men's thinking we are dealing with. For this at least is certain, and supports our hypothesis: writing *Death Sentence* during the war or after it, completing it in 1947, and publishing it in June 1948, Blanchot—unlike in 1940 when he perhaps wrote an initial version of it—was certainly aware of the narrative of Laure's death. He was certainly aware of the concern, the new developments, the historical climate (the aftermath of Munich), he was certainly aware of the key stages, the remorse of the lover who had stayed away too long from the dying woman and blamed himself for running away, the couple's incompatibility with the family group, the vision of the rose. And knowing all of the above perhaps led him to attempt the impossible: "*reconstructing death*," as Claude Rabant writes.[6]

It is a triple wager. To reconstruct death on the authority of friendship is to confront at once History, love, and literature. These are the stakes that give life to *Death Sentence*. This tale of friendship past and to come stands in the shadow of Bataille, Laure's lover; in that of Levinas, the Jew who had suffered during the war; in that of Antelme, who had survived the concentration camp. Reconstructing the death disfigured by the aftermath of Munich and the "final solution" is the task of the *récit*'s first part, which attempts to restore its singularity and extremity without making it exemplary. A *récit* of friendship, *Death Sentence* would be even more so in Bataille's footsteps, because it is also a passing on of Denise Rollin, who is sometimes said to have met Laure, and who is often said to have been fascinated by her; such a passing on also transmits "the suffocating, impossible ordeal" of mourning. The book's second part is triggered by reconstructing the death that was always betrayed by the resurgence of love, by the ensuing series of love stories. These stories are as if justified by N.'s fidelity to J. (N. is a translator), by Denise's assent to Laure, by Prince Myshkin's approval of all women as of their absence, his "excessive, endless Yes," his always sovereign words of welcome: "'Come,' and eternally, she is there." Reconstructing the death would thus also be to attempt to make it available once again to poetry, to narrative: *Death Sentence* would be written with other debts to death, too, with debts to other moments and forms of death—for instance, Ligeia's eyes in Rowena's face, Nastaysia's eyes in Rogozhin's face—J.'s eyes and the mask of death in N.'s face.[7]

We can understand how Blanchot saw it as necessary to construct this *récit*, to superimpose dates, experiences, and history. We can also understand that it was impossible for him to write it, at least in its final form, before the years when he knew Denise Rollin and Georges Bataille.

Having been diverted, and as if trapped, the autobiographical can only be revived by imagining that the nonbiographical was plain for all to see. A guide to the body of the fiction, it is the shadow of that fiction, or what lies in that shadow. Because the second death is only ever a citation of the first, because every event is double, repeated, only becoming pure when altered, the autobiographical regains its ability to create pressure, to cause terror. It is not to be found in the small facts of life, but instead allows one to grasp bodily powers, capacities for listening, sensitive zones of communication. Thus it tells us much more about what people like to call the writer's body than any other self-portrait or any other *récit* ("never again"[8]). We must simply accept the rhythms imposed by disordered time, which allow the distancing necessary for the requisite attentiveness and acclimatization to night, and allow the *there is* to become available in the darkest space ("I saw it distinctly, that dead and empty flame of her eyes"). "A great deal of patience is required if thought, driven down into the depths of the horrible, is to rise little by little and recognize us and look at us." A great deal of patience is required if the event is to be welcomed without fear, the new intensity of perception, the enormous movement of the infinite, the choreographies of desire, of the blood, of breathing. Regarding the silence of the gaze, "he who hears it becomes other."[9] The few singular, violent, mad events that traverse the narrative only tolerate being read in this single, withdrawn mode, and readers will be able to appreciate this according to how able they are to give themselves over to this listening, which is infinite, eroticizable and empty, insane and delicious, warlike and monstrous. The violence of certain scenes, of gestures and cries which seem unlikely to deliver up their meaning except through discretion, a discretion that will be commented on infinitely, will henceforth punctuate Blanchot's *récits*, beginning with *When the Time Comes*.

CHAPTER 37

Quarrels in the Literary World
Publication and Reception (1948–1949)

The turn of the screw given to narrative writing seems to have sat uneasily with the regular production of articles. These years of intense literary activity (1948, 1949) saw Blanchot, who was so disenchanted with critical writing as to feel it to be worthless, abandon commentary little by little.

He was most often in Èze, only returning to Neuilly for a few months at a time, as in summer 1948 or spring 1949. In May 1949, he again left Paris at the same time as Bataille, who had got a job as librarian at the Carpentras library. In July, however, he was back. He gave up his apartment in Neuilly, which for some time he had felt to be unnecessary, and agreed with his brother René and his sister-in-law Anna that he was to stay with them when in Paris, at 18 Rue Violet, close to La Motte-Picquet metro station. In September, he was in Èze once again.

His relationship with Gallimard was tense. Having been submitted in May 1947, and with printing finished on May 12, 1948, *The Most High* would not appear before the summer, at the same time as *Death Sentence*. Blanchot wrote the two *prières d'insérer* in June. He was furious at the delay and considered moving to the Minuit publishing house, where Bataille had a new series named "The Use of Riches." His idea was to publish his forthcoming *récits* in this series, beginning symbolically with the second version of *Thomas the Obscure*. But Gallimard retained all of its rights over Blanchot's books and was extremely condescending when it did allow Minuit to publish *Lautréamont and Sade* the following year. Bataille had already announced the work in April and May with a double article in *Critique* named "Happiness, Eroticism and Literature," which also commented on what Blanchot had already published on Sade. Gallimard invoked the June publication of *The Work of Fire* and asked Minuit to delay until September that of *Lautréamont and Sade* (which would sell only around eight hundred copies in its first year). Blanchot had to accept the situation as it was: Gallimard had the upper hand over Minuit, the latter having decided on a strategy of calmness and tolerance.[1]

In any case, the promises of summer 1948 (when Blanchot was in Neuilly) would not be kept. Gaston Gallimard published *The Most High* at the beginning of August, and promised Blanchot that *The Work of Fire* and *Thomas the Obscure* would appear before the end of the year. In actual fact, these books would have to wait longer than that: the first appeared in June 1949 and the second . . . in spring 1950.

Three works of fiction and two critical books in less than two years: At the turn of the decade, such an intense rhythm of publication, which like his journal pieces included both cohesive and diverse elements, definitively placed Blanchot center stage. The main journals commented on his works. The reign of mediocrity also began, with many stupid judgments about a body of work that was said to be "haughtily hermetic" or so much "intelligent trickery."[2] The critics thought they were being sarcastic, witty, disdainful.[3] While Blanchot's talents were recognized for the most part, they were immediately said to have been wasted. This view applied most of all to the works of fiction. But in fact opinions were divided to the extreme, and some glowing endorsements shone through. For instance, Luc Decaunes in the *Cahiers du Sud* situated *Death Sentence* "at an equal distance from Edgar Poe and André Breton."[4] Above all, the first major readings emerged: in *Critique* by Bataille, of course, but also in *Combat* by Nadeau, in *Les Temps Modernes* by Klossowski. By February 1949 the pattern of the future reception of Blanchot's narratives was established: Some readers resisted and would continue to resist their paradoxical and demanding readability, whereas others did not resist, and would continue not to resist, the strong attraction they felt for work which left them naked, dispossessed, which comprehended them without ever having the last word.

The *récit* is richer, but it is also more obscure. Through it we come into contact with mystery independently of our comprehension, because we belong to this mystery, and what in us belongs to it thus remains as ungraspable to our reason as the incommunicability of lived and related fact does. Maurice Blanchot's art thus consists in putting a part of ourselves into relation with what he says. As soon as we read what he says to us, we do not understand it, we understand all the less because we are already included in his sentence. And this is not because we do not understand that we are being led to push further, but because we are constantly in search of this part of ourselves alienated by the *récit* that we want to recuperate at any price. As readers we also try to grasp what the *transcribed* experience of facts—to which we adhere—abolishes; we try to grasp a *real presence* even beyond this abolition.[5]

PART IV

1949–1959

Some beings have a meaning that eludes us. Who are they?
Their secret comes from the deepest secret of life itself.
They approach it. Life kills them. But the future they have thus
awakened with a murmur, in foretelling them, creates them.
O labyrinth of sheer love!

RENÉ CHAR, *The Word as Archipelago*

CHAPTER 38

Invisible Partner
Èze, Withdrawal (1949–1957)

Maurice Blanchot's life is not only a story of withdrawal. However, two periods do correspond to the image of a writer who was solitary, withdrawn from the world, devoted to literature. The first of these periods began in fall 1949, when Blanchot returned to Èze after having given up his apartment in Neuilly. It lasted eight years.

To withdraw was not to be a recluse, and Blanchot continued to be a public man. He published regularly: books for Gallimard (at a steady rhythm of one every two years)[1] and, beginning in 1953, an article per month in the *Nouvelle Nouvelle Revue Française*. In this decade, during which he gained considerable notoriety, the absence of any face, voice, or body on the social or media scene created an image of mystery.

Blanchot did not remain permanently in Èze. His life there was punctuated by several periods in Paris at his brother René's apartment on the Rue Violet, or in Chalon with his sister and mother, or in Quain, often alone.[2] When his health allowed, he liked to go to Germany to start his *récits* there. But being away from the literary circles of Paris also meant that he was far from his friends, removed and often exhausted, as is shown by his 1953 dedication of *The One Who Was Standing Apart from Me* to Georges Bataille: "the only one who is close in extreme distance."

Bataille was no longer in Carpentras: in June 1951, he got a job at the library of Orléans. He and Blanchot sometimes went a year without seeing one another. From Èze, one June, Blanchot wrote to him that:

> Yes, all winter I have felt sadness and anxiety at the silence that seemed to be between us. I was responsible for it, but beyond my responsibility was perhaps that of the silence between me and myself, as well as a difficult period of waiting, accepting a time without future. Even now I cannot begin any projects. To live from one day to the next is all that I am permitted to do, and even that is a struggle.³

Blanchot was indeed most often ill and exhausted. Fatigue, weakness, physical strain would become the major themes of his *récits*, sometimes even their origin. Illness undermined his everyday vitality, his attentiveness to friendship, and even his ability to write. Blanchot regretted not being able to write as much as he wanted to. He could not manage any articles beyond the monthly column for Gallimard, for which he was paid. "I would like to be able to give something to *Critique* too. Unfortunately, my activity is severely limited," he wrote to Bataille around 1953 or 1954. Death entered every part of his existence, his concerns, his readings. He read a book by Paul-Louis Landsberf, *Essai sur l'expérience de la mort*, and another by Camille Schuwer on *La signification métaphysique du suicide*.

This despair passed through—and passed away because of—his correspondence. He managed to disappear into his relation to friendship, which provided a measure of this despair. The community of friendship went further even than a shared relationship with illness (in this, Blanchot was close to Bataille, whose health declined irreversibly from 1955 on). Time became the exhausting framework of a mortality remedied by letters, by the painless and sometimes even joyful presence of a faraway face. Blanchot's letters were countless. They exhausted their already exhausted author, but gave a meaning to this exhaustion, measured it, defied and subjugated it. Most often, his letters were sent to Emmanuel Levinas, Georges Bataille, Denise Rollin, Jean Paulhan, René Char, and Roger Laporte. He asked Pierre Prévost for news of his friends from Jeune France, even if they had not followed his political journey: Lignac, Ollivier, Petitot.

In 1955, René Char wrote the first of his poems for him, ending with these lines:

> Some beings have a meaning that eludes us. Who are they? Their secret comes from the deepest secret of life itself. They approach it.

Life kills them. But the future they have thus awakened with a murmur, in foretelling them, creates them. O labyrinth of sheer love![4]

The deep friendship that linked Char to Blanchot is expressed in poetry here in a way that resembles the future thinking on friendship, effacing all arbitrary boundaries between the public and the private, between the political and the personal. It also evokes conceptions of friendship based on presence (attentiveness, listening, generosity) or based on correspondence (density, murmur, forgiveness). Through the poem, friendship once again is revealed as a gift, the metamorphosis of disenchanted despair into an even deeper version of itself, a despair that offers no salvation but makes one complicit and frees up the force and energy of the work. "Consenting to a time without future" becomes a creative future, a childhood, "innocence and forgetfulness, a new beginning, play, a self-propelling wheel, a first motion, a sacred Yes."[5] The friend is the witness, the guide, and the authority providing this power. He acts as the source of *expiation*. The friend is the future, an awareness of the murmur. He is named "the moral partner" since such a friendship possesses and excuses the languages of knowledge and desire; it is created by the fact that two voices are equal to one another, the fact that they wait for one another and challenge one another to remain at the same high level: namely, that of death, of what death enjoins us to think, to defy, to *refuse*. "Dying," writing the interminable and incessant process of "dying," is therefore the essence of friendship. The poem recalls the poet's partner to the "blank surface" of his name, to the power of the struggle with death, to the inexorability of a bodily struggle. Char paints Blanchot as a "well-toned boxer, imposing and powerful at the center of his legs" with their aggressive and defensive geometry."[6] Death's opponent "challenges it, advances toward its heart." This unrepentant opponent, who is the only one who knows which words could harm death ("words so perfectly offensive, or appropriate, or enigmatic"), only fights, only establishes an advantage in order to withdraw. This withdrawal, more than any fight, is what awakens the future. In this way Char allows us to understand the withdrawal of "the incomprehensible combatant." He makes visible the partner who is thunderstruck, brought down to earth: He gives the invisible its visibility.

CHAPTER 39

The Essential Solitude
Writing the *Récits* (1949–1953)

All the evidence suggests that Blanchot's two new *récits* were conceived between 1949 and 1951, for *When the Time Comes* (which appeared in December 1951), and around 1952, for *The One Who Was Standing Apart from Me* (published in spring 1953). Both were announced by the prepublication of an excerpt in *Botteghe Oscure*, and both come from Blanchot's most secret and certainly most painful period of withdrawal, during which he published very rarely: a dozen critical articles in four years. The two *récits* are all the more unusual insofar as they complete a period of intense literary activity: after a novel and five *récits* written in seven years, the next *récit* would come four years later with *The Last Man* in 1957, and the one after that five years later—*Awaiting Oblivion* with which, in 1962, Blanchot brings his fictional work to a close.

Written in the solitude of Èze, and themselves solitary within his work, these two *récits* emphasize the author's image as faraway and exhausted. They depict him in withdrawal and absence, in an apartment that he might have inhabited, in a house in which he wrote, before the beings he might have loved, before the apparitions that occupied his dwelling (*demeure*). The *prière d'insérer* of *The One Who Was Standing Apart from Me* publicly signaled this solidarity in solitude, asking that the new books share it with the first of them, *Death Sentence*, which like them mentions its own genre, its nature as *récit*, on the title page. The *prière d'insérer* reads: "*The One Who Was Standing Apart from Me* is the third panel in the triptych following *Death Sentence* and *When the Time Comes*. They are three distinct *récits*, but they nonetheless all belong to the same experience." This shared experience gave the new narrative voice the stubborn autobiographical status already tested in *Death Sentence* and *The Madness of the Day*. The autobiography in question is the adventure of the *writer*, and this is how Bataille presents them, in a formulation that is curiously similar to that of the *prière d'insérer*: these three *récits* (this "triptych," he wrote) relate to the same experience, that of the writer, and "in this way they form a myth of literary creation."[1]

"The essential solitude" was being carved out at this time. It is not unimportant that Blanchot marked his return to regular criticism, in January 1953, with an article that, written as early as June 1952, evokes his solitude in Èze, and which supplies something like the theoretical argument behind his *récits*. Blanchot placed it at the start of *The Space of Literature*. This article invites us to perceive how private space morphs into literary space. That this space is initially that of the room and more generally of the house in Èze, opening onto the sea, is something that we must recall before immediately forgetting again: This movement of distancing guides the author. Even if the site of writing cannot be reduced to this site of existence, at the same time not just any living space can become a space for writing, and this was a space that counted—Blanchot must have grown attached to it. Duras's remarks about her ten years of solitude in her house in Neauphle might stand in for Blanchot's ten years of residence in Èze: "It is only in this house that I am alone. In order to write. In order to write differently to how I had done up to then. But to write books as yet unknown by me and never yet determined by me and never determined by anyone."[2] We see that Blanchot wanted to evoke the house in Èze in *The One Who Was Standing Apart from Me*, just as Duras more pointedly but with the same impulse, would immortalize the one in Neauphle.

"The Essential Solitude" speaks volumes about the source of solitude, the notion of solitude, and the solitude of the work.[3] The essay is presented as a general reflection on the modern writer and their relation to their work, a reflection that, despite its references to Valéry, Kafka, Rilke, and Rimbaud, is largely inspired by Blanchot's experience. The "essential solitude" is first of all his own. But here, speaking of himself only serves to move toward effacing himself. While still founded on Hegelian or

Heideggerian positions, the critical discourse moves away from them to translate an aesthetic thinking close to myth and poetry, in a narrative tone visibly influenced by the experience it theorizes. Of course, the figure of the ideal writer (whose activities are glossed in various ways: "Writing is the interminable, the incessant" (26), "writing is making oneself the echo of that which never stops speaking" (26), "writing is to surrender to the fascination of the absence of time" (30) also comes from a controlled interpretation of certain journals or correspondences of writers he admires, beginning with Kafka and Mallarmé. But the article is also informative about the way Blanchot lives his own experience as a writer: It is like a fragment of the *Journal* that he did not write. It seems important that it was written at the same time as the triptych of Èze *récits*. "It is perhaps striking that from the moment the work becomes the search for art, from the moment it becomes literature, the writer increasingly feels the need to maintain a relationship with himself" (28), writes Blanchot. But "maintaining a relationship with [it]self" is what the article does, with the single difference that it does so *in the name of the other*, in the name of the ideal writer it describes. Blanchot's critical work is this other journal written in the name of the Other. It accomplishes, term by term, the destiny of the writer's journal as Blanchot conceives it: "The journal represents the series of reference points that a writer establishes so as to be able to recognize himself when he begins to suspect the dangerous metamorphosis to which he is exposed" (29). From the 1930s, Blanchot's critical work embodies the displacement of these points, of these axes, of these stakes of recognition. It is "the Chronicle" of the choices made and all that was left behind on his itinerary.

Thus when Blanchot explores the meaning of the word "solitude" at the beginning of the article, we already know that he was not content with evoking melancholy or stillness, for "there is no need to comment" (21) on these sentimental ramifications of solitude, whether personal or public. "The essential solitude" is that of the body of work, that which removes all protection from the writer as he faces this terrifying, always incomplete work; this solitude beneath all other solitudes, which his own solitude allows him to locate and to complete, by way of a demanding path, is what he would describe in the "southern *récits*." The *tone* is thus all that can still be perceived of the writer's effacement, "the intimacy of the silence he imposes upon the word, which means that this silence is still *his*—what remains of himself in the discretion that sets him aside" (27). The tone provides the authority of effacement that can be seen in the tension of the sentences, the fallen block of the text, the decision to begin. The *récits* provide this tone. They describe how real space (the house, the room in Èze) makes itself absent in order to give rise to an evaded, diffuse, diffracted, disseminated, and sometimes hallucinated space, that of writing, the *space of literature*, the eternal return and glorious *jouissance* of the "primal scene," a space that allows one to enter into "the silent emptiness of the work" and "the absence of time." This impressionism of personal description ("personal" because although it describes the impersonal forces acting on the person as he writes, here it is the critical voice, attributed to the first person, that exposes, explains, recuperates it) allows Blanchot to develop his thinking of the work's impersonality and neutrality (its anonymity, its endlessness).[4] And Blanchot takes the true authority of his discourse, its real *tone*, from an experience that, even if it is one of dispossession, remains radically personal. We know how marked he is by the fantastic experience of multiple apparitions, and particularly the apparition of death; Èze is where these events take place; and he takes pleasure from reading about them in Thomas Mann, Hermann Hesse, or Henry James. In the same way that he makes this link in his *récits*, in his critical discourse too Blanchot ties together the conception of the work and the fact of seeing apparitions. A vocabulary of the fantastic acts as a paradigm for elaborating concepts. Like an apparition, the work "escapes" the writer, it "always leaves him or her wanting"; it is "what is there . . . but is withheld—the harsh and scathing void of refusal" (24); it makes the writer "the survivor, the idler [*désoeuvré*], the unoccupied, the inert" (24), who finds himself in "the errant intimacy of the outside from which he could not make an abode" (24). The work that Blanchot would figure via the character of Eurydice, an evanescent apparition over which Orpheus has no power, addresses to its author a *Noli me legere* that parodies the *Noli me tangere* of Christ's apparition. Beyond these equivalences, what is most surprising in the text's rhetoric is that the final pages, nearly a third of the article, entirely avoid the theme of writing (which Blanchot has nonetheless just glossed with multiple anaphoric phrases: "Writing is . . ."). These pages move away from critical theory *stricto sensu* and only return to it in the final paragraph, in the meantime developing the themes of fascination and childhood.[5] It is as if Blanchot were suddenly describing the nature of the fantastic rather than the nature of the work, as if he only theorizes the experience of writing by borrowing from that of apparition. The absence of time is one of the conditions of the work; Blanchot describes it as the *there is*, as what allows the appearance of "Being beyond the absence of Being, which *is* when there *is* nothing, which *is* no more as soon as there *is* something" (30). The being that becomes present in the absence of time escapes any presence; it is a ghost:

> What is present presents nothing, but represents itself and belongs henceforth and always to the return. It *is* not, but comes back, comes already and forever past, so that I do not know (*connais*) it, but I recognize (*reconnais*) it, and this recognition destroys in me the ability to know, the right to grasp, making what is ungraspable also the inescapable, the inaccessible that I cannot stop reaching, that which I cannot grasp, but only grasp *anew*, never to let go. (30–31)

And there is also this, which bears witness to the intensity, the significant presence of this figure of apparition precisely where and when Blanchot has set himself the task of describing the work:

> When I am alone, I am not alone, but, in this present, I am already returning to myself in the form of Someone. Someone is there, where I am alone. . . . Someone is what is still present when there is no one. . . . Someone is the faceless third person (*le Il sans figure*, 31).

When what is seen *touches the gaze* in this way, the work is not far from imposing itself on the author as his *invisible partner*, and this is what a *récit* such as *When the Time Comes* tries to show.[6] For what is then seen "does not belong to the world of reality" (32), no one "strictly speaking sees it" (33), not even the child ("childhood is the moment of fascination," 33). The abrupt, conclusive, and decisive comparison of the author to a child evokes the world of a writer such as Henry James or the very particular tenderness with which Blanchot himself describes children (starting in Èze, as we have said, with the figure of Julie Bataille). Finally, there is this:

> What fascinates us robs us of our power to give meaning, abandons the world, draws back behind the world and lures us there. It no longer reveals itself to us and yet it affirms itself in a presence foreign to the temporal present and to presence in space. (32)

This attraction turns the work into an initiation into a "vision" by which the author himself becomes "the phantom of an eternal vision."

The greater this fantastic or mythic anthropomorphization of the work, the less the author is neutralized. Such an anthropomorphization demonstrates the turns and condensations that intensify the experience whose genesis Blanchot explores in his three Èze *récits*. An experience of the fantastic is thus the model for the experience of writing. It is not a question of seeing this as a simple rhetorical strategy, literary convention, an unremarkable belief. Instead, the *récits* seek to show how *real* this experience is, how the life that experiences it gradually negates itself as it discovers the law governing the world of the work. The *récits* contain the genesis of this literary experience, which transforms a man into a writer and sees him becoming a being of solitude and of language.

CHAPTER 40

The Radiance of a Blind Power
When the Time Comes (1949–1951)

"I said to her: 'Come to the South with me.' She shook her head. 'It's impossible.' 'Come!'"[1]

It's impossible. For her and for him, alike. Sharing in this refusal by restating it makes the narrator of *When the Time Comes* into a writer, one who has withdrawn to his house in the South, an empty house containing only the presence of the woman whose apparition he will hallucinate at the foot of the stairs (as the author had previously). He meets Claudia in a Parisian apartment, unexpectedly, on a visit to a Jewish woman he once loved, Judith. The two women are now living together in a relationship. Every kind of jealousy will be provoked. This jealousy will lend violence even to apparently minor events, leading to brusque gestures, unexpected appearances, sudden about-turns, cries. It will be a question of listening to them, at the limit of what cannot be perceived.

The woman appears, possessing and dispossessing. Her image at the foot of the stair illuminates the suffering and the *jouissance* of her absence.

> I cannot say that I am always conscious of it, of this glimmer, I would probably have to admit that it often leaves me free, but, how shall I put

> it, this glimmer is freedom in me, a freedom which destroys all bonds, which abolishes all tasks, which lets me live in the world, but on the condition that there I be almost no one. So if I have now seen myself reduced to the transparency of a being that one does not encounter, it is because little by little the glimmer has relieved me of myself, of my character, of the serious and active affirmation that my character represented. (72–73)

She holds the authority of transparency, her law is the effacement of the person. She has pushed so far as to encounter the creative joy of sacrifice.

When he gave Denise Rollin a copy of *When the Time Comes*, Blanchot wrote these words on the title page: "this book, written for you in proximity to danger."[2]

"I burned, but this terrible fire was the shudder of the distant to which no task corresponded. I grew more silent (and since I was alone, that meant silent toward myself)" (63). In the dispossession that makes desire possible, each character retains an element of creativity and beauty. Claudia is a singer, the narrator writes. Their meeting at a point of annihilation will be experienced as a demand to annihilate everything leading up to this point. As a demand for the disappearance even of what has already disappeared, even of appearance itself.

> How terrible things are, when they emerge from within themselves into a resemblance in which they have neither the time to become corrupted nor the origin to find themselves and in which, eternally their own likenesses, they do not affirm themselves but, beyond the murky ebb and flow of repetition, they affirm the absolute power of this resemblance, which is no one's, which has no name and no face. That is why it is terrible to love and why we can love only what is most terrible. To bind oneself to a reflection—who could agree to that? But to bind oneself to what has no name and no face and to give that endless, wandering resemblance the depth of a mortal instant, to lock oneself in with it and thrust it along with oneself to the place where all resemblance yields and is shattered—that is what passion wants. (71–72)

Passion leads from empty resemblance to the smashing of resemblance, by a movement that is the movement of death.

A figure appears, in order to disappear. It only appears because it has already disappeared, and in order once again to take everything away. "Something is happening" (64). "Someone is there who is not speaking, who is not looking at me" (72–73). In "The Essential Solitude," Blanchot would use the same words to refer to the depths of being, the neutral presence that imposes itself on the writer: "Someone is there, where I am alone. . . . Someone is the faceless third person."[3] *When the Time Comes* has the task of describing how this writer comes about, how his personality is effaced in the withdrawal of writing, which allows it access to the "unraveling of time."[4] In this sense it is the first Èze *récit*, that of the passage from "I" to "He/It," from subjective speech to anonymous rustling; that of the oblivion of the café terrace or the room as they are converted, flattened, and incorporated into the night of *literary space*. It represents real space, which has become the site for a graceful, joyful, dignified encounter with distress. It recounts the appearance of the *neuter*.

> That I should descend so far from myself into a place one can, I think, call the abyss, and that it should only have surrendered me to the joyful space of a festival, the eternal glitter of an image, I would be surprised by this too, if I had not felt the burden of this untiring lightness, the infinite weight of a sky where what one sees remains, where the boundaries sprawl out and the distant shines night and day with the radiance of a beautiful surface. (71)

The autobiographical mode of narration would impose itself as a violent, precise, persistent, rigorous rumination on lived experience.[5] Sometimes only the portrait of a character is torn away from life like a citation from a text. "There is, in my need to name her," the narrator warns early on in speaking of Judith—there is, in the need to name her and "to make her appear in circumstances which, however mysterious they may be, are still those of living people," "a violence that horrifies me. That is the reason for my desire to abbreviate; at least that is the noble part of this reason." (5) With a tone that calls to mind the beginning of *Death Sentence*, Blanchot makes the mystery more plausible and credible, legitimizes its autobiographical borrowing by this concern for conviction, justifies its oblique and partial treatment as a matter of discretion. It is a question of producing a new image of fantastic conviction, of reinforcing literature's terrible right to death, to give shape to the emergence of death (Judith greatly resembles J.), to expose the ravages of the personal. This implies that a less noble element is at play, to which the text alludes without comment. The "desire to shorten" that belongs to the nature of the *récit* is the desire to cut into the event, the desire for language to remain untouched by bareness, the necessary collusion of language with destitution. It is a way in which the sentence can work as if with a scalpel, with a refined sense of sacrifice which, as Blanchot said about Lautréamont and Sade, is the best guarantee of the consciousness, gestures, movement, fear, offerings, and desire that are present between the characters, the true performers of the *récit*. Blanchot's particular narrative dramatization stems from here; as does his almost technical mode of listening to the varying movements of the body, his attentiveness to the smallest gestures of unveiling and turning, his rhythm of slowing down time in order then to jump forward quickly and suddenly move to the *dénouement*, and—particularly in *When the Time Comes*—the theatricality implicit in the dialogues, the scenography always invented by the gaze.

The spaces disarticulated by this mise en scène are those that best capture our attention. They are the ones that reveal how the personal is shared, how torn-apart immanence and real but ultimately impossible encounters are shown. There is intense and almost telepathic communication between the narrator and Judith but the latter, unlike previously, violently rejects any bodily relationship. Judith's defeat by Claudia, whose fraught relation to the narrator mixes eroticism and suffocation, is compensated by lucid knowledge, by the presence of emptiness, and is lightened by the knowledge that the other two bodies will also in turn separate. "I was there in flesh and blood, but Judith continued to watch me in a sterile way through the window" (41). In itself, this sterility is only meaningful insofar as it provokes Claudia's unhappiness. Between the disaffection of the past and the destruction of the present, the narrator realizes that he is simply a pawn in the two women's desire for one another: "calm in the midst of furious desire" (35). "And what about me, was I in on the secret? At the very most, I was the secret, and for that reason quite far removed from having anything to do with it" (42). In making the narrator the blind spot of the narration, Blanchot traps the reader in the same way he had announced in *The Most High* and *Death Sentence*. He closes the door on the autobiographical idealization he had previously suggested. This narrative detour is just one more fictional illusion, part of the autobiographical game of fiction. While he protects what is secret and brings all biographical readings into his game, that of fiction, he makes this fiction the very place, the literary space in which the truth of the secret can be grasped with its layering. Perhaps he therefore forces us toward a new kind of biography, an invisible partner not wholly accompanying its subject, remaining ignorant about the man in question but not about his genius, recognizing the way in which this man did not know himself and created the writer-character that he became.

Maurice Blanchot was always highly attentive to the men and women he knew and loved.[6] He makes use of the same nocturnal, profound and exhaustive capacity to listen with his fictional characters, in the circumstances he creates for them, which, "however mysterious they may be, are still those of living people," (5) and which were often those experienced by friends in real life. Such listening can seem cruel at first, although ultimately it is fascinating, dazzling, prone to fill one with joy. This is what is staged by the opening of *When the Time Comes*, with Judith opening a door, which immediately becomes her opening to an absence—a divine absence.

The familiar figure (*connaissance*) immediately becomes a figure of recognition (*reconnaissance*) in the following extract:

> I was extremely, inextricably surprised, certainly much more so than if I had met her by chance. My astonishment was such that it expressed itself in me with these words: "My God! Another familiar figure [*encore une figure de connaissance*]!" (Maybe my decision to walk right up to this figure had been so strong that it made the latter impossible.) (1)

The narrator recognizes Judith, a Jew, as his God from the beginning of the *récit* (he will later say that she is detached from the passage of time). It is in the gap provided by this recognition, in the distance from the expression "my God" to Judith, that the relation to the divine and the feminine is sketched out, and that the possibility of the gaze arises. Judith, a woman, a body, is negated as soon as she is perceived, and the narrator's gaze focuses on the horizon, like the gazes exchanged between Dorte and the "Most High," like the other visions that characterize the Èze *récits*, those from behind a window or from the foot of the stairs. The narrator's gaze immediately settles not on Judith but on a figure of Judith, just as later it will settle on Claudia's apparition. The doubled figure that Judith helps to set up from the beginning of the *récit*, to which she gives form, belongs to a fantastic or mystical type of vision.

In fact, without this doubling the narrator would remain in the vertiginous world of *appearances*. Only this rupture projected by the gaze helps discernment and identification. It is precisely because nothing is yet written in Judith's "different seeming" appearance, because her face has remained indifferent to time, that the old face projected beyond her, in order better to recognize her and her past, opens a space of memory and oblivion, of divinity and welcome (anything can happen in this space). The *apparent otherness* created in this way clears the way for the dramatic movements in the *récit*: between the door and the back of the apartment, or between the door and the window, the space of the studio will be occupied by the *récit*'s most violent irruptions and by its happiest movements.[7] This choreographic opening makes Judith's divine, defied, deified face, in the words of the dancers, the face of the *invisible partner*.

The fact that Judith resists this *apparent otherness*, which manifestly marks both the singer and the writer, makes it necessary—according to the law of this *récit* which makes itself a *récit* on the very possibility of *récits*—to produce this figure, and to do so in a way that is not exactly cathartic. On the contrary, the narrator's astonishment and distress are effaced before the radiance of a blind power, a neutral power of dispossession, the sudden blaze of an appearance that brings things together as much as it forces them apart, and that ultimately suffocates one. Because he is unable to inscribe this divine, inviolable figure in the real, and due to this nature's destructive violence, the narrator disappears into the intermediary space he has created, which is named as the space of *thought* (3). This is a neutral, cold, and suffocating space, which forces the following question, a motif of the Èze *récits*: "Give me a glass of water."[8] Is that what it means to be a subject? To be for another, to face the other, to face the divine face of the other? This space of thought becomes the paradoxical site of the subject's intimacy, a way of inscribing one's body (or the shadow that precedes one's body) in the other space of the air, a way of beginning to give oneself over to dying.

Judith is abstracted from the space of thought that she has violently helped to create. Scattered everywhere, she is not visible anywhere. She is the possible receptacle for all emotions, a divine, dismembered body made of words, organs, emptinesses. She is invisible, ungraspable, unnarratable. She is the possibility of the *récit* from which she herself is immediately excluded. She is the possibility of the work, but as Cupid only appears at night, the narrator can never know whether to rely on her is to rely on a word, an organ, or an emptiness. She is the ground of all experience, of all danger to come. She is the ground of space or of the gaze, from which all spaces or all gazes are possible. "I saw certain parts of the room very clearly, and it had already renewed its alliance with me, but I did not see [Judith]" (5). If Judith's room is the site of exodus, the tent for the new covenant, it is because her face is the neutral, invisible, and dazzling ground through which all other possible faces will be inscribed. All other possible faces, that is, starting with that of the narrator, which takes its meaning from this transfiguring radiance. How could a photograph capture this transformation, this ground of the face? Blanchot already believes that the writer's face must remain invisible.

This power of figuration, whether it is divine, corporeal, or feminine, explains the narrator's repeated fainting, his fights and his *jouissances*, the erotic, suffocating back-and-forth he engages in with Claudia. Claudia thaws the cold, suffocating, uneasy space presented by Judith's gaze. She is the one who, when suffering a coughing fit, places the narrator's chilled hands on her hot throat, "to enjoy a colder touch," a touch charged with Judith's presence (54). The swelling of her chest, the movement of her suffocation changes its meaning little by little, and eroticism takes over from the choking fit:

> I felt a terrible, convulsive storm pass between my arms, and in order to stay (*demeurer*) with her, I had to respond to the awesome call that rose from the depths of the day at this instant, I was filled with rage, I passionately seized her, and now that I had caught hold of her again in the midst of unsteadiness, the static falling of our two bodies together, I held her firmly out of reach of limitlessness. (54)

The indistinctness retained through these bodily ravages is fueled by an obsessive idea: the fear of the other coming close. There is a risk of something so strong that it immediately provokes apprehension, suffocation. It is as if the characters had no protective skin, and all contact between their bodies were infinitely violent; even the slightest appearance is a confrontation. This coalescence of open flesh makes all images impossible. This perhaps concerns the bodies' gender: Blanchot's *récits* place a man between two women too often for us not to raise this question. Is it simply a way of heightening man's ability to bear death? For him to know that he is "an arc between two deaths"?[9]

In his existence, Blanchot had encountered women's strength in withstanding the work of death.[10] This strength is what separates the narrator of *When the Time Comes* from Judith and Claudia. Blanchot's inability to withstand dying had lasted too long not to become the timid law governing his character, he who would only find grace and joy in "the essential solitude," that of writing. After a long, difficult, painful journey through exhaustion, writing would henceforth always be the moment when the time comes.

A few years earlier, Blanchot had cited Nietzsche in an article in *L'Arche*: "Die at the right time" (*au moment voulu*). His commentary is that the cruelty of death never allows us to know, once we are dead, what the right moment will have been, "so that finally the choice of the moment of death assumes that I leap above my death and from there gaze down on my whole life, assumes that I am already dead."[11]

This gaze has a name: writing.

CHAPTER 41

Are You Writing, Are You Writing Even Now?

The One Who Was Standing Apart from Me (1951–1953)

It is tempting to attract the unknown to oneself, to attempt to bind it by a sovereign decision; it is tempting, when one has power over the distant, to stay inside the house, to summon it there and to continue, during this approach, to enjoy the calm and the familiarity of the house.[1]

The house in Èze offered Blanchot a double possibility. On the one hand, "the little garden—hardly a garden, a few feet of earth enclosed within walls," this "reservoir of space and of light," was the space for the day, a way of drawing on the rich, peaceful outdoors, of making time for breath, recovery, the horizonless spread of suffering. On the other hand, "the small room" had a clear view onto "the splendor of the limitless" and, even as it retained the calm familiarity of the indoors, in other ways "made [one] think of it as the unique moment and sovereign intensity of the outside" (298–299). The house in Èze frames the *récit* from beginning to end and, apart from the explicit mention of the "regions of the South" (274), is described in a way consistent with the descriptions in *When the Time Comes*, *A Voice from Elsewhere*, and several other autobiographical texts. The description of the copious light entering the "small room," a kind of "watchtower open on two sides" (284), filled by the presence of nothing more than a table, chair, and sofa, chimes with the description which opens the book on Louis-René des Forêts. This is the room where Blanchot "most often stayed."[2] It is the site where the narrator, again a writer, comes to sit in order to write, where he is "offered the right to speak of [himself] in the third person" (318). It is the site where true silence can be listened to. Down below, at the foot of the stairs where the narrator often places himself, in the place where in the previous *récit* he saw Claudia's apparition, the room offers a "poorer, more desolate" silence (286). The room creates a true space for writing only by filling itself with the apparitions glimpsed through the three large bay windows.[3] The house in the *récit* is even more truly the house in Èze in real terms in that it is also its imaginary form, which was probably the way Blanchot saw it, recreated it, loved it. In *When the Time Comes*, it condenses other spaces dear to the author, certain windowpanes, a kitchen, a storeroom that recall the rooms of the apartment in the Rue de la Victoire.

The house in Èze was not the site that created Blanchot's solitude, but it did allow it to be made "essential." "Little by little and under the constraint of this concealment," which made him abandon a certain kind of political public relation and offered him the suffocating shelter of literary creation, "I had withdrawn from everything," explains a narrator whom we are encouraged to confuse with Blanchot by the first person of the title, "so that now I no longer lived in the world, but in concealment" (302–303).[4] From simulation to dissimulation, from semblance to dissemblance, fiction gives the author's political and literary itinerary the shape of destiny, in which the end refers back to the beginning, as if under the intense authority of the "primal scene." The triptych of southern *récits* prolongs the movement of contradictory and even paradoxical introspection that defines Blanchot's relation to the act of writing; it prolongs the movement in which journalistic responsibility is abandoned in favor of the abyssal commitment of the narrative form adopted. The triptych prolongs and accentuates this movement. Little by little, the characters become fewer. Ultimately only the narrator remains, alone face to face with himself, with the charged power of the work he is writing: with writing, with dying. There has to be an end to this return to the origins of the possibility of writing. Blanchot's *récits* revolve around a confrontation with a single subject, namely, how the possibility of writing comes about. This mythical *récit* of a solitary adventure, this fiction of fictitious happenings, is the sole witness to the experience of writing. It is lucid about its appearance and its language, and ultimately makes a point of returning to the world, of trying to set what is extremely personal (the genesis of creation) in relation to what is extremely public (the demand of refusal and the possibility of community). Ultimately it meets its own first—and thus final—demand: the fragmentary. The completion of the cycle of *récits* can now be envisaged.

The One Who Was Standing Apart from Me is the first of Blanchot's *récits* directly to confront the figure of the neuter, an unnamable figure (as the title indicates in its exhaustive efforts not to name it). Inscribing in language what precedes all speech and all writing, describing the writer's solitary confrontation with the work, shutting oneself in one's writing room and removing all entertainment: the *récit* is formed around such objectives. Starting from such thoughts, the narrator engages in a fantastic dialogue with this "He/It [*Il*]," this other self, the anthropomorphic work or apparition against which he protected himself during the "extraordinary" time of the novels, and that now must be brought to the presence of the image, made to emerge on the surface of language, the essence of dissimulation.[5] "I sought, this time, to approach him [*le*]" (263): the decision is made, as is thus indicated with the opening words of the *récit*. While this "he" or "it" seems to be a divine figure, and while openly going to meet him or it does not come down to defying satanic temptations but instead to "erecting the tent of exile" (299), envisaging the apparition does not allow for any imagery (with the ethical exception of an invisible, Judaic God). Such an envisaging attempts to open itself to everything that has disappeared and disappears anew with it, and it must raise itself to the level of infinite attention required for the fate of ghosts returning from the dead, of the last men, who have been—as it were—rendered godly by their astonishing return from the death camps, from the impossibility of dying.

What is at stake is the very possibility of conversation, of the attentiveness necessary in order to listen to the other, once one has reached a level of exhaustion that makes language—producing language, analyzing or deconstructing it—difficult. How can one find a path through words, how can one remain open to what remains unsaid in dialogue, how can one make one's words immediately accessible to others; the *récit* surveys these forms of vigilance, weighing up, dissecting, *providing commentary on* each expression chosen, without ever totally aligning itself with an institutional listening, whether that of the Socratic dialogue, the confessional, or psychoanalysis.[6] The other: the "he/it," the neuter, the absent party: all of these embody vigilance regarding one's own language. Thus, writing imposes itself as "the best way of making our relationships bearable" (264). Writing is the platform for an infinite listening that could never really "limit and circumscribe the void" (the ordeal of dying) (267), and that is therefore forced to reach such a limit. Writing leads us to endless forcing of and regular denials of the presuppositions of any speech that takes itself to be homogeneous. In a sense, the *récit* has no object except to deconstruct, unfold, explain its own beginning: "I sought, this time, to approach him" (263). What does it mean to take this risk? Why now? Why does such an attempt seem to be destined to fail, ruling out in advance any catharsis? Is it possible to see this phantom, this *invisible partner of writing*, to which Blanchot is giving form here (and doing so in a unique exception in his work, as the main character of a *récit*)? Or is it even possible to hear it, to hear "some of his words which I could not distinguish, once they were said, from my own" (320), that is, to hear these words that register writing as a distancing, as an equivalent to the visions with which it seduces us and to the movements to which it condemns us, by which it causes an abandoned body to be listened to?

If the narrator's absence from himself, registered by an abundance of narrative omissions, sometimes makes him unaware of how he moves in space—so much so that he finds himself unexpectedly and almost instantly a few steps away from where he thought he was—and if he thus gives the impression of having been lifted up and swept along by an unknown force, he owes this to what, describing the apparition of the neuter in *When the Time Comes*, he calls "the burden of this tireless frivolity."[7] Such spatial breaks are experienced as a doubling of bodily perception, accompanied by cries and falls. It is the experience of the withdrawal of Judith's face applied to oneself, as it were, experienced as a painful force within the body that shares and alters it in a void charged with presence.[8] Such unexplained movements do not render any less mysterious the apparitions of a third party behind the window panes or on the staircase, described as they are in the manner of Henry James, a third party who will be shown to be the narrator *himself*, or rather the element *within him* that escapes his power, challenges his capacities of recognition, and calls for writing.[9] These visions are sovereign and frightening,[10] and it is impossible to coexist with them, as Blanchot would often put it via a Cratylic play on words.[11] They give the sensation of having one's body *operated on*, of a vertiginous movement being *opened up* within it, and also of making it not into a "metaphor" (as had already been ruled out in *Thomas the Obscure*), but into the *work* itself.

Bearing an attentiveness to dying that Blanchot redefines here as "the uninterrupted and the incessant" (317), another proof (as if it were necessary) that the critical essays indeed derive from a shared experience, the narrator can hear words which seem to him to come from outside and therefore to pass through him, confirming his dying, but without yet being writing. The thirty or forty last pages of the *récit* recount precisely the move *from dying to writing*, in an address—beyond the mirror—to words themselves, with the pronoun "they" [*elles*] that replaces the "he/it" [*il*] and lyrically imposes itself on the narrator's fascinated attention. "Risen, as if from their graves" (324), words bury the dead body of the subject, who has disappeared into writing. They are the tomb of his desire, the forgetting of his secret, the unlocatable site of a prophet now without prophecy. They dispossess him of what he did not yet have, of what they had promised to him. They provide him with shelter.

Literary space becomes the space in which the subject can advance, sheltered from the world, but also, at the same time, the space in which the world of shelter can take shape. In the very depths of solitude, it is charged with the community to come. "In this space, there were still knots and tensions, strong areas where everything was a demand, others where everything leveled out, an interlacing of waiting and forgetting that incited one to continuous restlessness" (303). How can community with the last man be founded? The next *récit* will address this question.

Little by little, writing returns to gaiety, to "a joyful pleasure, a strange enthusiasm" (271), to the strength of sand and the power of wind. This does not mean that there are not endless reversals, from the "anxiety of the void" (305) to the "pleasure of having broken out of the depths" (306). In the disappearing absence toward which he is led, the subject always seems to be waking from a dream or from an exile, from suffocation or from insomnia, and to hear this pressing question: "Are you writing, are you writing even now?" (307).

This question, the leitmotif of the *récit*, is the enveloping force of night.[12] It gradually takes over the space and time of this house in the south, as if it were a matter of showing that the narrator is doing precisely nothing other than writing; as if it were a matter of constructing an image that hides life in the sometimes anguished, sometimes delicious ordeal of writing; as if it were a matter less of giving shape to the image of effacement than of effacing a terrorized subject. This total projection of the narrator in literature onto the very site of fiction is itself a fiction. Ultimately, it speaks to the very power of fiction itself, which is real, and which invites us to resist being taken in by the immediate circle of fascination. Being no one has no meaning unless *someone* is no one, even if this someone is the last man.

CHAPTER 42

The Critical Detour
A Few Articles of Literary Criticism (1950–1951)

During the years when the "southern *récits*" were written, Blanchot's critical activity decreased as a result of illness and what he described as his loss of interest in commentary. The origin of this disenchantment is itself the subject of fictional writing: the origin and the creation of the oeuvre, which weakens critical discourse by taking that discourse's object for its own.

In quantitative terms, Blanchot rarely contributed to journals during this period. Only one article appeared in 1949; in 1950, no substantial critical text came out before October. Beginning that month, he published in four of the next five issues of *Critique*, with texts on Thomas Mann and Hölderlin (each opening its issue), and a double article on Malraux's *Le musée imaginaire*. In spring 1951, the *Cahiers de la Pléiade* published "The Two Versions of the Imaginary," which would be appended to *The Space of Literature*. Then, again, there was nothing, at least not until March 1952.

Meanwhile, Blanchot had been contributing sporadically to the weekly paper *L'Observateur Politique, Économique et Littéraire*. Founded by Roger Stéphane in April 1950, this predecessor of the *Nouvel Observateur* was linked to *Les Temps Modernes*, where Stéphane, who had joined the journal in 1948, quickly took on an important editing role. Blanchot contributed seven articles between May and August, more or less regularly every other week: these were full-page literary columns, and alternated with pieces by Léon Pierre-Quint. The articles addressed Mann, Goethe, Lowry, Parain and the Russian nihilists, Cayrol, Hölderlin, and Adamov. This brief journalistic column would be Blanchot's last.

The small number of texts published tells us nothing about the amount of original material published, however. The article on Thomas Mann that appeared in *Critique* in fall 1950 repeats the one from *L'Observateur* almost word for word (although it also added considerable material). The reflection on the image undertaken in various passages of the Malraux article prefigures "The Two Versions of the Imaginary." But what may look like Blanchot cutting corners in fact indicates how insistent and firm his thinking was becoming. This is the period when the first major ideas appear, circulating from one text to another: the neuter (still in adjectival form), the outside, the "faceless someone," "the absence of time." These ideas are established within recurrent, deconstructed concepts and themes, pushed as far as they will go, to the limits of what paradox can make them signify, sometimes so much so that their everyday meaning gets lost: the image, the work, the Open (*das Offene*), the initial, solitude, silence. The critical texts do not so much offer commentary on the books they take for their object as lean on them in order to exceed the reflection carried out there, putting this excess toward a personal quest, toward the creation of the work. This can be seen particularly in two articles: one on Malraux, where Blanchot feigns a student/teacher relationship ("as Malraux says," "as Malraux has taught us") in order to underline the meaning and the authority of what he himself is trying to demonstrate (he concedes as much: "perhaps we are going a little further than Malraux's formulations would allow");[1] and the *Critique* text on Hölderlin, presented in the journal as a review of Jaspers's book on Strindberg and Van Gogh but that in fact moves away from the philosopher's thinking to confront it with Hölderlin's life and poetry.[2] Blanchot is one of the few who can allow himself the luxury of deviating from the genre of the review, and later he would use this authority, notably in his pieces for the *NNRF*, to bypass the need to refer to recently published books (and indeed to do without Gaston Gallimard's judgment—finding Blanchot's articles austere and incomprehensible, he allegedly wanted to drop them as early as the first year of the relaunched journal).[3]

This period of infrequent criticism was when Blanchot constructed his own theory. By historically questioning the status of the modern work of art and by denying the sacred value of antiquity and the aestheticizing idealization of classicism, Blanchot opposed Malraux's humanism with what had by then been his view for almost ten years: an art reduced to being "nothing but its passionate contestation," "the refusal of the world and the affirmation of solitude," divine dissimulation.[4] In the same article, he calls into question the belief in the mimetic status of the image, a belief that he paints as narrow-minded and comforting. Beginning with a meditation on dead bodies, he moves toward another "version of the imaginary": "One must wait for the cadaverous appearance, the idealization by death and the eternalization of the end for a being to take on the great beauty that is its own resemblance, the truth of itself in a reflection." Blanchot adds that in portraits "the face is not there, it is absent, it appears only from the absence that is precisely resemblance, and this absence is also the form that time seizes upon when the world moves away and when there remains of it only this gap and this distance."[5]

This was the end of 1950. The following spring saw the simultaneous publication of *When the Time Comes*—which opened with the captivating apparition of Judith's face, steeped in the divine nature of its resemblance to itself and made absent by the projection of a gaze that sets it apart—and of the article in the *Cahiers de la Pléiade* in which Blanchot completes this theory of the image: "In the rare instances when a living person shows similitude with himself, he only seems to us more remote, closer to a dangerous neutral region, astray in himself and like his own ghost already: he seems to return no longer having anything but a life in echo."[6]

In this way, J.'s dying face, the deathly masks of *Death Sentence*, Anne's abandoned body, Judith's surprising, frightening face, the impersonal face of *The One Who Was Standing Apart from Me*, all speak to the same experience of the image in question. This experience, having begun with the *récits* for which it provides an *initial* appearance (an inaugural or central scene, even if a disarticulated one, always needing to be caught up with and then moved beyond), is prolonged in the critical texts that offer a detour to the turn of the screw carried out by the fiction. The better-known, better-selling critical works would mask the *récits*. This redoubled masking would form the basis of much of the criticism leveled at Blanchot about his theoretical justification for hiding his own image. Above all, this criticism stems from a blindingly impoverished way of conceiving time, which, preferring linear time to the unfolding, complicated, cyclical time of the *récit*, deprives itself of its own absence, its own personal shadows, making abusive use of too much clarity.

This means surely that the *imaginary museum*, that of our time, has imposed itself upon the *space of literature* that attempted to open it up to itself. The article on the psychology of art ends by casting a decisive light on the contradiction Malraux falls into by limiting himself to a view of art based on consciousness and control, refusing to recognize that a child's drawing or the narration of a dream can have aesthetic qualities. "This may be," Blanchot comments, "but then one must give up the Museum," for the *Psychologie d'art* also states that the Museum can rule de facto on the artistic value of an object. If the space of the work is imaginary, it is not because it allows one to "negate nothingness" and to construct a counterdestiny, but rather because "the image . . . is also the gaze of nothingness upon us."[7] According to Blanchot, the space of the imaginary is not one to which presence can be transferred with any guaranteed result, but instead one of deracination from presence, the courage of absence, prophecies without future, visions without object.

Not to be afraid of fear, to open up to "madness par excellence": this is where Blanchot's *récits* and commentaries come together. Perhaps because he had experienced it several times, a proof—if ever there were one—of his unshakeable confidence in life, Blanchot believes in the existence of Ariadne's thread, of Orpheus's incantations. Being lost is never a state entirely outside comprehension. It demands a "tense awareness."[8] Instead of the different theories on Hölderlin, which see the rupture of madness as essentially motivating his poetry, Blanchot prefers "the simplest words, those of the carpenter Zimmer": "if he has gone crazy, it is from being so learned." Because poetry preexists madness and continues to exist in it, Blanchot insists on "the continuity of Hölderlin's destiny, the movement that raises him to an always-clearer consciousness." He believes that these different fates are continuous with one another even before one or the other is present, and he believes that these personal movements are persistent, that they prune away any false modes of refusal, any illusory solitudes, since they are created by the grace of encounter, and in turn create true thinking. To some extent, they are his fate too. Encounters with the gods can have a sense only if they are proffered onward, if they offer "the tranquil light of community."[9] If thought turns to the community, it does so because it is so solitary.

Critical solitude, too, finds meaning in being shared. Blanchot does not let go of the question of community. He does not yet know when or how he will respond to the way literary experience tears him away from the present, a response that would come in the shape of more violent, insubordinate, and trenchant public intervention. He probably does not even know whether this event would come to pass. But he continues to refuse "illusory communities." The challenge of the death camps to thought is taken up silently, discreetly, in a muffled way. In July 1950, Blanchot reviewed Jean Cayrol's book, *Lazare parmi nous*. The article in question, in *L'Observateur*, mainly praises the Russian nihilists, who had been among the first to undergo the humiliation of deportation. Blanchot had not yet thought through how exceptional Auschwitz was. For him, the pain of the camps stands in a general way for the previous century of history. "Who would dare to compare such equally extreme ordeals?" he writes.[10] However, he would soon find himself thinking about what made them different. For it was probably during this year that he became aware of Robert Antelme's book *The Human Race*, in a reissue by Robert Marin rarely mentioned today.

CHAPTER 43

The Author in Reverse
The Birth of *The Space of Literature* (1951–1953)

Although it was published in summer 1955, *The Space of Literature* was in fact almost entirely complete by June 1953.[1]

It benefitted from the years largely dedicated to narrative creation, from the more regular publication of critical texts in 1952 (five important articles in *Critique* and *Les Temps Modernes*), and in 1953 from the platform offered by the *Nouvelle Nouvelle Revue Française* beginning with its first issue in January. Blanchot's involvement with this journal, on a monthly basis for more than six years, then more or less fortnightly, represented an important turning point in his career, fame, and—more fundamentally—his research.[2]

The period of scattered publication was over. This was only 1953, and yet the vast majority of Blanchot's future critical articles would appear in the *NNRF*, this "pure site," in Paulhan's words, a "privileged place where words are permitted to retain their meaning." Sharing the editorship with Arland, Paulhan had come back to his journal. After the purges, the climate had become less fractious, and the status of the former *NRF*, the folding of *L'Arche*, and the relative decline of *Les Temps Modernes* made Paulhan's return almost natural. In accordance with the line pursued by the *Cahiers de la Pléiade*, and not content with distancing himself from Sartre, Paulhan aimed to open his journal to "writers with the most divergent tastes, opinions, and even party allegiances. It asks those it publishes neither to be engaged, nor *not* to be engaged. . . . *French* through its concern for universality, it will also be French because it will recall and defend the highest values of a civilization."³

These points were vague enough for Blanchot to be able to see himself there, or not see himself there but nonetheless to agree to be part of an undertaking that gave his research the greatest freedom, guaranteeing a modest but regular salary, and bringing with it the fidelity of a choice readership. Blanchot's column was supported by Paulhan, who saw him as the journal's best writer, paradoxically "so admirable when he speaks of authors that he does not like, or does not much like."⁴ Many readers—often major figures themselves—would feverishly await this column before each issue. This "Research" (which was the title of the column) would mark an entire generation of writers, philosophers, and artists.

At the time, Blanchot was publishing almost all of his books with Gallimard. Alongside Camus, Malraux, and Queneau, he belonged to the review panel, for which he was paid. Difficulties with Gaston Gallimard remained (in 1951 Blanchot almost exercised his right to buy himself out, in order to move his books to Minuit), but they seem to have smoothed themselves out. His move away from *Critique* was due to a variety of reasons involving money, health, and editorial freedom. And he was not sad to leave *Les Temps Modernes*, or entirely unstrategic in doing so. He was fairly close to Merleau-Ponty, who also left *Les Temps Modernes* the year that Blanchot joined the *NNRF*.

The 128 articles given to the *NNRF* would mostly be collected in Blanchot's four main volumes of criticism: *The Space of Literature*, *The Book to Come*, and later *The Infinite Conversation* and *Friendship*, in 1969 and 1971. In following his thinking as it advances, we can track both his progress and the moments it becomes sidetracked; we see it developing original and essential ideas such as the "outside," the "neuter," the "other night" or "infinite distance." The rhetoric of paradox merges into the poetics of dissimulation, and then into fragmentation and interruption. The attentiveness to the origin of the work, to the experience of writing, the patience required by the negative, Hegel and Heidegger's critical legacy, a permanent dialogue with the thought of Levinas and Bataille, endless meditation on the works of Mallarmé and Kafka, renewed debates with Malraux, Sartre or Camus, an unshakeable conviction in the excessive nature of literature, an infinite approach to death by way of dying and to the work by way of the book, analytical praise for the new criticism, new philosophy or *nouveau roman*. All of these elements gave this anonymous enterprise an exceptional place in twentieth-century aesthetic thought, impressing the young readers who in the 1960s would become the most decisive figures of the new modernity: Barthes, Deleuze, Derrida, Faye, Kristeva, Lacan, Sollers, and others. This was the period when Foucault "dreamed of being Blanchot."[5] Each article was experienced as a new rupture in literary, philosophical, and political thought. Alongside Bataille, although differently from him, and often against Sartre, Blanchot opened literature up to philosophers and psychoanalysts, introduced them to Broch and Beckett, even to Jaspers and Artaud. He allowed them to hear this decisive and neutral, personal and shared speech, which within all language resounds with insanity, transgression, powerlessness, restlessness. What was most imposing was that this speech was his own speech, and it troubled the greatest minds all the more because it seemed to condemn them to silence.[6] At this time, few were aware that Blanchot experienced this apparent ease in writing and this penetrative strength as a secret struggle, the repeated experience of thought wrested from ill health and weakness.

The Space of Literature is probably the most unified of Blanchot's volumes of critical essays, thanks to its simultaneously progressive and cyclical movement. Described on its cover as a rich and rigorous meditation on "creative behaviors," it stems from the personal experience of writing, which by this stage was drawing on twenty years of research and maturation, as well as from an empathetic attentiveness to the creative experiences of Malraux, Rilke, and Kafka, an attentiveness that was also—already— longstanding but had counted more than ever in the preceding years. Indeed, when, more than at the beginning of the 1950s, could Blanchot have identified with these sayings by Kafka: "I am nothing but literature," or "my unique aspiration and my sole vocation ... is literature ... Everything I have done is a result of solitude alone"?[7] Or with this one, by Mallarmé: "I am now impersonal"? The critic, he says, is an "author in reverse," and therefore he is speaking about himself in the long, lyrical pages on the journals, letters, and autobiographical essays of these writers.[8] Even allowing for the grace of chance, he tacitly recognizes fabulous coincidences, fierce complicities, between the eternal return of his own birth and the mystical night of Kafka's decisive revelation about the form and rhythm of writing. Blanchot twice cites the night on which this ordeal took place, September 22, 1912; it is said to mark "the demand of the work."[9]

The book takes its strength from highly personal meditations on these writers' experiences. Blanchot listens to, reads, and analyzes the simplest of personal experiences, but also the most tragic and the most foundational: married life, solitude, death. Here "personal" can only be understood in terms of personality melting away, through a violent and often unpredictable rupture, into the impersonality of time: the other, "interminable and incessant" time of *dying* and *writing*. Struck by how the experiences of death and writing seem analogous when taken to their limits, Blanchot turns the screw even more tightly on his fiction, a turning that—here—he attempts to halt.[10] But on each occasion the Other, whether Kafka, Mallarmé, or Rilke, offers violent resistance on behalf of the work, which always avoids being grasped. The moments when discourse falls down serve to relaunch the search. At such moments it confronts the opening-out of what is intimate to its own rupture, to the assimilating forces of myth and history. This is the subject of the pages on "the gaze of Orpheus," which Blanchot saw as the center of the book, as well as the final chapters on communication and the future of art. "The eternal torments of dying" return each time, the exhausting and yet inexhaustible search for the work, which is never reached, which always withdraws into the depths of the night, of the other night; not the night that provides relief from the ordeals of the day, but the one that welcomes the artist's insomnia, the artist who is henceforth open to the dissimulation of being, for what appears to him is the essence of disappearance, the absence of being as the ground of being, what is anterior to the beginning of time, the origin of the speech that is still nothing but a murmur, a rapid and incessant prose to which the essence of the poem will move ever closer. This is the artist to whom nothing appears, however, because he is open to this "rustling of the eternal outside," because he is carried away by this neutral speech that ties together some of the obscure points where shared, anonymous understanding can emerge, because he is doubled in the dissolute, infinite space from which the gods have withdrawn and whose overwhelming horizon makes the body hallucinate and blinds all representation—starting with the artist's own. This artist writes a poem that inscribes this invisible encounter only to efface itself immediately, effacing itself as a poem and effacing the artist as a poet, subsisting as an encounter of the untouched work with a reader who affirms it anew, via the light, transparent grace of a "yes" belonging only to him, a reader watched over by the possibility of writing, a faraway but still probable invitation, that of no longer escaping dying, a reader thus entering into the "joyous, free" dance with the tomb, into the dance with the *invisible partner*. Such is the vocabulary that returns, because returning is its essence, in the "essential solitude" that is Blanchot's, that belongs to him alone because it also belongs to others, to Kafka, Mallarmé, or Rilke, which means mythically that it belongs to a single impersonal figure, Orpheus turning around to see Eurydice's face because he can and wants to grasp her only in night. On the level of history, this means that any belonging is collective and is all the more communitarian because it is solitary, and that "the essential solitude" indeed finds that it has taken the path of shared thinking, by the very force of its original disengagement. We must all make up our own minds about whether this is a dream or utopia, but the force of this thought comes from not belonging to what such a mode of meaning could concede to it, but instead in affirming "the overabundance of refusal," which has no other power or guarantee than that of passing via "the vain overabundance of worklessness [*désoeuvrement*],"[11] and which would inscribe in history the marks—private and collective, present and future—of its insubordination.[12]

For *The Space of Literature* is indeed driven by a thinking of history, the movement of the book carrying it toward that confrontation. It is a book that was finished before it was written. "Literature and the Original Experience," the final part of its development, was at once its future and—as its title recalls—its origin. Indeed, these pages had been published in the spring of 1952 (only the section on Kafka is older) in two consecutive issues of *Les Temps Modernes*, a choice of journal that underlines how political their theoretical commitment was.[13] They would be continued a year later, for two consecutive issues of the *NNRF*, with an article entitled "Where Is Literature Going?" only a part of which is collected in *The Book to Come* (and with good reason: it repeats the reflections of the preceding article, provides the same commentaries on the same citations). Blanchot answers the question "Where is literature going?" by responding, following Heidegger: back where it came from, back toward what is originary. However, we must also recognize the political aspect of this return and admit that there is no better commentary on the work, on the movement that takes solitary space toward public space—a movement that can be seen in 1952–53 when Blanchot refers the genesis of texts back to the structure of thought, and more generally in the demand that the political never be forgotten, however far literature might carry us.

Thus literature returns to the political, but not to the same site nor via the same paths. The terms of this movement are still very vague: they are situated in and around communism, as the December 1953 article on Mascolo's book indicates. However Blanchot, struck by the "remarkable coincidence" of the artistic demand and the communist demand, expresses regret that art and communism too often shy away from this coincidence.[14] This is to admit how difficult the task of responding to these permanent demands is: for "the work is history; it is an event, the event of history itself, and this is because its most steadfast claim is to give all its force to the word beginning."[15] And more: "Nothing is more important than this sovereignty which is refusal and than this refusal which, through a change in sign, is also the most prodigious affirmation, the gift, the creative gift."[16]

The ideas of beginning, refusal, affirmation, the creative gift still remain groundless. Prodigality remains in reserve, available, ready to be used in order that one day refusal should give "all its strength to the word *beginning*." In 1952, at the height of the Cold War, the apogee of Stalinism, the middle of the Korean War, Blanchot writes from what seemed a faraway space:

> *The time of distress* designates the time which, in all times, belongs to art, but which, when historically the gods are lacking and the world of truth is wavering, emerges in the work as the concern in which the work has its reserve, threatening it, making it present and visible.[17]

But this reserve for him carries the greatest risk, one that is always active even when it is not permitted, is defeated, or seems useless. This reserve is not concerned simply with the day, action, usefulness, necessity, value, but also with the night, with the other, the wholly other, the essence of mankind: with "its right to truth, and, even more, its right to death," a death that is never individual, that has to be maintained even in anonymity, dignity, neutrality, collectivity (to put it brutally: for Blanchot, death is at the origin of community).[18]

Blanchot gives another name to this reserve of prodigality: prophecy. This is prophecy with no prophet except a poet who has disappeared behind his prophecy, with no authority except the distress left by the flight of the gods, without any message beyond its formulation for the future of an absolute beginning.[19] This politics of disappearance might seem to be a mask for evasion, but in truth it demands that we think through the conditions of its appearance, its practical resurgence, its particular speech. Later, Blanchot would refer to the "*freedom of speech*," the "everyday poetry" that would stimulate the communication, the "being-together" of 1968.[20] Poetic speech is the reserve on which this political speech draws. Char's authority is invoked here, the Char cited in the article in *Les Temps Modernes*: "At the center of this hurricane, the poet will complete the meaning of his message by renouncing himself, then will join the side of those who, having lifted from suffering its mask of legitimacy, assure the eternal return of the stubborn burden-bearer, the smuggler of justice."[21] This is the Char on whom Blanchot wrote a significant article in April 1953, which five years later became a book thanks to Guy Lévis Mano.

> [Char the poet] binds, in the space that premonition reserves, speech firmly to an upward movement and, by virtue of this upward movement of speech, reserves the coming of a broader horizon, the affirmation of an inaugural day. The future is rare, and not every day that arrives is a day of beginning. Rarer still is the speaking that, in its silence, is the reserve of a speaking still to come, and that turns us, even though we may be on the brink of our own end, toward the force of the beginning.[22]

The advent of this speech is the future of thought. In this sense, *The Space of Literature* strongly critiques Heidegger's thought. Blanchot's aesthetic reflection is shot through with Heideggerian notions, but it turns them round in a historically aware way, and no one has been better able than Levinas to show the philosophical, ethical, and political implications of this, as he did in 1956. "Does Blanchot not give art the role of deracinating the Heideggerian universe?" he asks in conclusion to his essay.[23] As is well known, Levinas always reproached Heidegger for his ontological dogma of the anteriority of Being in relation to beings, and his consequent indifference to the ethical position that Levinas judged indispensable. He recognized that "Blanchot, too, refuses ethical preoccupations" but only when they take on "explicit form." Thus his reading consists, already, via unequalled complicity, via friendly and prophetic knowledge, in reconstituting the implicit, nascent form of ethical thought that would soon occupy center stage in Blanchot's reflections. He returns to the sharing of the *there is*, which is still present. The pages in *The Space of Literature* on insomnia refer back to *Existence and Existents*, and Levinas is cited twice in the book, in footnotes; but in fact the whole work refers to this experience. Mallarmé's *it is* and Kafka's *dying* are made to chime with the *there is*. For Blanchot, the impersonal nature of rapture is a prior condition for the rapture of the community. It opens out onto the light of exile, is never a magnifying glass held over a fixed position. For art is not capable of installing truth in being, only the wandering of truth (Blanchot had been saying so since *Death Sentence*), the wandering that makes it authentic.[24]

Levinas recalled—this was 1956, and the terms were just barely veiled—that

> the Heideggerian world is a world of lords who have transcended the condition of needy and poor men or a world of servants who think

only of these lords. There, action is heroism, and dwellings, princely palaces, and divine temples sketch out the landscape before they serve as shelters. A life of mortals consoled by the visiting gods and their magnificence. A life of hard work on ancestral ground that no cataclysm could ever remove from under their feet. This calm possession, this pagan rootedness marks all Heidegger's evocations of things, whether he speaks of a bridge, a pitcher of water, or a pair of shoes.[25]

Literary space as Blanchot sketches it out allows for no territory save that of exile, it allows for no pagan restoration in a world where the divine only occupies the empty space of the community's needs, it allows for no sovereignty that does not accept its own annihilation. It accepts no ground that is not, and does not remain, shaken.

Still effacing any explicit response to the political nature of its eponymous question, the article "Where Is Literature Going?" concludes with a parable from Kafka. An old merchant is only able to get up by expending all his bodily strength. At night, he calls on the Devil to save him from the shadows—a strange move. There is a knocking at the door. Blanchot narrates and explains as follows:

> The writer of today, this old merchant drained of all strength, was long ago a man of enterprise and exchange; to break free from the night, he can appeal only to the night. It is a wonderful thing indeed now that the outside, at his appeal, trembles; and that, in the innocence and jubilation of distress, the writer joyfully makes one last effort to open literature out to this shaking of the immense outside. What is the result for him and for literature, what happens to the old merchant? This is what the interrupted *récit* does not say, unless it does so by means of interruption.[26]

Literature is the interruption of weakness, the old merchant's weakness, the community's weakness. It is the interruption of community. It is written, found, and lost in this interruption that is Blanchot's (and that he constantly began anew). The old merchant is also the "well-toned boxer," this "mortal partner" who hits the mat only in order to spring back up again. He constantly confronts death, in his name and in the name of the other, every month and every night, *in order to be able to write*, as he has Kafka say (misquoting him, and recognizing that he was doing so, recognizing that this was the overabundant law of his commentary and his narration). He sometimes worries about the hurtful judgment of time ("our modern, Occidental world," "our late Occident," Blanchot writes with a hint of sarcasm).[27] The times were now less concerned with literature. The day was ignorant and warned the partner that his indefatigable prose had no future. As for him, he immediately saw this as nothing more than the future of this ignorance. Burning with impatience, he was also infinitely patient.[28] Any initiative from him would be suspect. And he had also aged, grown tired. He waited, but the parable was not over. There were a few more words to make the narrator say, as others might make children say something. It still needed to be said that the book, that the action was still to come, and that the outside (Godot, perhaps) still needed to be awaited (this was 1953, and Blanchot was commenting on Beckett). The work (refusal) still had to be brought to the light of day. Readers still had to be dispossessed of their history, their religion, their occupation. "Everything must become public. The secret must be broken."[29] For what is broken is already public.

CHAPTER 44

Always Already (The Poetic and Political Interruption of Thought)
Toward *The Book to Come* (1953–1958)

These were years of plenty. From July 1953, with the first of the articles of what would become *The Book to Come*, to November 1958, with the last, Blanchot wrote one piece per month, all—with one exception—for his column at the *NNRF*. Thirty-three of these sixty-four articles would be collected in *The Book to Come* (1959).[1] The coherence of this book should not obscure the fact that today we can read thirty-one of these articles elsewhere (thirteen pieces in *The Infinite Conversation* and eight more in *Friendship* also belong to the same reflective movement, or temporality). Often, those included in the latter work could have featured in *The Book to Come*; the reasons for Blanchot's choices seem random or unclear. The selections made for *The Infinite Conversation* can be explained more easily: these pieces generally address philosophical aspects of the books discussed (by Camus, Pascal, Freud, Weil, and Nietzsche). In any case, all of these articles—including the few not included in collected volumes—are deeply linked.

An unprecedented critical movement is underway in Blanchot's oeuvre. Increasingly unable to limit its subjects to particular works, his thought is gaining autonomy and dictating what he publishes. It progressively abandons autobiographical references and begins to construct a political subjectivity.[2] And while his thought remains obsessed with "creative behaviors," it moves away from the external productions of those behaviors, focusing on the point when one loses touch with overarching narratives, when "everything disappears." His thinking forms a paradoxical consciousness in the way it moves away from the world and *interrupts* thought. This is to say that his thought focuses on the interruption of thought (as well as the thought of interruption). This shift from the vocabulary of dissimulation to that of interruption moves away from references to dialectics ("it is not the end of the affair when the word 'dialectic' is uttered") and toward phenomenology (Heidegger is increasingly criticized).[3] This aesthetic move already gestures toward fragmentary writing. In being repeated, insisted upon, and in creating a detachment, it brings literature closer to the world: closer to its historical essence and political consciousness. *The Book to Come*, despite the straightforward meaning of its structure, does not make this explicit. It is a publication that sets aside the most philosophical texts and keeps the most literary ones, and therefore downplays the untiring, endless work of exposing different discourses to one another: literature, politics, philosophy.

How is literature impossible? This could be the question at the origin of such thought. The ever more violent gesture of a world closed to literature makes Blanchot determined to open literature to the world, and to open up the world through literature. Following *Lautréamont et Sade*, he repeats that literature belongs to a region "where morals grow quiet." This region does not exclude literature from the world: the writer's irresponsibility does not shelter him from social judgment.

> Whoever comes up against, when writing, a truth that writing could not address is perhaps irresponsible, but must answer all the more for this irresponsibility . . . : the innocence that saves him is not his own; it is that of the place that he occupies, and occupies by mistake, and with which he does not coincide. (28)

The world of moral, partisan, or religious judgment imprisons, denatures, and pacifies art, makes it into an imaginary museum, a cultural example, a protective sovereignty. Such worlds strip art of its ability to ask questions, to raise the stakes, to take absolute risks. They make it into the site of a sedentary truth that lessens the authenticity of its wanderings. They are based on values that Blanchot sees as nothing more than "the pretences of those who abide."[4] They attempt to impose bourgeois and arbitrary values, passing them off as natural: they attempt, as Roland Barthes showed at the same time with *Mythologies*, to "dress the conventional up as *natural*." Resisting any discourse of values, Blanchot admires Barthes's "formalist study of ideologies" which by studying "the relationship between the order of values and the proliferation of 'signs'" shows how one discourse can surreptitiously enter into another, denouncing "this "consumption" of signs" and "the frightful pressure that values exert upon us."[5]

The sense of refusal is a permanent one. "There is certainly a great price in trying to create humanity at all costs," writes Blanchot on Max Brod's staging of *The Castle*.[6] "There is in Claudel a cruelty of thought that is perhaps responsible for his dramatic genius and to which one regrets that he did not give freer rein" (255), he writes in opposition to that writer's faith, to his fear of the infinite and measureless.[7] Hesse had confided that harmony and beauty were words that "made [him] laugh" (172), and Blanchot himself, apropos of Bataille's *Madame Edwarda*, opens "beauty" to scandal (189). He recalls an idea that had been dear to him since the beginning of the 1940s: over and against the traditionalists' view that all modernity was "futureless," the idea that tradition cannot survive by being faithful to itself, by reproducing itself. Instead, rupture is what renews it and allows it to remain alive. In literature, the exception becomes the rule.[8] Blanchot sees the writer becoming a value—a relative value—made and unmade by publicity.[9] This publicity reveals the type of language that was now dominant, a language that founded its nihilistic power on a discourse of values. For the domination of values was nothing more than a trick played by nihilism. It was necessary to oppose "all speech of certainty that decides, all substantial truth, all traditional knowledge—and generally, all speech predicated on a relation of power."[10] It was this nihilist discourse that thought had to *interrupt*.

From the three articles on Camus, first published in spring 1954 and then collected in *The Infinite Conversation*, where they became "Reflections on Hell," to the articles on Nietzsche that appeared in summer 1958 and featured in the same collection as "Reflections on Nihilism," Blanchot pursued the same argument. Nietzsche had called for the transmutation of values, but his strategy was judged to be insufficient: even the word itself had to be eradicated. *Value* was always "the mask of nihilism itself," its protective mask.

> What we call nihilism [is] at work in this obscure constraint that turns us away from it; . . . it [is] the very thing that hides it, the *movement of detour* making us believe we have always already put nihilism aside.[11]

It was necessary to repeat these condemnations. Blanchot probably had little choice. His care in discrediting nihilism rivaled what seems to have been others' enthusiasm in accusing him of it.[12] He knew that the space of literature, its power to fascinate and to create vertigo, could lead hasty readings into confusion, depriving the critical movement of its strength and reducing it to a type of nihilist disengagement. Neutral speech is risky. It always risks giving the impression that the question of politics—not to mention the question of philosophy—is neutral or has been neutralized. This risk is even greater in that it cannot be defended by being made more moderate, more receptive to the discourse of commitment and of values. On the contrary, only fully accepting it enables its true strength of refusal. In July 1958, Blanchot made this question felt when writing on André Gorz's book *The Traitor*. Gorz engaged with the movement of neutral speech without completely giving himself over to it. "Not having accepted it, nor even perhaps suffered it, he succeeds in saving himself from it, which leaves the experience inconclusive." Blanchot's commentary (and conclusion) is that "this, I think, is the problem of nihilism—we do not know whether its power comes from our retreat before it or whether its essence is to withdraw before us: that is to say, whether this essence is always posed, deposed by the very question of the detour."[13]

Nihilism depends upon the false choice between a terrorizing domination of values and an agonizing threat of disappearance (of faithlessness), this complementary movement, this repeated detour. It infects literary ambiguity (that of an absolute confrontation with death through language) with its own ambiguity (that of a hidden will to power). Blanchot identifies nihilism as the malady of modern politics, philosophy, and literature.[14] If this is the case, it is no longer enough to simply be close to communism, nor to phenomenological language.[15] Blanchot creates a *break* in his own itinerary, in his own language, the better to *interrupt* any value-creating (nihilist) effect, the better to introduce his—broken—voice into the political break, whose agent, initiator, or militant he would declare himself to be. The book is *to come* not because it is the Book or the Oeuvre, but because it does not exist in absolute terms, because it denies itself the book's quality of being-there, because the book can *be* only on the condition of putting into practice a political refusal, a rupture of and by the community.

Creating such a rupture within discourse also marks its continuity, persistence, insistence. The "wound of thought which had ceased to think itself" of *Thomas the Obscure*, the wound of "thought taken ironically as object by something other than thought" is precisely what is now being given or given back to thought.[16] Thinking the wound, the interruption of thought, is the new object of a reflection that assumes a critique of the languages that previously authorized it. This is signaled by a *"violent gap,"* an "always already" being introduced as a breach in the logic of the origin, an interruption of thought from before the beginning.[17]

Blanchot finds "this *nothing* that divides thought" (65) at work in extremely different writers, in the most radical wagers they take. For instance, he sees it in Pascal, whose belief in God is dependent upon a probabilistic reasoning which also sets the latter forever apart, and which would have to be interrupted if he wished to truly believe.[18] Interruption characterizes modern dialogue: dialogue with the hidden God, but also psychoanalytical dialogue ("the doctor does not claim to act upon the one who is ill. Power is situated in neither; it is between them, in the interval that separates them by bringing them together and in the fluctuating relations that found communication").[19] It also characterizes dialogue in novels (such as with the neutral speech which breaks down understanding for the characters in *The Square* by Marguerite Duras, leaving them with an impersonal, profoundly solitary, and exiled language).[20] Prophetic speech is "a momentary interruption of history" (81), poetic language is the power of dispersal (Mallarmé, but also Dupin, Du Bouchet),[21] Brecht's theater aesthetic opens an "interval" in the audience's passive absorption by the stage.[22] Artaud's pain makes him touch the point at which thought is interrupted: Through it, he understands that he had not previously even begun thinking, and that he has to maintain this point—dig into it, as Mallarmé did with verse—and take it toward the most unbearable pain, the most unbearable thought.[23] Ultimately, these are the trial of what is originary as literary language is created, as time—the other time—"separate, tears, divides," or as the unreality of imaginary space, given shape by the irrecoverable distance that exists between Achilles and the tortoise, between the land surveyor and the Castle (95–96), which puts this interruption of thought to work, turns it toward the book.[24]

The examples mount up, article after article and month after month, interrupting the space of thought in such a way that no value can be forged, but neither can any nihilism take root or act as simple catharsis over and against the promising openings of thought. This demands constant vigilance and permanent movement. Continuing his commentary on the aesthetics of movement proper to Sade or Lautréamont, irreducible to the fixed categories of literary criticism, Blanchot now allies himself with Nietzsche's demand, by which "the essential movement of . . . thought consists in self-contradiction." This endless dialectic opens the text to the "fragment" and thought to "the play of the world." Nietzsche names this thinking that of "the last philosopher" because it breaks, finishes, interrupts philosophy. Blanchot's texts on Nietzsche at this time recall those that Bataille had written for *Acéphale* twenty years earlier. It is still a question of reclaiming this thinking from its perversion by the Nazis, from its alignment with "the will to power." "The eternal return is not of the order of power."[25] This philosophical thinking of interruption opens a world that does not seek "the all-powerfulness of the person or the subject," but "makes us attain an order to which the notion of value no longer applies."[26]

Such considerations can seem somewhat removed from the space of politics. Blanchot's efforts were directed entirely toward fracturing—via a double gesture of solidarity—his philosophical and literary thinking, and in preparing a political thinking. This was never more evident than in 1957. In the summer and fall of that year, Blanchot wrote two articles successively on Simone Weil, later collected in *The Infinite Conversation*, and then two on Mallarmé which would precede "The Power and the Glory," the final essay of *The Book to Come*; the latter article was overtly political and was published in April 1958, a month before De Gaulle returned to power.

Blanchot's attentiveness to Simone Weil stems from his interest in Jewish mysticism, which he discovered through Levinas, and from Gershom Scholem's book *Major Trends in Jewish Mysticism*, which henceforth he would cite regularly.[27] With these two articles, for the first time since the end of the 1930s—and from an altogether different perspective—Blanchot's text contains an explicit interest in Jewishness. It is not insignificant that this return narrowly predates the return to politics: indeed, it prepares the way for it.

Blanchot approaches Simone Weil's texts through a reading of Isaac Luria, a sixteenth-century Jewish mystic.[28] He is impressed by Luria's "forceful idea" of Creation as an act of abandonment by God:

> In creating the world, God does not set forth something more, but—first of all—something less. Infinite Being is necessarily everything. In order that the world *be*, this Being would have to cease being everything, make space for it via a movement of withdrawal, of retirement, and by "giving up something like a region within itself, a sort of mystical space."[29]

Blanchot finds the same idea in Simone Weil, in many passages presenting creation as a withdrawal, a renouncement, an abdication. But for him it is above all an opportunity to conceive a new relationship between thought and what is originary: thought as the withdrawal, abandonment, interruption of thought. The care with which he announces this analogy does not hide the decisive strength and historical necessity that it seems to lay out for him:

> It may be (and is this experience not continually ours?) that the further thought goes toward expressing itself, the more it must maintain somewhere within itself a reserve, something like a place that would be a sort of uninhabited, uninhabitable non-thought, something like *a thought that would not allow itself to be thought*. . . . But it so happens, rightly or wrongly, that this sort of blind spot of thought—this *impossibility* of thinking that thought is for itself in its reserve—can appear to us to be not only present in all things, all speech and all action in a certain negligible way, but also, by this negligible presence, able to take up always more space, to be extended to the entirety of experience and little by little to entirely alter it.[30]

We shall see as much: this small element of agitation means that experience is no longer limited to "inner" experience. It means that nothing should be named (whether God or a dictator) that would in any way illuminate this blind spot. Here, the thinking of absence and oblivion provides guarantees for the thinking of interruption.

And Blanchot recognizes the same thinking in Mallarmé (224–244, esp. 226–229). "I have created my work by *elimination* alone," the poet wrote to his friend Lefébure.[31] Thus the space of creation, poetry, or literature acts as a palpable representation of thought as it opens to the "pure movement of relations" via the rhythm of words and sounds, and via the *interruption* of language on the page and in the air (the interruption of everyday language, but also of poetic language, language as it is read, written or linear language: for Blanchot the Book to come is not the posthumous manuscript published by Scherer, but *A Throw of the Dice*). The theory of creation by elimination will come to found theories of the effacement of the author and of his individual prophesying, to which Blanchot was laying claim more than ever. His public engagement should of course be read in the light of this effacement, which existed in order to free up "the pure movement of relations." The poet disappears into words, which themselves disappear into this movement. This model—which also applies to political discourse—sees Luria's thinking meeting that of Georges Bataille, with his thinking of sacrifice (Bataille speaks of it in fairly similar terms in his *Manet* of 1955).

Blanchot defines Simone Weil's thinking as one of misfortune and attentiveness. Having aligned it with Jewish mysticism, he links it to Robert

Antelme's thinking of misfortune:[32] "To think through affliction is to lead thought toward this point at which force is no longer the measure of what must be said and thought; it is to make thought one with this impossibility of thinking that thought is for itself, and is like its center."[33] This impossibility of thinking affliction, this impossibility of thinking the camps, is *a large-scale interruption of thought*. It also gives this interruption the possibility of sovereignty: a point at which it is so strongly affirmed that any nihilism becomes unthinkable (the nihilism that always hangs over the "Yes" of Nietzsche and Artaud). This is because this interruption, when accompanied by a thinking of attentiveness, allows political thought—the thought of controlling the other—to be interrupted, and replaced with friendship and community. Attentiveness is an "emptiness of thought oriented by a gentle strength," terms that are used to describe Antelme: "the perfection of attentiveness which, by means of others' gaze, opens a path toward the closure of affliction."[34] For Blanchot, this attentiveness to the other is "always already" an attentiveness to language (to the other's political language, to the political language of all). "Language is the site of attentiveness," he concludes in the article on Simone Weil.[35] Poetic language is the advent of political language. According to Blanchot, this is also what Mallarmé's poems teach us: In an "undefined tension in which a new time seems to develop, the pure time of expectation and attentiveness," thought watches over "the brilliance of the poetic impulse" (234).

"This frail literature, barely existing, is not much to count on in the struggle against the great hoax."[36] Blanchot expects this kind of objection, which he anticipates in his article on *Mythologies*. A month before the first text on Simone Weil, he set in opposition to the nihilist power of values "this frail literature," this modern, frail literature of "the very last" (*de toute extremité*). In it he sees "the affirmation most staunchly opposed to myths" (and we must note that reading myths, for instance with Orpheus and the *Odyssey*, is a way of *interrupting* them). "True, it is not much," he concedes. "But here weakness, and the language that models itself on what lies short of all force, impede the trickster more than strength, his inevitable accomplice." Weakness bothers those who seek to deceive; it bothers the dictator who is denounced as early as March 1955 ("the man of *dictare*, of imperious repetition" (220), whom he did not yet distinguish from "the providential man" (221)); it bothers those who sought to impose "the cult of the individual" (248). Political vigilance, undeniably and cruelly supplemented by Blanchot's experience, is another aspect of the interruption at the heart of his thinking of language. The political returns to the political through language. To be more specific: sometimes it would use the same words as before (the return, then the *refusal*), but without any submission to rhetoric and fully aware of the interruption of speech, of thought. And although weakness does not easily trouble power, this interruption needs still to be linked to collective practice, in order to do more than just trouble those who hate thought and who can say only that Voltaire must not be thrown in jail.[37]

During these years, Blanchot also pursued this demanding, obliging line of thought by drafting *The Last Man*. "Language is the site of attentiveness." In it, dialogue, conversation, speech, silence are the sites of attentiveness. They also provide its strength, its desire, its quality as an oeuvre, they create and continue to endlessly create the desire to be attentive: to be attentive to the other. The impossibility of any last word, the impossibility of death are theirs alone, they do not fear any return of nihilism. The last word, death, has already come and gone: the last philosopher has died. Perhaps there remains only the silence left by he whom in March 1955 Blanchot calls the "last writer."

Blanchot would offer literature a new form of dialogue, a new form of conversation. They are not unconnected to the way in which, in the same period, he starts (again) to intervene politically. The limitations imposed by discourse and by genre were rejected, as Blanchot is well known for having called for. It is perhaps in this "triple metamorphosis"—political, philosophical, literary—where Blanchot sought to transcribe the new truth.

"When one is forced to give up oneself, one must either perish or begin again; perish in order to begin again."[38] Such is the movement that Blanchot named "the leap of the future."

Guy Lévis Mano published fewer than six hundred copies of the reprint of the *NNRF* article of April 1953 as *The Beast of Lascaux*, a discreet homage to René Char, in 1958. *The Book to Come* would appear in early summer 1959, and the critics were far from won over. Their disorientation led them to varying judgments, from accusations to defensiveness, from circumspection to occasional admiration.[39] They had already reacted similarly to the *récits*, *The Space of Literature*, and the *nouveau roman*, a label that they were making popular. The climate seemed even to approach exasperation. The 1960s were approaching, the decade that saw lightning bolts from the Sorbonne rain down upon Roland Barthes, as well as the agitations of *Tel Quel*, a journal whose first issue of March 1960 gave one of its highest "marks" to *The Book to Come*.

Between the major figures for whom Blanchot was a decisive influence and the bureaucrats of criticism whose obscene stupidity was often more tragic than farcical, perhaps Roger Judrin best expressed the gap that Blanchot's books sought to create, in a piece on *The Last Man*: "This book makes me fearful as would a precious object that I cannot avoid breaking. . . . Ultimately, I admit that—to speak Blanchot—this *récit* is closer to me than I am to it."[40]

CHAPTER 45

Of an Amazing Lightness
The Last Man (1953–1957)

An epilogue to the trilogy? In *The Last Man*, a *récit* published at the beginning of 1957, we find another narrator who is a writer—but is he still writing?[1] On the table in the room, "there [are] some written pages."[2] What are we to make of them? What are we to make of the self, the self that has written? What happens when the last writer encounters the last man?

This encounter takes place in a sanatorium in the mountains, a place from "where we could see the sea, very far away" (38). If it is still possible to situate a *récit* in Blanchot's life, we might place this one in Cambo, not far from the Atlantic. The supposed age of the characters might confirm this. The last man is slightly older than forty. The young woman and the narrator are markedly younger, and yet old enough for the woman, who has been at the sanatorium for many years, to be known as the "queen of the place" (67). Perhaps she has even been there since childhood. The narrator, who is much less ill and who has recently arrived, is perhaps thirty years old.

There are descriptions of the gardens, the buildings, the corridors, the rooms. Grievances, coughing, cries violently interrupt the night, each night, leading to a terrifying indifference. "The moans, the calls, at night, still had something dry about them that didn't arouse pity" (53). The last man's suffering is among the most intense. "He is a man alone, a stranger, gravely ill. For a long time now he has not left his bed, he doesn't move, he doesn't speak" (11). His silence is the zero state of suffering, the cry's final moments.

Who are these exhausted characters? In terms of names and identities, we never find out. We know only that they are narrator who writes or has written, a young woman with whom he has a relationship. A "last man," sometimes referred to as "professor," who has no characteristics of the last inhabitant of the planet or a master of morals. He bears no resemblance to the last man of Nietzsche's *Thus Spake Zarathustra*: he who razes space, the offspring of the old morality. In Nietzsche's terms, he is something like the "last philosopher."[3] In Kafka's, he is the man who loves great city in the East, as well as his own anguish, and writes a *Journal* whose questions he reformulates ("Are you altogether forsaken? Can't you speak for yourself? Must we think in your absence, die in your place?" 7).[4] For Hermann Hesse, he would be the wolf from the steppes who constantly surveys his room, the solitary and ill man, the "genius of suffering"—he who twice compares himself, explicitly, to a wolf.[5] For Thomas Mann, he would be the inhabitant of the magic mountain.[6] After Beckett, and also after Michaux, he could a fantastic, glorious, exhausted figure. In Levinasian terms, he has patience, and in Antelme's, there is the thought of misfortune. "The bare presence of suffering" recalls Antonin Artaud.[7] These various links, sketched quickly here, have a single aim: approaching a point of lightness where life, suddenly and finally, is soon to be spent. This is one reason why, along with *Death Sentence*, this is one of Blanchot's most admired *récits*.

The last man is like the last of literature's characters, composed of the most sovereign characters—of their very shapelessness, of their anteriority to any shape, of the gulf from which they only emerge when the book is to come. "Often, what he told of his story was so obviously borrowed from books" (6). But if the last man is the man of books, if he is Kafka, if he is a wolf, if he is Castorp, he is also Blanchot, that figure who constantly tells his story by borrowing from books: *in and from the name of the other*. Having an extraordinary fate makes one fearful, it makes one feel guilty and ashamed. To meet when one is "dead, then ... dying" (4) is both terrifying and paralyzing. Having to borrow one's words rules out glorification; effacement rules out the question of reputation. Via a long journey, a long detour, all of these situations return the man in question to life, a life that has continued, meanwhile, in a displaced manner, masked, in the other time belonging to literature.

The figure of the last man had haunted Blanchot for almost twenty years. Bataille attests to this in *Inner Experience*:

> Blanchot was asking me: why not pursue my inner experience as if I were the *last man*? In a certain sense.... However, I know that I am the reflection of the multitude and the sum of its anguish. In another sense, if were the last man, the anguish would be the most insane imaginable! I could in no way escape, I would remain before infinite annihilation, thrown back into myself, or even: empty, indifferent. But inner experience is a conquest, and it is such *for others*![8]

There could be no better commentary on *The Last Man*. Only one point remains: the contradictions raised by Bataille are all dissolved by the last man of the *récit*, so completely that his various anguishes come together with his severe neutrality and his boundless generosity at a point of exhaustion and overthrowing.

It is by reaching an extreme state of sensibility, even by disinterring such a state (when the nocturnal companion takes on the stiffness of a corpse),[9] that the *récit* attempts to indicate the minimal but also originary nature of a life of exhaustion. The last man is an *almost* man: "almost nothing distinguished him from others" (1), but this "almost nothing" allows for a precise, rigorous, minute description: distilled or instilled, and foggy, extending into the far reaches of perception and of sensibility. His "near stammering" (3) places him at the boundary of speech and silence, confrontation and pain, giving and withdrawal, the repeated murmur and the forgetful world. His face, which is "of a radiant near-invisibility" (12), returns from death as if from a divine sojourn. This *almost* is the *always already* of the critical texts. Both represent interruption into fatigue, the possibility or the attempt to reflect upon it, to think it. Both introduce the same rupture within language: for both *almost* and *always already*, time is broken down. Placed before a noun, *almost* acts adjectivally, weakly, almost invisibly, discreetly questioning the force that all noun-forms convey. Paradoxically, passivity toughens, separates, hermeticizes language, not by making it difficult to comprehend vocabulary or syntax, but by introducing an indifference to figuration (what is a face when it is invisible? what is speech when it stutters?). "As soon as I was given to use that word" (1): the *récit* begins with such a presupposition, with a presupposition that will never be dislodged. This passive form acts on behalf of mystery alone: chance, the power of chance set in opposition to any will to power.

This passivity brought into language is the mark of the last man's gift and sovereignty. "Retiring" and "imperious" (1), "worn out by knowledge as one who knows things can be" (24–25) and yet divinely childish, he still manages to be reserved in such a way as to take others into his charge. He is not the "first man" that Thomas was, he no longer has the same mythical capacity, the gift of being able to metamorphose.[10] He is the last man: the man of "the absence of myth" in the language developed by Bataille at the time, the man of the absence of poetry, of the impossibility of poetry, of the interruption of thought. "I can't think about myself," (2) he confides: No one can now think of himself or herself without thinking of *humankind*.

Such a gentleness is at the mercy of all desire for violence; the narrator's does not escape this (55–56). But it also has a strength of its own, taken from the gulf of a solitude abundantly offered to the other's becoming. It opens up an unexpected ability to listen:

> someone other than me was listening to him, someone who was perhaps richer, vaster, and yet more singular, almost too general, as though, confronting him, what had been "me" had strangely awakened into an "us," the presence and united force of the shared mind. (2)

It creates a virtual feeling of belonging to a community, paradoxically but efficiently suited to a new affirmation of singularity. This gentleness also allows for "the happiness of saying yes, of endlessly affirming" (4). This is not without pain, nor without demands. "Why is that all you think? Why can't you help me?" (1). In truth, these are not questions; they are necessary admissions that something is lacking, and they impose an ethical transcendence on thought. To think *beyond* then becomes a way of helping a singularity that no longer thinks of itself. To think *beyond* is to help humankind insofar as it is represented by the last man. The last man is the thinnest point of humanity; he is the last man (*dernier homme*) in the sense that one speaks of the very latest thing (*du dernier cri*). To think *beyond* is thus to think "at the very last" (*à toute extrémité*, 23), the very lastness of death, of the human race. The formulation just cited also refers, when used in an article of February 1955 and therefore contemporary to the writing of *The Last Man*, to the lastness of art and, more specifically, of the novel, whose end has been predicted for centuries, says Blanchot. Adorno's statement on the impossibility of poetry has nothing to do with the traditionalists' attempt to salvage something.

> Art is always, in every artist, the surprise of what *is*, without being possible, the surprise of what must begin at the very last [*à toute extremité*], the work of the end of the world, art that finds its beginning only where there is no more art and where its conditions are lacking.[11]

The *récit* therefore has to think "at the very last" or "at every extremity," where there is no more art, no more world, no more death.[12] The interruption of thought is the interruption of the *récit*; it is also its genesis, and this is what *The Last Man* accomplishes, this *récit* of how the interruption of the *récit* takes hold.

The Last Man provides a figure for what, outside myth, outside the symbolic and outside narration itself, can still be transmitted by a *récit* in a world quite prepared to live without narratives. What, then, can be made of miraculous experiences? How far-reaching can the damage caused by mankind's cultural death be (would this be a culture stripped of all types of belief)? Could it reach the heart of its body and its thought? Why is such a death blindly tolerated, to what state of fatigue, exhaustion, illness will we allow ourselves to be reduced? Is the thought of death itself mortal? Into what death does it plunge us? How workless does it leave us? Is that what we must henceforth communicate? This risk?

Now, in the mid-1950s, Blanchot can finally risk the last man in the *récit*. The last man is he whose withdrawal allows the world to be recreated. It is he who allows the writer to attempt to enter a new, Mallarmean space, in which at once the origin (the last man) and the site of withdrawal (the narrator) can be given shape. It is he who thinks the limitlessness of suffering, who suffers the limitlessness of thought (and he helps the narrator to think it, to suffer it). "When he thinks," the young woman says of him, "he suffers, and when he doesn't think, his suffering is naked" (51). Let us recall the end of the article on Artaud, published in November 1956, when *The Last Man* was being readied for publication: "suffering and thinking are linked in a secret way.... Do extreme thought and extreme suffering open up the same horizon? Is to suffer ultimately to think?"[13] Any response to these questions would be singularly reductive. We could say that suffering is already thinking, is the interruption of thought; that thinking is suffering, if one manages to remain faithful to that interruption; that not thinking is to increase suffering if it consists in laying suffering bare by depriving it of any language, which is to say of any community. But if to think is to sacrifice thought (to sacrifice: to alter without neglecting, says Bataille), staying faithful to sacrifice also demands that we stay faithful to refusal, and that we think the affirmation that sacrifice, joy, and refusal all represent.[14] The last man is he whose strength (his faithfulness to sacrifice) and gentleness (his faithfulness to refusal) will allow the thinking of misfortune to be a thinking of joy; they will allow the narrator to write this, and the author to complete the cycle of novels in order to begin his ethical and political interventions (or interruptions).

Completing the fictional cycle allows the fragmentation of writing to begin. In *The Last Man* the sheer number of noun phrases is striking, as is the fracture that they impose on the *récit*, their dryness, the effect they have as a block that does not conform to the movement of creation, irreducible to the cycle of metamorphosis, a splintering of the world and deterioration, even of silence. These "calm blocks here fallen from obscure disaster" always appear in unexpected ways, providing constant danger for the continuity of the narrative thread, which they deprive of any verb, even as they accrue in numbers, providing a stippling effect.[15] The narration—the relation, the communication—is constructed by both retaining flow and at the same time (but in another temporality) placing alongside it various forms of confrontation, withdrawal or brokenness. The tensions between separation and attraction, oblivion and memory, invisibility and figurability, loss and discovery, limitlessness and claustrophobia are what elevate the *récit*, raising it to a high level of thinking (though without relying on any notion of purification). As in the space of criticism, in this space where death strikes, where each group of nouns represents a crude and devastated drive, even the appearance of disappearance disappears, and interruption and fragmentation set in.

The last man is therefore also he who is capable of opening a space of gentleness within himself, a gentleness held out over and against the worst violence, sometimes even encouraging the illusion that he might be able to think everything. He is capable of effacing himself before this space that he creates, that he delivers unto us, and unto which we are delivered. This happens in the second part, which is really a sort of long epilogue, less than a third of the total length of the *récit*. Alone, the narrator confronts a space that has no center and seems to be searching for something within him: "something hungrily obvious" (66). Stripped of anything that might align it with mysticism, this space of *writing* exercises a mad pressure, echoes with nocturnal noises, and exalts the impossible elevation that it promises: "I stayed on the crest of that narrow drunkenness, cramped against a phantom of lightness, controlling a feeling of pain, of joy, not controlling it. It was light, joyous, of an amazing lightness" (66). This feeling has a limitless communitarianism about it. *Writing* is what takes us back to the community, "that chorus whose bedrock I situated over there, somewhere in the direction of the sea." "That was where we all were, over there" (67).

It is above all in this second part that these groups of nouns and this impossible syntax fill the text, and that it fragments and breaks into short dialogues printed in italics, announcing the fragmentary aesthetic that for Blanchot is powerfully linked to communitarian feeling, and that is the aesthetic of his last major works. In this section, he erases the differences between characters, allowing what is said to be readable in various ways, as if the last man were dying in and through all of the words written. This second part, a veritable interruption of the *récit*, gives to us fragmentary, neutral, free, shared speech: a "we" that is alone capable of evoking glory, Thomas's inverse hypostasis, the effaced shadow of the last man. This "We" is not immanent, but is made up of the encounters opened by the last man, the interruption of the personhood present in each of us. "When someone stops speaking it is hard not to go looking for the missing thought" (9).

"The spirit of lightness" has the virtue of giving one over to the "innocence of the worst" (5). The narrator is given over to this. The relation to the last man is goes for all speech. It returns the guilty subject to freedom, to lightness. The *récit* constructs—as if by transference—such a companion of writing. This construction always threatens, of course, to sink into idealization, into a redeeming divinization. Accepted, this risk would limit the last man, assuming that he also waits for an admission, "the unreserved admission that would put an end to everything" (25). But the feeling of community—friendship—is created precisely by such an admission's being recognized as impossible. It is precisely because community is founded on the impossibility of the admission that it is shameful. A dangerous model of friendship, we might say, a way of granting a pardon without having any guarantees; or at least if we had forgotten the last man's sovereignty, the convictions it leads to, the demands it imposes (the thought of misfortune, the interruption of thought), the values it refuses (purification, salvation). The friendship thus created exists only by placing last men in relation to one another; the community thus created exists only by relating to the lastness present in each of us. For Blanchot, the last man is also what is most originary: "perhaps he is only me, from the very beginning me without me, a relationship that I don't want to embark upon, that I push away and that pushes me away" (26). A relationship henceforth open, a relationship ultimately opened up by *dying* and *writing*.

CHAPTER 46

Grace, Strength, Gentleness
Meeting Robert Antelme (1958)

A little over a year after having published *The Last Man*, Maurice Blanchot met Robert Antelme.¹

Perhaps their paths had already crossed in the corridors at Gallimard, as had been the case with Blanchot and Dionys Mascolo. Probably Blanchot had already discussed the author of *The Human Race* with Louis-René des Forêts, whom he met in 1953 on the panels of various prizes, or with Georges Bataille, who was linked to the Rue Saint-Benoît group in 1955, with the formation of the Comité d'Action Contre la Poursuite de la Guerre en Afrique du Nord (Committee for Action against the Continuation of the War in North Africa). But the events of the spring and summer of 1958 took place before Blanchot met in person the man whose book he had read almost ten years previously.

He had read his work, liked it, been so impressed by it that he remained silent and wrote *The Last Man* before speaking to him. When they did finally meet, there was little risk: Their friendship was already certain.²

It was a strange encounter: a man possessed of a rare authority, one acquired through the grace, the strength, and the gentleness of a sovereign narrative; an authority that was not to be atoned for, and yet that had given him no renown. And another man, responsible for a past no longer spoken about, and recognized as the leading figure of French critical intelligence. Robert Antelme alone, probably, could disregard the writer's status, reminding him of his responsibility and giving him his own grace, as if it shone through from one to the other. In any case, he did not need to do so (and would not have done so). When they met, this grace had already made its appearance.

This grace ruled out any possible reappearance of nihilism, freed up an infinite attentiveness to the other, gave back the possibility of public action and closeness to the community. It led Blanchot to what the word "Judaism," from Strasbourg on, had meant for him (or perhaps it facilitated his access to this).[3] It led to a careful vigilance.

As early as 1945, although he was saved only in June, Antelme wrote several articles taking positions on the war, on prisoners, on the concentration camps. In 1947 the first edition of *The Human Race* appeared, with a publishing house that he had founded. He joined the Communist Party in 1946, was excluded from it in 1950, and cofounded the Comité d'Action in 1955. During this time, despite the confirmation in his written work that he had changed course, despite his various displays of solidarity, despite the formation of a thinking capable of relating to real experience, Blanchot had not yet performed any public action nor adopted any position regarding contemporary affairs. The potential authority of his *refusal* was entirely theoretical. Only privately did he avow his disenchantment, his disgust, his feeling of being politically fragmented. Antelme, for his part, felt entitled to take a range of actions due to perhaps the most legitimate principle that history could produce: "Anything that resembles, even vaguely, what we saw there literally destroys us."[4] This was the case with Stalinism and with the war in Algeria, neither of which he could condone, and against which he was already rebelling.

The authority that a book such as *The Writing of the Disaster* would give Blanchot would only have meaning and possibility because they were given to him by Levinas and Antelme. And the authority that his new political refusals would give him would consist solely in the grace of having been by Antelme's side, with a sense of duty and nobility similar to those this friend had already explored: "To the madness of vengeance, to secret abstention, to the cowardliness of those who were unharmed, we say: no."[5] Perhaps Blanchot only came across this sentence after meeting Antelme, whose few articles were little known at the time. But its meaning is everywhere in *The Human Race*, as well as in what Blanchot knew about its author from his friends. For Antelme was precisely the person who had been able to carry out this prodigious about-face: no longer leaving things at "secret abstentions, the cowardliness of those who were unharmed." He alone could teach Blanchot how much he had become his own prisoner, prisoner of his past, of his judgments. In the same article, Antelme had written that the prisoner is "a sacred being because he is a being surrendered, who has lost any chance he once had." Antelme was precisely he who brought deliverance, not removing the burden or providing salvation, but giving Blanchot the strength to carry it. After the *interruption* of thought, after writing *The Last Man*, the *14 Juillet* project came at the right moment to force Blanchot to return to the contemporary. Without falling into the spectacle of public statements, he took seriously the responsibility of showing—initially to itself—how necessary his trenchant stance, his refusal, his presence was. Antelme's authority echoed within Blanchot as a demand that was at once terrifying and pacifying: to act thus was the only way to relive the past *totally*.

Antelme therefore allowed another link to death, to dying, to be made ("humanity as a whole was called upon to die through the ordeal suffered by some of its members," Blanchot would write).[6] The fact that this new friendship was founded on this link, in a space that was foreign both to vengeance and forgiveness, via an immediate gift, is what gives it its grace. In Daniel Dobbels's words,

> This grace was weightless, it left no impression on whoever experienced it; it opened this "miraculously most neutral space" where differences of thought, of rhythm, of times recognize what they share that is unique, irreducible, held in common. This grace was the unshakeable awareness that a link exceeds or precedes all judgment, one so just that it was like the need or desire for justice that shines through all speech.[7]

Such is the grace that came down to Maurice Blanchot at this time, shining through speech.

This grace did not arrive thanks to any supernatural force, however. Blanchot had travelled a long way, as his *récits* show. This *space of literature* is the site of the recognition they gained. All of his friends bear witness to this: Maurice Nadeau said that Antelme was a "character of Blanchot's," and perhaps we can take this to mean not that Antelme could have featured in Blanchot's fiction, but that Blanchot was the figure made possible by his own fiction. He was a character-version of Antelme in the sense that his fiction had created his persona. Effaced even in their first meeting, these characters produced two silent, accepting presences who were similarly convinced of the necessity of refusal and commitment (and a particular type of commitment). In this light, what Marguerite Duras said of Robert Antelme becomes a portrait of Blanchot too: "He did not speak and yet he spoke. He offered no advice, and yet nothing could be done without consulting him. He was intelligence itself and yet he hated the discourse of intelligence." And this: "I am unable to name this: perhaps it is grace."[8]

Robert Antelme's role in the return of Blanchot's narrative oeuvre to silence was probably not a small one. *The Last Man*, "their" most fully shared *récit*, was also almost the last. *Awaiting Oblivion* oscillates between being narrative and fragmentation. The encounter with the pure song of the sirens was abandoned. Nadeau even states that for Blanchot, Antelme always represented the refusal to write; he was the author of only one narrative. Michel Surya recalls this forcefully: "Because literature could not live up *more than once* to what he wanted it to say. *The Human Race* belongs to literature in a way that condemns literature. Which is to say that it is happy to leave literature to those who have nothing else."[9]

And for his friend, it was as if Blanchot were the only writer, as Antelme said himself: "If I wrote something . . . it could only be something that resembled the *récits* of Maurice Blanchot."[10] Neither wrote any further; no more *récits*. For Blanchot, the misfortune of thought still had to be thought through, the interruption of speech still had to be written: ever-renewed loyalty had to be commented upon, in the movement of refusal and the presence of friendship.[11]

CHAPTER 47

In the Gaze of Fascination
The Return to Paris (1957–1958)

On September 25, 1957, Maurice Blanchot's mother passed away. She was nearly eighty-three years old. Had she returned to Quain in order to die there, or simply for the end of the summer? She died in the dwelling where she, as well as all her children, had been born. A few days previously, Blanchot had still been in Èze. He was with his mother when she died. These are difficult moments, as we are reminded by the scenes in *Thomas the Obscure*, *Death Sentence*, and even the few texts that subtly evoke a mother's presence. In 1943, in the *Journal des Débats*, Blanchot had written about an autobiographical book by Jouhandeau, and he had not failed to emphasize a chance occurrence of the inverse image of his own mother: Jouhandeau's family called their mother Marie, although she "was baptized Alexandrine." Praising the author's unashamed depiction of a son's love, he saw it as a reflection of maternal love and the necessary legacy of a temperament necessary "to defy the abyss."[1] More recently, he had evoked the "force of the maternal figure" in "The Essential Solitude": "if the Mother exerts this fascinating attraction it is because, appearing when the child lives totally under a fascinated gaze, she concentrates in herself all the powers of enchantment."[2]

For many years, Maurice Blanchot's mother had lived with her sister Élise, in her daughter Marguerite's house. Élise had died on September 28, 1953, in Chalon. Fate was stubbornly symbolic: Many of Blanchot's relatives died on similar dates, shortly after his birthday on the twenty-second of that month. When his mother died, he had been fifty for three days.

Marguerite had taken her two elderly relatives into her care, her powerless mother, handicapped by coxalgia, and her aunt who had gone blind. While for day-to-day, domestic reasons she thought it necessary for her mother to be there and not elsewhere, this made for a heavy load; relatives sometimes said that the daughter remained unmarried out of to devotion to her elderly mother. The three women lived together in relative financial comfort: Marguerite's piano lessons, renting out the ground floor of the house, the rent from the tenant farming at Devrouze, which had been invested profitably in small bonds, together brought in enough money to allow the purchase of an apartment in a former hotel at the tip of Cap Martin, close to the Èze property, which itself proved profitable through holiday rentals. Demanding, cautious, *bressanes* (from the Bresse region), as they say in Chalon, the three women managed their land themselves and authoritatively. Although they could have had a telephone, they did not get one installed: The few messages that did arrive were passed on by their neighbors, Mr. and Mrs. Herbinet.

Their mother's death seems to have deeply affected the children. Maurice Blanchot spent the winter with his brother René at Rue Violet in Paris.

At this time he considered moving back to the capital for good. In 1958, no later than Summer, he moved to a one-bedroom apartment in the Rue Madame, on the corner of the Rue de Vaugirard. It would become his best-known address: it corresponded to the new period, around fifteen years, in which he was much more present on the public stage. He would meet people in the Café de la Mairie on the Place Saint-Sulpice; he would go to Marguerite Duras and Dionys Mascolo's apartment in the Rue Saint-Benoît; he would even almost be George Bataille's neighbor, for the last few months of the latter's life. Some of his friends visited him: Dionys Mascolo remembered a large library, full of books, and Louis-René des Forêts recalls being shown into an austere room, furnished at random, with subdued lighting. For his part, it was the total absence of books, even on the table, that surprised him: "I felt slightly that I was entering the room of Monsieur Teste," he recounted.[3] Blanchot used to say that in Paris he was not in his own city, but in that of his brother René. Did he ever feel at home? Was he not always at his brother's house, in one way or another? This was a family link that was never broken.

CHAPTER 48

Refusal, II: In the Name of the Anonymous
The *14 Juillet* Project (1958–1959)

And so Blanchot experienced the political events of 1958 in Paris.

Dionys Mascolo and Jean Schuster responded to the generals' insurrection in Algiers on May 13, and to the Fourth Republic's call of distress to De Gaulle, with a manifesto that was made public on May 17 and that took note of the demystification underway: "nothing equivocal remains about De Gaulle." It called for the people to act, for a general strike, for the formation of committees to fight against fascism. Such were the preludes for the project named *Le 14 Juillet* that took shape in the following weeks.[1]

The friends of the Rue Saint-Benoît group, which met in the apartment Marguerite Duras had been living in since the war, and centered on her, Dionys Mascolo, and Robert Antelme, would play a major role in Blanchot's political undertakings from 1958 onward. These included Edgar Morin, Maurice Nadeau, Claude Roy, and Elio and Ginetta Vittorini, as well as Monique Régnier, Robert Antelme's partner. At the end of the war or shortly after, some belonged to the communist party and were expelled from it because they were anti-Stalinist (or anticonformist, the freedom of their lifestyle having a bad reputation in the Communist Party). "The place where we live together is a place permanently open to friends, a glass house, like the one Breton dreamed of," in Mascolo's words. Through community links, the feeling of responding to the same demand—a refusal not infatuated by communist or existentialist post-war ideas of treason— Breton brought the surrealist group closer to the group in the Rue Saint-Benoît in the 1950s. This was the moment of the first postcommunist militant stirrings, notably the Committee of 1955, which also included Bataille and Des Forêts. What Mascolo would name "communism of thought" and with Hölderlin was "the life of the mind [*esprit*] between friends," was indeed already at work in this communist-leaning communal space: "for our part, we were already living as if after the revolution, and in a sense we had got a head start over it."[2]

With De Gaulle taking power, the group stayed together after the disbanding of the 1955 Committee against the Continuation of the war in North Africa (meanwhile, the Committee of Revolutionary Intellectuals had failed). In May Mascolo and Schuster, from the Surrealist group, decided to found *Le 14 Juillet*. The journal's title, as well as those of the first editorial and of Mascolo's first text, indicate clearly enough what type of engagement this was: it proposed a faithfulness to the *revolution*, a return to the *resistance* which had been hijacked by Gaullists and Stalinists, an unconditional *refusal* of providential power. Fear of fascism, hatred of personal power, refusal of the "supreme savior," insurrection against the Petainism threatening the French people: all of these motivated Mascolo and Schuster to call for new links to be created between intellectuals and the working class in order to prepare for "the revolutionary task." For this first edition, published on July 14 itself, they gathered together no fewer than nineteen texts, including pieces by Antelme, Breton, Duras, Duvignaud, Des Forêts, Lefort, Morin, Nadeau, Parain, Péret, Pouillon, and Vittorini.

On his return to political events, Blanchot would later write that:

> There is, finally, for the person whose vocation is to remain in retreat, far from the world (in that place where speech is the guardian of silence), the pressing necessity to expose himself to the "risks of public life" by discovering a responsibility for someone who, apparently, means nothing to him, and by joining in the shouting and the clamor, when, on behalf of that which is closest, he has to give up the sole demand that is properly his own: that of the unknown, of strangeness and of distance.[3]

The word "finally" signals both that he had been released from a long-standing stance, and that his thinking was now open to the future. It is a fact: Blanchot's critical writing had been growing more and more political since the Liberation, although without specific outlets (without reproducing a borrowed, more or less appropriate rhetoric). In doing so, it reflected on itself, on its own origin and possibility. He now gave himself to this other vocation, but did so in the name of the demand that he only renounced in order to accomplish; this other vocation, other appeal or other voice was that of "shouting and clamor," was carried out in the name of an Other that escaped comprehension as soon as it was identified, in the name of the anonymous and the rumble of its presence.

The first "other" in whose name Blanchot "opened up" had a name: Dionys Mascolo. Mascolo has stated how dazzled he was, a few days after the first issue of *Le 14 Juillet* appeared, to receive the following short note from Blanchot: "I want you to know that I am in agreement with you. I accept neither the past nor the present."[4] He perhaps did not suspect how far these few words also concerned the past and the present of the person who had written them. Mascolo would later annotate the letter with the words "great joy"; this was an overwhelmingly positive piece of news, "more than if a whole crowd had joined the movement."[5] This great joy also speaks volumes about what Blanchot's status as an intellectual must have been in 1958; but it responded to another sense of astonishment, which was no less striking. Blanchot would speak of it later in almost mystical terms: "It was political responsibility and exigency that somehow made me return and turn toward Dionys, who, I was certain of it (or felt it), would be my recourse. In receiving *Le 14 Juillet*, I hear its call and respond to it with resolute agreement."[6] Having recourse in this way to Mascolo, a go-between who became a friend, was all the more significant because it gave him access to Robert Antelme, whom Blanchot now met; and it brought him closer again to Emmanuel Levinas who now saw him as totally "judaized."[7]

Blanchot was astonished for other reasons too. A few years earlier, he had written in detail on Mascolo's book on communism, which accorded with his own political as well as philosophical and literary concerns. He even risked concluding that "one must go further than he does along the path set out by his thinking."[8] He knew of Mascolo's interest in Marx, but also in Nietzsche and Hölderlin, and what linked them even more was their thinking of what linked these figures. In July 1958, the similarities or convergences of his thought with those of Mascolo, Antelme, or Des Forêts could not have failed to strike him when he read their articles.[9] His attentiveness to Des Forêts's writing, with his denunciation of the nihilist and tendentious political rhetoric that abused language and betrayed thought;

the interruption of reason announced by Antelme, who even with his principles being radically put to the test "says that everything is always possible but that today nothing is possible"; his appreciation of the silence heard in the cries of the May 28 demonstration ("just and fraternal, not aggressive, not cruel, aware"); all of these culminated in "Unconditional Refusal," the title of Mascolo's article which Blanchot would adopt for his own in the journal's second issue. Omitting the adjective, he named it "Le Refusal"—the unconditional or absolute nature of this concept is nonetheless clear thanks to the definite article and the first lines of the text.[10] The twin nature of these titles indicates well enough how Blanchot saw his return to politics. This was a return in the sense of the politics being drawn up at the time by Robert Antelme, in a tone that was at once Hegelian, post-Hegelian, and marked by the thinking of *The Human Race*: "The story of each individual is written by his limitless need for recognition; friendship designates this infinite capacity for recognition." The demand for the independence of Algeria was made in the name of his principle.

Blanchot was not content with demonstrating that he was in agreement. A few days after his first letter, he wrote a second one, accompanied by "Refusal"—for publication. Stripped of three short sentences, the letter itself was also published as an introduction to the text. Mascolo, who must have again been "dazzled," telephoned Blanchot. They met, drew up shared plans, wrote to one another. Blanchot joined the group in the Rue Saint-Benoît; soon he would be helping to edit the journal.

"Refusal" was the first text after the editorial of the second issue, which appeared on October 25, a month after a "special communication" that, following a remarkable line of reasoning, declared "De Gaulle's government illegal and Charles de Gaulle an intruder," as well as refusing in advance to recognize the results of a referendum in which nearly 80 percent of the French population would approve the new Constitution, and calling for "the union of free thinkers to put UNCIVIC-MINDEDNESS [*incivisme*] on the agenda" and "the spreading of the spirit of insubordination." With its letter of introduction and an image by Daumier, Blanchot's text took up a whole page. It was, however, fairly short, and Mascolo's typographical largesse in relation to it showed how much store he put in opening this new issue with this strong, authoritative, radical stance that was so foreign to individual debates on which strategies to adopt, how Marxist and Leninist strategies were to be adapted, or detailed commentary on the rebellion in Algeria. Blanchot's task in his piece was to justify his return. "Something has happened," he wrote in the letter; "a rupture has occurred," responds the text; De Gaulle had returned to power, "this time carried not on the shoulders of the Resistance, but of mercenaries," he added in a note when the text was republished in *Friendship*, thirteen years later.[11] It was important for Blanchot to distinguish refusal from any appearance of nihilism, and he shows that this "certain, unshakable, rigorous No," this "absolute, categorical" refusal, is open to the future, its power (and its difficulty) lying in what "henceforth each of our assertions should confirm." Blanchot thus distinguishes refusal from nihilism, following Robert Antelme, in the spirit of *The Human Race* and more explicitly of the text he published in the first issue, defining refusal as a "movement without contempt, without exaltation, and anonymous, as far as possible, for the power to refuse cannot come from us, nor in our name alone, but from a very poor beginning that belongs first of all to those who cannot speak."[12]

Exaltation and contempt: precisely what had characterized his previous refusals. Distinguishing refusal from nihilism can also be seen as a way of reclaiming language from the other extreme, from the far right that had been his home in the 1930s, to the very word "refusal." Down to the very word, and to the word alone, if indeed we accept that at that time Blanchot had been overburdened with rhetoric and did not put in place any thinking as such, and that all of his efforts since that time had consisted in abdicating (atoning for) this language with thought, in order to manifest a refusal that was now capable of receiving not the modesty of ideas and the rigor of speech, but what his conclusion to this 1958 text calls the "rigor of thought and the modesty of expression."[13]

The third issue of *Le 14 Juillet* was set for December, at the height of the election campaign and as De Gaulle was about to be inaugurated as president of the Republic. Fearing imminent censorship and dismayed at the passivity of French intellectuals, the editors decided to produce a questionnaire aimed at the latter. Signed by Blanchot, Breton, Mascolo, and Schuster, it was made public on April 10, 1959, and sent to a hundred writers; the twenty-eight responses would be published in what would be the journal's last issue, sarcastically brought out on June 18.[14]

There were some problems in preparing this issue. The correspondence between Blanchot and Mascolo shows that vague ideas of abandoning the journal had already been raised. The feeling of isolation seemed to play a considerable role; it depressed Dionys Mascolo who, reading a letter in a bistro on the Avenue du Maine, scribbled these words on the back of the envelope: "I am henceforth as if on a voyage, a solitary voyage (this explains my carelessness)." It affected Blanchot less, who saw the failure of the movement as the confirmation of the reasons that had given rise to it, and thus as one more reason to continue it by other means. It is thus remarkable that

Blanchot's return to politics was neither vain nor ephemeral; on the contrary, he was totally oriented toward the future and the possibility of building that future. He would also be behind the thinking on the group's various methods of intervention: the questionnaire of 1959, the Declaration of 1960, the project for an *International Review*. Each failure was immediately seized upon as the means of coming up with a new intervention. Each new intervention attempted to get intellectuals on board, with a violence thought necessary to get them out of their reserve, to leave a mark on public debate and to redefine a link with the working classes that had grown stale. Interrupting intellectuals' isolation (their withdrawal, entrenchment, self-sufficiency, self-importance), taking them away from their own glory in order to get them to speak *in the name of the anonymous*, breaking the "essential perversion" with which they acquiesced in advance to the perversion of politicians (with all their attraction glory, their providential certainty); such were the difficult tasks that needed to be taken on. Thus Blanchot continued thinking, even on the political scene, that it was necessary to efface oneself in order to think, to withdraw—like Luria's God—in order to create.

The questionnaire was put together primarily in February. The list of addressees and the five questions formulated by Mascolo and Schuster were put to Blanchot, then to Breton. Blanchot suggested a few names and changed the text in a number of places. Notably, he insisted on a term in the first question, the word "ensemble": "What happened on May 13, 1958, and what has happened since constitute an ensemble whose importance seems to us to have been generally underestimated." It was indeed as an ensemble, as a total and pseudo-sovereign action, that De Gaulle's seizure of power was to be understood, though without being reduced to a single dimension, whether economic, colonial, national, military, or psychic. Blanchot's remark, which was developed at length, in fact constituted the premises of his own response, which he developed in his article in the third issue, "The Essential Perversion."

Blanchot, then, had taken a key role at the journal. Following the responses to the questionnaire, the final issue contained only three texts: those by the two editors-in-chief, and "The Essential Perversion." From a strictly personal point of view, the text responds to the first article given to the *NNRF* six years earlier, "The Essential Solitude." The link is not only a superficial one. For while Blanchot conceives of political action in the light of a discretion that links the author back to his or her initial anonymity, to "the essential solitude," thus recalling that the theory of effacement stemmed from a reading of historical rather than aesthetic sections of Hegel's *Phenomenology*—those conceptualizing the definition and ultimately the annulling of the worker by the work—it must be noted that the "essential perversion" describes exactly the opposite situation. This is to say that historical agents glorify themselves through their works and project their being, providentially, beyond themselves, a being that is completed in history and that itself completes history. The resolute man who is without myths (a rather tragic man, Mascolo would say) is set in opposition to the man who allows for a belief in the resurgence of myths (in their epic form). The providential man is therefore above all he who perverts sacred values. And yet the essence of perversion is not to be found in this alone: just as Blanchot in his January 1953 essay distinguishes the "essential solitude" and "solitude in the world," here it is important to him to distinguish a form of perversion that is more perverse, more insidious, precisely the one that perverts solitude, donning a mask in order to project the image of a magician, a sovereign, an aesthete. "The main feature remains the transformation of political power into a power of salvation."[15] This is the first thing he seeks to demonstrate, the one that proves the raison d'être of the journal and the questionnaire: denouncing the power that makes use of the fascination of the sacred for reductive purposes, such as salvation or the nation. But the essential point is the huge difference between dictatorship and this false sacralization. Blanchot is all the keener on making this distinction since he is convinced that his views on dictatorship, which he had been repeating since March 1955 and his article "Death of the Last Writer," are correct (this thinking was often repeated, often word for word, in his correspondence with Mascolo).[16] De Gaulle was not a dictator, because he did not act.

> The omnipotence that fell to this man alone from the beginning was quite extraordinary; everyone wondered: what *won't* he do with it? But one had to notice with surprise (and cowardly relief) that he wasn't doing anything with it. . . . Hence the following situation gradually became clear: De Gaulle can do everything but, in particular, he can do nothing. He is omnipotent, but the respect that he has for this omnipotence (the feeling of being the whole of France, the sense not only of representing her, but of making her legible and distantly present in her timeless reality) forbids him from using it for any determinate political decision. Thus even if he had political ideas, he could not apply them. . . . We are far from a simple and profane dictatorship. Dictators are constantly parading; they do not speak, they bawl. . . . De Gaulle appears, but only out of duty. Even when he appears, it is as if he were foreign to his appearance. He is withdrawn into himself. He speaks, but secretly.[17]

The article repeats that De Gaulle "is not a man of action." This "bizarre passivity" proper to him parodies the "essential solitude," just as his vanity parodies sovereignty.[18] De Gaulle parodies withdrawal, solitude, invisibility, writing. Blanchot does not attribute De Gaulle's lack of activity to a respect for the rules of democracy: instead, it is said to be the mask for underhand activity, that which—while dictatorship always has a "human" face, which does not worry writers because it leaves their thinking intact— here invisibly corrodes, surreptitiously paralyzes the capacity for reflection, refusal, and insubordination. He does not act, but he allows others to act. This reflection, which was complete by spring 1959, would be richly explored over the next ten years. Following Blanchot, Francis Marmande would say it forcefully: Gaullism was constructed "from hatred for thought."[19] Hatred always pretends to be close to what it hates, even if it knows it has no hope of even identifying it.

Blanchot, and with him *Le 14 Juillet*, was mounting an essential defense of thought. Mascolo's joy and astonishment were also linked to his suspicion (or certainty) that thought would now provide a basis for insubordination. Blanchot's sense of wonder also led to the certainty (or the suspicion) that insubordination would now provide a basis for thought. This exchange of authority or this sharing, in which atonement could be forgotten thanks to an activity that needed no explicit avowals, led to a mutual recognition, a coming-together that defined friendship and politics as the search for a community link (in Antelme's words: infinite recognition). This friendship (this politics) had a name, which Mascolo and Schuster had emphasized in their appeal of September 1958: uncivicmindedness, civil disobedience as a form of citizenship. This spirit of insubordination, which would preside over the Declaration of 1960, was paradoxically attached to the law of the Republic, an ephemeral but necessary transgression that regularly reforged the community link, and that only remained true if it could be based on essential principles: "respect for the living and the dead, hospitality, the inviolability of the human being, the inalienability of truth."[20]

Blanchot had already been adopting these positions "at the very last" (*à toute extrémité*) for several years in the *NNRF*. There, they were linked to the aesthetics of philosophical or literary commentary and had not yet broken out into contemporary events. His involvement with *Le 14 Juillet* did not go unnoticed. It earned him a closely argued rebuttal from Mauriac in *L'Express*. He received troubled letters from Paulhan, a fierce opponent of decolonization and public admirer of how *le général* was able to embody the nation—he defended De Gaulle in *Le Figaro*. In June 1959, when Blanchot probably gave "The Essential Perversion" to Paulhan to read, it was confirmed that the two men were now incompatible. It even seems that they did not see each other again. Blanchot would continue to contribute to the *NNRF*, but less frequently. Other concerns, notably that of collective writing, moved him away from a friend who wrote to him at this time to say that it was enough, if one wished to lose sight of truth, "to group together in an attempt to think it."[21]

Friendships were being broken and formed, lost and found. Char approved of "The Essential Perversion," on which he wrote a magnificent text in 1964, published in *Recherche de la base et du sommet*.

> Politically, Maurice Blanchot can only go from one disappointment to another, which is to say from one courage to another, for he does not have the forgetful mobility of most great contemporary writers. Blanchot is fixed at the depth that distress determines, which is also electrified but not knocked by revolt, the only depth that will count when everything is dust or ashes, taking its cold value, in a new present, from the past alone.[22]

The prose poem also reveals to what extent Blanchot's literary work and political courage are linked. They commit him to the future; they open up unsuspected spaces; they offer to time true seasons and inexhaustible plenty. They prepare one for a "true eternal theater," with the challenge proper to hypnosis, to terror and to cunning; with their ability to inspire confidence in "supreme slowness": the profound rhythm of friendship's knowledge, toward the action in which it is always more rapidly engaged.

When Blanchot saw the complete final issue of *Le 14 Juillet* when it appeared in the summer, his remark to Mascolo brooked no argument: The journal's lack of success and the awkward responses given by writers showed that a new era for the intellectual had begun.

PART V

1960–1968

Sharing distress with you is a happy thing. To walk toward failure, if it is with you, is not to fail. I have sometimes thought that being in step with you would make it not difficult to die. You can see that I am being dragged into saying something about the unknown that can exist in friendship, or about what—within friendship— is stronger than it. Forgive me.

DIONYS MASCOLO, letter to Maurice Blanchot

CHAPTER 49

Note That I Say "Right" and Not "Duty"
The Declaration on the Right to Insubordination in the Algerian War (1960)

At the beginning of 1960, the public face presented by the Gaullist regime was more ambiguous than ever. The events of the fall would begin to dispel this ambiguity. In the spring, when it became known that the trial of the "Jeanson network" would take place after the summer, Dionys Mascolo felt it necessary to intervene. But what form would this intervention take? That, quickly settled upon, of a collective manifesto, the "Declaration on the Right to Insubordination in the Algerian War."[1]

Still, the mask of ambiguity remained: This meant that in Algeria the terror of torture and the desire for indifference, the politicization of military affairs and the militarization of political affairs could continue untroubled. It is true that on September 16, 1969, in an address broadcast on radio and television, De Gaulle did indeed recognize for the first time that Algerians had the right to self-determination, but this was issued in terms unacceptable to the FLN (National Liberation Front). In March 1960, he reaffirmed France's right to remain in Algeria, while also speaking of an "Algerian Algeria" and preparing for the first secret negotiations. The Jeanson network, which helped the Algerian FLN, had recently been exposed; insubordination and desertion were spreading though the French army. Mascolo's aim was to give the men concerned a sense of legitimacy and thus to support Jeanson's cause and his right to do what he had done, as well as to allow writers and thinkers to be insubordinate.

There are at least fifteen versions of this text, which was initially called the "Address to International Opinion." They were all written between April and June 1960. The way the declaration evolved closely resembled *Le 14 Juillet*. The first versions were drafted by Mascolo and Schuster, and the overall scheme did not change greatly. Breton looked at version four, Blanchot at the ninth and subsequent ones. The definitive version was shown at the beginning of July to Sartre and Nadeau, who immediately endorsed it.

The changes made by Blanchot make him, along with Mascolo and Schuster, the third author of the Declaration. As Mascolo noted in the margin of the ninth version, these changes "attenuate what was abrupt in the previous versions": The phrasing was made less clunky, the attacks against the army were moderated. This stylistic and strategic attenuation did not affect the basic intransigence of the text, however: it was Blanchot who replaced "autonomous community" with "independent community," it was he who, in line with his wish to eradicate nihilism, introduced the last expression "not to be taken in by the equivocal aspect of words and values"; last, it was he who—against Mascolo and with Schuster—restored the word "duty" in place of "right" in the key phrase justifying insubordination: "the refusal to serve is a sacred duty."[2]

It was the same Blanchot who, worried about the weakness of the Declaration's title, proposed in a letter of July 26 a new one that Mascolo immediately accepted and then imposed on all those who had signed the text bearing a more neutral title. Blanchot even wanted to add the phrase "and to desertion" to "Declaration on the Right to Insubordination in the Algerian War," although he suspected that the formulation would become less clear and that semantically the addition was unnecessary, as insubordination implied desertion. Curiously, the text became both more intransigent and gentler thanks to Blanchot's new title. The title became a political, provocative, illegal act in itself, responding to the army's provocations and to the illegitimacy of torture. But restoring the word "right" allowed it to avoid any sense of moral obligation. The title was as subtle as it was authoritative; it placed each reader directly before his or her human responsibility. Removing the references to the French Revolution and to the Declaration of the Rights of Man, which had been imposed by Mascolo in the early versions against the wishes of the surrealists, served a similar function: doing so avoided constraining or placing obligations upon one by any system of values which simply by being cited would result in a moralizing effect. The Declaration was proposing a rigorous formulation of a right to recognition with a grace and authority that recalled Robert Antelme's book. It moved away from a notion of "sacred duty" and imposed itself as an illegal act of refusal, as universal respect, as justified conviction (these were the final three phrases of the Declaration, in which strictly speaking it consisted).³ Blanchot would address this in the interview with Madeleine Chapsal in the fall:

> Note that I say Right and not Duty, as some thoughtlessly wanted to hear in the Declaration, undoubtedly because they believe that the formulation of a duty goes farther than that of a right. But this is not so: an obligation refers to an anterior moral that enfolds, guarantees, and justifies it.... A right, on the contrary, is a free power for which everyone is responsible, by himself, in relation to himself, and which completely and freely engages him: nothing is stronger, nothing is more serious.⁴

Later, the authors of the Declaration and those that were close to them would unanimously recognize the good fortune of Blanchot's reintroduction of the word "right" to the title, instead of any "unreflective" formulation, including also his own initial one. The choice of the title forged another link with Antelme, Duras, and Mascolo, who twenty years later would recall the issue almost aphoristically: "Always a *right*, never a *duty*."⁵ This link offered recognition based in strength and in gentleness. The singularity of Blanchot's style and of his face were—as it were—superimposed on to the stormy, interrupted, and collective writing of the text, if the first witnesses of the era are to be believed: for instance Claude Roy, who saw Blanchot as responsible for the shape of the Manifesto's thinking ("the tone of this enigmatic, crystalline writer had given the affirmation of a principled position the clearness of a calm statement of fact. It now expressed in simple terms the conclusions reached by everybody's complex reflections"), or Madeleine Chapsal, who after interviewing Blanchot found him to be "the gentlest of men":

> I was touched by their gentleness, by their awkwardness at suddenly finding themselves in the eye of the storm, by their resolve to face up to things. There is Robbe-Grillet who is no fierce revolutionary.... There is Simone Signoret, aware and courageous.... There is Maurice Blanchot, the writer, the gentlest of men.⁶

Perhaps the Declaration allowed for the osmosis between public affirmation and personal reserve that Mascolo had spoken of;⁷ to the writer whose "essential solitude" was the most abyssal fell the task of prizing the text away from belonging to anyone in particular, to any of those who had signed it.

The Declaration had a number of other singular points about it. For instance, Blanchot observed that "for the first time, words have arisen from the depths of a people to lay claim to the right *not to oppress*, with the same strength that has previously led all peoples to claim the right *not to be oppressed*."[8] He believed that this conscience could only belong to the post-Auschwitz period. The words of Robert Antelme, "anything that resembles, even vaguely, what we saw there literally destroys us" now forms the basis for Blanchot's thinking. This analogy raises the stakes of intellectual, political, and legal responsibility. For example, the Manifesto explicitly compares the "institution" of torture in Algeria to the Nazi concentration and extermination camps.[9] Blanchot recalled that the military court in Bordeaux in 1953 had condemned German soldiers for not having disobeyed their superiors' orders to perform terrifying acts, and used this precedent to legitimize "the right to military disobedience." He also invoked Nuremberg and confirmed that the end of the history of patriotism had come, an ideology that was essentially perverse and blind. "The principle that recommended serving one's country, whether it was just or unjust, was buried in the concentration camps alongside the victims of those who were not able to choose disobedience and reason over obedience and madness." This reasoning, fundamental to the Declaration, legitimized the right to refusal, this "ultimate recourse to the ability to say no." What it did not do was to blindly condone all revolutionary ideologies or strategies. Thus Blanchot refused to explicitly support the FLN, just as he said that he was reserving judgment on the emerging revolutionary power of China.[10]

Reversing the official interpretation of events and attributing the responsibility for the anarchic situation to French politico-military power, the call for illegal action had a profound effect, for it broke from the innumerable intellectual declarations and petitions that appeared after the Liberation.[11] Initially, it disturbed a number of potential signatories contacted by Mascolo, Schuster, Nadeau, Pouillon, Péju, and Leiris during the summer. Some refusals to sign were surprising: not without prevarication, close friends such as Barthes, Duvignaud, and Morin refused to support illegal action and ended up drafting their own resolutely pacifist "Appeal to Public Opinion," which was published by the Fédération de L'Éducation Nationale (a trade union group) on October 5, a month after the Declaration had appeared. Led by several members of the *Arguments* group, with

Claude Lefort and Colette Audry, a few dozen intellectuals signed it, including Domenach, Étiemble, Merleau-Ponty, and Prévert.

The summer was therefore spent collecting signatures. A few dozen by the end of July became, just by chance, 121 by the end of August: This number would remain almost as a fetish, and the Declaration almost immediately came to be known as the "Manifesto of the 121." The number and diversity of intellectuals committed was impressive.[12] Some of the writers contacted wanted to modify aspects of the text, and Blanchot, like Mascolo, was extremely attentive to this desire to write collectively. While it was too late to modify the Declaration, for a number of weeks both contemplated adding a section that would allow either certain figures to speak in their own names, or allow all to signal that there was no consensus and that each signatory was able to retain an individual position. But ultimately the idea was abandoned, in the name of a unified effect. It is true that it would have made the Manifesto much less effective. But the care that Blanchot took over this question would not be without consequences. He was completely sold on the idea of writing as a community, enthusiastic about the way that the Declaration was drafted (with as many versions as there had been authors, texts constantly going back and forth, the series of "countless, almost daily meetings").[13] When in September the judicial system would call the signatories to appear before it, he based his thinking on the collective and anonymous authority of the Manifesto for reasons going beyond simple defense. In July, he proposed to Mascolo that the undertaking should be continued after the Declaration was published. Mascolo accepted immediately, but on condition that the roles be reversed, with Blanchot having the task of defining this new project for which he declared himself available.[14] Blanchot replied evasively that concerning "this Algerian thing" one day it would be necessary to "bring together, around a text, writers in all languages, on condition—it is true—that this text should not simply be vague, but that it should express why their *shared* truth of being writers *also* obliges them to participate in such a project."[15]

The project of the *International Review* was born.

To write with Dupin and Char, who during the summer both wanted to rework the text, opened this political undertaking up to the demands of poetry, the infinite attentiveness to language that also infinitely welcomes the speech of the other. In mid-July, Blanchot met René Char, who revealed his main objection to the text: that it asked young conscripts to become insubordinate without providing them with any collective or judicially valid support. Robert Antelme had already expressed the same concern a few weeks earlier. Char said that he was struck by the collapse in morale of some deserters and by the lack of responsibility of certain leaders of underground networks. "We are encouraging them to take this extreme path by saying to them: Here is the truth, but without doing anything to make it *viable in practice*," Blanchot added when he related the meeting to Mascolo.[16] This infinite attentiveness, which was immediately adopted by Mascolo, would remain as an open wound in the demands made by a publication that could no longer be delayed, although it is true that it proposed no less a risk than the trauma of battle or death, not to mention that of being forced to inflict torture. Nonetheless, the indirect effect of publishing it—magnified by Sartre's support during the trial—was precisely to put an end to a war that the very person who was both president and a general had declared absurd— "a statement that ought to have destroyed him there and then" ("can a people be mocked in any crueler a fashion?").[17]

Between July and September, there followed correspondence with the two poets about which Blanchot kept Mascolo informed, sending him copies of the letters. But Char and Dupin would not sign the Declaration. This dialogue raised the possibility of a Review; their refusal to sign already provided a glimpse of its failure. Blanchot and Mascolo would never truly get over this failure, having together set in motion this infinite writing with the questionnaire, with the Declaration, with their correspondence which was sometimes doubled and repeated in other correspondences, other articles or other books. They would always insist on the "collective character of the Declaration": "The version made public is rigorous in having no identifiable author," Mascolo told *L'Autre Journal* in 1985; and when *Gramma* was considering republishing it in a special issue on Blanchot, Mascolo would ask Christian Limousin to remember that "its collective responsibility must be preserved."[18]

The text of the Manifesto was printed on September 1. It immediately fed into the trial of the Jeanson network, which began on September 5 without the accused party, who was still hiding from the law. Mascolo mailed more than two thousand copies of it; among those to receive it were government ministers and the president. Under the threat of censorship, no mainstream press outlet dared to publish it.[19] Only its final phrases appeared in *Le Monde*, on September 7—the part that was, strictly speaking, "declarative." The Manifesto was creating waves. It provoked other intellectuals, who assembled to publish two countermanifestos a month later, which were also opposed to one another: the Appeal of the FEN, and the "Manifesto of French Intellectuals for Resistance to Desertion," which was in favor of French Algeria and was published by *Le Figaro* with 185 signatures, including Thierry Maulnier's (in fact the final number of signatures was closer to five hundred, including those of Andreu, Boutang, Massis, and Paulhan). Thierry Maulnier was among the fiercest opponents of the original Declaration, contrasting "the real France" to "the France of Sartre," whose provocative authority he could not stand.[20] It was an irony of history that by strongly attacking the latter, Maulnier was attacking Blanchot's vision, was attacking what he saw as a betrayal of his own past and his own authority.

Above all, it was the Manifesto's presence in the trial that gave it its notoriety. On September 14, the defense demanded that the 121 be called as witnesses in solidarity with the accused. The signatories were initially interrogated and painted as guilty. The day's proceedings on September 20 were given over to them. Immediately after Claude Lanzmann appeared as a witness, the defense lawyer, Roland Dumas, interrupted proceedings to read a letter that he claimed he had just received from Sartre, who was in Brazil at the time. In fact it was a text written by Péju, in agreement with Lanzmann and Pouillon, that already had Sartre's blessing when he had left at the beginning of August. The letter made explicit the previously missing link between the Jeanson affair and the Manifesto. "If Jeanson had asked me to pass on materials or to host Algerian militants, and if I had been able to do it without risk for them, I would have done so without hesitating," read the letter which ended with a diatribe against the French government and its notion of justice, "an ephemeral power that . . already represents nothing."

Sartre's letter provoked a national outcry and accusations of guilt began to rain down. In the following days, Antelme, Duras, Frénaud, Lanzmann, Mascolo, Nadeau, Pouillon, Schuster, and Geneviève Serreau were charged with inciting insubordination and desertion. On September 22—for his fifty-third birthday, or the day after—Blanchot too was charged via a letter. He had been cunning when being interrogated: patiently, insolently, hiding an anger that he would say was the greatest of his entire life, Blanchot had constantly irritated Judge Braunschweig, criticizing his arbitrary power and systematically opposing the imprecise, indirect transcriptions of his own statements.[21]

On the same day of September 22, government ministers increased the punishment for inciting insubordination and for hiding deserters; the FLN put out a communiqué supporting the 121. On September 29, an order allowed the provisional suspension of state employees who supported insubordination or desertion or who encouraged soldiers to disobey orders. The signatories were banned from being cited on radio or television. On

October 3, one of them, Robert Barrat, was arrested; this caused all the signatories to claim that they were authors of the text in an individual capacity and to demand that they be arrested too. Finally, on October 4, a new charge—encouraging soldiers to disobey orders—was applied to the 121, and initially to Nadeau and Blanchot, who seems to have been chosen as a main activist and a main writer, respectively, linked to the Declaration.

The charges led to further signatures; the number rose to 246 by October 29, the day the third and final version of the Manifesto was published.[22] Their primary effect was to outrage the majority of newspaper, radio, and television journalists, the worlds of teaching, trade unions and associations, and even the assembly of cardinals and archbishops who, although they did not always support the Declaration, resolutely defended the victims of government repression (this was the moment when De Gaulle abandoned his prime minister, Michel Debré, by publicly recalling his attachment to freedom of speech for major intellectual figures: "Voltaire must not be thrown in jail," he said to his prime minister). Added to this was fact that Simone Signoret, Alain Resnais, François Truffaut, and their works disappeared from the airwaves: The whole of public opinion was affected. The media coverage of the Manifesto succeeded in attracting public attention where *Le 14 Juillet* had failed. It also made clear its limitations, for instance in the huge change brought about by Sartre's intervention. The reading in court of a letter at least attributed to Sartre—even when he was out of the country—meant sections of the press erupted in anger, with veterans' associations marching in the streets to demand that the philosopher be shot and the signatories found guilty. When Sartre returned from Brazil at the start of November, the charges were dropped and the new sentences not applied. There was no way Blanchot and Mascolo could not write to him, which they did a month later, trying to involve him in their new project.

On October 27, the meeting called by UNEF (National Union of Students in France)—which had supported the Manifesto—protesting against the war in Algeria brought nearly twenty thousand people to the Mutualité building in the Latin Quarter. The fact that the meeting had officially been banned led to police intervention—a rather heavy-handed one. In what would turn out to be a rehearsal for 1968, Nadeau, Blanchot, Mascolo, Monique and Robert Antelme, and Paule Thévenin left the meeting together and were chased into the Rue des Bernardins and violently beaten on the shoulders or the head.[23] We should also remember that eight years later, Blanchot would take part in all the demonstrations. "Step up the pace" was what Mascolo and those close to him often had to ask him, and it was what he could not do, being ill and short of breath; and yet sometimes he managed it, as he knew that the march of refusal requires a patience that does not exclude its step beyond, and even calls for it to hasten on to the end.

The manifesto accelerated the shift in public opinion and Algeria's march toward independence; it played a key role in the trial, which little by little became less Jeanson's than the army's. Above all, it had changed the position of intellectuals and the extent to which they were listened to. Sartre had become "the Untouchable one." The affair had been compared to those of Calas and of Dreyfus. Thinking men had discovered that they had an authority, Mascolo would write in 1985:

> It was a truly inaugural moment when a right claimed back from the void of values was loudly declared, and whose energy, which had seemed to dissipate, would reconvene, infinitely diversified, in the happy effervescence of 68, from which nothing positive or tangible would ultimately come, as has been clearly said—from which nothing less was to be expected than a general renewal of sensibility whose effects are still being felt.[24]

Twelve years after even this statement, the continuing influence of this moment saw a collective of 121 people with "difficult to pronounce" names calling for disobedience against a proposed law on immigration presented by a government led by Jean-Louis Debré. Among the 155 writers who supported the initiative were Edgar Morin, Maurice Nadeau, and Maurice Blanchot.

After the failure of *Le 14 Juillet*, the latter had written to Mascolo that a new era had begun. Jean-Paul Sartre would be the first to remind Blanchot of the meaning of those words.

CHAPTER 50

Invisible Partners

The Project for the *International Review* (1960–1965)

When in the fall of 1960 Blanchot, Mascolo, and Vittorini decided to launch the project for an *International Review*, they knew that it could gain broad and quick success only through Jean-Paul Sartre. A meeting took place at the end of November; the charges against them all still stood. A few days later, on December 2, Blanchot wrote to Sartre: "You have reminded me of what I must have said at times and what I have always thought privately: that the Declaration would find its true meaning only if it were the beginning of something."[1] At this time, everyone was thinking of a new review. Sartre was considering changing *Les Temps Modernes*, Nadeau thinking of transforming *Les Lettres Nouvelles*; but Blanchot was not satisfied with "a more literary *TM*, a more political *LN*." "Experience shows that, not without risks, one can update a review, but one cannot make an old review a new one," he wrote to Sartre. For a true beginning, a "new platform" was needed.[2]

Everyone agreed that the Manifesto affair and the trial had changed matters greatly. A larger number of intellectuals saw how necessary their involvement, as well as their political radicalization, had been, conceiving of them in terms of an almost immediate extension of their activity, beyond a simple feeling of responsibility. They saw how strong an impact their speech could have, a speech that was all the stronger because it defended itself collectively, anonymously. This change exalted Blanchot who saw in it, for the first time in his life, the possibility of using speech to respond to radically new events of history. This speech was meaningful only if it was now thought of as the interruption and the neutrality of speech; this response was only meaningful if it attempted to "represent as we should, unequivocally, the change that we are all sensing."[3] The political calling of the new review was therefore to *represent change*. It had to be public, to mobilize people; for that reason, it could not do without Jean-Paul Sartre. Blanchot told him this in a letter, without flattery, suddenly referring to him in the third person to underscore how his name was now able to represent change.[4]

> If Sartre, and others among the 121 with him, are seen deciding to express themselves in this form deliberately chosen as new, everyone—and I am thinking not only of writers and the general public but also of the intellectual youth as a whole—will understand that we are entering into a new phase and that something decisive is taking place and trying to find expression.[5]

Sartre would not become involved in the project, and from the beginning the review's survival was therefore threatened.

The first six months of the following year were spent putting together the project and looking for editors, correspondents, and publishers all over the world. British, Polish, American, Mexican, and Argentinian intellectuals were interested but unable or unwilling to participate in it fully.[6] Three national committees were formed. In France, the committee consisted of Antelme, Blanchot, Butor, Des Forêts, Duras, Leiris, Mascolo, and Nadeau, with Julliard as the publisher (Barthes would join them actively later); in Italy, there were Calvino, Pasolini, Vittorini, with Einaudi as publisher; in Germany, Bachmann, Enzensberger, Grass, Johnson, Walser. Few of the names on this impressive list, however, contributed much real work. Those who did threw themselves into it with body and soul for more than three years.

Blanchot worked on it frenetically. He edited the best texts from all the committee meetings and during this period provided far fewer articles to the *NRF*. His energy stemmed both from conviction and despair. Sartre had refused to take part. Bataille was sinking into illness. Algeria was becoming a tragedy, between the generals' coup and terror attacks by the OAS (Secret Army Organization); relations with Tunisia were broken off after the Bizerte crisis. The first delays with the *Review*, the fact that his closest friend was no longer near, French politics, and general indifference: All of these suffocated him with "personal misfortune" which he compared, in a letter to Dionys Mascolo, to the misfortune of a driver seeing a child throw itself beneath the wheels of his car.[7] This an unbearable image reveals the pain Blanchot felt assailing him from all sides, like an impossible cry, a permanent nightmare, a disorientation of all projects. It was like an infinite, silent, absurd death that had raised its head in innocence and happy oblivion; it was like a lightning bolt of truth. "I believe that we are all living in fear," he wrote to Bataille; "but that we cannot know it: only in certain moments—and then it is as if truth moves through us."[8] The image of the slaughter of an innocent child spoke to him as truth; it left him with the feeling of a "world falling apart."[9] The only thing at this time, as in the future, that gave him back his strength was Robert Antelme's book. Again to Bataille, he wrote:

> I can see nothing that would dissuade me from saying together with you that ultimately things lead nowhere; I would only add that this "nowhere" can only be affirmed in the necessity of always leading somewhere, doing so through the inexorable decision never to give up. In recent days I have been remembering Robert Antelme's book (the narrative of his time in the camp), and I have been remembering, almost with horror, the type of hope that never abandoned him even when hope was absolutely absent and that made even the basest human needs sacred for him and his companions: this hope seems terrible to me, perhaps even awful; it is hope without hope.[10]

This thought was working away at him: the previous day, Blanchot had written the same letter (even with some of the same words) to Dionys Mascolo. It was working away at him because it set free a feeling of lightness even in the depths of despair. "An 'absolute' backdrop of hopelessness sits behind my readiness to affirm human truth and futurity."[11] Robert Antelme's book and even his face were what brought Blanchot back to the *Review*, what made it possible to write the texts preparing the committee's collective reflection in July 1961.

Blanchot was personally utterly convinced that an interruption of history had taken place, that one period had ended and another begun, and the *Review* had to respond to this new period: "We are approaching an extreme movement in time, what I could call a change of times. . . . It is therefore necessary that such a project be ceaselessly focused on its own gravity, which is the attempt to respond to the grave enigma that is the passage from one time to another."[12]

This was why he could not stand any traditional form of commentary or review. "There is nothing more illegitimate [*bâtard*] than political commentary expressed by an individual who believes he has something to say and who wishes to say it," he wrote to Mascolo.[13] Political rupture and historical revolution brought the *Review* into being: they also forced it to adopt new forms. "This review will not be a review": it would not review contemporary literary, cultural, or political activity (there would be no *reviews*, precisely). "This review will not be a review": it would be collective, fragmentary writing, centered on a new column, the "Intellectual Course of Events."[14]

Collective writing did not mean seeking out equally shared solutions. The "communism of thought" was also the interruption—the fragmentation—of such a communism of writing. On the contrary, by bringing together problems belonging to each language, to each nation, to each political situation, to each culture with its differing view of literary endeavors, the idea was to seek out the literature that was "*more* than literature."[15] In the same way that the international perspective acted upon national ones, so did poetics upon politics, fragments upon totality, community upon solitude. Collective writing had to allow one "to internally go beyond [one's] own thoughts" and "to give rise to new ones." Each writer was to be effaced by his own thinking and by that of others. Each was to share responsibility for affirmations whose author he became, without actually writing them; he was more than a cosignatory, even more than a coauthor: He was an author of excess, an interrupted author. "This is the sense of the review as a collective possibility. It is an intermediary status between author and reader."[16] Each was to write in the name of the other, each to become the other's partner. This *International Review* was a review (a dance) of invisible partners.

Seven years earlier, at the beginning of his work with the *NNRF*, Blanchot had called for a light, innocent reader freed of all religious devotion and all cultish respect, capable of "dancing quickly round the text," the best way of relocating the meaning of true gravity.[17] The author-reader of the *Review* was just such a creature, freed of all political cults, of all literary schools, of all ideological "platforms"—of all nihilism. Instead, this author-reader was to use collective writing to "answer for a knowledge that he does not originally know himself."[18] Such at least was the dancer that Blanchot hoped for, since this review was to do more than simply juxtapose individual concerns, instead drawing on permanent exchange, adjustment, on constantly changing approaches and projects, on international and therefore collective standpoints; he wanted the dance to resemble a difficult accomplishment, a truncated, doctored relation with death, where the concern for visibility and the fetish for having a visible partner would not overwhelm the expectations of its too-numerous contributors.

The very first event it addressed—the construction of the Berlin wall on August 13, 1961—caused difficulties for the project. Beyond the clear dismay and the "impersonal misfortune" they once again shared, the German contributors—notably Enzensberger—would see their preoccupations shift. A month after the event, the latter wrote to Mascolo: "Berlin stinks of war and of fear: of the end of free alternatives, of rational analysis." What appeared to the French group as another reason to continue and even to speed up the *Review* was seen by Enzensberger as a historical trap closing around him. He noted the political differences within the group, the fact that the majority wanted to disengage and abandon the project, and explicitly resigned. He emigrated to Norway. The only one in the German group who could draw on friendships with some of the Italians and French, Enzensberger left and was replaced by Uwe Johnson who, after waiting nearly a year to decide whether to become involved, proved to be extremely cold, attempting to base the relationship with the other groups on contractual terms.

Winter 1961 and spring 1962 were thus spent in despair over whether the *Review* would ever come to anything. The French and Italians both refused to contemplate a review that was exclusively Franco-Italian and waited for the Germans to decide; they were depressed and regularly discussed giving up. Louis-René des Forêts tried to reanimate the group by taking over the secretarial duties—"a guarantee of vigilance and reserve in relation to so many passions."[19] Although Gallimard eventually did offer to publish the review, even considering replacing the *NRF* with it, the discussions were long, painful, and bothersome, and Maurice Nadeau therefore offered to make his review available, "which is to say to replace it with the one we are imagining."[20] Blanchot was considerably moved by the offer.

Events were not helping: Algeria won independence against a backdrop of further atrocities: for instance, the massacre on February 8 at Charonne metro station in Paris during a demonstration against the OAS, for peace (a peace that the government would agree to a month later, in Evian), or that of partisans of French Algeria on March 26 in Algiers. The Charonne murderers were not sought by the police. Proclaimed on July 3, Algerian independence proved only a short-lived relief for Blanchot. Georges Bataille died five days later.[21]

In summer 1962, Blanchot was perhaps more depressed than ever. On July 18, Johnson sent Louis-René des Forêts an incredibly haughty, distant, indifferent letter, overturning many points originally agreed about the project. The crisis ran from July to the end of the year. In effect, Johnson demanded that texts be ready before the international meeting scheduled for mid-December in Zurich. "There is a great misunderstanding," Blanchot wrote to Mascolo. Johnson wanted to remove the collective writing of "The Course of Things." He explicitly told Louis-René des Forêts on October 6, adding in imperturbable fashion (and in the formal mode of address): "Dear Mr. Des Forêts, allow me to remark that we do not see as opportune an interview such as that given by Mr. Mascolo to the representative from *The Observer* which appeared on September 23 in that [British] newspaper." Mascolo was asked to explain himself—to explain what was the responsibility of the publishers, who had contacted the press at the Frankfurt book fair.

Such failures of understanding and such complaints left Mascolo and Blanchot in despair. Moreover, at the end of the year they were forced to abandon the project of publishing with Gallimard. In this fall 1962 and winter 1963, the two friends were in turn fairly seriously ill. Then, at the beginning of January, Mascolo was laid low by the death of his niece, only a young girl.

The Zurich meeting finally took place in mid-January 1963. Meanwhile, having newly arrived as an Italian editor and taken charge of that committee, Francesco Leonetti had tried—with the agreement of Enzensberger and Vittorini—to mediate between the French and German groups. He criticized the utopian vision of one side and the traditionalist vision of the other. However much the Italians supported "The Course of Things," and despite the friendship that still linked Vittorini to Mascolo and Blanchot (even when they disagreed), before the Zurich meeting the crisis came to a head rather than disappearing. The French only attended "unwillingly," Mascolo wrote. The *Review* was at an impasse. The meeting was a disaster. Des Forêts would remember leaving it furious, sickened, outraged, then "sadder and more depressed than the others."[22] He recalled the Germans' refusals, Johnson saying *Nein* repeatedly as each French text was discussed. Certain texts, for instance those by Char and Genet, were even censored rather than discussed, or criticized in the name of cultural values or ideological criteria, which were precisely what the French wanted to avoid. The Italians attacked the "ontologism" of Barthes, Blanchot, and Mascolo. A letter from Vittorini to Blanchot, dated March 1, 1963, explained the basis of these Italian objections fairly well. Beyond a disagreement on the definition of literature and the demand that it represented, the divergences grew out of the Italians' inability to see notions such as silence or absence as anything but mystical. Calvino would admit a few years later how Vittorini "stiffened" as soon as he heard discussion of such notions, which he still saw as values, in a way that Blanchot condemned as nihilist.[23]

After Zurich, the crisis deepened and hastened the end of the *Review*. Des Forêts withdrew the texts of his that had been accepted. Blanchot blamed Johnson for having closed the meeting too early. Faced with German inflexibility, he could do little more than express simple moral truths, solicit the most elementary tolerance. Correspondence proliferated: Blanchot, Mascolo, Vittorini proclaimed how sincere their friendship was, which also enabled them to air their negative remarks. Viewpoints were becoming incompatible. In April 1963, after a meeting in Paris, an ensemble of texts formed a first issue; the publishers, Einaudi, Suhrkamp, and finally Julliard, were ready, but nothing appeared.

The *Review* ultimately failed on the question of its form. Was collective writing utopian, impossible? It did not seem so. This writing already existed: it was partly Blanchot's own, that which he had often practiced, in the free indirect discourse of his "critical journal," in the authority — shared in friendship — of *Death Sentence*, in the shared, repeated work of the political interventions made alongside Mascolo. It was no longer a question of condensing the text written with the other or in his or her name, of appropriating the creativity of the dance with an invisible partner. On the contrary, it was a question of freeing up this creativity, of returning it to the invisibility it had come from. This required attentiveness, multiple encounters, infinite mutual recognition. This attentiveness also had to be attentive to the constant movements of history as it was interrupted and disoriented; this recognition provided a maximal access to the most accursed and the most withdrawn share, to the most essential and the most personal solitudes. Enzensberger and Mascolo were able to put it in infinitely simple terms: "Absolutely in agreement: no 'machine' can replace immediate contact between friends who know each other well and who run no risk of their encounter becoming a quasi-diplomatic one."

So the *Review* could exist, it just could not be "international." But that was the condition that everyone had agreed on: even a Franco-Italian review would have been meaningless, as Blanchot would say one day. This is what Nietzsche had written: "For the hermit the friend is always the third person: the third person is the cork that prevents the conversation of the other two from sinking to the depths."[24] The community of writing could only exist if it allowed each participant to do more than meet only one partner at a time. Even the infinite meetings and letters between Bataille and Blanchot, or between Blanchot and Mascolo, took place through the presence of a third party: this was language, whose invisible presence we *are*, happily, sometimes indiscreetly, but in the certainty that we cannot give up on this interruption of community relation (if we still want our own interruption to exist, if we still want to think it).

The historical and political factors that caused collective writing to emerge provided a reason why it could only begin in relation to a third party. After Auschwitz, and as the Berlin wall was being constructed, the presence of a German group was a necessity. It would have made palpable the "Course of Things," which according to Blanchot was destined to become "the central column, around which the rest of the review should be organized' and which "must run throughout the issue."[25] It was to be an exploded and yet coherent chronicle, infinitely readapted, readjusted, a fragmentary writing open to discontinuity, citations, information, aphorisms; it was to be open to a thinking of the relationship between authors and between ideas accumulating, being denounced and contested, working and unworking each dialectical reduction, making all totalities impossible, suspending meaning, a movement of passage, relaunch and relay, a nomadic production of truth.[26] It was to be a column in which approaches to political events or reviews of books would bring each fact and each work out of their solitary context, whether national or ideological (whence the rule that books should be analyzed by someone from a different national tradition), placing them in the movement of reading, of alteration, of community, of languages, and of history.[27]

> The "fragment" is linked to the necessity of giving expression to numerous different reflections, that is to say, to connecting the plural multiplicity of objects and possibilities of the world through this diverse plurality, without threatening the review with formlessness, which would happen if the diversity of these multiple texts could not be composed and articulated into an overall project.[28]

Blanchot's description of fragmentary and collective writing sometimes sketches out what a postsurrealist adaptation of the reflection on the imaginary undertaken by *Documents* might have looked like. It might have introduced a type of formal dissemblance into the heart of continuity and the semblance of thought, a dissemblance excluded from any type of "formless resemblance." Or it could even have been a way of opening up *Critique*'s synthetic approach to both personal and collective writing, to the predominance of short over long forms, to the endless interruptions of commentary—involving a risk for this journal "which would live or die by its seriousness." For Blanchot, the *Review* could therefore have been something like an opening of Bataille's thought, and more particularly a transformation of the review that they created together and that he had so often blamed himself for no longer supporting, a prolonged homage to the friend who had recently died. A few years later, this homage would become "only" a book, *Friendship*.

The *International Review* could also have been responsible, as an open response or infinite renewal, for the movement of Blanchot's work and for its worklessness, for the transformation of convictions and for the insistency of thought expended. It could have been—after the "death of the last writer" or of the last solitary writer—this work's "infinite conversation," or its book always to come, a book ever more distant as speech was multiplied, repeated, interrupted. It would have offered to this work the unfolding of paradox, anonymous expiation, the interruption of thought. In its unrealized state, the project instead collapsed, made the foundations of the book collapse; it fragmented its own thinking with a fragmentation that was suffocated, melancholic, and meditative rather than selfless, plentiful, or political. Only the movement of May '68 could attract Blanchot once again toward this fragmentary, collective, anonymous writing; he threw himself into it heedlessly, but was already torn apart. In other words, this new failure made room for a definitive withdrawal that was sometimes tempered by the mysterious grace of return to the past, both his past and that of friendship (such returns would explain the books written for Bataille, Duras, Des Forêts, Mascolo).

Despite its failure, the *Review* project was therefore continued in Blanchot's work. No one was ready to abandon it altogether: three years would be spent trying to "save something of our project," as Mascolo put it to Leonetti. Various solutions were proposed without success, Blanchot and Mascolo refusing any publication that did not retain a collective and impersonal character. The only concrete object to appear was in April 1964, under the title *Gulliver*, upon which everyone had eventually agreed, a number zero in Italian that took the place of the seventh issue of *Il Menabò*, the review founded five years earlier by Vittorini and Calvino. It included texts by the editors but also by Jean Genet, Kateb Yacine, Jean-Louis Schefer, and Claude Ollier. Even in 1965 the Italians were proposing to "keep the project alive" by suggesting that collective books be edited; this was not especially meaningful for the French. Antelme, Barthes, Blanchot, Des Forêts, and Mascolo met to study the proposal. But Mascolo soon wrote back to Vittorini to let him know that they had rejected the idea: "We all agree that it would be *possible*, but that it would be a completely different project. A book, even a collective one, has a definitive, closed, solemn character and needs a different reader than a review does.... In short, it could no longer be a 'movement.'"

A book *obviously* could not address what Blanchot, in one of the four articles he gave to the *Menabò* issue, names "the problem of division."[29] It probably fell to Blanchot to write a text reflecting on the *Review*'s failure, tracing the movement back to its origins, grasping it as an event (as paradox, incongruence, interruption) and spinning out its future, like that of a symbol, developed, dramatized, and confronted with the pitfalls of time across a narrative. That was part of his method. Blanchot therefore returned to the first serious obstacle the review had faced, the building of the Berlin Wall. When he begins with the words: "For everyone, Berlin is the problem of division," we must take them to refer to this community as well as to Berliners and the whole world, insofar as the division of each reflected the division of the others too. This was a division that the raising of a wall, in its abstract force, only confirmed as intensely real. Berlin spoke to "the necessity and the impossibility of unity," the permanent equivalence between "a dwelling place" and "the absence of dwelling"; most of all,

> Berlin poses the problem of two opposing cultures within the same cultural whole, of two unrelated languages within an identical language, unusually, and therefore calls into question the intellectual serenity or the possibility of communication that one imagines is available to men who have the same language and the same historical past.[30]

To write this was to repeat that the obstacle of the wall ought to have called for rather than hindered the *Review*, ought to have made necessary an inflexible and apparently heterogeneous coherence, reflected the fracture of bodies, words, and thoughts, imposed the fragmentation of languages, styles, and modes of knowledge: not in isolated despair but in direct confrontation of the wounds between them. To write this was to establish a still-uncertain future meaning, in the thinking worklessness of a community where the sublime could not reappear without all authority being atoned for, all property effaced, all unquestioned unity renounced.[31]

The *Review* would take a long time to die; its contributors' writing would obey what Blanchot conceived of as the law of the work. In the same letter to Vittorini cite above, Mascolo wrote:

You can be sure that as far as I am concerned (and as far as Maurice is concerned—as well as Robert, in his own way) I shall never *definitively* give up on the project. Writing on one's own is necessary, inevitable. It is also sad and perhaps frivolous (but no less necessary) when one has thought of realizing something of the communist idea, at least in the form of a "communism of writing." Therefore I shall never give up on the *hope of one day escaping* this sadness.

The "considerable, almost terrible" amount of work that Blanchot had done over these years was disappearing into the disaster of his life and the frivolous sadness of his books, and with it disappeared the proximity of friendship, which had never previously led to such long, frequent, and personal encounters. This was a dark moment. Indeed, Blanchot did not recover from it; the failure of the *Review* left him exhausted, at death's door. He was only kept going by the demands of politics, of friendship, of the politics of friendship. Antelme, Mascolo, and Des Forêts were now infinitely dear to him, infinitely close. "To speak is our peril and our necessity," he wrote the same words to both Vittorini and to Johnson in February 1963. "Friendship is the truth of disaster," he had already written to Bataille in January 1962. It was friendship, to which Antelme's book would constantly return him, that continued to allow for hope. Perhaps this supplement which meant that "literature is always *more* than literature" was friendship; perhaps it was the third party, this invisible share that does not accompany one and that his narrative had sketched out; perhaps it was the unthinkable distancing that henceforth fragmented his writing, indifferent to which particular genre it belonged to; perhaps it was the silent possibility of personal death (*disparition*). In whichever case, Blanchot cared resolutely about these matters, and although none of the *Review* projects said so explicitly, this demand lay on the far side of collective writing: the fragment had to be anonymous, had to be the site where death was accomplished. Again to Vittorini, he wrote: "It is as if my entire life has almost disappeared in a searching movement which is perhaps the experience of writing, the responsibility for which I am trying to bear, poorly but absolutely." This responsibility would also be that of a few books; but the disgust he shared with Mascolo for individual writing explained why his articles now grew rarer, why collections were published only to get them out of his mind, and why his writing now opened to fragmentation. For Blanchot this was no complacency or wallowing in pain, but a demand for faithfulness. Quite simply, this force of refusal no longer seemed to be able to give rise to the sovereignty or the extravagance of a beginning.

"He held the rose at the summit until the protestations had ceased": Perhaps this phrase by René Char, written in October 1965, refers to the importance Blanchot placed on the political and passionate demand of collective writing.[32]

CHAPTER 51

Characters in Thought
How Is Friendship Possible? (1958–1971)

After the friendships of the 1930s and the exceptional encounters with Emmanuel Levinas and Georges Bataille, Blanchot's life progressed into a new mode of relation and thought as his work became structured by the temporality of the oeuvre and by political urgency. It was punctuated—in the absence of the collective writing proposed by the *Review*—by a book published in 1971, *Friendship*.

Maurice Blanchot's correspondence reveals that friendship, for him, always appears against a backdrop of loss; it is promised in advance to death and also beyond it, a way of responding to death or of preparing oneself for moments of weakness or exhaustion, of picturing death as a shameful, terrible, untamed accomplice in order to maintain the singular demand to remain attentive to all those whom it surrounds and strikes. On multiple occasions this correspondence demonstrates feelings of joy and of privilege, with small cards sent intermittently, as if as a form of embrace, or in epilogues to letters that suddenly change their tone, like melancholy smiles in which fatigue produces dependable, pitiless compassion.[1] Blanchot was a letter writer who became more prolific even as he met his correspondents more frequently, but who in this period was forced to deal with destiny's relentless campaign against those close to him: Georges Bataille died in 1962, Elio Vittorini in 1966, Paul Celan in 1970, the daughter of Louis-René des Forêts in 1965 (she "returns in the night to shatter his heart"), the child niece and adolescent nephew of Dionys Mascolo.[2] Some friends went through endless mourning; others became ill. At a greater remove there were the deaths of those he had had dealings with—Camus in 1960, Breton in 1966, Paulhan in 1969. Such recurrence of death gives some justification to the choices and the structure of a book such as *Friendship*, which is at once a homage and a tomb, mixing in equal number the dead and the living in a collective memorial for Georges Bataille, with whom the book opens, and who allows it to open out at its end. This book draws on Bataille even for its title, which was originally considered for what became *Guilty*, as if friendship once again were nourished by a friendly borrowing of authority.[3] The book's title, its two epigraphs, and the way its closing text—first published in a journal shortly following Bataille's death—functions as an epitaph all discreetly demonstrate how present the friend in question was. "Friendship: here I remember that Georges wrote this word and that he gave it to us."[4]

Friendship is always, always-afterwards or always-already, given by a friend moving away, in the process of moving away, who before one's defeated eyes is in the process of moving their speech, body, and thought away. It is also the gift of a body, one that is dying or being carried off, still strangely and irreducibly similar. Blanchot wrote as much to Bataille, nearly a year before the latter's death:

> It has long seemed to me that the nervous difficulties you suffer from—to speak in terms of medical objectivity—are only your way of living this truth authentically, of remaining at the level required by this impersonal misfortune which the world ultimately is. And doubtless this movement has acquired some complicity of its own, but how could things have been otherwise, if our bodies are also our pitiless truth, a truth that admittedly is sometimes sordid, not always however—and here "sordid" is just as significant as "glorious." If here I speak indiscreetly of things that are your concern, it seems to me that I too belong to them, through friendship but not through it alone: here, silently, we share something.[5]

There is no doubt that Bataille and Blanchot's bodies went through long declines, and that they saw this as their way of showing that disaster was unbearable, as well as—whether this was their crowning glory or an act of complacency—their way of rising to the level required by death. They even found here, in compatible but distinct forms of eroticism and the eroticization of language, a beginning for literature, a literary authority. The death of one, in suddenly revealing the other's secret, sickly indiscretion, reduced that other's style to nothing more than an imitative rhetoric, mixed together their art of formulation ("here 'sordid' is as significant as 'glorious'"). This, however, belonged to the breathless and almost passionate movement of friendship by which each was dispropriated of his body and language and used this abandonment to accompany the other's suffering (we know how much time and effort were expended by Bataille in writing his last book, *The Tears of Eros*, in the face of death). A groveling shame, a vigilance in the face of silence: Here speech bears the weakness of thought and the strength of commitment that confirm friendship.[6]

Was that what made friendship possible? "An *ecce homo* without subject"? Theirs were dying, despairing bodies abandoned to the thought of community, neutral bodies so naked as to be anonymous, bodies so strong that they felt the gentleness of difference and of equality, that they were the final traces of "impersonal misfortune" which bore in their own absence, in their hollows and folds, the essence of the world and the silence it imposed. They were walking Thomases, walking forward in a restaurant (Anne was there, as all of us who will die were there), a Thomas who was now truly the twin of a Lord without divinity, made absent and effaced but who through his effacement brought community together, created friendship. The friendship that took this form always arose in the name of the other, invisible, last man, suffering alone in his room, without speaking, no longer or not yet speaking, suffering from exhaustion, remaining discreet in order to listen. Maurice Blanchot crossed paths with such figures of friendship in his life; they took form thanks to the "complicity of the organic" with Robert Antelme, who had died through his book before Blanchot met him, as well as Georges Bataille as he died among the flames, deeply submerged by the tears of Eros. Thus it seems that Blanchot always needed a third, absent body, an empty and invisible body placed at a distance by death, illness, and discretion. It seems that it was always necessary for a body to be offered to community, abandoned without being sacrificed, an absence of sacrifice that responds to the absence of myth that gives a true idea of the action necessary. This was a *political* body, an escapee from Numantia, responding to collective thought, to the closeness, listening, and equality of thought.[7] Robert Antelme had given his silence, his intransigence regarding humankind, his immediately nocturnal attention, and had continued to make them available. He could—he wanted to—be all the more effaced for it.[8] Each of these friends—Bataille dying, Des Forêts mourning, Blanchot in exile—would in turn occupy this empty, formidable place, this "way of sharing death, of sharing questions." Each of them, in an infinitely reversible movement, forced the others to retain their hope even in shame, their awaiting even in oblivion, to both elevate and ground their love by endlessly confronting death. "Without your presence," Mascolo concluded in a magnificent letter to Blanchot, who was away from society at the time, "we would not be able to love each other very much."[9] The "Forgiveness" with which he closed another of these letters of friendship speaks volumes about how he was almost ashamed of the meeting of indiscretion and the joy of affirming how much grace touched the path they trod together, which always emerged from the desert.[10]

In turn, each withdrew from the world and created it, and with this distancing created a new community, at the same time claiming themselves back from death and thus creating *themselves* ("an infinite responsibility," Mascolo would say), returning to the edge of silence only through words aimed at a small—albeit open—circle of friends.[11] Each occupied the place left empty by the divine, even in their radical atheism, each suffered because the world was possible on its own terms but impossible to write, confronting politics and poetry, losing hope of opening up personal politics through collective poetics.

Their letters responded to books and explained them. After Blanchot had sent him *The Infinite Conversation*, Mascolo responded as follows:

> I feel that I must tell you, lacking the propriety that you are so able to apply to everything you touch, and despite the crassness of all the words that I can think of, how often I have felt extraordinarily lucky to be your friend and how, due to that alone, I can have no cause for complaint; and it would not be enough to say that you have constantly helped us to live. The marvelous thing, what's more, is that you have never helped by way of reassurance, on the contrary. I was saying this to Robert the other day. Sharing distress with you is a happy thing. To walk toward failure, if it is with you, is not to fail. I have sometimes thought that being in step with you would make it not difficult to die.[12]

This was a subjectless act of faith, a sublimation of the marvelous in the face of death, a drunkenness of connection that gave unmatched strength precisely because it refused any consolation, finality, salvation, or abdication. It was an absolute affirmation of the present and a trusting in the return, an innocence that did not make predictions. Blanchot then responded, mocking religion so as to make his own this face of friendship in the name of a "present God." This meant that it was no longer Blanchot who was writing, but friendship within him, the equal speech of community. "I welcome your letter by thinking that I might have sent it to you, to you both, to Robert" was how he began, recalling that friendship, this word "friendship" had been given to them by Georges Bataille. The friend always allowed the other friend to be evoked, even if he could no longer be reached, in a movement that would be taken up in the book *For Friendship*.[13]

Friendly presence was an extraordinary presence; the friend was the invisible partner of creation, of dance, of innocence, of affirmation. He would appear as the pure invisible presence of a dream, as Mascolo recounts at length, or as a type of vision, as Blanchot wrote to him from a trip to Greece where Vittorini had been shortly before his death;[14] he imagined him by his side beneath the Delphi sky as an "almost presence" that resembled that of the *récits*' companion or last man. The friend was becoming the character of the fiction, he was becoming the character of thought.

He had always been that. Always: since Bataille had shown them the way toward this figure. Blanchot and Mascolo often spoke of the dramatic, silent, terrifying, anonymous way that Bataille had cited Blanchot's authority in *Inner Experience*. Whether it is the open heart of inner experience or in relation to mourning or death, the friend provides more than a body, a speech, an empty site: he is the very possibility of thought. The friend is not only the subject of philosophical searching; he becomes effaced as a subject in order to lend authority to thought. Blanchot allows this very movement to be thought: friendship, the possibility of thought, becomes the object of that thought. Friendship comes to stop the breach opened by thought's interruption, without ever entirely filling it: it retains "the interruption of being which means that I have never have the authority to do with [my friend] as I please." Friendship lies in renouncing the feeling of shame concerning the friend's "complicity of the organic" in relation to his other friend, or concerning their agreement in the face of death ("the blinding marvel," in Bataille's words). It is the reverse side of the indiscretion to which correspondence bears witness, that organic or metaphysical dive into form forced upon one by the happy illusion of knowing about one's friend. "We must give up trying to know those to whom we are linked by something essential; by this, I mean we must greet them in the relation with the unknown in which they greet us as well, in our estrangement."[15]

This time, it is the other way around: the movement of narration returns to the movement of thought. The *récit* with its inexhaustible search for its own beginnings, with its narration of itself and of what made it possible, had arrived at the figure of the "last man" or the figure of friendship.

Thought, nourished by the collective practice of politics and sickened that the writing of community had failed, now espoused the movement that would try to lead it back to the origin of its own thinking. What figures were encountered along the way? Two friends, two friends who conversed in near-exhaustion, exhausting all the possibilities of friendship, all the possibilities of thought. Two friends on the edge of the indiscretion that held them facing one another, exhausted by the need to maintain this indiscretion. Friendship itself was then effaced and gave shape (the shape of a dialogue) to the exhaustion and indiscretion from which friendship arises. As if *indiscretion about who or what has been exhausted* were the origin of thought. As if trying to glimpse the invisible partner of dialogue (of writing) were at once what elevated and what broke thought—except if one oneself enters, insubordinate, into the gravity of the scandalous, the innocence of dance, the exhaustion of silence and discretion.

CHAPTER 52

Act in Such a Way That I Can Speak to You
Awaiting Oblivion (1957–1962)

The publication of *Awaiting Oblivion* in the spring of 1962 occasioned great amazement, even for Blanchot's staunchest supporters. The book, which had been written over nearly five years, mixes together fragments of narration, description, and commentary to such a degree that no one could identify the object being offered to readers. And yet *Awaiting Oblivion* remains a *récit*, with its location, duration, and characters; it belongs to the succession of *récits* begun by *Death Sentence*. Like each previous *récit*, it fulfills a contract in autofiction and furthers this previous line of research.[1] What is therefore surprising—more obscurely perhaps—is the way it draws on this research so as to explode it, exploding not only the *récit* but its origin too, the place it "always already" opens to thought. "Suddenly, forgetting has always already been here" (45), Blanchot writes at the beginning of the second part. In a final Nietzschean gesture, this break at the origin of memory's relation, the *entretien*, and love makes one free for the interplay of patience, attentiveness, listening, and the possibility of thought.[2]

We are presented with a hotel, a narrow, long room, a sofa, an armchair, a table, two windows, as in Èze, and a man and a woman who talk—sometimes distantly, sometimes wrapped around one another—without tiring. The man tries to uncover a secret that the woman has, a secret comparable with "the reserve of things in their latent state" (85), but that nonetheless does not belong to her, which she perhaps does not possess. The man *is* attentive, listening to the way oblivion allows this memory to be given space, but never does the woman recognize what he believes he can tell her about herself. Between them, successive movements of attraction and of withdrawal, advance and retreat, take place. We learn little by little that the two figures met well before this encounter, and that this presence of images from their past invades their memory, burdening their minds. What place can be given to this awareness? Is there any justification in believing that it can act as a foundation, or is it just another obstacle to the secret being told? As for the writer, who begins by putting down his pen ("he was obliged to stop," 1), what will he be able to say or not say about it? How far is attention capable of piercing, sculpting, marking, supporting, caressing, nourishing oblivion? How far is awaiting capable of waiting for oblivion without its force causing it to disappear? What succinct, spare speech can still exist, still breathe without being forced to participate? How to access violence, tenderness, love, friendship? What is this *entretien* that contains everything and maintains nothing, if not the permanent possibility of an event that does not come about? How can its radicality, a point on which neither character gives any ground (this is their constancy, their seduction, their marvel), claim to open onto thought?

A natural extension of *The Last Man* and a critical reworking of the previous *récits* from which it borrows constantly, *Awaiting Oblivion* brings such questions together without organizing them, disperses them through the fragmentation of a language divided and unfolded in a thousand ways. In this way it interrogates the source of all possible utterance, the flux of previous narration, and the pertinence of its own thinking. The latter stretches the verisimilitude of the events recounted, causing a crisis for what Levinas named a "condensation in opposition to erosion" in order to see what remains of it: what remains of the encounter with the other, the other sex, how can this forgotten relation still give rise to speech, to thought?[3] What is this constantly interrupted and yet unshakable duration? How do things stand with these depths of being, of which there is no better image than that of the two bodies together on the sofa and their untiring disinhibition, which is exquisite and yet almost atrophied? How do things stand with this intimacy, returning to its own source to better allow for writing, to allow for what makes writing possible? And how do they stand with what today makes it possible to comment on *entretiens* that stem from different intimacies, as well as being given over to *entretiens* on commentary? What of the infinite resource of the *entretien*'s fatigue, the exhausted breathing of a fragmentary thought clawed back from the violence of disaster, from long-standing misfortune?

Awaiting Oblivion provides a mode of access, still timid and yet already scandalous, to the dramaturgy of fragmentary writing, showing the very real effects of—and the distance traveled by—the previous *récits*. It takes up their discreet theatricality, elevates their vocal sensuality. The scenes and the characters had always moved from one text to another; now they are brought together in confrontation. Thus the feeling of nakedness produced by fascinating encounters, the fantastic callings, and the nocturnal appearance of bodies in doorways, the ability to resurrect by uttering a name, or the insistent repetition of "Come"; all of these are replayed identically, repeated intensely even as they are torn apart.[4] The man and the woman are those of *When the Time Comes*; Claudia's rough, seductive phrase "no one here wants to be connected to a story" is cited as the narrator remembers "words that had one day burst into his life" as an "almost faded memory that, nevertheless, continues to haunt him" (9).[5] They are also the characters from *The Last Man*, which *Awaiting Oblivion* extends, almost like a serialization. The final words of the *récit* published in 1957 are a caesura of speech and give a feel of potential to the suspension they represent: "Later, he asked himself how he had entered the calm. . . ." "Later, he . . ."[6] The same words are taken up here in a retrospective tone, the return to a previous event: "Later, he woke calmly, cautiously, facing the possibility that he had already forgotten everything" (45). This is done in such a way that this shared questioning seems to suggest that the same character is present, conversing with the same young woman who has returned from death, gone back to her final agonies (for like in *Death Sentence*, "the dead came back to life dying," 28).

Thus the narrator attempts to listen in a condensed way to the other, to this woman with whom he shares his room more and more often, and thus also listens to the other women in the previous *récits* (but perhaps it was always the same one), as well as—ultimately—listening to his own experience as a narrator which has led him in turn to J., to N., to Judith and to Claudia, to the last man and his female friend, to his own companion. This listening is so condensed that it becomes a pure listening to the self, or to the very capacity to listen, a listening to one's own listening, called into question by the presence of a partner who now does not stand apart from one, before ultimately being effaced. This listening is so condensed that it saturates one's sense of suffocation, inviting speech to be constantly taken up again, breathlessly, with words and fragments. Doing so allows the pressure of dialogue to alternate with the repetitions of commentary, the dialogue becoming serious due to the light and rapid nature of the exchanges, the dizzying commentary adding layer upon layer of waiting as attentiveness (*l'attente comme attention*), and of attentiveness as "opening onto . . . the unexpected in all waiting" (21), so much so that it is barely tolerable and difficult to listen to, thus forcing the reader to return to a slow rhythm, deciphering these aphorisms as if they were poetry.[7] If Bataille stated that he could not read *The One Hundred and Twenty Days of Sodom* in one sitting, what reader would claim to be able to read *Awaiting Oblivion* without the breaths provided by the pauses (allowed for by the fragments)? The two works share the same ceaseless recitations, the same constant reworking of a limited vocabulary, the same almost technical but always poetic, rhythmic, sometimes incantatory language, the same infinite attentiveness to the other, to the other's body and to what their memory can bear, sometimes the same violence in trying to learn a secret, the same infinite movement leading away from any mystical center ("the center as center is always intact," 69). How, in this tension of listening and this saturation of respect, having nearly arrived by imposing one's concern at the break from ethics, how "to act in such a way" that speech can come about? And what can the nature of this speech be, a speech "as if behind," "a different utterance with which hers had almost nothing in common" (11). Can this speech of withdrawal and thus of creation even have a nature? "Act in such a way that I can speak to you"—the demand that provides the motif running throughout the *récit*—is repeated six times (10, 11, 11, 28, 43, 57), worn down until it is negated: "Act in such a way that I cannot speak to you" (82), with this last version throwing doubt on how it originated and on the space reserved for it. To what extent is it a command? And does it come from the site of speech or a site prior to speech? What tone would allow a body to speak it, a voice to utter it? Does such a tone even exist? Is it not open to all tones? Are these not the words that any woman, any being or any work could speak to those who—whether out of powerlessness, ignorance, or clumsiness—make listening their profession or their faith?

It is the major question asked of the writer; he is asked whether he knows in what "way" he would be able to respond to it. The *récit* is the most unsuitable format of all: its space is worn down, deficient if it excludes poetry (this had been Blanchot's deep conviction since the beginning of the 1940s; he refers to it in the *prière d'insérer* written for *Awaiting Oblivion*).[8] To be open to the poem is to be open to the space of the poem. As these two worlds meet, what is shared most of all is fragmentation. Blanchot quotes this phrase from René Char: "in the breakup of the universe that we experience, how prodigious! The pieces that come crashing down are living."[9] This phrase is something like the model for the literary event represented by *Awaiting Oblivion*, with the writing of these blocks that are juxtaposed even in the title, of these groups of nouns already seen in *The Last Man*, these fragments leading into fragments in a stifling way, ultimately giving way to the broken writing of the epilogue, where citations from the dialogues and from the narration finally fuse together in the *entretien* of commentary: "*'Face to face in this calm turning away.'—'Not where she is or where he is, but between them.'—'Between them, like this place, with its great staring look, the reserve of things in their latent state'*" (85).[10]

Fragmentary writing gives tremendous new vitality to a speech that it does not allow to come about, but whose misfortune and secrecy it speaks to. It is the writing that almost breaks with ethics: that borders on indiscretion. It is indeed the space of thinking that opens up here, beyond any aesthetic laziness or cover-up, in its desire to know that goes as far as hatred,[11] in the violence of nakedness,[12] in the indiscreet attention to the other's exhaustion (the other, which here meant the woman: "what an extraordinary state of weakness she was in," 11). The two characters are armed with waiting as a possibility of thought and with oblivion as the interruption of it; they are confronted with a suddenly neutral space in which speech has rejected the categories of the visible and the invisible (it is nonetheless invisible, not because it has no appearance but in the manner of the gaze of a present body that blinds all sight, touching without touching); carried along on a nonknowledge that strips them of all knowledge, and yet they remain superior to this knowledge through the community of their understanding ("I do not know it," says one, "Together we know it," the other responds, 41).[13] As an inheritance for writing, they bequeath the care they take in setting out their speech and in exposing how the folds of their memory allow for multiple strands of discourse. For instance, the monologue or dialogue sometimes appears in the narration; inversely, the latter sometimes features in the dialogue, voices come from all sides, condense spaces, superimpose different times, dispropriate one's imaginary and divide people, creating a vast echo chamber in which attentiveness to the other's body is constantly undermined by the void of possibility, by true oblivion. How then can we rely on such attentiveness? How can it be represented beginning with a point of suffering that often becomes empty, returns as eternally empty? The written word, that in literature which is always *more*, has the simple task of saying this, of indicating "the space of a different speech, always interrupted" (79); it is a silent word masking a secret piece of knowledge, refusing to shelter itself from the story, indicating the unknown power of whoever possesses it, making the relation of one to the other possible. The writing describes how this singular, extraordinary, decisive attentiveness to the other makes thought possible, beginning with this real movement whereby difference appears at the heart of proximity.[14] The object of this abstract movement of writing is what is most concrete: nothing less than what makes it appear. "What you have written holds the secret" (37).

With the patient, untiring movement by which Samuel Beckett recognized himself in the words of *Awaiting Oblivion*, writing suddenly discovers its object through this infinite attention, this always improbable listening, this indiscretion of the exhausted woman.[15] What she is still recounting by this stage, even as she seems to be about to stop, is the characters' long death, "speaking instead of dying" (73), speaking in the very *stead* of dying, offering their fictitious bodies in order to allow the origin of thought to be exposed. A digging into thought by means of the *entretien*, in this way made possible by the *récit*, is palpable in the dialogues of the final pages which no longer set two fictional characters—the two characters of all Blanchot's fiction—in opposition to one another, but instead the two characters of thought by whom they have been effaced. "Motionless, they went, and allowed to come, presence.—Which, however, does not come.—Which, however, has never yet come.—From which, however, all future comes.—In which, however, all presents disappear" (84). This rapidly developed power whereby thought moves by way of advances, confrontations, contradictions, jumps, returns, and *steps-beyond*, is enough to make one mad: a "madness par excellence," a redoubling of strangeness through the alienation by the void that is created by disalienation to all stories (perhaps what Blanchot calls, in the *prière d'insérer*, "a certain rupture of internal linkages"). However, this final movement of Blanchotian narration opens on to a new adventure of the *cogito*, which should now be conjugated in the neuter or the plural; it opens on to an eidetic reduction where oblivion remains ("being is yet another word for forgetting") as the endless guarantor of thought's fragmentation, as the unceasing demand to think this fragmentation of thought (for "the other" is another name for oblivion).

The characters' disappearance into oblivion is their true gift to thought. Such is the movement of this research, returning to an extreme state of vigilance thanks to the friendships it has had (let us cite here Levinas, Bataille, Antelme, all three of whom are present in the new indiscretion that the rupture of history has imposed on thought). "Ask[ing] so calmly to do the impossible" (44); such was the ethical demand imposed on the violence and gentleness of thought. At this time Blanchot can think only of bringing it back to the play of friendship from which he had taken it, of giving it form through collective writing. This latter put into play the infinite attentiveness demanded by history's dead-end, the rupture of time, the rifts in the real. "No stories, never again": The prophecy, if you will, of *The Madness of the Day* has now been fulfilled. The *récit* can now only find a meaning by losing its singularity, by allowing itself to carry the fragmentary, international, collective demand of the Review, of its columns: All that remains is for it to be the *récit* of thought.

In this sense, *Awaiting Oblivion* is the most sublime "preparatory text" ever written for the *International Review*. It matters little whether its form was decided upon before or after the project began. The necessity of opening speech to a violent, indiscreet, clear-eyed intelligibility, in the gentleness of friendship and the terror of what is most literary, responds to the development of Blanchot's thought. "It is gentle and attractive, it attracts one constantly" (80). "It": this understanding beyond all understanding, this oblivion of everything except the movement for equality. Blanchot's research had arrived at this point by making the characters of his thought bear this demand: "As if their words were searching for the level where, even with each other, they would allow to be established between them the silent evenness, the one that comes to light in the end" (80). It was this provisional point of arrival that he allowed to speak through the dedications he wrote in *Awaiting Oblivion* for his closest friends. To Bataille: "Thinking of the goal that we share"; to Mascolo: "Thinking of all that we share"; to Antelme: "The vestiges of a journey, the premises of a speaking." One day, this speech of equality would rise up.[16]

CHAPTER 53

The Thought of the Neuter
Literary and Philosophical Criticism: The *Entretien* and the Fragment (1959–1969)

The end of the 1950s—specifically, the final months of 1959—saw a new transformation in Blanchot's critical writing. The political, editorial, and literary movement of his thinking is accompanied by the nominalization of the Neuter, articles written in the form of *entretiens* between two voices or in juxtaposed fragments, a large proportion of texts addressing those close to him, and the increasingly evident abandonment of interpretative criticism in favor of a discourse more closely resembling the philosophical essay (albeit one interrupting philosophy).[1] Chronologically rereading the articles written by Blanchot between 1959 and 1969 collected in either *The Infinite Conversation* (1969) or in *Friendship* (1971) allows us to underscore how, perhaps more than in any other period, he emphasizes repetition and accentuation.[2] These notions apply to a thinking constantly subjected to life's trials by fire, the thinking of literature, of philosophy, of their communitarian possibilities, whether directly or indirectly political. From 1959 to 1962, the critical texts echo the repetitive, dislocated speech of *Awaiting Oblivion*; identical versions of the phrases themselves are found indiscriminately in the *NRF* columns and in the *récit*.[3] Suddenly and irregularly, between April 1960 and July 1963, ten articles were written in *entretien* form. They open critical discourse to a double voice, holding the work discussed at a distance by attempting to use the to-and-fro of dialogue to listen to that work in a multiple fashion. The juxtaposition of the replies makes no attempts to interpret or make decisions about a work, instead giving shape to the murmur of the neutral voice that has given rise to it. During these years of endless encounters and *entretiens*, Blanchot thus offers this singular, experimental attempt at fragmentary writing, dislocated yet directed, as if it were an advance and openly deficient version of the collective speech of the *Review*. From 1961 to 1963, he frequently comments on the works of his closest friends, often those involved in the international project; almost one article in three is dedicated to them. Written at once in homage to their presence, in close relation with their thought, and against the backdrop of their shared despair of ever coming to anything (this "goal that they shared"), today these texts appear as the last moments of good fortune enjoyed by critical writing. From 1964 and 1965 on, with the *Review*'s failure now confirmed and Blanchot in a despondent state, the critical texts grow rarer and become fragmented. Blanchot seems able to carry on only by writing about his fatigue (a true exhaustion—it is the subject of a *récit* published in 1966 and which opens *The Infinite Conversation*). The return to fragmentation, a type of writing that had been proposed and justified as best suited to the *Review*'s central column, now speaks to the inevitability of thinking exhaustion, first of all in the shape of exhausted thinking. What Blanchot would later call "the writing of the disaster" now finds its necessity in fragmentation.

With his health in danger, visits to hospital, the deaths and suffering endured by his closest friends, the collective failure of the *Review*, the violence of a world that seemed ever closer to its end (the Cuban missile crisis then the Vietnam War marked these years), despondency might have set in like thought's dramatic external destiny. Instead, it became above all the matter of the drama inherent to thought. For a thinking that had raised itself to the high level of *indiscretion for the exhausted*, nothing that happened—even what was most tragic personally—could be wholly foreign. But this thinking of exhaustion (both one's own exhaustion and the exhaustion of possibilities) becomes, as René Char puts it, a thinking of courage, an exhausted thought, due to the way it forces itself to think misfortune, as well as the possibility of still speaking and acting, even in the depths of failure. The *force* of this demand is what so overwhelms the person who takes it on. He is an author defeated by his own thought and by a thought pushed to the breakdown to which the *entretien* and fragmentary writing now refer. This is where the movement of his research—critical, philosophical, political research, most of all research by writing—has led.

In January 1959, Blanchot writes, "The search for creative criticism is this same wandering movement, this same laborious process that opens up the darkness and is the progressive thrust of mediation, but which also risks being the endless recommencement that ruins all dialectics, procuring only failure and finding therein neither measure nor appeasement." He adds: "Criticism is connected to the search for the possibility of literary experience, but this search is not only a theoretical pursuit, it is the very process constituting the literary experience."[4] Creative criticism would not have any theoretical meaning if it were not doubled, or much rather preceded, by literary experience: its attention to the movements of creation only repeats the creation within narrative—the lived experience of narration that takes itself for its own object. Thus the whole narrative research of the 1950s, which is turned into an attentiveness to the origin of thought in *Awaiting Oblivion*, finds echoes in the critical forms of the *entretien* and the fragment. This is not unimportant for the type of recognition that this work would gain for a long period during the 1960s. Blanchot's extremely strong influence on writers, philosophers, and also artists, is to a large extent due to his writing and thought's capacity endlessly to address what it had evoked in the figure of Eurydice: a venturing into what is darkest, most distant, most anguish-inducing, most overwhelming about the origin of creative power. Each article and each *entretien* is more or less marked by thought's exhaustion as it confronts, beyond both the visible and the invisible, in withdrawn, faraway, and accursed areas of singular experience, what is most naked and most harrowing, what can still be clawed back from the impossible, so as to offer—whether exposed or not—the brutality of its beginning and the eternal return of its fire to the work and the anonymous part of the work that is its audience, its public element, its invisible neutrality. In this way Blanchot writes his thought, and does so *beyond* any expectation of salvation by means of catharsis, immanent effusion, or dialectical completion. In doing so he attracts, submits, and breaks those who, by pushing their own experience to the limit, suddenly read the clear return of the figure which Blanchot for a second time in his work names "the partner invisible" (*l'invisible partenaire*), and which here is the Neuter in him, and in itself, that which always "*sounds strangely for* me."[5]

What attracts the reader here, certainly in order to more easily break him, beyond any notion of safe distance, is the same thing that Blanchot despairs of. It is not certain that he wants the Neuter to become a thought in its own right: in any case, this extremity of thought is not thinkable in itself, and Blanchot *writes* it more than he theorizes it. But writing this thought comes to replace the collective writing of the *Review*, the happiness of friendship, shared authority, and political ambition that that project might have provided. Readers would have to wait until 1994 for Blanchot's next *récit*, *The Instant of My Death*, thirty-two years after *Awaiting Oblivion*. And yet the *récits* offer a happy, sometimes lyrical denouement, always opening onto thought. Their effacement in favor of the *Review*, which ultimately offered little to thought beyond the failure of the interruption it proposed, means that thought has to deal with a doubly unhappy experience. The exhausting movement of thought therefore repeats its capacity for exhaustive reflection. This dive into the depths of anguish once more returns Blanchot to the poverty and sadness of writing in the singular. In this (double) sense, *The Infinite Conversation* offers both the least unjust approach to, and the most desperately frustrating idea of, what the *International Review* could have been.[6] Writing individual contributions to literary journals becomes a way of writing that Blanchot is no longer interested in, that he barely sees as legitimate.[7] At the end of the 1960s, after the events of May 1968 and the death of Jean Paulhan, he would give up doing so. Having written, on average, almost ten articles a year, he would contribute only four pieces to the *NRF* in 1965, then two in 1966, four again in 1967, and only one in 1968 and in 1969. His regular production of authored articles was dead. The replacement of this activity by the enthusiasm with which Blanchot writes anonymous texts for the Student-Writer Committee of the revolution of May 1968 says much about what periodical writing now represents: the *jouissance* of writing is linked to its impact on the collective thinking of the rupture of history and of political revolution. Four years earlier, Blanchot had cited a few words by René Char—let us hear what the anonymous writer states: "An unknown being is an infinite being—one likely, in intervening, to change our anguish and our burden into arterial dawn."[8]

Between the Manifesto and the Revolution, and still under De Gaulle, Blanchot's thinking remained deeply political. A few passing references underscore his interest, for instance, in "a journal like *Arguments*, put together by political writers and by intellectuals who are ready for the future"; elsewhere, discreet allusions repeat his sarcastic condemnation of "the providential man" (261) who "monologues imperiously" (75);[9] the criticism of "depoliticization" (240) persisted.[10] These remarks decompartmentalize the literary genre of the article and the journal by opening them to a political dimension integrated within a wider reasoning. Little by little, even at the *NRF*, the stances Blanchot took were becoming clear. His interest in Marxism continued to grow, and through a reading of Henri Lefebvre's development, he denounced the conditions imposed by the Communist Party on the philosopher (and on philosophy), namely that he be submissive and ultimately leave the party. Blanchot closely understood how an intellectual could make concessions, provisionally, despite and against himself, to the only organization that gave itself the task of making thought *real*.[11] He was still tracking nihilism in all of its forms, as if this were at the secret heart of how all philosophy and all praxis could be articulated: It was the essential threat, what remained unthought in dialectical negativity, the enemy of the most equal thought and the most wary language. It was an insidious face that could appear unexpectedly behind anyone's face, a radical, insurmountable impurity, whose major success in the twentieth century Blanchot denounced: Its destructive irruption onto the political stage "with what was called Nazism or fascism." (402)

These readings of the century's most widespread ideologies also intersected with questions he was asking himself: How to find the site of a *praxis* that would be critically faithful to Marxism ("communism being still always beyond communism"; xii)? How to analyze his own mistakes, what he had agreed to in the past? Blanchot states that nihilism increases its destructive force not by declaring itself explicitly, but by giving its energy to the affirmation of "positive values it advances and that rouse other opposing but related values (the values of race, nationalism, force, the value of humanism and, on both sides, the value of the West)" (402). In doing so, he bears witness to his own former, unknown nihilism, as well as to the inevitably alienated struggle he had waged against it and against Hitler in the name of these "positive values" into which a force that truly assisted nihilism had crept. This had been a way of supporting the ideology that he condemned, whose most visible acts of destruction he condemned, and now he wanted to lay the blame—in a repeated, now-lucid movement of thought and in a mixture of necessary calm and past passion—the blindness that consisted in "playing into the hands of nihilism and its most vulgar replacement, anti-Semitism?" "Why . . . are we so uneasy as we reflect upon it?" he asks, thus underscoring the contemporary malaise whereby any defense of Jewish identity first had to pass through a condemnation of anti-Semitism, thus obscuring the very essence of this identity.[12] This is what he criticizes Sartre for, who "aims to recognize Jewish difference, but only as the inverse of anti-Semitism";[13] and it is also the point upon which he criticizes the writers of the previous century who were fascinated with Hebraic mysticism without trying to understand it (this "frightened admiration" was nothing but "the counterpart to anti-Semitism").[14] Nothing now would shift him from this position: no thinking of misfortune—which is to say no interruption of thought— could go without reflecting on both Judaism and anti-Semitism.

In Blanchot's reflections, this new imperative imposed on thought dates from the period of 1959 to 1963. His anti-Heideggerian position grows more radical toward the end of this period. This can be seen in his sarcastic remarks about legitimizing a sedentary truth, as he denounces the ontological positing of being's luminosity, or as he destroys the eternally new myth of what is initial or original ("to which we remain unreflectively subject"), or reassesses inauthentic speech and anonymous rustling (against "the willing and eager approbation that has been universally given to Heidegger").[15] These criticisms, which he broadly shares with Emmanuel Levinas, most greatly discredit not only on the political attitude of the 1930s university rector, but also the philosopher who was "responsible for a writing that was compromised," and what in philosophy is vulnerable to such compromises—on the nihilist power of this philosophy.[16] Remaining faithful to the thought of the Neuter, that impossible object of knowledge is only ever present through withdrawal, and thus is alone in escaping nihilism's traps. This demands that one radically extricate oneself from the "completion of metaphysics" which, like all philosophy, remains a way of *domesticating and refusing the neuter*.[17]

The discovery of (or attentiveness to) the Neuter forces Blanchot to situate his discourse, if not in relation to the history of philosophy, then at least in relation to *philosophical possibility* itself. This is why he is constantly discussing its margins (Antelme, Bataille, Foucault, Klossowski, Levinas, Sade), its origin (Heraclitus, Plato, Socrates), and its end (Hegel, Nietzsche, Heidegger). This is why he opposes all forms of conceptual stabilization representing "the great refusal" (that of death as death, of nothingness as nothingness, of the neuter as the neuter: this refusal is "all that leads men to prepare a space of permanence where truth, even if it should perish, may be restored to life" (33), or "the great reducers" (in all its instrumentalizing guises, this gigantic "work of inclusion," culture).[18] Interpretation itself is a form of negation; "the critic is a man of power" (327);[19] and the philosopher, Blanchot says after Bataille, a fearful man (49–50).

Perhaps things had come to what Hegel theorized as the end of history; perhaps they were already beyond that end and in the fourth period, outside the dialectic, of "negativity without use" the suggestion of which on the face of the philosopher had marked Bataille so strongly. The "departure from historical space" indicated, minimally, by our "material power to put an end to this history and to the world," to put an end to all debates on the end (in the absolute necessity of putting an end to all debates on the end of values), the "change of epoch" that according to Blanchot uncovered a radical ethical demand (269). Blanchot would not discover the naked place to give to the Other, and ultimately to give to the Wholly Other, without the experience of these exits from history, with the experience of his closest friends Levinas, Bataille, Antelme. The "great refusal" could not be broken without marching before and beyond fear, without paying attention to the possibility of violence—less the violence the thinker might suffer than that which he might inflict. Here, in this site of thought without any stakes except its direct realization, the foundation of all historical responsibility ("anything that resembles, even vaguely, what we saw there literally destroys us") legitimized critical interruption—philosophical interruption.

Thus can be heard the appeal made by dialogue, by the infinite dialogue of thinkers who had been put to the test, to the "relation of the third kind," beyond any sham transcendence and any misplaced immanence. This appeal alone is "not a relation from the perspective of unity, not one of unification" (67); it alone gives the other as other, in the relation of infinite distance or separation, outside any horizon, in language as the measure of separation. Transcendence has to be allowed to accomplish its work, and immanence to win its followers. But only this sovereign relation has their measure, it alone can recognize the equality of one and the effusion of the other, retaining for its part "the absence of any common measure that is my relation to others" (64) as well as the "relation with the unknown that is the unique gift of speech"[20] (212). For Blanchot, this ethical principle regulates the law of all relation, beginning with the relation to the figure of the Jew who, precisely because he carries the burden of such rejections, reductions, domestications, and criticisms, is all the more subjected to them.[21] This is a communitarian principle that regulates the law of the work and worklessness, of political law and poetic law, and to which Blanchot often refers in these terms: *naming the possible, responding to the impossible*. And it is a principle of writing that demands that searching obeys "the demand for discontinuity," which since *Awaiting Oblivion* at least has been regulating—and would regulate for a long time—the form of Blanchot's thought, whether *entretien* or fragment, whether "interruption as meaning" or "rupture as form" (8).

For Blanchot, the exit from history imposes an exit from ontology that alone might be able to found a relation to the other based on what separates us (54).²² This relation is a real *"interruption of being*—an alterity whereby for me there is no other me, nor another existence, nor any modality or mode of universal existence, nor any superexistence, god or nongod, but only the unknown in its infinite distance." This would be a relation to "an alterity that stands in the name of the neuter" (77). Here the strong influence of Levinas's thinking is clear, the Levinas of *Totality and Infinity*, a 1961 thesis whose defense at the Sorbonne Blanchot attended before commenting on the published version (and notably on what it says about the radical exteriority and interruption of ontology that are prerequisites for any ethical position). But equally clear is what goes beyond Levinas: radical atheology, the interruption of all subjective thought. Blanchot believes that he is able to take further, *and on his own account*, the workless nudity of all human relation, the asymmetry of all language. Nominalizing the Neuter stems from this need as it is revealed through the exit from history. The Neuter resides—faraway, errantly, nowhere—in this workless nakedness and in this linguistic asymmetry: points reached in what Blanchot names after, with, but also at some distance from Robert Antelme, as "the indestructible" (130–135). The thought of misfortune—the interruption of thought—touches on the Neuter, which immediately escapes: on the Neuter or on the indestructible that can be destroyed, on what remains unknown about humankind, the far point of sovereignty that escapes, even and especially when it is most naked, from power. This sovereignty is affirmed only in communitarian consciousness, which, beyond any restoration of the subject for another subject, welcomes the other in the name of the other, as all symbolic links are interrupted.²³

The Neuter for Blanchot is an unfinished response to the impossible, a definitive response to the traps laid by nihilism. At the limits of possible witnessing, it therefore avoids both "the great refusal" and "the great reducers," both philology and theology, both culture and—therefore—the book. The perspective of the *book to come* is now replaced by the invisibility of the *absence of the book*. The absence of the book steps away from an authority of knowledge based in oneness; it opens radically onto "the exteriority of inter-saying [*l'entre-dire*]." (431) While in spite of everything the absence of book can only be expressed though the book, or can only be—as it were—inter-said by "fragmentary plurality," it is always-already to the book what worklessness is to the work. This is to say that it is a "movement of detour," an active and senseless ruse of writing, a violent entry into the book, into the order of phrasing and of discourse, into the way a signature is endowed with authority; it performs these actions in the name of a wholly other authority, in the name of infinite responsibility, in the name of the other. It is the part of the book that escapes being burned, because it has always-already created a community of readers brought together by what escapes them and separates them: the indestructible which cannot be destroyed. In addition to not having any center, even a displaced one, there are no poles in the *space of literature*. The book's materiality becomes its own interruption. It is remarkable, from this point of view, that the article named "The Absence of Book" that closes *The Infinite Conversation* should have interrupted the business of publishing the work: it was given to Louis-René des Forêts for the journal *L'Ephémère*, and also given to Gallimard at the same time, after the rest of the manuscript. It closes the work at the last moment.

The interruption of thought: During these years, Blanchot therefore ultimately looked for a form to give to this interruption. The first article written as an *entretien* dates from April 1960. It retains the traditional *entretien*'s distinction between a questioning voice and one responding, immediately placing the latter in the position of authority.[24] Not without some awkwardness or naivety in the commentaries on how the speech is divided up, the *entretien* gradually moves away from this professorial model. With the third article written in this genre, a year later, the exchange is made equal and little by little would leave space for the most neutral (the most narrative) element within each voice in the discussion: "if there is this back-and-forth of words between us—we who are ourselves nothing but the necessity of this back and forth—perhaps it is to avoid the sentence [*l'arrêt*] of a last word"[25] (326). Later, when the texts were republished and when new pages were added to some of them, Blanchot would admit that he heard these two voices as being as distant from one another as they were from his own, his own which is never his own, if not to the extent that this engagement with dialogue dispossesses him of any ownership of words, replies, questions (72–73).[26] Authority resides in this neutral movement, which moves from one voice to the other and back again, indeed perhaps between multiple voices, and is only meaningful if seen in the light of collective authority, in the sense that the authority of the *Review* might have had. Little by little, fragmentary form is thus grafted on to the *entretien*'s lack of horizon. The four lozenges fitting into the absent frame of an interrupted lozenge (❖), used in *Awaiting Oblivion*, are replaced by these pairs: ±±, as if each algebraic sign suspends and makes neutral what is proposed, under the sign of separation, of the two juxtaposed, anonymous voices. These suspensions (more or less) and neutralities (neither more nor less) are conjugated by the spacing made available by punctuation and which, by being ignored, would cause speech to fail by condemning it to indecisive relativity (more or less) or to be misled by what seems obvious (neither more nor less). The movement whereby any individual authority is interrupted thus leads Blanchot not only to adopt the form of the *entretien*, not only that of the fragment, but to use each to disconcert the other.[27] If "fragmentary speech knows no contradiction, even when it contradicts itself" (153), it never accomplishes this lack of knowledge better than in interruption's infinite creation of gaps. It is also responsible for *the erosion of authority* by a wholly other syntax of phrase and utterance. A wholly other authority is what gives the poet over to the distant speech that translates experience. Blanchot, as we know, reserves a special category for René Char's language as capable of this.[28] In Char's poetry, not only does the neuter give its form to a number of substantivizations, which are so important that they take from it something like the strength of verbs, but it also represents the power of a "fictitious" root" that spreads and disseminates through language. Blanchot describes this syntax of the relation without relation as precisely as he would the syntax that starts to be imposed at the end of *The Last Man* and that neutralizes *Awaiting Oblivion*: for Char and Blanchot, the same "islands of meaning" "posed next to one another," "of an extreme compactness and yet capable of an infinite drift." This "arrangement that does not compose but juxtaposes, that is to say, leaves each of the terms that come into relation *outside* one another"; this "arrangement at the level of disarray," this "immobile becoming," is a "pure detour in its strangeness."[29] They are so much the same that they share—albeit at a distance—the authority of the same phrases. For if Blanchot says that this "pure detour ... allows one to go from one disappointment to another," it also leads "from one courage to another," Char happens to give a parallel formulation the neutral authority of the poet in a poem dating from the same year (1964) and dedicated to his friend: "Politically, Maurice Blanchot can only move from one disappointment to another, which is to say from one courage to another."[30]

This is an infinite authority, going beyond the name of the author and above all beyond the contingency of the book and the independence of the work: Blanchot places his last two major critical books under the sign of a *friendship* that responds to the impossible chasm left by the vanishing points of *the infinite conversation*. The friendship of all the partners is authoritative in itself; even if it means always returning to itself, this movement of negation is not without the beauty, strength, and withdrawal of utopia. Neither is it without weakness. In this way of engaging with exhaustion, there is an avowal of powerlessness that opens up in Blanchot a period that we may term *the recognition of the biographical*. Biography:

Blanchot has managed to *unavow* in a thousand ways quite how far his critical and narrative work was spent addressing his absence, how far it permanently challenged the unaddressable elements it contained, and thus how far it left traces in writing without ever emphasizing them or recognizing them as such. If he now recognizes this movement, as one would one's childhood, he does so from the depths of extreme weakness. This recognition can only come about by way of Kafka. The infinite passion that brings Blanchot back to Kafka had no equivalent in his critical texts; from the "last word' to the "very last word," *from Kafka to Kafka*, it is constantly found in the most personal parts of the work, with an ever more marked biographical indiscretion: the indiscretion of friendship, the indiscretion for the exhausted. In May 1968 Blanchot wrote that possessing many documents and hundreds of pages of letters means that "we are closer, but also almost deflected from asking the true questions, *because we no longer have the strength to let them come to us in their innocence, to hold them away from the biographical reports that attract and engulf them by giving them fuel.*"[31]

Biographical rumor, neutrally, attracts the work toward it as anonymously and fascinatingly as does the Mother, as does "the immense, faceless Someone."[32]

A final stirring of indifference, a final attempt at rigor in exhaustion leads the work to try to retain its force of insubordination and nonreference to rumor. However, opening oneself up to the shared authority of friendship demands too much energy not to create some visible signs. The *récit* that opens *The Infinite Conversation* perhaps demands to be read for what it points to rather than for what it says directly, as a mask worn by two voices exhausted by the demand to share their murmuring. First published in March 1966 by the *NRF* in isolation from the other texts of that decade (nothing else by Blanchot was published in the four preceding months, nor in the eight subsequent ones), it had already appeared as if from weakness. It came out of this period when illness was again troubling its author and forcing him to withdraw. This sketch of powerlessness, however exaggerated it might appear, still allows for the description of the lessening of strength, the extension of fatigue: "The forces of life suffice only up to a certain point ... the experience of fatigue that constantly makes us feel that our life is limited; you take a few steps in the street, eight or nine, then you fall." Blanchot clarifies that in saying as much, he is "thinking of something very simple"[33] (379). The allusion is becoming transparent, such ultimately is the weakness—now laid bare—of the narrative voice.

The liminal text of *The Infinite Conversation* (xi–xxiii) seems to be directed by an absolute contraction that kills being—perhaps a being that in the bosom of fatigue had still been able to believe that it was possible for the subject to be indefatigable (even if this possibility was a sacred one). "Only a being whose solitude has contracted through suffering, and in relation with death, takes its place on a ground where the relationship with the other becomes possible."[34] This phrase from Emmanuel Levinas nicely states the movement of truth that legitimizes, at this narrative threshold, the step toward the other that each critical article would repeat.[35] Perhaps it also suggests how real this movement is. The encounter between these two exhausted beings, whose exhaustion nonetheless finds a final strength consisting of placing them in relation to one another, imposes the greatest respect. The two beings (they could be Blanchot and Antelme, or Bataille, or Levinas) whose weakness has laid bare—via a cadaverous thinking—the indestructible, and has allowed it to speak. This is speech clawed back from the impossible and therefore one that is often interrupted and always without external references, which comments only on its own movement, its own capacity to still push its thinking forward. It also speaks to what a gift it is to be able to work within such a rhythm of exposition. It speaks to what remains of the *récit*, of the *entretien*, of friendship; that only the ending of all these, their most essential part, remains, and that it remains on the cusp of an old age that can see their sovereignty moving off into the distance. It speaks to the even more intense solitude that marks those who have been exhausted by returning, and it also tells us how far companionship, though cooled, can survive between solitudes distanced from one another (and between whom the *entretien* has always begun). This speech rejects all forms of consolation and complacency, keeping its eyes exclusively on the site where the sky appeared. It seeks neither causation nor periodization and, even when it "doesn't know what is to become of it" (*ne sait que devenir*, xvi), it puts a stop to the tragedy it went into exile in order to forget, it confronts the weight of significant silence. Its situation is one of gallows humor (how can the truth of fatigue be grasped when one is fatigued?), except that it can tell, recount, continue to speak for the third party, the one who brings them together without being there, the condemned man, the deserter, the insubordinate.

> They take seats, separated by a table, turned not toward one another, but opening up, around the table that separates them, an interval large enough that another person could be thought to be their true interlocutor, the one for whom they would be speaking, if they addressed him. (*viii–ix*)

This community refers to no one. It exists, it is conjugated in the neuter. The Neuter is the depths, the name, the alterity of the invisible partner, of the "*fictitious partner*" (311) who takes on authority where fiction had done so previously. Its beauty (has the beauty of the Neuter ever been mentioned?) lies in the smile of this partner, this memory of vertiginous speed, of unheard-of mobility, of a "light dance" (which any playfulness now deserts). Its beauty is in this brief slowness of the fiction; it is like a piece of news clawed back from creative vigilance, more disposed to write but less capable of doing so than ever. The past speaks for the two men present.

> He moves toward the shelves where—it is now noticed—a great number of books are arranged. . . . He does not touch a single volume, he stays there with his back turned and utters in a quiet but clear voice: "How will we manage to disappear?" (xiv)[36]

The past speaks for them and in their name. But the biography of the work they tease out speaks for the movement that their death, their gift, represents: it speaks for the effacement that presides over the community that little by little, now and then, invalidating the nihilism that reigns elsewhere, they assemble through the meaning of, and in order to protect, their worklessness.

CHAPTER 54

A First Homage
The Special Issue of *Critique* (1966)

"*How will we manage to disappear?*" Standing in the way are books, and books written by others. In the absence of collective writing and despite the impossibility of forming a school, Blanchot's thinking—beyond the influence that it was broadly exerting at this time—was beginning to give rise to new modes of thought. At first unaware of one another, little by little these modes of thought would cross-pollinate, creating the spaces necessary to further the thinking that had been given over to them. In the 1970s, conscious of this transfer of authority, the voice of Maurice Blanchot changed and pushed toward a new phase of withdrawal.

The singular quality of this recognition began in the 1960s and persists today. "No writer is more underrated, and yet none has been so carefully read over the last 25 years by a large number of *writers*," Dionys Mascolo observed in 1966. He attributed this lack of public awareness to Blanchot's work's endless demand for knowledge, which nonetheless opens onto acceptance of the impossible and attentiveness to nonknowledge. Unlike Sartre or Camus, whose agitations concern the realm of what is immediately possible, and who demand answers, Blanchot like Bataille denies himself "any possibility of acting *quickly* on the minds of others."[1] The radical, extreme elements of their approaches need to be read, ingested, digested, meditated upon. They cannot rely on writing alone. The young writers of the 1950s who had been touched by this ultimate avowal, this authority of friendship, would take up the task of making it known, of communicating it.

In 1959, Maurice Blanchot met Roger Laporte. Five years earlier, this young writer had sent him his first book, *Souvenir de Reims*, and an exchange of letters had begun (despite the imperfections of this text).[2] In 1957, it was Blanchot's turn to send a book: *The Last Man*, and the following year, Laporte wrote *Le Partenaire*, which Blanchot recommended to Maurice Nadeau. When the two writers met, one was writing *Awaiting Oblivion*, the other *La Veille*. Three or four years later, both books would cause a stir. Written in the neuter, under the watch of an impersonal authority traversing and constituting the subject of writing even as it irremediably and irrevocably opposes it, Laporte's narrative is the most Blanchotian and the most sovereign of all those that would be placed under the nameless sign of Blanchot. It is at once the most faithful and the most independent of them. Michel Foucault immediately wrote a prominent article on it in the *NRF*; a new friendship was born.

Laporte and Foucault shared a huge admiration for Blanchot, and both would voice it endlessly. The two men were around the same age.[3] Like Laporte, Foucault read Blanchot at the end of the 1950s. This reading produced a radical break: It moved him definitively away from university institutions, above all from their language and discourse. Blanchot led Foucault to Bataille, who led him to Nietzsche; alongside Artaud and Klossowski, these would be the tutelary figures of the thinking that the young philosopher would elaborate. Foucault gives them a revolutionary place in the history of thought—in the history of the way thought itself has been conceived. In these figures, he sees a new break from Western culture, he sees "extreme forms of language" that represent "the summits of thought." In Blanchot, he glimpses "a philosophy of nonpositive affirmation," an untiring, limitless contestation of ontology, which sees marginality as able to speak directly about being. This forces the subject toward what lies outside its thought, a thought in which Foucault sees—through neutral writing, whose madness he notes, as Levinas had done—"the narrative of imminence and withdrawal, of danger and of promise." He sees in it the appearance of the very language of thought, something capable of breaking the order of Western philosophical discourse by opening a "space indefinitely explored," in which the impurity of speech endlessly gestures toward silence. Foucault produces many statements of support and praise around 1963 and 1964, in articles on Bataille, Laporte, and Klossowski that are still read today.[4] These articles express endless gratitude, for which there was now an extra reason. For in 1961, Caillois had given Blanchot the manuscript of *History of Madness*, still in thesis form. When the book was published, he was one of the few to state how new and important it was—in fact, he was the only one (alongside Roland Barthes), something that would leave Foucault with feelings of both amazement and bitterness, as he would often recall.

In an interview with Raymond Bellour in 1967, Foucault would even go so far as to recognize that the figure who had initiated "the thought of the outside" was the most sovereign of all authorities: "it is Blanchot," he stated, "who has made possible all discourse on literature."[5] This is an unprecedented claim, which shakes the foundations of criticism, and makes Blanchot into the transcendental thinker of literature, he who defines the a priori conditions of his own practice and thought. It makes Blanchot the equivalent and the other of Hegel; for Foucault, the philosopher of the end of history and the writer of the indefinite neutralization of the end share the ability truly to bring to life Plato and *Rameau's Nephew* on the one hand and Hölderlin, Kafka, or Mallarmé on the other.[6] It is as if the third party gave the work its accessibility, and authors their authority, which suggests—in Blanchot's case—that he only abdicates his own authority in order to give it to the other, *to the name of the other*, in the free and infinite play of writing.

Despite these statements on the importance he gave to Blanchot, Foucault would always think that, "more from shyness than from ingratitude," he had not repaid the recognition and knowledge given to him by this thinker.[7] Thus, when in 1965 Jean Piel asked him and Roger Laporte to prepare an issue of *Critique* in homage to Blanchot, Foucault was swift to agree and to take the project forward, despite the risk of failure.[8] At the time, few authors had tried to write on Blanchot, and contributors would prove difficult to find. Neither was the editorial conception of the issue guaranteed to succeed, even if it did follow an issue in homage to Georges Bataille, for at the time *Critique* had only very rarely published issues dedicated to a single topic or author. However, the issue would be one of the journal's finest. It was praised by Mascolo in *La Quinzaine Littéraire*, by Jacques Réda in *Les Cahiers du Sud*, by Tzvetan Todorov in *Le Nouvel Observateur*, and brought together contributions by Jean Starobinski, Paul de Man, Emmanuel Levinas.[9] It opens with a poem by René Char which is followed by a outstanding critical study by Georges Poulet, "Maurice Blanchot, Critic and Novelist," one of the first to emphasize the unbreakable link between the two genres within the work and to show that this link was nonetheless dissolved by the creation of a language that "slithers in reptilian fashion."[10] The issue's contributors are in unanimous agreement: They protest the scandalous lack of studies addressing Blanchot's work, perhaps due to the "both tranquil and unstoppable energy" with which it constantly goes beyond itself and deprives criticism of tools, and therefore also due to the authority and fascination it exerts,[11] perhaps even due to the risks it takes in addressing experiences on the limits of what can be communicated, thus depriving interpretation of certainty.[12] They try to show that in constantly working with ambiguity and the unsayable, in the bosom of the obscurity that he had the rare courage to inhabit, this author nonetheless is still "the clearest of all."[13] They often attempt to shatter images that prevent approaches to the work, for instance that—already a common one—of its sadness and despair. On the contrary, in his essay in the middle of the issue, Foucault underscores Blanchot's serenity in expelling the subject from the neutral arena of language (in this gesture language opens on to the distance where the experience of thought is formed, an experience that is constant even in interruption). On the contrary, also, Foucault underscores how strong this "thought of the outside" is, which not only bears witness to its origins (Sade, "the rendering-naked of desire in the infinite murmuring of discourse," Hölderlin, "the discovery of the turning-aside of the gods in a fissure in language as it is abandoned"), but through which Blanchot's work takes itself as its own object. This takes place before the imaginary and reason are dissociated from one another, through the figures of attraction (madness, radicality, obsession, endlessness, oblivion), which are necessarily brought together with those of negligence (which was also absolute, indifferent, incalculable). And ultimately, Foucault underscores how the law becomes the only thing that can present the neuter's nihilist threat, how the relationship with the companion becomes the only compromise—albeit an invisible one—with death.[14] Bringing this strength to light, at the very moment when Blanchot had just published the *entretien* on fatigue (which a few years later would open *The Infinite Conversation*) allows Foucault's thinking to end on a note of gratitude, in a rapport that rises above distress, in the only movement able to access the outside: that of friendship.

This first collective publication in homage to Blanchot was a turning point in the critical reception of his work. It led to the first university theses and prefigured the first books, which would appear between five and eight years later. Françoise Collin, who in 1971 became the first author to publish a book on Blanchot, already featured in the issue of *Critique*. Bernard

Noël and Roger Laporte, whose text closes the issue, would publish theirs in 1973. From the more scholarly approach of Collin or Wilhelm to the readerly experience of Laporte, Noël, or Madaule, the variety of the first books dedicated to Blanchot can already be glimpsed in June 1966. No writer would fail to avow their fidelity, humility, and weakness: the "absence of book" that traverses them speaks volumes to the strength of this work's resistance to all forms of cognitive reductionism (which it denounces), as well as to the fact that even leading figures had been in two minds over whether to propose it as an exception in the intellectual landscape. Blanchot's paradoxical position, on the margins of literature, served him badly in terms of institutional recognition. The opposition to charisma represented by his invisibility in public and his dazzling language led those faithful to him to share a blind fascination. The resulting cultishness provoked as much idolatry as it did disdain for that idolatry, surrounding the work with chatter to which it remained indifferent but which did not allow it to be received in the most "neutral" way possible. Paradoxically, at first it was the success of this singular body of work that condemned it to have only a discreet public presence. Erasing the limitations of speech, being receptive to its mad, anonymous rustling, writing its movement which—whether in *récit*, fragment, or essay—dispossesses the subject in the name of the other, and thereby traces the truth of this dispossession: all of this spoke *most immediately* to those who practiced it: writers and artists. It illuminated what made their existence possible. It seemed to allow their consciousness, the consciousness of their unconscious, the archaeology of their creative power, to shine forth. Progressively, an author had effaced himself and a work had unworked itself, had always more assuredly, always more madly, withdrawn interpretation from his criticism and fictionality from his fiction, in order that others might be able to continue writing themselves, but he still held them due to this very fact, due to this demand to carry on.

Many authors would see Blanchot's literature as the labyrinthine description of the creative processes that were both most proper or improper to them—both their own, and ones that exceeded their control. Foucault put it as follows in 1967: Blanchot establishes "between the author and the work a mode of relation that had remained unsuspected."[15] For certain artists, when the question was raised of writing or filming something on the very possibility of this relation, Blanchot's name would represent the obvious authority. He marks the paradoxically "biographical" itinerary of Roger Laporte deeply. He exercises an ever-greater influence on Marguerite Duras's syntactical fragmentation and on her method of autobiographical exposition. He is a major reference in Jean-Luc Godard's self-portrait.[16]

He represents the guarantee of refusal, the vigilance of the outside, the uncompromising speech that consists in a demanding relation to the wholly other. His effacement offers no model, his creativity exposes the very conditions of the creative demand, and his thinking gives a clear narrative of the possibilities of thought. It is probably in this sense that, on being asked about the time "proper" to literature, literature's own, Roland Barthes—whom it is difficult to suspect of getting swept up in a mythology—would situate Blanchot "in the realm of what cannot be equaled, imitated, or applied."[17] He is irreproducible, and yet at the source of all possibility of reproduction.

Having interrupted his critical work in the mid-1960s, and only reviving it sporadically afterward, Blanchot would remain silent in the debates opposing traditional criticism and *nouvelle critique*. He himself would never adopt the lexicon of structural or functional analysis.[18] While some of the thinkers close to him adopt its methods, in Foucault's case this always goes hand in hand with an absolute vigilance that consists of thinking the subject through its margins, and in Barthes's case these new methods would always be subtly undermined. For both these thinkers, the domain of scientific enquiry remains useful, while authority always flows from the one discourse that makes the others possible—and this discourse is Blanchot's. *Criticism and Truth*, which Barthes published in 1966 as a response to the accusations of "new pretense" by the Sorbonne professor Raymond Picard, is full of references to Blanchot, who is thus pushed center stage in the polemic (a striking fact, given his attempts to remain absent from it).[19]

After the failure of the *International Review*, Barthes moved closer to Sollers and to *Tel Quel*: he must have overcome his great wariness of this group which he had regarded as too "literary."[20] But Blanchot remained, both for Barthes and for the *telquelliens* who since the early days had been asking him for a text (without success), a major reference point. Sollers cited him regularly, especially in a foundational 1965 article "The Novel and the Experience of Limits," stressing the revolutionary implications of Blanchot's research and thereby acknowledging his debt to him.[21] Genette does not discuss him directly; he simply cites him as the main authority.[22] In France, Blanchot often passed, without wanting the title, for "the master of the new criticism."[23] In following years, in Italy, his name alongside those of Bataille and Klossowski, was at stake in vigorous attacks against the faith in structuralism as a science.[24] Blanchot's fame was now international; this was particularly the case in Germany, where the 1962 translation of *The Book to Come*, under the title *Der Gesang der Sirenen* had gained enormous coverage across the press. Nowhere, however, were his ideas truly discussed: generally they were either ignored, or adopted wholesale.

This other type of authority—which Blanchot would never worry about, not from disdain but from indifference, because it did not flow from friendship—was perhaps due to the double reach of his work, literary and philosophical, work that dissuaded even leading thinkers from ever engaging in any real examination or commentary. Foucault would state that he "considered the literary and philosophical work [of Bataille, Blanchot and Klossowski] to be much more important than what he himself [could] produce," and that he felt extremely shy in relation to their achievements.[25] For Deleuze, Blanchot's influence would act in a subterranean, restless, and untiring way, without ever being openly declared or remarked upon; he barely cites the work in question.[26] Figures such as Levinas and Bataille had their entire personal intimacy with Blanchot behind them when they spoke about him. Over the following decade, only one philosopher would break the silence: Jacques Derrida. Like Foucault and Laporte, Derrida— born in 1930—began reading Blanchot in the late 1940s. Having discovered his work thanks to Sartre's article on *Aminadab*, he felt shaken by the grace of a language irreducible to any historically recognizable literary or philosophical discourse. Blanchot's authority over Derrida would mark even the syntax of their shared research, in the latter's extreme prudence over the meaning of particular signs, of particular words or phrases, the constant vigilance regarding the grammatical power and the contextual reach of given propositions, the irreducibly repeated statements that this incredulity is part of how creativity operates, the opening of all concepts to the spread of their possibilities, the regular return—despite the knottiness of the impossible—to truth. All of this finds its place in the decentered writing of this unfolding thought.

Beginning in 1962, Derrida had published a book and several articles, which were widely noticed. In December 1965, a text in *Critique*, "Writing avant la lettre," laid the foundations of the *Grammatology*, which was still to come. "La parole soufflée," published in *Tel Quel* in winter of the same year, opens with an extended reading of Blanchot's texts on Artaud and Hölderlin. During this time, the two thinkers had begun to appreciate one another's work—to put it mildly. Blanchot had been reading Derrida since "Force and Signification," which appeared in *Critique* in June 1963. When he wrote to him after the publication of "Violence and Metaphysics," a long essay on the thought of Emmanuel Levinas published in 1964 in the *Revue de métaphysique et de morale*, he made clear his joy, his recognition; he wanted to follow the developments of a thinking that, after the death of

Bataille and the failure of the *International Review*, brought him the support of a new friendship. In this early correspondence, he drew a lengthy parallel between his own questioning—both in writing and in theory ("Speaking is not Seeing")—of the optical metaphor which ruled over so much thinking, and Derrida's critique of the photological model of Western epistemology. When Blanchot read in Derrida that "the force of the work, the force of genius, the force, too of that which engenders in general is precisely that which resists geometrical metaphorization and is the proper object of literary criticism," how could he not have focused on a striking closeness of thought, which meant that he only had to substitute the word "force" for the word "neuter" in order to wholly identify with the statement?[27]

In 1967, Derrida published three books denouncing the theological and philosophical predominance given to the representation of speech (as the possibility of speech) rather than to writing. This "post-Heideggerian" gesture of an unprecedented ontological opening would in its turn exercise such authority over Blanchot that he would correct, as if commanded by these three books, all of the articles contained in *The Infinite Conversation*, inserting inverted commas around some concepts, or even replacing them with their antonyms, in order more strongly to defer or differ them, setting them at a distance from any effect of presence or of immediacy.[28] Thus it was not in the *nouvelle critique*, but in the thought of Foucault, Derrida (then also of Jean-Luc Nancy) that Blanchot would recognize (and he would say: happily, and not without grace) the true debate with thought that he had inscribed in his books: *thought's dissemination, its worklessness, its disappearance.*

CHAPTER 55

Between Two Forms of the Unavowable
The Beaufret Affair (1967–1968)

Another year, another homage: In 1967, François Fédier proposed a collective volume in honor of Jean Beaufret, whose prestige was considerable at the time. Of all French philosophers, he was the closest to Heidegger, and the one who had worked most after the war to rehabilitate the German thinker and recognize his greatness. Fédier asked for contributions from Kostas Axelos, Maurice Blanchot, René Char, Michel Deguy, Jacques Derrida, Roger Laporte, and Roger Munier. All initially agreed to contribute to the volume that would eventually be named *L'endurance de la pensée*.

Over lunch, however, Laporte informed Derrida of the deep unease that had quelled his admiration for Beaufret since he had heard him make an anti-Semitic remark in private.[1] The remark related to nominations for a post in philosophy at the university in Clermont-Ferrand, and Beaufret had stated, "If I had to choose between Clémence Ramnoux, X, Y, and a Jew, naturally I would vote for Clémence Ramnoux." Beaufret's known antipathy for Ramnoux, and his various subsequent denials that he had intended to vote in such a way, did not—in Derrida's eyes—alter the seriousness of the situation: a man, what's more a professor in the educational

370

establishment and a close ally of Heidegger, had qualified such a leaning as "natural." Paying homage to him suddenly became unthinkable. And what's more: beyond its racist generality and lack of attention to detail ("a Jew"), the statement was particularly aimed at a Jewish philosopher whose fate could not leave Derrida indifferent: Emmanuel Levinas.[2]

As surprised as he was absolutely shocked, Derrida immediately informed Fédier. "*It is absolutely impossible for me*, despite my stupefaction, to call into question the authenticity of what has been reported to me," he stressed, without revealing the name of the informant. Thinking the statement both serious and vulgar, without any possible ambiguity, he decided (he said irreversibly) to withdraw the text he had already submitted.[3]

It was November 27, 1967. Having known Derrida for some time (he especially admired *Voice and Phenomenon* but felt more negatively about *Of Grammatology*), Fédier responded the following day. With an equally weighty feeling of affliction, he protested the allegation of anti-Semitism, which he interpreted as a sign of a new, warped plot against Beaufret, of whom he painted an astonishingly angelic portrait based on his innocence and radical opposition to all forms of fanaticism and of ill-feeling. Meanwhile, Laporte had written to Beaufret, who informed Fédier: The "informant" (this was the term both used) was uncovered. Beaufret also wrote to Derrida, lamenting that with his blind faith in Laporte's assertion he had not taken the trouble to ask Beaufret for his account. Fédier then relayed to those he had in mind for the collection news of what became, by that very token, "the affair." Those close to Fédier immediately accused Laporte of slander.

In December, a first meeting was held in Derrida's office at the École Normale Supérieure in the Rue d'Ulm, featuring Laporte and Beaufret, who continued to deny the accusations. At the end of December or beginning of January, another meeting brought together various contributors to the work in the apartment of Michel Deguy, who, although he was not part of Fédier's entourage, had offered to "mediate." The discussion took a more general turn, calling into question Heidegger's anti-Semitism and the intolerable political extremism inscribed in his philosophy. At this juncture, the true roots of the conflict were revealed: Wahl and Levinas's attacks on the anti-Semitism of which Heidegger's philosophy was accused, condemnations that Beaufret, Fédier, and those close to them could not stand, and therefore rejected as lies. For these figures, the entire affair flowed from the tyrannical, delirious capacities they attributed to Laporte's "mind." Feeling pressured from all sides, and experiencing a real sense of persecution, the writer was less and less able to bear the fact that his word was doubted (this affair, he would say later, would remain the most painful of his life). Someone close to him therefore approached Maurice Blanchot on January 23.

Protected by the silence surrounding him, Blanchot was not aware of anything; nobody had yet contacted him. When they did, he wrote immediately to Fédier and received a response whose vehemence he found troubling. He therefore contacted Derrida and asked to see him. Thus the first meeting took place, in late January or early February, between Blanchot and the young philosopher he had been reading for several years. For a year they continued to see each other regularly, most often in Derrida's office at ENS Ulm.[4]

When he learned that the statement in question related to Emmanuel Levinas, and thus struck, via anti-Semitism, at the heart of friendship—this friendship, which was closer to him than he himself was—Blanchot decided to respond to Fédier. However, he did not wish to do so without considering Laporte and Derrida, to whom he sent copies of his letter and whom he asked for their opinions on this response. While he was considering withdrawing his text, he had not yet made any decision, and above all wanted to act in concert with his two friends. This letter, sent by Blanchot in mid-February, received no response from Fédier.

In March, the question of whether to publish or withdraw was far from decided. The proofs of the volume were sent to all the contributors. Laporte wrote to Fédier informing him that he would not be sending back the "Notes on Giacometti" that he had initially intended to contribute, even while saying that he was ready to reconsider his position, which was due more to the aggressive attitude of Fédier and those close to him than to Beaufret's statement; he still considered Beaufret his friend and recognized what he owed him intellectually. As for Blanchot, he returned to Fédier the proofs of "The Fragment Word," a text addressing René Char that had already appeared in Italian in the issue of *Il Menabò* given over to the *International Review*.[5] Along with the article he sent a letter or rather a warning, which took an exceptionally severe, unfriendly, and inflexible tone. It gave two conditions for the article being published: that it be accompanied by a dedication to Emmanuel Levinas,[6] and that all the authors of the volume be sent a letter explaining what actually happened, as well as the aim of his own participation in the project. At the same time, Derrida sent Fédier a similar letter in which he declared that he would cosign with Blanchot the future letter of explanation, whose definitive version of April 2 reestablished—over and against the rumors spread by Fédier—the "full confidence" that the authors had always had in Laporte.[7] The letter bore witness to a concern for friendship just as it did to the impossibility of knowing the whole truth. It therefore justified the choice to continue with publication; faced with the gap between (even absolute) confidence and the proof that was lacking, the only intervention that could be made was in the form of texts accompanied by preambles that changed their orientation in a striking way.

Once more, authority belonged to friendship alone and, as with the failure of the International Review, this new mode of division and sharing (*partage*) would be destined to secrecy. At least Blanchot experienced this "affair" in happy proximity to Derrida. He wrote to him on March 23:

> In any case, I shall be happy to sign this letter alongside you, for what together we are carrying today is fairly heavy, and I am sure that later (if our lives allow a "later") it will belong to the truth and perhaps to the fortune of friendship

To this, Derrida responded the following day:

> I am about to try to write this project of the shared letter, and then will send it to you. Among all the marks that this story will have left behind it, this shared signature will be the only gesture that I shall recognize in full.

A few days later, Blanchot left Paris for a period. "Sign in my name the text that you will write," he reassured Derrida, adding an extra chapter to the story of giving and receiving, of the effacement and sharing of authority.

Among all the impersonal justifications and unavowable dignity, the honor of secrecy and wariness over creating a stir, Blanchot and Derrida faced a question: should Emmanuel Levinas be informed of the affair? On the one hand, it was a question of not upsetting him, not creating a fanfare over the demand for justice that takes its strength from discreet responsibility and shared reflection. On the other, it was a matter of giving truth its due and of showing that they remained vigilant, as the affair seemed to be coming to an end, and could have become known to Levinas. In the face of Beaufret's "unavowable," which was unavowable in its essence or its nature, Blanchot and Derrida proposed a different sort of purely Levinasian unavowable, consisting in an ethical necessity. In Blanchot's life, the refusal to communicate pieces of information was not new. Until this point, he had always pulled back from speech that sees itself as transcending acts and works, which perverts responsibility by claiming subjectivity and by making compromises with the demand for public knowledge, which claims to break out of the silence of meditation; he had always preferred "to give [him]self over to silent awaiting." This is what he wrote to Derrida on March 27, citing an ethical demand: "We have to accept that we will not be *personally* justified."

Both therefore decided to wait; their "silent awaiting" that would not last long, as a few weeks later, Levinas was informed of the situation in an incomplete and indirect way. Meeting with him was now a necessity, making any scruples impossible.

Blanchot and Derrida went to see Emmanuel Levinas at home. It is probable that Blanchot had not seen his Strasbourg friend for almost seven years, since the defense of the thesis that became *Totality and Infinity*.[8] After this, he would not see him often, perhaps ever. In any case, their paradoxical proximity was complete. Whether it was personal or public, no event in the life of one would pass without a sign from the other. Michaël Levinas, the philosopher's son, would bear witness to the "sacred character" of a correspondence that would never end between his father and Maurice Blanchot.

In Blanchot's trembling, anguished, and solemn presence, Levinas showed little external reaction to an affair that, despite himself, made him smile. His position was simple: All drama was to be avoided, even while vigilance was to be retained; the texts ought to be published, in order that Beaufret not be tainted with anti-Semitism. Blanchot and Derrida's position was just as simple: they had to bear witness on behalf of their friends, as well as for one another and for themselves. Beaufret's denials continued. Blanchot and Derrida were the only ones who were still confident in Laporte's account, Char and Munier having dropped away. Others had agreed to believe him even as they played down the nature of the language in question. Those who were closest to Fédier were still proclaiming their outrage.

The book was published by Plon in October 1968; even though his text was included in it, Laporte's name had been erased from the table of contents. "The Fragment Word" opened as foreseen with a dedication to Emmanuel Levinas. On receiving the book, Blanchot sent the publisher the cosigned letter, to be forwarded to all the volume's contributors; none ever received it.

The encounter with Emmanuel Levinas had taken place at the beginning of May. The weight of the unavowable was exploding in France. Other forms of authority and of community were being sought, and Blanchot was taking part in these revolutions.

CHAPTER 56

The Far Side of Fear
Political Disillusionment (May 1968)

For Maurice Blanchot, the events of May 1968 unfolded against the backdrop of a profound disillusionment with politics matched only by that of the 1940s. Both he and Mascolo would state that they did not take part in setting up the movement and that their role in it remained negligible. However, far from being at a distance from the spirit of insubordination that was claiming and imposing its due, they kept in step with the *événements*, quickly undertaking the task of thinking them, and acting as chairs of a Committee. May '68 would be something like the "other time" at the heart of time, the incarnation in bodies, cries, and writings—and in absence too—of a different form of community.

Since 1965, the failure of the *International Review*, his personal distress, and new health problems had left Blanchot sidelined from everything, or from almost everything—except from "community." He traveled only at the suggestion of his brother René, following in the footsteps of friendship (Egypt in 1965, Greece in 1966, where he evoked memories of Elio Vittorini). Each time, he returned to find his disenchantment confirmed.[1] He nonetheless signed the petition, begun by Robert Antelme in May 1967, in favor of an American defeat in Vietnam; on Mascolo's demand, he wrote a manifesto for the boycott of the ORTF (Office for Radio and Television in France) after the elections of May 1967 (which gave the right a majority of only two seats in the Assembly); but at the end of the same year, his personal abandonment of any public profile seemed stronger than ever. He would therefore not go to Cuba in January 1968 alongside Mascolo, Des Forêts, or Leiris, not thinking that he had any authority to speak in a Congress of intellectuals, to abandon silence and produce culture as its own object. He did not see that he had any right to impose himself as a player in the liberation of Cuba (he did not believe that it had yet been "liberated"), nor did he have any desire to represent Western culture, which he saw as dead and as a bearer of death (alienating as it did its subjects, even the contestatory ones, right up till death). This refusal nonetheless caused him discomfort. Disillusioned with the possible and fixed on the impossible, he insisted that it was necessary to create swiftly and radically the new project for a bulletin alongside Duras, Mascolo, and Schuster. "It is not enough to stay on the sidelines."[2]

On March 22, when students were occupying the administration tower at the University of Nanterre, Blanchot was living through the most decisive days of the Beaufret affair (sending his proofs to Fédier, setting out the conditions on which the text could be published). At the end of April or beginning of May, when the *événements* were gathering speed, he visited Emmanuel Levinas for the last time. His closest friend would have harsh words for the student revolt.

From May 5 onward, after the first demonstrations, occupations, expulsions and condemnations, Schuster and the surrealists made themselves "available to the students." The same or the following day, using the text written by Blanchot in spring 1967, Mascolo and the group of the Rue Saint-Benoît reiterated the call for writers, artists, and scholars to boycott the ORTF. Intellectuals were organizing themselves, but being careful not to take over the movement; in any case, the students did not wish to have any figurehead or leader, and were prepared to say so if necessary. On May 8, thirty-five writers and philosophers made public a text in solidarity with the "student movement throughout the world," "this movement that in a few explosive hours has shaken the so-called welfare society perfectly embodied in the French world."[3] They encouraged the students to refuse any concession to the press, to power and to the political parties who for months had been playing down or slandering their actions; they called for the rejection of "any premature affirmation"; for the students to "oppose and maintain a power of refusal that we believe is capable of opening up a future." The text ended with these words, which provided the title when it

The Far Side of Fear 377

was published in *Le Monde*. It had been written in secret by Blanchot. Among the signatories were those close to him (Antelme, Nadeau, Des Forêts, Duras, Schuster, Leiris, Roy, Mascolo) as well as Klossowski, Sarraute, Lacan, and Blin, and names better known to the wider public such as Sartre and Lefebvre, who gave the text a certain reverberation.

The declaration was published the day before the first night of the barricades, which took place on May 10–11: Blanchot took part in this event and said that it "shook" him. He was shaken, as was the entirety of public opinion, by the fierce violence of the police charge, which injured hundreds. He was shaken by how quickly the situation turned, meaning one could no longer look beyond the barricades and to the future, but had to fall back behind them. And he was shaken by how the "exit from the space of history" he had been speaking of for several years had suddenly come into play as something real.

One of the more astonishing things about Blanchot's participation in these few weeks of "the May revolution" was that his health seemed to hold up, his energy levels maintained, despite his weakness and fatigue.[4] His body and thought came together to allow him to be present for confrontations at night and demonstrations during the day, endless committee sessions and the massed crowds of public meetings. Rarely would he shout, and those close to him often had to support him physically and sometimes wait for him anxiously, with a police attack imminent. But he liked letting himself get carried away with the students, in the short bursts of running set off by the sound of "hup! hup! hup!" which would regularly increase the pace of the demonstrations. He spoke in assemblies, chaired committee sessions with the gentle authority of a slow, dry voice often short of breath but that, perhaps due to this very weakness, immediately captured listeners' attention. He analyzed events, observed the movements of bodies and the growing body of graffiti, wrote treatises, addressed everyone as *tu*: everyone except his friends. Each day, he accompanied Dionys Mascolo, Robert and Monique Antelme, Louis-René des Forêts, Maurice Nadeau, Marguerite Duras, and often Jean Schuster and Michel Leiris too.[5] He marched until near-exhaustion on May 13 from the Place de la République to Denfert, in the largest demonstration that Paris had seen since the one at the Charonne metro station in 1962, or even the Liberation. He was also at Charléty stadium on May 27, when in the late afternoon nearly thirty thousand people gathered in the stands in order to listen to student and trade-union leaders, as well as waiting to hear Pierre Mendès-France (who ultimately did not speak). He was at the Renault factories in Flins, where from June 6 onward it seemed conceivable that the students would rally to the workers' cause (despite the prohibitions of the CGT), and where it seemed to him that the entire realm of the possible was coming together.[6] He was at the Sorbonne where one day, in June or July, he thought he saw Foucault.[7]

On May 21, a group of writers in solidarity with the student movement gained control of the Massa building, the seat of the Société des Gens de Lettres. On May 23, the first general assembly of the new "writers' union" took place, led by Michel Butor, Jacques Roubaud, and Jean-Pierre Faye. All three had been present for the creation of the "Student-Writer Action Committee" on May 20 at the Institut de Philosophie. Having founded *Change* in Cuba in January, Faye and his friends had joined together with Mascolo and his group: Antelme, Blanchot, Duras. Other members of the committee were Christiane Rochefort, Nathalie Sarraute, Jean Schuster, Georges Sebag, Jacques Bellefroid, and Daniel Guérin; Maurice Nadeau and Claude Roy were less constant presences. The Committee's adherents would immediately oppose the corporate nature of the Union, where "an a-communitarian specificity was reforming." Mascolo would later reiterate that what was really at stake was calling into question the writer's singularity, mastery and authority: "We wanted to write well, but without putting forward the specificity of writing, which is nothing but the poverty of the isolated mind."[8] And in Blanchot's words, "each person recognized himself in the anonymous words inscribed on the walls and which, in the end, even when on occasion they were the result of a collective effort, never declared themselves the words of an author, being of all and for all, in their contradictory formulations."[9]

Mascolo and Blanchot took on the roles of the main organizers of the Committee, falling into their usual pattern of working together, their shared authority, which by being shared was also abolished. The question therefore immediately arose of whether to write a treatise or declaration, in view of a fragmentary, public, and communitarian interruption of authority.[10] Blanchot knew that the texts in question were "necessarily insufficient": this is to say that he sometimes recognized what is paradoxical about such a division, burdened by its insufficiency and lightened by its necessity, made incomplete by its subjective element and pushed to insubordination by being shared publicly. (The ambiguity caused by these various elements not coinciding with one another saw Blanchot asking Derrida, during this period, whether he would agree to write political treatises.)[11] But in this necessary insufficiency of the texts, Blanchot also saw something like a truth, one that had almost immediately appeared on the walls of the city, in the hands and the voices of the movement of abandon, of dispersion, of flight and of oblivion that writing is—"the becoming-other that it is."[12] Blanchot saw something here—as far as possible, because these texts were doomed to be disseminated and most often lost—of the death of the author being prefigured as truth, of the evolution of the oeuvre, the abolition of the name, the leveling of memory. These texts are something like the impersonal awareness of an exchange that could not be summarized in any slogan. They are something like the political awareness that disorder is necessary and that power is in vain, given that it appears to be durable but is in fact constantly ephemeral, inexistent. Blanchot sees power as having an existence shorter even than the words of treatises or graffiti. For this dispersal alone is able to guarantee that it might return, happen, become present, and then disappear again, and in this detour that always takes place it accomplishes its own kind of truth. It is movement as the truth of the political, the political embodied in detour. It is a conception of the political that tied the possibility of the political to the ethical possibility of praising dispersion, the crowd, and movement—a possibility that only arose in the crowd and the movement whipped up by an "insurrection of thought."[13] Thus the essence of the political is embodied in words, in the power of saying no, in refusal, the only power "irreducible to any power," and "language . . . watches over it," if language is indeed this possibility of welcome, the space opened to the wholly other.[14] From this shared right to insubordination in the name of the other, of the wholly other, flows something like a foundation of all possible politics—as if here had been fixed the liberation not only of discourse on literature, but of all discourse on community (and in this sense Blanchot would be understood by Derrida and Nancy, above and beyond Foucault's statement).

Blanchot sees sovereignty in this refusal of power, in the "abeyance of history," the return of "the pure time of suspended history marking an epoch, this time of between-times when between the old laws and the new there reigns the silence of the absence of laws."[15] This revolutionary time he describes in 1965 as that of Sade is encountered anew in May 1968. This movement upsets the order of gravity, setting up a frenetic waltz of subjects (in their atomized state), a situation in which the crowd can shift with the suddenness of an earthquake, where between festival and sacrifice, between attempts at leveling-down and the besieging of key strongholds, in an emptiness of always differing density, certain words embody the community, against a backdrop of equality that is all the more desired because the repetitive nature of struggle forces one to forget it. The words being used are like the excessive and terrifying element of reason; they are limited only by the impossible, and create—in the bodies present, in turn tightly massed together and then suddenly dispersed—an absent, invisible community already of the future, a community of thought.[16] This is the sharp edge of revolutionary desire, the still-rational reverse-side of the light of reason: such words have an always secret and necessarily invisible relation with history, proportionality, and the law. They allow one to cross over "to the far side of fear":[17] far from the fear caught up with all associative movements (which had helped to paralyze Blanchot's imitative rhetoric of thirty or forty years earlier), far even from the "fear of fear itself" of the philosopher's consciousness. These words, their language written on walls, drown fear because no prohibitions now rule the body, because consciousness is now flesh, because one can now immediately come to the aid of those who are wholly other—but still one's equals.

"Whatever the detractors of May might say, it was a splendid moment, when anyone could speak to anyone else, anonymously, impersonally, welcomed with no other justification than that of being another person," Blanchot would write at the beginning of *Michel Foucault as I Imagine Him*.[18] By drawing attention to itself, such a hiatus draws attention to the justness and importance of its form: a parenthesis in law, a secret fold in language, a suspension of history.[19] He also analyzes it as a parenthesis of communism even in the bosom of communism, or rather as a parenthesis of communism *external* to communism, for here the parenthesis is more an externality than an inclusion, an interruption rather than a subtraction; it is the parenthesis of a "communism of thought," in Mascolo's words, or of a "communism of writing," in Blanchot's—it is outside ideological communism.[20] Of course, Blanchot is aware that "to believe that one is sheltered from ideology . . . is to give oneself over, without the possibility of choosing, to the worst ideological excesses."[21] What the parenthesis opposes is therefore not such a shelter, nor the body (of the phrase, of the text), but instrumentality, utilitarianism, submission. Blanchot would also see May as the parenthesis of the revolution and therefore as the truth of the movement, the repetition that drove it:

> Contrary to "traditional revolutions," it was not a question of simply taking power to replace it with some other power, nor of taking the Bastille or the Winter Palace, or the Elysée or the National Assembly, all objectives of no importance. It was not even a question of overthrowing an old world; what mattered was to let a possibility manifest itself, the possibility—beyond any utilitarian gain—of a *being-together* that gave back to all the right to equality in fraternity through a *freedom of speech* that elated everyone.[22]

Of the moment itself, he wrote admiringly to Derrida that sites overtaken by the "revolution" were not sites of power, but the sites of knowledge and of expenditure, demonstrating the essential nonutility of consciousness and of freedom. Blanchot's reading of May '68 is curiously prophetic, not coming at the time expected for looking back, as if he had known how the *événements* would pan out, as if he lived through them both as a stranger (only being present in *the other time*, though the *speech* and the *poetry* present in it and that according to him made its truth present), and as a convalescent (in the time of an upturn in his health, a parenthesis of illness allowing him to enjoy this parenthesis in history). In this prophecy of defeat announced before its time, according to his reading of prophecy as the withdrawal of the present, Blanchot downplays the stakes of the possible (the strike, the particular demands made, the struggle) in order to privilege something like the backdrop of the possible (the possibility of the political, of the outside, of parenthesis), the return of the "demand for the impossible."[23] The possible in its entirety is improbable, and the impossible in its entirety is both constantly at stake and constantly deferred. On May 19, 1968, Blanchot observed to Derrida that "the event at which we are present or think we were present is inscribed in at least two separate spaces": the space of transgression, which clashed with the laws of the Republic as well (and most notably) with those of the Communist party; and the space of refusal, the background and the truth of transgression, the sometimes-suspended play of political decision. But if no event actually occurs in the space of transgression, it is because it is prevented from doing so by the confrontation of the two principles (or the secret discussion between them). And if no event occurs in the space of refusal, it is because in its very nature the notion of the event is foreign to it.[24] "The event? And had it taken place?" Blanchot would ask in *The Unavowable Community*, again suggesting that the event lies elsewhere, precisely where no event seems to be occurring.[25] The ground for this always silent crowd, in a place where no avowal is necessary or needs to be "suggested," and in a place where everything is accountable to justice, eludes the justice of the powerful and all "suggestions" that avowals be made.

Between May '68 and its later reverberations at a great distance, Blanchot's thought is so persistent that it forces us to state that the revolution took place at once in the time of sameness and in a wholly other temporality, experienced as much as thought, not only in the way possible actions were carried out, but in the demand of what is necessary and impossible. If the first bulletin of *Committee* appeared only in October, it was because the events experienced and dreamed in May left no time or space for anything to take the form of a publication. Because writing, for its part, belongs to the temporality of the *événements*. "Tracts, posters, bulletins, words of the streets, infinite words . . . they belong to the decision of the instant. They appear, and they disappear. They do not say everything; on the contrary, they ruin everything; they are outside of everything," wrote Blanchot, adding that "there is no difference between tracts, posters, books, bulletins, films, etcetera etcetera."[26] Thus, when he adds that "in May, there is no book on May," it is because what is written is written in "the absence of book," this absence that is announced a year later in the pages of *The Infinite Conversation*. May is the time of worklessness, of the abolition of culture; after all, "even an open book tends toward closure, a refined form of oppression."[27] May is the time when writing outside the Book is exalted, its essential fate being better served by the shared urgency to produce such writing and to make it disappear, as well as by the desire for it constantly to return, the desire for the refusal it embodies to be reiterated. May stands for the time where negativity is no longer made useful by the book; the absence of book stands for the time when the book vacates the sacred space in whose name its sovereignty is inscribed in forms subordinated to power, placing writing in a site now swept clear, and which can be either profane or sacred. Asked to define "the possible characteristics of the publication" for the Committee, Blanchot specifies that it would have to tend toward "bring[ing] about rupture," and "bring[ing] it about in a mode of rupture." "Hence the necessity of breaking with the traditional habits and privileges of writing": this would be accomplished by the anonymity of the texts (for a "communism of writing"), by the fragmentation of speech (in order to "never arrest the process itself," the better to explode meaning by way of "conjunction-disjunction," "placing together," "relations of difference"), by new and previously published texts sitting side-by-side, by commentary punctuated by the "brute force" of information, by the bulletin being "first and foremost" open to nonwriters. In short, it is a question of "maintain[ing] the incessant work of questioning." Thus the bulletin has to respond to three criteria: "the movement as a demand for rupture"; "the possibilities of rupture in the workspace"; "the international demand."[28] And for this reason Blanchot proposes to the Committee the following series of titles: *No, The Impossible, Rupture, Refusal, Commune, Prohibited, The Movement, Black Red, Disorder*, including one that is not the least poetic nor the least immediately public: *The Against One* (*Le contr'un*).

Ultimately, the bulletin would be called simply *Committee*. Only a single issue would appear (even if a second was prepared), and by no means all the demands formulated by Blanchot would be included. However, it does have something of this "movement as demand for rupture" and of these "possibilities of rupture in the workspace." It retains the principle of anonymity, except for the dozen or so citations spread throughout the issue.[29] The fragmentation of some texts and the dispersion of all of them do not prevent the inclusion of some more theoretical discourse. The thinking, occasionally incomplete, would move between the texts, and the same expressions were reiterated. We now know, Dionys Mascolo having cleared up the mystery of the texts' attribution, that he and Blanchot wrote almost the whole issue.[30] While Blanchot's texts are mostly easily recognizable, the stump-speech tone he adopts explodes the cyclical or paradoxical prose of his writing of previous years. He is much more paratactic than usual, more lyrical and hot-tempered, even at the level of the typescripts where certain words—the ones set in bold type—are written in red ink (red and black: these loose sheets bear the colors of the flags of May); he tends toward exclamative phrasing. His writing sometimes borrows from the formulations of a certain activist language, then widespread but now ideologically and historically marked. It does not shrink from using virulent slogans, for instance casting De Gaulle as "a ghostly old man" whose only remaining good action could be to die. Enemies are therefore clearly indicated as such: again De Gaulle is called "a man politically dead," "the delegate of our own political death," an actor "believing that he is magnifying the present, whereas he is parodying the past," the president of a Republic "to which he is just as foreign as he is to any living political future". "a ghostly old man who always seems to be wondering whether he is in the Pantheon or not and whether his memory, which forgets nothing, has not simply forgotten the imperceptible event of his own demise, which is to say, the demise of a puppet."[31]

Blanchot declares a state of "war" with liberalism, capitalism, and patriotism, a patriotism that he also sees in the perversion of communist revolution by the Stalinist system ("a repressive management apparatus and state superpower").[32] He denounces the invasion of Czechoslovakia in August, and draws links between "the May of Prague and the May of Paris."[33] He even says that he believes in the Cuban revolution, but does note that Castro is "capable of speaking against [it]." He reproaches the latter with "allowing himself to be misled by a false conception of internationalism."[34] He finds the true, other, wholly other conception of internationalism in words from the street the day after the expulsion order aimed at Daniel Cohn-Bendit, the evening of May 22: "we are all German Jews." This formula, slogan, cry, which has remained famous, would always find an echo in Blanchot's thought, these words which give something like an advance commentary on the meaning of the fragmentary discourse on Jewishness that he would constantly repeat. Already he recognized that "never had this been said anywhere, never at any moment: inaugural speech, opening and overthrowing the frontiers, opening and disrupting the future."[35]

The sessions of the Committee would continue all summer, but the group was veering toward breakup. Some of its members were unable to live with all of the consequences of the absence of the particular, with the shared impersonality of the desire for rupture, and this would lead to the failure of the Committee as it had already led to that of the *International Review*. As early as the beginning of August, Antelme, Mascolo, and Schuster were worried about this. Blanchot proposed that they continue but in a different format, arguing that an action committee could only have meaning in relation to a particular action and must therefore remain constantly mobile, in permanent evolution.[36] He remarked that this already meant any publication of a bulletin was in vain, except if it was clear that the permanent nature of the group was necessarily a betrayal of the truth behind publishing its texts: A bulletin is no longer entirely the absence of book, in it, the treatise is no longer a treatise, no longer permits the same revolutionary reading. With the return of the book and the person as concerns, thought disappears. In order to reorganize the movement, Blanchot therefore proposed a solution, the same he had already proposed but which had not been acted upon, neither in May nor several years later: making the Committee international. He would never give up on internationalism as the only way of eradicating all forms of nationalism, of fragmenting language and knowledge.

The invasion of Prague by Soviet tanks on August 21, undertaken with Castro's approval, played for the Committee a role that was slightly less clear but nonetheless parallel to the construction of the Berlin wall for the International Review: it reinforced internal divisions, so much so that all coexistence became impossible.[37] It played an even more serious role for Blanchot, who in mid-August considered going to Prague with German friends: it put an end to any hope for communism, plunged him once more into sadness, brought back his health problems. When the issue of *Committee* appeared, despite and due to the energy he had expended in contributing to editing the publication, Blanchot could only see further forms of struggle against the backdrop of disillusionment. The ground of the impossible was falling away. Already, words were withdrawing.[38] At the end of 1968, exhaustion struck again. November and December passed by: it seems that none of the authors of the collective volume for Beaufret received the letter signed by Blanchot and Derrida. On December 30, he wrote to his friend in the following, barely thinkable terms: "We are being dragged toward a realm so base that we can only refuse to remain there." This refusal would last for many long years. In February, Blanchot decided to abandon any form of engagement with the Committee. But in the obscurity that was again troubling his health, in the misfortune that was again striking those close to him, an event on April 28, 1969, an event that came a year too late, would help to lighten his mood.[39] "I admit that for a moment I found myself breathing more easily and, waking in the night, asking myself: 'What is it? Why this lessening of a burden? Ah yes, De Gaulle.'"[40]

PART VI

1969–1997

In this way, Blanchot's voice understands—or declares—itself to be the voice of someone alive, yet already reported missing or believed dead: dead, that is, while still living on in his own words, according to the sameness of those words that still persist (even though history itself may have been broken in two), and yet who can speak only with that break in his throat. And what sustains such a voice is the "absolute responsibility" of having to be responsible for what is always without guarantee and without response. . . .

But [this voice] restores to each one of us, strangely, the chance and duty of risking ourselves in our turn . . . amidst a world that is made up no longer (at least not immediately) of the violent contrast between fever and shame, but of a care that is itself uncertain of what it means, and hesitates as to whether "literature" still has any sense, even the sense of casting suspicion upon itself, or whether sense does not now run somewhere else (but certainly not through religion, science, or philosophy), given that it always runs somewhere, even if it is against the flow, in its own absence, or furtively.

JEAN-LUC NANCY, "In Blanchot's Company"

CHAPTER 57

Life Outside

The Step Not Beyond, a Journal Written in the Neuter (1969–1973)

The narratives aside, *The Step Not Beyond* was Blanchot's first work that, on publication, was composed mainly of new texts. When it came out in fall 1973, it produced great astonishment among its readers, if only due to its form. Yet Blanchot had been repeating since 1969 the *impressions* made by this *pas*—a step, a negation, a passing-away, impressions without any transcendence except the undialectical one of the wholly other.[1] These impressions were made in a temporality outside time, withdrawn from the present and inscribing the return of what never was, what would only ever occur through exposure, through the vacuity of the subject; this temporality could only be written through traces that were immediately erased. This first fragmentary book still addresses inner experience, a mass of inner experiences that in their fragmentation are foreign to themselves and, due to their natures, to the time in which they take place. This return to the disorder of what is torn apart, to the truth of impossible witnessing, breaks any links to the *récit* and, in this nonfictional(or not only fictional) exposition of thought, gives rise to Blanchot's first noncritical, nonfictional work. This speaks volumes to the movement that this author gives his work after 1968 in order to remain faithful (at a distance) to the demand for anonymous *tutoiement*,

389

for the unworking of authority, thus remaining as close as possible—even in apparent solitude—to rupture, and as far away as possible from fruitless wandering. Everyday decisions and the sheer chance of existence also have their part in this thoughtful writing, which represents a *mise-en-abyme* in the body of life.

This concern for fidelity, this permanent quality of a thinking carried out *in the name of the other*, the life of this thinking which ends up pushing one to extremes, to the point of irreducibility and invisibility, this attention to the *wholly other*: None of these can find a place in another "author's book," at this time when the only meaning to be found in individual authority is in denying it, and opening it up to anonymous community. In 1969, as he is about to publish the longest book of his lifetime, *The Infinite Conversation*, Blanchot gives himself over to the movement of writing's exteriority, which, beyond all the possibilities of transgression, puts his name to his past body of work by taking on its authority and responsibility for it, but also prevents it being straightforwardly attributed to him as an individual thinker. He is careful to indicate, in a final note, that the texts collected in this volume are already old, "for the most part written between 1953 and 1965": in doing so, he sets their author at a distance and underscores, however vain it is to do so, the welcome that the movement of writing extends to the "fictitious partners" of thought.[2] The fact that there are many texts and that they are diverse assists in this process; criticism's desire leads it to take on the forms of the *entretien*, the dialogue, the fragment. Any additions Blanchot makes to the preexisting articles comes in the form of short italicized texts named "Parentheses" and which, shifting the commentaries from their critical role, repeatedly throw the work off center. He also writes, a year and a half after the apparently final text, a last piece glorifying "the absence of the book," "the attraction of (pure) exteriority," "the exteriority of saying-between" that the Law has not given up on.[3] He makes space for some notes, like the two that close the volume, displacing critical homages in the name of the other, and moving toward what, in each individual author, meets the nameless name of what is wholly other: Thus, the texts of *The Infinite Conversation* do not belong to any subject, any critical subject or any object of criticism, but to what within them touches on the "lack of a name" or on the "nearly anonymous."[4] Almost as if it were a treatise—though this "almost" is important—criticism takes to the streets; to follow the metaphor of *The Step Not Beyond*, it plays out in the city. Blanchot declares that the movement that attempts to gain exemption from the order of unitary discourse is fully possible, and opens to what he once named the "Course of Things." This movement is separated from any faith in immediacy by the book's status as a site of knowledge that is also open to nonknowledge; it traces something like the embodied future of writing in a disseminated, although sometimes gathered, community. Blanchot imposes on his public existence as a subject this same *step beyond the law* as a repeated decentering.

The "step (not) beyond' therefore refers both to a movement of rewriting and of publication, a way of leaving behind a situation in which one can be trapped by the struggle for the possible, even when it is carried out in the name of the impossible. This is a new disengagement seeking a new way of engaging. From 1969 on, Blanchot would again dedicate himself to literature, even as he set himself the task of setting it free by intensely playing with and displacing genre: publishing books and denouncing the book, returning to the work in order to reaffirm its worklessness. There are few entirely new texts, although such fragments confirm that his thought is advancing, albeit only every few months (on average, in the years up to 1973, Blanchot published only two new texts per year).[5] And yet almost a hundred articles had been published in the space of two years, from fall 1969 for *The Infinite Conversation* to fall 1971 with *Friendship*. However much they were criticized for their encyclopedic effect and their show of authority, these books add to Blanchot's work, giving it a new form, sometimes referred to as revolutionary: that of completion. From 1970 on, Blanchot's novels and *récits* were gradually reprinted, but he continued firmly to oppose Robert Gallimard's suggestion that they be grouped together in a single volume. Thus a few months before the publication of *Friendship*, in spring 1971, *Thomas the Obscure*, *The Last Man*, and *Death Sentence* were simultaneously reprinted. But this movement recognizing the work was met by its author, who abdicated a certain form of sovereignty. In the reprint of *Death Sentence*, Blanchot removes the reference below the title to its status as *récit*; he also removes the final page of the text that, separated from the main body of text, superimposes the voice of someone who is implicitly the author, challenging the reader to escape the trap that has been laid in the *récit*. Not providing the book with any future, interrupting any assurance that might have been found in solitude, Blanchot delivers the author's voice, in a sentiment of nakedness and weakness, unto the presence of a reader that he can no longer define as his "prey," but as his *invisible and fictitious partner*, he who, as he said twenty-three years earlier, "in the darkness, would see me."[6] Last, in February 1973 another *récit*, largely unknown because it had been published in 1949 in a journal, was published by Bruno Roy on the suggestion of Roger Laporte, with a frontispiece by Bram Van Velde: *The Madness of the Day*. No modifications were made, except that it now had a title. The last line of the *récit* announces, belatedly and not unparadoxically, that it is the final one: "No. No stories, never again."[7] (This publication also announces, at the very moment when Blanchot is again withdrawing, a movement of autobiographical secretion within the work: something is secreted while still being kept secret.)

Thus gathered together, acknowledged, denounced, republished, modified, retitled, the text attempts to free itself of any rootedness in the sedentary nature of books ("only the *nomadic* affirmation *remains*").[8] It appears against a backdrop of silence, it is torn away from—or a fragment of—forbidding absence. It is its author's public manifestation, and the dispersed form it takes upon publication refers back to the demand of return. The disseminated variety of languages would never be as marked or as panicked in their rhythm as in a book such as *The Step Not Beyond*; the few sections of it published beforehand allow us to follow its genesis and to emphasize how exceptional it is. Blanchot wrote its first passages in a text published in homage to Jean Paulhan in May 1969, formulating what would become the title, but was still—being between dashes—a way of referring to overcoming the possibilities prescribed by the law: That is to say, the title is a way of referring to transgression.[9] In one of *Friendship*'s few texts *not* to have been previously published, and in scare quotes as if to announce that the author is particularly concerned with the term and the work it carries out in the margins, the "step (not) beyond" still refers to transgression, but insofar as it "is always incomplete and always allows itself to be thwarted further still because incompletion is its only mode of affirmation."[10] Meanwhile, two extracts from the future book had appeared in journals; "The Exigency of Return" and "Fragmentary Pieces" (*Fragmentaires*) bore witness to how the research they flowed from was advancing, if only by way of their titles, the way they are set out, their form. The next extracts, very short ones, would only appear in December 1972. None of these pieces sets out its statements in the complex manner of *The Step Not Beyond*, which constantly splices together narrative speech and the discourse that—beyond the obvious division of the fragments into those in italics and those in roman type—initially seems to associate some with the *récit* and others with commentary, only to offer different declensions of language and different attributions of the voices. The different modes of speech are made to flow into one another (commentary into *entretien*, fictitious *récit* into discourse), suspending any preeminence of one language over another and preventing the work from presenting itself as a spectacular literary event within narrative, just as it neutralizes any pretention of the critical work toward spoken monologue. The lines become blurred instead of the dialogues progressively illuminating meaning, these being dialogues in which no particular standpoints can be identified, and in which opinions and values are constantly switched. The neutral layout of the fragment takes to its extreme the fragmentary demand that refuses to align with the dogmatism of aphorisms or the moralism of the nicely turned phrase. It constantly sets aside any self-recognition by language, makes the surfaces of its narratives uneven, with fragments that always seem to be simply present, without justification. The authority of all speech is diffracted, withdrawn from the historical grasp of the negative, and the disquiet, irritation, and misfortune of the everyday is transposed into a different type of journal, one open to welcoming, to listening, and to using any speech it can in the name of seeking what is wholly other.[11] This "step beyond" serenity does not submit thought to misfortune (which would be to return to the historicity of "unhappy consciousness"); instead misfortune is given over to the possibility of thought, the unfulfillable demand for the impossible as the condition absolutely necessary for thought's exercise.[12]

Thus following the rhythm of the days over four years, torn away from the life and the becoming of the work, and demonstrating the latter's radical independence, the fragments of *The Step Not Beyond* appear like notes taken for a journal fictitiously written in the neuter. Blanchot sets out something like a governing agreement in the first pages: "If I write *he*, in denunciation rather than in reference and far from giving him a rank, role or presence which would elevate him above whatever might signal toward him, it is I who thereby enter into the relation where *I* agrees to adopt a static fictional or functional identity" (4).

"*He*" (*il*) is the neuter, which does not refer but allows itself to be referred to, does not occupy any position of oversight but instead welcomes the mobile workings of the subject. As a "partner" in "play," in Blanchot's words, this "*he*" become a noun as the grammatical partner of writing provides—in the name of anonymity—the history of a subject in terms of its relation to transgression and the law. It is also referred to as an "inhospitable host" (37), the clandestine partner of what is most personal for us. "*He*" prevents the passion of the relation engendered by desire or fear being amalgamated into the self. Feeling that there is no hope of unifying one's existence, or even of explaining what makes it so varied, something in this book nonetheless *recognizes the biographical*. First of all, the "*he*" serves to withdraw the subject from any statement that would confirm a straightforward chain of events, instead offering the only grammatical trace accounting for the strangeness of the fictional subject, that subject that is withdrawn from life, from others and from itself in the violent intimacy of the "primal scene," that is alone facing the "opening of the sky," and then in the blinding light of the "primal scene" of writing, in which not only is the writer's work inaugurated but—after years of wandering—the underlying possibility of that work as well ("Thomas sat down and looked at the sea").[13] These two secret moments, which are not present in the opening text of *The Step Not Beyond* on its first appearance in *L'Arc*, interrupt it like a parenthesis in the book version: "Whence comes this power to uproot, to destroy or change, in the first words written facing the sky, in the solitude of the sky, words by themselves without prospect or pretense: '*he—the sea*'?" (1). In a sequence of fragments that exemplifies the constantly varying utterances throughout the collection, second-person narration holds sway over the autobiographical turn to the birth of the writer, to his expulsion from the family milieu and paternal order:

> Writing as the question of writing, a question that bears writing that bears the question, no longer allows you this relation to being—understood first as tradition, order, certainty, truth, all forms of rootedness—which one day you received from worlds past, a domain that you were called to administer the better to strengthen your "Ego" [*Moi*], even though it had as it were cracked open, the day the sky opened onto its emptiness. (2)

Here the mysterious strength of the movement of writing is what is most at issue, over and above the question of the origin, and without any description of the scene of the opening of the sky that *The Writing of the Disaster* would address a few years later. Blanchot makes the concession of one of the few strictly autobiographical passages in his work, albeit one rigorously without references, to this "step (not) beyond" whose authority he underscores: "I will try in vain in represent to myself he whom I was not and who, without wanting to, began to write, writing (and knowing it then) in such a way that the pure product of doing nothing was introduced into the world and into his world" (2).

Here and there in the book we encounter the room in Èze, the pane of glass from *The One Who Was Standing Apart from Me*, the study of *The Infinite Conversation*.[14] *The Step Not Beyond* imposes on them a recognition of the biographical that is sometimes allusive, sometimes literary, but always draws on friendship and on reservedness. This is because however confidential they are, events, objects, and places only ever refer back to language. The discretion that Blanchot imposes even on those closest to him means that he allows them no recognition except in the realm of the imaginary. Fragmentary writing demands that everyone accept the vacuity of images. "Let us enter into this relation," the first fragment proposes, the only one that is not preceded by the lozenge-shaped sign. The existence of this relation is signaled by this mark's absence on this occasion, in this preamble destined to disappear, and signaling within all affirmations of life the slipperiness of death, the neutral version of the image, the exposition of the cadaver. From the unwritten autobiography—which had already forced writing to the demand of more than one return—the "journal" of the 1970s retains what, given the precariousness of Blanchot's health, thought is forced to call a "last thought" (1).

Between 1970 and 1973, Blanchot experienced various further health scares, including a serious hospitalization that would ultimately force him to leave the Rue Madame in order to follow his brother René and his sister-in-law Anna, who were now living in a house in a small town in the suburbs outside Paris.[15] While he still sometimes went to Quain or Èze, when his health was bad, he returned more frequently to the suburbs. From 1970 on, he had to give up seeing most of his friends regularly, and, mortified, he wrote to them to say how much he regretted this; Emmanuel Levinas, Jacques Derrida, and Roger Laporte would never see him again. At his brother's request he spent several weeks with him in Marrakech in January 1971, but rarely left the Mamounia Hotel, the comfortable residence where they were staying, which made him fear that he was slipping into laziness and therefore—he added with humor—might end up like Raymond Roussel. A year later, in January 1972, those close to him received letters that he had written consecutively, and that took the tone of a last will and testament, taking as their witness the grace that had allowed him to meet them and that had therefore made his existence a happy one (to the point of the "last thought," as the opening of *The Step Not Beyond* would say, 1). By the spring, however, he thought he would be able to return to Paris. He had to move out of the apartment in the Rue Madame, which was on a high floor and had no elevator. He quickly found a new place to live in the Rue Jean-Bart, which was close to his previous address; the old apartment had been neglected for several years and after being renovated, served as a *pied-à-terre* for René and Anna. He moved into his new dwellings in the summer, rather secretively, only giving his address and telephone number to his closest friends, although he was happy to do so in such cases. He even considered seeking a second job with Gallimard to help him with the rather high costs of the new apartment. It would mainly serve him as a *pied-à-terre* in Paris: from the end of this year, or at the latest from early 1973, Blanchot went to his brother's house in the suburbs more and more often. There he spent long weekends, which would eventually become long years.[16]

"*The more he shuts himself away, the more he says that he belongs to the Outside*" (102). The movement of withdrawal, which is both inexorable and contested, is therefore also behind the repetitive nature of fragmentary speech, it is the expression given to the pace [*pas*] marking dying's incomplete and arrhythmical work, "like a beating heart whose every beat would be illicit, unnumbered" (96). It is not a new demand in Blanchot's work for writing to have to escape death's ubiquity; but here it has to escape Dying itself, the substantivization of the dying that had for a long time been set in opposition to the pure transcendence of death.

> Dying, in the discretion that is attributed to this word while it is distinguished from the obviousness and the visibility of death, in its turn becomes extremely visible, like an entity (Dying) hiding its capitalized form that illness and ageing help us—as if thanks to a reagent or to being heated up: as if thanks to the fever of life—to reveal. Dying of an illness or old age, we do not just die ill or old, but deprived of or frustrated by what seems to be secret in dying itself: we are thus reduced to not dying. (98)

The everyday anguish of the early 1970s surfaces in the writing (in 1973, Blanchot was sixty-six years old); in so doing it, also staves off any dissolution, any shying-away from anxiety, any acceptance of "dying," a concept that too often became synonymous with the simple, visible decline of the body. "Dying" has to be denied if the rigor of the movement of separation is to continue, that movement that—even in an empty anguish sometimes touching absolute absence (an invisible but tenacious form of paralysis)—preserves death from any possibility of being thought. For several years already Blanchot had been calling this emptiness fatigue or weakness. "Weak thoughts, weak desire: he felt their force" (3). Writing attempts to inhabit this force—it attempts to inhabit it, in an everyday way, as its subject, for "on the far side of weakness" the bottomless nature of exhaustion has an ultimate resource, an ethically charged one: through an infinite emptying-out movement it infinitely heightens its attentiveness to the slightest gesture of the other.[17] One voice says to the other:

> "You are not yet at the limit, nor impaired enough, still having and being, nor vulnerable enough, not reaching the point of passivity in which the other would tack toward you without you being an attack on the other, nor plaintive enough for your cry to carry the plea of all to all."

The other responds: "I know, I still exist too much, via a too-little that is too much" (131).

This demand for humility is held in a secret, immanent cache for speech, desire, and encounters (9–10). None of these three precedes the others, and each escapes the others. For Blanchot, the passive ground of attentiveness opens onto ways of imagining the broadest virtual qualities of the space of community: that which proposes and fixes, although without any axis or center, fragmentary writing. (Indeed, there could be no fear of fixing it in one place, when such a fixing would allow it to be glimpsed but nothing more, when through the dance of the text's italics or through the emptiness of its interstices, it shows the reader its slightest movement, its slightest vibration.) The writing at hand sets out to create a space of waves, of returns and inversions, a space less visible than musical.[18] In this sense, the constant irritation provoked by paradoxically inverted phrases only inscribes *an openness to what is hidden about the other*, something to which the infinite attention enabled by weakness is attentive. The journal of dying is inscribed between these two poles: the possibility of the relation to the other maintained by analysis's constant to-and-fro, and the impossibility of any trace of this being written without vanishing.[19] If "writing is only written at the limit of writing" (57), it is because writing is destined to repeat itself, to erase the marks it has made, to remain the only erasable mark. "Everything must be effaced, everything will be effaced. It is in accordance with the infinite demand of effacement that writing takes place and takes its place" (53).

Such an "accordance" is not without fear. It is even in this fear, conceived of as a dead organ that is part of a broader flesh (language), that one can find the extreme difficulty of the demand of writing; a difficulty linked to its atheist foundations. "Fear is a piece of language, something that it would have lost and that would make it entirely dependent on this dead section" (59). Occupying the invisible place of absent divinity, an absence of divinity only present in fragmented language and depriving that language of any salvation, piercing it even when given over to it, fear is inevitably found "on the far side of weakness," as the condition on which thinking can be carried out. This is an absolute fear that disarms all hope, eradicates all beliefs (however nihilistic they might be). This fear is not the fear of the philosopher, that which gives up on confronting fear. It opens the domain of the impossible to an endlessly repeated necessity for effacement (in the sense that the latter cannot *not* take place, even if it has to erase singularity). It constrains the possible to the following reading: "That the fact of the concentration camps, the extermination of the Jews and the death camps where death carries out its work are for history an absolute which has interrupted history: this one *must* say without however being able to say anything else"[20] (114). This means that fear makes it all the more necessary not to abandon attentiveness and concern.

"The most serious of idolatries: to take into account that which does not take into account" (134). And the most serious not-taking-into-account is that of fear, that of the fear deep down in those who show no fear. Such is the inflexible limit that Blanchot would henceforth place on all thinking of misfortune. Consideration of the "dark, ruined sovereignty" of the other afflicted by the misfortune of the camps (125) finds here, after the article on Robert Antelme's *Human Race* and after the more recent text written in response to a Polish magazine's investigation into war and literature, its first major expression.[21] Various passages in *The Step Not Beyond* explicitly refer to "the roll-call in the camps" (38), to "the horror of the death camps, of those dying by the thousands" who were tragically condemned to feel guilty for their deaths, "to *die* of the very abjection of *death*" (96–97), to feel the ruin of all presence, even the presence of friendship (114).

Concern for this limit would now constantly preoccupy Blanchot because "the gravest of idolatries" had appeared where he could never have imagined it: at the heart of the political group he belonged to. The anti-Zionist and pro-Palestinian positions adopted by intellectuals of the far left, which inevitably became more radical in September 1970 ("Black September") when royal troops expelled Yasser Arafat's organization from Jordan, led to an immediate rupture. For while he did not overtly defend Zionism, Blanchot was unable to tolerate what he saw as a de facto alliance between anti-Zionism and anti-Semitism, an alliance built on ignorance, lack of awareness, or disowning. On several occasions Emmanuel Levinas would bear witness to this rupture, notably by publishing a letter that he would only later reveal had been sent to him by Blanchot.[22] The letter asks: "Isn't this a strange reversal, which proves that the absence of anti-Semitism is not enough?" This is said to be a reversal, or a rather a perversion, of the words of May: "We are all German Jews." For these "young people who are acting violently, but also with generosity" were the same, spontaneously identifying with the fate of a community that was a victim of genocide, but without having "any idea of what anti-Semitism was and is." Blanchot's reasoning is paradoxical; he tries to demonstrate that such arguments do not stand up, refuses to see anti-Zionism as "the anti-Semitism of today" and yet also denounces "a perhaps innocent ignorance, but one that is henceforth gravely responsible and deprived of innocence." His reasoning is persistent, refusing to follow "those who are completely ignorant of what it is to be Jewish" and using the same objection to them that Sartre and others had used in the 1960s. Last, his is a reasoning that initiates a "last thought" (1), a concern to be vigilant over anti-Semitism that would preoccupy him for long years to come, with the name of Auschwitz as an "absolute" of history, as its erasure, as its interruption, instead of what he had been calling, since the *International Review*—its suspension.[23]

The Step Not Beyond therefore touches on the absolute of all political, community, historical reflection, becoming its fragmentary echo. It inscribes the "line drawn through" the Committee as the final limit of what is tolerable, instead and on the reverse of which affirmation and refusal can take place.[24] It continues the reflections of May 1968 on the relative quality of all forms of possible transgression. It unmasks all the ways in which an authority or a power can profit from the activities of a group.

> We are not taken in by the present that would make us believe we had any authority or exercised any influence, and still less are we taken in by the past, and still less again presumptuous of any future. We see right through the impersonal responsibility claimed by groups affirming, secretly or directly, the right of some to lead in aggrandizing their name with that of a group. (36)

The book's allusions remain anonymous but for Blanchot also represent a way of drawing a line, a line to follow in one's approach giving over "the acts of the day" to the fragmentary, which is constantly being thought in relation to the "absolute" of history. They therefore leave a trace of the disagreements that marked these years, from the break with the Committee and the refusal of anti-Zionism to his irritation over the ways in which the names of Artaud, Bataille, and Breton were being reappropriated, in quarrels over intellectual inheritance that were in full flow, by the groups led by Philippe Sollers and by Jean-Pierre Faye.[25] Blanchot seems to regret having left, for health reasons, the committee charged with publishing the *Complete Works* of Georges Bataille.[26] However, he would not follow Dionys Mascolo in his project for a declaration denouncing such abuse of names and works that should have been placed far out of the reach of such political or literary instrumentalizations; this was because he refused to see himself as representing any authority over these works or these names.[27] Letting the name of the other play itself out, letting the works of the other take their course; such are the risks of the way writing evolves, and they do not allow for writing to be reduced to a manifesto ultimately coextensive with strategic positioning only meaningful in the political arena of the possible. The writing of *The Step Not Beyond* would be faithful to the demand for the impossible, contrasting on the one hand the breakup of political discourse and of literary strategy, and on the other its own fragmentary demand. In its narrative—even poetic—passages, its shards represent Blanchot's political itinerary, the itinerary of that subject doomed to traverse "the city," to frequent the silent members of a dispersed community, to traverse in the words of a detached fragment that functions almost as free verse: "*the eternal, straight streets, under an erased sky*" (80). This writing bids farewell to the memory of the possible ("*I crossed [the City] as one passes distractedly over the graves in a cemetery,*" 83), also chiming with its most personal or secret manifestation, like in the dream that Blanchot spoke of in a letter to Dionys Mascolo and to which he now returns: "At night, dreams of death in which one does not know who is dying: all, all those who are threatened by death—and oneself, *into the bargain*" (115). This "oneself" is now caught in a fracturing of the political that Blanchot is tempted to carry—*to the limit*.

The space of the *récit* is invaded by the thought of misfortune. The fictitious room able to include the entire city now also includes the space of the camps, "*the crumbled city*": "*All around, there were men who seemed to be sleeping, lying on the ground, blankets thrown over them like earth is thrown into a pile, and these innumerable little knolls, thoughts of the crumbled city, were leveled out until they became the bare floorboards of the room*" (112). Such poetic attention to a community space traversed by war was already at hand in the "*récit*" published in 1949, which had been reprinted a few months before *The Step Not Beyond* as *The Madness of the Day*. The aphasic impossibility of avowal, the then-affirmed and now-fragmented absence of any possibility of narrative, the blinding (through glass crushed into the narrator's eyes) that prophetically withdraws the present and authorizes a completely different type of gaze, one of speech where speaking goes beyond seeing: through all of these the wind of the most despairing madness, the dominion of the most unbearable impersonal hell takes priority over any serene acceptance of tragedy. There are some memories of this "mad writing" (22), ratcheting up its own patience, in *The Step Not Beyond*. This atmosphere of madness again surrounds Blanchot during these years when dying is less than fully present and yet not entirely absent, and repeatedly justifies the move toward the limits (of interruption, of fragmentation) over the writing of attentiveness and of misfortune. This madness is the parenthesis of the "new reason," the externality of return, the empty reiteration of the absolute of history. Madness is the poetry of those who are the "last to speak."

It is not wholly unrelated that Blanchot's most silent and maddest text of these years addressed Paul Celan. On April 20, 1970, Celan had joined the "unknown girl" whose portrait always hung in Èze: in the Seine. Shortly following the thirtieth anniversary of the death of his parents during the deportations, Celan's suicide shocked Blanchot. *The Step Not Beyond* resonates with the echo of May 1970, when the body was searched for at length and then finally identified. The fragments further inflect the reflections in *The Space of Literature* on suicide, especially its characteristics of *indiscretion* and *impossibility*, which give it a double meaning on which, in the words of *The Step Not Beyond*, "nobody has the power to pass judgment" (123; see also 97–98). Thus indiscretion with regard to those who have exhausted possibility becomes a Blanchotian figure of friendship touching the poet-suicide precisely where he had refused the patience of dying. Through discreet anonymity, the figure of Paul Celan must be seen as one of the possible interlocutors of the *entretiens* of friendship that run throughout the book, of these dialogues between two who are "*the last to speak*" (92–93). *The last to speak*: Blanchot takes this formulation from Celan's poem, demonstrating how much they share in terms of the exhaustion of speech, and uses it as the title for a 1972 homage to him in the *Revue de Belles-lettres* in the form of a commentary that he would turn into a book twelve years later. This commentary stands out in Blanchot's critical work, abolishing as if definitively the analytical format and instead presenting itself as an *entretien* within friendship, in the now-convergent, now-divergent friendship of two voices.[28] Like a collection of epigraphs or epitaphs, Celan's verses are cited sometimes in detached form, sometimes intermingled with the words hearing and translating them in an infinite attentiveness to their resonances, to their "shrill sound beyond what can become song," at the limit that they constantly cross in the other's language, that of the attackers, that of fear.[29] Friendship alone attests to the lack of witnesses for death (or for madness) and in this lack, which it does not accompany, it dictates the law of separation. If self and language are indeed being destroyed, as Celan's critics have often tried to argue, then this never takes place without preserving otherness: such is the ethics of witnessing that Blanchot reads in this poetry.

"The responsibility of and for friendship" henceforth irreducibly inflects Blanchot's critical writing, his writing in the name of the other. Such a situation, which flows from a politics of writing, is decisive for the years of accompaniment and rupture that followed the moment that Blanchot would continue to name simply as the month of May. And thus even the decision to publish was submitted to friendship. This was the case in terms of who the texts were addressed to: of the few articles between 1969 and 1973, three were given to Louis-René des Forêts for *L'Ephémère* and one to Maurice Nadeau for *La Quinzaine Littéraire*.[30] It was also the case concerning the gift that publication could offer: "The Exigency of Return" was dedicated to Pierre Klossowski, "The Last to Speak" to Henri Michaux.[31]

And it was also the case in terms of the subjects chosen: all the texts concern friends, either as part of a collective homage (Celan, Jabès, Merleau-Ponty, Parain, Paulhan) or as a commentary on their latest book (Duras). None of the articles published goes without one or another of these relations to friendship. Beyond their persons—far from the exile into which he must have been considering withdrawing at this time—it is to the friendship in his friends that Blanchot addresses each of his texts, like faraway speech. Friendship is also part of this movement of confronting the absolute: "Friendship: friendship for the unknown without friends" (133). It is made more important by each death, each withdrawal of a friend, thus moving ever closer, beyond all separation, to wholeness. Blanchot used a passage from his letters of January 1972 here, in another parenthesis: "(*In the night that is coming, let those who have been united and who are effaced not feel this effacement as an injury that they would inflict on one another*)" (137).

These penultimate lines of *The Step Not Beyond* have the ring of an epitaph. For almost a year and a half, Blanchot would dwell in silence.

CHAPTER 58

Friendship in Disaster
Distance, Disappearance (1974–1978)

In February 1975, a few lines bearing a date from the past (October 1974) appeared on the final page of an issue of the collective journal *Change*, like a discreet epitaph. They were curiously signed Maurice Banchot; the letter "l" had disappeared. There was no doubt, however, that this first prepublication from *The Writing of the Disaster*, this "fragment" that was declared "previously unpublished," did indeed come from the pen of the author who had remained silent since the publication of *The Step Not Beyond* alongside an article in *La Quinzaine littéraire* in September 1973. The laws of chance and return would mean that it was in issue 22 of the review.

A few further publications would follow, establishing the rhythm adopted in the 1970s: around two texts per year. Until 1980, except for two texts written in homage to the friends that were then closest even while faraway, Emmanuel Levinas and Roger Laporte, all of these publications would concern the major book that Blanchot was to spend nearly six years writing, which, like his previous ones, would appear in the fall, bearing a final date of September 18, 1980, just before its author's seventy-third birthday.

It is an understatement to say that these years were unhappy ones, and it seems too easy just to say that they were filled with a constant thinking of disaster, of sadness, of distance. And yet they were that, in real and personal ways. Frequently retreating to his brother's house, little by little giving up his stays in Paris itself, Blanchot barely saw his friends anymore—they regretted this, even secretly resented him for it. When he and his friends wrote to one another, it was often to signal their bad news: Blanchot reserved this signaling for what he named "the innocence of the disaster."[1] In her correspondence with Michel Fardoulis-Lagrange, Denise Rollin described a being "in a state of such infinite fatigue that it does not allow him to be present."[2] She added that this being was exhausted by his work as a reader for Gallimard. But what saddened Blanchot above all was his absence from others, which was not a matter of choice, and which meant that most often he felt himself unable to write, even to his friends. This powerlessness overwhelmed him. He resigned himself to sending only the following few words by Nietzsche to Jacques Derrida as a sign of deep friendship, of tragic humor, and of precarious refuge: "We do not speak to one another, because we know one another too well: we are silent with one another, we laugh at our knowledge." In the same period, Dionys Mascolo recounted to him the following astonishing dream, which gives a sense of the silences flowing from friendship and the works:

> I am telephoning you. At the same time, I can see you a little bit, backlit, backlit but still visible so that you are something more than a silhouette, I can see something of your features (at the beginning; then this vision withdraws). I have no idea what I am saying to you. I only know that it is plaintive, perhaps even sentimental (I am slightly ashamed). You respond a little, trying to pacify me, then less and less (what I am saying is in vain—vain is not even the word: this is a lament about nothing—and there is no thought behind your responses: this pacification comes from your voice). Ultimately, you grow silent. I too stop speaking, but don't hang up. You don't hang up either. I don't know how long this lasts. My dream doesn't end. Has this wait actually lasted a minute, or two hours? It continues to infinity. And it doesn't wake me. On waking, I find it intact. Nothing else has happened in it, no image or thought has traversed it. Not even any words. Just "speech." It is absolutely pure. I cannot remember ever having had a dream like it.[3]

This silent listening, this infinite presence in the density of absence, this voice preceding the vanity of its words attests to the exceptional nature of

Maurice Blanchot's rarest, most faithful friendships. These friendships could only limit the pain of waiting in benefit of the grace that constantly traversed them. Blanchot would reiterate to all those close to him during these years of absence how much his—much regretted—lack of presence was nothing compared to silent faithfulness, to the *impossibility of separation*. As an embodiment of the "relation without relation," friendship preserved one from the most terrible of fates. At the heart of a tragedy that was sometimes graceful but often marked by death, it alone provided atheist salvation.

This grace also made demands. The fate that had been pursuing the two friends for twenty years continued its work. In January 1978, Dionys Mascolo lost his mother. The writing of the disaster was at this time also that of correspondence, which gave voice to a shared powerlessness to provide consolation (but there was some consolation in this sharing: "each one restrains himself, clinging to an other, an other who is himself and is the dissolution—the dispersion—of the self").[4] For on January 9, a few days earlier, Maurice Blanchot had lost his brother, René, to cancer. His silent complicity with death had only allowed him to spend two weeks watching over the agony of the one who had protected him his whole life—the one who, in an irony of fate, had so often cared for him on the brink of death. Lacking any protective parental figure, Blanchot would share the solitude of his sister-in-law, Anna, for almost twenty years.

A few days later, on January 23, 1978, the time came for Denise Rollin to pass away.

CHAPTER 59

The Last Book
The Writing of the Disaster (1974–1980)

For many years, Blanchot had often thought that he would not finish the book that he believed, when it was finally published, to be his last. Although it could be argued that this was the case with many other books, his feeling was exceptionally strong with this one. From the depths of this silence, of this belief in disappearance come, exploding, jostling together and dispersed, sometimes as testaments and sometimes against autobiographical backdrops, the discreet revelations, the final words clawed back from illness, death, knowledge, dying: the fragments of the *Disaster*. "Public matters" proved more attractive to Blanchot than ever. But he was powerless to act on that realm, even to participate in it.

    This infinite attention given to the other, to what is wholly other, to the self insofar as it is effaced by responsibility for the other (even in the case of its "murderous Will," which does not meant that one cannot refuse, resist, combat it) guides the almost daily or weekly rhythm of these fragments.[1] There are 403 of them, or a little more than one for each week of this period: we must remember this writerly rhythm, and compare it to the rhythm with which we read. How can we relate to these fragments without our attentiveness to the disaster of the other simply being the same on each occasion? How can we give ourselves over to reading them without being immediately and repeatedly placed at a distance, given our concern for the infinite responsibility to which each new possibility of thought constrains us? How can we read them without rereading them, how can they be torn away from the book that gathers them together in a linear space that is necessarily foreign to the other time that disperses them? The density, brevity, and completed nature of each forces upon us separations and returns, the rhythm of an insistent discontinuity beyond oblivion; they are a gift that does not belong to us, or no longer belongs to us, a time given over to the infinite so that we might suddenly come across the site of entry, the place for the body that thinks, writes, initiates some kind of reflection of language. This poetic writing of thought, which defies any presumption of language, overwhelms us, opening up, suggesting, laying out the terms available to it.[2] Each fragment—as it were—*disasters* all notions, frees them from having to revolve around a central star (or aster), whether ontological or ethical, theological or metaphysical, whether a being (*être*) or a being (*étant*), whether a God or a subject. They do so in order to avoid any rootedness in the substantiality of language, to avoid stratifying this block carved from the intensity of pain, threaded through with many readings, experiences, and so much knowledge. Each fragment imposes its own code, its own origin, its own reversibility of notions; each therefore forces the reader to call into question her own interpretive knowledge, or better: her own way of questioning. How should we approach each fragment? By means of what palpable aspect, what salience of pain, of disaster, of weakness?[3] In these fragments there is something solitary, something unable to express the unavowable, except by saying why it is also impossible to keep to a perfect silence. There is also something atemporally solitary: curiously, all these texts—sometimes written six or seven years apart—give the impression of synchronicity, of a stability that is both assured and tormented by the slow movement of patience.[4] There is something solitary in refusing to take refuge, only being receptive to the disaster of thought. This disaster has a name, Blanchot would henceforth always repeat: Auschwitz. This is the name of anonymous monstrosity and senselessness, a site that struggles to find its place in memory, belonging as it does to a time that is separate to what it is normal to call—localizing and closing it in the process—"history." "How is it possible to say: Auschwitz has happened?" (143). This shattering question undoes all the possible relations of memory and oblivion.

"*The holocaust: the* absolute *event of history*" (47): These few words introduce a fragment of around ten lines, picking up an idea that had been stated multiple times since the beginning of the 1970s. The entirety of this fragment appeared, like a leitmotif, in two prepublications before being included in *The Writing of the Disaster*. It is separated, as if *absolutely*, from all others, and it seems that thought is powerless to say anything beyond this. Instead it is limited to emphasizing the detached nature of this fragment on its various occurrences: sometimes at the end of the published text (in the version published in 1975), sometimes by italicizing it, sometimes by placing *absolute* in roman script in an italicized setting. Thought is already powerless to retain the event, as is underscored by the only change made in the book version: "*how can it be preserved, even by thought?*" became "*how can it be preserved, even in thought?*" (47). Thought can neither be what carries out this preservation, nor its essence. It can only use its emptiness to ask why absolute knowledge is so powerless, and to call on the depths of this disaster, which it becomes.[5] It is unable to develop it, and infinitely sets aside any messianic hope, any politics of the possible, any complete reflection on history. Henceforth it cannot be satisfied with any response limited to the category of presence. The event that had taken place without yet taking its place establishes the disaster as the ground of all thought; its *absolute* character means that thought can only be thought if it is a thought of disaster, of *the* disaster. "To think would be to name (to call) the disaster the way one reserves, in the back of one's mind, an unspoken thought" (4). If the disaster is the thought in the back of the mind of all thinking, Blanchot is once again attempting to address—to enunciate, to name, to appeal to—the possibility of thought itself, and of contemporary thought. It is a question of seeking out what, through thought and writing, can provide an echo to this, can face up to it; a question of seeking out a place for thought, "where there is no room even to introduce a question" (31). A question of knowing what kind of book to add to all the others, and most of all to his own, in such a way as to face the unthinkable quality of this event.

Such is another point of view from which *The Writing of the Disaster* can be considered Blanchot's *last book*. All the other books, smaller in volume, more uniform because they return to the continuity of discourse and the linearity of reason, would be nothing but detached fragments of this one; fragments always give over to a figure of friendship, always attempting to welcome the absolute in a new way by means of another, often close thinking (his friends were thoughts that took on the names of Bataille, Duras, Nancy, Foucault, Des Forêts, Mascolo). It is therefore this final book that engages writing's responsibility in view of its other, namely the personal nature of history, which is *wholly other* and which writing can never reach or account for, but which it can accept in its distant nature and whose demand it can signal and repeat, a demand reinforced by the event that is absolved, detached, separated from it, a demand that this book forces one to recognize in the law of knowledge and of the book. Writing has discovered how to make possible such a welcome for the other: after critical language, after the *récit* and reflection on its various metamorphoses, it welcomes the other through *the regime of the fragmentary*. Having been in gestation since *Awaiting Oblivion*, the fragmentary does not impose itself as a genre, exactly, but as a subtitle or something with no title whatsoever, a necessity for a certain layout of words. Various eponymous titles were published by Blanchot at this time. "Fragmentary Pieces" (*Fragmentaires*) had already been the name of an ensemble of fragments published in 1970 and collected in *The Step Not Beyond*. The few lines published by *Change* in 1975 were entitled "Fragment"; and the text of the same year in a collective homage to Bram Van Velde was named "Fragmentary." In 1976, "A Child is Being Killed" bore the subtitle "(fragmentary)"; it was something like an interruption of the realm of argumentation. More often in the singular than the plural, these titles refer to the absent reason governing the appearance of the text, rather than to what is written in it. Given that it follows explorations dating back more than twenty years and is made to chime in ever more personal ways with the impossibility that interruption (the absolute, that which is absolutely separate) brings to thinking, *The Writing of the Disaster* cannot be seen as surprising; instead, it confirms the firmness of the choice to write like this. And yet something is conspicuously absent, something has been boldly excluded: A major difference from *The Step Not Beyond* is that narrative fragments are now extremely rare. While the demand for the interruption of space remains, with the fragments once again divided between those in italics and those in roman type, now it simply serves to differentiate two distinct modes of abstraction. The roman fragments are more numerous and affirm both a proximity to non-systematic philosophies (whether the pre-Socratics or Nietzsche) and a distance from everything in those philosophies that can still lead one to establish a form of moralism, dogmatism, or nihilism. The constant nature of the fragmentary form immediately destroys any sense of a genre being achieved, and thus Blanchot would not need to later return to dismantle it. The texts in italics replace narrativity with a poetic or citational mode of language: a few paragraphs in prose, a few verses, a few isolated lines of free verse, which are often jarringly uneven—or a citation used to set in motion discourse, the moving-off of discourse, discourse as thought running away with itself (*le discourir*). In this sense, this last book also signals the distancing of speech: old now, Blanchot writes essays and even public letters that are shorter and shorter, filled with silences, but all the more dazzling for it. This is the distancing of a thinking that remains present by being said, present in the world, in publishing, in republishing, in the constant solidity of what the author still has to fill his solitude: the endless pursuit of reading.

The Writing of the Disaster is one of the finest ever homages to reading: to what reading imposes on us, not as abandonment of origins, but as abandonment of the center, of power.[6] It is a homage to the distances reading establishes, the better to return to itself and to the movement within it that opens onto what is wholly other; to reading's ability to capture the knowledge of books and to use it to interrogate what is beyond knowledge; to what, in disaster, it allows to come to patience; to what it gives unknowingly to the writing of the reader—to the part of the reader that it "inflames" (44). The homage to reading is therefore also homage to its infidelity, its indiscretion, its dispropriation. More than sixty writers are cited by name in the book. They are not limited to canonical authors or to Blanchot's friends in thought; many are highly contemporary writers or philosophers. This number and this diversity might conspire to make the reflections less weighty; but each time Blanchot seems to manage to welcome the thinking of the other, compressing it into a knotty question, transforming it into one of the folds of his own disaster. The citations given are often free or from memory, like faraway echoes which, even when they lack precision, ask precise questions of the established quality of the fragmentary work; they dispossess all thought in order to illuminate it anonymously. Unlike the articles of the past, which were always short essays that developed in the manner of the book and the possibility of the book, these fragments depart from a more unstable point in thought and aim at a point—a weak point, necessarily—of the thinking that they welcome. There is no direct refutation; even the most sovereign concepts are instead rendered fragile. There is no dialectical opposition, but a movement of distancing which reveals the disastrous reverse side of the notion discussed, the fear it draws on, its primal trembling which precedes all the feelings of safety provided by systematicity, catharsis, or sublimation (this is the case with "early Hegel," in whose case Blanchot emphasizes an early conception of infinite, permanently destructive death, unsuited to sublimation, alien to the dialectical role that it would later hold in the historical construction of the knowledge of Spirit—68).[7] Beyond the name and beyond citation, the fragment bears witness to the wholly other movement that all thinking could always have followed. Such is its weakness, which some would name its strength, for here weakness is an unlimited listening to the other, responding to the exhaustion that Blanchot was encountering in his life, when he was most attentive to his interlocutors. In his withdrawal, Blanchot makes each fragment into the site of an *entretien*, a repetition of weakness: "the extreme of discretion, offered to the point of effacement" (54).[8] "Nothing extreme except through gentleness" (7). This is an offer or gift that draws on exhausted attentiveness, on a loss of limitation that the self does not suspect and that has neither the maneuvers of the desire to possess nor the calculation of generosity. It is an invisible gift, a "suspension of self" that is surprisingly incomplete and prone to confession, allowing the other to be seen as a *beyond* because it is anonymous, an anonymous disaster that is "unassignedly strange." To say this is not to glorify the other nor to strip it of its own resources, but to imbue it with transparency though the discreet guarantee of presence alone; the absence of this presence speaks to the strength of thought, its pure temporality (purer even than dying itself), its exteriority to all duration, its blinding dazzlement, its sheer sensibility. This is time in its essence as separation and tearing, in its vertiginous absence, in its disastrous gaping, felt in the flesh, disobeying gravity, then *falling*.[9] All fragments reproduce a falling movement, as Blanchot had already announced through the weakness of *The Infinite Conversation*. They also avoid closure, knowledge, anything based on oneness: the obscurity of which the fragments of *The Writing of the Disaster* are sometimes accused only signals that the accusing parties have carried out a reading that is hasty, consumerist, impatient to forget itself, and *unwilling to search for* any point of weakness. For Blanchot, to divide up the fragments, to order and reorder them is therefore also to search for what place should be given to the other, in order that it might be heard. This is how the variations of the book's prepublications should be read: as so many inversions, separations, groupings, entanglements, changes of character.

Perhaps such thinking sets out to speak the possibility of others by interrogating its own possibility. It is in *The Writing of the Disaster* that Blanchot chooses, not without hesitation (for there is something testamentary about addressing one's childhood, addressing the possibility of retaining childhood), to narrate and to comment on in three sections the "primal scene" of the opening of the sky. The possibility of an infinite attentiveness to the other opens up when one places oneself at a distance, already in childhood, through this absolute availability recognized in the disaster, distributed across one's gaze and one's flesh and then forgotten, tormented, defied, little by little opened to the possibilities of narration, put into the form of the essay or of the fragment's unworked work, in any case never killed off. The pages that take Serge Leclaire as their starting point (*A Child*

Is Being Killed) seem offered to this personal disaster, which has already responded to the impossible (not claiming any knowledge of it, but simply a listening), has already responded to the attempt to sustain a death that is originary, repeated, and always-already past.[10] These pages were published as an article in *Le Nouveau Commerce* in 1976, then included in the book in the form of three long fragments preceding the *récit* of the "primal scene?" whose devastating, deracinating strength they do more than suggest, designating an initial experience of dying, even if its initial status is only a screen effect. For while the movement of writing is recognized in the recognition of this immemorial death (the original and repeated dying, the attractive and obliging void, the invisible in the depths of the sky), in the traces that "call upon one to *exclude oneself from the cosmic order*" (66), this recognition contains no therapeutic element, no sublimation, no transference or even work of mourning. To kill the child, but also to kill childhood within one, in the double impersonality of the act of killing ("*A* child *is being* killed" [*On* tue *un* enfant]: Blanchot accepted this double neutrality, insisting on its "indecisive force," 71), is to agree to be accompanied by a "companion, but of no one, whom we seek to particularize as an absence" (72), in a "primal scene" of writing.[11] The *disaster* lies and comes about in *discovering* this murder and its constant repetition, in the face of which all knowledge of the origin disappears. To write is to continue to open up the sky, to move from the blue sky to the void of the sky: "*the disaster as withdrawal outside the sidereal abode, and as refusal of nature's sacredness*" (133). This is a sunless blue, a blue of disaster, a blue in which disaster has replaced the sun, signaling both dazzlement and lack of origin, signaling that all coordinates have been lost. Not least among the virtues of the disaster is that it annexes, in its obscure poetic luminosity, the sun—as appears in the various versions of the book's final fragment, "*shining solitude, the void in the sky, a deferred death: sun*" becoming "*shining solitude, the void of the sky, a deferred death: disaster.*"[12]

In any case, a striking new confidence in the autobiographical transparency of writing—even if in the neuter, in the name of the other or of the anonymous—is apparent in what is most personal, most secret, most childish experience being confided in this way. Such is the case even if this is an experience of the impersonal, of the other, of the infinite reserves of weakness that channel writing's evolution toward an impossible response to an original "ravaging joy" that poses questions and opens to the disaster.[13] In the following years, Blanchot would never renew this confidence without sideways glances and suspicion. And yet he would do so, more and more freely and not without pleasure, with no other protection for his own weakness than the concern to manifest the truth regarding the unsayable: the concern that makes life possible.

To hold, to hold on: to hold insofar as one has held on so far: this is what is now required. To hold on to fear beyond any catharsis, beyond any blinding by knowledge, to hold strong in the face of apathy, to undergo the greatest pain (this "saturation by impropriety" that Blanchot even discusses in terms of Sade [45]); such imperatives are only meaningful if one thinks through Levinas's view that "others [*Autrui*] are always closer to God than I," if one holds on to the demand it makes, "whatever might be meant," Blanchot adds, "by the unnamed name of God." The neutral welcome given to the broader responsibility for others comes down to holding on to the thought of what Levinas, similarly, names "*in*discretion with respect to the *in*effable," which he makes into a task for philosophy (114). Blanchot recalls this in an article dedicated to him for a collection of homages in 1980, which he closes in these terms:

> How can one philosophize, how can one write in memory of Auschwitz, of those who told us, sometimes in notes buried near to the crematories: know what happened here, do not forget, and at the same time you will never know. This is the thought that traverses, and bears, all of Levinas's philosophy and that he proposes to us without saying it, beyond and before every obligation.[14]

To hold on to philosophy while thinking Auschwitz, philosophy which Blanchot names a "clandestine companion" in a gesture toward his friend: this is the demand with which Blanchot constantly aligns himself henceforth. It is a movement that imposes itself on the development of his thought: the infinite attentiveness, the nonreciprocity of the relation to others (the subject's responsibility even for the violence of the other), the coming-together of the movements represented by Levinas (Judaism as a humanism) and by Mascolo (Judaization through the experience of war), the conviction that history is being left behind, and the political engagements: All of these make it necessary to place this *absolute* at the heart of interrogating the end of historical dialectics. But his growing and sometimes seemingly exclusive interest for Judaic culture would have greater surprises in store. To find them surprising, however, is to forget that this interest is continuous with the rest of his thinking. Blanchot reproached others many times for only thinking Judaism in terms of anti-Semitism; he had intensely, and as it were blindly, experienced a thinking of Judaism as a culture of refusal of all mythical thought; in the 1930s he had touched on it through his writing accompanying Levinas and at *Le Rempart*. Judaism as a thinking of errancy, of the demand to constantly relate to the Wholly Other: that much can be traced back to the articles of the 1960s. But what now makes itself felt, under the pressure of the memory of the political experience associated with them and in the state of division that allows this experience to be thought through all the more—faced with the course of history that saw the Middle East in flames and the appearance of the first accounts of French anti-Semitism—is the strong necessity of uprooting events from the realm of the possible with its causes and effects and evaluating them according to a wholly other type of duration.[15] From this point of view, Judaism for Blanchot represents a culture of resistance capable of envisaging, beyond the dialectical oeuvre of death, infinity without anguish—or more precisely, an infinity able to hold on to anguish given the lack of any site, of any end.[16] In this framework, the State of Israel would often be trivialized and yet at the same time over-estimated: it would be seen as the return of events immemorial, as the simple reflection of the West's inability to sustain the existence of a culture that refuses all historical closure. Paradoxically, Israel and its limitations are recognized in the name of the impossible without limits.[17]

He who had never tried to be present in representation (through the reproduction of his voice or image), who had tried to remain absent to the point of effacement in order to guarantee his long-term, even infinite capacity to listen to the other-the wholly other—and who henceforth in his retirement could only be present through text and letters ("absence in its vivacity," 51): This man would leave the struggle for the possible to others, a struggle that he thought as necessary as ever (72–74). On the question of anti-Semitism itself, this was palpable in 1976 with the Boutang affair. Blanchot discreetly but firmly, with the entire weight of his friendship, supported Jacques Derrida.

On March 17, 1976, the board of the University of Strasbourg had elected Pierre Boutang to a post as *maître de conférences* in philosophy, against the wishes of the specialist advisory committee. He was a fiery polemicist who had been a Maurrassian journalist before the war and responsible for various nationalist mouthpieces since; he had been barred from teaching after the Liberation and reinstated in 1967 after rallying to Gaullism, something that did not exclude a long-standing sympathy for Nouvelle Action Française. A petition signed by around one hundred academics denounced the procedure used by the university management, the criteria used, and the choice of Boutang, which it linked to the nonrenewal of Heinz Wismann's contract the same month and in the same department. On June 15, 1976, *Le Monde* published this petition and a response by Boutang. On July 1, Derrida published in the same newspaper a text named "Where Are the Witch-Hunters?" in which he expressed some reservations about secondary aspects of the declaration that he had nonetheless signed, and whose principles he defended, even as he called for Boutang's work to be read in the first instance. The accusation of "witch-hunting" was aimed not at the declaration but at Boutang's actions under Vichy, and Derrida denounced this figure's persistent anti-Semitism and "overt racism," with citations as evidence. The same evening, Blanchot wrote to Derrida after having read the article, expressing his unreserved support. He did so with the same suddenness, the same decisive mindset with which he expressed his "agreement" to Dionys Mascolo in 1958.

In this way, at a moment when he was gaining immense recognition, Blanchot let it be known that the weight of his oeuvre concerned him less than ever.

CHAPTER 60

Forming the Myth
Readings and Nonreadings (1969–1979)

In the 1970s the gap grew more palpable between, on the one hand, a critical thought that was becoming a thing of the past, increasingly recognized as *the* thought of the postwar era and even the twentieth century, abundantly evident in print and radio literary journalism, both at home and abroad, and used in university commentaries (for there was barely any contemporary writer on whom Blanchot had not written a few lines); and, on the other hand, the fragmentary work of this period that was difficult to digest, less and less analyzed, and sometimes even downplayed. There was already a desire to summarize his work even as it was still unfolding and metamorphosing with each new text. For the first time, one and then several more works dedicated to Blanchot appeared; even in this decade they would outnumber the works by the author himself. As each of his books came out, and as each gained more admiration than the last, there were those ready to defend him in the press (André Dalmas in *Le Monde*, Maurice Nadeau in the *Quinzaine Littéraire*, and even—despite some reticence—Claude Mauriac in *Le Figaro*). It was a curious situation that his detractors, for whom the task of criticism was limited to clarity, reproached him for his difficulty, while this same difficulty earned the praise of others, for whom it proved that he refused to make concessions to the vulgarizing tendencies of the times, that his thought was strongly unique. On the publication of *The Step Not Beyond*, Nadeau underscored how challenging it was for criticism to provide any commentary on it: "To describe or to restate, yes, to make oneself the more or less faithful echo. But it is impossible, even with great efforts, to do better than this. Let us therefore quite simply listen." With these words he closed a note introducing a parallel publication: Two pages of the *Quinzaine* reproduced various fragments from the book.[1]

The importance of his work only seemed to be recognized when no commentary was provided. University-style approaches were rare; *critical* essays were not always critical, strictly speaking.[2] There seemed to be unanimous agreement: "It is as if Blanchot wrote from a point of view that presupposed—without revealing it—a rigorous mode of textual analysis that is still to be invented."

> Would it be possible to write on Blanchot without affectation, which is to say without fear? Without such trembling, such preliminaries, such guarantees, such anxious questions over the possibility, pertinence, or irreverence of a reading—without all this excessive, misguided critical gesticulation, which makes reading into a fetishist ritual of transgression? ... The fascination that these texts exert easily forces reading to become a mimetic parade sent mad by the withdrawal of any "model."[3]

Reinforced by the reception of books by Bernard Noël, Roger Laporte, and Pierre Madaule in 1973, the idea of work made sacred—under the paradoxical protection of the Author as an absent God—began to spread in public:

> Thus Maurice Blanchot's readers appear to belong to a sort of secret community. They are unaware of one another but the presence of the author of *The Most High* within them unites them. They officiate in solitude and in anguish, but are fortified by the solitude and anguish of their peers. They address this *maître* who has no power or knowledge, who does nothing but produce a strength that forces one to imitate him.

Jean Frémon wrote this in *La Quinzaine*.[4] The hour of the myth—"a living myth"—had arrived.[5]

This hour was not without misunderstandings; it even increased them. In 1972 Roger Laporte formed a project for a book uniting accounts of reading Blanchot by himself, Pierre Madaule, and Bernard Noël. In "By an Obscure Hand" Noël recounts how he was overwhelmed by reading *Death*

Sentence on a train from which he suddenly had an almost unmanageable desire to throw himself: "What would our relation to books be, if reading violated our bodies?" In "A Passion," Laporte examines his inability to write on Blanchot and speaks of the influence on his own itinerary in writing of work that he had been reading since 1944. He formulates various realizations about the narrative work and situates Blanchot's conceptual reflections in relation to Levinas and Derrida. Last, Pierre Madaule, in a book that would eventually appear separately from the two other accounts, recounts how his reading of *Death Sentence* is interchangeable with his life. However real it might have been, such a dramatization of reading (the reading of a silent, invisible, withdrawn author and the reading of work on which only one other book had been published at this stage) provoked widespread incomprehension, and contributed to or even created—if it did not already exist—the myth of the Great Absent Author taken to be sacred, even the myth of an idolatry of the Void.

Perhaps these accounts lacked the nakedness that had marked the experiences of their authors. Their books had followed in others' footsteps. Of the *Two Readings of Maurice Blanchot*, only Bernard Noël's would be reprinted (in 1980); it was probably the denser, briefer, tighter of the two. Roger Laporte would refuse to allow "A Passion" to be reprinted: "I so detested that text, I was ashamed of it," he would write in 1994 upon publishing a completely new version of it, taking the public reception of the first version badly (it has been seen as blind idolatry) and fearing that the awkwardness of certain remarks might have hurt Blanchot, "my friend of friends."[6] Pierre Madaule would displace into his fiction his fascination for the figure of Veronica, whom he sees as key to the secret of *Death Sentence*. This displacement reminds us once again that writers repay their debts to Blanchot through misunderstandings that are much less patent in creative work than in simple homages. Perhaps Benoît Jacquot's first film, an experimental adaptation of chapter 10 of *Thomas the Obscure* (the death of Anne), fails due to its inability to decide between homage and creation; it is based on a reading by Michael Lonsdale and consists of sixty-five mostly fixed shots, showing a garden, a villa, furniture and objects, sometimes a woman's body—not without eroticism and a mawkish relation with death—and representations of illness, medicine, suffering. The fifty-eighth shot focuses on a typed text and declares the filmmaker's desire: to see "cinema as the unique ability to grasp death at work."[7]

The richest readings of Blanchot's work continued to flow, if not from cinema, then from the area of creative work, writing, and thought—these readings were not afraid of remaining close to the new, fragmentary, invented forms he was using. Such an understanding led Edmond Jabès, with whom Blanchot had been corresponding regularly for several years, to name an important section in the first volume of his *Book of Margins* after an expression in *The Step Not Beyond*, which is recalled at the end of the work: "it goes its way." Consisting of various poetic fragments, the text "The Unconditional" addresses both mankind (present as subtitle in the French version) and its "infinite, unconditional" absence, or rather the work: "Writing unconditions." It also addresses what links the two authors: "Silence too links us.... The tearing-apart of thought on the limits of the unthinkable links us.... Centuries of unquiet and the small glimmer on which our male energies converge—*dissidence*—link us."[8] In a different way of accompanying or taking part in the continuation of their shared thinking, Emmanuel Levinas conversed with André Dalmas on the philosophy of Blanchot's writing, wrote several pages on *The Madness of the Day* for an issue of *Change*, and the same year gathered together the four texts he had published on his friend in a volume called *On Maurice Blanchot*. Between 1976 and 1979, Jacques Derrida also produced many texts, international lectures, and seminars on Blanchot, thus contributing to the recognition of the oeuvre abroad.[9]

With the interventions of Derrida and Levinas, academic recognition also increased. As early as 1971, Levinas had recognized the first book to appear on Blanchot's work, *Maurice Blanchot and the Question of Writing* by Françoise Collin.[10] The book is above all an invitation to situate in the history of philosophy various notions that Blanchot had worked on: the subject, the gaze, alterity, the body, illness, sexuality, the law, the imaginary, the negative; and to emphasize the originality of the concepts he had elaborated in a spirit of "resistance to totality and to the system," an originality that was guaranteed by the close interrelationship between his thinking and his fiction. The book emphasizes this questioning's constant—albeit sometimes distant—relation to the reflection of Emmanuel Levinas. Presented on the flyleaf as a homage to the two friends together, the book was criticized, sometimes even violently, as *Blanchotiste* or imitative; the same attacks would be made—with varying degrees of justification—against the university works that would follow in its footsteps, all of which were situated in proximity to thinkers who themselves owed much to Blanchot (and to whom he also owed much).[11] For instance, Daniel Wilhelm's 1974 thesis was linked to Barthes, Genette, and Foucault;[12] Evelyne Londyn's of 1976, which attempted to show the fantastical nature of the narrative work, relied on Todorov's work; the following year, Georges Préli's book *The Force of the Outside* bore the influence of Deleuze and Guattari; last, there was Claude

Lévesque's work on Nietzsche, Freud, Blanchot, and Derrida, *The Strangeness of the Text*.[13]

With its absence of commentaries, imitative reproductions, unreflective quarrels, baseless miscomprehensions, creative research, faithful admiration, and the works of thought that accompanied it, the reception of Blanchot's work was perhaps more diverse than that of any other major body of work of its time, of any time. However, it always lacked free discussion unhindered by creative ambitions or by complacent reiterations of the "themes" at its heart. Such a discussion might identify where research could begin, bracketing the traps of circular language, signaling its debts to various tempos or models of reflection. The void created by this lack of responsibility, which is generally that of academic discourse, inevitably increased the impatience of commentators who, without always knowing what irritated them about Blanchot (or those whom they saw as his adoring disciples) and without always trying to think about this, hastened to mock the formation of a myth of divine, esoteric, oracular, disembodied speech. Henri Meschonnic was the only one in this period to undertake this task critically, in a long article in *Les Cahiers du Chemin*.[14] He raises questions about "the 'magic' exercised [by Blanchot] over young writers," adding that "what is at stake is not unimportant. We cannot dismiss it out of hand. We must clarify what is implied by certain literary practices and by their historicity." With less goodwill, he also writes "'to what point . . .' 'toward what . . .' 'and yet how can we avoid . . .' let us bid farewell to all that." After recognizing that Blanchot is rigorous to an extreme and very rare degree, Meschonnic denounces his inadequacies, the contradictions or half-pursued thoughts of

> the conception of language that is at work in Blanchot and which shows that it governs a conception of literature as well as all the relations between living and writing, life and death, the individual and the social; in so doing, it produces a circularity which is the greatest *temptation* and in which, paradoxically, what is most difficult leads to what is most facile, characterizing a mode of literature that has grown more widespread.

He is referring to the dramatizations and contrary readings of Mallarmé, to the bypassing of contemporary linguistic theories, to the mythology of absence, to the discreet neonominalism, to the infinitely metaphorical instrumentalization of death as paradigm. "The language of myth and of experience has placed esthetics and politics within an unlocatable poetics"—and therefore within something that cannot be reproduced without falling into sterile imitation. Meschonnic therefore sees in Blanchot a desire for a single language for thought and a complacency regarding the painfully immanent view that writing is impossible, even when one is writing. He misrecognizes the work of the neuter, which he sees as part of the allegorical creation of narrative simulacra, and as drowned out by the unnuanced identification of the unconditional state of writing with Jewishness. In all of this, Meschonnic ignores the way this thinking, which he encloses within the hypothesis of self-mythologizing circularity and within that of a verbal and ideological fascination in which truth remains hidden away, had in fact developed over many decades. "Blanchot's experience and thinking bear witness to a crisis in the Hegelian dialectic and, implicitly, in Marxism. The only possible development was revealed to be Nietzsche. The only possible outlet was myth": such is the conclusion. It is trapped within both phenomenology and theology, and the misunderstandings of Blanchot's nihilism that were already apparent twenty years earlier are still present. Respected but rejected by the thinker it attacked, Meschonnic's argument would remain unanswered (unlike various future misinterpretations).

In 1976, two years after this article by Meschonnic and ten years after the special issue of *Critique*, the journal *Gramma* dedicated two consecutive issues (including one double issue) to Blanchot. This is a different approach, emphasizing its Lacanian or Derridean ties and the question of identity, with the aim of provoking critical debate over Blanchot's work. The editors' opening statement sets out a clear desire to make a clean break:

> Some have thought it best to follow Maurice Blanchot in his path of effacement: they have done little but fall into the trap of fascination. It is necessary—as this issue shows—to take the opposite approach and to have no qualms: to write Blanchot into the history that surrounds him and which he somehow troubles or corrupts.[15]

The fact that most of the major specialists of the time are not part of the issue signals this desire to renew the discourse; Françoise Collin provides a text very different to her book of 1971. The operation—the word is not misplaced—was a large one: more than one hundred pages by Derrida, two previously unpublished texts by Bataille, the most complete bibliography ever published, three recent letters by Blanchot, two attributions of texts from *Committee* and, for the first time, the reprinting of some political articles from the 1930s preceded by "Topography-Itinerary of a (Counter)Revolution," a long and precise study by Michael Holland and Patrick Rousseau lacking any moralizing misappropriation and concerned only with analysis and truth. The two issues did not pass without notice. *Le Monde* briefly declared that: "The journal *Gramma* has published the second installment of the ensemble entitled 'Reading Blanchot.' It includes political texts from the 1930s by Maurice Blanchot and articles by Christian Limousin, Françoise Collin, and Alain Coulange." No other information was provided and, publicly, no debate ensued.

Although the publication was politically discreet, it still voiced strong critical reservations. Numerous elements of what looked like a dossier could no longer be ignored. Literary society was doubtless aware that before the war Blanchot had belonged to circles on the far right; and yet no public revelation had filtered through. It was the historians who had little by little raised this question: in 1962, in his vast work on Action Française, Eugen Weber had briefly mentioned Blanchot's contributions to *L'Insurgé*; in 1969, most notably, Loubet del Bayle had begun more specific investigations into Blanchot's role in *The Nonconformists of the 1930s*. But readers had had to wait until 1976 to read the beginnings of an analysis of the author's "transformation of convictions." What is even more astonishing is that the same year, introducing the Blanchot special issue of the North American journal *Sub-stance*, referring to the *Gramma* dossier and therefore in full awareness of the existence of the 1930s articles (which were also mentioned in the bibliography that he put together), Steven Ungar not only did not address the political question at all, but he also linked—in a flagrant anachronism—Blanchot's work of the 1930s with that of Bataille, Klossowski, and Leiris.[16]

Similar gestures, barely concealed in their increasing hostility, would for many years refuse to engage either with Blanchot's political past or with his contemporary thinking. In April 1979, clearly regretting his enthusiasm of the 1960s, Tzvetan Todorov masked his first political attacks on Blanchot with the veil of a supposedly hermeneutic approach, which might appear to follow Meschonnic's line of thinking; it was called "Reflection on Literature in Contemporary France."[17] After this ambitious title, Todorov immediately clarified that his interest lay in only two of the main critical thinkers: Barthes and Blanchot. His analysis is initially detailed before becoming allusive and misleading on its final page (certain texts are ignored, citations are truncated or decontextualized); hot-temperedly and without rigor, he sets about denouncing a double mystification that he attributes to Blanchot. He denies the clear legacy of romanticism in the latter's work, condemning fusionalism and stating that it is necessary to recognize "the otherness of the other"; he can thus critique a cultural "egocentrism" (an ethnocentrism) said to be at the heart of the critical work due to the attention it allegedly pays to thinking similar to its own.

> These pages are inhabited by sameness as Western European consciousness has constructed it over nearly two hundred years. And for us Blanchot's work no longer provides the diagnostic of a literature and a culture, but instead seems to be a symptom of it: it is like the things that it describes, and there is no place within it for what is foreign to it.

This attack on the critical work in the name of a political principle, which was new and totally unfounded, would prefigure others in the decades to come. For his enemies, collapsing the entirety of Blanchot's thought into the ideology of the 1930s was the best way to avoid any true debate about the work, given that this work could then be swiftly denounced for its supposed historical closure and for its so-called nihilistic, outdated literary influence.

CHAPTER 61

Making the Secret Uncomfortable
Blanchot's Readability and Visibility (1979–1997)

Blanchot was always secretive and secluded. Early in his life, illness forced him to spend long and frequent periods in isolation: the "primal scene" made him almost a stranger to his family; his writing at night remained unknown to the journalists and activists he frequented in the 1930s; in the Rue de Lille or Rue Saint-Benoît he most often remained silent; and in Èze or later in the suburbs of Paris, he lived a withdrawn life. For him, care and patience were necessary for truth, authority, the kind words that could appear—which could then be decisive, creative, mysterious, revelatory of their improper secrets, even if it meant making the perfection of his silence uncomfortable. Sometimes almost a society figure, at times suddenly called upon to show his presence and at others annulled by anonymous crowds, he often thought face-to-face meetings were important, speaking little about others or the past, paying exhaustive attention to the friend before him and the secret that this other held. His ability to withstand resolute solitude can sometimes seem astonishing, but this is to forget that he was neither the only author nor the only human being to have confronted the void, the intensity, the fragmentation, the strength, and the duration of this solitude; and that the body of the most forgotten writer is also—even in its secret folds and its open flesh—the most exposed. His solitude was uncompromising partly because he maintained intimate relationships through the love of thought (the *récits* state this clearly enough). This was an exemplary position, and one that was not without obstacles or scandals; it was a fragile, defenseless position that over the years became such a familiar one that the slightest encroachment on silence could easily disrupt it, or undermine it through powerlessness, refusal, and anger—sometimes even through writing.

Maurice Blanchot's refusals of requests for interviews and photographs, his refusals of the pressure exerted in the attempt to get him to recognize his early political standpoints, were never the unshakeable prohibition that is often attributed to him in an ignorant and facile manner. While, especially from the 1970s on, outrageous failures of discretion would occasionally catch him, proving costly and sometimes hurting him deeply, ultimately he would always recognize the freedom of the other—even if it was ill-intentioned—and in this he would remain faithful to the demand of his thinking. His pain and anger would most often remain private, with the exception of the greatest source of his intransigence: "that utter-burn where all history took fire."[1] Whenever anything resembling anti-Semitism arose, it would provoke firm and prompt reactions, in public. For the rest, his indifference concerning the reception of his work did not stem from any affected disdain but from a reciprocal concern, between the forgotten author and the ephemeral reader, for freedom.[2] After all, he had written long ago that the work belongs only to the future, which is to say to the spacing-out, effacement, and anonymity of time.

If the mystery and the myth had by now taken shape, this was perhaps due to the dazzling nature of the work, perhaps to the chance that made its author an effaced and discreet being who placed the guarantee of discretion in literature, or last perhaps to the obligation to protect his necessary fragility felt by those close to him. It must be admitted that this concern for reservedness sometimes led to extreme forms of meticulousness, even fetishistic obsession and unreal excess. The attempts to make Blanchot sacred and profane thus shared a sort of strategic alliance, some critics even occupying both camps in turn, which had the effect of creating an edict of obscurity and inviolability around a work that could be accessed only by the initiated. This meant only that Blanchot would be all the more the victim of his reputation, of his unbearably poetic renown. Indeed, how could fate have been kinder to his critics than by making possible all the barbs concerning the *blancheur* (whiteness) of he who was effaced?[3] Lacking any reality beyond its own sonorities, any body beyond work that was more and more distanced, any life except the disembodied sadness attributed to his thinking by inattentive readings blind to their own secret, the *blancheur* of Blanchot provided fodder for a certain type of criticism, but for a short time only. Such criticism, having yielded the first readings of his work as a succession of mystical revelations, would soon find other metaphors for him: for instance, a hermit, a ghost, or a block of granite.[4] And even in literary circles he is sometimes, with ignorant or calculated violence, forgotten. When Marguerite Duras at the height of her fame in the 1980s and 1990s eventually agreed to do television interviews, she thought it necessary to maliciously recall that yes, Blanchot was still alive.[5] Up in arms against the pretense that Sartre was the greatest writer of the century, she placed all the weight of her fame behind the view that only two writers in the century had ever really *written*: Bataille and Blanchot.

Even before it had been thought through ethically, in terms of infinite responsibility, *in the name of the other*, authorial effacement had become caught up in the politico-social game of spectacle and secret (at least for the commonplace, mystified observer). It had become something like the cultural double, the imitation of that game. In Blanchot's old age, withholding his presence was a strange way of falling into the trap of frenetic public demand, which makes the author into the only image and guarantor of the work. "*Communication of the incommunicable*" has become the new watchword of the cultural sector and, beyond it, of the political and mediatized world that has taken the place of social relation. All breaches, crises, the entire power of rupture are immediately neutralized by this. The incommunicable, the absolute, the unsayable, the impossible, the neuter, death, dying: so many words that die as soon as they are placed in the language of this world, which has become one of "generalized aesthetics."[6] For instance, the order of commentary most often dictates reading (the consumption of reading) according to the mechanisms described by Guy Debord in terms of the military-industrial complex:

> The reasonably well-known fact that all information on whoever is under observation may well be entirely imaginary, or seriously falsified, or very inadequately interpreted, complicates and undermines to a great degree the calculations of the inquisitors. *For what is sufficient to condemn someone is far less sure when it comes to recognizing . . . him.*[7]

Ultimately only the oeuvre can fight against what is thus produced alltoo spontaneously—or perhaps only commentaries that accept that they must bear witness "to the absence of attestation," outside the dialectic of retention or revelation which, dragging reception into a spiral of error, continues to falsify the rival, viral falsifications that the secret has already produced, the self-authorizing accounts of endless data.

The long end of the twentieth century—the 1970s, 1980s, and 1990s—had the greatest trouble *imagining* Blanchot. It grew more ignorant of him the more it searched, in the first instance, for nothing except concrete figuration; finding only an absence of images, it often then gave up on reading a language that everything about this period encouraged it to set aside.[8] This period was exasperated, titillated, astonished by this language. "No one ever met him," wrote Jean-Louis Ézine of Blanchot in 1980. "No photos, no interviews, no biography, nothing." Jude Stéfan writes as follows: "Perros was once beside Bl. in the Rue Vavin and had a moment of fright in *realizing*, as the English say, that he had approached this living shadow whose stature towered over him!" And Georges Perros himself: "Tall, tall, so incredibly tall that the present eternity of his work makes no change on him, he was there. . . . It must therefore have been Blanchot's hand that I shook."[9] The slightest sighting of the writer therefore seemed to make him into a figure similar to Proust's Bergotte. In 1996, the showy narration of a failed "visit" to Blanchot (who had recently left hospital and was recovering) would further develop a particular hypothesis concerning him; the epilogue to a book presents the story of someone inheriting from the dying writer, from whom a few crumbs of speech were snatched against the odds, words that are cited without dignity (without dashes, full stops, *capital letters*) in a violently exhibited, deceptive suggestion of vulnerability.[10]

For a long time, Blanchot seemed to challenge the photographers and caricaturists of the literary press. Over so many years, attempts to sketch his likeness were very rare, and minimalist when they did come about: in 1962 in *L'Express*, a hand held a book in a beach scene; in 1979 in *Libération*, a square in the middle of the page was left blank, bearing as its only legend the name "MAURICE BLANCHOT" and a citation from *The Infinite Conversation* ("[a] gap in the universe: nothing that was visible, nothing that was invisible").[11] In 1986, Blanchot refused to send a photograph to the Vu Agency, which was organizing an exhibition of seventy portraits of writers; he asked that instead of the photograph should appear his letter to the editor, Blandine Jeanson, in which he reiterated his concern to "appear as little as possible, not so as to privilege [his] books, but to avoid the presence of an author with a claim to an existence of his own."[12] The previous year, however, Bernard Pivot's magazine *Lire* had published for the first time a photograph of Blanchot, taken without his knowledge. In it, he was about to get into a Renault 5 in a parking lot, on the passenger side (which is referred to in French as *la place du mort*, the dead man's seat, an occasion that was too tempting for a paparazzo).¹³ In 1987, organizing a special issue on "untamed authors" (Char, Gracq, Blanchot), *Le Nouvel Observateur* reprinted the photograph, this time accompanied by a "report" by a young journalist, Jean-Marc Parisis, who had spoken to the writer's neighbors.¹⁴ It would appear again, ten years later, on the homepage of an Internet forum bearing Blanchot's name.

The "scoop" was all over literary Paris. While they all condemned the methods used, the photograph itself divided Blanchot's friends; many of them kept a copy and valued it highly. In 1987, for a book of interviews with François Poirié, Emmanuel Levinas provided various photographs dating from his studies in Strasbourg, and featuring Maurice Blanchot. One of them shows the two friends, surrounded by three others including two elegant young women, visiting one of their university professors: in years to come it would often be reproduced in the press and even on television.¹⁵ In it we see Blanchot as a young well-dressed Maurrassian leaning on the hood of a luxury car, trying to seem more relaxed than he was, with a somewhat condescending look. It recalls the caricature dating from *L'Insurgé* that Etienne de Montety published in his biography of Thierry Maulnier in 1994.

"Throughout his life he never allowed his photograph to be published, and he rejected the most tentative overtures of modern publicity with icy politeness": in 1942, Blanchot had written these lines about Taine.¹⁶ His resistance had been successful for more than forty-four years. It had given rise to all sorts of theories: for instance that it was exemplarily coherent with the theory of the author's effacement, of course, but also that it was a refusal of all literary, worldly vanity and of romantic or surrealist self-satisfaction; that it showed disdain for photographers, that it was simply narcissistic, fetishizing and fearful, a way for Blanchot to protect himself against the resurrection of face being put to the *instant* of death, the death sentence (*arrêt de mort*). Does the question of invisibility not pose that of the secret? If to write, to publish is indeed also to deliver a face, a face facing the fixed moment or the instant of death, which sees death as imminent, on the face of the dying—or killing—other of the living being that bears it over an entire lifetime, then this being can only exist *beside itself* (in Bataille's terms).¹⁷ If it can only give over its face, to whom is it to be given, and how? With what attentiveness? Creating what possibilities of incarnation or disincarnation? On the basis of what divided, dispossessed, disappropriated body? On what boundary of the unavowable? And above all: to whom, to what *invisible partner*? Perhaps this restless spacing is what displaces a *récit* of 1937 to 1948, one of 1944 to 1994 (not to mention "The

Idyll," "The Last Word" and, to think of his friend Georges Bataille, *Blue of Noon* where Blanchot's name figures, written in 1935 and published in 1957). Perhaps there is an element of someone who finds his own face unbearable, haunted by the presence of a face from the past, like Veronica and the likeness, in the image of a face that Levinas resurrected *after the fact*, from the past. How can this face be offered further assistance? How can it hold in a different community—in another form or thinking of community? How can one avoid fearing an excess of light, of daylight, if it is true that my photograph only ever resembles other photographs and that this resemblance relates only to my civil or legal identity?[18] To allow the face to be photographed, painted, sculpted would have been to claim an authority that it is not possible to atone for, and could probably not be *envisaged* for Blanchot (we know from Roger Laporte that he refused the idea of a portrait by Alberto Giacometti). Does Blanchot lack the friendship for sculptors, painters, and photographers necessary to give them such a task? Or rather, does he believe that friendship is incapable of this task, that friendship is to be found in accepting such a responsibility as a limit that cannot be transgressed? Or—last—does he wish to be other to himself, to take on the responsibility of being other, according to a demand proper to him, that of writing (to the point of silence), by which, by which alone, he shades in this too-pale face?

A snapshot, in the strong sense of a shot, a death sentence, the return of the event, of the event insofar as it is impossible, as a taking-charge of the event that is unimaginable and yet put into play in writing. With Blanchot, such an image achieves what Marie-Claire Ropars-Wuilleumier names his "disfiguring logic," his "placing of language in worklessness."[19] Death is present for the image, at each step overtaking it, breaking it up, doing violence to it: its "pure abstract invisibility" gives the image a power that allows us to access "a different region where we are held by distance," grasping us the better to release us, both from objects and from ourselves.[20] "No sooner would we begin to tell our story than we would be choking over it," in Robert Antelme's account.[21] How can one not be fearful in bearing witness to the extreme? How can one not immediately want to make the secret readable? How can writing bear witness to this, bear witness to the secret, to the unimaginable—*to the biographical*?

"Thought is incapable of writing its own history. Let it at least admit this, before consciously taking the risk of attempting to write it," warns Dionys Mascolo in 1987, before recounting the friendship that linked him to Robert Antelme.[22] This is a necessary risk, because making the secret uncomfortable does not mean accepting "the secret" (traps, prison, solitary confinement); instead, it demands attentive, prudent, and infinitely responsible speech. How can expression be given to the speech that is "beyond the living and the dead, *testifying to the absence of testimony*"?[23] How, in Jacques Derrida's words, "to testify where testimony remains impossible," how "to give in the name of the other, to give to the name of the other . . . thus bringing responsibility unto itself"?[24] How can the mythology of the secret be broken, when Blanchot himself had always known that "everything must become public," that "the secret must be violated," for "how vulgar it would be . . . to put forward confidences"? In such cases, how can this distance from the friend be maintained, "the pure interruption of Being that never authorizes me to use him, or my knowledge of him (even to praise him), and that, far from preventing all communication, brings us together in the difference and sometimes the silence of speech"?[25] How can the secret be allowed to meet itself, to give us the secret as secret, in the responsibility that consists of giving it over with all the violence of its uncertain opening?

How, except "in the name of the other"? When Georges Beauchamp and Dionys Mascolo saved Robert Antelme from death, taking him away from the camp at Dachau and returning to France, with a pause at Verdun where they took him into a restaurant where the prisoner's frame (77 lbs/35 kilos) brought the entire room to attention and silence ("when he entered the mess all the officers stood up and saluted him"), this obscure choreography or luminous displacement, these questioning gazes, this form of attention in the face of near-death and of responsibility for death—all of these were given over to writing, because they were immediately given to a third party.[26] When, in the Rue Saint-Benoît apartment where around forty people had gathered to debate the Manifesto, Maurice Blanchot suddenly and momentarily looked away to watch the child Jean Mascolo cross the room, Jean's father Dionys noticed the gaze and thought that the scene constituted an event, something that would remain with him thirty-five years later as a precise, clear memory of Blanchot's sensibility to "the grace of childhood." This third-party gaze, this witness's gaze, maintained to the point of exhaustion or indiscretion, necessarily sensitive to the slightest blinking of an eyelid—to the pain of withdrawal, to the rupture of history—represents something like the threshold of an ethics of witnessing. A witnessing of writing, of commentary, of the biographical. Far from any soothing principle or belief in charity, Blanchot gives himself and us the responsibility of thinking—living—this *"responsibility for the other before the other."* "To give in the name of, to give to the name of, the other is what frees responsibility from knowledge—that is, what brings responsibility unto itself, if there ever is such a thing."[27]

As the threshold for an ethics of witnessing and therefore of reception, this responsibility was unsurprisingly first taken up by writers, artists, and thinkers working creatively. Thus in the 1980s and 1990s it would find responses in the theatre with Pierre-Antoine Villemaine, in fiction with Pierre Madaule, in thought with Jacques Derrida, Sarah Kofman, Philippe Lacoue-Labarthe, and Jean-Luc Nancy. Each year, the life of Blanchot is further elucidated by valuable, crisscrossing accounts given in statements, books, interviews, and articles by Duras, Laporte, Mascolo, Nadeau, Prévost, by the appearance of the first biographies of Bataille, Levinas and Maulnier, by the publication of the literary correspondence of the twentieth century.[28] In particular, the work carried out by and in the vicinity of Michel Surya, Daniel Dobbels, and Francis Marmande at the journal *Lignes*, which has dedicated three issues to Blanchot, Antelme, and Mascolo, has allowed an essential relation between work and life to be conceived in a more immediate, insistent way. For instance, Daniel Dobbels introduces the double issue of 1990 on Blanchot (it contains critical studies extending the seminar organized by Laporte the previous year at the Collège Internationale de Philosophie, unpublished texts concerning the projects and correspondence associated with the *International Review*). He writes:

> The movement and the meaning of this issue can be illuminated, beyond the restlessness that haunts them, as follows: to observe the transparency of daylight is to remain, unwithdrawn, in the course of things and to attempt to seize things "by the middle" as Deleuze would say (after Kafka).[29]

In different formats, a long radio program by *France Culture*, produced by Didier Cahen and broadcast in 1994, a conference in London the same year, and an issue of *Ralentir Travaux* in 1997, would respect the same "restlessness," through similar convictions.[30]

There followed university theses (sometimes published) and special issues of reviews.[31] These had the effect of more and more palpably fracturing the intellectual domain. Roger Laporte approached first *Poétique* and then *L'Arc*, proposing in vain that they dedicate issues to Blanchot. On behalf of the former, Genette responded that the editors had themselves had the same idea, but that it had been abandoned; and the second refused to consider an issue that would not feature the author's photograph on its cover. Another dossier, conceived by Nancy and Lacoue-Labarthe for the *Cahiers de l'Herne*, remained broadly unfinished; it aimed to go beyond straightforward commentary and to appeal to writers who would contribute texts taking Blanchot as a starting-point, but most of the responses received were evasive, often based on feelings of intimidation. After seemingly endless delays, Didier Cahen's project for a conference at Cerisy also fell by the wayside in 1996. At the heart of the tensions and disagreements from 1982 onward was the interpretation of political questions. This interpretation also had distorting effects due to its straightforward refusal to read, or due to its conjuring tricks presenting boorishness as a pseudo-hermeneutics.[32] In its summer issue, *Tel Quel* had published an article by Jeffrey Mehlman denouncing what he named Blanchot's right-wing extremism and anti-Semitism before the war and at least until 1942. Despite the presentation of some new information and a letter from Blanchot himself, the article contains far fewer revelations than it claims. It seems to be unaware of the issues of *Gramma* six years earlier. Above all, it is clear that it relies only on incomplete, partial, and often wrongheaded readings of the ideas and the texts. It inaugurates a mode of interpretation indexed on a memory of the political writings of the 1930s that is said to be at work in many ways in Blanchot's later texts. A year later, in a note sent to the review that had meanwhile changed its name to *L'Infini*, Mehlman would cite the extremely rare instances of anti-Semitism from *Combat* as the heart of his argument, letting it be believed that all the 1930s texts were in a similar vein. Meanwhile, Mathieu Bénézet had published an energetic reply in *La Quinzaine Littéraire* taking aim at the editors of *Tel Quel*, displaying indignation at their silence over Blanchot that had lasted twenty years even though they had taken an ever-greater interest in the work of Céline, even his anti-Semitic texts. Claiming that he had been badly translated, Mehlman sent a list of errata to *Tel Quel*. He reestablished the precise version of his text—although it barely modified the positions adopted—when it was published in his 1984 book *Legs de l'antisémitisme en France*.[33] The same year, Todorov returned to and expanded his 1979 article in a new work, *Criticism of Criticism*. In an essay on "Fascist Ideology in France," the Israeli historian Zeev Sternhell also attacked Blanchot, who he said gave "the perfect definition" of "the fascist mindset."[34] The positions of such players would only harden: in 1994, Mehlman gave an interview to *Le Monde* in which he ratifies Sternhell's thesis and undertakes a reading of *Death Sentence* as the sacrificing of a "pure fascist ideology." At the end of the same year, *L'Infini* published an article by Philippe Mesnard, a sort of preamble to his book *Maurice Blanchot: The Subject of Engagement* which would be published in 1996, alongside a new book by an American scholar, Steven Ungar, which aimed at an "articulation of the literary and the political in interwar France," which it attempts to begin with the "case" of journalist Maurice Blanchot.[35] Between 1995 and 1997 there were many frontal attacks in *L'Infini* and in *Art Press*, in books by Bernard-Henri Lévy and by Marcelin Pleynet, on Blanchot's political extremism and on the mystification that his work allegedly represented. While Leslie Hill's book *Blanchot: Extreme Contemporary* (1997) at last looked at the question seriously and as a whole, it was not translated into French and therefore remained isolated. The Jewish intellectual community, for its part, paid little attention to these debates. It commented on and welcomed Blanchot more and more often: with Salomon Malka in *L'Arche* and *Globe*; Rachel Ertel in her book *In Nobody's Language* on "Yiddish poetry of annihilation"; Sarah Kofman, who looked at what was shared by the texts of Antelme and Blanchot, seeing in the *récits* of *Vicious Circles* many figures for what happened in the camps; she read her father's final hours of freedom—who was deported and died in Auschwitz—in the words and the thinking of the *Disaster*.

Thus, certain sections of the intellectual landscape took part in the vast denial and denigration of Blanchot's importance. More or less explicitly, these moments often shared a suspicion that Blanchot was intensely adept in psychological "disguise"; numerous false connections in analyzing the political, intellectual, and journalistic situation of the 1930s; the view that right- and left-wing political extremism is one and the same;[36] the accusation of thorough-going nihilism, and sometimes of persistent anti-Semitism; the—sometimes exclusive—emphasis on the ideological positions allegedly behind political and literary itineraries, which were distinguished only in order to be linked; the resulting superficial, mechanical periodization of the life of a man and of a body of work (from engagement to disengagement, from reengagement to silence); a functionalist conception of Blanchot's literary criticism and even of his writing (which is placed in the service of his so-called identity quarrels and reduced to a process of purification or work of mourning, as if "history had been cleansed by literary language" and "the political digested by literature"); hermeneutic extrapolations (the illusions of allegorical commentaries or of "superposed readings"); the *penalization* of literature by which it was reduced to a political or legal rhetoric and treated like one language among others, as a minor phenomenon, denied the right to have any real implications for political, historical, or ethical thought; and ultimately the *denial* of politics, which are set aside from the philosophical implications at hand whenever they are present.

At a distance, a great distance from the comforting mediocrity of such thinking, at the same time as Mehlman was publishing (but was it in the same temporality?), Blanchot continued to think—through the notions of friendship and of community—the irrefutable and indissoluble link between the literary and the political, their possibility and necessity for the impossible, inscribing his life and the lives of those close to him into the unavowable and secret forms that he has passed on to his "invisible partners."

CHAPTER 62

With This Break in History Stuck in One's Throat
The Unavowable Community (1982–1983)

Friendship, with the reading of inebriation, is the very form of the "inoperative community" Jean-Luc Nancy has asked us to reflect upon, though it is not granted to us to pause over it.[1]

One has to talk in order to remain silent. But with what kinds of words? That is one of the questions this little book [*The Malady of Death*] entrusts to others, not that they may answer it, rather that they may choose to carry it with them, and, perhaps, extend it. Thus one will discover that this question also carries an exacting political meaning and that it does not allow us to lose interest in the present time which, by opening unknown spaces of freedom, makes us responsible for new relationships, always threatened, always hoped for, between what we call work, *oeuvre*, and what we call unworking, *désoeuvrement*. (56)

Published in December 1983, *The Unavowable Community* takes the form of a diptych, an open response to two books of friendship, or rather an incitement to speak according to historical necessity and political responsibility. Between "ethics and love," between ethics and violence, in the occasional violence of the ethical gesture, the impossibility of Blanchot

435

remaining silent after the publication of such noteworthy texts bears witness to their roughness and their incompleteness. The new book, the third book (*le tiers-livre*), adds to the two others and provides them with their impossible echo, with an infinite distancing but also with agreement on what matters most, namely bringing together free transmission, and shared refusal. It provides a signature for the absence, for the wound represented by the two books, and for the links between them. It accomplishes what must be seen as the law of their worklessness, if by "worklessness" we mean the constant, indestructible movement toward the name of the other, a movement carried out in the name of the other. This movement can only be grasped—and even then, barely—by the repeated, replayed relation of writing, if by "law" we mean the obligation (Bataille would have said: *the constraint*) to expose the necessity of this community relation, of what within it is endlessly played out, presented as a gift.

This composite work consists of "The Negative Community," the first section of *The Unavowable Community*, which responds to "The Inoperative Community" by Jean-Luc Nancy (a long article that had appeared in the journal *Aléa* in spring 1983), together with "The Community of Lovers," the second part, written in homage to *The Malady of Death* by Marguerite Duras (published by Minuit the previous year). It is a composite work because it is composed of these two others, or rather of the movement whereby each composes the other, and Blanchot wanted to include many gestures of gratitude in it. Even in the early publication of a few fragments of the second part in *Le Nouveau Commerce* that spring, a final note refers to Nancy's piece, "which should become a landmark among approaches to the thought of Georges Bataille, still so misapprehended, whether despite or due to his renown."[2] In the book, a quotation from Jean-Luc Nancy is symmetrically used as the epigraph opening the section on Marguerite Duras. To weave these threads together to create an encounter that might have appeared unlikely is to respond to a secret movement, extending and revealing the work that Blanchot had been undertaking. Having learned of a thesis on Bataille that in his view silenced what was essential about the latter's view of community, he had returned to such reflections, as a letter to Bruno Roy which appeared in 1982 in a homage to Guy Lévis Mano had already suggested. Nancy's reading therefore must have seemed all the more fortuitous and striking. It came several months after Blanchot's agreement that Nancy could "translate" and publish "The Name: Berlin." Splicing together the two homages therefore took on a political meaning: It meant the politics of thought and the politics of friendship, allowing a return to the two figures who are present (Nancy, Duras), but also going beyond them to what was made necessary by certain essential responses to the contemporary rupture of historical space. These responses were *Contre-Attaque* and Bataille's thought, May '68 and the presence of the people (after an introduction of a few lines, the section on Duras soon abandoned *The Malady of Death* to address, in a surprising way, marches and committees, as well as the protestors and deaths at Charonne).

It was not the first time that Blanchot had written on his friends' books. But until this dedicated and quickly-produced publication he had never confronted them with one another like this. Something of the personal movement of history was at stake here. And above all, something of the movement of their personal history. Some passages extend the speech used in *The Infinite Conversation* and *Friendship*, in homage to this "shared agreement" between Bataille and Blanchot ("be it the momentary accord of two singular beings, breaking with few words the impossibility of Saying which the unique trait of experience seems to contain," 18). Others seem to belong to the fiction of the amorous relation in *The Malady of Death* ("He does not answer," Blanchot writes of the male character, adding "I will be careful not to answer in his stead, or else, coming back yet again to the Greeks, I would murmur: But I know who you are," 45).[3] These unshakable links also seem to retrace the sometimes-uneven history of political agreements and disagreements from Bataille to the friends of the Rue Saint-Benoît group, in order more strongly to tie together such displacements of thought as had been foundational for Blanchot's persistent, continuous political presence since the 1940s.

This book moves back and forth across the traces of past friendships and reveals those of his current friendships. It therefore contains many marks of incredible violence with which politics became personal for Blanchot. It condemns Heidegger's political consent to and philosophical recognition of Nazism (13) and distances Bataille's name from any suggestion that he can be seen as a mythological or immanentist thinker, as one concerned with a sacrificial, fusional imaginary. On the contrary, this book sees, in his work's trajectory, an ever more radical claim that all relation *is lacking* (that myth, immanence, sacrifice were lacking), that community is *interrupted* by the infinite nonreciprocity of the relation to the Other as conceived by Levinas, the other friend.[4] At the same time, it displaces Levinas's thinking toward a political demand that remained alien to him, although it became the ethical foundation for an oppositional communism: that of Antelme, Duras, or Mascolo. Blanchot inscribes this thinking of community as a memory of the collapse of the communist model, in the legacy of the venture of *Le 14 Juillet*, of the Manifesto, of the *International Review*.

The Unavowable Community marks Blanchot's return to Minuit, which published Bataille and Duras, and which nearly became his publisher too at the end of the 1940s; Minuit did indeed publish *Lautréamont and Sade*, which the structure of this book recalls. But it is above all *Death Sentence* that this structure evokes, both in the way it sets out—beyond the appearance of duality—multiple figures of thought (his characters, his friends), and in the secret, unavowed place occupied by a personal account of the relation to history. Blanchot describes the communitarian illusions in which he had once been able to place his trust. He demonstrates how at that time he gave himself over to the demand of literature alone, even if it was susceptible to orient and situate his return to a politics of the gap. The comparison of *The Malady of Death*, "a *récit* that also says in its own way: no more *récits*," (42) with *Madame Edwarda* and *The Madness of the Day* is not an anodyne one: they similarly evoke an interruption of History, the opening of a new historical space.[5] Perhaps this book also represents a personal malaise, insofar as it poses political questions, its questioning being carried out by way of friendship, and asking questions of a person who remains absent or delayed. This would explain why the work seems to have two beginnings, with its double avowal that something has been forgotten: "In the wake of an important text by Jean-Luc Nancy, I would like to take up again a reflection never in fact interrupted, although surfacing only intermittently, concerning the communist demand" (1); and in the first version of the text on *The Malady of Death*: "I had not read a book by Marguerite Duras for a long time: perhaps because I lacked the ability to read, or because I wanted to remain close to the books of hers that I loved so completely and therefore lacked the power to go beyond. For other reasons too: reasons are never lacking."[6]

Indeed, reasons were hardly lacking for a return to the political discourse that had been somewhat effaced by notions of ethical necessity in the 1970s. In May 1981, the election of François Mitterrand and the formation of a left-unity government resurrected feelings of lightness and hope. New intellectual spaces were opening up too: Lacoue-Labarthe and Nancy founded the Center for Philosophical Research on the Political in November 1980;[7] at Cerisy in 1981, Derrida presented "Of an Apocalyptic Tone Adopted Long Ago in Philosophy," a lecture published two years later (and to which *The Unavowable Community* was also a type of response).[8] At the beginning of 1983, Hélène and Jean-Luc Nancy proposed a "reconstitution" of "The Name: Berlin," which Blanchot immediately authorized. Blanchot would approach the question of intellectuals and politics in the 1980s and 1990s through such spaces of reflection on the possibility of a different thinking of community, of which he and Bataille were the founders but not the proprietors. This question would be passed back and forth between him, Derrida, and Nancy, in a play of gifts and exchanges. The latter's article from *Aléa* would be published in book form by Christian Bourgois in 1986, expanded to include a series of lectures given in Berlin, "Myth Interrupted," and a new text, "Literary Communism." Four years later, a new edition would be further extended by two texts that had appeared in journals in the interim. These extensions of the work's interrogations bring one back to worklessness, which comes and goes between the texts, whose movement never stops, and whose necessity for the community Nancy willingly agrees has been defined by Blanchot.[9] These interrogations of the possibility of witnessing had grown more pronounced in Blanchot's writing and even in his shorter interventions. They were accompanied by *Parages* by Derrida (1986), *Smothered Words* by Kofman (1987), *Around an Attempt to Remember* by Mascolo (1987), and *Georges Bataille: An Intellectual Biography* by Surya (1987), all books that bear witness in different ways to the very necessity of witnessing, in a period marked by the abandon of any hope based in community.

Perhaps such a necessity to bear witness, to bear witness to one's own witnessing, is what makes Blanchot cite himself frequently for the first time.[10] Perhaps too the pressure exerted by this possibility of bearing witness is what allows the influence of fragmentary writing to diminish. From this fragmentary writing, this new work retains only the brief nature of its twenty-six chapters (something like long fragments with titles) and its discontinuous structure, its workless movement that halts, fractures, or overspills any accumulative, linear exposition—"with this break in history stuck in [one's] throat," as Jean-Luc Nancy would later put it.[11] This break is transmitted from one text to another, this commonly felt need to avoid any model of immanence (any communitarian or totalitarian model: the total presence of the community to itself) or any model of transcendence (any individualist or liberal model: the individual as "the absolutely detached for-itself, taken as origin and certainty").[12] The necessity of relation is to be found first of all in its interruption. Rather than any direct link, which he sees as part of a social order, Nancy proposes a conception of *coappearance* (*la comparution*) (even if it takes place from a basis of separation, of breach, of love, of death): he proposes that we conceive "the passage of one through the exposed limit of the other."[13] More than love or death themselves, it is the ethical impossibility of making love or death into a work that founds the demand of community. The resulting notion of community is thus founded not on mourning or on death, but on its self-mourning and self-death: on its own impossibility. This impossibility, this mourning, this death are improper in a proper way, and this is what makes this foundation possible. Community is only community if it is an impossible community. Such are the relations that Blanchot and Bataille, or Blanchot and Mascolo, named friendship. Although it is absent in Nancy's book, the term reappears several times in Blanchot's, who adds: "friendship ... is the very form of the 'inoperative community' Jean-Luc Nancy has asked us to reflect upon, though it is not granted to us to pause over it" (23). Friendship is thus the equivalent of grace, a way of sustaining absence that has always been deferred and inverted since it became clear that death is impossible; it is fidelity to the unknown, the only certainty held in language to the point of all uncertainty, thus remaining what bears witness to the impossibility of witnessing. It also confronts the absolute of history: "against a backdrop of disaster," Blanchot repeats here (1). It is what leads to the "presence of the people," (31) what links without linking the demonstrators of 1968 or Charonne: the exception that makes for "one of those moments when communism and community meet up and ignore that they have been realized by being lost immediately," (32) Blanchot writes in a political paraphrase of the final words of *The Malady of Death* ("live that love in the only way possible for you. Losing it before it happened").[14] All forms and conceptions of community henceforth have to face "the malady of death." Ethical witnessing has to make its refusal clear, a refusal based on impossible community. "It is because no community is possible with the SS that there is also the strongest community, the community (of those) without community," Sarah Kofman would write.[15] A community that continues to weave together modes of speech that bear witness both to the impossibility of community and to the absolute uniqueness of humankind. A community to which the literary community bears witness when it agrees to recognize ambiguity between the work and worklessness, between experience and infidelity, between memory and effacement: when there is an opening of "the groundless ground of communication." (17) With such "literary impropriety," (20) Blanchot insists that the only fitting impropriety is Bataille's, to whom a debt is owed (we can recall that a related formulation saw Blanchot attributing to Sade "the major impropriety"). Literature is neither suitable nor does it bring people together. It calls on the unavowable to appear, doing so via "nocturnal communication ... that which is not avowed" (20). This communication is what the narrative by Marguerite Duras remains faithful to, what it attempts to give voice to.

Concerning death, this narrative establishes that one can only ever be ill, something that explains both its sly, sovereign interiority and its radical exteriority, its total lack of relation. For the woman in the narrative tells the man that he is stricken with illness, and that she is unable to cure him: His illness stems from what he does not possess, but she remains unable to give him what she possesses. There is no way that what she possesses could be any foretaste of death (any collection of relatable experiences) which she could somehow access; she just might, however, be linked to the appearance of dying. Anything that is avowed is avowed by death; it cannot be avowed by any subject.

Blanchot's relation to Duras is surprising—as is the solidarity with which he speaks of her, the backdrop of silence against which she appears, and his avowal of this solidarity and this silence at the beginning of the version published in *Le Nouveau Commerce*. Also surprising is his analysis that the text in question is a declaration: "it is a declarative text and not a *récit*, even though it appears as such" (35), when conversely everything seems to point to the text as a narrative playing fictionally with its mode of address. This seems to be confirmed by the Freudian slip Blanchot makes in removing the conditional tense from a citation he gives ("you shouldn't have known her [*vous devriez ne pas la connaître*]," the opening phrase of *The Malady of Death*, becoming "you won't have known her [*vous ne devez pas la connaître*]," 35).[16] No more expected is his silence over the strange enunciative setup of the text, which creates an unequal relation between the two characters, the man cited by the text as "you," the woman more conventionally as "she"; or the remarks attributed to the (neutral or neuter) narrative voice, "a voice whose origin escapes us," (59) and which is sometimes reduced to a divine metaphor, that of "the supreme Director: the biblical 'You'" (35), but at other times is merged with the female character.

In a long footnote on *The Ravishing of Lol V. Stein*, Blanchot had previously reproached Duras for choosing to attribute "the narrative voice" of the *récit* (that which at the time he called "the *it* [*il*], the neuter") to a character, a man, Jacques Hold—and had done so in the sentiment of indecisiveness that seemed so decisively to be his when he spoke of a book by Duras ("perhaps rashly, perhaps rightly," he wrote).[17] Over and against this "slightly shameful" attribution, it had seemed better to him to have a female character speak in that voice, a female character of which he stated only that,

> the one [a woman or a thought? Lol or Duras?] who cannot recount because she bears—this is her wisdom, her madness—the torment of impossible narration, knowing (by a closed knowledge anterior to the

scission of reason-unreason) that she is the measure of this outside where, as we accede to it, we risk falling under the attraction of a speech that is entirely exterior: pure extravagance.[18]

Blanchot was always interested by the third-party element in Duras, stemming from:

> the need (the eternal human vow) to place in another's charge, to experience once again through another, third party, the dual relation, the fascinated, indifferent relation that is irreducible to any mediation, a relation that is neutral, even if it implies the infinite void of desire.[19]

These words could also apply to the young woman in *Destroy, She Said*, a narrative that Blanchot would also pause over, or to the lack of inhibition of Madame Edwarda's taxi driver, to whom Blanchot refers twice in *The Unavowable Community* (41, 48).[20] In *The Malady of Death*, these words can only be understood to refer to an invisible form, the "You" of the voice.

In this nonreading to which he sometimes consents, everything is connected.[21] Everything seems to make this text appear or reappear in the form of true speech, imitating what the interruption of the book would be for community, and everything seems to flow from a dialogue between Blanchot and Duras. Strangely, Blanchot hesitates over reading in "this *récit* devoid of anecdote" (43) what is most "Blanchotian" about it (what makes it the most "Blanchotian" of Duras's *récits*: therefore also the most communitarian, and perhaps the most unavowable).[22] The misunderstandings suggested by Duras's public—even violent—refusal to accept elements of his interpretation would only superficially concern questions of the male figure's homosexuality and the sexual encounter between the two characters.[23] Perhaps with the woman there remains something of a belief in the ability to "impose death" which suspends her sovereign indifference to her own ability to be summoned before death. At the same time and in the same site, Blanchot is fascinated by the torment undergone by the sovereign voice which is embodied then immediately set aside, made absent in this *feminine third party*: It is a torment of recognition offering the space of fiction to community.

What Duras herself attempts to do for (and with) Blanchot in her fiction should be studied with precision, given that she, more than any other, occupies the neutral place made possible by community (Mascolo liked to recount how she withdrew in order not to impinge on friendships with Antelme).[24] Duras turns all those close to her into fictional characters, for instance with the name of the character Andesmas, which brings together the first letters of the names of Antelme, Des Forêts, and Mascolo. *Abahn Sabana David* (1970) was dedicated to Antelme and Blanchot. Certain depictions in this narrative and in *Destroy, She Said* (1969) are not alien to the extreme closeness that—as Mascolo confirms—Duras felt for Blanchot (we think especially of the mysterious, imposing figure of Stein, the Jewish insomniac writer haunted by the end of history, and of the use made of the picture windows of the hotel, a site of convalescence away from the world).[25] In Blanchot's original article on it, "Destroy," which uses the same title but minus the attribution of this word to a woman, he distances himself from any possibility of narrative appropriation. He only remarks on the elements of the *récit* that are close to his own:

> Characters? Yes, they are in the position of characters—men, women, shadows—and yet they are immobile points of singularity, although the path movement takes through a rarefied space—in the sense that almost nothing can take place in it—can be traced from one to the other, a multiple path, along which, fixed, they constantly change.

Or again: This place "is there, it seems, before the action of the book begins, the questioning of the film, that death—a certain way of dying—has done its work, introducing fatal worklessness into it."[26]

This is not to say that Blanchot is not fascinated, worried, troubled by the figure of the young woman Alissa who disturbs the characters' conjugal relationship, as a new figure of the third person. In the *récit* Stein loves her, as does Thor. Blanchot concludes his article with her, as if in homage: "the innocent young companion henceforth with us at our side, she who gives and receives death, as it were, eternally."[27] The same figure attracts him thirteen years later in *The Malady of Death*, proving decisive for the movement of writing: this eroticism of "this young woman, so mysterious, so obvious, but whose obviousness—the ultimate reality—is never better stated than when she is about to die"; she whom he identifies quickly, "somewhat offhandedly," he admits, "with pagan Aphrodite or with Eve or Lilith" (53–54). This harmful, young innocence, which here has no name and no face, is the invisible, fleeting knot at the heart of community, even as the fiction recounts its disappearance.

The Malady of Death stages an exhibition of singularities in which—with their respective finitudes appearing alongside one another, all finitude disappears as soon as it has appeared—the "with" of this coappearance is a confrontation of flesh with flesh; it exhibits the dislocation whereby they form a community, a *being-in-common*, what is precisely *not* a common being, and is the inaccessibility of communion for them. Here love is recognized as that which opens onto an abyss where love has no object—where there is no love.

CHAPTER 63

Even a Few Steps Take Time
Literature and Witnessing (1983–1997)

Then followed long years measured out in difficult days and nights of insomnia, lived out facing the near-total density of the void, spent no longer writing but still being there, now and again demonstrating his presence through a few public letters, fragments, small works, and numerous reprints. There were signatures, stands taken, refusals, periods of anger, periods of acquiescence. There was an absolute presence in the world, in the publishing world, in public matters, in questions of who was to govern, questions relating to what was still supposedly the Left.[1] There were illnesses, falls, hospitalizations, returns to the isolation of his suburban house, the condemnation of solitude. Blanchot experienced this solitude as if it were his fate (how could the presence of such weakness be imposed on the other, on others?). There was the time of "disaster," without distress but during which the demands made by distress were held in an intimacy that only very few friends would share, and even then only barely. "It is not permitted to be old" a Hassidic master once said in a phrase that Blanchot now liked to cite: this encouragement to write (even if to cast light on or to efface all secrets), this dogma of resistance—for a person whose health ultimately became a major worry—to defeat each illness that temporarily incapacitated him: these would lead to some of Blanchot's sweetest smiles, some of his work's finest pages.² Only a few pages, or even a few lines, now appeared each year. They were sent as if from a great distance, from the ends of the earth and from outside time; they were sometimes prophetic and sometimes bore witness, but always related to an intense, febrile presence in the world. They had been—as it were—clawed back from the temporary ailments of the eyes, the voice, the hearing, from his trembling handwriting (writing became increasingly painful, and thus his ability to maintain relations with others diminished). His correspondence dropped away, he used the telephone less and less. But his tenacity remained, and he read endlessly. "The other, the Friend, always remained within reach of one's voice," wrote Roger Laporte. Yes, within reach, but silently; he was on the other end of the line, but said little, as in Mascolo's dream; "in unison, but each on a different shore." "Space brings us together, separates us forever."³

The century was drawing to a close. Almost all its great writers were dying, homages were the order of the day (most often in the deflated form of commemorations), lived experiences were becoming historical (even with those who had resisted this for so long). In such a network of texts, amid such resonances in place of memories, how could he not feel increasingly isolated? The litany of deaths had already included Barthes, Sartre (1980), Lacan, (1981); now it was those who had once been so close who were suddenly distant: Foucault (1984), Michaux (1984), Char (1988), Beckett (1989), Dalms (1989), Leiris (1990), Jabès (1991), Deleuze (1995), and Claude Roy (1997). Blanchot's generation was dying, but so too was a younger generation; so too were even his closest friends. In 1983, Robert Antelme had an operation on his carotid artery; a mistake in the surgery left him paralyzed on one side. He died seven years later, on October 26, 1990. Marguerite Duras died in 1996, Dionys Mascolo in 1997, Emmanuel Levinas on December 25, 1995. "I am sorry, but I must bury a few others before I bury myself": even the prophetic words of *The Madness of the Day* were too soft for reality, and this infinitely cruel softness ultimately enclosed Blanchot in silence.⁴

These words would hold true even for his family. In 1984, Marguerite Blanchot was admitted to hospital with heart problems, in a clinic in Chalon. Unable to play her beloved pianos, she wrote notes on musicology, notably on Chopin. She had almost ten years to live, but they would be spent shuttling between hospitals and rest homes. Initially, her brother George wished to have her close; she thus left Chalon and moved to the hospice in Montmerle-sur-Saône in the Ain *département*; she was not happy there. In an irony of fate, it was George who died two years later, on October 9, 1986. Marguerite left for a home in Belleville in the Rhône *département*. She had one of her pianos transported there, but was unable to play in her final years. She died on February 23, 1993. Four days later she was discreetly buried in the cemetery in Devrouze. When her death was announced in Chalon, it only proved how rapid and strong oblivion was (public remorse and urbane compassion followed several days later, as it always does). One of Blanchot's nephews, a son of George, died around this time.[5] One of this nephew's sons also died. Last, in December 1997, Anna—who had lived for nearly twenty years with Blanchot—also passed away.

And so these texts existed, which seemed to be sent out from time to time, these interfering voices, this shards of thought, this ethical absolute, that exist to one side of systematization or homage, *beside oneself*; these fragments that mime effacement, that impose a secret mode of commentary and of presence.

His works saw numerous reprintings: as early as 1981, a request from Gallimard led to the collection of texts on Kafka, preceded by "Literature and the Right to Death," in a low-cost edition called *From Kafka to Kafka*, which quickly gained an international audience. In 1982, in *The Beast of Lascaux*, Blanchot evoked the "fleeting memory" of René Char and of Guy Lévis Mano, who was the first to turn this short essay into a book. Bruno Roy, who took on this publication the same year that he produced a homage to Mano, also reissued two other articles by Blanchot: one in 1984 on Paul Celan (*The Last to Speak*), which had been written after the death of the poet, and one in 1987 on Joë Bousquet's *Translated from Silence*. This was followed by Bousquet's essay on *Aminadab*, thus creating a two-headed book with two texts of similar length, both written at the beginning of the 1940s.[6] For around twenty years, Bruno Roy became Blanchot's third publisher. He looked after shorter works, which were published in limited runs in a long, thin format and on tinted laid paper; sometimes they were illustrated (by Bram Van Velde, Pierre Tal Coat, and Jean Ipoustéguy).[7]

In 1986 and 1987 the Brussels publisher Complexe reissued texts by Blanchot on Sade, Restif, and Lautréamont in their new collection "The Literary Gaze." We can imagine why the author must have agreed to these publications, again in a low-cost format, which formed part of a book series that was more literary than critical, consisting of readings of writers by other writers (indeed, the text on Lautréamont features alongside two others, by Gracq and Le Clézio). A few critical texts written for defunct journals were sometimes reprinted by new ones. "The Paradox of Aytré" was taken from *The Work of Fire* to form part of a new, 1988 edition by Spectres Familiers of Paulhan's narrative *Aytré Losing the Habit*. In English, Michael Holland published a volume comprising many texts that Blanchot had not collected in his volumes.[8] And last, all of the *récits* were reissued in Gallimard's "The Imaginary" series.

The most striking republication of all these years would be one of the earliest: that of *Vicious Circles* by Minuit, followed by an afterword that gave its name to the work, *After the Fact* (1983). The two novellas had become almost impossible to find. Preceding *The Unavowable Community* by a few months and appearing the same year under the same imprint, their publication was not without major political significance. These *récits* written before but published after Auschwitz once more raised the question, forcefully: *How can we not write, after Auschwitz?* "There can be no fiction-story about Auschwitz," Blanchot says, but also: "no matter when it is written, every story from now on will be from before Auschwitz." And yet, "perhaps life goes on."[9] He notes that toward the end of *The Metamorphosis* when Gregor Samsa dies, his young sister becomes newly alive. This example casts its light far. The absolute event of History confronts us, tragically, with the task of thinking its withdrawal. Expressing this withdrawal is perhaps all that remains for literature: it is precisely its curious "idyll" and therefore its "last word," its "very last word." In the 1980s, when political, civil, legal, historical, and artistic life began to question this barely speakable past more than ever, it was necessary to reaffirm the radical impossibility and yet the infinite responsibility of all the avowals and trials, of all the necessary and possible revelations. Something like the *perforated site* of literature opens up to Blanchot through the occurrence of an event that, *after the fact*, becomes charged with the unsustainable weight of the disaster and the writing of the disaster. And this site opens up to him in the face of the blinding, always deferred perspicacity of narration and in the face of the infinite exhaustion of thought (of the *entretien*) that is foundational for it. This is a space offered to witnessing, the vigilant speech of memory, the demand for truth and fidelity, the practice of a consenting to weakness (nonetheless always placed under the double demand: *naming the possible, responding to the impossible*). Phrases such as "I remember," "I recall," "I was a stranger [*étranger*]," "I was writing," "we were [*étions*]" authenticate autobiographical memory, and a slippage into the imperfect tense now makes such statements possible. Of course, not a great number of past events would be recounted; but this rare quality made them all the more astonishing and precious. Blanchot had this tendency for many years: we can date it to 1965 when in an article on "The Great Reducers," he mentioned an encounter with one of his friends ("I remember, around 1946, a conversation [*entretien*] with Merleau-Ponty").[10] From then on such references became more frequent. Most of the texts of the 1980s and 1990s appeared under the sign of shattered memories, of fragments of memories. Even his critical essays would begin by evoking recollections, as if to avow that they had always drawn the unfolding of their speech from the memory of events and of experiences. There was a weakness inherent in all commentary and even in all narrative: The latter could only ever be a commentary after the fact, except in the event-status of a rare type of literature where it is the event itself (itself: in its separated relationship with the event whose equivalent in language it cannot avoid being). And this double weakness is avowed by Blanchot in an afterword written in proximity to the greatest writers, those closest to him, who shared—he recalls—the same weakness: Mallarmé, Kafka, Bataille. To comment on, to provide a reading of or a follow-up to the work is necessarily to adjourn it in the name of the false transparency of "life." And yet Blanchot now believed that his task was to bring about a witnessing, through a concern with "(indirectly) taking on responsibility" for presence, for writing or action as work.

This responsibility was also imposed on him by the deaths of those close to him, of those who had themselves taken it on. The prologue written by Boris Souvarine for a new edition of *Social Criticism* in 1983 was full of attacks on Georges Bataille, and as such forced Blanchot to respond. He did so in these terms: "As, with the passing years, witnesses to the period are becoming fewer, I cannot remain silent while there is still time, and allow credence to be attached to claims which I know to be incontrovertibly untrue."[11] In 1993 his "pre-text" for Dionys Mascolo's book *Searching for a Communism of Thought*, named "For Friendship," is—a first in his writing—rich with brief, laconic but precise memories. It concludes as follows:

> Friendship, comradeship, I would have liked, dear Dionys, to wonder from afar with you who are so present, as with those who are even more present, because having disappeared, they can respond to us only through their disappearance.[12]

This same principle would guide him for many years, as it had from at least 1983 or 1984 with his first autobiographical sketch, consisting in a few lines named "Encounters" given to *Le Nouvel Observateur* for an issue celebrating the magazine's twentieth anniversary.[13] While Blanchot would only rarely agree to reveal anything personal, whether relating to himself or to those close to him, he did engage in an indirect mode of witnessing in the name of the unavowable. His agreement that his article on Bousquet be published in a work setting two voices in such symmetry contains some highly personal descriptions of illness, solitude, and the experience of these in and through language. "We understand from various notes that long ago this man travelled far in absence and in silence."[14] But the necessity of witnessing would overwhelmingly be felt in relation to political matters, on multiple occasions in relation to May '68, and—always—to Auschwitz.

One such occasion was a work on political consciousness and intellectual ethics, published following Jean-Denis Bredin's book on the Dreyfus affair, described as "the sketch of a reflection" and yet an extension of the work that for some time Blanchot had been doing on the 1930s and the thinking of Georges Bataille: "Intellectuals under Scrutiny."[15] This is a long article that appeared alongside a previously unpublished text by Sartre in the journal *Le Débat*; "notes" given to Pierre Nora in an uneven, unordered state, and sometimes taking the form of an autobiographical narrative (albeit still under the sign of secrecy). Blanchot would not hesitate to publish this text in book form with Fourbis twelve years later (his request was behind its appearance alongside the new, 1996 edition of *For Friendship*). This shows how much he cared about this text, which provided another form of political testament, in a more or less veiled fashion. "I am not one of those who are content to seal up the tomb of the intellectual," he declares early on, immediately adding: "first and foremost because I don't know what is meant by the term."[16] Blanchot refuses the self-deprecation of the intellectual who, under the pressure of a certain understanding of history and of the breakdown of grand ideologies, abandons the object of his existence: the search for universal justice in the name of reason. Such an attitude belongs too closely to the "air of the time" that he denounces.[17] But this does not mean that the intellectual is "the man of commitment," nor, according to the terms of Foucault's call to vigilance, "the representative of the universal" or "the conscience of all."[18] Unlike Sartre, Blanchot does not give the intellectual any permanent status; ultimately, the intellectual does not exist, intellectuals are always "under scrutiny" and, as he writes in conclusion, "being questioned." Writers, artists, or scholars can only be intellectuals provisionally: "The intellectual is a portion of ourselves, which not only distracts us momentarily from our task, but returns us to what is going on in the world, in order to judge or appreciate what is going on there."[19] At the same time, the writer, artist, or scholar can never avoid this engagement. It is an ethical demand that constantly places them in relation with the domain of the possible. They have this duty but receive no rights in exchange, except perhaps the right of remaining insubordinate, in order better to become anonymous. Their sole concern is to lay claim to a "universal idea of what is just and unjust"; it is even their existence as artists, not intellectuals, that places this straightforward stubbornness within them (they defend "in the same impulse the demands of right and of justice and the demands of writing, considered as that which must submit to nothing but itself").[20] Therefore intellectuals do not take their authority from knowledge; Blanchot even takes care to show how many mistakes they made in the specific case of the Dreyfus affair, when the category of the intellectual was born. Péguy, Guesde, Blum, Jaurès: All of them, at one time or another, made mistakes. Like Valéry, their mistakes led them to follow a path extremely close to the one taken decades earlier by Blanchot himself. That intellectuals often make mistakes; and sometimes even take a long time to reestablish themselves after these mistakes, that despite their intellectual nature they lack thought and submit to the unsuspected power of their prejudices, or ultimately that they are *unable to explain themselves*—this is what this article, become a short work, would attempt to demonstrate. It immediately adds that the issue of anti-Semitism is often what ends up reestablishing the link to universal justice, the intellectual's "simple idea." "From the Dreyfus affair to Hitler and Auschwitz, the proof is there that it was anti-Semitism (along with racism and xenophobia) which revealed the intellectual most powerfully to himself."[21] From his alignment with *Rempart* to the time at *Combat*, from his wartime attitude to his meditations on the camps, it was indeed anti-Semitism that—not without provoking vexation—had revealed Blanchot to himself, in the infinite demand for the coming of the Other, the Wholly Other. "There would thus seem to be a moment, in every life, when the unjustifiable prevails and the incomprehensible is given its due," Blanchot writes, and we must also relate this to his life. In this, more than in the citation of René Char on which he ends, is to be found what he names "my personal confession."[22] This is the confession that no confession can be sustained except by constantly reflecting on the unjustifiable. That was what Heidegger, who was guilty of many other "errors," of what Blanchot himself here names "the fatal error" or of what in 1966 he named "the capital offence," refused to do.[23]

Strangely, this avowal of an impossible avowal is accompanied by the fiction of an avowal, the fiction of an autonomous, autobiographical and more or less secret avowal. For the pages on the 1930s and on the 1960s repeat the details of the positions that, as a journalist, then as a thinker, Blanchot had adopted (on democracy as an erosion, the denunciation of Hitler's anti-Semitism, the condemnation of pacifist antifascism; and, in the 1960s, on the necessity of intervening in favor of a "concrete cause," against the idea of mythical providence, for what is closest, and in the name of anonymity alone). These pages rehearse these positions without ever declaring that they had been Blanchot's own, simply making it possible to recognize them and to think the free and perhaps blind movement behind such recognition. This is proof, if proof is possible, that avowal is always absent, and ultimately that single avowal can be sustained.

If what can never be sustained nonetheless has to be attempted, and if it is necessary to hold to "the categorical imperative . . . which Adorno formulated more or less thus: *Think and act in such a way that Auschwitz may never be repeated*," then there are also the many times he takes a stand against anti-Semitism, and against Heidegger's in particular.[24] While Blanchot knew that he had been able to protect himself against any "naivety" with regard to Nazism, with its mythical thinking and its professed ideology of murderous racism, his tenacity in addressing Heidegger's engagement can only be understood in the light of the misdirection in thought of which he accuses the philosopher (and had done so for a long time). There is a note in *Intellectuals under Scrutiny* that exemplifies this, beginning as follows: "The more important Heidegger's thought is taken to be, the more it is necessary to try and clarify the sense of his political adhesion in 1933–34."[25] It provides a précis of everything with which Blanchot reproaches the philosopher of *Being and Time*. It shows the degree of tolerance he is prepared to assume in order to agree to understand and realign the boundaries of what is justifiable, although the latter never included the "political declarations" in favor of Hitler through which Heidegger placed "the language of his own philosophy . . . in the service of the worst of causes." "That, for me," Blanchot adds, "is the gravest responsibility: what took place was a falsification of writing, an abuse, a travesty and a misappropriation of language." These words applied not only to language but also to the language of thought. And further on, Blanchot recalls precisely what the demand of that thought is: "there is no greater courage than the courage of thinking."[26]

Such is Blanchot's position, restated each time in the same terms from the notes of *The Infinite Conversation* and the text of 1980 on Levinas ("Nazism and Heidegger, this is a wound to thought").[27] He feels that it is necessary to say and repeat that thinking is henceforth impossible, except when it thinks how to pass on the impossible witnessing: "How can one philosophize, how can one write in memory of Auschwitz, of those who told us, sometimes in notes buried close to the crematories: know what happened here, do not forget, and at the same time you will never know."[28] When he adds: "This is the thought that traverses, and bears, all of Levinas's philosophy and that he proposes to us without saying it, beyond and before every obligation," we can understand why the name of Levinas traverses all the texts written by Blanchot in the 1980s (very few do not cite him—as an appeal, a demand, a request).[29] Inversely, by refusing to interrogate this new "categorical imperative," by remaining silent and difficult to pin down about the past, Heidegger only allowed the deepest suspicion to be cast over his thinking. Blanchot would publicly accuse him on the basis of this silence, at the time of what he could not bring himself to name "the Farias affair."

In the fall of 1987, Victor Farias's book *Heidegger and Nazism* was published. The question was not a new one, but the new work gave space to the anecdotal, bore witness to several unknown facts, and polemically denied the philosopher any substantial importance. The literary press was bowled over and for the first time the subject was widely discussed by the media. Neither Levinas's older nor Lacoue-Labarthe's more recent reflection, both of which examine Heidegger's Nazism and anti-Semitism in much more pertinent ways, had succeeded in provoking such a "debate."[30] For *Le Nouvel Observateur*, Catherine David asked various writers and philosophers for statements on the topic. The title of Blanchot's response, which he wrote as early as November 10, 1987, is explicit: "Thinking the Apocalypse." This was precisely what he accuses Heidegger of not having done: "a sort of anti-Semitism was not alien to him and it explains why never, despite being asked to on several occasions, did he agree to make any statement about the Extermination." And later, in conclusion, he writes that: "Heidegger's irreparable fault is his silence concerning the Extermination."[31] The rest of the article barely refers to the national, sedentary essence of Heideggerian philosophy; above all, it attempts to show through numerous examples that Heidegger's rare avowals and standpoints on the question of his engagement and the engagement of his philosophy for National Socialism are as contradictory as it was possible to be. They are therefore untenable, and above all are inept in relation to the failure to think that they mask.

Blanchot makes the same accusation in another letter, responding to another request, from Salomon Malka for the journal *L'Arche* in May 1988.

"Know what happened, do not forget, and at the same time never will you know." This sentence from "Our Clandestine Companion," which even there had been borrowed from *The Writing of the Disaster*, and would be borrowed again in a 1986 article for *La Quinzaine Littéraire*, and later in a text in homage to Jabès, each time in exactly the same terms, this time was modified.[32] And yet at the heart of the formulation there remains the imperative "Do not forget," with Salomon Malka confirming that the use of these words for the title was requested by Blanchot (they had also been used for an article for the *Quinzaine*, two years earlier). To refer to "the unforgivable silence of Heidegger" is to bear indirect witness to Blanchot's own speech. His letter to Malka reveals his first memories of meeting Levinas, in the 1920s at the University of Strasbourg. It also refers to Blanchot's proximity to the Jewish community in Paris in 1933 (without explicitly citing the name of Paul Lévy or referring to the contributions to *Le Rempart*). A short autobiographical narrative confirms how long Judaism had been present in Blanchot's mind and emphasizes what his thinking owed to Buber and to Levinas. His desire to think Judaism philosophically, in relation to his meditations on anti-Semitism, is present everywhere. For instance, the responsibility for others (*autrui*), who in Levinas's terms are closer to God than I am, justifies the condemnation of Heidegger (what's more, Blanchot recalls in a note that Levinas himself had stated as much).[33] This thought or meditation is constant; after *The Step Not Beyond*, after *The Writing of the Disaster*, after Buber and Levinas, and now with *Shoah* by Claude Lanzmann, which he cites on various occasions (the book and the film appeared in 1985), Blanchot continues to meditate on Judaism, anti-Semitism, and the Nazi exterminations. It is his way of avowing: avowal as what comes about through what thinking found unthinkable, and through the impossible witnessing of literature, which was charged with "transmitting the intransmissible," as he says in the 1986 text in *La Quinzaine*. "He who has been the contemporary of the camps is forever a survivor: death will not make him die."[34] Such is the charge that the writer confides to the intellectual. "The heaviest blessing," as Blanchot wrote about Judaism in 1985 for the catalogue of an exhibition at the Grand Palais on the Dead Sea scrolls and contemporary Jewish artists ("From the Bible to our times"): Chosenness brings with it infinite responsibility, setting one aside only in order that one should watch over the principle of equality in relations with the other, with the stranger.[35]

Only this principle's demanding nature is able to hold off the malaise or discomfort that can seize us as we read the occasionally violent texts of this period, which take many positions even as they reiterate individual terms taken from Blanchot's thinking, as if only the same words could now be uttered, as if nothing new, nothing different, nothing more could be said. (This would explain his propensity to cite himself or those close to him such as Jabès or Levinas, especially on Auschwitz, repeating the litany of titles, formulations, almost verses; "nowadays I only have thoughts for Auschwitz," he would write to Bernard-Henri Lévy.)[36] These are texts which, *exhausted of literature*, give up on composition and sometimes give free rein to clarifying points of his autobiographical narrative, although without leading to the clarifications that many of both Blanchot's admirers and enemies would have liked to have seen him publish (clarifications that would later be attributed to him). Steven Ungar would allude to a rumor that in 1986 Blanchot had written a seven-page text on his early political articles.[37] Leslie Hill, for his part, would refer openly to a letter written to Roger Laporte in December 1984, in which Blanchot gave a detailed account of his political trajectory.[38] With Blanchot's permission, he would cite a long extract from it, signaling that the text should have appeared in the abortive issue of the *Cahiers de l'Herne* prepared by Lacoue-Labarthe and Nancy.[39] Similarly, he cites a letter from Blanchot to Laporte on December 24, 1992, after the latter had asked him to reread his own article from the *Journal des Débats* of March 1942 referring to Charles Maurras.[40] In both letters Blanchot attacks himself, using unequivocal expressions such as "detestable and inexcusable," "the texts . . . for which I am reproached today, and rightly so," and "the responsibility which is mine."

It is clear: These attempts to bring clarity to the past of the 1930s are part of Blanchot's autobiographical unveiling in the 1980s. His correspondence with other scholars such as Diane Rubenstein (in 1983) or William Flesch (in 1988) also bears witness to this. And it also clear that nothing can replace a clear-eyed reading of these old texts, which are mostly difficult to approach, a lack of accessibility that means that Blanchot's indirect, ambiguous, cryptic accounts sometimes are not fully appreciated for what they are. Instead they sometimes distort readings that, through ignorance, see them as amounting to lies (the rumors around the political texts of the 1930s rarely leave space, for example, for Blanchot's opposition to Hitler from 1933 onward). But what is also clear—last—is that nothing should lead us to forget the political and philosophical demand for thought to which Blanchot constantly bore witness. Such a demand, a "past without date," is reinforced by all the work of thought that went into *The Infinite Conversation* or *The Writing of the Disaster*, but which had also been at work since the first *récits* and the first novel. It is at the moment when friends, thinkers, and even witnesses were dying, at the moment when their death seemed to risk disincarnating such questions, that the rhythm of Blanchot's language and his publications set itself the task—not without weight, not without heaviness—of reincarnating, remarking some of their traces, cries, inscriptions.

He also committed himself to a political presence that, even in withdrawal, was never abandoned. On the invitation of Dominique Lecoq and Jacques Derrida, in 1986, Blanchot wrote a few pages that were published in a collection named *For Nelson Mandela*, connected to an international support committee that had been formed to assist the man who had once been the world's longest-standing political prisoner.[41] In it, Blanchot at moments rediscovers the tone of his texts for—fittingly—*Committee*.[42] Denouncing "the inertia of the European Community," giving voice to "a call, a denunciation, a cry and again a cry": he reduces the task of language to this, the largest of all tasks, if it is a question of engaging in it the feeling of infinite responsibility that leads to the "Judaism of thought." For he finds the impossible necessity of infinite witnessing precisely in what leaves no choice in these blind times, with apartheid as a new form of the disaster of Auschwitz:

> How can we speak, or write, in an appropriate fashion about the segregation of Blacks and Whites? What was experienced when Nazism excluded from life and the right to life an entire portion of humanity, thereby persists beyond the disaster which seemed to render such a wretched doctrine impossible or unformulable.

What was frightening and what one had to rise up against was this way in which Auschwitz seemed to have become a template, a concept, even as it called into question the practice of thought (Blanchot recalls precisely that "apartheid acquired its legal form at precisely the moment when the colonial nations were collapsing, as they recognized that they did not have the privilege of embodying the diversity of the human spirit"). That this system wanted to oppose the upheavals of History (its end, its opening, its tearing-apart, its uprising) is also what Blanchot denounces here. Only "the international demand" could respond to such upheavals. This was the context for a publication also signed by Nadine Gordimer, Mustapha Tilli, and Jean Goytisolo. Blanchot would not fail to point out to Bernard-Henri Lévy that it was also that of the 1960s *Review*: "there is no such thing as good nationalism"—all nationalism is totalitarian, he essentially added, including a reference to the dossier that had just been published by the journal *Lignes*: "the failure of our project did not prove it was a utopia. What does not succeed remains necessary. That still remains our concern."[43]

There were therefore multiple requests for publications, which did not fail little by little to prove troublesome for a man who always wanted to be present, and must have realized that he would not be able to respond as often as he wanted. Sometimes they came from his closest friends and concerned things that Blanchot saw as absolutely necessary. But often they were clumsier, and provoked a certain irritation through their inevitably mythologizing function: to collect the words of the great writer—a great *absent* writer. Therefore Blanchot would sometimes not respond, or do so to express his reticence, not without humor or—he admitted—sarcasm. A request from Geneviève Brisac and the editors of *Le Monde* who were asking writers what meaning should be given to literary glory in the contemporary world saw him pointing out how "old-fashioned" and lacking in "inner necessity" their questionnaire was (these were themselves old terms, which in the 1940s he applied to novel writing). He recalls with Kafka that the writer seeks less to write in order to die than he dies in order to be able to write; in doing so he sends back less a response than his own questions.[44] Jean-François Fogel and Daniel Rondeau, who wanted to know for *Libération* how writers wrote received only a few words, an apparently anachronistic citation of Luther followed by a commentary that seemed to turn its meaning on its head.[45] The editors of *La Règle du Jeu* were reminded that "it is better for a writer to try to ask new questions rather than to answer questions that have already been formulated"; and, a year later, were sent two enigmatic lines ("literature is a sort of power that takes account of nothing. But when is there literature?").[46]

At other times he would respond in an unconventional way. In response to the question "who comes after the subject?" he sent Jean-Luc Nancy a dialogue in the form of an interrogation, where one party analyzes the wording as if it were a school exam question, but does so knowing full well that he is "irritating the examiner" ("the tempter") by endlessly exploring what makes the questions possible instead of approaching them dialectically. And when "the tempter" suggests a series of answers—"the overman, or else the mystery of *Ereignis*, or the uncertain demand of the inoperative community, or the strangeness of the absolutely Other, or perhaps the last man who is not the last"—they are all close to Blanchot's own thinking, which he thus evokes in reference to his books which attempt to welcome and to carry these answers.[47]

In the same spirit of referring readers to his work, which carries the "heaviest blessing," public letters to editors increasingly replaced articles, letters that bear witness to the thinking already manifested, given, through books. The elegance of his responses served only to attest to the necessity of the silence that his thinking traversed, the result of bodily exhaustion.[48] The many notes of only a few lines, their willfully enigmatic, emphatic, prophetic tone would allow glimpses of the link between humor and the displacement of writing. For instance, the appeal to Salman Rushdie, who in 1989 had been condemned to death by a *fatwa* from religious authorities in Iran for his novel *The Satanic Verses*:

> I invite Rushdie to my house (in the South). I invite the descendant or the successor of Khomeini to my house. I shall be between the two of you, and the Koran also.
>
> It will decide.
>
> Come.[49]

The arrival and departure of this appeal, from and toward the most faraway place, are not alien to the choice of a site—that of his fiction— from which at the time Blanchot had been distant for many years, as he had been from the sea, rocks, and wind. It was an appeal to breathe openly beyond all notions of presence, an appeal to respect the Other, beyond any Orient or any culture, with—once again—the Book as the only guide.

His writing exhausted, Blanchot's texts were now dedicated to his friends. Twenty years after the issue of *Critique* and two years after the death of the philosopher behind it, Blanchot wrote a short book on Michel Foucault, *Michel Foucault as I Imagine Him* (Gilles Deleuze published his *Foucault* the same year, and these gestures of friendship contributed greatly to the recognition of a thinking against which there existed sharp animosity and many prejudices). The few articles published (averaging three per year between 1984 and 1991, one per year in 1992, 1993, 1994, none after that) can be traced back to friendship: they were afterwords, articles in the press or in journals; they followed the deaths of André Dalmas and Samuel Beckett, or addressed books by Vadim Kozovoï or Leslie Kaplan (two authors close to him, with whom he corresponded); or they were for his long-standing friends Roger Laporte, Jacques Derrida, Louis-René des Forêts, and Dionys Mascolo. Last, in January 1994, "In the Watched-Over Night" was a text for Robert Antelme, and heralded a long silence.

They are not commentaries ("ah, how Foucault hated commentaries," Blanchot recalls parenthetically, a hatred that was above all his own), but rather texts written in the margins, as accompaniments extending the poems, prose, or thinking whose movements, knots, folds, pains, rhythms, ruptures, agreements, and relations they follow.[50] They follow points of convergence that are fascinating but also kept at a distance by the displacement of the voice, the inadequacy of lived experience (and even sometimes of death), the infinite alterity of friendship. They are not homages ("such a word, which is not without ideas of glorification, was always alien to him," Blanchot wrote of Beckett), but instead awakenings, the awakening of tangential relations between experiences and words.[51] These are his own experiences and words, and also the words and experiences of those close to him, described in the language of a friend, most often in the first person: an empty or missing person or one without any higher perspective, who knows that he is just as inadequate as commentary was, but also that through this inadequacy it is possible to pierce through to—or to slide into—the personal pain of the other. This had never been as palpable as in the texts intermingled with those by Louis-René des Forêts, where there is constant interchange between citations, narrations, occurrences, indiscretions, suspensions, interrogations, hesitations . . . this is a faithful movement of both approach and withdrawal, which Blanchot musically names *anacrusis*:

> in the first, inaugural bar, nothing is heard, or else a tone so weak that it seems to fail and hence lasts without lasting, so that after it or starting from it the note that is finally struck rises up to a sometimes phenomenal burst, a burst or surge so strong it can only collapse—fall—into a new silence.[52]

In these intimate accompaniments, in playing a four-handed piece with death and marking the *ostinato* that Berg saw in Schumann and Blanchot in Des Forêts, there is an uneven demonstration of the strength of pain and insubordination that is perhaps the most unavowable element of community. Thus in attending unknowingly to his own illness, "a serious illness that he barely anticipated, ultimately the approach of death that opened him up not to anguish but to a new and surprising serenity," Foucault had observed points at which history became discontinuous: its irrational accelerations or—worse—its dizzying rationalizations of "the abominable."[53] "The *discontinuity* of a language interrupted through touching on extremity" is what fascinates Blanchot in Leslie Kaplan, the "*marvelous toothless smiles*" with which factory women address the end of time, permanently lacking being, and the rupture of history that marks this enclosure without remainder to the point of death. Poetic force flows from this vigilance that gives being an outside again, although this force itself is always interrupted. If Blanchot writes that *Factory-Excess* is "perhaps poetry, perhaps more than poetry," it is because poetry directs its being and its death toward political and historical vigilance. Such is the fatigue of ideas, "the infinite in pieces."[54] Such, too, is the "decapitated time" of Vadim Kozovoï, the harshness of a language that in its "rhythmic rupture" and its blinding rapidity, in a Rimbaldian mixture of vehemence and gentleness, infinitely rises up "against oppression," "against the oppressors."[55] Throughout this entire period the philosopher and the poet, who refused to recognize themselves as the creators of these shards of philosophy and of poetry (for to do so would have signaled a dialectics), evoke the figure of Moses, whom Blanchot would describe in a text of 1990, "Thanks (Be Given) to Jacques Derrida." He writes that this figure is "faltering, a heavy speaker (heavy of mouth), weary to the point of ruining his own health by the excessive service he does for others"—and that he has no (avowable) successor and no (locatable) tomb.[56] Illness in language (*la langue*), death in the mouth, only ever signaling trenchant, silent withdrawal: these notions recall the figure of Georges Bataille, who as he died represented the "complicity with the organic" within the travails of thought, as well as the figure of Maurice Blanchot himself.

This recognition of a community of writing throws up some strikingly forceful coincidences. Coincidence is neither injurious, nor pleasant, nor complacent—or at least is not so at first, or only ever at times, at the times when one grows weak (when one does not have the strength for one's weakness).[57] To fail to find the strength for weakness is precisely to hope to accept the death of the other, the other recognized by the displacements of one's speech. Blanchot cites an extract from *Awaiting Oblivion*, "because Beckett agreed to recognize himself in [that text]." Texts written on the death of such friends are neither tombs for the other, nor tombs for oneself. They are the impossibility of tombs, which *secretes* the speech of waiting, the powerlessness of the "Oh to end it all" at the heart of the notion of *having done with it*.

But in its strength, coincidence is revulsion, displacement, relation at a distance, an overwhelming that hides any resemblance and attempts to grasp or to read what in this distraction, alteration or dispossession allows one to arrive at the same place, at this place that an isolated mind forgetting friendship might have seen as singular. From 1984, with the appearance of the first fragments of *Ostinato*, then in 1988 with the publication of the *Poems of Samuel Wood*, Blanchot is profoundly affected by the incompletable work of Louis-René des Forêts, to which he would dedicate three articles between 1989 and 1991, collecting them in the book *A Voice from Elsewhere*. As in what he names apropos of Kozovoï "the relation between terror and speech . . . this terrible antecedence that calls for and devastates expression," also in Des Forêts there appear figures of fright, of childhood, of mourning, of death.[58] Each time, Blanchot says of them what he says of the vision that was "so similar to the apparition evoked by Henry James": that they are a "figure that troubles me, since I have met her too."[59] *Me too*: this is a new mode of speech, new in its autobiographical transparency. Blanchot employs it on several occasions. It speaks to the desolate relation of the child who "will live henceforth in the secret" and to the "silence to which [the poet] is DEVOTED and out of which, by an impossible challenge, he makes a VOW."[60] From the "primal scene" to the vow without avowal, writing holds within it the "biography" of a life that—precisely—had only begun with that writing.[61] Even if Blanchot conspicuously translates Samuel Wood as "Samuel la Forêt," he nonetheless keeps open a space in the poetry of Des Forêts for the displacement of an "I without I, a mode in which questioning and uncertainty [are] at play, the balance between the real and the imaginary." This "I" even recalls, in Des Forêts's narratives, that of a "me without me, a mode where contestation, uncertainty, oscillation between the real and the imaginary [are] played out"—in other words, yet another way of displacing any triumph of negative recognition.[62]

"Even a few steps take time," Blanchot writes of the strategies of avowal that, "from the confessional to the couch," "from secret murmur to endless chatter," govern Western discourse.[63] Blanchot would agree to take these steps, without gossip, in the company of his closest friends. He always invokes them in this period when he began releasing a few narrative shards of a life that had often been public (whether literary or political), but sometimes also private (as in the room in Èze beautifully evoked at the beginning of the Des Forêts book). And it is also in the presence of his friends that he would immediately erase these memories in order to bear witness in their name and *in the name of the other*. Daniel Dobbels recalls this: after the 1994 issue of *Lignes*, "Maurice Blanchot was the first one to propose that a collection of texts dedicated to Robert Antelme deserved to be a book."[64] Blanchot is again present in 1998 in the issue that the same journal gave over to publishing unknown texts and reprinting others by Dionys Mascolo, who had died the previous summer.[65] What's more, in the "pretext" written in 1992 for *In Search of a Communism of Thought* (the book appeared the following year), Blanchot gave more recognition than ever to memory, thus—a year before the publication of *The Instant of My Death*—allowing a testamentary tone to begin filtering through the witnessing. In November 1993, whether in a dream, during insomnia, or awake, "watched over at night" and using a dialogue to recall *after the fact* those of *Awaiting Oblivion*, *The Step Not Beyond*, and *The Infinite Conversation* (thus emphasizing *after the fact* that his friend had been present in them), Blanchot addresses the "unfathomable void" that Robert Antelme had always both signaled and deferred. Thus silencing all sympathy except that with death, after a few lines he moves from his commemorative words to the text of *The Human Race*, from which he takes two extracts. One is the haphazard execution of an Italian by an SS soldier ("a man, it does not matter which, in order that killing can be carried out") that forces the other prisoners to "picture themselves standing before the machine gun." Except for death's difference from an ongoing dying, the episode is strikingly similar to the one from his own life which Blanchot was then in the process of writing, for his first *récit* that would come so close to biography. Is a face struck at by death one that can be afforded recognition? Such is one of the questions posed by the second extract cited, in which a terrified Antelme feels unable to recognize a friend's face as, watched-over, he lay dying.

On 22 September 1994, the symbolic and perhaps the actual day on which *The Instant of My Death*—that narrative of being put before the firing squad in Quain—was printed, Maurice Blanchot turned eighty-seven.[66] This new and surprising act of narration was placed under the sign of his birthday. Fifty years after the events had taken place, for the first time Blanchot addressed his past, doing so in an apparently simple, immediately readable, and also staggering way. The narrative is extremely short: only a few pages long. But the sparse nature of its sentences should not mislead us. They place the subject and his literature in a voluntarily ambiguous situation: "my death," even in the title, refers in a both tempting and undecidable way to the author's name. Adopting a retrospective viewpoint, the narration itself is in the first person ("I know," repeats the narrator), but the subject discussed remains in the third person ("he," a "young man," a "man still young").[67] Nonetheless, an exception occurs in the final few lines, which occupy a separate page in the manner of an epilogue, and conclude thus: "All that remains is the feeling of lightness that is death itself or, to put it more precisely, the instant of my death henceforth always in abeyance."[68] Citing the title, these words suddenly project the narrator onto the character, thus attributing to the latter—who is said to be close to Malraux and to Paulhan—an identity at the last, an identity of lastness, an identity or sameness between death and this figure (but which figure: the narrator, the author?). This displacement, which protects literary speech from being reduced to autobiography, while also addressing the stakes of such a relation, speaks to the essence of witnessing, to its unquestionable lack of resolution: he *who cannot bear witness to death does bear witness to dying*. It sidesteps the greed of knowledge by providing only an episode of life's disappearance, of its "near disappearance," of what in life is absolutely separate from knowledge. It casts a particular light on the narrative of an event that had already been briefly related and almost summoned in *The Madness of the Day*, just as it had been corroborated by the written testimonies of Laporte and Nadeau.

Such an opening to witnessing also speaks to how far this witnessing is carried out *in the name of the other*: in the name of youth, of justice, of all those who in the summer of 1944 died in Blanchot's place, saved as he was by local renown for his lineage and by the imposing nature of his dwelling. At base, the book is as if dedicated to them.

This dwelling, this other writing-house which he thus evokes for the first time, after having done so with Èze a few years later, can be said—following Jacques Derrida—to be the central character of the *récit*.[69] As a sign, as a title, as a birthmark, Blanchot places center stage the cast-iron figures that decorate its façade: "On the façade was inscribed, like an indestructible memory, the date 1807," adding in the tone of someone writing a dissertation: "this was the famous year of Jena, when Napoleon, on his small gray horse, passed under the windows of Hegel, who recognized in him the 'spirit of the world.'"[70] But here the narrative shows a double "error," the double errancy of a witnessing that only makes its fiction truer. For it was in 1806 that the Emperor entered into Jena (perhaps followed by one of Blanchot's ancestors), and that Hegel saw fit to pronounce the end of history.[71] And it is 1809 that is clear for all to read on the façade of the house in Quain. It is not impossible that as a child, Blanchot had often dwelled upon those two missing years between his birth and the centenary of his family residence. It is not impossible that as an adult, he had dwelt upon the coincidence that meant that, but for a year or three, Hegel's end of history was humorously gainsaid by the start of his ancestral history, in the very place where a war at its end had violently challenged his own life, in this dwelling where he had been born and nearly died. It is not impossible that as a man henceforth "less young," and who since the death of his sister Marguerite a few months beforehand in 1993 was the only survivor of the events, he now wanted to leave a trace of a dwelling that was slipping away, one of whose rooms had seen him write a first version of *Death Sentence* which was snatched from him.[72] The pulse evoked in that work, the beating of the pulse and the flesh, was also what was moving into the distance. The lost manuscript now had no witnesses, it delivered writing back to writing alone: it has never been found. Its uninhabited site is secret and at the same time far from all secrecy. The uncertain date of a house outside time is now given over to the outside, to anonymous circulation, to inoperative community.

This ultimate consenting to a fragment of memory soon became a farewell to the narration of life. The man who bore it, worked through it, and wrote it is now given over to the traces of writing, to writing's *invisible partners*.

Amor
Blanchot since 2003
John McKeane

February 20, 2003, was the date of the event that Maurice Blanchot had described as "natural," as "more insignificant and more uninteresting than a little heap of sand collapsing."[1] Fulfillment, release, an "immense pleasure" for he who underwent it: such are a few ways of seeing this event.[2] But none of these ways speaks to the absolute unknowability of death that is the driving force behind his work, even and especially as its author attempts to think *the instant of his death*.

That instant is now fixed in cold marble. The grave of Maurice Blanchot can be found in the cemetery at Le Mesnil Saint-Denis, the suburb of Paris where latterly he lived in a cul-de-sac named Place des Pensées. He shares this grave with his sister-in-law Anne Blanchot (née Anna Wolf), and is remembered with the simple inscription MAURICE BLANCHOT 1907–2003. The tombstone's last word is AMOR: whether added at the author's request or not, it certainly echoes the openness and generosity of his work. *Amor, amour, amitié*: this loving friendship was offered to the near and to the far, it was offered to thought itself by a body of work that privileges not knowledge but understanding, not sophism or sophistry but philosophy in the most demanding sense.

This was the end for the thin, often unwell body that featured so prominently in Blanchot's narratives, and which was thought about extensively by a man medically trained. The body that was exposed or exhibited in this way was not fixed or easily comprehensible: as one critic writes, "there will always be a shoulder too many, an elbowing. . . . This type of physical event—shuddering, shivering, distress, vomiting—is what is constantly occurring in Blanchot's narratives."[3] But even such an unruly body eventually grew still. It was incinerated, and the ashes interred in a private ceremony. The eulogy was given by Jacques Derrida, who although he spoke elsewhere of incineration and inhumation, of the body's destiny or *destinerrancy*, here concentrated on the question of legacy: "Blanchot did not have what is called influence, and he did not have disciples. Something entirely different is in play. The legacy he leaves will have reserved a more internal and more serious trace: a non-appropriable one. He will have left us alone, he has left us more alone than ever with our endless responsibilities."[4]

Such a sense of Blanchot's legacy being not an order but a demand, not a duty but a right, to dedicate oneself to thought, was also present at a major colloquium, planned before his death, that took place the month following it, *Maurice Blanchot: Récits critiques*. Christophe Bident opened proceedings with the following words:

> Maurice Blanchot has died [*Maurice Blanchot est mort*]. His passing was not unthinkable. But I gave it no credence at all. Over these two years in which Pierre Vilar and I have prepared this conference, not for a moment did I imagine that Blanchot could die before this morning's opening, nor—therefore—that he would die so close to today, 34 days before. Whether in good or bad faith, but what does it matter now, we had good reasons to believe in another reprieve. But we had nothing but reasons. The reprieve has been withdrawn. This places our words in the temporality of a mourning that responds strangely to a future perfect: Maurice Blanchot has died, Maurice Blanchot will have died.[5]

Thus Blanchot's biographer became, as it were, his thanatographer: but he was well prepared for the role, given the constant meditations on death undertaken in *Maurice Blanchot: A Critical Biography*.[6] It is as if this work were a rehearsal for the uttering of the words "*Maurice Blanchot est mort*," which seem striking in their simplicity (and indeed were reiterated by Derrida in the title of his talk closing the colloquium, "Maurice Blanchot est mort"). When we come to translate them, however, we realize that there are in fact two possibilities in English: "Maurice Blanchot is dead" and "Maurice Blanchot has died."[7] I have chosen the second translation due to its greater emphasis on a connection to the present, whether that of 2003 or of today.

This connection to the present is very much alive, notwithstanding the death of Blanchot's body—a physical death which he referred to, citing Hegel sympathetically, as "the coldest and meanest of all deaths, with no more significance than cutting off a head of cabbage or swallowing a mouthful of water."[8] In the remarks that follow I wish to point out some of the ways in which Maurice Blanchot has continued to live (or continued to die) since the publication of Bident's work in 1998.[9] These include the controversial publication of a dossier of photographs of Blanchot, the appearance of several volumes of articles and correspondence, and some major critical interventions. The purpose of these remarks will be to signal the existence of various fault lines and debates, rather to enter into them: but even so, it will be necessary to point out modes of reading that have remained conspicuous by their absence.

First, though, a few notes on translation, which has certainly proved to be a tool for rethinking and rereading as Bident's work has been brought across into English. The sinuosity of French syntax has been apparent, particularly in the passages of the work when Bident demonstrates Blanchot's metamorphic effects on one's own thinking and writing (a writing that draws on a 1992 doctorate on Blanchot, Bataille, and Duras entitled *The Imaginary of Death*—much of its thinking is clearly present in this 1998 biography).[10] In any case, it is sometimes said of premodern English that—to parody this style—*the words any way round one can arrange*. This is less the case nowadays; for its part, formal academic French lies somewhere between the two. This mode of writing is in evidence in much of this work; however some of the more straightforward biographical passages go to the other extreme, and adopt the short, fragmented sentences of journalistic French, which is very different. I have sometimes stretched English syntax and expression to reflect Bident's French, but on other occasions simplified matters.[11] In short, it has been necessary to pay attention to the sometimes competing demands of both readability and accuracy.

The translation of tenses has proved a particular conundrum. Regarding historical events, Bident makes use of the possibility in French of referring to the past using the present tense: e.g., "*Blanchot ne se contente pas de témoigner son accord.*" In English, while it is possible to use the present to refer to past historical events—"Blanchot is not content with demonstrating that he is in agreement"—to do so is a stretch, adding a sense of strangeness not present for a Francophone reader of Bident's text. I have therefore used the past tense in English in such historical cases: "Blanchot was not content with demonstrating that he was in agreement." By contrast, with the French present tense when it relates to literary texts—"*Blanchot est Thomas au sens où Thomas n'est personne*"—there was the choice of either using the calm narration of the simple past—"Blanchot was Thomas in the sense that Thomas was no one"—or retaining the strange dislocation of the literary present: "Blanchot is Thomas in the sense that Thomas is no one." I have most often chosen the latter, so as not to relegate Blanchot's work to a reified, safely historical phenomenon, lacking the greater risks (and rewards) of the truth-claim made when literature speaks to us, here and now.

So two different approaches have been used in these two different areas. But where to draw the line between history and writing, politics and literature, the possible and the impossible? This is nothing other than the question of Blanchot's life and work. The latter is not disconnected from his life, and concurrently, a great deal of his life had an intensive relationship to the strange, irruptive temporality of literature (above all the *instant of his death* in summer 1944, an episode I have retained in the present tense). There is a delicate balance, given the importance Blanchot accorded—or accords!—to erasing the distinction between life and work. Thus, while events that are clearly historical have been rendered with the past tense, and discussions that are clearly literary with the present, there has inevitably been some shifting between the two. Sometimes the shifts come in quick succession or indeed within a single sentence (perhaps due to an adverbial phrase), when the balance moves from what *was* the case in the historical moment or context to what *is* discussed in the relevant Blanchot text. This balance often being very delicate, I have had—as it were—to *listen* attentively in order to discern the location of the tipping point. This is to say that I have had to listen for the moment when the literary comes together or coalesces: I have been able to better understand why Blanchot writes of literature as a metamorphosis or alchemical process. In this way, translation has provided an excellent tool for thinking about the challenge posed by the strange temporality of Blanchot's life-writing, by his life spent writing: the challenge of a thinking relevant not just yesterday or today, but tomorrow and tomorrow and tomorrow.

Whether it is in *Thomas the Obscure*, *Death Sentence*, *The Last Man*, or a host of other narrative and critical writings, in Blanchot's work, the boundaries between life and death are constantly moved where we do not expect them, or even removed altogether. In that spirit, let us begin to look at some of Blanchot's strange resuscitations and afterlives since 2003.

The first concerns the question of the author's image. Bident's biography is named *Maurice Blanchot, Partenaire invisible*, and even though *A Critical Biography* has been chosen as the subtitle for this translation, the notion of invisibility lives on in the choice to avoid using a photograph of Blanchot for the cover. This choice retains the public figure that Blanchot was—or rather wasn't—as a writer in twentieth-century France. He opposed all attempts to publish photos of him, even the few that appeared in the 1980s in circumstances recounted by Bident. Blanchot's readers therefore knew him—or didn't know him—almost exclusively through his work, something that gave it all the more power and insistency. While Roland Barthes has gone down as the name associated with the Death of the Author thanks to his short article of 1967 (if we are to play such a paradoxical game), surely the stronger claim is that of Blanchot, who in 1953 asked: "Isn't the writer dead as soon as the work exists?"[12]

The insistency, the weight of Blanchot's work is therefore indissociable from such a complex relationship with his own image. Over and against this, however, a stir was created in 2014 with the publication of a Blanchot issue of the *Cahier de l'Herne*, one of France's most prestigious literary journals. Its large-format cover bears a photograph of him, and two dozen more are included inside: passport photos, portraits, holiday snapshots. This is doubtless a significant event in the history of Blanchot's reception, and in that of his and others' efforts to write his (auto)biography, his (auto)thanatography. What's more, there is certainly an argument to be made that the time has come to make such images public: his statement that "no man alive ... yet bears any resemblance" draws on the view that such resemblance and death go hand. Since 2003, therefore, one cannot have the same reservations as before.[13] It even seems possible—just about—that Blanchot himself would not have resisted the images being published, just as he scrupulously sought to leave critics the freedom to comment on his work. One could maintain that losing control is precisely what is at stake when one dies.

The *Cahier de l'Herne*, however, argues very little, if anything at all. It justifies the publication of the images with just six lines of text, as part of a brief introductory page. These lines speak of "giving this writer back his historicized element," but without any assessment of how large this element is, or what the other, opposing elements in his thought and work are (for instance his immense resistance to the power of the image). This perfunctory approach does not seem to recognize the importance of the publication of these images of Blanchot; let us therefore briefly look at some of the arguments for and against the image, in Western thought in general and in that of Blanchot in particular.

First, the arguments for publishing images, these images. It is well known that "Thou shalt not make unto thee any graven image" features early on the Ten Commandments (it precedes "Thou shalt not kill" by several places).[14] Used as an argument to justify the breaking of false idols of the true God, this commandment suggests that not to make, retain, or publish images, icons, or likenesses of someone is to hold them in great respect, to set them apart as irreducibly singular.[15] Publishing the images of Blanchot would therefore be a way of answering criticisms that writing on him often tends toward praise rather than analysis, that is, that it tends to create a cult or a myth around him. Such a publication would be, as it were, iconoclastic (albeit, paradoxically, in the form of iconolatry, a praise of images). There is doubtless a cathartic pleasure in such a publication, and pleasure leads us on to our second example, also taken from religious thought. In traditional Catholic practice before Vatican II in the 1960s—the practice with which Blanchot grew up, speaking Latin to his father—among the pleasures denied during Lent was that of the image. Paintings, statues, crucifixes were veiled, turned to the wall, or removed altogether. While it might seem strange to think in terms of the image or likeness as a pleasure (whether denied or not), this can be better understood when we realize how an image can summarize and fix a given situation for us. Images—and photographs especially—define a moment or a person. And following this line of thought in relation to the publication of Blanchot's image, he can be found acknowledging this aspect when he writes of "the gratifying aspect of the image" or of "that ecstasy which is the image" (an ec-stasy because it takes one out of reality, but presumably also a pleasurable ecstasy).[16] He writes further: "In this way the image fulfills one of its functions which is to quiet, to humanize the formless nothingness pressed upon us by the indelible residue of being. The image cleanses this residue—appropriates it, makes it pleasing and pure."[17] In short, we like images because they summarize things for us, making them pure, simple, and easy: not requiring further thought.

So, there is an argument that publishing photographs of Blanchot lets cleansing light in on something that otherwise risks remaining obscure or mythical. But can we be sure that the immediate gains and pleasures of such a publication do not fall into the trap of the argument above: that images summarize, define, make things easy? For Blanchot's life, his writing, his thought may be many things, but they were never and are not easy. What's more, his work understands what Western thought has gained from preferring invisibility to images: For a long while, the lack of any author photo allowed this work to remain interpretable, mobile, flexible, open to new combinations and arrangements. In short, it allowed it to remain alive. And this is all the more the case because in his explicit and influential writing on images, he saw the power of the image or icon, likeness or resemblance, as a deathly, murderous power. Let us see how.

Blanchot wrote on the image, and wrote with and through images, on various notable occasions.[18] But one piece that stands out is "The Two Versions of the Imaginary" in *The Space of Literature*. The two versions of images and the imaginary in question are, first of all, the summarizing, definitive aspect of the image with its apparent ability to magically present us with an object that in reality is absent, elsewhere, even dead. The second is the fact that this object is not really present, but present in the form of absence, in a virtual and misleading copy of whatever the object might have been. He sets out these two senses as follows:

> The image, according to the usual analysis, is secondary to the object. It follows it. We see, then we imagine. After the object comes the image. "After" means that the thing must first take itself off a ways in order to be grasped. . . . Here the distance is at the heart of the thing. The thing was there; we grasped it in the vital movement of a comprehensive action—and lo, having become image, instantly it has become that which no one can grasp, the unreal, the impossible. It is not the same thing at a distance but the thing as distance, present in its absence, graspable because ungraspable, appearing as disappeared. It is the return of what does not come back, the strange heart of remoteness as the life and the sole heart of the thing.[19]

According to the representationalist "usual analysis," then, images are able to magically overcome time and space, rendering something present to us in a triumphant overcoming of worldly difficulty. If I see an image of something, then I can see that thing itself: again, the image makes things easy. But Blanchot goes on to emphasize the reproduced, *ersatz* quality of the image: even and especially when we have an image of something, it is "that which no one can grasp, the unreal, the impossible." While there is likeness or resemblance between the object and the image, this can only ever appear from a ground of difference.

Now, this discussion is doubly relevant to the publication of images of Blanchot following his death given that the analogy he uses for this resemblance is precisely the way a cadaver resembles the living body of the same person. We read:

> The image does not, at first glance, resemble the corpse, but the cadaver's strangeness is perhaps also that of the image. What we call

mortal remains escapes common categories. Something is there before us which is not really the living person, nor is it any reality at all. It is neither the same as the person who was alive, nor is it another person, nor is it anything else.[20]

While we can tell that a dead body is dead, we can also tell that it is the body of a particular person. It has undergone the most fundamental of changes, and yet there seems to be a connection across the two sides of the abyss. But Blanchot has chosen the analogy of the cadaver in order to show that this connection is only ever an illusion, that the nature of this particular abyss is that nothing can bridge it (or inversely: that this abyss is whatever cannot be bridged). While the cadaver resembles the living person, in fact this resemblance immediately starts to break down. The ease with which the image had appeared to resemble its object is shown to be false as the cadaver starts to be affected by inevitable physical decay, and in a more eerie sense, starts to wander through the minds of the living:

> We dress the corpse, and we bring it as close as possible to a normal appearance by effacing the hurtful marks of sickness, but we know that in its ever so peaceful and secure immobility it does not rest. The place which it occupies is drawn down by it, sinks with it, and in this dissolution attacks the possibility of a dwelling place even for us who remain. We know that "at a certain moment" the power of death makes it keep no longer to the handsome spot assigned it. No matter how calmly the corpse has been laid out upon its bed for final viewing, it is also everywhere in the room, all over the house.[21]

The cadaver will not remain where it is. Instead, it finds itself abroad, wandering, perhaps stumbling, as is made clear by an entire literature of the fantastic, and in Blanchot by *Thomas the Obscure*, *Death Sentence*, Orpheus returning from the dead, the repeated references to the resurrected Lazarus, and so on.[22] He gives a significant role to the fantastic, the gothic, the morbid. Keeping in mind that this is an analogy, his insistence on the mobility and instability of the dead body, its ability to haunt us, and the futility of trying to remove "the hurtful marks of sickness," is an insistence that relying on images is only ever a short-term strategy. The immediate pleasure we gain from them comes at the cost of any longer-term engagement with what they represent; we lose sight of the underlying forces, pulling this way and that, at work in any life and in any written work. So while one has every right to publish such images, we must also return to the first principle of why Blanchot touches us as a writer: and surely this is due to the way he conveys the suspension of the subject, effected by the anxious difficulty, the suffocating pressure, the *ressassement éternel* or eternal rumination of doubt. We must not be against the publication of images per se, for fear of falling into a mysticization of this author. But the *Cahier de l'Herne* falls down because it does not even attempt to offer the full and frank discussion of the question of the image—too rapidly sketched out here—that Blanchot and his readers deserve.

From the wandering cadaver we can move to another sense in which Blanchot's death remains unresolved: the changing profile of his corpus of writings. While his major works have all been published, there has been considerable other activity since his death. On the one hand, several volumes have collected his previously scattered, shorter texts.[23] The difficult-to-locate *Écrits politiques: Guerre d'Algérie, Mai 68, etc.* (2003) saw a second edition of sorts in *Écrits politiques, 1953–1993* (2008), and then a translation with *Political Writings, 1953–1993* (2010). *La Condition critique: Articles 1945–1998* (2010) brings together the vast majority of his postwar texts not collected elsewhere; many had already been translated either in *The Blanchot Reader* (1995) or in a special issue of *Paragraph* (2007). His wartime writings not featuring in *Faux pas* have given rise to a substantial volume, *Chroniques littéraires du Journal des Débats, avril 1941–août 1944* (2007), which is being translated in four volumes, *Into Disaster* (2013), *Desperate Clarity* (2013), *A World in Ruins* (2016), and *Death Now* (2018). And the first volumes of his voluminous correspondence have appeared: with Vadim Kozovoï (2009), with Pierre Madaule (2012), with German translator Johannes Hübner (2014), and a letter to Roger Laporte addressing the 1930s in Jean-Luc Nancy, *Maurice Blanchot: Passion politique* (2011). Further volumes of correspondence (Jean Paulhan) have been announced or are known to exist in the archive (Laporte, Gaston Gallimard, others), and the process of publishing Blanchot's correspondence will no doubt last many years. In time, enough material for a new or a rewritten biography may even appear.

Two purchases by Harvard University mean that the archive is slowly becoming available. The first was of the page proofs of *The Infinite Conversation*, and the second of twenty boxes of varied materials.[24] There seem to be several other caches of materials held by various private individuals in Europe. The *Cahier de l'Herne* presents a few materials and insights, but we still await a comprehensive and as it were scientific account or cataloguing of what the archive contains. Until then, the glimpses that are offered remain just that; among others, readers have been tantalized by references to Blanchot's practice as a translator, to his extensive note-taking, to a table he drew up sorting his works into categories for an abortive *Complete Works*, to *The Last Man* and *Awaiting Oblivion* being written concurrently in the same notebooks, to up to eight versions of *Thomas the Obscure* (each significantly different), and so on.

The Space of Literature reserves a central role for Orpheus, the legendary singer or poet who on his return from the underworld is ripped to shreds by maenads, with his song being disseminated around the world. In Blanchot's case, worldwide dissemination of his song certainly seems a laudable aim; it is, after all, a major motivation behind this translation. Let it not be accompanied by a bloodthirsty frenzy over a corpus.

Although his death was of course singularly his, Blanchot's political, literary, and philosophical signature was often tightly enmeshed alongside that of others. This is not to say that he had disciples or that one could convincingly write, after *Heidegger's Children: Arendt, Löwith, Jonas, Marcuse* (2003), a work with the title *Blanchot's Children*.[25] *Blanchot's Orphans* is perhaps more acceptable, but even then that supposes that his work is essentially fixed, static, dead, whereas in fact—perhaps uniquely for a twentieth-century writer of his stature—it remains alive, with many major areas still largely unexplored. The years since the publication of Bident's biographical essay have nonetheless seen many developments in the thinking in which Blanchot's work is enmeshed.

Much writing on Blanchot's work falls into one of two traps. The first is that of *académisme*, of being little more than the exegesis of the myriad implicit and explicit references in his works, of his moments of self-citation, or of the differences between subsequent versions of his texts (whether through contingency as with *Death Sentence*, or more systematically with the first and "new" versions of *Thomas the Obscure*, or with a very great percentage of his articles, much of his work was written *twice*). There is an infinity of textual detail to study, but just as infinite is the demand Blanchot makes on his readers, the void he creates and which one vainly tries to fill with information and knowledge. The second trap is the complementary one: to abandon rigor and to hone in unsystematically on one particular passage or work, before performing an often sub-Blanchotian analysis, an imitation or *mimétisme*. Such articles—and even books—often plunge into a self-regarding tailspin, leaving any concern for their reader far behind. Returning to Blanchot after such cases, one is reminded of the sobriety and force with which he thinks and writes.

An *état présent* of critical work on Blanchot was published in 2004, and remains a helpful point of reference.[26] Since then, there have been developments such as the proceedings of the 2003 conference *Maurice Blanchot: Récits critiques*, and of those of the weeklong conference at Cerisy-la-Salle for his centenary in 2007, *Blanchot dans son siècle*. There have been monographs and collective volumes dedicated to particular ways of reading his work: *The Dark Gaze: Maurice Blanchot and the Sacred*, *Blanchot Romantique*, and *Maurice Blanchot and Fragmentary Writing: a Change of Epoch*.[27] In English, there have been further important monographs (*Last Steps: Maurice Blanchot and Exilic Writing*) and collective volumes (such as *Clandestine Encounters: Philosophy in the Narratives of Maurice Blanchot*, and *Understanding Blanchot, Understanding Modernism*).[28] And in French there have been monographs too numerous to mention, and a slew of collective volumes.[29] Last—although I do not pretend to have been exhaustive—these years have seen the launch of a book series promising to publish elements from Blanchot's archive, and a dedicated journal, the *Cahiers Maurice Blanchot*. In what space remains I wish to briefly look at some of the major areas into which critical thought on and with Blanchot is—or, precisely, is not—advancing.

We discussed the notion of a wandering cadaver both *in* Blanchot's writings, and represented *by* them. To these two senses we can add a third, in which something refuses to die, haunting us spectrally but without being anything more than phantasmatic. This something is the question of Blanchot's politics.

Despite protestations to the contrary, it is well known and well documented that in addition to his postwar activities on the left (particularly in 1958–1968), he is the author of extreme, nationalist newspaper articles dating from the 1930s. It is doubtless shocking to discover this, but extensive documentation has been provided by the publication of several of the articles in the mid-1970s in *Gramma*, and the careful work of Leslie Hill's *Blanchot: Extreme Contemporary* (1997) and the French version of the present book, Bident's *Partenaire invisible: Essai biographique* (1998).[30] Blanchot himself has written that the extremist texts in question are "detestable and inexcusable;" he has spoken of "the texts . . . for which I am reproached today, and rightly so," and of "the responsibility which is mine."[31]

Many of the texts in question have recently been made more fully available in the volume *Chroniques politiques des années trente, 1931–1940*.[32] This means that we have avowals of responsibility from Blanchot (cited in Bident's final chapter), and we have access to the texts. That may well be all we are going to get.

The point is surely a crucial one in the light of several recent works criticizing Blanchot: Michel Surya's *L'autre Blanchot: l'écriture de jour, l'écriture de nuit* (2015), Jean-Luc Nancy's *Disavowed Community* (2014), and Henri de Monvallier and Nicolas Rousseau's *Blanchot l'obscur: Ou la déraison littéraire* (2015).[33] These texts are haunted by the idea of Blanchot's unpalatable past, but precisely they are *haunted* by it because there is not sufficient evidence to move to any full-scale condemnation (there is a clear difference of scale to the scandals surrounding Paul de Man and Martin Heidegger, for instance). There are indeed statements in Blanchot's work that he himself recognized as "detestable and inexcusable." But because they are so few, Surya for instance is often reduced to criticizing Blanchot's associates.[34] I will discuss some of the major hypotheses of how the writer's itinerary can be understood, and Surya and Nancy's works in particular are certainly substantial enough to require fuller response elsewhere. But it nonetheless seems necessary to comment on the way that Blanchot's politics continues to haunt critics: Forty years after the publication of selected 1930s texts in *Gramma*, and twenty years after the comprehensive accounts of Hill and Bident, we need to realize that this incomplete line of thinking has run into the sand. Perhaps in due course archival information will arise allowing a full-scale condemnation of Blanchot. But in the meantime, sufficient evidence is lacking, meaning we exist in a half-light where strange shapes are seen in the shadows, and where the debate is one of insinuation and guilt by association. Therefore it is surely time to banish these particular specters by switching on the lights of reading and analysis.

Carefully judged critical material on Blanchot's work does of course exist. For instance, the question of how (and whether) to divide his work into periods has given rise to several competing hypotheses. On the one hand, there are those for whom there is an underlying, second-order continuity between the assertiveness of the earlier texts and the infinite movement of the latter ones: Surya is among such critics. On the other, some argue that such divisions exist, his work moving around one or more turning point(s) or hinge(s). The precise location of these points is matter for detailed, ongoing discussion: did Blanchot move away from his early political period in 1937, later in the 1930s, or in the early 1940s? Was his return to politics in 1958 a sudden one, or had it been prepared by previous writings, readings, and encounters? Similarly, among critics who accept that such turning points existed, there is debate over how many of them there were. Are there ultimately two parts to Blanchot's career, his early, rightwing writings and his later, left-wing ones? Or are there three parts, with his novels and narratives constituting a distinct middle phase? Did 1958 open a communist period that ended in 1968 in order to give way to a new phase centered on Judaism, or was there continuity? Proper treatment of these questions requires greater resources than I have time to deploy here. But we can at least note the existence of the argument based on the existence of one or more turning points. One of Blanchot's major readers, Philippe Lacoue-Labarthe, has used the terms "break" (*coupure*, a cutting, caesura, break) and "transformation" to describe the death of a political voice discussed by *Death Sentence*, dating from the late 1930s.[35] Indeed, Blanchot's writings themselves provide us with the term "turning point."[36] And in a recently published letter from 1984, he speaks of "a sort of conversion." The context is a discussion of the 1930s, when he tells us that he engaged in political journalism during the day while writing completely differently—fiction, what would become *Thomas the Obscure*—at night. He states: "if there was a fault on my part, it was doubtless in this division. But at the same time it hastened a sort of conversion of myself by opening me to awaiting and to comprehending the overwhelming events that were underway."[37] The fact that the term "conversion" is qualified as "*a sort of* conversion" emphasizes the striking nature of this term, of course more usually encountered in a religious context. Doubtless this qualification speaks to the radical nature of the shift in Blanchot's thinking. But before there can be any discussion of the implications of the term "conversion," qualified or otherwise, we need to have greater clarity over the shift in question. There is no doubt that this is a shift *away* from a nationalist mindset: that never returns to Blanchot's writing. But what is it a shift *toward*: the novels and narratives, or a left-wing political activism?

Asking this question is a necessary stage for any serious work on Blanchot's writing. And of course, to properly ask a question, one must also critically assess it. In the present case, this means asking whether the division between narrative and politics post-1940 can truly hold water. On the one hand, there is a marked periodization, with the novels and narratives being produced predominantly in the 1940s and 1950s, and politics then taking the upper hand from 1958 through 1968. And similarly, what could be more different than the prose of *Thomas the Obscure* and the assertive fragment that is the Declaration of the Right to Insubordination in the Algerian War? On the other hand, however, texts including *Death Sentence*, *The Madness of the Day*, *The Most High* can be read as political, as concerned with the extinction of the desire to narrate the world, to raise one's political voice as an individual, to take back control. Once again, this is not the place to enter into these debates per se. But we can note that the two major and recent attacks on Blanchot's politics reserve little space for such a consideration of his fiction (or indeed, for any consideration of it at all). Michel Surya jumps straight from the politics of the 1930s to the period

1958–1968 and beyond, ultimately arguing against the existence of any turning point, on the basis that any "conversion" Blanchot spoke of did not alter the underlying extremism of his political engagement (whether on the right or on the left).[38] And Jean-Luc Nancy considers almost exclusively a single, later text, *The Unavowable Community*. While both works adopt methodologies that appear to be largely sound as far as they go—Surya comparing texts from two periods, Nancy looking at the detail of a single text—surely they are missing something bigger. Even if they can be said to be addressing the truth of Blanchot (something open to debate), they cannot claim to be addressing, as far as he is concerned, the *whole* truth. Even though it is challenging, and indeed precisely for that reason, we must look at the whole truth of the whole man.

After all, the ground underlying any controversy surrounding Blanchot is that his writings are among the most striking and influential of the twentieth century. That much is surely demonstrated by Bident's biography, with not only its mapping of that author's huge presence in the work of Derrida, Levinas, or Bataille (to mention only three figures), but also the way it shows us the radical transformations of Blanchot's writing as they are brought about by the sheer weight of his thinking of illness, death, and friendship. If we forget that it is first of all as a writer that Blanchot comes to us, and if we let insinuation and incompleteness govern our approach to him, then we risk remaining in the half-light. Without wishing or claiming to know how to read his work in any single way, we must be wary of readings that conveniently exclude what is challenging about it. Blanchot's work is not convenient, and it was never meant to be—but it is published, and the majority of it is translated: All that remains for us is to read.

ACKNOWLEDGMENTS

I would like to thank here all those who accompanied this work as it took shape.

This means especially those without whose acquaintance it would not have been possible: Daniel Dobbels, Virginie Pelletier, and Jean-Benoît Puech. My warmest thanks also go to Monique Antelme, Jacques Derrida, Roger Laporte, Francis Marmande, and Michel Surya. As well as to Dionys Mascolo, whose generous attentiveness contributed to the early direction of the project.

I wish to thank, for the interviews they granted me and sometimes for making private archives available: Jean Bazaine, Mr. and Mrs. Georges Bérardan, Jean-Pierre Boyer, Michel Deguy, Louis-René des Forêts, Jacques Dupin, Francine Fardoulis-Lagrange, Mr. and Mrs. François Forêt, Mrs Pierre Gauthey, Mr. and Mrs. Jean Herbinet, Leslie Kaplan, Vadim Kozovoï, Michaël Levinas, Xavier de Lignac, Pierre Madaule, Maurice Nadeau, Jean-Luc Nancy, Bernard Noël, Louis Ollivier, Jean Piel, François Poirié, Pierre Prévost, Jean Rollin, Claude Roy, Jean Suquet, Pierre-Antoine Villemaine.

I thank Bernard Desportes and all contributors to the issue that *Ralentir Travaux* dedicated to Maurice Blanchot (Winter 1997), as well as Hugo Santiago, Andès Jarach, and all those who took part in the film *Maurice Blanchot* produced by INA (Institut National de l'Audiovisuel) and broadcast on France 3 (1998).

I thank as well, for their assistance, David Amar, David Amar, Aliette Armel, Raymond Bellour, Philippe Blanc, Claude Burgelin, Didier Cahen, Hubert Déssolin, the Curate of Simard, Guislain Drot, Gérard Dufresne, the Baron of Marais, Claude Elly, Marina Galletti, Christophe Halsberghe, Leslie Hill, Michaël Holland, Viviane Jabès-Crasson, Charles Juliet, Patrick Kéchichian, Pierre Pachet, Sylvie Patron, Claire Paulhan, Liliane

Phan and Gallimard, Dominique Rabaté, Pierre-Paul Ryga, Tatsuo Satomi, Emmanuel Tibloux, and Pierre Vilar.

I would also like to thank, in particular, Geneviève and Marie-Christine Drot and Sabah Rahmani, with whom the bibliographies and (especially) the index were compiled.

NOTES

PREFACE

1. [Throughout, the term *récits* will be retained in French. The alternative translation *narratives* does not allow for the important distinction between *récits* and novels made by Blanchot. Also, I have usually translated *l'attention* (often used by Bident) with "attentiveness," its literal quality underlining the importance of this notion for Blanchot. —Trans.]

2. [Blanchot was still alive when this text was written and published. He died in 2003. —Trans.]

1. BLANCHOT OF QUAIN: GENEALOGY, BIRTH, CHILDHOOD (1907–1918)

1. Maurice Blanchot, *The Instant of My Death*, in Maurice Blanchot and Jacques Derrida, *The Instant of My Death / Demeure: Fiction and Testimony*, trans. Elizabeth Rottenberg (Stanford: Stanford University Press, 2000), 3.

2. The surname Blanchot, whose emptiness and whiteness would be commented on at length, is a derivative of the name Blanc (White), which is common in the South of France. It can also sometimes mean "white woollen fabric."

3. Half a century later, Élise would end her days at her goddaughter's house.

4. Isidore and Edmond Blanchot's younger sister, Marthe, born in 1866, had married a man named Jules Thevenot. She would die in 1922.

5. Interview given by Marguerite Blanchot to Philippe Merley, *Le Courrier de Saône-et-Loire*, July 27, 1979.

6. A great composer and organist, both as a theorist and a practitioner, Marcel Dupré, who was internationally recognized, would teach at the Conservatory in Paris beginning in 1926, eventually becoming its director. In 1936, the great organ of Saint-Sulpice was placed in his care. He died in Meudon in 1971.

7. Jean Suquet remembers a German teacher at the *lycée* in Châteauroux at the beginning of the Second World War. Wearing a long black cape, he

looked like the ghost of some German Romantic. The schoolchildren called George Blanchot "the corpse."

8. Blanchot, *The Instant of My Death*, 5. [The French noun *demeure* used by Blanchot means "dwelling," but it also suggests a conjugation of the verb *demeurer* (to remain) and of the verb *mourir* (to die; e.g., *il meurt*). The old French *demourance* is related to the sense of dwelling but recalls *mourir* even more strongly. Bident uses *demeure* regularly throughout the work. —Trans.]

9. Maurice Blanchot, *The Writing of the Disaster*, trans. Ann Smock (Lincoln: University of Nebraska Press, 1986), 72.

10. Rainer Maria Rilke, "Letters to a Young Poet" (VI, December 23, 1903), in *Sonnets to Orpheus with Letters to a Young Poet*, trans. Stephen Cohn (Manchester: Carcanet, 2000), 191.

11. Louis-René des Forêts, *Ostinato*, trans. Mary Ann Caws (Lincoln: University of Nebraska, 2002), 5, 123. There is no childhood to be rediscovered: "Genius is no more than childhood recaptured at will"—Charles Baudelaire in *The Painter of Modern Life*, trans. P. E. Charvet (London: Penguin, 2010), 11. Instead, we can see it as both a privilege and a letdown, a continual source or resource for the imaginary and the neuter. Blanchot uses quite extraordinary language, in a letter to Dionys Mascolo, to describe "impersonal misfortune [*malheur*]": "close to the feeling of personal misfortune one would feel in seeing a child throwing itself under the wheels of a car one was driving" (August 7, 1961).

12. Maurice Blanchot, "The 'Sacred' Speech of Hölderlin" (1946), in *The Work of Fire*, trans. Charlotte Mandell (Stanford: Stanford University Press, 1995), 117.

13. Georges Bataille, "Celestial Bodies" (1938), trans. Annette Michelson, *October* 36 (1986): 78.

14. Blanchot, *The Instant of My Death*, 9.

15. Maurice Blanchot, "Kafka and the Work's Demand" (1952), in *The Space of Literature*, trans. Ann Smock (Lincoln: University of Nebraska Press, 1982), 59; "The Very Last Word" (1968), in *Friendship*, trans. Elizabeth Rottenberg (Stanford: Stanford University Press, 1997), 280.

2. MUSIC AND FAMILY MEMORY:
MARGUERITE BLANCHOT IN CHALON (1920S)

1. Two children resulted from this marriage, the only two grandchildren of Alexandrine and Isidore.

2. Philippe Merley, presentation of the interview given by Marguerite Blanchot in the *Courrier de Sâone-et-Loire*.

3. Her cars were also a subject of conversation: a gray *traction avant* before the war, a Citroën 2CV after it. People in Chalon said she had a rather eccentric way of driving.

4. Maurice Blanchot, "*Le Docteur Faustus*" (1950), in *La condition critique: Articles 1945–1998*, ed. Christophe Bident (Paris: Gallimard, 2010), 168–171.

3. THE FEDORA OF DEATH: ILLNESS (1922–1923)

1. Maurice Blanchot, "The Turn of the Screw" (1954), in *The Book to Come*, trans. Charlotte Mandell (Stanford: Stanford University Press, 2003), 259 n.
2. Maurice Blanchot, "Story and Scandal" (1956), in ibid., 190.
3. Dionys Mascolo would invoke "Maurice Blanchot's grilled steak," a special diet reserved for him when staying at the Rue Saint-Benoît and ordered for him by Marguerite Duras. Georges Bataille makes an allusion to this in a letter to Mascolo: "I am myself in a bad way, and the diet that suits Maurice Blanchot will apparently be suitable for me too." In *Choix de lettres*, ed. Michel Surya (Paris: Gallimard, 1997), 577–578. Louis Olliver, who often ate lunch with Blanchot in 1940–42, confirms that the latter ate little, although without following any particular dietary regime.
4. Maurice Blanchot, "Sleep, Night," in *The Space of Literature*, trans. Ann Smock (Lincoln: University of Nebraska Press, 1982), 265.
5. "My existence is surprisingly solid; even fatal diseases find me too tough. I'm sorry, but I must bury a few others before I bury myself," in Maurice Blanchot, *The Madness of the Day*, trans. Lydia Davis (Barrytown, N.Y.: Station Hill Press, 1981), 9.
6. An expression used in a letter from Maurice Blanchot to Dionys Mascolo, July 10, 1972.
7. Interview in François Poiré, *Emmanuel Levinas*, 2d ed. (1987; reprint, Besançon: La Manufacture, 1992), 60.
8. Michel Butor in Didier Cahen and Jean-Claude Loiseau, "Sur les traces de Maurice Blanchot," a France-Culture radio show first broadcast on September 17, 1994.
9. [The affair concerning the rightist author Benoist is discussed in a note in the final chapter. —Trans.]
10. Letter from Maurice Blanchot to Dionys Mascolo, undated, 1960s.
11. Gilles Deleuze, *Essays Critical and Clinical*, trans. Daniel W. Smith and Michael A. Greco (Minneapolis: University of Minnesota Press, 1997), 3.
12. Georges Bataille, *Inner Experience*, trans. Stuart Kendall (Albany: SUNY Press, 2014), 85. In "My Properties," Henri Michaux writes: "At the stake where he finds himself, the atheist cannot believe in God. His health would not allow him to./But all this is neither determining nor clear for well people. Everything suits these crass individuals, *as it suits those with strong stomachs*." *La nuit remue* (Paris: Gallimard, 1935), 19; emphasis added. The atheist is the writer who writes "for reasons of hygiene," "for [his] health." "Doubtless one writes for nothing else," Michaux warned.

13. "I am forced to wait, without knowing how and when the waiting will end, a waiting which is surveyed here in the most affectionate and discreet way. It is as if, all of a sudden, all I have written has caught up with me and, to tell the truth, I have borne it badly. More simply, let us say what Robert once said: that illness and life are one and the same and that doctors can only give us provisional assistance in giving one the appearance of the other" (letter from Maurice Blanchot to Dionys Mascolo, July 18, 1965). This was a constant in Blanchot's life: his extreme—and understandable—mistrust of doctors, which would often lead him to consult several rather than just one, and on which the *récit* that is *The Madness of the Day* is more than eloquent. Nonetheless, he was extremely affectionate toward the staff dispensing care.

14. Maurice Nadeau, "Maurice Blanchot" in *Grâces leur soient rendues* (Paris: Albin Michel, 1990), 70.

15. Louis-René des Forêts in "Sur les traces de Maurice Blanchot."

16. Marie-Anne Lescourret in *Emmanuel Levinas* (Paris: Flammarion, 1994), 64, 68.

17. Pierre Monnier, *À l'ombre des grandes têtes molles* (Paris: La Table Ronde, 1987), 205–206.

18. From a study by his son, Jean-Luc Maxence, *L'ombre d'un père* (Paris: Hallier, 1978), 127.

19. Dominique Aury, "Propos," *L'Infini*, 55 (Autumn 1996): 21.

20. Claude Roy, *Moi je* (Paris: Gallimard, 1969), 244. Roger Laporte described Blanchot's voice as slightly lilting; for Michaël Levinas, it was unique and "very French," belonging to a time that no longer existed; for him it has always evoked passages from Couperin's *Tombeau*.

21. Georges Bataille, *L'être indifférencié n'est rien*, in *Oeuvres complètes* (Paris: Gallimard, 1954), 3:369 and 559. The second verse of the poem recalls the world of *Thomas the Obscure*, which is often quoted by Bataille.

22. Roger Laporte, "Un sourire mozartien," *Ralentir travaux* 7 (Winter 1997): 75.

23. Marguerite Duras, *Écrire* (Paris: Gallimard, 1993), 45. "I have known great writers, they were never able to speak about it [where writing came from]—I knew intimately Maurice Blanchot and Georges Bataille," she writes elsewhere. "They were never able to, they never spoke about it": Marguerite Duras, *Le monde extérieur*, in *Outside* (Paris: POL, 1993), 2:24–25.

24. ["Muffle" recalls the verb *feutrer*, a cognate of which is evidently chosen (and italicized) by Bident due to its association with the previous use of *le feutre*, a fedora hat. —Trans.]

4. THE WALKING STICK WITH THE SILVER POMMEL:
THE UNIVERSITY OF STRASBOURG (1920S)

1. Blanchot himself, in a letter he has made available, suggests the date of 1923. This date is nonetheless not certain, although it is the most probable.

2. For more details on the Strasbourg context and on meeting Levinas, we refer the reader to Marie-Anne Lescourret, *Emmanuel Levinas* (Paris: Flammarion, 1994), especially the first chapter.

3. Henri Carteron had died in 1929 at the age of thirty-seven.

4. Maurice Blanchot, "Do Not Forget" (1988), in *Political Writings: 1953–1993*, trans. Zakir Paul (New York: Fordham University Press, 2010), 124–129, at 124.

5. See Jacques Derrida, "Sur les traces de Maurice Blanchot," radio program.

5. A FLASH IN THE DARKNESS:
MEETING EMMANUEL LEVINAS (1925–1930)

1. Jacques Derrida, *Adieu—to Emmanuel Levinas*, trans. Pascale-Anne Brault and Michael Naas (Stanford: Stanford University Press, 1999), 8.

2. Emmanuel Levinas in François Poirié, *Emmanuel Levinas*, 2nd ed. (1987; reprint, Besançon: La Manufacture, 1992), 59–60.

3. Maurice Blanchot, letter of February 11, 1980, cited in *Exercices de la Patience* 1 (1980): 67.

4. Maurice Blanchot, letter to Pierre Prévost of November 16, 1987.

5. Maurice Blanchot, *For Friendship* (1993), in *Political Writings: 1953–1993*, trans. Zakir Paul (New York: Fordham University Press, 2010), 143.

6. Maurice Blanchot, "Do Not Forget" (1988), in ibid., 124.

7. Several accounts confirm that Emmanuel Levinas never considered his friend an anti-Semite. He saw Blanchot's monarchism as a curiosity, barely compatible with the rest of his personality, although a *thinkable* incompatibility.

8. [Aristide Briand (1862–1932) was a seven-time prime minister of France and joint winner of the Nobel Peace Prize in 1926. —Trans.]

9. Emmanuel Levinas, "Comme un consentement à l'horrible," *Le Nouvel Observateur* (January 22, 1988), 82.

10. Emmanuel Levinas, *Totality and Infinity*, trans. Alphonso Lingis (Boston: Martinus Nijhoff, 1979), 47.

6. THERE IS: PHILOSOPHICAL APPRENTICESHIP (1927–1930)

1. Emmanuel Levinas, *Ethics and Infinity*, trans. Richard A. Cohen (Pittsburgh: Duquesne University Press, 1985), 38.

2. Maurice Blanchot, "Thinking the Apocalypse" (1987), in *Political Writings: 1953–1993*, trans. Zakir Paul (New York: Fordham University Press, 2010), 123.

3. Maurice Blanchot, "Our Clandestine Companion" (1980), in ibid., 144.

4. Here and for the quotation above, Emmanuel Levinas's words are taken from François Poirié, *Emmanuel Levinas*, 2nd ed. (1987; reprint, Besançon: La Manufacture, 1992), 61–62.

5. Emmanuel Levinas, *Sur Maurice Blanchot* (Montpellier: Fata Morgana, 1975), 12. On the relations between Heidegger, Husserl, and Blanchot, see the articles by Francis Wybrands and Alain David in *Exercices de la patience* 2 (Winter 1981): 79–87, 131–138. The less well-known influence of Bergson (1927 Nobel prize winner) on the development of Levinas and Blanchot (via a writer like Massis) is found in a certain approach to time ("the infinite in us," Levinas would say); to duration (understood as pure and creative, i.e., when intuition completes the mind's movements); to substance and to Being, or even to a critique of language that "lets be lost the mobility of consciousness, the dream of inner life, all that has its source and reality in duration," thus leading to a theory of symbolism that nonetheless retains the abysses of Mallarmé's poetry; see Maurice Blanchot, "Bergson et le symbolisme" (1942), partly reprinted as "Bergson and Symbolism" in *Faux Pas*, trans. Charlotte Mandell (Stanford: Stanford University Press, 2001), 112–115.

6. Emmanuel Levinas, "Intentionality and Metaphysics," in *Discovering Existence with Husserl*, trans. Richard A. Cohen and Michael B. Smith, 2nd ed. (Evanston, Ill.: Northwestern University Press, 2000), 190.

7. Husserl's sometime assistant Eugen Fink would speak of a "nonknowledge of the Being of beings" characterizing astonishment in its "horrifying" (*entsetzend*) essence; see the French translation, *De la phénoménologie* (Paris: Minuit, 1974), 203. The fate awaiting such words in Blanchot is well known; he was first able to read Fink's work in 1939 in the *Revue Internationale de Philosophie* under the title "Le problème de la phénoménologie d'Edmond Husserl."

8. Emmanuel Levinas, *Existence and Existents*, trans. Alphonso Lingis (The Hague: Martinus Nijhoff, 1978), 63–64; *Ethics and Infinity*, 48.

9. Levinas, *Existence and Existents*, 63.

10. Ibid., 61; preface to second edition of *De l'existence à l'existant* (Paris: Vrin, 1986), 10–11, not included in *Existence and Existents*; *Ethics and Infinity*, 48.

11. Françoise Collin, "La peur," in *Cahier de l'Herne: Emmanuel Levinas* (Paris: Livre de Poche, 1991), 351.

7. ALIGNING ONE'S CONVICTIONS:
PARIS AND FAR-RIGHT CIRCLES (1930S)

1. Blanchot would return at length to skepticism in numerous fragments of *The Writing of the Disaster*, trans. Ann Smock (Lincoln: University of Nebraska Press, 1986)

2. [The "two hundred families" refers to criticism from the Left of the influence of the two hundred biggest shareholders of the Banque de France, who exercised disproportionate influence on it. —Trans.]

3. Pierre Monnier, *À l'ombre des grandes têtes molles* (Paris: La Table Ronde, 1987), 206. According to Xavier de Lignac, Blanchot earned 12,000 francs a month at the *Journal des Débats*—perhaps an exaggerated figure. According to another account, each month Blanchot earned 900 francs each month at the *Journal*, and later 300 at *L'Insurgé*.

4. For relevant background, see in particular Jean Louis Loubet del Bayle, *Les non-conformistes des années trentes: Une tentative de renouvellement de la pensée politique française* (Paris: Seuil, 1969); and Jeannine Verdès-Leroux, *Refus et violence: Politique et littérature à l'extrême droite, des années trentes aux retombées de la Libération* (Paris: Gallimard, 1996).

5. Maurice Blanchot, "Les français et le couronnement," *L'Insurgé* 19 (May 19, 1937): 4.

6. Claude Roy, *Moi je* (Paris: Gallimard, 1969), 242.

7. Maurice Blanchot, *Intellectuals under Scrutiny* (1984), in *The Blanchot Reader*, ed. Michael Holland (Oxford: Blackwell, 1995), 211. Maurice Barrès: The adolescent who read this author must have noticed that he had the same first name and the same initials.

8. According to Jean Rollin, Denise Rollin used to say that Maurice Blanchot had been seduced by Maurras's personality, more than he had been convinced by his ideology. We can have doubts about this, even if the first part of the statement should not be excluded. Similarly, the far-reaching influence of Barrès on Blanchot should not be excluded, with its egotism, the importance of the *terroir*, love for one's humiliated neighbor, a nationalism with roots.

9. Lucien Rebatet, *Les décombres* (Paris: Denoël, 1942), 127.

10. Étienne de Montety, *Thierry Maulnier* (Paris: Juillard, 1994), 181.

11. Thierry Maulnier, *La crise est dans l'homme* (Paris: Librairie de la Revue Française, 1932), 240.

12. Pierre Boutang does this in the interview related by Bernard-Henri Lévy in *Adventures on the Freedom Road: The French Intellectuals in the 20th Century*, trans. Richard Veasey (London: Harvill, 1995), 153 ("it is beyond question that Maurrassian ideas acted as a barrier," "preventing excesses" that could have led to fascism).

8. "MAHATMA GANDHI": A FIRST TEXT BY BLANCHOT (1931)

1. Maurice Blanchot, "Mahatma Gandhi" (July 1931), trans. Franson Manjali in consultation with Michael Holland in *Journal for Cultural Research* 16, no. 4 (2012): 366–370. Thirteen years later, Blanchot's position on Gandhi would remain unchanged: see "Le pèlerinage aux sources," *Chroniques littéraires du Journal des Débats: Avril 1941–août 1944*, ed. Christophe Bident (Paris: Gallimard, 2007), 536–540.
2. Blanchot, "Mahatma Gandhi," 366.
3. Ibid.
4. Ibid, 367.
5. Ibid. [Rendering the French *spirituel* and *esprit* poses difficulties: "spiritual" and "spirit," while they do align well with philosophical and religious traditions, also lose the connection to what in everyday English and in philosophy is identified as "(the) mind." —Trans.]
6. Ibid., 368.
7. Ibid., 369.
8. G. K. Chesterton cited in ibid., 370.
9. Ibid., 369–370.

9. REFUSAL, I. THE REVOLUTION OF SPIRIT: *LA REVUE FRANÇAISE, RÉACTION*, AND *LA REVUE DU SIÈCLE* (1931–1934)

1. Maurice Blanchot, "Le monde sans âme" (August 25, 1932), in *Chroniques politiques des années trente: 1931–1940*, ed. David Uhrig (Paris: Gallimard, 2017), 74–88, at 75. (Here and elsewhere, references to this volume relate to the pages in the untranslated French edition.) Several months later, on March 21, 1933, in the *Journal des Débats*, Blanchot would return to the work by Daniel-Rops and notably to its follow-up, *Les années tournantes*, this time in an article containing little reserve; see "*Les années tournantes*," in *Chroniques politiques*, 93–96.
2. Georges Bataille, "Materialism" and "Base Materialism and Gnosticism," in *Visions of Excess: Selected Writings, 1927–1939*, ed. Alan Stoekl (Minneapolis: University of Minnesota Press, 1985), 15–16 and 45–52.
3. Blanchot, "Le monde sans âme," 87.
4. Ibid., 81.
5. Maurice Blanchot, "Le marxisme contre la revolution" (April 25, 1933), in *Chroniques politiques*, 100–113.
6. Ibid., 105.
7. Ibid., 108.
8. Ibid., 110.
9. Ibid., 111.
10. Ibid., 112.

11. Ibid.

12. The journal would publish with "great joy," in its seventh issue, a telegram from the count and countess of Paris expressing thanks for the good wishes that had been published by the journal on the occasion of their recent marriage.

13. Maurice Blanchot, "Nouvelle querelle des anciens et des modernes" (April–May 1932), in *Chroniques politiques*, 47–54, at 54.

14. [Bident is referring to the slogan used under Vichy: "work, family, nation." —Trans.]

15. Blanchot, "Morale et politique" (May 1933), in *Chroniques politiques*, 126–133.

16. Ibid., 130.

17. Ibid., 129.

18. Ibid., 127.

19. Ibid., 133.

10. JOURNALIST, OPPONENT OF HITLER, NATIONAL-REVOLUTIONARY: *LE JOURNAL DES DÉBATS, LE REMPART, AUX ÉCOUTES,* AND *LA REVUE DU VINGTIÈME SIÈCLE* (1931–1935)

1. This may not have been Blanchot's first contribution to a daily newspaper. We have not been able to verify reports that he worked for *La Nouvelliste de Lyon*, one of the newspapers that covered the whole of France while retaining the name of a town or a region. None of its articles were signed, and nowhere is a list given of the editorial teams.

2. An article of August 18, 1931, bears the initials M.B. The next one, signed M.Bl. and attributable to Blanchot without too much doubt, is dated May 2, 1932. Two publicity announcements for the *Journal des Débats* in sympathetic journals list the paper's contributors, helping us to confirm Blanchot's role and his importance. One—in *Réaction* in April 1932—gives his name, unlike the second, from the last issue of the *Cahiers Mensuels* (July 1931). Finally, Emmanuel Levinas attributes to Blanchot the anonymous editorial of March 9, 1932: "Mr. Briand" (who had just died). The philosopher quotes from memory thus: "Each time he spoke he created a law, each time he acted he failed": see Marie-Anne Lescourret, *Emmanuel Levinas* (Paris: Flammarion, 1994), 112. The words actually written by Blanchot were even harsher: "Each time he spoke he always triumphed, his actions were always failures" in *Chroniques politiques des années trente: 1931–1940*, ed. David Uhrig (Paris: Gallimard, 2017), 44. In the article Blanchot provided a remarkable portrait of the "shared solitude" of Briand (44).

3. After the First World War he moved to the *Revue de Paris*, then to *Figaro*, as well as being the literary critic for the *Revue des Deux Mondes*, and

from 1930 being a member of the Académie Française, where he was influential. Chaumeix (1874–1955) was later accused by the collaborationist and pro-Nazi weekly paper *L'Appel* of having treated Maurice Blanchot as a "negro"; "Videz Thomas," *L'Appel* (May 28, 1942), 4.

4. He probably authored an article in the *Journal des Débats* of August 18, 1931, entitled "Comment s'emparer du pouvoir?" in which the technique of coups d'état is analyzed; it is collected in *Chroniques politiques des années trente*, 36–39. He argued for the relevance to the revolution of Daniel-Rops's work, *Les années tournantes*, in an eponymous article in the *Journal des Débats* of March 21, 1933; *Chroniques politiques*, 93–96. Daniel-Rops himself often contributed to the newspaper, thus ensuring that Ordre Nouveau was represented there.

5. Maurice Blanchot, "Un discours logique," as "Avant Genève—M. de Neurath expose les principes de la politique allemande—Un discours logique," in *Chroniques politiques*, 324–327.

6. Blanchot would return to the nature and necessity of the call for force in *L'Insurgé*, 10 (March 1937): 5, in terms of the work by Alphonse Séché, *Réflexions sur la force*. "That force should demand to be rehabilitated" is strange but necessary in terms of history, he wrote. "The moment a regime starts discrediting violence and recommending incapacity is also the moment when the society that accepts this becomes incapable and loses the will to do what is required for power." However, Blanchot criticized the more outrageous and fascistic aspects of a rehabilitation of force that "even Nietzsche would not accept," thus demonstrating a right-leaning but not extreme reading of the philosopher who wrote on the will to power.

7. Maurice Blanchot, "Les communistes, gardiens de la culture," *Journal des Débats* (March 25, 1933); *Chroniques politiques*, 97–99. The two following citations are from pages 98 and 99.

8. Maurice Blanchot, "Le rajeunissement de la politique," *Journal des Débats* (May 2, 1932); *Chroniques politiques*, 56.

9. Maurice Blanchot, "Au Congrès pour l'éducation nouvelle," *Journal des Débats* (June 23, 1932), and *Chroniques politiques*, 61; "L'histoire désarmée," *Journal des Débats* (July 21, 1932), and *Chroniques politiques*, 68.

10. Maurice Blanchot, "La doctrine catholique et les relations internationales," *Journal des Débats* (May 9, 1932), and *Chroniques politiques*, 59.

11. The library collection is incomplete (85 issues of at least 130). I have therefore been unable to read all Blanchot's articles for *Rempart*, while still having read enough (60) to be able to discern his political and ideological positions in 1933. In the remainder of this chapter, the numbers in parentheses provide page-references to the *Chroniques politiques*.

12. Jean-Pierre Maxence, *Histoire de dix ans, 1927–1937* (Paris: Gallimard, 1939), 257–258.

13. One of the early, biographical fragments of *The Step (Not) Beyond* can be read in this way. See Maurice Blanchot, *The Step Not Beyond*, trans. Lycette Nelson (Albany: State University of New York Press, 1992), 2.

14. *Le Rempart*, issue 50.

15. Maxence, *Histoire de dix ans*. Maxence is not completely wrong to discuss the "singular lucidity" of the era: "We were able to see the significance of everyday events. We underlined this popular movement, this movement of revolt that eventually would lead to the February events. . . . And *Le Rempart* was doubtless the only newspaper which, at the time, took up a position that was *at once* antiparliamentarian and anticapitalist." On Paul Lévy's friendship with Georges Mandel, see Bertrand Favreau, *Georges Mandel ou la passion de la République* (Paris: Fayard, 1996), notably 69, 80, 269–270.

16. [Although it seems clear that *salut* here bears a meaning distinct from "salvation," several alternatives remain. It could be translated as "safety," "security," or "well-being." I have chosen the first of these here in order to align with something that was doubtless in Blanchot's mind: the postrevolutionary Comité de Salut Publique to which Robespierre belonged, and which is commonly translated as the "committee of public safety." In a related (nontheological) register, a variant of the verb "to save" has been used in some cases. —Trans.]

17. Maurice Blanchot, reader's notes on *L'école du renégat* by Jean Fontenoy in *L'Insurgé* 30 (August 4, 1937): 5.

18. Blanchot would long remain close to Paul Lévy as a faithful friend, even to the point of seconding him in a duel. The affair is recounted in *Aux Écoutes* 1024 (January 1, 1938): 17. At the end of December 1937, Lévy learned from the press that he had been "violently offended" by Albert Naud in the high court in Paris. He straightaway sent two witnesses, Henri Israel and Maurice Blanchot, to demand "a formal apology or the chance to defend his honor by arms." According to the statement by Israel and Blanchot, as it is reported in *Aux Écoutes*, Albert Naud hid from them. On December 30, they drew up a legal claim against Naud following his lack of action. Paul Lévy excused himself to his friends thus: "Mr. Naud insults people and then runs away. Please excuse me for having disturbed you on account of this coward." We can note here that a certain confrontation with death is always present for Blanchot. We can also see the kind of aristocratic world, with its absolute and outmoded forms of dignity, to which he belonged.

19. In parallel to *Le Rempart*, Paul Lévy had launched a "great illustrated newspaper," *Aujourd'hui*, containing four full pages of photographic reproductions, which probably folded in 1934. A number of the editorial team from *Le Rempart* could be found there; the two newspapers even had the same headquarters at 17 Rue d'Anjou. It seems that unlike Maxence or Maulnier, Blanchot did not put his name to any article for this paper. This allows us to

reasonably suppose that a large part of his activity was now dedicated to *Aux Écoutes*.

20. Maurice Blanchot, "La fin du 6 février," *Combat* (February 1936), and *Chroniques politiques*, 364.

21. Paul Lévy, "La révolution nationale," *Aujourd'hui* 259 (February 8, 1934): 3.

22. Maurice Blanchot, note to "Nietzsche, Today," in *The Infinite Conversation*, trans. Susan Hanson (Minneapolis: University of Minnesota Press, 1993), 448–449.

23. Emmanuel Levinas, "Some Reflections on the Philosophy of Hitlerism," trans. Seán Hand, *Critical Inquiry* 17, no. 1 (Autumn 1990): 62–71.

24. This is the title of one of the two articles, "Le dérèglement de la diplomatie française," *La Revue du Vingtième Siècle* (May–June 1935); see *Chroniques politiques*, 355–362.

11. THE ESCALATION OF RHETORIC:
THE LAUNCH OF *COMBAT* (1936)

1. Jeannine Verdès-Leroux usefully underlines the radicalization of tone that took place between *Réaction* and *Combat* and how it can be understood in terms of the demands of the era and the pressure of history. She also shows how the vehement "juvenile and tragic" indignation of Blanchot and Maulnier differed from the vulgar extremism of a figure such as Brasillach. She quite rightly discusses their "national-revolutionary" mindset, which was separate from the fascist grouping that fell out with *Combat* in 1937, and that a few years later would become involved in collaboration. Verdès-Leroux, *Refus et violences: Politique et littérature à l'extrême droite, des années trentes aux retombées de la Libération* (Paris: Gallimard, 1996), 70–73.

2. It is nonetheless important to point out that the contributors' positions differed from one another: from the Maurrassian orthodoxy of Gaxotte, who above all was concerned to keep France's borders and therefore also its culture intact, to Fabrègues's confused timidity on the subject of Nazism, or Maulnier's fairly unequivocal condemnation of Hitler's anti-Semitic policies (which were said to be unacceptable from a humanitarian point of view, but also because they prevented "the Jewish problem" from being posed).

3. Keeping his paradigms coherent, eight months later Brasillach would write an article named "The Machine for Kicking Asses" before quitting a journal that for him had become "absurd"; Robert Brasillach, letter to Jacques Brousse, February 12, 1940, cited by Verdès-Leroux, *Refus et violences*, 71.

4. [The meaning of *Marchenoir* is unclear. It does not seem to be a typo for *marché noir* (black market), since this would have been noticed from one issue to another, though it could be a deliberate play on that expression

(though one whose meaning is unclear). It may refer to a small village of the same name in central France (although it is not clear why it would). —Trans.]

5. Maurice Blanchot, "La fin du 6 Février" (February 2, 1936), in *Chroniques politiques des années trente: 1931–1940*, ed. David Uhrig (Paris: Gallimard, 2017), 363. In the remainder of this chapter, the numbers in parentheses provide page references to the *Chroniques politiques*.

6. Later, Blanchot would see the invasion of the Rhineland as the crux of the Second World War. March 1936 already equaled September 1938: Munich.

12. TERRORISM AS A METHOD OF PUBLIC SAFETY: *COMBAT* (JULY–DECEMBER 1936)

1. Maurice Blanchot, "Le terrorisme, méthode de salut public" (July 7, 1936) in *Chroniques politiques des années trente: 1931–1940*, ed. David Uhrig (Paris: Gallimard, 2017), 379. In the remainder of this chapter, the numbers in parentheses provide page references to the *Chroniques politiques*.

2. Maximilien de Robespierre, extracts from speeches of July 15, 1791, and February 5, 1794 (17 pluviôse year II).

3. Maurice Blanchot, "La grande passion des Modérés," *Chroniques politiques*, 383–387.

13. PATRIOTISM'S BREAKING POINT: *L'INSURGÉ* (1937)

1. Maurice Blanchot, "Réquisitoire contre la France," in *Chroniques politiques des années trente: 1931–1940*, ed. David Uhrig (Paris: Gallimard, 2017), 393–395. [In the rest of this chapter, the numbers in parentheses are the page references for *Chroniques politiques*. —Trans.]

2. On *L'Insurgé*, see notably Etienne de Montety, *Thierry Maulnier* (Paris: Juillard, 1994), 126–136; Marie-Anne Lescourret, *Emmanuel Levinas* (Paris: Flammarion, 1994), 65; Eugen Weber, *L'Action française* (1962; reprint, Paris: Fayard, 1985), 585–562. According to Pierre Monnier, who was an associate of Deloncle and contributed to *L'Insurgé*, Blanchot knew Deloncle; he had at least made "approaches," but he never carried out any activities for *La Cagoule*, and neither did Maxence or Maulnier; Pierre Monnier, *À l'ombre des grandes têtes molles* (Paris: La Table Ronde, 1987), 193.

3. The text is included in *Chroniques politiques*, 413–414.

4. Was he even the editor-in-chief? Pierre Prévost suggests that he was; see Michel Surya, *Georges Bataille: An Intellectual Biography*, trans. Krysztof Fijalkowski and Michael Richardson (New York: Verso, 2002), 546.

5. Pierre Viénot was undersecretary of state at the Foreign Ministry in Blum's government.

6. Like Action Française, Blanchot spoke of Blum in the feminine.

7. In fact, given the venue in which Blanchot was publishing, this diplomacy was nonetheless situated in relation to Maulnier's thinking of "national revolution." It was therefore positioned in relation to a particular theory—albeit one lacking any practical consequences.

8. Should we read this date as symbolizing that this break was made in the name of the Republic? Should it be linked to the recent fall of Blum's government? These readings are both tempting and unlikely. As we shall see, other events had a role to play.

9. Letter from Thierry Maulnier to Charles Maurras, July 23, 1937, quoted by Etienne de Montety in *Thierry Maulnier*, 135. According to a brief anonymous article in the collaborationist weekly paper *L'Appel* on May 28, 1942, it was Blanchot who "sank [*L'Insurgé*] together with the aforementioned Thalagrand [Thierry Maulnier]."

10. Blanchot would write to Diane Rubenstein on this point: "I remember that, being totally opposed to Brasillach, who had been utterly won over by fascism and anti-Semitism, I had stipulated as a condition for my collaborating on the journal that he would not be involved with it"; letter of August 20, 1983, in Diane Rubenstein, *What's Left?* (Madison: University of Wisconsin Press, 1990), 187. This condition was granted only with difficulty. Relations with Maulnier at the time were fraught. Blanchot would later say that his texts were sometimes altered at *Combat* and *L'Insurgé* without his view being sought. They were thought to be too anti-Nazi or not anti-Semitic enough. He demanded corrections, which he did not receive; he then brought his participation to an end.

11. Maurice Blanchot, "On demande des dissidents," *Chroniques politiques*, 474–478.

14. THESE EVENTS HAPPENED TO ME IN 1937: DEATH SENTENCES (1937–1938)

1. Maurice Blanchot, "Hommage à Claude Séverac," *Aux Écoutes* 997 (June 26, 1937): 11.

2. "The only date of which I am sure is the 13th October, Wednesday 13th October"; Maurice Blanchot, *Death Sentence*, trans. Lydia Davis, in *The Station Hill Blanchot Reader: Fiction and Literary Essays*, ed. George Quasha (Barrytown, N.Y.: Station Hill Press, 1999), 129–187, at 133. For our reconstruction of the chronology, all subsequent quotations are taken from the first part of the narrative and indeed from the first fifteen pages.

3. Blanchot, *Death Sentence*, 173.

4. The narrator of *Death Sentence* spends several weeks in an establishment being treated for "illness of the lungs"; ibid., 160. We can also think of the sanatorium in *The Last Man*, and of the descriptions in *The Madness of the Day*, trans. Lydia Davis (Barrytown, N.Y.: Station Hill Press, 1981), 7, 11–12.

5. Blanchot, *Death Sentence*, 163.
6. Blanchot, *The Madness of the Day*, 6.

15. ON THE TRANSFORMATION OF CONVICTIONS: A JOURNALIST OF THE FAR RIGHT (1930S)

1. Maurice Blanchot, "M. Briand" (March 9, 1932), in *Chroniques politiques des années trente: 1931–1940*, ed. David Uhrig (Paris: Gallimard, 2017), 46. This editorial is not signed, but it is attributed to Blanchot by Emmanuel Levinas.

2. The advent of Hitler was "for us and above all for the Jews the interregnum when all rights, all recourse ceased, when friendship became uncertain and the silence of the highest spiritual authorities left us without guarantee, not only threatened but anxious about not responding as one should to the silent call of others"; Maurice Blanchot in "Do Not Forget" (1988), in *Political Writings: 1953–1993*, trans. Zakir Paul (New York: Fordham University Press, 2010), 127. Such incompatibilities were opening up an ever-larger fissure in his thinking. At the time, he remained silent on the attitude of Catholic and Jewish authorities. He would later say that this objectively undeniable lack of engagement was in line with the wish most shared by the Jews that he knew: "The most commonly shared view was: let us not exaggerate anything, we must be prudent, reserved, warn the Jews about the consequences of any action"; Maurice Blanchot, letter to Roger Laporte, December 9, 1984, cited in Leslie Hill, "Introduction," in *Maurice Blanchot: The Demand of Writing*, ed. Carolyn Bailey Gill (New York: Routledge, 1996), 9.

3. We can therefore better understand what, beyond the absence of any partisan or institutional involvement with fascist parties, distinguished his position from that of Heidegger. Blanchot did not have *Being and Time* behind him, but rather *Thomas the Obscure* ahead of him, a work whose form he was searching for, slowly and with difficulty. He had not developed any thinking that he could put forth as his own because neither he nor anyone else recognized any theoretical authority in his writing, and because in parallel fashion he was struggling to assume a literary authority that was as yet unknown to everyone. He accused Heidegger on the contrary of compromising his language and his thinking: Heidegger's main "political" text of 1933 "put in Hitler's service the *very* language and the *very* writing through which, at a great moment in the history of thought, we had been invited to participate in the questioning designated as the most lofty—that which would come to us from Being and from Time"; in *The Infinite Conversation*, trans. Susan Hanson (Minneapolis: University of Minnesota Press, 1993), 451. See also Jean-Michel Rabaté's "Le scandale de l'après-coup," *Critique* 594 (November 1996): 921–922: "There was nothing comparable to Heidegger's attitude here . . ."

4. Maurice Blanchot, letter to Raymond Bellour in *Cahiers de l'Herne: Henri Michaux* (Paris: L'Herne, 1966), 88; Maurice Blanchot, "Intellectuals Under Scrutiny" (1984), in *The Blanchot Reader*, ed. Michael Holland (Oxford: Blackwell, 1995), 223.

5. "The story of the transformation of convictions! In the whole realm of literature there is no other story of such thrilling interest!" Lev Shestov cited in Michel Surya, *Georges Bataille: An Intellectual Biography*, trans. Krysztof Fijalkowski and Michael Richardson (New York: Verso, 2002), 504, 506.

6. "Is it simply an accident, for example, that Blanchot distanced himself from the far right and from journalism at the same time? Ought one not ask whether the message is to some degree determined by the medium? Could one not say that an entire sector of French literary production became simultaneously fascist and journalistic? That the temptations of fascism had a lot to do with journalistic exaggeration?" Denis Hollier, "Fahrenheit 452 (Below Zero)," *Critique* 594 (November 1996): 934.

7. Beyond the stakes in politics, economics, social questions, or war, Georges Bataille recognized the power of fascism, as early as 1933, in what he named this power of "irrational attraction" in "The Psychological Structure of Fascism," trans. Carl R. Lovitt, *New German Critique* 16 (Winter, 1979): 64–87; see also "Le fascisme en France," ibid., 2:205–213).

8. Maurice Blanchot, *The Step Not Beyond*, trans. Lycette Nelson (Albany: State University of New York Press, 1992), 2.

16. FROM REVOLUTION TO LITERATURE: LITERARY CRITICISM (1930S)

1. We know how highly Maulnier—a personality who at the time was clearly much better known—thought of Blanchot. Their postwar relations were more distant but still continued, probably until the end of the 1950s. See also Pierre Monnier's remarks in *À l'ombre des grandes têtes molles* (In the Shadow of the Great and Spineless) (Paris: La Table Ronde, 1987), 192.

2. Claude Roy, *Moi je* (Paris: Gallimard, 1969), 244.

3. Monnier, *À l'ombre des grandes têtes molles*, 223–224.

4. Maurice Blanchot, "After the Fact," in *The Station Hill Blanchot Reader: Fiction and Literary Essays*, ed. George Quasha (Barrytown, N.Y.: Station Hill Press, 1999), 490–491.

5. There is also a 1973 text that addresses Valéry, "La comédie d'avoir de l'ordre." The beginning of the article suggests what attracted the young reader of the 1920s: the "pressure of the morning mind which demanded—to the point of suffering, or exaltation—that [Valéry] think quickly, too quickly, that he think everything and also what is beyond everything." We can also infer what gradually distanced this young reader: the tendency toward academic

stiffness in the organization of thought, the search for and publication of the "System," the desire to insert the slightest morning jotting into it, to use even what was unusable, to erase nothing. See *La condition critique: Articles 1945– 1998*, ed. Christophe Bident, 339–342 (Paris: Gallimard, 2010).

6. Maurice Blanchot, "De la révolution à la littérature," *L'Insurgé* 1 (January 13, 1937): 3.

7. Maurice Blanchot, review of *La dentelle du Rempart* by Charles Maurras, *L'Insurgé*, 7 (February 24, 1937): 5. Along with Denis de Rougemont, Maurras was the only author to whom Blanchot dedicated two columns over the ten months (the other appeared on July 28, 1937).

8. Bl. (Maurice Blanchot), review of *Médée* by Léon Daudet, *Aux Écoutes* 895 (July 13, 1935): 30.

9. We know of the existence of a letter from Drieu to Blanchot, dated March 28, 1937, which is to say a good month before the appearance of the article on *Rêveuse bourgeoisie* in *L'Insurgé*. This letter is referred to by Pierre Andreu and Frédéric Grover in *Drieu La Rochelle* (Paris: La Table Ronde, 1989). Blanchot himself confirms that he met Drieu on this occasion in *For Friendship* (1993) in *Political Writings, 1953–1993*, trans. Zakir Paul, 135–136 (New York: Fordham University Press, 2010).

10. Maurice Blanchot, review of Alain, *Souvenirs de guerre*, *L'Insurgé* 24 (June 23, 1937): 5.

11. Bl. (Maurice Blanchot), review of Maeterlinck, *Avant le grand silence*, *Aux Écoutes*, 864 (February 8, 1934): 35.

12. Maurice Blanchot, "La culture française vue par un allemande," *La Revue Française* 10 (March 27, 1932): 363–365.

13. Today, who knows Georges Reyer, Guy Mazeline, Hubert Chatelion, Jean Guirec, Jolan Foldes? Who still reads Louise Hervieu, Thyde Monnier, or even Charles Plisnier (the Goncourt Prize winner in 1937)? These are only a few of the now obscure names to whom Blanchot dedicates texts as long as those treating Virginia Woolf or Thomas Mann.

14. Maurice Blanchot, review of André Rousseaux, *Âmes et visages du vingtième siècle*, *La Revue Universelle* 18 (December 15, 1932): 742–745.

15. Maurice Blanchot, "Les communistes, gardiens de la culture" (25 March 1933), in *Chroniques politiques*, 97.

16. Maurice Blanchot, review of Daniel-Rops, *Deux hommes en moi*, *La Revue Universelle* 21 (February 1931): 367–368.

17. Maurice Blanchot, review of *Penser avec les mains* by Denis de Rougemont, *L'Insurgé* 3 (January 27, 1937): 5.

18. See notably the end of the reading of Ramuz, *Le garçon savoyard*: "This is also what makes admirable language such a gift in this writer who, today, through the rigor of his refusals, the purity of his innovations and through

his heightened awareness most makes us think of what could be, in the novel, the work of a new Mallarmé." *L'Insurgé* 37 (September 22, 1937): 6.

19. Maurice Blanchot, review of Rilke, *Letters to a Young Poet*, *L'Insurgé* 33 (August 25, 1937): 4; of Mann, *Joseph and His Brothers*, *L'Insurgé* 14 (April 14, 1937): 5; of Woolf, *The Waves*, in "Time and the Novel" (1937) in *Faux Pas*, trans Charlotte Mandell (Stanford: Stanford University Press, 2001), 248–251.

20. Maurice Blanchot, review of Martin du Gard, *L'Eté 1914*, *L'Insurgé* 4 (February 3, 1937): 5. Eight years was also the interval separating the beginning and the publication of *Thomas the Obscure*, another work constructed in silence.

21. Maurice Blanchot, review of Mauriac, *Journal*, *L'Insurgé* 20 (May 26, 1937): 5.

22. Blanchot, review of Rilke, *Letters to a Young Poet*. Blanchot already addressed the "impure elements of biography" and "the abolition of the writer" on December 15, 1932, in a reading of André Rousseaux, *Âmes et visages du vingtième siècle*. It is therefore one of his few points of convergence with the Surrealists. In the *Journal des Débats*, he railed against the false science of surveys, most of all surveys sent out in search of literary anecdotes, "the wish to know others' secrets," the search for intimacy and "scandalous anecdotes"; "Les faux-semblants du savoir" (February 27, 1933), 1. However, in June 1939 in a reading of Haeden's work on Nerval, he rehabilitated— already in Bataillean mode—Nerval's attempt "to give existence the necessity, the rigor, and the quality of absoluteness that befit the work of art" in "Un essai sur Gérard de Nerval," *Journal des Débats* (June 22, 1939), 2.

23. Maurice Blanchot, "Les écrivains et la politique" (July 27, 1932), in *Chroniques politiques*, 73.

24. Maurice Blanchot, review of Denis de Rougemont, *Penser avec les mains*.

25. Maurice Blanchot, "De la révolution à la littérature."

26. Blanchot distinguished between "allegory, the poison which condemns all symbolism to the most certain death" and the symbol, "the burning center of a dialectics that devours what it completes until it has brought forth from the enigma itself the light of clarity" in a reading of Claudel, *Les aventures de Sophie*, *L'Insurgé* 25 (June 30, 1937): 5.

27. Maurice Blanchot, review of Chardonne, *Romanesques*, *L'Insurgé* 9 (March 10, 1937): 6.

28. Maurice Blanchot, "Time and the Novel," reading of Mann, *Joseph and His Brothers*.

29. Maurice Blanchot, "Interior Monologue" (1937), in *Faux Pas*, 244–247.

30. Maurice Blanchot, review of Bernanos, *Nouvelle histoire de Mouchette*, *L'Insurgé* 23 (June 16, 1937): 5.

31. Maurice Blanchot, review of Daniel-Rops, *Ce qui meurt et ce qui naît*, *L'Insurgé* 12 (March 31, 1937): 5; Maurice Blanchot, review of Mazeline, *Bêtafeu*, *L'Insurgé* 11 (March 24, 1937): 5.

32. Maurice Blanchot, review of Petit, *Un homme veut rester vivant*, *L'Insurgé* 18 (May 12, 1937): 5.

33. Maurice Blanchot, review of Rougemont, *Journal d'un intellectuel au chômage*, *L'Insurgé* 32 (August 18, 1937): 4.

34. Maurice Blanchot, "Interior Monologue."

35. Maurice Blanchot, "The Beginnings of a Novel" (1938), in *The Blanchot Reader*, 33–34. For their part, Maxence and Brasillach railed against Sartre: see Annie Cohen-Solal, *Sartre* (Paris: Gallimard, 1985), 237–238. Sartre had not yet made public any political commitment, although he was close to Paul Nizan, who was a member of the Communist Party. Nonetheless, he had already come out against Mauriac's Catholic, academic, and conventionally moralistic literature.

36. Maurice Blanchot, "François Mauriac et ceux qui étaient perdus," *La Revue Française* 26 (June 28, 1931): 610–611.

37. Georges Bataille, *Inner Experience*, trans. Stuart Kendall (Albany: SUNY Press, 2014), 9.

17. MURDEROUS OMENS OF TIMES TO COME. WRITING THE *RÉCITS*:
"THE LAST WORD" AND "THE IDYLL" (1935–1936)

1. Pierre Prévost recounts that Pelorson introduced Blanchot to him as follows: "He was so acutely demanding that he had destroyed his manuscripts several times." In Pierre Prévost, *Pierre Prévost rencontre Georges Bataille* (Paris: Jean-Michel Place, 1987), 86.

2. This is if we believe Pierre Monnier, who depicts Blanchot's editorial activities at *L'Insurgé* thus: "We knew that he was writing his first book. Kléber Haedens had seen extracts from it, and told me that *Thomas the Obscure* would be a masterpiece. Guy Richelet and I, a little intimidated, used to watch Blanchot and admire him." Monnier, *A l'ombre des grandes têtes molles* (Paris: La Table Ronde, 1987), 205–206. His supposed correspondence with Drieu was that of two novelists discussing the preoccupations and certainties of their creative processes. This rare passage speaks to this correspondence: "What we need, I believe," wrote Drieu, "is for all our characters to be within the very movement of our most quotidian and our most profound reflexes, that they should be tied to our difficulties in living. They are the temperature charts of our two or three illnesses—and also of our *recoveries*" (letter of March 28, 1937). Finally, Georges Bataille would later confirm (around 1954) that "novels and tales of an excessively strange character" existed before 1940, in "Maurice Blanchot . . . ," *Gramma* 3–4 (1976): 218.

3. Maurice Blanchot, "After the Fact," in *Vicious Circles: Two Fictions and "After the Fact,"* trans. Paul Auster (Barrytown, N.Y.: Station Hill Press, 1985), 64.

4. Paul Valéry, *Monsieur Teste*, trans. Jackson Matthews (London: Peter Owen, 1951), 4–5.

5. Maurice Blanchot, "After the Fact," 64.

6. Maurice Blanchot, "The Idyll," in *Vicious Circles*, 5.

7. "At a time when you are already beginning to worry about middle age, do you know what it is like to find a young woman who has more gaiety and freshness than all the others?' Ibid., 7. This presence of parental figures is all the more worthy of attention for being very rare in Blanchot's narratives, except for *The Most High*, where the father figure is absent and replaced by a hated stepfather.

8. "The Idyll," 4.

9. "The burning of libraries will always be the calamity that foretells the death of the mind," Blanchot would write in "The Book" in *A World in Ruins: Chronicles of Intellectual Life, 1943*, trans. Michael Holland (New York: Fordham University Press, 2016), 29. "The Last Word" opens with the disappearance of the library and closes with the tower in flames.

10. Maurice Blanchot, "After the Fact," 65. "These innocent texts in which echoed the murderous omens of times to come," he would also write. Ibid., 64. It is possible to be struck in a similar way on reading poems by Robert Antelme written prior to his arrest, but which according to Daniel Dobbels provide "an unexpected form of premonition"; see Robert Antelme, *Textes inédits* (Paris: Gallimard, 1997), 52–57.

11. See in particular "L'Allemagne nouvelle ou le triomphe de la Prusse," *Le Rempart* 17 (May 8, 1933): 2.

12. For some time yet, Blanchot would continue to live this life of a journalist of the far right, which he was nonetheless beginning to disdain. He would later recognize the same paradoxical fate at work in Tocqueville: "Yet he devotes himself to this [political] life that he does not like and that is beneath him. He sacrifices his projects as a historian to it. He allows it to jeopardize his health. In order to live it, he gives up being fully what he ought to be." In "Tocqueville's *Recollections*" (1943), in *A World in Ruins*, 61.

13. Blanchot, "The Last Word," in *Vicious Circles*, 39. Citations in the rest of this chapter are taken from the three texts collected in *Vicious Circles*.

14. [*Le mot* can be translated both as *word* and as *saying* (as in a *bon mot*). —Trans.]

15. Maurice Blanchot, *The Step Not Beyond* (Albany: State University of New York Press, 1992), 57.

16. Ibid., 83.

18. NIGHT FREELY RECIRCLED, WHICH PLAYS US:
THOMAS THE OBSCURE (1932–1940)

1. Perhaps it is this indulgence that he is commenting on obliquely, in a 1947 article on Julien Gracq's "magical world," when he underlines that it might so happen that a writer could "desire to be weighty. It is perhaps necessary for him to move forward along a path that he blocks to the precise degree that he clears it" (such a way of moving forward describes that of Thomas, and even more that of Thomas in *Aminadab*). The abundance of adjectives clouds one's vision and places events at a remove. "Grève désolée, obscur malaise" (1947), in *La condition critique: Articles 1945–1998*, ed. Christophe Bident (Paris: Gallimard, 2010), 95–100. Nonetheless, we must add that from the outset Blanchot fights against this tendency, and that it is less the abundance of adjectives than the abundance of "movements" that characterizes the precision of his prose.

2. Maurice Blanchot, "Lautréamont," *Revue Française des Idées et des Oeuvres* 1 (April 1940): 67–72. This article was republished, with a few modifications, in *Faux Pas*, trans. Charlotte Mandell (Stanford: Stanford University Press, 2001), 172–176. The expression "the cancer of the French novel," for instance, does not feature in this later version.

3. Although mentioned in the apostolic lists, Thomas or Didymus (twin) only appears in the New Testament in the gospel of John. Arrogant and unbelieving, trusting touch more than sight, he would also be the only apostle to recognize Christ's divine nature, calling him "My Lord and my God" (John 20:28). In the Oxyrynchus papyrus, discovered in the third century, the Lord says to Thomas: "whoever listens to these words shall not taste death." In the *Acts of Thomas*, a Syriac text also of the third century, Thomas who in the dividing-up of the world had received India is killed with spears; but even once dead, his body continues to perform miracles. In the *Gospel of Thomas*, an apocryphal book once again of the third century (and discovered in 1947), Thomas's full name is Didymus Jude Thomas, the "twin brother" of the Lord. He would be the only one to respond correctly when Christ asks what he looks like—the answer is that he is Ungraspable, Unknowable. He is the only one who knows the secret words of Revelation.

4. Letter from Hegel to Niethammer, quoted by Jacques Derrida in *Glas, II* (Paris: Denoël-Gonthier, 1981), 247.

5. Daniel Wilhem, *Maurice Blanchot: La voix narrative* (Paris: UGE, 1974), 276; *Pierre Klossowski: Le corps impie* (Paris: UGE, 1979), 228–229.

6. Jacques Derrida, *Parages* (Paris: Galilée, 1986), 39.

7. Maurice Blanchot, *The Step Not Beyond*, trans. Lycette Nelson (Albany: State University of New York Press, 1992), 1.

8. This is the paradox of Gracchus, which repeatedly appears in Blanchot's fictional and critical work. From the 1930s, through the character of Thomas, and from the first texts on Kafka: "We do not die, it is true, but because of that we do not live either; we are dead while we are alive, we are essentially survivors"; Maurice Blanchot, "Reading Kafka" (1945), in *The Work of Fire*, trans. Charlotte Mandell (Stanford: Stanford University Press, 1995), 8, or on Lautréamont: Maldoror's "*definitive* impossibility of *having done* with things"; *Lautréamont and Sade*, trans. Stuart Kendall and Michelle Kendall (Stanford: Stanford University Press, 2004), 106.

9. [For the remainder of this chapter, references in parentheses refer to the first version of *Thomas the Obscure* (reprint, Paris: Gallimard, 2005), which is untranslated. —Trans.]

10. Drawing notably on the scene of being devoured by the rat (which Lacan would address), Frédéric Nef reads not the impossibility of contact ("fear before the threat of a mortal contact") but the presence in this literary experience "of fascination as a way of living through the phantasm"; "Le piège," *Gramma* 3–4 (1976): 71–88. There is indeed no need to prove that the novel is full of phantasmatic scenes or scenarios. The a priori concerns of any reading must surely be dialed down a notch by the idea that writing is the unfolding of such phantasms, their still-secret opening, that it investigates their movement even as it abstains from providing a single figure for it, and that is elaborated (whether through a phobic or joyful relationship to the same, through the immanence of the double, the transcendence of metamorphosis) as the unending analysis of an originary scene.

11. Maurice Blanchot, "Roman et poésie" (1941), in *Chroniques littéraires du Journal des Débats: Avril 1941–août 1944*, ed. Christophe Bident (Paris: Gallimard, 2007), 43–48.

12. Emmanuel Levinas, *Time and the Other*, trans. Richard A. Cohen (Pittsburgh: Duquesne University Press, 1987), 64.

13. René Char, "Even if . . . ," in *Poems of René Char*, trans. Mary Ann Caws and Jonathan Griffin (Princeton: Princeton University Press, 1976), 259.

19. THE UNIVERSE IS TO BE FOUND IN NIGHT: RESISTANCE (1940–1944)

The epigraph from James Joyce is cited by Maurice Blanchot in *Chroniques littéraires du Journal des Débats: Avril 1941–août 1944*, ed. Christophe Bident (Paris: Gallimard, 2007), 609.

1. See Edmond Buchet, *Les auteurs de ma vie ou ma vie d'éditeur* (Paris: Buchet-Chastel, 1969), 65.

2. Maurice Blanchot, "Lautréamont" (1940), in *Faux Pas*, trans. Charlotte Mandell (Stanford: Stanford University Press, 2001), 172–176.

3. From 1938 to 1940, Blanchot did not put his name to any texts of a political nature. But he was responsible for numerous editorials in the *Journal des Débats*, which we can identify stylistically. They regularly denounced Germanic nihilism and particularly Hitler's totalitarianism.

4. Pierre Drieu La Rochelle on May 3, 1940, in *Journal 1939–1945* (Paris: Gallimard, 1992), 180.

5. If we are to believe *Death Sentence*, 1940 was a year of pain. In any case, what Blanchot's narrative states regarding his shock corroborates the accounts we have heard. See *The Station Hill Blanchot Reader*, ed. George Quasha (Barrytown, N.Y.: Station Hill Press, 1998), 131.

6. When exactly? It is not impossible that Blanchot could have written until mid-October the daily "Letter from Clermont" on the front page of the *Journal des Débats*. The author of this column did not forgo praising, at first moderately and then clearly under external pressure, the regime and the figure of Marshal Pétain. Brought to heel from the outset—as sometimes he contradicted his own writing from the previous day—for a certain period this author set out to justify each government measure historically and ideologically.

7. Another question must be asked: to when is the religious "transformation of convictions," the abandonment of faith, to be dated? Did it not give rise to a more radical rupture? Had it already taken place around 1937 or 1938? Was there, would there ever be anything like Pascal's night, but in inverse form? Can we not see this night, charged with the return of the "primal scene," in the dedication to Lignac? Did the *death sentence*, providing the unbearable image of a corpse left to rot, "remove this man's faith" like the Holbein painting that so astonished Prince Myshkin?

8. "Private assistance for the middle class continues to fulfill a task in which it cannot be replaced. It alone reaches the social categories that official aid cannot, because the poverty they suffer is a hidden poverty. It has its own methods, tried and tested through long experience. It intervenes when necessary and its intervention is like the concern of a friend," in M. Bl., "Une oeuvre à sauver," *Journal des Débats* (June 5, 1941), 1. This text is not included in *Into Disaster: Chronicles of Intellectual Life, 1941*, trans. Michael Holland (New York: Fordham University Press, 2014).

9. Paul Lévy, *Journal d'un exilé* (Paris: Grasset, 1949), 29–30.

10. See Emmanuel Levinas in François Poirié, *Emmanuel Levinas*, 2nd ed. (1987; reprint, Besançon: La Manufacture, 1992), 59; Maire-Anne Lescourret, *Emmanuel Levinas* (Paris: Flammarion, 1994), 121–122, 138; Maurice Blanchot, "Do Not Forget" (1988), in *Political Writings, 1953–1993*, trans. Zakir Paul (New York: Fordham University Press, 2010), 124; and a reader's letter in *Le Monde* signed Simone Hansel, née Levinas, "J'ai lu votre article . . ." (December 1–2, 1996), 10.

11. See also Roger Laporte, *Maurice Blanchot: L'ancien, l'effroyablement ancien* (Montpellier: Fata Morgana, 1987), 56. Claude Roy even places Blanchot, as early as the war, among former right-wing extremists now "close to the Communist Party," in *Moi je* (Paris: Gallimard, 1969), 200.

12. Quain was in the so-called free zone, around 25 miles (40 km) to the west of the demarcation line and around 60 miles (100 km) from the Swiss border.

13. Maurice Blanchot, *Intellectuals Under Scrutiny* (1984) in *The Blanchot Reader*, ed. Michael Holland (Oxford: Blackwell, 1995), 222.

14. Jacques Derrida, *Politics of Friendship*, trans. George Collins (London: Verso, 1997), 148.

20. USING VICHY AGAINST VICHY: JEUNE FRANCE (1941–1942)

1. Regarding Jeune France, the reader is referred to Pierre Prévost, *Pierre Prévost rencontre Georges Bataille* (Paris: Jean-Michel Place, 1987); Pierre Schaeffer, *Les antennes de Jéricho* (Paris: Stock, 1978); Véronique Chabrol, "Jeune France: Une expérience de recherche et de décentralisation culturelle" (PhD thesis, Université de Paris, Institut d'Etudes Théâtrales, Bibliothèque Gaston-Baty, June 1974). (Véronique Chabrol is Paul Flamand's daughter.) See also Serge Added's book on *Le théâtre dans les années Vichy* (Paris: Ramsay, 1992). We owe a lot to interviews with Jean Bazaine, Louis Ollivier, and above all Xavier de Lignac, who lent us precious archives. The chapter that Marc Fumaroli dedicates to Jeune France in *L'etat culturel: Une religion moderne* (Paris: Librairie Générale Française, 1992) ascribes too much importance to the ideological and strategic role played by Mounier (for whom Jeune France was a "working tool" whose "soul" was provided by the team from Esprit). Fumaroli does not mention the existence of a faction that was radically opposed to that of Flamand or Schaeffer, namely that of Lignac and Blanchot, who, as we shall see, would provoke the breakup of Jeune France in 1942.

2. The publisher Edmond Buchet confirms this, but in different terms: "A few days ago, Maurice Blanchot took me to an exhibition of young painters that he is praising. I was not able to hide my disappointment from him. How could a mind as sharp as his be duped by such mediocrity? It is true that he is literary above all else"; note of December 5, 1942, in *Les auteurs de ma vie ou ma vie d'éditeur* (Paris: Buchet-Chastel, 1969), 91–92. This taste was not new. In the 1930s, he was interested in surrealism. Pierre Roy, the only contemporary painter mentioned in the first version of *Thomas the Obscure* (Paris: Gallimard, 2005), 205, alongside Da Vinci and Titian, belonged to this movement. He is known for his trompe-l'oeil pictures.

3. Blanchot would admit: "The situation was too ambiguous. Jeune France, which had been founded by unknown musicians who would later

become famous, was subsidized by Vichy, and our naïve project to use this association against Vichy . . . failed because of this contradiction," in *For Friendship* (1993) in *Political Writings*, trans. Zakir Paul (New York: Fordham University Press, 2010), 135.

21. ADMIRATION AND AGREEMENT: MEETING GEORGES BATAILLE (1940–1943)

1. Maurice Blanchot, "The Play of Thought," in *The Infinite Conversation*, trans. Susan Hanson (Minneapolis: University of Minnesota Press, 1993), 212–213. Another singular similarity is demonstrated by the 1944 portrait of Bataille by Henri-François Rey, which seems to retain only those characteristics which could also be attributed to Blanchot: "a very handsome face, a quiet voice, a very abstract way of moving in space, both absent and present at the very same time. . . . He was the most fascinating man I have ever met, who had his mysteries, his ambiguities and his contradictions. I have never seen or experienced the existence of a being who unceasingly pursued the same quest, that for the absolute, which so much sheer passion, so much suffering and unhappiness, so many hopes and doubts" in *Le Magazine Littéraire* 44 (January 1979): 58.

2. Georges Bataille, *Inner Experience*, trans. Stuart Kendall (Albany: SUNY Press, 2014), 104.

3. Letter from Maurice Blanchot to Georges Bataille, May 9 (1961?), quoted in Georges Bataille, *Choix de lettres*, ed. Michel Surya (Paris: Gallimard, 1997), 594.

4. Maurice Blanchot, *Intellectuals Under Scrutiny* (1984) in *The Blanchot Reader*, ed. Michael Holland (Oxford: Blackwell, 1995), 226. Bataille presents the encounter as follows: "At the end of 1940, he met Maurice Blanchot, to whom he soon became linked through admiration and agreement." In "Notice autobiographique," in *Oeuvres complètes* (Paris: Gallimard, 1976), 7:462. Everything or almost everything it is possible to say about the relationship between Blanchot and Bataille has been said in Michel Surya's biography, to which we refer the reader: *Georges Bataille: An Intellectual Biography*, trans. Krysztof Fijalkowski and Michael Richardson (New York: Verso, 2002).

5. We can note that due to their multiple acquaintances, Bataille and Blanchot could have met earlier. Drieu frequented the Collège de Sociologie; Denis de Rougement spoke there. Pelorson edited a journal, *Volontés*, to which Queneau was a regular contributor. Denis Hollier also remarks, "Curiously, the first time the names of Blanchot and Bataille were associated was in 1938, without either of them knowing about it, in *Commune*, the communist publication whose press review was written by Sadoul. Sadoul took apart in a very insulting way the dossier by the Collège de Sociologie from the July 1938

Nouvelle Revue Française, before moving—without a pause—on to a detailed denunciation of a long Blanchot article from *Combat*, the far-right newspaper of the era." Denis Hollier, in *Art Press* 204 (July–August 1995): 47–48.

6. Georges Bataille, *Guilty*, trans. Stuart Kendall (Albany: SUNY Press, 2011), 10.

7. Ibid., 97.

8. Bataille met Blanchot at the end of 1940. He contracted pulmonary tuberculosis in 1942. Later, in 1955, he was doomed by cerebral arteriosclerosis: he would suffer more and more intensely over the final seven years of his life.

9. Bataille, *Guilty*, 28. [In this and the following quotation, the switching between tenses is Bataille's own. —Trans.]

10. Ibid., 15.

11. Ibid., 4. Blanchot would return to this phrase in the homage paid to Bataille after his death in *Critique*. This fear is clearly what enabled their immediate understanding. It is a shared, physical, concrete, oral fear; it is the fear to which their dialogue leads them, not a dialogue of construction, confrontation, or contestation, but a movement at once resolute and uncertain, a cavernous and spoken word, "a neutral, infinite, powerless speech, where the limitlessness of thought . . . is at stake," "it is thought itself that is put at stake by calling upon us to sustain, and in the direction of the unknown, the limitlessness of this play." Thus "between two men speaking, bound by what is essential, the nonfamiliar intimacy of thought establishes a boundless distance and proximity. . . . Relations that are strange, privileged, sometimes exclusive, and that can only with difficulty withstand being shared with others; relations of invisibility in full light that are guaranteed by nothing and which, when they have endured over a lifetime, represent the unforeseeable chance, the unique chance in view of which they were risked." *The Infinite Conversation*, 215–217.

12. Bataille himself would underline how close the three men's thinking was: "Levinas's thinking . . . did not seem to me to differ from that of Blanchot or from my own." "L'existentialisme au primat de l'économie" (1947), in *Oeuvres complètes* (Paris: Gallimard, 1979), 9:293. Even before the war, Levinas must have read passages of *Thomas the Obscure* and must have recognized in it what he and Blanchot had lived through and thought together in Strasbourg, which he named the *there is*; between the submission and publication of the book, Bataille must also have read it and have seen in it the demand of experience (he quotes a long section of the second chapter in *Inner Experience*). After the Liberation, Levinas published *Existence and Existents*, in which he refers to the same chapter, which he sees as an admirable description of the *there is*; trans. Alphonso Lingis (The Hague: Martinus Nijhoff, 1978), 63. For Bataille,

the word "description" "is not wholly just: Levinas describes and Blanchot somehow cries the *there is*. . . . Levinas describes as an object, through a formal generalization (in other words through *discourse*) what, in Blanchot's *literary* text, is the pure cry of an existence." "L'existentialisme au primat de l'économie," 292–294. In this article, Bataille calls into question whether discourse can be external to experience, in Levinas as in all existentialists and in almost all philosophers. Nonetheless, he recognizes that Levinas "retains to some degree the quality of a cry in his writing." Finally, we can recall the "incident" whereby Heidegger, referring to the person he thought to be "the best French mind" confused Bataille and Blanchot; see Georges Bataille, *Choix de lettres*, ed. Michel Surya (Paris: Gallimard, 1997), 582.

13. Bataille's expression quoted by Blanchot in the epigraph to *Friendship*, trans. Elizabeth Rottenberg (Stanford: Stanford University Press, 1997).

14. "Now, 'the basis of communication' is not necessarily speech, or even the silence that is its foundation and punctuation, but exposure to death, no longer my own exposure, but someone else's, whose living and closest presence is already eternal and unbearable absence, an absence that the work of deepest mourning does not diminish. And it is in life itself that the absence of someone else has to be met; it is with that absence . . . that friendship is brought into play and lost at each moment, a relation without relation or without relation other than the incommensurable." *The Unavowable Community*, trans. Pierre Joris (Barrytown, N.Y.: Station Hill Press, 1988), 25. "The community of friendship, with Blanchot, would no more be founded on this specular similarity, but on the necessary, definitive dissimilitude into which its death causes me to enter." Michel Surya, "Les hommes mortels et l'amitié," *Lignes* 11 (September 1990): 69.

15. The metaphor is Blake's in *The Marriage of Heaven and Earth*. Bataille would also say that "one must be a god in order to die." *Inner Experience*, 75.

16. Blanchot believes, and there seems to be no doubt about this, that he was "one of the first" to read *Madame Edwarda*, a *récit* written by Bataille in September–October 1941.

17. See Jean-Luc Nancy, *The Inoperative Community*, trans. Peter Connor, Lisa Garbus, Michael Holland, and Simona Sawhney (Minneapolis: University of Minnesota Press, 1991). "I have seen too many things and I have suffered too much to bother myself with what does not cause major problems for our everyday understanding. I no longer know—or no longer am—anything but an unlimited force of negation that divinizes everything I have not emptied of meaning. And to divinize for me also means to 'empty of meaning.' It is difficult to imagine how silent I have become, so much so that I tell myself that any word would break if it touched me (it would either fall apart or become so comical that the sentence could only finish with an outburst of

laughter). As for the rest: I am walking oddly, as gaily as ever and if I slip, I hold the rope of silence." Letter of February 3, 1942, from Georges Bataille to André Masson in *Choix de lettres*, 179.

18. Jacques Derrida, *Politics of Friendship* (London: Verso, 1997), 10.

19. "Aimer *avant* d'être aimé," ibid., 291.

20. Ibid., 296. "These two are not in solidarity with one another (*solidaires*); they are solitary (*solitaires*), but they ally themselves in silence within the necessity of keeping silent together—each, however, in his own corner." Ibid., 54–55.

21. Blanchot, *The Unavowable Community*, 24.

22. This exception of belonging to two groups, alongside Bataille, recalls the similar case of Breton in the Marat and Sade groups of *Contre-Attaque*. Authority and recognition had their obligations.

23. Pierre Prévost, *Pierre Prévost rencontre Georges Bataille* (Paris: Jean-Michel Place, 1987), 102.

24. Michel Fardoulis-Lagrange, "Le Collège socratique," unpublished text of May 27, 1987, read at the Collège de Philosophie.

25. Bataille, *Inner Experience*, 14, 104, 19. In a letter of January 31, 1962, to Jérôme Lindon, he wrote: "I shall then declare that the impossible is literature, and that one cannot grasp the meaning of literature without seeing this. But above all, philosophy is the meaning of the impossible, though philosophy insofar as it is the impossible ceases to have anything in common with the dominant formal philosophy. In this sense, the impossible is better stated by Blanchot and me. Blanchot has written on Sade. Myself." *Choix de lettres*, 582.

26. What Bataille states about his and Blanchot's positions regarding a book by Alexandre Marc, in 1946, nicely reflects what could be said about all their positions: "You know what Blanchot thinks: I would gladly think it too, if I did not see that it risks being impossible. But above all I *fundamentally* think what Blanchot thinks." *Choix de lettres*, 283.

27. Letter from Maurice Blanchot to Dionys Mascolo, September 1966.

28. Michel Surya has found in "La folie de Nietzsche," a 1939 text, this phrase by Bataille: "the very love of life and of fate means that from the outset he himself commits the crime of authority which he would atone for [*expiera*]." *Georges Bataille: An Intellectual Biography*, 317.

29. Whether these statements were "philosophical" or literary, they addressed as in Blanchot's writing the essence of the *récit*, of its power and its readability: "My *récit* does not live up to what one expects of a *récit*," says Charles C.; "If I say what is essential about it, if I allow it to be understood, if I speak about it—it is ultimately only in order to leave it all the more in shadow" in *L'Abbé C.* in *Oeuvres complètes*, 3:338–339. This recalls the moments in which the reader is addressed (in the epigraph and the final

note) in *The Most High* or in *Death Sentence*, which were both published two years later.

30. See the text of Georges Didi-Huberman, *La ressemblance informe* (Paris: Macula, 1995), notably 216–252.

31. In a letter to the Gallimard publishing house of December 29, 1948, Bataille announced the existence of a book named *Maurice Blanchot and Existentialism*. Subsequent projects tended to take the form of long chapters as part of larger ensembles rather than that of books. In March 1950, Bataille wrote to Queneau in order to inform him of a vast project named *The Atheological Summa*, including republished and new texts. In it, *Maurice Blanchot* appeared after *History of a Secret Society*, in the second part of the *Summa* named *Friendship*. In 1958, in an overarching plan for *Pure Happiness*, he intended to add *Alleluiah* and *The Narratives of Maurice Blanchot* to *Guilty*, in the same section of the *Summa*; see *Oeuvres complètes*, 6:361–364; 7:610; 12:645. Blanchot was something like the impossible authority of the *Summa*. Instead of remarking on this, Bataille would eventually settle on ... an epigraph. *Oeuvres complètes*, 8:582.

32. Maurice Blanchot, *The Step Not Beyond*, trans. Lycette Nelson (Albany: State University of New York Press, 1992), 1.

33. Georges Bataille, "Collège socratique," in *Oeuvres complètes*, 6:279–291.

34. Blanchot, *The Unavowable Community*, 18.

35. Maurice Blanchot, "After the Fact," in *The Station Hill Blanchot Reader*, ed. George Quasha (Barrytown, N.Y.: Station Hill Press, 1998); Georges Bataille, "Maurice Blanchot ... ," *Gramma* 3–4 (1976): 220.

22. IN THE NAME OF THE OTHER: LITERARY CHRONICLES
AT THE *JOURNAL DES DÉBATS* (1941–1944)

1. [*Chroniques* can be translated as either "chronicles" or "column." In this chapter I have largely chosen the former in order to align with the recent, multivolume translation of these texts. —Trans.]

2. Blanchot's column, which became shorter in 1944 because of difficulties in paper supply that forced the newspaper to reduce its length, stopped in the penultimate issue of August 17. The newspaper had become more and more favorable to Pétain and to Hitler. In June 1944, it did not run headlines on the "Anglo-American" landings (i.e., foreign, enemy landings) or on the actions of "the ex-General de Gaulle," instead choosing to focus its coverage on the reactions of Marshal Pétain and Prime Minister Laval. The accounts given of the operations were favorable to the Nazi troops. The newspaper definitively ceased publication in the midst of the fighting for the liberation of Paris.

3. "The habitual critic is a sovereign who avoids immolation, claiming to exercise authority without atoning for it [*l'expier*] and to be the ruler of a

kingdom over which he rules without danger. There is no more poorer sovereign than this, and none who—because he has not refused to be something—is in fact closer to being nothing." Maurice Blanchot, "Le mystère de la critique" (1944), in *Chroniques littéraires du Journal des Débats: Avril 1941–août 1944*, ed. Christophe Bident (Paris: Gallimard, 2007), 533–536.

4. Blanchot asked himself this question apropos of a novel by Raymond Dumay, *L'herbe pousse dans la prairie*, which he addressed in one of his first articles: "Whence then does the pleasure it provides originate? Quite clearly, from the hum of idleness and musing, the murmur of lazy absent-mindedness that rises faintly from the meadows, woods, and water." In *Into Disaster: Chronicles of Intellectual Life, 1941*, trans. Michael Holland (New York: Fordham University Press, 2014), 25. In one way or another, this type of reading must also have been *imposed* on Blanchot: by the editors of the newspaper, by the need to make concessions to his readers, by the dizzying lack of awareness, by the wish for respite, for humor, or for freshness.

5. Maurice Blanchot, "Charles Cros" (1944), in *Chroniques littéraires*, 618–622.

6. Maurice Blanchot, "Tales and Stories" (1942), in *Desperate Clarity: Chronicles of Intellectual Life, 1942*, trans. Michael Holland (New York: Fordham University Press, 2013), 32.

7. Claude Roy, *Moi je* (Paris: Gallimard, 1969), 408.

8. Maurice Blanchot, "Fils de personne" (1944), in *Chroniques littéraires*, 660–663.

9. It would be interesting to read more precisely into the respective influence of these authors in the forming of Blanchot's judgment. The genesis of Blanchot's readings is still to be established, notably these 1930s readings, which come into the open at this stage. It is often (too often) said that he had read everything. He did read an enormous amount, and not only Kafka or Mallarmé; no one has yet determined how influential the silenced voices of Giraudoux or Valéry were for him (whether he admired or rejected them). Such a reading would perhaps allow Blanchot to be seen, as if in a mirror, as a critical memory of the century's literary history.

10. In *Faux pas*, the superlatives on Péguy disappear, either because the article in question was not collected (as with "Chronicle of Intellectual Life II" (1941), now available in *Into Disaster*, 18–22), or because less extreme expressions are used: "overbrimming purity and ripe inspiration, of which there is no greater example" becomes "a kind of pure tranquility and the calm concern of his salvation," in *Faux Pas*, trans. Charlotte Mandell (Stanford: Stanford University Press, 2001), 282. Regarding Claudel, "what is divine in his own mind" became "what is 'divine' in his own mind" (ibid., 295), the inverted commas setting the lyrical judgment at a distance and likening it to a metaphor that can be found in Bataille. Numerous references to the thought

and the work of Giraudoux disappear from the articles in *Faux Pas*; see also the articles from which the quotations in the text are taken: "The Art of Montesquieu" (1941), in *Into Disaster*, 34–39; "The Man in a Hurry," ibid., 119–124; "Charles-Louis Philippe" (17 February 1943), in *A World in Ruins: Chronicles of Intellectual Life, 1943*, trans. Michael Holland (New York: Fordham University Press, 2016), 45.

11. Blanchot, *Faux Pas*, 55.

12. [In the English version of *Faux pas*, the chapter entitled "Le jeune roman" is rendered as "The New Novel." —Trans.]

13. Maurice Blanchot, "Chronicle of Intellectual Life 1" (1941), in *Into Disaster*, 8–12; "The Writers' Silence" (1941), ibid., 13–17.

14. Blanchot would take sides just as openly in an article of September 1941 against the theater policy of Vichy and Jeune France, which was said to be "a dangerous temptation, aimed at luring the artist away from his essential vocation" and distorting the theatrical act, reducing it in a crude and artificial way to what appeared to be "an unrivaled means of creating unity" in "Theater and the Public" (1941), in *Into Disaster*, 82–87, at 87.

15. Maurice Blanchot, "The Search for Tradition" (1941), in *Into Disaster*, 41–45, at 45.

16. Maurice Blanchot, "The Writer and the Public" (1941), ibid., 107–112.

17. Maurice Blanchot, "The New Novel" (1941), in *Faux Pas*, 183–186; see also "The Enigma of the Novel" (1942), ibid., 187–191, and "The Angel of the Bizarre" (1941), ibid., 222–226.

18. Maurice Blanchot, "Mythological Novels" (1942), ibid., 196.

19. Maurice Blanchot, "The Angel of the Bizarre," in ibid., 224.

20. Maurice Blanchot, "The Misfortunes of Duranty" (1942), in *Desperate Clarity*, 84.

21. Jean Paulhan, *The Flower of Tarbes or, Terror in Literature*, trans. Michael Syrotinski (Urbana: University of Illinois Press, 2006), 91–92.

22. Ibid., 24.

23. The opening of Laurent Jenny's book *La terreur et les signes* is thus very Blanchotian: "The space of expression, which cannot be reconciled with itself, is the space of terror." *La terreur et les signes* (Paris: Gallimard, 1982), 11. In the period in question, this irreconcilability denotes the impossible for Bataille and Blanchot. The subsequent inevitability of Terror and its status as "*a regulated violence*" (20) are the starting points for the movement that directed Blanchot toward language; he would submit it once again to an infinite contestation, whose various critical movements bear the names of Mallarmé, Sade, and Lautréamont.

24. Maurice Blanchot, "How Is Literature Possible?" (1941), in *Faux Pas*, 76–84.

25. We must also note the role played by Brice Parain, who provides an intermediate point between Paulhan and Mallarmé. "As Brice Parain writes in a remarkable formulation about invention in language, it is not the object that gives the sign its meaning, but the sign that imposes on us the necessity of finding an object for its meaning" in "Studies on Language" (1943), ibid., 87. This justifies anew the law of inner necessity and opens the path to the conception of language autonomously creating a universe. Parain, Mallarmé, and Valéry allow Blanchot to recognize the specificity of poetic language: "to communicate silence through words and to express freedom through rules," "to be evoked as having been destroyed by the circumstances which make it what it is"; ibid., 90. Blanchot would often cite—either directly or allusively—an expression by Valéry which must have been the object of debate between him and Bataille: "poetry is the attempt . . . to reconstitute via the means of articulated language these things or this thing which cries, tears, embraces, sighs obscurely try to express."

26. Maurice Blanchot, "The Secret of Melville" (1941), ibid., 240.

27. Maurice Blanchot, "Is Mallarmé's Poetry Obscure?" (1942), ibid., 109.

28. 28 Maurice Blanchot, "After Rimbaud" (1943), ibid., 145.

29. Maurice Blanchot, "De Jean-Paul à Giraudoux" (1944), in *Chroniques littéraires*, 548–552. See also "The Pure Novel" (1943), in *A World in Ruins*, 262–268.

30. Maurice Blanchot, "Mallarmé and the Art of the Novel" (1943), in *Faux Pas*, 165–171. "We dream of a writer, a symbol of purity and pride, who would be for the novel what Mallarmé was for poetry, and we glimpse the work that this poet wanted to make into an equivalent of the absolute. But how are we to feed such a dream?" In "The New Novel," 186. Blanchot dreamed that he was this impossible writer.

31. Maurice Blanchot, "On Hindu Thought" (1942), ibid., 36.

32. Maurice Blanchot, "Reflections on the New Poetry" (1942), ibid., 128–131.

33. Maurice Blanchot, "Master Eckhart" (1942), ibid., 23–27; "On the Subject of *The Fruits of the Earth*" (1942), ibid., 296–300; "The Myth of Sisyphus" (1942), ibid., 53–58. In the same period, in two articles of late November and early December, the first two references to the myth of Orpheus in Blanchot's critical work can be found. It was also at the end of 1942 that the military and political situation became clearer: the Allies landed in Algeria on November 8, the Germans invaded the free zone on November 11.

34. Maurice Blanchot, "On the Subject of *Fruits of the Earth*," 296–297. What Blanchot says about the essay, beginning with Montaigne (an essayist who did not shy away from self-portraiture), can be applied to any of his pieces: "the essay is above all the effort of a mind that goes from personal

secrets to thoughts, from the concrete to the abstract, and that offers itself as an example in order to go beyond itself. The essay is an endeavor that is focused less on the subject it is concerned with, Corneille or his style, than on the author who is in search of himself through writing it, and wants to discover himself there in the most general form possible. It is an experience during which, sometimes indirectly, the writer does not only become involved, but opens himself up to dispute, presents himself as a problem, leads his ideas to a point where he is rejected by them, derives from his personal ordeals a meaning that is acceptable to everyone, in short, makes himself the hero of an adventures whose significance lies beyond him." In "Mediterranean Inspirations" (1941), in *Into Disaster*, 88–93, at 89. Writing is thus a continuation of *inner experience* (it will have been noted that the same language is at work), where the writer only locates the other and himself in order to lose himself and to give himself over to the others, the readers, the invisible partners of the written work.

35. For example, a passage on landscapes and beings in Bosco seems to be a description of *Thomas the Obscure*: "It seems that a mysterious hand has withdrawn from the trees, the houses and the marshes the physical appearance that they usually take on for us, and instead reveals them as they really are, sites of pure mind [*esprit*], fields where light itself can be perceived, regions that are bizarrely conscious of the gaze that contemplates them and of the thought that penetrates them. There, [mankind] compares itself to emptiness, to absence, to the perpetual exhaustion that is its ultimate fate. Without rest, without consolation, it detaches itself from all that appears. It goes to the most intimate part of itself, having no object save waiting and only finding in this waiting the expression of a frivolous fatedness." In "Birth of a Myth," in *Faux Pas*, 195; the article was written in June 1941. Again regarding Bosco, the following sentences evoke *Aminadab*, which was being finished at the time: "We have abandoned the universe of abstract forms where we truly seem to touch the order of profound things. However, we are not in the mystery of the banal world, since the reality we enter remains distant and extraordinary" (194), and this: The beings who come and go "seek the unique image of which they are a distant reflection. They try to rediscover the radiant meaning that is their true life through a rigorous series of experiences," 195. This research is mentioned only in order to then say immediately that Bosco has not succeeded in it, thus raising the possibility of another novel. And as early as May 1941, we read this which evokes the narrator of *The Most High*: "A yearning for prison, a familiarity with solitude, an unease when confronted with anonymous crowds, a need to live a dutiful life as if one were above the world: these are all products of the anxiety in which everyone has lived and sometimes continues to live" in "Chronicle of Intellectual Life II" (1941), in *Into Disaster*, 22.

36. Maurice Blanchot, "The Silence of Mallarmé" (1942), in *Faux Pas*, 99–102.
37. Maurice Blanchot, "Goethe and Eckermann" (1941), ibid., 270. In the name of such demands, Blanchot showed his anger at a biography of Rimbaud by Pierre Arnoult, inventing scenes "to make him come alive," distorting the poems, amalgamating them into the overall story, etc.; "Après Rimbaud" in *Journal des Débats* (September 15, 1943), 2, in a passage not retained in *Faux pas*.
38. Maurice Blanchot, "Molière" (1942), in *Faux Pas*, 259.
39. Maurice Blanchot, "An Edition of *Flowers of Evil*" (1942), ibid., 157.
40. Maurice Blanchot, "The Silence of Mallarmé" (1942), ibid., 101.

23. A TRUE WRITER HAS APPEARED: THE PUBLICATION AND RECEPTION OF *THOMAS THE OBSCURE* (1941–1942)

1. Maurice Blanchot, *For Friendship* (1993), in *Political Writings, 1953–1993*, trans. Zakir Paul (New York: Fordham University Press, 2010), 136. The printer's *achevé d'imprimer* (completion of print) date for the first edition of *Thomas l'obscur* is given as September 5, 1941.
2. Letter from Jean Paulhan to Claude Roy of November 9, 1941; letter 207 in Jean Paulhan, *Choix de lettres, II: Traité des jours sombres* (Paris: Gallimard, 1992), 248. It was not Brasillach but probably Rebatet who reviewed the novel in *Je Suis Partout*: "Mr. Blanchot, who was editor-in-chief on behalf of the Jew Lévy, has made his debut in what he calls the novel, just as he previously made his debut in what he must have called a political newspaper. He brings to the task the same sort of bad faith. Indeed, in the same way that he refused to see reality in order to align himself with his employers' ethics, so he refuses to know what the art of narrating and the art of writing are about. If the reader does not give up before the end, prodigiously bored by this shapeless little book, he will have time to notice the faded influences upon it: here is some lymphatic Giraudoux, here is some bland Surrealism, here is some Rilke without poetry. These are all colorless larvae crawling through a sort of humid fog, around a Thomas who would have appeared boring twenty years ago, and who today adds to his other graces that of being as out-of-date as the Jewish art to which he lays claim. In a period where there is a crisis in the availability of paper, the publication of *Thomas the Obscure* is an affront to common sense as well as to art. It is a superb monument of pretentious imbecility—R." In *Je Suis Partout* 534 (October 18, 1941): 8.
3. Letter from Jean Paulhan to Roger Caillois, number 102, December 25, 1941, in *Correspondance Jean Paulhan-Roger Caillois, 1934–1967* (Paris: Gallimard, 1991), 147.

4. Letter from Monique Saint-Hélier to Jean Paulhan, number 49, 3 March 1942, in *Correspondance Jean Paulhan-Monique Saint-Hélier* (Paris: Gallimard, 1995), 120–122.

5. Albert Camus, *Carnets* (1942), in *Oeuvres complètes* (Paris: Gallimard, 1983), 6:221–222.

6. Thierry Mauliner, review of *Thomas the Obscure* in *L'Action Française* (January 28, 1942), 3. See also "Quelques romans," *La Revue Universelle* 30 (March 25, 1942): 464–467.

7. Marcel Arland, "Chronique des romans," *La Nouvelle Revue Française* 335 (January 1, 1942): 94.

8. August Rivet, review of *Thomas the Obscure* in *Confluences* 7 (January 1942): 103–104.

9. Jean Mousset, "Un roman de M. Blanchot, *Thomas l'obscur*," *Journal des Débats* 30 (October 1941): 2–3.

24. LIFT THIS FOG WHICH IS ALREADY OF THE DAWN:
THE PUBLICATION OF *AMINADAB* (1942)

1. Letter from Jean Paulhan to Drieu La Rochelle (January 1942); letter number 219 in Jean Paulhan, *Choix de lettres, II: Traité des jours sombres* (Paris: Gallimard, 1992), 263.

2. Georges Bataille, notes on "La religion surréaliste," in *Oeuvres complètes* (Paris: Gallimard), 7:610. Thierry Maulnier's brilliant article also insisted on the tragedy of knowledge staged by the novel, this new mythical search for the Golden Fleece or Grail; review of *Aminadab* in *L'Action Française* (November 26, 1942), 3.

3. Albert Camus, *Carnets* (1942), in *Oeuvres complètes* (Paris: Gallimard, 1983), 6:222.

4. Ultimately, this is what Sartre could not stand, writing as he did in 1943 in the *Cahiers du Sud* two powerful articles against Bataille and Blanchot: "Un nouveau mystique" and "*Aminadab* ou du fantastique considéré comme un langage," collected in *Situations I* (Paris: Gallimard, 1947). Beyond Bataille's influence, on which he says nothing, he criticizes the "extraordinary resemblance [of *Aminadab*] to the novels of Kafka." Blanchot is thus said to have established a "cliché of the fantastic 'à la Kafka.'" The two criticisms rely heavily on each other: Although they seem to address fairly different literary questions, they end up denouncing the two books' archaicism, artificiality, and mystification. Regarding Blanchot, Sartre is not wholly wrong in underlining the similarity with Kafka; but the reflex of attributing the narrative to a "world turned upside down" reduces and constrains the reading to nothing more than an imitation of every reading of Kafka. After the war, Maurice Nadeau would say both how exact and how limited Sartre's criticism

was: "He placed himself as a 'consciousness' before another consciousness: that of the novelist." *Le roman français depuis la guerre*, new ed. (Paris: Gallimard, 1992), 75. Sartre's positioning makes him both closed to Blanchot and Bataille's work and mockingly heretical toward them. He sets in opposition transcendence and immanence, limits his interest to the reader's relation to the character (an upside-down character who in an upside-down world could only appear the right way up), criticizes Blanchot for not having chosen between identifying with or distancing himself from Thomas, and carries out a literary investigation that does not fully suit his aims. In all of these ways, Sartre closes down his reading of the narrative at the point where it begins to be interesting: the reversals in the status of the body and in the interpretative positions.

We must also recall that Sartre's critical intervention was part of his strategy of eliminating potential rivals on the intellectual scene; see Anna Boschetti, *Sartre et 'Les Temps Modernes': Une entreprise intellectuelle* (Paris: Minuit, 1985), 18–19, 53, 176–177, which interestingly outlines his strategies, despite making multiple mistakes of judgment regarding authors. In this light, it is necessary to consider the following points:

> Blanchot was the first to publicly express a "judgment" on Sartre in *Aux écoutes*, and the mixture of negatives and positives in this judgment was returned to him with an additional touch of irony and severity, sometimes even word for word (the alignment with the fantastic replaced that with the mythical; the overreliance on Heidegger became an overreliance on Kafka; where the undertaking had been called "imperfect," the mode of writing was now "uncertain"; whereas one writer had been said to lack rigor and to conform to the "usages" of "habitual psychology," the other "only had to find his own style" in order not to remain limited to "some banal ideas on human life"). Sartre replied by taking things apart more violently and a little less briefly; at the beginning—with a touch that only *appeared* to be anodyne—he recalled Blanchot's Maurrasian origins (this was 1943). At the end of his article, and more seriously because it was not without slander, he began the much later tradition of forced readings of Blanchot's narratives in light of his extreme right-wing activities by evoking his "transcendence tainted with Maurrassism." Leiris would tell Sartre how harsh this was (as he would confide in a letter to Bataille on July 6, 1943).
>
> In May 1941, Blanchot produced another unfavorable judgment on Sartre's novel writing by placing it, alongside Bernanos and Drieu, among the disappointments of the French novel, which was said to be too conventional in its desire for change. "They have used up as

much energy trying to conform to novelistic habits as they would have creating new ones. They have done violence to themselves and, having desired much less than they could have accomplished, they have ended up exchanging themselves for more modest authors." "Le Jeune roman," *Journal des Débats* (May 14, 1941), 3. The whole passage can be found in "The New Novel" in *Faux Pas*, trans. Charlotte Mandell (Stanford: Stanford University Press, 2001), 186, but lacking the direct references to the names of the authors discussed. We should add that in the meantime, Sartre had published his article.

Blanchot, like Bataille, would always see Sartre as too moderate, and even in the largely laudatory article on *The Flies* in July 1943 would conclude on the mediocrity of the world of the gods as depicted by Sartre; in "The Myth of Orestes," in *Faux Pas*, 63–64. Moreover, Blanchot confesses to Bataille by letter that this praise was strategic in the first instance, a reply to the generally "discouraging" criticism that had greeted the play: "I therefore decided to discuss it while silencing my reservations." We can imagine that there must have been many of the latter.

In October 1945, Blanchot gave a very positive view of *Nausea* (see "The Novels of Sartre," in *The Work of Fire*, trans. Charlotte Mandell [Stanford: Stanford University Press, 1995], 196), just as he would in July 1946 on the entirety of Sartre's novels (see "Translated from . . ." in ibid., 187). But in March 1947 his piece in *L'Arche* on the Baudelaire book, which followed Bataille's piece in *Critique* (January–February), and then at the end of the year several passages in "Literature and the Right to Death," would be extremely harsh. Sartre would nonetheless publish a Blanchot text on Sade in *Les Temps Modernes* in October 1947.

Blanchot refused the existential, secretly nihilist, and paradoxically cathartic goals (*finalité*) of Sartre's criticism. Thus in October 1953 he would be fairly reticent regarding *Saint Genet* (see "Where Now? Who Now?" in *The Book to Come*, trans. Charlotte Mandell [Stanford: Stanford University Press, 2003], 210–217), in which Sartre cited him as a Mallarmean advocate for Being's unavoidable reduction to nothingness in language. Something of the two men's lack of understanding can be found here, just as it can in the gap between their positions on the "act" or the "versions" of the imaginary.

5. Aminadab is also the name of two biblical characters with minor roles. One is Aaron's father-in-law (Exodus 6:23), and the other belongs to David's line (Luke 3:33). He is also a demon discussed by the *Spiritual Canticle* of St. John of the Cross. As the shadowy, voiceless, and faceless guardian

of subterranean spaces, the character in Blanchot's narrative appears only in the course of a single conversation at the end of the narrative: Maurice Blanchot, *Aminadab*, trans. Jeff Fort (Lincoln: University of Nebraska Press, 2002), 145. We can also add that in Arabic *Adab* refers to a discursive and humorous literary genre, which grew with the expansion of the Islamic empire and evokes the diversity of peoples and culture. Last, Michael Holland looks at the importance of a Nathaniel Hawthorne tale, *The Birth-Mark*, in which a character named Aminadab appears in "La marque de naissance" (1998), in *Avant-dire: Essais sur Blanchot* (Paris: Hermann, 2015), 381–386.

6. Joë Bousquet, "Maurice Blanchot," collected in *Maurice Blanchot/Joë Bousquet* (Montpellier: Fata Morgana, 1987), 47.

7. This quotation and the one that closes the paragraph in the main text are taken from several passages in *Guilty* in which Bataille refers to the ending of *Aminadab*: *Guilty*, trans. Stuart Kendall (Albany: SUNY Press, 2011), 216 n., 71–72, 221 n., 126. He would also quote the novel in the epigraph to *The History of Eroticism*: "Soon we'll be united for good. I'll lie down and take you in my arms. I'll roll with you in the midst of great secrets. We'll lose ourselves, and find ourselves again. Nothing will come between us any more. How unfortunate that you won't be present for this happiness!" *Aminadab*, quoted in *The Accursed Share: An Essay on General Economy*, trans. Robert Hurley (New York: Zone Books, 1991), 13. We can see all that proved attractive to Bataille here, between death and *jouissance*, immanence and transcendence. What is more, he was not the only one to be marked by this ending: Michel Leiris was too—he wrote about it in a letter of July 6, 1943. Where Bataille saw "feverish humor," Leiris read "sinister joking," which recalled "the gaiety of Socrates as he lay dying."

8. Maurice Blanchot, "Encountering the Imaginary" (July 1954), in *The Book to Come*, 9–10.

9. Blanchot, *Aminadab*, 68. Thus, once again, Thomas is unable to name the beings and things that surround him; he is constantly on the lookout for signs. He does not know whether a person he encounters should be addressed as a staff member (ibid., 71, 143), he hears "poorly" the answers he is given (a paucity of meaning: what does "free" mean, he asks himself, when I am told that I am free even though I am being chained up? [24]). Citations in the rest of this chapter are taken from *Aminadab* unless otherwise stated.

10. This "syntactical torsion and twisting" is the object of Derrida's analyses in "Pas," in *Parages* (Paris: Galilée, 1986), 33. Derrida was probably the first to be so attentive to Blanchot's syntax, notably to the paradoxical links of the "without" and the "*pas*" that place the sign beyond the reach of "the logic of identity, even of the dialectics of contradiction." This is to say that the narrative sign is never fully present or on display; it is not given over to read-

ing as such, but always spliced with its own negation, for instance being suspended because it is logically incompatible with neighboring signs or because the fact of being uttered makes it virtual. This is another trace of the provocative aspect of *l'écriture*, which disallows any reading seeking to memorize the entire narrative, and which a fortiori blocks any representation through the imaginary. [*Pas* can mean "not," "step," "nots," "steps." —Trans.]

11. Bousquet, "Maurice Blanchot," 48.

12. Ibid., 35.

13. The expression is Rilke's concerning El Greco's saints, which he calls "giant plants" that "flower at the highest point" and "open themselves to storms of visions."

14. Maurice Blanchot, *The One Who Was Standing Apart From Me*, trans. Lydia Davis, in *The Station Hill Blanchot Reader*, ed. George Quasha (Barrytown, N.Y.: Station Hill Press, 1988), 261–339, at 315.

25. WRITERS WHO HAVE GIVEN TOO MUCH TO THE PRESENT: NRF CIRCLES (1941–1942)

1. See Maurice Blanchot, "The Ease of Dying" (1969), in *Friendship*, trans. Elizabeth Rottenberg (Stanford: Stanford University Press, 1997), 149.

2. Claude Roy, *Moi je* (Paris: Gallimard, 1969), 312–314.

3. José-Flore Tappy, "Présentation," in Jean Paulhan and Monique Saint-Hélier, *Correspondance Jean Paulhan-Monique Saint-Hélier* (Paris: Gallimard, 1995), 21.

4. Maurice Blanchot, *For Friendship* (1993), in *Political Writings, 1953–1993*, trans. Zakir Paul (New York: Fordham University Press, 2010), 135.

5. Cupid, the lover of this mortal woman whom some believe to be more beautiful than Venus, visits her nightly, on condition that she always refuse to see him; he leaves as soon as day comes.

6. Letter from Jean Paulhan to Monique Saint-Hélier, no. 11 (November 22, 1941) in *Correspondance Jean Paulhan-Monique Saint-Hélier* (Paris: Gallimard, 1995), 47–48. Paulhan adds: "You will think that these articles pay me a lot of compliments. They do not; in fact, there is above all (I believe) a tragic tone that gives me confidence." Paulhan would not always appreciate this "tragic tone." For example he would write to Maurice-Jean Lefebvre on April 15, 1948: "There is a certain *je ne sais quoi* that I find revolting in Blanchot's philosophy (a sort of pessimism). But it would be a hellishly long task to explain why." Letter 32 in Jean Paulhan, *Choix de lettres, III, 1946–1968: Le don des langues* (Paris: Gallimard, 1996), 60.

7. Letter from Jean Paulhan to Jean Prévost, no. 209 November 22, 1941) in *Choix de lettres, II: Traité des jours sombres* (Paris: Gallimard, 1992), 252–253. See also the letter to Henri Pourrat, no. 210 (November 24, 1941), ibid., 253–254.

8. *The Flowers of Tarbes* and Blanchot's articles were bound to interest Ponge, both because of his friends and especially for literary reasons. Was Paulhan trying to retain his influence over the poet? "I am irritated at not having the three articles from *Débats* (!) on the *Fleurs*, which I am told are greatly superior to the *Fleurs*," were his words to Ponge, who replied happily: "[Blanchot] is quivering before what you have discovered (in your prudent but inexorable way). Ultimately, he is placing you where I want you to be placed (as a new Copernicus, if you allow me to say so)." Letters 257 and 258 in Jean Paulhan and Francis Ponge, *Correspondance 1923–1968* (Paris: Gallimard, 1986), 1:263–264.

9. Letter from Jean Paulhan to Francis Ponge, no. 260 (January 29, 1942), ibid., 268.

10. Letter from Jean Paulhan to André Dhôtel, no. 216 (January 10, 1942) in *Choix de lettres, II*, 259.

11. Letter from Jean Paulhan to Monique Saint-Hélier, no. 24 (December 22, 1941) in *Correspondance Jean Paulhan-Monique Saint-Hélier*, 67.

12. Letter from Jean Paulhan to Drieu La Rochelle, no. 219 (January 1942) in *Choix de lettres, II*, 262.

13. Paul Léautaud, *Journal littéraire, III (février 1940–février 1956)* (Paris: Mercure de France, 1986), 596–597. At the end of August, Léautaud relates a meeting with the head of production at the *NRF*: "Mr. Blanchot? That (*ça*) no longer exists," he was told by Festy, for whom Blanchot had only replaced Drieu "for a short time." Ibid., 687–688.

14. Letters from Jean Paulhan to Drieu La Rochelle, nos. 239 and 240 (June 9 and 10, 1942), in *Choix de lettres, II*, 280. On this whole episode, see also Pierre Andreu and Frédéric Glover, *Drieu La Rochelle* (Paris: La Table Ronde, 1989), 489–492; Maurice Blanchot, *For Friendship*, 135–136.

15. Letter from Jean Paulhan to Monique Saint-Hélier, no. 75 (June 25, 1942) in *Correspondance Jean Paulhan-Monique Saint-Hélier*, 169.

16. See Pascal Fouché, *L'édition française sous l'Occupation* (Paris: Bibliothèque de littérature contemporaine de l'Université Paris-VII, 1987), 280; Jeffrey Mehlman, *Legacies of Anti-Semitism in France* (Minneapolis: University of Minnesota Press, 1983), 116–117.

17. Maurice Blanchot, "The Writer and the Public" (1941), in *Into Disaster: Chronicles of Intellectual Life, 1941*, trans. Michael Holland (New York: Fordham University Press, 2013), 107–112.

18. Montherlant and Goethe, cited in ibid., 111.

19. Maurice Blanchot, "On Insolence Considered as One of the Fine Arts" (1942) in *Faux Pas*, trans. Charlotte Mandell (Stanford: Stanford University Press, 2001), 306–309.

20. Montherlant cited in ibid., 308–309.

21. Ibid., 309.

22. Maurice Blanchot, "A User's Guide to Montherlant" (1942) in *Desperate Clarity: Chronicles of Intellectual Life, 1942*, trans. Michael Holland (New York: Fordham University Press, 2013), 114–121.

23. Maurice Blanchot, "From the Middle Ages to Symbolism" (1942), ibid., 15–20, at 16.

24. Ibid., 17.

25. Ibid., 18.

26. Ibid., 19–20.

27. Maurice Blanchot, "Literature" (1942), in *Faux Pas*, 91–95.

28. Ibid., 91ff. The article nonetheless still contains some strange populist and demagogic moments: "what is furthest from Montaigne and Marivaux is the well-read Frenchman, but what is closest is the Gascon wine-grower or the Parisian milliner." *Faux Pas*, 95. We might think of this as some kind of humor, but a few years previously Blanchot made similar statements much more seriously (or perhaps ironically).

29. Maurice Blanchot, "Machiavelli" (1943), in *A World in Ruins: Chronicles of Intellectual Life, 1943*, trans. Michael Holland (New York: Fordham University Press, 2016), 99.

30. Maurice Blanchot, "French Suite" (1943), ibid., 141–147.

31. Maurice Blanchot, "The Myth of Orestes" (1943), in *Faux Pas*, 64.

32. Maurice Blanchot, "Considerations on the Hero" (1942), in *Desperate Clarity*, 122–129.

26. FROM ANGUISH TO LANGUAGE: THE PUBLICATION OF *FAUX PAS* (1943)

1. Maurice Blanchot, *For Friendship* (1993), in *Political Writings*, trans. Zakir Paul (New York: Fordham University Press, 2010), 136.

2. Pierre Prévost, *Pierre Prévost rencontre Georges Bataille* (Paris: Jean-Michel Place, 1987), 100.

3. See Pierre Assouline, *Gaston Gallimard* (Paris: Balland, 1984), 351.

4. See ibid., p. 328; Blanchot, *For Friendship*, 134–136.

5. On 30 August 1943, Dionys Mascolo wrote to Marguerite Antelme (later Marguerite Duras), on the Control Committee: "the text of 'DIGRESSIONS' agreed in May (no. 18159) will appear under the title 'FAUX PAS'"; letter in Marguerite Duras, *Romans, cinéma, théâtre* (Paris: Gallimard, 1997), 16.

6. Maurice Blanchot, "France and Contemporary Civilization" (1941), in *Into Disaster: Chronicles of Intellectual Life, 1941*, trans. Michael Holland (New York: Fordham University Press, 2013), 29.

7. Maurice Blanchot, "Realism's Chances" (1942), in *Desperate Clarity: Chronicles of Intellectual Life, 1942*, trans. Michael Holland (New York: Fordham University Press, 2013), 88.

8. Maurice Blanchot, "A World in Ruins" (1943), in *A World in Ruins: Chronicles of Intellectual Life, 1943*, trans. Michael Holland (New York: Fordham University Press, 2016), 287–290.

9. Maurice Blanchot, "How Is Literature Possible?" (1941), in *Faux Pas*, trans. Charlotte Mandell (Stanford: Stanford University Press, 2001), 83.

10. Maurice Blanchot, "On Hindu Thought" (1942), ibid., p. 35.

11. Maurice Blanchot, "L'expérience magique d'Henri Michaux" (1944), in *Chroniques littéraires*, pp. 663–67.

12. Maurice Blanchot, "From Anguish to Language," in *Faux Pas*, 2.

13. Ibid., 3–6.

14. There is little of note in the reception of *Faux pas*. There was little chance of the major players, who were already familiar with the quality of the articles, expressing their views on a collection of this kind. The few articles that did appear often took issue with the conception of language and literature that Blanchot was developing, but nonetheless recognized his as "the only original and profound criticism" in the French press (Anglès, in *Confluences*), and saw this author as "nonetheless the best of our young critics" (Blanzat, in *Poésie 44*). This praise came from the Resistance press.

27. THE PRISONER OF THE EYES THAT CAPTURE HIM: QUAIN (SUMMER 1944)

1. See Georges Bataille, "Discussion sur le péché," in *Oeuvres complètes* (Paris: Gallimard, 1973), 6:315–359; Pierre Prévost, *Pierre Prévost rencontre Georges Bataille* (Paris: Jean-Michel Place, 1987), 111–115.

2. Prévost, *Pierre Prévost rencontre Georges Bataille*, 115.

3. Maurice Nadeau, "Maurice Blanchot," in *Grâces leur soient rendues* (Paris: Albin Michel, 1990), 71; Prévost, *Pierre Prévost rencontre Georges Bataille*, 116; Maurice Blanchot, *The Madness of the Day*, trans. Lydia Davis (Barrytown, N.Y.: Station Hill Press, 1981), 6.

4. Maurice Blanchot, "Des diverses façons de mourir" (1944), in *Chroniques littéraires du Journal des Débats: Avril 1941–août 1944*, ed. Christophe Bident (Paris: Gallimard, 2007), 632–636.

5. The letter to Prévost, a written source and the closest to the event, seems the trustworthiest. It places the firing squad in June. June 29 is the most likely date according to local memories of the fighting. But there may not have been any direct battles the day Blanchot was placed before a firing squad. Ultimately, June 20 seems to be the most likely date. Derrida mentions a letter written by Blanchot on July 20, 1994, described as being fifty years to the day after the event; *Demeure* in Maurice Blanchot and Jacques Derrida, *The Instant of My Death / Demeure*, trans. Elizabeth Rottenberg (Stanford: Stanford University Press, 2000), 52. There seems to be little

doubt that Blanchot's memory was mistaken by one month, and yet perhaps the day is correct. This would allow us to explain the content of the article published in the *Journal des Débats* on June 29.

6. Maurice Blanchot, *The Instant of My Death / Demeure*, 2.

7. André Malraux, *Antimémoires* (Paris: Gallimard: 1967), chapter 6, esp. 217–218).

8. Blanchot, *The Instant of My Death / Demeure*, 5.

9. Bataille finished this book in August 1944; it would therefore presuppose that Blanchot had told him of the event by letter, which he did rarely at the time, there being multiple obstacles to delivery. We read the sentence quoted, from *Sur Nietzsche* in *Oeuvres completes* (Paris: Gallimard, 2007), 6: 23, as a chance echo of the astonishing proximity of these two friends' "experiences," and of their similarities in written expression.

10. Blanchot, *The Instant of My Death / Demeure*, 11.

11. [Blanchot, in *The Instant of My Death*, and Derrida, in his response to it in *Demeure*, insist upon the term *demeure*: meaning dwelling, but recalling *demeurer* (to remain), and of course *meure*, the third-person singular subjunctive of the verb *mourir* (whence the term *demourance* in Bident's text). —Trans.]

12. Blanchot, *The Madness of the Day*, 6.

13. Maurice Blanchot, "Reading Kafka" (1945), in *The Work of Fire*, trans. Charlotte Mandell (Stanford: Stanford University Press, 1995), 8.

14. Blanchot, *The Madness of the Day*, 5, 6.

15. Emmanuel Levinas, *Sur Maurice Blanchot* (Montpellier: Fata Morgana, 1975), 60–61.

16. Blanchot recalls this almost offhandedly in an article of July 1946; see *The Work of Fire*, 183.

17. Maurice Blanchot, *Death Sentence*, in *The Station Hill Blanchot Reader*, ed. George Quasha (Barrytown, N.Y.: Station Hill Press, 1998), 173–174.

28. THE DISENCHANTMENT OF THE COMMUNITY:
EDITORIAL ACTIVITY AFTER LIBERATION (1944–1946)

1. Maurice Blanchot, *Intellectuals under Scrutiny* (1984), in *The Blanchot Reader*, ed. Michael Holland (Oxford: Blackwell, 1995), 223).

2. See Vercours, *Cent ans d'histoire en France*, *III* (Paris: Plon, 1984), 53–54.

3. Maurice Blanchot, "L'énigme de la critique" (1946), in *La condition critique: Articles 1945–1998*, ed. Christophe Bident (Paris: Gallimard, 2010), 53–56.

4. Blanchot published an extract from *The Most High* in the third issue of *Cahiers de la Table Ronde*, in July 1945. However, he would keep his distance

from the later journal of the same name, founded in 1948 by Mauriac, published by Plon and coedited by Maulnier, which quickly adopted a reactionary line.

5. At this time Blanchot's political positions were in agreement with those of Bataille. Only the awareness of past responsibility seemed to constrain him to silence on contemporary matters. This much is suggested by a parenthesis in a letter from Bataille of late April 1946: telling Prévost to allow Blanchot free reign regarding the choice of subjects he wrote on in *Critique*, he added: "(perhaps it is also necessary to be attentive to the unfortunate question of politics)" in Georges Bataille, *Choix de lettres*, ed. Michel Surya (Paris: Gallimard, 1997), 209–291 (and 316, note 1); Pierre Prévost, *Pierre Prévost rencontre Georges Bataille* (Paris: Jean-Michel Place, 1987), 133, 135.

6. Ibid., 117.

7. Maurice Blanchot, *For Friendship* (1993), in *Political Writings, 1953–1993*, trans. Zakir Paul (New York: Fordham University Press, 2010), 136–137.

8. "Is not the most singular thing in the case of Maurice Blanchot that as a withdrawal—a paradoxical withdrawal—from the absence that is attributed to him, people are generally unaware that all his life he bore witness to an intense *public* presence. . . . There is no movement in Blanchot allowing us to claim that he withdrew from the world that is not accompanied by an inverse and often simultaneous movement linking him to it all the more firmly; which is to say, all the more politically" Michel Surya, "Présentation du projet de revue internationale," *Lignes*, 11 (September 1990): 161.

9. In 1945, Blanchot was still part of the panel for the Prix de la Pléiade. In November, he volunteered his services for the Prix des Critiques, which had been founded by the Pavois publishing house. He thus joined Arland and Paulhan; Nadeau, Bataille, and Maulnier would also later participate. This panel would award the prize to Romain Gary, Albert Camus, and Françoise Sagan (against the latter, Blanchot voted for André Dhôtel). Char and Prévert refused the prize, which would eventually come under the influence of Paulhan and Gallimard. It continued to be awarded until the 1970s, gradually falling into distaff (*quenouille*), as Maurice Nadeau put it (the members stopped meeting). Blanchot seems to have remained until the end (he was still present in 1970 when the prize was awarded to Jabès).

In 1947, he was also part of the first panel of the Prix Sainte-Beuve, with Queneau, Nadeau, Aron, Fouchet, Buchet, and Paulhan. This was meant to be a sort of alternative prize: Edmond Buchet reported that its purpose was "to select each year a novel or a work of criticism that had not been considered by the numerous prizes, which are generally badly awarded"; *Les auteurs de ma vie ou ma vie d'éditeur* (Paris: Buchet-Chastel, 2001), 139. Later, at the end of the 1950s, he would refuse, as did Beckett, to sit on another jury, which had been dreamed up by Nadeau and Pingaud, intending to use the springtime to evaluate books that had been overlooked by the end-of-year prizes. He would refuse humorously, telling Nadeau that the prize would only succeed if it were awarded by members of the Académie Française. Nonetheless he did take part in the first Prix de Mai, in 1957, although not without hesitations, and he remained uncertain about its long-term prospects; see the article that he gave to *L'Express*, "Is Something Happening?" (1957), trans. Leslie Hill in *Paragraph* 30, no. 3 (November 2007): 12–14. In fact, two letters from Bernard Pingaud confirm that it was Blanchot's doing that on March 6, 1961, the Prix de Mai fell on its own sword, calling into question less the prize itself than "the very notion of prizes." We know how much Blanchot would approve of Sartre's refusal of the Nobel Prize three years later.

10. This paper was *Paysage Dimanche*, a weekly, Sunday publication founded in June 1945, which would exist under various titles for just over three years. Opening with a text by Jules Romains, "Démocratie et grandeur," its aim was to restore the faith and pride in the nation necessary for all democracies. The cultural dimension had an important role (three pages of six), and the other material addressed political and economic current affairs. The books column was initially written alternately by Marcel Arland and Henri Thomas. For several months, between October and December 1945, Blanchot replaced Thomas; in November, Arland stopped his contributions, leaving his place for Roger Giron. Lacking any coherent aesthetic line, *Paysage Dimanche* had room for both the most modern and the most conventional viewpoints. Blanchot would publish seven texts with this paper, on Giraudoux, Sartre (a twin article to the contemporaneous one for *L'Arche*), Dhôtel, Du Bos, Melville, and Malraux (the latter was reprinted with hardly any variations in *The Work of Fire*, and contemporaneous to the one given to *Actualité*).

11. See Michel Surya, *Georges Bataille: An Intellectual Biography*, trans. Krysztof Fijalkowski and Michael Richardson (New York: Verso, 2002), 364–367; Georges Bataille, *Choix de lettres*, ed. Michel Surya (Paris: Gallimard, 1997), 243, 251, 256.

12. Maurice Blanchot, "*Days of Hope* by André Malraux" (1946), trans. Michael Holland in *Paragraph* 30, no. 3 (November 2007): 5–11. Blanchot himself had insisted that Bataille allow an article on Malraux to be included: "I really find it impossible that we discuss neither Malraux nor the question of communism," he had written to him on May 8, 1945.

29. THE YEAR OF CRITICISM: *L'ARCHE, LES TEMPS MODERNES,* AND *CRITIQUE* (1946)

1. Sometimes he would not see his friends for a year (he wrote as much to Bataille, sometimes complaining about it in a very moving way).

2. Leiris and Merleau-Ponty were Blanchot's main supporters with regard to Sartre.

3. On *Critique*, see Pierre Prévost, *Pierre Prévost rencontre Georges Bataille* (Paris: Jean-Michel Place, 1987), 119–149; Michel Surya, *Georges Bataille: An Intellectual Biography*, trans. Krysztof Fijalkowski and Michael Richardson (New York: Verso, 2002), 368–375.

30. RESPECTING SCANDAL: LITERARY CRITICISM (1945–1948)

1. Maurice Blanchot, "Reflections on Surrealism" (1945) in *The Work of Fire*, trans. Charlotte Mandell (Stanford: Stanford University Press, 1995), 85. References in brackets in this chapter are henceforth to this work.

2. Maurice Blanchot, "Quelques réflexions sur le surréalisme," *L'Arche* 8 (August 1945): 93–104; "Reflections on Surrealism."

3. Maurice Blanchot, "Du merveilleux" (1947), in *La condition critique: Articles 1945–1998*, ed. Christophe Bident (Paris: Gallimard, 2010), 128–129.

4. Blanchot, "Reflections on Surrealism." The article on René Char published in October 1946 addressed the relation of literature and politics in the same terms. "The struggle of the partisan in the world" belongs to poetry, which "puts us in contact with all that is sovereignty in the world." This sovereignty places us on the path to "Terror" since poetry "is itself in everything, the presence of everything, the search for totality": "it alone has the ability and the right to speak of everything, to speak everything" (105–106). It is also in this text that Blanchot first uses the term "community" in the sense he will later give to it, drawing on both presence within a struggle, and the distance of an interruption: in the sense of uncommitment in the mode of commitment.

5. Although Blanchot was now closer to Sartre regarding politics *stricto sensu*, he would not hesitate to affirm this particular understanding of commitment. And it was precisely during an analysis of "Sartre's novels" that he would cite, not by accident, this passage from the *Paths of Freedom* in which the character Mathieu reflects his own image back at him: "you have spent 35 years cleansing yourself and the result is emptiness. You are a strange body ... you live in the air, you have cut your bourgeois attachments, you have no tie to the proletariat, you float, you are an abstract, an absentee" (204). Blanchot wrote the article for the October 1945 issue of *L'Arche*; he had just turned thirty-eight. Of course, the portrait captured in this citation does not correspond exactly to Blanchot's reality; it nevertheless remains suggestive: it is doubly sarcastic, first toward Sartre (Blanchot using his fiction as a mirror) and second toward Blanchot himself (because he was anything but a floating body, but far sooner a cumbersome, withdrawn body). The citation is therefore significant in terms of his critical, public, and resolute commitment as early as the summer of 1945.

6. "It is quite clear that reality does not exist in order to provide a guarantee for extravagance, but that it exists because it is the very site of the unreal which endlessly interrupts it, tears it apart, which is its deepest manifestation and guarantee"; Maurice Blanchot, "Du merveilleux" (1947), 119.

7. Ibid., 115–129. Blanchot would later abandon the term "fantastic" when referring to this sovereignty of the invisible, of inner experience. He would replace it with the "imaginary," an imaginary infinitely open to the subterranean figure of the unimaginable. For instance, in 1947 he wrote: "Unreality begins with the whole. The realm of the imaginary is not a strange region situated beyond the world, it is the world itself, but the world as entire, manifold, the world as a whole" (316).

8. See "Literature and the Right to Death," in *The Work of Fire*, 341–344. It must be added that the privileging of the ambiguity of literature is not without relation to the debate with Sartre. The notion is already present in "From Anguish to Language," notably regarding Kafka; here it comes to the fore. In *Faux Pas*, trans. Charlotte Mandell (Stanford: Stanford University Press, 2001), 9–11. It can be found twice in the critical articles of *The Work of Fire*: apropos of Baudelaire ("we can think along with Sartre that . . . poetic creation is pure only in the equivocal," 141) and of Sartre himself ("the novel has its own moral, which is ambiguity and equivocation," 207); the first version in *L'Arche* 10 (October 1945): 134, evoked Sartre's respect for "the statute of bad faith which is the moral [of the novel]." Ambiguity also plays against Sartre's concept of bad faith; this informs the strategy of the article "The Novel Is a Work of Bad Faith" (April 1947), in *The Blanchot Reader*, ed. Michael Holland (Oxford: Blackwell, 1995), 61–73. It turns that concept's immorality and its relative indifference to ethics back on themselves and, agreeing with the thinking of Bataille and Levinas, transcends it in poetic (semiological), aesthetic and ethical dimensions.

9. This approach was all the more influential given that it was repeated almost forty years later and in the same terms: see "After the Fact" in *Vicious Circles, followed by "After the Fact,"* trans. Paul Auster (Barrytown, N.Y.: Station Hill Press, 1985), 59–60. On Blanchot's relation to the Hegel of Kojève (whose work appeared in 1947), and on the influence of this strand on Lacan, see Mikkel Borch-Jacobsen, *Lacan: The Absolute Master*, trans. Douglas Brick (Stanford: Stanford University Press, 1991), 192–194 and 272–273.

10. Martin Heidegger, "The Origin of the Work of Art," trans. Albert Hofstadter in *Poetry, Language, Thought* (New York: Harper & Row, 1971), 73, 55. This lecture was first given in November 1935 in Freiburg, before being updated and given again in 1936 in Zurich, and then divided into three lectures at the end of the same year in Frankfurt.

11. Ibid., 45–46.

12. Stéphane Mallarmé, "The Tomb of Edgar Poe," in *Collected Poems: A Bilingual Edition*, trans. Henry Weinfield (Berkeley: University of California Press, 1994), 71.

13. See Maurice Blanchot, "From Lautréamont to Miller" (1946), in *The Work of Fire*, 174–175. On what this lack means for his differences with Heidegger, see Leslie Hill, *Blanchot: Extreme Contemporary* (New York: Routledge, 1997), 77–91.

14. See notably the openings of "Reading Kafka" (1945), in *The Work of Fire*, 1, or of "Gide and the Literature of Experience" (1947), ibid., 212.

15. The organization of the texts in *The Work of Fire*, which does not separate them into groups, responds to this notion: the chapters on the relation between literature and the secret or silence are followed by several on poetic language (from Char to Lautréamont), then by others on the experience of the prose writer. On the whole, there are few alterations from previous versions. Some of them are important, however: a full study of them is still to be carried out. Mostly it is simply a question of style: simplifying syntax, removing passive forms, overloaded adverbs, and peremptory formulations (for example the frequent "it is clear that"). Sometimes the changes make the thinking seem more swift, the contradictions more vertiginous and the statements more effective. The corrections aim to produce spontaneity on the basis of complete control (notably in the case of "Reading Kafka," which becomes prodigiously jubilant in the collected version). The collection's title is linked to Bataille. It can be found in his writing, in a manuscript for *The History of Eroticism*, contemporaneous with Blanchot's publication: "the accursed share must be sacrificed, it must be that given unto *the work of fire*" in *Oeuvres complètes* (Paris: Gallimard, 1976), 8:553; passage not included in *The Accursed Share*, vols. 2 or 3. *The Work of Fire* replaced the title originally planned, which in the first edition of *The Most High* (1948) the publisher announced as being soon to appear: *Between Day and Night* (*Entre chiens et loups*). While Blanchot chose the Bataille citation over the one from Hölderlin, he nonetheless used the famous extract by the German poet as the epigraph to the book, and would cite it on two further occasions, in the articles on Paulhan and on Hölderlin himself: "It behooves morals/To speak with restraint of the gods. / If, between day and night [*entre chien et loup*], / One time a truth should appear to you, / In a triple metamorphosis transcribe it; / Though always unexpressed, as it is, / O innocent, so it must remain" (xi).

16. See Blanchot's very fine reading of Nietzsche's confrontation with the thought of God, which, touching on Bataille's reading of the Incarnated, rejoins the infinite movement of "inner experience"; "On Nietzsche's Side" in *The Work of Fire*, 291–297.

17. Letter from Maurice Blanchot to Dionys Mascolo, January 12, 1971.

18. "Each time that the "is" or the "it is" takes form in this text, it does so in order to withdraw from the logic of identity, even from the dialectics of contradiction," Derrida writes in *Parages* (Paris: Galilée, 1986), p. 32. This is the injunction of *come*, the imperative of the *pas* (the *step* and the *not*). The event is that which happens endlessly. The coming of the wholly other prevents any full manifestation of essence. This leads to the interplay between *without* (*sans*) and *not* (*pas*) in the texts, which "disarticulates any logic of identity or of contradiction" (ibid., 46), and which therefore disarticulates dialectics as well as the *récit*, "in which the presence of the present is paralyzed" (74).

19. See Michel Surya, "Pour une matériologie sadienne," preface to D.A.F. de Sade, *Français encore un effort si vous voulez être républicains* (Paris: Fourbis, 1996), 21.

20. See Maurice Blanchot, "The 'Sacred' Speech of Hölderlin" (1946), in *The Work of Fire*, 126.

21. Maurice Blanchot, *Lautréamont and Sade*, trans. Stuart Kendall and Michelle Kendall (Stanford: Stanford University Press, 2004), 7–8. Blanchot called for the same respect to be given to Rimbaud (who had in him "something howling and ferocious that one finds again exactly in the Marquis de Sade" in "The Sleep of Rimbaud" (1947) in *The Work of Fire*, 158.

22. Blanchot, *Lautréamont and Sade*, 14.

23. Ibid., 41.

24. Ibid., 153. Bataille would state as early as spring 1949, announcing in *Critique* the publication of *Lautréamont and Sade*, that Sade's thinking pushes that of Blanchot to the point of completion, and likewise Blanchot's thought completes that of Sade; see *The Accursed Share*, vols. II and III, trans. Robert Hurley (New York: Zone, 1991), 174–175. He would remain impressed by Blanchot's work on Sade, sometimes citing entire pages from it.

25. Blanchot, *Lautréamont et Sade*, 69.

26. Ibid.

27. Ibid., 117.

28. Ibid., 145.

29. Ibid., 143.

30. Ibid., 94, 109, 105, 117.

31. Ibid., 153–154.

31. THE BLACK STAIN: WRITING *THE MOST HIGH* (1946–1947)

1. The surnames in *The Most High* are strangely rare and sometimes hard to understand. Most of them, even those of secondary characters or those only mentioned once, are formed of four or five letters. Sorge, the name of the narrator, means "care" in German and is a fundamental notion in Heidegger's philosophy. It is also the name of a German expressionist dramaturge who

died at twenty-four, who was strongly influenced by Goethe and Nietzsche, and whose hero, Unruh, is searching for the new man and seems ready to bear the entire weight of the world on his shoulders ("Unruh" means disquiet, agitation, and even riot or revolution; see *The Young Man*, a work published posthumously in 1925). Dorte evokes death (*la mort*). Bouxx evokes the English word *books*; Sorge even tells him: "you are a book" (Maurice Blanchot, *The Most High*, trans. Allan Stoekl [Lincoln: University of Nebraska Press, 1996], 48); or the mouth (*bouche*) if the *x* is pronounced as in Basque. Blanchot feigns astonishment over the strangeness of the name in a letter to his Japanese translator: see *Exercices de la patience* 2 (Winter 1981): 107. Bouxx might also recall the name of a person and a building in Beausoleil, Roux (pronounced "Rouks"), which was inscribed on a building that must have faced the villa Margot where Blanchot stayed; he cannot have missed the fact that the name is immediately followed by a stylized letter, probably a V which, the way it is written, gives the strange feeling of reading: "Rouxx" . . .

2. Blanchot, *The Most High*, 1. Citations in the rest of this chapter are taken from this text unless otherwise stated.

3. There is something of Myshkin in Sorge, and also something of Dostoevsky's chatty characters, who agitate for evil, in Bouxx.

4. Maurice Blanchot, *Aminadab*, trans. Jeff Fort (Lincoln: University of Nebraska Press, 2002), 6.

5. Let us recall that there are two tombs, probably both empty, in the garden of the house in Quain. There are no surnames among the inscriptions on the family tomb in the church cemetery at Devrouze. Yet we know that the body of Blanchot's father was taken there after being exhumed from the cemetery in Chalon at an unknown time.

The scene of the grave's desecration is overtly Bataillean. We can think of what Michel Fardoulis-Lagrange says about it: to desecrate a grave, "the last site of desecration," is "to give more room to absence." In *G.B. ou un ami présomptueux* (Paris: Le Soleil Noir, 1969), 92.

6. Maurice Blanchot, "Musil II" (March 1958), in *The Book to Come*, trans. Charlotte Mandell (Stanford: Stanford University Press, 2003), 148.

7. Maurice Blanchot, *The Madness of the Day*, trans. Lydia Davis (Barrytown, N.Y.: Station Hill Press, 1981), 13.

8. [Bident's phrase is a play on the last line of *The Madness of the Day* (18), which reads, "No. No *récits*, never again." —Trans.]

9. This was underlined by Levinas: "the face, behind the countenance it gives itself, is like the exposure of a being to death, it is the defenselessness, the nudity, and the poverty of those who are always the others. It is also the command to take others into one's charge, to not leave them alone; in this the word of God is heard. If you understand the face as the photographer's object, then of course you are dealing with an object like any other. But if

you *meet* the face, then the responsibility lies in this strangeness and poverty of the others. The face offers itself to your mercy and obliges you." François Poirié, *Emmanuel Levinas*, 2nd ed. (1987; reprint, Besançon: La Manufacture, 1992), 83.

10. Blanchot, *The Madness of the Day*, 15, 16. ["*Elle*" referring to the law should be rendered as "it"—however, here it is clear that, as elsewhere, Blanchot is playing with the idea of female personalization. —Trans.]

32. THE PASSION OF SILENCE: DENISE ROLLIN (1940S)

1. When he was in Paris, Blanchot regularly went to the Rue Vaugirard, where Denise Rollin lived. A child at the time (he had just turned five at the Liberation), Jean Rollin remembers a very kind, humorous man who was also ill and extremely weak. You had to be quiet when he came. Jean Rollin also reports an anecdote: The concierge, an old, difficult woman, did not look favorably on this man who regularly visited a woman living alone with her child. Every time, she would open the door as he arrived and would ask him where he was going. Blanchot would reply with unfailing politeness and go up to the sixth floor. Every time Denise Rollin would get angry at this inconvenience.

2. She would remain close to Michel and Francine Fardoulis-Lagrange, to whom she would write regularly. This correspondence is of value, and we thank especially Francine Fardoulis-Lagrange for having made it available to us. Unfortunately it is neither dated nor catalogued: the extracts cited therefore usually lack references.

3. We are drawing on Michel Surya's interviews with Michel Fardoulis-Lagrange and Laurence Bataille; *Georges Bataille: An Intellectual Biography*, trans. Krysztof Fijalkowski and Michael Richardson (New York: Verso, 2002), 281. We can read Fardoulis on Rollin's silent nature: "she was the woman who incarnated silence. She metaphorically recorded ideas. . . . We were astonished by the echoes they had produced in her." And Bataille stated: "I have never felt, except with Laure, such easy purity, such silent simplicity"; "such a fragile illusion would dissipate over the slightest thing, at the slightest relaxation of *inattention*." In *Carnets pour Le Coupable* in *Oeuvres complètes* (Paris: Gallimard, 1973), 5:509.

4. Ibid., 521, 515, 524.

5. Maurice Blanchot, *The Work of Fire*, trans. Charlotte Mandell (Stanford: Stanford University Press, 1995), esp. 232–237.

6. Ibid., 237.

7. Ibid., 235.

8. Not only is there no doubt that Denise Rollin knew the book and the character, but they were also popular at the time: on June 7, 1946, Georges Lampin's film showcasing Gérard Philipe came to cinemas. The character

Myshkin and notably his Pascalian *skillfulness* (everything that brings Blanchot into proximity with Pascal is important) are discussed in an article by Georges Philippenko, "La sainteté impossible," *Le Nouveau Receuil* 37 (December 1995): 88–98.

9. "His experience is certainly the most atrocious, the most inhumane that it is possible to undergo, for me it is the experience of God, you must feel what I am trying to say because it absolutely cannot be explained in the meaning of words it is absurd, but it is true."

"I use the word 'God' *after* the sense of Nietzsche's 'God is dead'" (Letter from Denise Rollin).

10. Blanchot's relative silence on Dostoevsky is remarkable. Also remarkable are the final pages of 'On Nietzsche's Side' (1945/6) in *The Work of Fire*, 285–286, which first appeared in *L'Arche* in December 1945. Blanchot was reviewing a critical work by Father De Lubac containing several studies, including one on Dostoevsky, "the most remarkable thing," he states, but still without spending more than a few lines on it, is that "the characters are always different to what they are, and when they are relatively simple, they share with each other and receive from other characters reflections that make them invisible" (298). And when he cites Myshkin, it is in order to underline his ambiguity as an expression of anguish: "Raskolnikov, Kirilov, Stavrogin, Prince Myshkin answer, in the dramatic richness of their story, to an emptiness without history, to something frozen that the burning of their passions makes unbearable" (ibid.). The *récits* of the 1950s will evoke this burning cold of passion.

11. Maurice Blanchot and Denise Rollin would continue to correspond until the latter's death. Perhaps ultimately they spent more time corresponding than in one another's company. But this takes nothing away from the intensity of their encounters and their love. Indeed it adds a great deal to their stories of solitude, to the sensation of having been burnt that marks their readings, of Dostoevsky for Denise Rollin, of Kafka for Maurice Blanchot. After the article on Constant came "L'échec de Milena" (November 1954), another great critical text in which Blanchot addressed passion, and which would remain almost secret, kept out of *The Book to Come*, *The Infinite Conversation* and even of *Friendship*, only being republished after Denise Rollin's death in *De Kafka à Kafka* (Paris: Gallimard, 1981). Although he did not see them as a model, Blanchot approached Kafka's loves in light of the tragic, uncertain, and hasty manner in which he lived through his own. "His relations with the young woman are first and foremost established on the level of *written notes*," he wrote in "The Very Last Word" (May 1968), thus using an expression fetishized by Denise Rollin apropos of Felice. In *Friendship*, trans. Elizabeth Rottenberg (Stanford: Stanford University Press, 1997), 273; CB's

emphasis. As with Kafka, and in proximity to Bataille, it is certain that other women featured in Blanchot's life, just as the need for discretion imposed by the passing of time is also certain.

33. THE MEDITERRANEAN SOJOURN: THE WRITING OF THE NIGHT (1947)

1. Maurice Blanchot, "The Inquisition Destroyed the Catholic Religion . . ." trans. Michael Holland in *Paragraph* 30, no. 3 (November 2007): 43.
2. Letter from Maurice Blanchot to Pierre Prévost, October 15, 1947.
3. Maurice Blanchot in *A Voice from Elsewhere*, trans. Charlotte Mandell (Albany: State University of New York Press, 2007), 5.
4. Pierre Fedida in "Sur les traces de Maurice Blanchot," *France-Culture* radio show broadcast on September 17, 1994.
5. The theoretical importance Blanchot gave to the distinction between novel and *récit* is well known: "the *récit* begins where the novel does not go." In "Encountering the Imaginary" (July 1954), in *The Book to Come*, trans. Charlotte Mandell (Stanford: Stanford University Press, 2003), 6; see also "Autobiographical Narratives" (1943), in *A World in Ruins: Chronicles of Intellectual Life, 1943*, trans. Michael Holland (New York: Fordham University Press, 2016), 223–229, an article originally published on October 13, 1943, a highly important date in *Death Sentence*.
6. Maurice Blanchot, *The Madness of the Day*, trans. Lydia Davis (Barrytown, N.Y.: Station Hill Press, 1981), 15.

34. SOMETHING INFLEXIBLE: *THE MADNESS OF THE DAY*, A NEW STATUS FOR SPEECH (1947–1949)

1. Maurice Blanchot, *The Madness of the Day*, trans. Lydia Davis (Barrytown, N.Y.: Station Hill Press, 1981), 11. All future references in this chapter are to this translated version, unless otherwise indicated.
2. Jacques Derrida, *Parages* (Paris: Galilée, 1986), 139, 150.
3. "Whoever has seen the madness of the day is unable to tell the tale of having done so, for he will have lost the thread of the story, the ability to set the negative to work, to leave an impression on the ordeals undergone, to lay out any figures," Emmanuel Tibloux writes in his fine study "Dérives du génitif," *Lignes* 11 (September 1990): 119–121. The narrator plunges into the madness of the essence of light, which is still brimming with the dawn that contains and fills everything, refusing to be sublated; Hegel named it "the holocaust of being-for-itself." Having been plunged into mud by the doctors, the narrator rediscovers the fire of the earth and remains insensible to the *development* of light (which produces light thanks to pacification).

This point of visibility, beyond (or before) Hegel, also breaks with all technological thought, any dialectical interrogation, any "Platonism." This is what Sarah Kofman implies in stating that the expression that both opens and closes the *récit*, "I am not learned; I am not ignorant," describes the Eros of the *Banquet*. She concludes her book *Comment s'en sortir* (Paris: Gallimard, 1983) with long citations of *The Madness of the Day*, the same passages that Tibloux would analyze. How to get out (*s'en sortir*)? How, without getting out (*sans sortir*)? Only a few autobiographical notes are added to the "aporia" that closes the book without providing closure. What kind of autobiographical narrative is possible? It is well known that this will also be the question asked by Kofman's *Smothered Words* (1987), trans. Madeleine Dobie (Evanston, Ill.: Northwestern University Press, 1998). What then remains is nothing but to inscribe death (*la disparition*) in writing, if "the work which is its drifting from the outset gives up on making an work, indicating only the space in which resounds, for all and for each, and thus for nobody, the always-yet-to-come words of worklessness." Maurice Blanchot, *The Unavowable Community*, trans. Pierre Joris (Barrytown, N.Y.: Station Hill Press, 1988), 46. From this point of view too, *The Madness of the Day* is indeed the rupture inaugurating Blanchot's final *récits*.

4. Blanchot, *The Madness of the Day*, 9.

5. The link established between power and the *récit*, a theme shared by *The Most High*, will leave its mark on the 1950s generation of readers, among them Jacques Derrida and Michel Foucault.

35. THE TURN OF THE SCREW: THE SECOND VERSION OF *THOMAS THE OBSCURE* (1947–1948)

1. Maurice Blanchot, *Thomas the Obscure* (1950 version), trans. Robert Lamberton (1973; Barrytown, N.Y.: Station Hill Press, 1988), 1. On the relation between the two versions, Blanchot wrote as follows to Bataille as early as January 1948: "In recent days I have been working on a different version of *Thomas the Obscure*. It is different insofar as it reduces the first version by two thirds. And yet it is a true book and not just sections of a book; I can even say that this project is not dictated by circumstances or by the vanities of publishing, but that I have often thought of it, having always wanted to see through the thickness of my first books—like the very small and very far-away image of the outside can be seen in opera glasses—the very small and very far-away book which seemed to be their kernel." See also what Jean Starobinski writes about the imaginary demand of disappearance (*la disparition*); "*Thomas l'obscur*, premier chapitre," *Critique* 229 (June 1966): 502.

2. This question of the relation of parts to the whole as part of a mobile search for a center would frequently guide Blanchot's criticism. It is

not surprising to find it resurfacing regarding his own fiction given that it had been one of his interests for some time. Examples can be found as early as 1941, at the start of a chapter in *Faux pas* on Bosco (192); or in "Paradoxes on the novel," December 30 the same year: "What can best reveal the validity of a novel ... is thus a particular orientation, a mysterious magnetization, the rotation of all the elements of the work around an invisible and constantly mobile center." He then lists the questions that must be asked of the most remarkable works: "What did the book want? Did it want it completely? Where is it headed in that secret state of supreme tension that is its true soul and its primary reason for existing?" In *Into Disaster: Chronicles of Intellectual Life, 1941*, trans. Michael Holland (New York: Fordham University Press, 2013), 135. [Gallimard reissued the first version of *Thomas l'obscur* in 2005. —Trans.]

3. Maurice Blanchot, *The Unavowable Community*, trans. Pierre Joris (Barrytown, N.Y.: Station Hill Press, 1988).

4. Blanchot, *Thomas the Obscure*, 83, 76.

5. Ibid., 96, 98, 91, 93.

36. THE AUTHORITY OF FRIENDSHIP: THE COMPLETION OF *DEATH SENTENCE* (1947–1948)

1. Georges Bataille, fragment of an autobiographical note, in *Oeuvres complètes* (Paris: Gallimard, 1973), 6:486.

2. Georges Bataille, Foreword (1957) to *Blue of Noon*, trans. Harry Mathews (New York: Penguin, 2001), 127.

3. Bernard Noël's intuition concerning the link between the deaths of J. and Laure is therefore not without foundation, despite what he modestly claims. He himself condemns it as a protective "antifiction," and he does so in the unconscious humility of not claiming to enter into the friendship that is at stake in the case of Bataille. This leaves wide open the possibility of sinking into, or being sunk by, this *récit*; "D'une main obscure," in Roger Laporte and Bernard Noël, *Deux lectures de Maurice Blanchot* (Montpellier: Fata Morgana, 1973), 25. Let us recall that in February 1956 Blanchot would evoke Laure by name in an article on Michel Leiris; "Battle with the Angel" (1956), in *Friendship*, trans. Elizabeth Rottenberg (Stanford: Stanford University Press, 1997), 139.

4. Maurice Blanchot, "Kafka and Literature" (1949) in *The Work of Fire*, Charlotte Mandell (Stanford: Stanford University Press, 1995), 21.

5. Let us remember that in one of Blanchot's earliest critical texts the expression "death sentence" (*l'arrêt de mort*) referred to the effacement of the author. It was also the title of a novel by Vicki Baum translated into French in 1933, prefaced by Ramon Fernandez, and announced in large type against

a pink background in an advertisement in *La Revue du Siècle*, in May 1933, an issue containing a contribution by Blanchot. Such are the reasons why Blanchot probably must have known about this title, even though it belonged to an insignificant novel with no other link to his own text. Finally, the expression can be found in the second epistle to the Corinthians: "Indeed, we felt we had received the sentence of death": 1 Corinthians 9 (the French version reads "*arrêt de mort*"). Here it is a form of recognition preceding divine reassurance.

6. Claude Rabant, "Cette mort dure encore . . ." *Lignes* 11 (September 1990): 25.

7. [Bident's first two examples are taken from Edgar Allan Poe's *Ligeia* and Dostoevsky's *Idiot*. —Trans.]

8. Maurice Blanchot, *The Madness of the Day*, trans. Lydia Davis (Barrytown, N.Y.: Station Hill Press, 1981), 18.

9. Maurice Blanchot, "Death Sentence," in *The Station Hill Blanchot Reader*, ed. George Quasha (Barrytown, N.Y.: Station Hill Press, 1998), 177–178.

37. QUARRELS IN THE LITERARY WORLD: PUBLICATION AND RECEPTION (1948–1949)

1. On the relationship between Gallimard and Minuit, see Anne Simonin, *Les Éditions de Minuit, 1942–1955, le devoir d'insoumission* (Paris: IMEC, 1994), esp. 420–422.

2. These assertions were made by Henri Hell at the start of his article "À propos des romans de Maurice Blanchot," *La Table Ronde* 12 (December 1948): 2051. Another critic, Gabriel Venaissin, thought *Thomas the Obscure* too simplistic, with its rhetoric "that anyone can reproduce, once they know the rules of the game" in "Le suicide du roman," *La Vie intellectuelle* 44 (April 1951): 152.

3. Blanchot? Nothing more than an "alchemist who will doubtless one day notice that to get water, it is best to turn on the kitchen tap. And that in order to say: "it's nice weather," the best way of proceeding is to say: "it's nice weather"," J.P.—Jean Paulhac?—reader's notes on *Death Sentence* in *Cahiers du Monde Nouveau* 5 (May 1949): 125. As for the far right, it continued to settle scores with the writer who had betrayed it; see Pierre Boutang, "A propos du *Très-Haut* de Maurice Blanchot," *Aspects de la France et du Monde* 22 (December 9, 1948): 3–4.

4. Luc Decaunes, review of *Death Sentence* in *Cahiers du Sud* 291 (second semester 1948): 377–378.

5. Pierre Klossowski, "On Maurice Blanchot," in *Such a Deathly Desire*, trans. Russell Ford (Albany: SUNY Press, 2007), 89 n.

38. INVISIBLE PARTNER: ÈZE, WITHDRAWAL (1949–1957)

1. To this should be added the 1951 publication by Minuit of "The Idyll" and "The Last Word" under the title *Le ressassement éternel*.
2. In this vein, he wrote to Bataille: "I have been here for about a month, in a fairly hidden spot in the countryside, in a solitary house, and myself alone. Your thought is thus doubly present for me" (no date).
3. Letter from Maurice Blanchot to Georges Bataille (June 9, 1958 or 1959), in Georges Bataille, *Choix de lettres*, ed. Michel Surya (Paris: Gallimard, 1997), 589.
4. René Char, "The Fatal Partner," in *The Word as Archipelago*, trans. by Robert Baker (Richmond, Calif.: Omnidawn, 2012), 69. Blanchot was already the author of two articles on Char: one appeared in *Critique* in October 1946, the other in the *NNRF* in April 1953. In a letter to Bataille, Char states: "I believe Blanchot to be indispensable to the field in which he works, as you are indispensable to yours. An entire, major region of mankind *today depends on you*"; letter of December 7, 1946, cited in Bataille, *Choix de lettres*, 402.
5. Friedrich Nietzsche, "Of the Three Metamorphoses," in *Thus Spake Zarathustra*, trans. R. J. Hollingdale (London: Penguin, 1961), 55.
6. Char, "The Fatal Partner," 69.

39. THE ESSENTIAL SOLITUDE: WRITING THE *RÉCITS* (1949–1953)

1. Georges Bataille, "Maurice Blanchot ... ," *Gramma* 3–4 (1976): 221. In an article of 1955, Blanchot referred to the way a fictional *récit* can give a better account than a journal of the author's most personal experience, and therefore has an autobiographical content; this article referred to *Hope*, *Nausea*, and *Nadja*. "Sur le journal intime," *Nouvelle Nouvelle Revue Française* 28 (April 1955): 683–684. He removed the three paragraphs making this claim when he included the article in *The Book to Come*.
2. Marguerite Duras, *Écrire* (Paris: Gallimard, 1993), 13. An incidental remark: we know that for several years, before the revolution of 1979, the village of Neauphle was where Ayatollah Khomeini lived. When Blanchot would "invite" his successor to Èze, perhaps some memory of Khomeini's stay was in his mind.
3. Maurice Blanchot, "The Essential Solitude" (April 1953) in *The Space of Literature*, trans. Ann Smock (Lincoln: University of Nebraska Press, 1982), 19–34. Citations in the rest of the chapter are taken from this article.
4. "The Essential Solitude" was the first article in which, with an almost prophetic density, the notion of "neuter" appeared. This adjective, however, had not yet been turned into noun form.
5. A similar approach, although more justified this time, would be used in the article on "The Two Versions of the Imaginary," with the abrupt,

unexpected appearance of the theme of magic during a reflection on the image (see *The Space of Literature*, 262); the first version of the text dates from 1951, but this passage comes at the end of the much longer development which only appears in the new, book version). The link between children and the universe of the fantastic and more particularly to magic is a frequent one in Blanchot (it is explicitly addressed by a citation from Kafka in "L'échec de Milena" (November 1954), in *De Kafka à Kafka* (Paris: Gallimard, 1994), 162.

6. This expression can also be found in Maurice Blanchot, *When the Time Comes*, trans. Lydia Davis (Barrytown, N.Y.: Station Hill Press, 1985): "[It] touches me with its gaze," 73.

40. THE RADIANCE OF A BLIND POWER: *WHEN THE TIME COMES* (1949–1951)

1. Maurice Blanchot, *When the Time Comes*, trans. Lydia Davis (Barrytown, N.Y.: Station Hill Press, 1985), 57. Citations in the rest of this chapter are taken from this text unless otherwise stated.

2. Denise Rollin had several friendships with women; it is difficult to rule out love. For example, she was strongly linked to a singer from Lorraine, Marianne Oswald, to whom the character of Claudia seems to owe a great deal (her singing, her language, but also her temperament). Denise Rollin's husband, whom she left for Georges Bataille, was named Claude.

3. Maurice Blanchot, *The Space of Literature*, trans. Ann Smock (Lincoln: University of Nebraska Press, 1982), 31. See also "The Essential Solitude and Solitude in the World," in ibid., 253.

4. "Things happened to me, to me and to the story, events that were more and more curtailed (in the sense that, just as I had become no one or almost no one, the traits of my character weakened, the world was readily merging with its limit), but this sort of unraveling of time disclosed above all the exorbitant pressure of 'Something is happening,' a possessive immensity that could only curtail or suspend the natural progress of the story" (63–64). We can compare this to "the absence of time" from "The Essential Solitude."

5. In *When the Time Comes* there are even some precise references to places and events which allow us to think that the apartment in the *récit* is in Paris, and more precisely in front of the synagogue on the Rue de la Victoire (no. 44), which suffered an arson attack on the night of October 2–3, 1941. The fire is referred to on several occasions in *When the Time Comes*, and information on it can be found in Michael R. Marrus and Robert Paxton, *Vichy France and the Jews* (1973; Stanford: Stanford University Press, 1995). The quarter around the Opera is always the one mentioned in Blanchot's *récits* featuring Paris.

6. Dionys Mascolo would say that he was: "incomparably attentive to the smallest things, the least abstract of men" in "Parler de Blanchot" (1981), in *À la recherche d'un communisme de pensée* (Paris: Fourbis, 1993), 441.

7. This is a recurrent motif in the reading proposed by Bataille: "no novel describes happiness more," in "Silence et littérature" (1952), in *Oeuvres complètes* (Paris: Gallimard, 1988), 12:174. The commentaries on *When the Time Comes* and *The Last Man* published by Bataille in *Critique* in 1952 and 1957 are both intensely visual. Both begin by evoking apparently arbitrary images: a scene from H. G. Wells's *Invisible Man*, or photographs published by the journal *Life* on the origin of the world. Both constantly set aside the normal visibility of these images in order to see in them what Bataille calls "apparent otherness": something dazzling, invisible, for Bataille "the gaze on (the gaze open to) death" in "Ce monde où nous mourons" (1957), *Oeuvres complètes* (Paris: Gallimard, 1988), 12:460.

8. We also find this in *The One Who Was Standing Apart From Me* and again in *When the Time Comes*, 15.

9. "Dance, then, lay in an arc between two deaths," Doris Humphrey, cited at https://www.britannica.com/biography/Doris-Humphrey (consulted July 8, 2016).

10. "Yet I have met beings who have never said to life, 'Quiet!' who have never said to death, 'Go away!' Almost always women, beautiful creatures" in *The Madness of the Day*, 7.

11. Maurice Blanchot, "On Nietzsche's Side" (1945–1946) in *The Work of Fire*, trans. Charlotte Mandell (Stanford: Stanford University Press, 1995), 298. Blanchot cites this phrase again in *The Space of Literature*, with the same meaning, but in a different translation: "Die at the given time," 116.

41. ARE YOU WRITING, ARE YOU WRITING EVEN NOW? THE ONE WHO WAS STANDING APART FROM ME (1951–1953)

1. Maurice Blanchot, *The One Who Was Standing Apart From Me*, in *The Station Hill Blanchot Reader*, ed. George Quasha (Barrytown, N.Y.: Station Hill Press, 1998), 329. Citations in this chapter are taken from this text unless otherwise stated.

2. Maurice Blanchot, *A Voice from Elsewhere*, trans. Charlotte Mandell (Albany: State University of New York Press, 2007), 5.

3. "It seemed that only the presence of someone could transform [the silence of the room] into true solitude" (286). Only this could transform it into an "essential solitude."

4. Just as *Death Sentence* cites Vicky Baum and a biblical formulation, just as *When the Time Comes* and *The Last Man* allude to Nietzsche, the title of this *récit* is taken from a Rilke passage also cited in *The Space of Literature*: "O seek

to understand that he must disappear! / Even if the anguish of it dismay him. / While his word extends this world, / Already he is beyond, where you may not accompany him . . . / And he obeys by going beyond"; Maurice Blanchot, "Rilke and Death's Demand" (1953) in *The Space of Literature*, trans. Ann Smock (Lincoln: University of Nebraska Press, 1982), 156. Rilke is announcing Orpheus in this figure, who here becomes the partner of the writer-narrator.

5. "'I have been doing a lot of thinking lately. I have the impression that you used to remain more hidden. You were perhaps something extraordinary, but I lived with the extraordinary without being disturbed by it, without seeing it and without knowing it.' 'Do you miss those days?' 'No, I do not miss them'" (300).

6. "I wish (for example) for a psychoanalyst to whom the disaster would beckon [*ferait signe*]," Blanchot would write in *The Writing of the Disaster*, trans. Ann Smock (Lincoln: University of Nebraska Press, 1986), 9. Pierre Fedida underscores this: "Language is the true interlocutor of such speech. Language as it exists in this form of the silent other who is listening. Might language be the reverse-side of speech? . . . It is not certain that psychoanalysts have wholly comprehended what Blanchot has said." In "Blanchot pose cette question de la mémoire," *Ralentir Travaux* 7 (Winter 1997): 67.

7. Maurice Blanchot, *When the Time Comes*, trans. Lydia Davis (Barrytown, N.Y.: Station Hill Press, 1985), 71.

8. "I was surprised that I was now very near the windows and yet felt that I was still in the middle of the room" (276).

9. "He turned to the window and, without pausing on me, stared rapidly, with an intense but rapid gaze, at the whole expanse and depth of the room" (275). "The figure was over there, I saw it motionless, it seemed to me that it was almost turned away, and I had the feeling that at the moment my eyes were fixed on it, it was preparing to climb the last steps and disappear. . . . It was nevertheless stopped and suspended under my gaze, as though the fact that my gaze was riveted to it had, in fact, riveted it to that point" (289). The bay window and the staircase are also the sites where specters appear in *The Turn of the Screw*, a *récit* that Blanchot discussed in 1954 in an article for the *NNRF*, in a way strangely resembling the analogy that he himself drew between his critical essays and his *récits* (and his life): "The ambiguity of the story is explained not just by the abnormal sensitivity of the governess but also because this governess is the *narrator*. She not only sees ghosts, which perhaps haunt the children, it is she who also talks about them, drawing them into the indistinct space of the narration"; "The Turn of the Screw" in *The Book to Come*, trans. Charlotte Mandell (Stanford: Stanford University Press, 2003), 130. Blanchot adds that the subject

of the *récit*, like that of James's *Notebooks*, is indeed the turn of the screw, "the pressure to which he submits the work," "the pressure of the narration itself." Ibid., 133.

10. "Someone who has disappeared completely is suddenly there, in front of you, behind a pane of glass, becoming the most powerful figure." Maurice Blanchot, *Death Sentence*, in *The Station Hill Blanchot Reader*, 161.

11. "What had been there was frightening [*effrayant*], was what I could not associate with [*frayer*] and, in this shift, it seemed to me that I myself could no longer associate with anyone, not even with myself" (294). Etymologically, *effrayer* comes from the Vulgar Latin *exfridare*, literally "expel from peace," and *frayer* from *fricare*, "to rub."

12. It is also found in *The Space of Literature*, in a form using the informal "you," as part of an imaginary inner dialogue attributed to Kafka, and to all authors: "Are you writing? Yes? Might you be writing?" in "Kafka and the Work's Demand" (1952) in *The Space of Literature*, 57.

42. THE CRITICAL DETOUR: A FEW ARTICLES OF LITERARY CRITICISM (1950–1951)

1. Maurice Blanchot, "The Museum, Art, and Time" (1950), in *Friendship*, trans. Elizabeth Rottenberg (Stanford: Stanford University Press, 1997), 34, 18.

2. Maurice Blanchot, "Madness *par excellence*" (1951), in *The Blanchot Reader*, ed. Michael Holland (Oxford: Blackwell, 1995), 113.

3. See Frédéric Badré, *Paulhan le juste* (Paris: Grasset, 1996), 294.

4. Blanchot, "The Museum, Art, and Time," 17, 24.

5. Ibid., 32. As if in echo to this, Blanchot would repeat and comment on these passages in "The Two Versions of the Imaginary": "to *resemble himself* . . . is this not an ill-chosen expression? Shouldn't we say: the deceased person resembles who he was when he was alive? 'Resembles himself' is, however, correct. 'Himself' resembles the impersonal being, distant and inaccessible, which resemblance, that it might be someone's, draws toward the day." In *The Space of Literature*, trans. Ann Smock (Lincoln: University of Nebraska Press, 1982), 257.

6. Maurice Blanchot, "The Two Versions of the Imaginary" in *The Space of Literature*, trans. Ann Smock (Lincoln: University of Nebraska Press, 1982), 258. The interrogative form of the phrase is dropped in the move from article to book.

7. Blanchot, "The Museum, Art and Time," 39, 40.

8. This emerges from his readings of Hölderlin, Mann, or Lowry, whose novel "is at once marvelously lost and controlled in a sovereign way," just as its hero is "awfully dominated, although master of himself until the end";

"Au-dessous du volcan" (1950), in *La condition critique: Articles 1945–1998*, ed. Christophe Bident (Paris: Gallimard, 2010), 175–177.

9. Maurice Blanchot, "Madness *par excellence*," in *The Blanchot Reader*, 125, 125, 119, 115. However, in an article from January 1955, Blanchot would place more emphasis on the theory of a "turning point" in Hölderlin's poetry (see *The Space of Literature*, 269–276). Michel Foucault would cast light on the paradoxical break in this discourse: the way that "*the absolute of rupture*" is found in the "inseparable unity" of madness and writing; "Le 'non' du père," *Critique* 178 (March 1962), reprinted in *Dits et écrits* (Gallimard, 1994), 1:199–200. Jacques Derrida would also address it at the beginning of "La parole soufflée" (Winter 1965), in *Writing and Difference*, trans. Alan Bass, 2nd ed. (London: Routledge, 2001), 212–245.

10. Maurice Blanchot, "Les justes" (1950), in *La condition critique*, 180. This might seem rather late for Blanchot's first mention of the extermination camps. It does not mean that he had not felt a pain that he had preferred to keep secret, or that he was not asking questions that as yet had led nowhere. Bataille was the first to be made aware of this pain and this questioning: in a 1946 letter to Prévost, he cast doubt over whether Rousset's *Univers concentrationnaire* could form the object of an article for *Critique* by Blanchot, "also, it is perhaps at the opposite pole to what Blanchot wishes to discuss" (May 7, 1946). In *Choix de lettres*, ed. Michel Surya (Paris: Gallimard, 1997), 318.

43. THE AUTHOR IN REVERSE: THE BIRTH OF *THE SPACE OF LITERATURE* (1951–1953)

1. Only one of the constituent articles appeared in 1951. The first important text was published in March 1952. A fairly regular series of articles followed until June 1953. Two further ones would appear in November and December of that year, and a final one, much later, in January 1955.

2. Was it a sign of his glory? Blanchot's research caused critics to think conservatively. In 1956, the jury of the Prix de la Critique was unanimous that they should not consider *The Space of Literature*, owing to their hesitations over whether it belonged to the genre of criticism.

3. "Introduction" to the first issue, signed *NRF* (January 1, 1953): 2–3.

4. Letter from Jean Paulhan to Roger Caillois, no. 178 (July 12, 1957) in *Correspondance Jean Paulhan-Roger Caillois, 1934–1967* (Paris: Gallimard, 1991), 232.

5. Remark reported in Didier Eribon, *Michel Foucault* (Paris: Flammarion, 1989), 79.

6. If we set aside Bataille's two articles on the *récits* and Levinas's on his critical thought, no major writer or philosopher wrote on Blanchot in the 1950s. Although these texts are no less remarkable for this reason, they were nonetheless written by his two best friends.

7. Kafka cited by Blanchot in "Kafka and the Work's Demand" (March 1952), in *The Space of Literature*, trans. Ann Smock (Lincoln: University of Nebraska Press, 1982), 64, 61.

8. "This way of reading—this presence to the work as a genesis—worsens, and thus produces the critical reading through which the reader, now the specialist, interrogates the work in order to know how it was made, asks it the secrets and the conditions of its creation, then examines it closely if it responds well to these conditions, etc. The reader, having become the specialist, becomes an author in reverse"; "Communication" (December 1953), in *The Space of Literature*, 203; this passage was added in the 1955 version.

9. Blanchot, "Kafka and the Work's Demand," 58–60.

10. Blanchot here cites Hegel as cited by Bataille (the article was originally published in *Critique*): life "does not fear surrendering to the devastation of death, but endures death, supports death, and persists in death"; "Death as Possibility" (November 1952) in *The Space of Literature*, 101.

11. [*Le désoeuvrement* is an important term in Blanchot's writing. In normal French it means "idleness" or "unemployment." But Blanchot uses it in close proximity to his notion of the work, *l'oeuvre* (itself always impossible and withdrawn), playing on its literal meaning, *dés-oeuvrement* being an "un-oeuvreing" or "un-working." —Trans.]

12. "The ordeal which always destroys the work in advance and always restores in it the futile overabundance of worklessness"; "Mallarmé's Experience" (July 1952), in *The Space of Literature*, 46. The work "is always in excess, it is the superfluous quality of what is always lacking, what we have called: the overabundance of refusal"; "Characteristics of the Work of Art" (1952), in ibid., 221–233, at 228; see also 215.

13. The editors of *Les Temps Modernes* placed the first installment of the article at the start of the May issue.

14. Maurice Blanchot, "On One Approach to Communism" (December 1953), in *Friendship*, trans. Elizabeth Rottenberg (Stanford: Stanford University Press, 1997), 93–96. What was described as only a "strange coincidence" in December 1953 became the "remarkable coincidence" in the version published in 1971.

15. Maurice Blanchot, "Literature and the Original Experience" (May–June 1952), in *The Space of Literature*, 228. The word "beginning" was underlined in the first version in *Les Temps Modernes*.

16. Ibid., 215. The words "the gift" were underlined in the first version.

17. Ibid., 246. In the book version, "present and visible" replace a more Bataillean vocabulary (the article used the words "impossible and sovereign").

18. Ibid., 238.

19. The article from *Les Temps Modernes* closes with these words: "the poem is solitude's poverty. This solitude is an understanding of the future,

but a powerless understanding: prophetic isolation which, before time, forever announces the beginning" ("Literature and the Original Experience," 247). A few years later, Blanchot would say strikingly that prophetic speech does not give the future, but takes away the present; *The Book to Come*, trans. Charlotte Mandell (Stanford: Stanford University Press, 2003), 79.

20. Maurice Blanchot, *The Unavowable Community*, trans. Pierre Joris (Barrytown, N.Y.: Station Hill Press, 1988), 30; see also *Michel Foucault as I Imagine Him*, in *Foucault—Blanchot*, trans. Jeffrey Mehlman (New York: Zone Books, 1987), 63–64.

21. René Char cited in "Literature and the Original Experience," 214.

22. Maurice Blanchot, "The Beast of Lascaux," trans. Leslie Hill, in *Oxford Literary Review* 22 (2000): 9–18, at 12–13.

23. Emmanuel Levinas, "Le regard du poète," in *Sur Maurice Blanchot* (Montpellier: Fata Morgana, 1975), 22–26. The aim of this essay is to demonstrate this process of reversal, this deconstruction; it begins by recalling the heritage of the 1936 lectures. In Blanchot, he writes, "the accent with which the word *Being* is offered is Heideggerian" (12).

24. Blanchot would return to this critique of Heideggerian thought as a "philosophy of rootedness" (and as the thought of a "slightly shameful Neuter") in "L'étrange et l'étranger" (1958), in *La condition critique: Articles 1945–1998*, ed. Christophe Bident (Paris: Gallimard, 2010), 278–288.

25. Emmanuel Levinas, "Le regard du poète," 24.

26. Maurice Blanchot, "Où va la littérature?" *NNRF* 8 (August 1953): 303.

27. Blanchot, *The Space of Literature*, 94, 220.

28. "Impatience is the failing of one who wants to escape the absence of time; patience is the ruse that seeks to master this absence of time by making it into a different time, measured otherwise. But true patience does not exclude impatience, it is intimacy with impatience, it is impatience suffered and endlessly endured"; Maurice Blanchot, "Orpheus's Gaze" (June 1953), in *The Space of Literature*, 173.

29. Maurice Blanchot, "Inspiration, Lack of Inspiration" (March 1953), in *The Space of Literature*, 187.

44. ALWAYS ALREADY (THE POETIC AND POLITICAL INTERRUPTION OF THOUGHT): TOWARD *THE BOOK TO COME* (1953–1958)

1. Maurice Blanchot, *The Book to Come*, trans. Charlotte Mandell (Stanford: Stanford University Press, 2003). Unless indicated otherwise, references in this chapter henceforth refer to this translated work.

2. "How can one speak of oneself?" The question was still a valid one, but it was no longer a major concern. Blanchot returned to this formulation in articles of February 1956 (on Michel Leiris; "Battle with the Angel" in *Friend-*

ship, trans. Elizabeth Rottenberg [Stanford: Stanford University Press, 1997], 129) and June 1958 ("Rousseau" in *The Book to Come*, 45). See also the article on Hesse: "Not all his books are autobiographical, but almost all speak intimately about him"; "H.H." (May 1956) in *The Book to Come*, 167; indeed, the elements shared by the *Steppenwolf* and Blanchot's personality are not without interest. Last, some purely anecdotal allusions can be found. In the article on Caillois's and Huizinga's books on gambling, Blanchot evokes chance in games of luck. The example of roulette given is not accidental: "that 22 should be the number that emerges, I cannot expect this, it is the unexpected," he writes with secret humor; "L'attrait, l'horreur du jeu" (May 1958), in *La condition critique: Articles 1945–1998*, ed. Christophe Bident (Paris: Gallimard, 2010), 269–278. Choosing his birthday in a nod to chance is itself a game—or a way of believing in magic. It is sometimes said that Blanchot liked gambling (games of chance, casino games; he did live near Monte Carlo for many years). Could this explain the conclusion of the article on Caillois and Huizinga? "We will be better able to understand how gambling can lead to great passions and why the greatest passion is that of games of chance." Ibid., 278.

3. Maurice Blanchot, "Reflections on Hell: 2" (May 1954), in *The Infinite Conversation*, trans. Susan Hanson (Minneapolis: University of Minnesota Press, 1993), 181. This sentence, which offers a summary of the critical thought of the 1950s, nonetheless only appeared in 1969.

4. Maurice Blanchot, "The Fall: The Flight" (1956) in *Friendship*, 205.

5. Maurice Blanchot, "The Great Hoax" (1957), trans. Ann Smock, in *The Blanchot Reader*, ed. Michael Holland (Oxford: Blackwell, 1995), 157–166.

6. Maurice Blanchot, "Kafka and Brod" (1954), in *Friendship*, 246.

7. The tone has significantly changed since the article from *Faux pas*, which concluded with the "divinity" of Claudel's mind (288–295). The phrase cited here appears as such only in 1959, and in a note to the text (the number of the *NNRF* of 1955 was, it is true, a homage to Claudel).

8. See notably "A toute extrémité" (1955) in *The Book to Come*, 107–110. [This chapter title is translated as "At Every Extreme," but might be better rendered "At the Very Last." —Trans.]

9. Maurice Blanchot, "The Power and the Glory" (1958), in *The Book to Come*, esp. 245–246.

10. Maurice Blanchot, "L'étrange et l'étranger" (1958), in *La condition critique*, 279.

11. Maurice Blanchot, "Reflections on Nihilism: 2" (May 1954), in *The Infinite Conversation*, 177. The expression "movement of detour" was added in the 1969 version.

12. For example, Gaëtan Picon's accusation that Blanchot was an "ontologist of non-Being" is not far from suggesting as much. Even in recognizing

that the experience of literature in his critical oeuvre has "the greatest authority," Picon denounces its incomplete logic, the lack of a final stage where "negative transcendence" would open onto "living transcendence," thus freeing art of its subordination to the void of nothingness; see "L'oeuvre critique de Maurice Blanchot II," *Critique* 113 (October 1956): 845–854.

13. Maurice Blanchot, "The Terror of Identification" (1958), in *Friendship*, 216. The final words, on detour, are found in the book version only.

14. "Nihilism has become the commonplace of thought and of literature." In "Reflections on Nihilism: 1" (August 1958), in *The Infinite Conversation*, 143.

15. References to Marxism become increasingly common in this period, as do signs of sympathy. For instance, Blanchot even sees the meeting of Breton and Trotsky as "an exalting sign"; "There could be no question of ending well," in *The Book to Come*, 29. He translates *The Man Without Qualities* as "the man without particularities": "is he not essentially the proletarian, if the proletariat, characterized by not-having, is directed only toward the suppression of any individual mode of being?" He thought it a shame that Musil had avoided this question; "Musil: 2" (March 1958), in *The Book to Come*, 260 n.

16. *Thomas the Obscure* (1950 version), trans. Robert Lamberton (Barrytown, N.Y.: Station Hill Press, 1988), 14.

17. The expression "always already" appeared in April 1953 in an article ("Rilke and Death's Demand") collected in *The Space of Literature*, 141; it is found four times between 1954 and 1958. It was used widely in the texts of the 1960s. It is well known how much it would influence Derrida's thinking. On the "violent gap," see "Man at Point Zero" (April 1956) in *Friendship*, 82.

18. See "Tragic Thought" (August 1956), in *The Infinite Conversation*, 96–105.

19. Maurice Blanchot, "The Speech of Analysis" (September 1956), in ibid., 455. Blanchot nonetheless adds that this situation is a fragile one, and always tends to be reappropriated by institutions.

20. Maurice Blanchot, "The Pain of Dialogue" (March 1956), in *The Book to Come*, 155. Blanchot evokes similar modern modes of interrupted dialogue regarding Malraux, James, Kafka, and Camus.

21. Maurice Blanchot, "The Book to Come: 2" (November 1957), in ibid., 233–244; "The Effect of Strangeness" (February 1957), in *The Infinite Conversation*, 360–367 (the two contemporary poets are only cited in the 1969 version).

22. Ibid., 363.

23. Maurice Blanchot, "Artaud" (November 1956), in *The Book to Come*, 34–40. In its review version, the text is preceded by a page that sets out in the form of four fragments the relations between suffering and thought. "Forgot-

ten" in *The Book to Come*, this page is nonetheless not dissimilar to various passages in *The Last Man*.

24. Maurice Blanchot, "Museum Sickness" (April 1957), in *Friendship*, 48. This conception of the power to separate time was shared by Blanchot and Bataille; Sartre judged it to be illusory in "Un nouveau mystique."

25. Maurice Blanchot, "Reflections on Nihilism" (May 1954), in *The Infinite Conversation*, 149.

26. Ibid. When he reworked these pages written in summer 1958 for publication in *The Infinite Conversation*, Blanchot set himself in clear opposition to Heidegger (see particularly the end of the footnote on 449–451). Among the Heideggerian strategies he rejected was the undeniable conflation of an implicit discourse (regarding the philosopher's rejection of Nietzsche) with an explicit one (his commitment, the commitment of his discourse to Nazism).

27. It also came indirectly from Mr. Chouchani, the mad teacher-figure and nomad of thought from whom Levinas learned a lot about Jewish mysticism between 1945 and 1949. Blanchot did not meet him in person, but heard reports through his friend as well as through his brother René and his sister-in-law Anna, who also met Chouchani.

28. Maurice Blanchot, "Affirmation (Desire, Affliction)" (July–August 1957), in *The Infinite Conversation*, 106–122.

29. Ibid., 116–117.

30. Ibid., 119.

31. Stéphane Mallarmé in *Selected Letters*, trans. Rosemary Lloyd (Chicago: University of Chicago Press, 1988), 77.

32. As early as April 1954, Blanchot develops a reflection on misfortune, with a veiled reference to the camps ("these overwhelming, so vast upheavals produced in our time"; in its original version it read "these overwhelming, so vast upheavals that our times have unveiled"). It would be interesting to compare this reflection with one by Robert Antelme, named "Pauvre-Prolétaire-Déporté" and published without fanfare in a Christian journal in 1948. Maurice Blanchot, "Reflections on Hell: 1" (April 1954), in *The Infinite Conversation*, 171–176, at 173; Robert Antelme, *Textes inédits* . . . (Paris: Gallimard, 1997), 25–32.

33. Maurice Blanchot in "Affirmation (Desire, Affliction)" (July–August 1957), in *The Infinite Conversation*, 120.

34. Ibid., 121, 122.

35. Ibid.

36. Maurice Blanchot in "The Great Hoax" (1957), in *The Blanchot Reader*, 166.

37. [This refers to an episode concerning "the Manifesto of the 121," a petition against conscription for the Algerian war, which was signed by

Sartre. De Gaulle, wary of the implications of arresting this leading writer, declared: "Voltaire must not be thrown in jail." Of course, Voltaire *was* thrown in jail. —Trans.]

38. Maurice Blanchot, "Man at Point Zero" (April 1956), in *Friendship*, 82. In 1956, he had written, "perish in order to begin."

39. Some of the pearls are as follows: "a fierce determination to perform intellectual gymnastics," "a sort of swindle" (Claude Ernoult in *Les Lettres nouvelles*), "a sample of hardline obscurantism" in which he "persists in following his friend Bataille" (Ed Ewbank in *La Lanterne*). "Paradox can be positive, it spices things up, adds salt to the mixture. But Mr. Blanchot adds salt by the spoonful, by the ladleful, an avalanche of salt" (E.B. in *La Libre Belgique*). *The Space of Literature* was said to be "a curious, picturesque text, which could prove interesting to any reader who, wishing to win the Great Prize for Translation, might attempt to turn it into lucid and clear French" (anonymous reviewer in *Phare Dimanche*). *The Last Man* "beats all records for hermeticism in the genre of the novel" (Albert Loranquin in *Le Bulletin des Lettres*).

Fortunately, we find some more fortunate texts by Butor, Carrouges, Dalmas, Dufrenne, Pingaud, Poulet, or Rida, as well as a very good commentary by Jean Pfeiffer, "L'expérience de Maurice Blanchot," *Empédocle* 11 (July–August 1950): 55–64.

40. Roger Judrin, review of *The Last Man* in NNRF 52 (April 1957): 725–726.

45. OF AN AMAZING LIGHTNESS: *THE LAST MAN* (1953–1957)

1. Printing was completed in January. Four excerpts appeared in *Botteghe Oscure*, the *NNRF*, and *Monde nouveau* between 1955 and January 1957. The "new version" that would appear in 1971, even though it would carry this description only from 1977 onward, seems only to have minor differences.

2. Maurice Blanchot, *The Last Man*, trans. by Lydia Davis (New York: Columbia University Press, 1987), 18. References in the remainder of this chapter are to this work.

3. See Jacques Derrida, *Parages* (Paris: Galilée, 1986), 176–179, note. It must also be said that for Blanchot the Nietzschean "last man" is "he who does not want to be the last man": "the man of the last rank, the man of permanence, of subsistence." In *The Infinite Conversation*, trans. Susan Hanson (Minneapolis: University of Minnesota Press, 1993), 155.

4. See Franz Kafka, *Journal* (Paris: Grasset, 1954), 3.

5. "Like a wolf, he said" (3, 19). Let us recall that Blanchot published a double article on Hesse in May and June 1956, when he was likely to have been about to finish his *récit*.

6. Indeed, Michel Gauthier picked up a large number of similarities between the two fictions. See "La montagne magique" (Fall 1983), 16. We can also think of the links possible between Claudia in *When the Time Comes* and Clavdia Chauchat in *The Magic Mountain*.

7. In November 1956, Blanchot published an article on Artaud in the *NNRF*, which would be collected in *The Book to Come*—apart from four fragments which, in the third person and without ever naming Artaud, describe the relation he felt to suffering and to thought. Three months before the *récit* was published, the phrases were strikingly similar. For example: "For him, each thought was the greatest suffering, and not to think, the absence of thought, was the bare presence of suffering. It seems that he wished to encounter a small thought that, in giving some time to pain, would have allowed him to suffer it." "Artaud," *Nouvelle Nouvelle Revue Française* 47 (November 1956): 873. And in *The Last Man*, the following words are spoken by the woman character: "When he thinks, he suffers, and when he doesn't think, his suffering is naked. . . . He must be given a little thought that isn't a thought of pain, a brief moment, I think that would be enough." The narrator remarks, "So she tried to procure for him that little bit of time—that single moment that might allow him to recover the pain, to suffer it?" (51).

8. Georges Bataille, *Inner Experience*, trans. Stuart Kendall (Albany: SUNY Press, 2014), 65–66.

9. "Her body seemed incredibly hard to me, more so than any truly hard thing could be. Scarcely had I even grazed her than she leaped up, crying out indistinct words which surely expressed an excruciating ignorance and rejection. I didn't have time to study them, I wanted only to grab her again, and in fact, she immediately collapsed into my arms, everything in her that was hard melted, became soft, of a dreamlike fluidity, while she wept and wept" (47). This scene, which recalls J.'s collapse in *Death Sentence*, mixes together the motifs of jealousy, guilt, and incommunicability. Above all, it marks the absolute, intense, unbearable toughening imposed by entering alone the passive experience of dying.

10. Maurice Blanchot, *Thomas l'obscur, première version, 1941* (Paris: Gallimard, 2005), 191.

11. Maurice Blanchot, "At Every Extreme" (February 1955), in *The Book to Come*, trans. Charlotte Mandell (Stanford: Stanford University Press, 2003), 107. This article, like that of the following month, "Death of the Last Writer" (March 1955) in ibid., responds implicitly to a text by Cioran, "La fin du roman," published in December 1953 in the *NNRF*, which only praised Blanchot as a novelist in order to paint him as a nihilist, although this was in fact to be reductive in relation to his thinking, which constantly condemned nihilism.

12. [*À toute extremité* means "at the last moment" or "at death's door." In the pages that follow, Bident plays on this sense of extremity, which, for Blanchot, links the thinking of death to extreme models of writing and thought. —Trans.]

13. Blanchot, "Artaud," 40. We should also compare the two articles on Simone Weil and the thought of misfortune, of July and August 1957, to passages such as the following: "he had the weakness of an absolutely unfortunate man, and that measureless weakness struggled against the force of that measureless thought, that weakness always seemed to find that great thought insufficient, and it demanded this, that what had been thought in such a strong way should be thought again and re-thought on the level of extreme weakness" (16–17).

14. Georges Bataille, *Manet*, in *Oeuvres complètes* (Paris: Gallimard, 1979), 9:157.

15. See Stéphane Mallarmé, "The Tomb of Edgar Poe," in *Collected Poems: A Bilingual Edition*, trans. Henry Weinfield (Berkeley: University of California Press, 1994), 71.

46. GRACE, STRENGTH, GENTLENESS: MEETING ROBERT ANTELME (1958)

1. Blanchot succinctly describes the encounter in *For Friendship* (1993), in *Political Writings, Political Writings, 1953–1993*, trans. Zakir Paul (New York: Fordham University Press, 2010), 137.

2. "Do we know when it begins? There is no friendship at first sight; instead, it develops little by little, in a slow labor of time. We were friends and we did not know it," Blanchot writes as he begins a text dedicated to Mascolo; ibid., 134. These words also apply to Robert Antelme.

3. Mascolo said that he, Duras, Antelme, and a few others had been "Judaized" by the war.

4. Robert Antelme, "Vengeance?" (November 1945), collected in *Textes inédits* . . . (Paris: Gallimard, 1997), 17–24.

5. Ibid.

6. Maurice Blanchot, "After the Fact," in *The Station Hill Blanchot Reader*, ed. George Quasha (Barrytown, N.Y.: Station Hill Press, 1998), 494.

7. Daniel Dobbels in Antelme, *Textes inédits*, 9.

8. Marguerite Duras in ibid., 252.

9. Michel Surya, "Une absence d'issue," in ibid., 114–119.

10. Robert Antelme, "broadly" remembered by Dionys Mascolo in interview with Aliette Armel, *Le Magazine Littéraire* 278 (June 1990): 38.

11. This is what he wrote to his friend Georges Bataille: "That something which can be called misfortune, but which we must also leave nameless, can in a sense be shared; it is a mysterious, perhaps misleading, perhaps unsayably

true thing"; letter of August 8, 1961, cited in Georges Bataille, *Choix de lettres*, ed. Michel Surya (Paris: Gallimard, 1997), 592.

47. IN THE GAZE OF FASCINATION: THE RETURN TO PARIS (1957–1958)

1. Maurice Blanchot, "On Jouhandeau's Work," in *A World in Ruins: Chronicles of Intellectual Life, 1943*, trans. Michael Holland (New York: Fordham University Press, 2016), 107–110, at 109. Parts of this article were included in "Chaminadour" in *Faux Pas*, trans. Charlotte Mandell (Stanford: Stanford University Press, 2001), 227–233, but not these words on the mother.

2. Maurice Blanchot in *The Space of Literature*, trans. Ann Smock (Lincoln: University of Nebraska Press, 1982), 33.

3. Louis-René des Forêts in "Sur les traces de Maurice Blanchot," France-Culture radio show first broadcast on September 17, 1994. Were there no books or many books, then? With Blanchot, who sold many of his (too) numerous books, and who would say more than once that in order to stop writing it was necessary to write (too much), absence and presence always go in hand. [Des Forêts is referring to Paul Valéry's *Monsieur Teste*. —Trans.]

48. REFUSAL, II. IN THE NAME OF THE ANONYMOUS: THE *14 JUILLET* PROJECT (1958–1959)

1. This manifesto was published as an annex to the complete reedition of the *14 Juillet* journal in *Lignes*, in an unnumbered special edition of 1990.

2. For a more precise history of the Rue Saint-Benoît group, see Dionys Mascolo, *Autour d'un effort de mémoire* (Paris: Maurice Nadeau, 1987), and his interview with Aliette Armel in *Le Magazine Littéraire* 278 (June 1990): 36–40.

3. Maurice Blanchot, "Intellectuals under Scrutiny" (1984), in *The Blanchot Reader*, ed. Michael Holland (Oxford: Blackwell, 1995), 217. The conditions in which the Republic was trying to save itself recalled the summer of 1940 too closely for Blanchot not to emerge from his withdrawal.

4. Maurice Blanchot, letter to Dionys Mascolo, trans. Michael Holland in ibid., 107.

5. His joy was all the greater given that, the same day or very nearly, Mascolo received a letter from Bataille that was equally unexpected, but for different reasons; see Georges Bataille, *Choix de lettres*, ed. Michel Surya (Paris: Gallimard, 1997), 491; see also 481–483.

6. Maurice Blanchot in *For Friendship* (1993), in *Political Writings, 1953–1993*, trans. Zakir Paul (New York: Fordham University Press, 2010), 137.

7. This sense of *passage* explains, it seems to us, the two moments of *For Friendship* that are indirectly quite "harsh" toward Mascolo. Having just discussed how their friendship began in 1958, Blanchot adds: "It was doubtless then that I met Robert Antelme," *For Friendship*, 137. And concluding the

book, which originated as a preface that Mascolo did not dare request from him (leaving Maurice Nadeau to pass on his request), he recognizes Emmanuel Levinas, "the only friend—ah, distant friend—whom I call *tu* and who calls me *tu*" (ibid., 143).

8. Maurice Blanchot in "On One Approach to Communism" (December 1953), in *Friendship*, trans. Elizabeth Rottenberg (Stanford: Stanford University Press, 1997), 97.

9. Robert Antelme, "Les principes à l'épreuve," *Le 14 Juillet* 1:11–12; Dionys Mascolo, "Refus inconditionnel," ibid., 19; Louis-René des Forêts, "Le droit à la vérité," ibid., 20.

10. The similarity of the two titles is proof less of borrowing than of recognition. In fact, the word "refusal" belongs to the vocabulary of all Blanchot's political periods. It came back into force in 1958, having also been used in "The Power and the Glory" (April) in *The Book to Come*, trans. Charlotte Mandell (Stanford: Stanford University Press, 2003), 249, and in "L'étrange et l'étranger": "Literature, like thought, is nothing but the experience of itself and for itself: this experience of strangeness nonetheless only grasps or institutes the movement of refusal that tirelessly constitutes it and tirelessly fails to constitute it" in *La condition critique: Articles 1945–1998*, ed. Christophe Bident (Paris: Gallimard, 2010), 288.

11. Maurice Blanchot, "Refusal" (October 1958), in *Friendship*, 112, 297.

12. Ibid., 7.

13. Let us recall the sentence with which Blanchot signed off, in December 1937, from his militancy on the far right: "The true communist dissident is he who leaves communism, not in order to move closer to capitalist beliefs, but in order to define the true conditions of the struggle against capitalism"; *Combat* 20:155. It defines rather well the situation of this new group of friends.

14. [June 18 was the date of De Gaulle's famous radio broadcast in 1940. —Trans.]

15. Blanchot, "Refusal," 10–11.

16. For example this phrase: "[the dictator] is the man of *dictare*, of imperious repetition, the one who, each time the danger of an unknown language appears, tries to struggle against it with the rigor of a commandment without rejoinder and without content," in "Death of the Last Writer" (March 1955), in *The Book to Come*, 220. The phrase was repeated in a letter to Mascolo of November 29, 1958 (which is to say, when the article was being readied for republication in *The Book to Come*).

17. Maurice Blanchot "The Essential Perversion" (1958), in *Political Writings*, 10.

18. Ibid., 9.

19. "The prodigious hatred for reflection, the hatred focused on revenge against thought, are revealed in the reactions of the *sheep* [*veaux*] . . . those

Notes to pages 310–316   553

that De Gaulle delicately called *sheep*"; Francis Marmande, "Par haine de la pensée" (From Hatred for Thought) in the introduction to the republication of *Le 14 Juillet* 1:10. [De Gaulle's term was *veaux*, the sense of which seems best rendered in English by reference to a different animal. —Trans.]

20. Etienne Balibar was the one who formulated or reformulated these principles, in circumstances analogous to those of 1959 or 1960, during the movement of winter 1997 against the Debré law on declaring foreigners' periods of stay in France. At the height of the Algerian war, at the height of reactionary Gaullism or neo-Gaullism (mimicked by Debré), at the height of power's arrogance (claiming for itself the right of surveillance, of casting suspicion, of potentially making guilty any citizen acting as host), a community of artists and intellectuals demonstrated its refusal of the law's ignorance by using principles that are like the "higher laws of humanity"—the very same ones, if we read those listed by Balibar, backed by Robert Antelme; "État d'urgence démocratique," *Le Monde* (February 19, 1997), 1, 13.

21. See Blanchot, *Friendship*, 149; Jean Paulhan, letters 162 and 163 in *Choix des lettres, 1946–1968, Le don des langues* (Paris: Gallimard, 1996) 3:181–183.

22. René Char, "Note à propos d'une deuxième lecture de 'La perversion essentielle' dans "Le 14 Juillet 1959'" (1964), in *Recherche de la base et du sommet* (Paris: Gallimard, 1971), 124–125.

49. NOTE THAT I SAY "RIGHT" AND NOT "DUTY":
THE DECLARATION ON THE RIGHT TO INSUBORDINATION
IN THE ALGERIAN WAR (1960)

1. This account is based primarily on four sources, the fullest and most reliable. They are: Dionys Mascolo's personal archives (notably fourteen of the preparatory versions of the final text); "Le droit à l'insoumission: Le dossier des '121,'" in *Cahiers Libres* 14 (January 1961), including an interview given by Blanchot to Madeleine Chapsal for *L'Express* in fall 1960 but censured by the editors at the weekly paper; a section of Anne Cohen-Solal's *Sartre* (Paris: Gallimard, 1989), 694–717; and an MA thesis by Fabien Augier on the manifesto, from University Paris-VII in 1988: "La résistance française à la guerre d'Algérie."

2. Maurice Blanchot et al., "Declaration of the Right to Insubordination in the Algerian War," in *Political Writings, 1953–1993*, trans. Zakir Paul (New York: Fordham University Press, 2010), 15–17. In an unpublished text (from Dionys Mascolo's archives and only referred to, to our knowledge, by Fabien Augier in "La résistance française à la guerre d'Algérie"), Blanchot qualified the political and military situation of France and Algeria precisely as "of a nihilist character." This text dates from 1960, probably from the fall.

3. "The undersigned . . . declare:

—We respect the refusal to take arms against the Algerian people, and we judge this to be justified.
—We respect the conduct of the French citizens who consider it their duty to bring help and protection to the oppressed Algerians in the name of the French people, and we judge this to be justified.
—The cause of the Algerian people, which contributes to ruining the colonial system in a decisive way, is the cause of all free men." "Declaration of the Right to Insubordination," Ibid., 16–17.

4. Maurice Blanchot, "First I would like to say . . . ," in ibid., 33–34. This interview took place several months before the one between Georges Bataille and the same journalist, in February 1961 in Orléans. It is also significant that it was the only interview Blanchot ever gave, and that it was rejected by the editors of *L'Express* and not published.

5. Dionys Mascolo, "Aux heures d'un communisme de pensée," in *À la recherche d'un communisme de pensée* (Paris: Fourbis, 1993), 441. See also the interview with Aliette Armel, *Le Magazine Littéraire* 278 (June 1990): 39. Marguerite Duras, too, would state in 1985: "The Declaration on the right to insubordination did not order men to rebel against the state. It gave no orders. It did not and does not demand that the individual disobey the orders of the state. It teaches him that within him he has, both clearly and intelligibly, all the reasons needed to be insubordinate and also all those needed to not be so. . . . It places the men who are 'called' before their essential responsibility: their sovereignty"; she added that this was probably "an absolute text.'" In "Écrit pour tous les temps, tous les carêmes," in *Outside* (Paris: POL, 1993), 2:79.

6. Claude Roy, *Somme toute* (Paris: Gallimard, 1976), 285; Madeleine Chapsal, *L'Express* (October 6, 1960).

7. "The approach that led us to say these words together, in response to this question for our consciences, was no different to the approach that leads the solitary writer to speak—to write—on his own account. Or if you will, the thinking man here (by intervening in things) was only following his own thinking." Mascolo, *À la recherche d'un communisme de pensée*, 441.

8. Unpublished text of fall 1960 from the archive of Dionys Mascolo; quoted in Augier, "La résistance française à la guerre d'Algérie."

9. "Is it necessary to recall that fifteen years after the destruction of Hitler's order, French militarism as a result of the demands of this war has managed to reinstate torture and to make it like an institution in Europe once again?" "Declaration of the Right to Insubordination in the Algerian War," 16. Blanchot was the one who came up with the definitive version of this phrase, adding notably the word "like."

10. Unpublished text of fall 1960 from the archive of Dionys Mascolo; quoted in Augier, "La résistance française à la guerre d'Algérie."

11. "Anarchy lies in the fact of letting the army become a political power as well as in the fact that the current regime owes its rise to a military coup d'état that thereby sealed from the beginning the illegality of the imperious order that in its august manner it claims to represent and to impose upon us. Since May 1958 we have been in a situation of anarchy, this is the truth that everyone has vaguely grasped." The army introduced the trap of dictatorship, which made the people the prisoners of their own children: "because their sons are participating in it—albeit automatically, by the automatism of military service—they can no longer recognize that this war is unjust, and they make themselves its accomplices." *Political Writings*, 34, 35.

12. Among the 121 signatories, beyond the "main authors" of the text, were Adamov, Blin, Boulez, Damisch, Dort, Lefebvre, Lévy (Paul), Lindon, Losfeld, Malraux (Florence), Maspero, Masson, Monod (Théodore), Mounin, Pontalis, Resnais, Robbe-Grillet, Sarraute, Signoret, Simon, Vercors, and Vernant.

13. Maurice Blanchot, *For Friendship* (1993), in *Political Writings*, 137.

14. Letter from Dionys Mascolo to Maurice Blanchot, July 31, 1960. "If you wish, something will be done, and I shall stand close by you as you may desire, to help you, if I can. Beyond simple respect, of which it is ashamed, this is a type of necessity that can only be imposed through rare individuals such as yourself, I am sure of it."

15. Letter from Maurice Blanchot to Dionys Mascolo of August 8, 1960.

16. Letter from Maurice Blanchot to Dionys Mascolo of July 22, 1960.

17. Letter from Maurice Blanchot to Jacques Dupin, July 1960 (between the 23rd and the 26th).

18. Mascolo, *À la recherche d'un communisme de pensée*, 440; Maurice Blanchot, letter to Christian Limousin, July 28, 1975, trans. Michael Holland in *Paragraph* 30, no. 3 (November 2007): 17.

19. Three periodicals with small readerships, sometimes quasi-clandestine ones, would publish the Manifesto in full: *Témoignages et Documents*, which published dossiers on the Algerian war, defined itself as a force of opposition and the site of freedom of expression and was seized on September 20 for having printed the piece; *Vérité-Liberté*, a review created in May 1960 by opponents of the war in Algeria, coming from *Esprit* as did Jean-Marie Domenach or from *Les Temps Modernes* as did Jean Pouillon, and whose editorial committee had roughly as many signatories as nonsignatories; and *La Voie Communiste*, which was Leninist, anti-Stalinist, and opposed to the Communist Party, placed the manifesto on the front page of its September issue. The September–October issue of *Les Temps Modernes* would appear with two blank pages and the list of 121 signatories, and it was also

seized. The manifesto was reproduced in great numbers abroad (Germany, Belgium, Great Britain, Holland, Italy, Sweden, Colombia, the United States, and elsewhere).

20. Thierry Maulnier, editorial in *Le Figaro* (September 30, 1960).

21. Blanchot recounts the scene in *For Friendship*, 139. He had already alluded to it discreetly in "A Plural Speech" in *The Infinite Conversation*, trans. Susan Hanson (Minneapolis: University of Minnesota Press, 1993), 81.

22. Among the new signatories were Châtelet, Debord, Danièle Delorme, Bernard Frank, Limbour, Clara Malraux, Olliver, Madeleine Rebérioux, Sagan, Siné, Terzieff, Truffaut, Tzara, Vildrac, and Wahl.

23. The event is briefly described by Maurice Nadeau in *Grâces leur soient rendues* (Paris: Albin Michel, 1990), 71.

24. Mascolo, *À la recherche d'un communisme de pensée*, 443.

50. INVISIBLE PARTNERS: THE PROJECT FOR THE *INTERNATIONAL REVIEW* (1960–1965)

1. Maurice Blanchot, letter of December 2, 1960 to Jean-Paul Sartre in *Political Writings, 1953–1993*, trans. Zakir Paul (New York: Fordham University Press, 2010), 37. The richest dossier on the *International Review* was published in number 11 of the journal *Lignes* in September 1990. It contains an ensemble of documents written by the editors in 1961 and many letters from between 1960 and 1965, which came from the archives of the Italian publishing house Einaudi (the Gulliver collection) and from those of the cantonal library in Lugano (Vittorini collection). In this issue the letters are arranged in chronological order.

2. Ibid.

3. Ibid.

4. Blanchot's reservations regarding Sartre are well known. They did not prevent him from truly admiring the "generosity of spirit" that he saw, as it were, incarnated in him ("Sartre's readiness to make affirmations makes many of his thoughts polemical ones, but it expresses his generosity of spirit, for if he offers up even his most instantaneous affirmations unhesitatingly, as if his whole life had always revolved around them," he wrote in "L'étrange et l'étranger" (1958), in *La condition critique: Articles 1945–1998*, ed. Christophe Bident (Paris: Gallimard, 2010), 278–288). Blanchot appealed to Sartre in the name of this generosity on the subject of the *International Review*.

5. Blanchot, *Political Writings*, 37.

6. Iris Murdoch, Leszek Kolakowski, Richard Seaver, Carlos Fuentes, and Ernesto Sabato were the *Review*'s correspondents, although they (co)responded with varying levels of interest.

7. Letter from Maurice Blanchot to Dionys Mascolo, August 7, 1961.
8. Letter from Maurice Blanchot to Georges Bataille, without date (1960?), cited in Georges Bataille, *Choix de lettres*, ed. Michel Surya (Paris: Gallimard, 1997), 593–594.
9. Letter from Maurice Blanchot to Georges Bataille, postscript, August 19, 1961.
10. Letter from Maurice Blanchot to Georges Bataille, August 8, 1961, cited in Bataille, *Choix de lettres*, 591–592.
11. Letter from Maurice Blanchot to Georges Bataille, May 16, 1962.
12. Blanchot, *Political Writings*, 56. Blanchot used exactly the same terms in a letter to Dionys Mascolo. The commentaries that follow cite the preparatory texts written by Blanchot and published in *Political Writings*, 56–69.
13. Letter from Maurice Blanchot to Dionys Mascolo, June 29, 1961.
14. Blanchot, *Political Writings*, 57, 59. The International Review would also be different to any other international review, such as *Botteghe Oscure*, the trilingual (English-French-Italian) review edited by Margeurite de Bassaiano, to which Blanchot, Bataille, and most of all René Char had contributed; these contributions bear witness to their longstanding interest in confronting texts, languages, and modes of knowledge.
15. Blanchot, *Political Writings*, 59.
16. Ibid., 56–57.
17. Maurice Blanchot, "Reading," in *The Space of Literature*, trans. Ann Smock (Lincoln: University of Nebraska Press, 1982), 197.
18. Blanchot, *Political Writings*, 57.
19. Maurice Blanchot, *For Friendship* (1993), in ibid., 140.
20. Maurice Nadeau, *Grâces leur soient rendues* (Paris: Albin Michel, 1990), 71 (on the meeting with the publisher, see 460). In a letter of November 1962, a furious Blanchot would speak of Gallimard and its "ways of doing things which would be more suited to a lunatic asylum"; letter to Dionys Mascolo published in *Lignes* 11 (September 1990): 258. The negotiations bear witness to how publishers failed to understand the *International Review*, which aimed to end the territorial logic of the world of reviews.
21. Maurice Blanchot attended his funeral in Vézélay. Jacques Pimpaneau does not mention his presence, but Jean Piel confirms that he was there, alongside himself and Michel Leiris; see "*Critique*, l'histoire souterraine de l'intelligence contemporaine," *Libération* (December 13–14, 1980), 20–21. Other, private accounts confirm Piel's. Blanchot went to Vézélay with his sister-in-law. He took with him a wide wreath of flowers.
22. Letter from Elio Vittorini to Louis-René des Forêts, February 1963, in *Lignes* 11 (September 1990): 272.

23. Italo Calvino, article in *Menabò* quoted by Marina Galletti in "Le monstre souterrain," in *Georges Bataille après-tout* (Georges Bataille After All), ed. Denis Hollier et al. (Paris: Belin, 1995), 251. Concerning collective and fragmentary writing, Vittorini let it be understood that only a centralized country such as France had the luxury of thinking the interruption of a relation which was not yet established between friends in a country whose geographical separation and linguistic difference (Blanchot himself remarked upon this) made it necessary to "hold the relation" before any other absolute. This was an interesting objection that applied above all to the Germans, now separated by a wall. However, it should have been one more reason to begin and then continue the *Review*, as it offered precisely something like the siteless site where the absolute could be related to the demand of thinking separation.

24. Friedrich Nietzsche, "Of the Friend," in *Thus Spake Zarathustra*, trans. R. J. Hollingdale (London: Penguin, 1961), 82.

25. Blanchot, *Political Writings*, 57, 61.

26. "The fragment linked to the mobility of seeking, of the traveling thought that fulfills itself in separate affirmations and demands this separation (Nietzsche)"; "Truth is *nomadic*," the project stated, leaning on Nietzsche and Levinas against "Heideggerian paganism, the poetic paganism of *rootedness*"; *Political Writings*, 63, 64.

Another remark: This column would have been the best in which to address texts' translatability. Blanchot had thought about this both explicitly (see "Course of Things" in *Political Writings*, 62) and in more general terms; "Translating" (September 1960) in *Friendship*, 57–61; and previously, "Translated from . . ." (July 1946), in *The Work of Fire*, trans. Charlotte Mandell (Stanford: Stanford University Press, 1995), 176–190.

27. As early as the end of the 1950s, Blanchot had already suggested to Queneau to ask a foreign critic to write the chapter on French literature in the Pléiade *Histoire des littératures*.

28. Maurice Blanchot, letter to Dionys Mascolo, in *Political Writings*, 50.

29. Maurice Blanchot, "Berlin" in ibid., 73.

30. Ibid.

31. Missing in French until 1983, Blanchot having lost the original manuscript, *The Name Berlin* was republished in a bilingual edition by Merve Verlag in Berlin thanks to Hélène Jean and Jean-Luc Nancy's proposal to "reconstitute a French text from the foreign versions," with the author agreeing to "sign this text [as] his text" (see the preface by the translator-editors, 4). The first French edition was therefore fulfilled according to the law of the text and the spirit of the review. Once more, the *authority* of a "Blanchot text" goes beyond any singular attribution and lays claim to a communitarian essence.

32. René Char, "Maurice Blanchot, nous n'eussions aimé répondre...," in *Le nu perdu* (Paris: Gallimard, 1968), 57; in 1966 this poem opened the issue of *Critique* in homage to Blanchot.

51. CHARACTERS IN THOUGHT: HOW IS FRIENDSHIP POSSIBLE? (1958–1971)

1. A little less than a year before dying, Georges Bataille wrote the following to Dionys Mascolo: "I have written several times to Maurice Blanchot for whom my friendship counts more and more. His letters have counted a lot for me" (September 5, 1961) in *Choix de lettres*, ed. Michel Surya (Paris: Gallimard, 1997), 576.

2. Louis-René des Forêts, *Poems of Samuel Wood*, trans. Anthony Barnett (Lewes: Allardyce, 2011), 9. "An immense, infinite, irremediable catastrophe," "the abyss, absolute disaster"; Maurice Blanchot, *A Voice From Elsewhere*, trans. Charlotte Mandell (Albany: SUNY Press, 2002), 11.

3. Georges Bataille, *Le coupable*, translated as *Guilty* by Stuart Kendall (Albany: SUNY Press, 2011).

4. Letter from Maurice Blanchot to Dionys Mascolo, December 7, 1969.

5. Letter from Maurice Blanchot to Georges Bataille, August 8, 1961, cited in Bataille, *Choix de lettres*, 591–592.

6. We can also read the following, written barely a month after the previous letter cited: "It seems to me that, in these days of distress, therefore ordinary days, something has been given to both of us, to which we also have to respond together, as if we were both tasked, at the limits of our strength, with keeping silent watch over this relation with I know not what, and which is so lowly (perhaps physical, perhaps metaphysical, necessarily both one and the other)"; letter from Maurice Blanchot to Georges Bataille, September 2, 1961.

7. [Numantia was an ancient settlement in what is now Spain, famously besieged by troops of the Roman Empire. — Trans.]

8. He wrote as much to Dionys Mascolo: "Dionys, I would like to tell you that I do not think that friendship is a positive thing, I mean something like a value, but much more than that, something like a state, an identification of death and therefore a way of sharing it, of sharing questions. It is the most miraculously neutral site from which the constant unknown can be seen and felt, the site where what is most acute about difference is fully experienced — as it would be at 'the end of history' — only in its opposite; the proximity of death"; letter of 1949 or 1950, cited in *Autour d'un effort de mémoire: Sur une lettre de Robert Antelme* (Paris: Nadeau, 1987), 23–24.

9. Letter from Dionys Mascolo to Maurice Blanchot, March 11, 1981.

10. Letter from Dionys Mascolo to Maurice Blanchot, November or December 1969, published in *Ralentir Travaux* 7 (Winter 1997): 33. Mascolo

would speak of "the friendship of No" in "Sur les traces de Maurice Blanchot," France-Culture radio show broadcast on September 17, 1994.

11. Mascolo, *Autour d'un effort de mémoire*, 52.

12. Letter from Mascolo to Blanchot, November or December 1969.

13. Perhaps we should see this movement beyond direct address as the meaning of the untranslatable words attributed to Aristotle: "O friends, there is no friend," discussed by Jacques Derrida in *Politics of Friendship*, trans. George Collins (New York: Verso, 1997).

14. See Dionys Mascolo's singular dream where Maurice Blanchot appears as an empty, continuous presence on the other end of the telephone line; in *Ralentir Travaux* 7 (Winter 1997): 34.

15. Maurice Blanchot, "Friendship," in *Friendship*, trans. Elizabeth Rottenberg (Stanford: Stanford University Press, 1997), 291.

52. ACT IN SUCH A WAY THAT I CAN SPEAK TO YOU: *AWAITING OBLIVION* (1957–1962)

1. At this start, the narrator warns us that this "is not a fiction, although he is unable to utter the word *truth* in connection with all of that. Something happened to him, and he can neither say that it is true, nor the contrary. Later, he thought that the event consisted in this way of being neither true nor false." Maurice Blanchot, *Awaiting Oblivion*, trans. John Gregg (Lincoln: University of Nebraska Press, 1997), 4. In this chapter, references in brackets refer to this translation.

2. [*Entretien* in French sits somewhere between interview, dialogue, and conversation; I have therefore retained the French term. —Trans.]

3. Emmanuel Levinas in "The Servant and Her Master," trans. Michael Holland, in *The Levinas Reader*, ed. Seán Hand (Oxford: Blackwell, 1989), 154.

4. The description of the woman entering the man's room (29) recalls those in *Death Sentence*. The image of resurrection is evoked as a memory ("if I were to die, you would not fail to call me back to life," 17). The "Come," which is already present in *The Most High* (53, 55, 238) and also in *Death Sentence*, now punctuates the *récit*: it is the speech of awaiting and of the quest for oblivion.

5. Maurice Blanchot, *When the Time Comes*, trans. Lydia Davis (Barrytown, N.Y.: Station Hill Press, 1985), 47.

6. Maurice Blanchot, *The Last Man*, trans. Lydia Davis (New York: Columbia University Press, 1987), 89.

7. There is something of Heraclitus in the aphoristic and paradoxical phrasing of certain fragments; in January 1960, Blanchot published a text on the philosopher in the *NRF*.

8. "While poetry is dispersion itself which, as such, finds its form, the work of the novel can also claim to be struggling against the spirit of disper-

sion and to be starting from that spirit"; reprinted in *La condition critique: Articles 1945–1998*, ed. Christophe Bident (Paris: Gallimard, 2010), 301–302.

9. René Char in *Word as Archipelago*, cited by Blanchot in *The Infinite Conversation*, trans. Susan Hanson (Minneapolis: University of Minnesota Press, 1993), 458.

10. [The French title, *L'attente l'oubli*, provides a starker juxtaposition (referred to above by Bident) than the English one *Awaiting Oblivion*, where the first word *can* be read as a noun, but more naturally functions as a verb. —Trans.]

11. "And he could see how much he had wanted to know" (6). "As if the proper dimension of pain were thought" (10). "Stagnant waiting, waiting that at first took itself as its object, complacent with itself and finally full of hatred for itself. Waiting, the calm anguish of waiting; waiting become the calm expanse where thought is present in waiting" (29).

12. "When I speak to you, it is as if the entire part of me that covers and protects me abandoned me and left me exposed and very vulnerable" (10), the woman tells the narrator.

13. "Lying down and showing herself through a passion to appear that turns her away from everything visible and invisible" (67).

14. "In proximity, touching not presence, but rather difference" (61).

15. See Maurice Blanchot, "Oh All to End" (1990) in *The Blanchot Reader*, ed. Michael Holland (Oxford: Blackwell, 1995), 299. Alongside Bataille, Blanchot had been the first to write on Beckett's work; alongside Blanzat and Nadeau, he had tried in vain to give him the Prix des Critiques, in 1951. Suzanne Dumesnil states how important this recognition was for her husband: "to have been defended by a man such as Blanchot, that will have been the main thing for Beckett, whatever happens"; letter to Jérôme Lindon, May 25, 1951, archives of the Éditions de Minuit, quoted by Anne Simonin, *Les Éditions de Minuit, 1942–1955* (Paris: IMEC, 1994), 378. Gilles Deleuze, for whom reading Beckett and Blanchot was decisive as early as the 1950s, is one of the few who have compared them, even if he did so fugitively: see notably "The Exhausted," trans. Anthony Uhlmann in *Sub-Stance* 24, no. 3/78 (1995): 3–28. The way in which both writers constantly pursue an exhausting of literary speech calls for them to be brought together in greater depth. With infinite attentiveness, there is at work an awaiting ultimately without object except speech itself (a speech lived with or for the other, and beyond this, with the question of the possibility of companionship, of friendship), an interruption of thought, an exhaustion of bodies without cause, a constant dying of these bodies, a repetition carved out until it becomes a murmur, an insomnia, a certain *community of thought and of writing*.

16. *Awaiting Oblivion* could be for Blanchot what *Phaedra* was for Racine, at least according to what he himself had written about that play twenty years

earlier: "*Phaedra* is there to remind us of the meaning of silence and to admit, at the same time as its own ruin, the effacement of the mind that has tried to use this meaning to understand night. Although she expires in an almost peaceful death because she surpasses the torments of ordinary misfortune, it is only natural that she seems to drag down with her the one who has touched the mystery of what cannot be unveiled, and whom henceforth cannot represent in the world anything more than its silent secrecy." In *Faux Pas*, trans. Charlotte Mandell (Stanford: Stanford University Press, 2001), 70.

53. THE THOUGHT OF THE NEUTER: LITERARY AND PHILOSOPHICAL CRITICISM—THE *ENTRETIEN* AND THE FRAGMENT (1959–1969)

1. The first article where the notion of the Neuter is substantivized is "L'étrange et l'étranger" (October 1958), in *La condition critique: Articles 1945–1998*, ed. Christophe Bident (Paris: Gallimard, 2010), 278–288. [*Le neutre* can be rendered either as "the neuter" or as "the neutral." I have usually (but not always) chosen the former, in line with Blanchot's thinking of a relation of a third gender or kind (*genre*), and also to avoid the suggestion of neutrality in the sense of indifference. —Trans.]

2. Setting aside those written in 1968 for *Committee*, between 1959 and 1969 Blanchot wrote nearly seventy articles, the vast majority of them for the *NRF*; forty-four were collected in *The Infinite Conversation* and seventeen in *Friendship*. In both works they were placed alongside other, less numerous texts from the 1950s.

3. There are extremely notable similarities between the *récit* and two articles in particular: "Speaking Is Not Seeing" (July 1960), in *The Infinite Conversation*, trans. Susan Hanson (Minneapolis: University of Minnesota Press, 1993), 25–32; and the opening of "Forgetting, Unreason" (October 1961), ibid., 194–201.

4. Maurice Blanchot, "What Is the Purpose of Criticism?" (January–March 1959), in *Lautréamont and Sade*, trans. Stuart Kendall and Michelle Kendall (Stanford: Stanford University Press, 2004), 5. [This article, entitled in French "Qu'en est-il de la critique?" is better translated as "How Do Things Stand with Criticism?" since "purpose" is foreign to Blanchot's understanding of criticism. —Trans.]

5. On the Neuter as "partner invisible," see *The Infinite Conversation*, 460. The *récit* that opens the work also features the phrase "*the neuter, the neuter, how strangely this sounds to* me" (xxi), which is also found later, in an article of 1962, "The Relation of the Third Kind," 71.

6. The final note of *The Infinite Conversation* underscores this: these "already posthumous" and "nearly anonymous" texts do not have any authority stemming from a single author; "belonging to everyone, even and always written not by a single person, but by several: all those to whom falls the task

of maintaining and prolonging the demand to which I believe these texts, with a stubbornness that today astonishes me, have constantly attempted to respond even unto the *absence of book* that they designate in vain," 435.

7. He had already written as much to Bataille, probably at the end of the 1950s: "I am wearied by this work which I find a burden, perhaps because I have not managed to make it essential" (the fact that others *did* find it essential means that Blanchot's aim was really to say that he had not managed to make it so *for himself*). He also wrote as much to Sartre: "knowing the strong aversion that I have . . . to participating in the kind of literary reality that a review is . . . I would feel capable of overcoming this repulsion only if the project were strong enough to maintain and develop all the reasons that made me participate in the Declaration," in *Political Writings, 1953–1993*, trans. Zakir Paul (New York: Fordham University Press, 2010), 38. He also wrote to Vittorini, indicating an essential reason which is another proof of the immense renewal he was expecting from the *International Review*, whose failure confirmed that his judgment was correct: "All the journals are dying, the 'journal' genre is dying" (February 8, 1963) in *Lignes* 11 (September 1990): 277.

8. Maurice Blanchot citing René Char in "René Char and the Thought of the Neutral" (Summer 1963), in *The Infinite Conversation*, 302. Henceforth and unless otherwise stated, references in brackets refer to this volume.

9. Maurice Blanchot, "Le bon usage de la science-fiction" (January 1959), in *La condition critique*, 289–298. There was another allusion to De Gaulle: "We are still living under a First Consul" (229).

10. Blanchot does not use the term "depoliticization" without precautions; he gives it scare quotes. For in the very use of the word there is a risk of nihilism.

11. Maurice Blanchot, "Slow Obsequies" (August 1959), in *Friendship*, trans. Elizabeth Rottenberg (Stanford: Stanford University Press, 1997), 84–85. See also his refusal of Jaspers's liberal anticommunism, "The Apocalypse Is Disappointing" (March 1964), in ibid., 101–108.

12. Maurice Blanchot, "The Indestructible. 1. Being Jewish" (August 1962), in ibid., 123. The citation is an addition of 1969.

13. Ibid., 124.

14. Maurice Blanchot, "Gog and Magog" (June 1959) in *Friendship*, 229.

15. Maurice Blanchot, "The Absence of the Book," in *The Infinite Conversation*, 343; "Idle Speech" (1963) in *Friendship*, 125.

16. Blanchot, *Friendship*, 125; *The Infinite Conversation*, 437 n.

17. "In a simplification that is clearly misplaced, the entire history of philosophy can be seen as an effort either to acclimatize and domesticate the neuter by replacing it with the law of the impersonal and the reign of the universal, or to refuse it by affirming the ethical primacy of the Self-subject, the

mystical aspiration to the singular Unique." Blanchot, *The Infinite Conversation*, 299.

18. Maurice Blanchot, "The Great Reducers" (April 1965), in *Friendship*, 68.

19. Denouncing the power of criticism, notably in its journalistic and academic forms, therefore becomes often wisely and rationally, sometimes comically and meanly, vigorous: see, notably, "What Is the Purpose of Criticism?" (1959), in *Lautréamont and Sade*, 1–6; "Forgetting, Unreason" (October 1961), in *The Infinite Conversation*, 194–201; "The Great Reducers" (April 1965) in *Friendship*, 64–65. Let us recall that the climate in the 1960s was particularly lively, setting traditional and new critics against one another. Blanchot would not intervene directly in the debate; what's more, he had little faith in the new disciplines' purported scientific status (see his sarcasm over the "already outmoded distinctions" of the signifier and the signified, the only time these notions occur in his work [261]). However at the time he himself was using logical and geometrical models. He would still cite—confirming his positive view of them—Barthes, Damisch, Dort, Doubrovsky, Faye, Poulet, Marthe Robert, and Starobinski, as well as Lacan, of course, and philosophers such as Deleuze, Derrida, and Foucault.

20. Blanchot hears this relation with the unknown in all "narrative voice," just as he does in its backdrop and even in its possibility, the latter reflected by the contemporary *récits* that he would come to write on in the 1960s, including those by Marguerite Duras, Roger Laporte, and Louis-René des Forêts.

21. In Blanchot's eyes, "the feeling of a distance never abolished, but on the contrary kept pure and preserved" is what characterizes Hebraic mysticism (*Friendship*, 231) and, beyond it, the entirety of Jewish experience. Not without the obvious influence of Levinas, the figure of the Jew now begins to give shape to the very existence of the "third relation" in Blanchot's work: Judaism "exists in order that the idea of exodus and the idea of exile can exist as a just movement; it exists, through exile and through this initiative that exodus is, in order that the experience of strangeness may be affirmed near to us in an irreducible relation" (125). The essence of these affirmations could not be reduced to the political question of the Zionist state (Blanchot's first public stance on this subject dates from this article; see the long note in "Being Jewish" in ibid., 447–448, lines that in 1962 were part of the main text, which they concluded). These affirmations are closer to the poetic demand that Blanchot would see as if embodied in the work of someone such as Jabès, by reflection on this kind of equivalence between condition, speech, and writing; "Traces" (May 1964), in *Friendship*, 223.

22. See also Maurice Blanchot, "Thought and the Exigency of Discontinuity" (9–10). The section from "but what does this mean?" to the end was added in 1969.

23. We could also say: in the interruption of any fusional link. For in posing the question of community by beginning with the hospitality of lovers (Klossowski), the same formulation, this difference aside, could be used. Roberte was "a great figure who will say nothing, and even when she lets herself be seen in the most provocative manner, will continue to belong to the sovereign invisibility of the sign"; in "The Laughter of the Gods" (July 1965), in *Friendship*, 174.

Here, in any case, the question of community arises—Blanchot would return to it. What influence can the thought of the Neuter have on that of community? The question is asked for the first time as follows: "if the question 'who are others [*autrui*]?' has no direct meaning, it is because it must be replaced by another: 'how do things stand with human "community" when it has to respond to the strange relation between man and man that the experience of language allows one to sense: a relation without common measure, an exorbitant relation?'" (71).

24. See Maurice Blanchot, "On a Change of Epoch: The Exigency of Return" (April 1960), in ibid., 264–281 (the final part of the text published in 1969 had not appeared previously).

25. In Blanchot there seems to have been something like a wish to overturn the proposed structure that Genette was preparing at the time, according to which "narrative inserted into discourse becomes an element of discourse, while discourse inserted into narrative remains discourse"; "Frontières du récit," *Communications* 8 (1966): 161. Here, the narrative voice sheds light on the backdrop against which speech is used, what is actually said remains subject to the law of a time that is other; discourse remains neutral.

26. This would mark a whole generation of writers and philosophers, beginning with the twin, "unrecognizable" authority of Deleuze and Guattari.

27. See notably the end, added in the book version, of the article "On a Change of Epoch," in ibid., 271–281.

28. See "René Char and the Thought of the Neutral," 298–306, and "The Fragment Word" (1964), in ibid., 307–313. See also the attention he gave to Heraclitus's language; "Heraclitus" (January 1960), in ibid., 85–92.

29. Blanchot, "The Fragment Word," 308, 310.

30. Ibid., 310.

31. Maurice Blanchot, "The Last Word" (May 1968), in *Friendship*, 266.

32. Maurice Blanchot, "The Essential Solitude" (January 1953), in *The Space of Literature*, 33.

33. This weakness grows more extreme, this ability to walk lessens further: "*Taking three steps, stopping, falling.*" *The Step Not Beyond*, trans. Lycette Nelson (Albany: State University of New York Press, 1992), 135.

34. Emmanuel Levinas in *Time and the Other*, trans. Richard A. Cohen (Pittsburgh: Duquesne University Press), 76.

35. Moreover, the *récit* contains a fairly long passage describing the situation the author of the book it introduces finds himself it: "*he has lost the ability to express himself in a continuous manner. . . . This makes him neither happy nor unhappy*" (xxi).

36. [*Disparaître* has the double meaning of "to disappear" and "to die." The voice that speaks in this dialogue plays on this double term, as Bident will regularly do in the remainder of the work. I have most often chosen "disappear" as the translation, but its usage in referring to a death, which is relatively common in French, is one to bear in mind. —Trans.]

54. A FIRST HOMAGE: THE SPECIAL ISSUE OF *CRITIQUE* (1966)

1. Dionys Mascolo, "Hommage à Maurice Blanchot," *La Quinzaine Littéraire* 12 (September 15, 1966), collected in *À la recherche d'un communisme de pensée* (Paris: Fourbis, 1993), pp. 205–10.

2. See Roger Laporte, "Un sourire mozartien," *Ralentir Travaux* 7 (Winter 1997): 74.

3. Roger Laporte was born in 1925, Michel Foucault in 1926.

4. Michel Foucault, "Préface à la transgression" (1963), in *Dits et écrits, 1954–1988* (Paris: Gallimard, 1994), 1:240; "Guetter le jour qui vient" (1963), in ibid., 267–268; "La prose d'Actéon" (1964), in ibid., 336. See also the later "De l'archéologie à la dynastique" (1973), in ibid., 2:412.

5. Michel Foucault, "Sur les façons d'écrire l'Histoire" (1967), in ibid., 1:593.

6. "If Hölderlin, Mallarmé, Kafka fully exist in the language that we speak, it is precisely thanks to Blanchot. He is therefore the Hegel of literature, but at the same time Hegel's opposite." Foucault then develops the opposition between a dialectical conception of the historical existence of works of art (which makes them available to the memory addressing and uniting them), and the free establishment of a relation without relation that exposes works of art to the exteriority that terrifies them and disperses them into the infinite neutrality of oblivion. See "Folie, littérature, société" (1970), in *Dits et écrits*, 2: 124.

7. We can read what he said about it to Watanabe in "La scène de la philosophie," in ibid., 3:589. Here Foucault invokes his debt to Bataille, Blanchot, and Klossowski. But having been taken aback on several occasions by students' ignorance even of Blanchot's existence (this did not happen with Bataille or Klossowski), he emphasizes how much work of recognition still needed to be done in terms of the man and his work being known.

8. After Bataille's death, Foucault had joined the editorial committee of *Critique* alongside Roland Barthes and Michel Deguy, here too taking up the invitation of Jean Piel, who had taken over the editorship.

9. Twenty years later, Todorov would show much less enthusiasm, accusing Foucault, Levinas, all the authors of the issue, with the exception of Poulet and de Man, of paraphrasing; "Les critiques-écrivains," in *Critique de la critique* (Paris: Seuil, 1984), 66–67.

10. Georges Poulet, "Maurice Blanchot, critique et romancier," *Critique* 229 (June 1966): 485–497. This text expands an article of fifteen years earlier in *Yale French Studies* 7 (Fall 1951): 77–81.

11. These are the remarks of Jean Starobinski, "*Thomas l'obscur*, chapitre premier," *Critique*, 229 (June 1966): 506–507, 513.

12. A remark made by Emmanuel Levinas in a note at the beginning of his article, collected in *Sur Maurice Blanchot* (Montpellier: Fata Morgana, 1975), 77–78.

13. See the opening of the article by Paul de Man, "La circularité de l'intepŕetation dans l'oeuvre critique de Maurice Blanchot," *Critique* 229 (June 1966): 547.

14. Michel Foucault, "The Thought from Outside," trans. Brian Massumi in *Foucault—Blanchot* (New York: Zone Books, 1987), 7–58.

15. Foucault, "Sur les façons d'écrire l'Histoire," 593.

16. "With *JLG/JLG*, I wanted to make a film similar to the books I read as a teenager, those by Blanchot, by Bataille" Jean-Luc Godard in "Il est de règle de vouloir la mort de l'exception," interview in the journal *Théâtre de la Bastille* 7 (September 1995): 28. Blanchot's work always watches over Godard, being his "clandestine companion" (Godard cites the text of that name on Levinas in *For Ever Mozart* in 1996).

17. Roland Barthes, "On *The Fashion System* and the Structural Analysis of Narratives," in *The Grain of the Voice: Interviews 1962–1980*, trans. Linda Coverdale (Berkeley: University of California Press, 1985), 51. See also "Literature and Signification" (1963) in *Critical Essays*, trans. Richard Howard (Evanston, Ill.: Northwestern University Press, 1972), 261–264.

18. He wrote hot-tempered outbursts such as the following: "You theoreticians, know that you are mortal, and that theory is already death in you," in a fragment of *The Writing of the Disaster*, trans. Ann Smock (Lincoln: University of Nebraska Press, 1986), 43. The accent here recalls Valéry's famous phrase: "As for us, civilizations, we now know that we are mortal." In another fragment, Blanchot stated that "theories are necessary (the theories of language, for example): necessary and useless.... We must pass by way of this knowledge and forget it"; ibid., 75–76. A little later still, evoking structuralism in *Michel Foucault as I Imagine Him*, Blanchot would reduce the scope of his silence, not without malice: "I realize that until now I have never pronounced, either in approval or disapproval, the name of that ephemeral discipline, despite the friendship I bore certain of its adherents." *Foucault—Blanchot*, 70.

19. Beyond the explicit references to Blanchot's name and to his investigations of the absence of work or the essential solitude, the entire tone is imbued with the pages of *The Space of Literature* on reading; Roland Barthes, *Criticism and Truth*, trans. Katrine Pilcher Keuneman (1966; New York: Continuum, 2004), 38–40.

20. On the relation between Barthes and *Tel Quel*, see Philippe Forest, *Histoire de Tel Quel* (Paris: Seuil, 1995), notably 195–199.

21. Philippe Sollers, "Le roman et l'expérience des limites" (1965), in *Logiques* (Paris: Seuil, 1968), 226–249. Like in *Criticism and Truth*, the last pages of the article take up Blanchot's theories about reading as developed in *The Space of Literature*. Furthermore, Philippe Forest shows how Sollers's new novel *Drame* of the same year owes much to Blanchot's conception of literature: see *Histoire de Tel Quel*, 233. Sollers's Blanchot is therefore close to Foucault's: he guarantees the awareness, in language itself, of what is radically external to language.

22. In the first volume of *Figures*, every sentence following a citation from Blanchot is interspersed with an "indeed" or an "evidently"; *Figures* (Paris: Seuil, 1966), 1:61–63, 79.

23. A radio show by France-Culture on September 15, 1970, presented him in this way. The same year, Jean Pfeiffer prepared a show dedicated to Blanchot for Belgian Radio.

24. See Tito Perlini, "Maurice Blanchot: L'opera come presenza-assenza," *Nuova Corrente* 45 (1968).

25. Michel Foucault, "La scène de la philosophie," in *Dits et écrits*, 3.

26. Deleuze only ever cites Blanchot's critical work, and often the same passages return multiple times. For example he uses Blanchot's distinction between dying and death in his discussion of Freud's theory of drives; in *Difference and Repetition*, trans. Paul Patton (1968; New York: Continuum), 138–139; he returns to the same thinking for his analysis of "the event" in *The Logic of Sense*, trans. Mark Lester (1969; New York: Continuum, 2001), 172–174. In the same works, Deleuze also addresses an "eternal scintillation," in terms of the Blanchotian reading of the image and of "the absence of origin" (respectively 162–163, 318).

27. Jacques Derrida, "Force and Signification" in *Writing and Difference*, trans. Alan Bass (London: Routledge, 1978), 20.

28. Roger Laporte has underscored this importance of Derrida and his authority on the very manuscript of *The Infinite Conversation*. Blanchot modified numerous passages of the articles collected in the volume after reading *Writing and Difference*, *Voice and Phenomenon*, and *Of Grammatology* in 1967. See Roger Laporte, *À l'extrême pointe* (Montpellier: Fata Morgana, 1994), 40–42; see also Leslie Hill, *Blanchot: Extreme Contemporary* (London: Routledge, 1997),

127–142. This preoccupation was taken up and—if you will—*signed* by multiple fragments of *The Step Not Beyond*, trans. Lycette Nelson (Albany: State University of New York Press, 1992), 10–12, 30–32.

55. BETWEEN TWO FORMS OF THE UNAVOWABLE: THE BEAUFRET AFFAIR (1967–1968)

1. It seems that Laporte did so without imagining what the consequences would be; for him, Beaufret's comment had not seemed so serious as to prevent him from contributing to the volume.

2. There were also other less serious statements, slippages in the rhetoric of everyday conversation, hot-tempered Freudian slips. While Blanchot and Derrida agreed at the time—not without difficulty—to "attenuate" their seriousness (recognizing only that they could not take such statements as "a declaration of anti-Semitism"), these lapses in language nonetheless did not paint a favorable picture of a philosopher whose attitude, during the whole affair, remained unchanged. Although Beaufret agreed to explain himself regarding these remarks, whose context could attenuate their scope and their offhand nature, he never accepted that he had made the statements aimed at Emmanuel Levinas. We must also recall that following Beaufret's death it was revealed that he had supported the Holocaust denier Robert Faurisson.

3. The text was already almost written when Fédier had approached Derrida, because he was working on Heidegger at the time. It would be collected in *Margins of Philosophy* (Paris: Minuit, 1972).

4. They would not see each other again thereafter, but they would often write to and telephone each other.

5. Maurice Blanchot, "The Fragment Word" (1964) in *The Infinite Conversation*, trans. Susan Hanson (Minneapolis: University of Minnesota Press, 1993), 307–313.

6. "For Emmanuel Levinas / with whom, for forty years, / I have been bound by a friendship / which is closer to me than myself: / in a relation of invisibility with Judaism."

7. "At no moment did we cease to have full confidence in Roger Laporte, never having doubted either his good faith or his sense of truth."

8. Maurice Blanchot had attended the defense and went to see Levinas three days later.

56. THE FAR SIDE OF FEAR: POLITICAL DISILLUSIONMENT (MAY 1968)

1. From the Nile, close to Aswan, he wrote to Mascolo: "Everything is different, but does one ever forget? Yes, for a few moments, only for harsh

memories to then return" (postcard from Maurice Blanchot to Dionys Mascolo, January 4, 1965).

2. This is what Blanchot wrote in the text that he proposed for a call for a boycott of the ORTF; noting that all forms of artistic and intellectual expression, even the most critical, were immediately recuperated by power (by De Gaulle) as "proof of 'national' prestige," he called on "all men of thought, writers, scholars, journalists to refuse to work together with the services, organizations, institutions, or mouthpieces controlled by the government, and without any true autonomy, such as the ORTF" (unpublished text).

3. Maurice Blanchot et al., "The Solidarity That We Assert Here," in *Political Writings, 1953–1993*, trans. Zakir Paul (New York: Fordham University Press, 2010), 79.

4. Maurice Blanchot, "On the Movement" (1968), ibid., 109.

5. Leiris did write a laconic note (September 12, 1968) on "the ridiculous aspect of Mascolo, Blanchot, Schuster, etc." *Journal* (Paris: Gallimard, 1992), 628. But he had taken part in several demonstrations (see *For Friendship* [1993], in *Political Writings*, 141), and the following year would express his deep admiration for Schuster when he appeared before a correctional tribunal after having reproduced in *Coupure* an issue of *La cause du peuple*, which had once again been banned by the ministry of the Interior; see Jean Schuster, *Magazine littéraire* (February 1992): 51–52.

6. [The Confédération Générale du Travail is one of France's largest confederations of labor unions. —Trans.]

7. "I addressed a few words to him, he himself unaware of who was speaking to him," in *Michel Foucault as I Imagine Him*, in *Foucault—Blanchot*, trans. Jeffrey Mehlman (New York: Zone Books, 1987), 63. Foucault would say that he never met or recognized Blanchot. And in any case that spring and early summer the philosopher was most often in Tunisia. There were several possible dates when they could have met, however: on May 27, for example, Foucault was at Charléty, and at the end of June he was indeed at the demonstrations and assemblies at the Sorbonne.

8. Dionys Mascolo, cited in Marianne Alphant, "Une présence secrete," *Libération* (January 28–29, 1984), 23.

9. Maurice Blanchot, "Intellectuals under Scrutiny" (1984), in *The Blanchot Reader*, ed. Michael Holland (Oxford: Blackwell, 1995), 224.

10. Mascolo recounts how one of the most famous slogans of May, "Be realistic/Demand the impossible," originated in a discussion at the Renault factory in Billancourt. A trade unionist said to two members of the Committee, "We must be realistic, we must not demand the impossible." Mascolo stated that that afternoon, at Censier, "We had some paper, and a print worker available to us, and we were searching for themes. It was spontaneous, I can only

present it as a collective intuition." The trade unionist's statement was inverted. *Naming the possible, responding to the impossible*: we also know that for several years this had been the major formulation in Blanchot's thinking of both the necessity of dialectics and the demand of the wholly other.

11. Blanchot retained the greatest respect for Derrida's reservations over the "fusional spontaneity" of May '68, reservations which in his eyes only confirmed the necessity of retaining a distance in all friendships within thought. This paradoxical essence of friendship meant that 1968 was both the year when they were continuously present for one another, and that when they did not converge politically (in this sense, there is a symbolism in the fact that they took part separately in the march of May 13: Blanchot with Antelme, Mascolo, Nadeau; Derrida with Goux, Sollers, Baudry).

12. Maurice Blanchot in "The Most Profound Question" (February 1961), in *The Infinite Conversation*, trans. Susan Hanson (Minneapolis: University of Minnesota Press, 1993), 22 ("this being-other that it is," read the first version). See the lines written by Blanchot in 1961 on revolutionary speech, something that would be embodied in the movement of May (ibid., 22–23); as well as, six months before the *événements*, the final pages of "Atheism and Writing. Humanism and the Cry" (November 1967), ibid., 246–263, quoted by Levinas in an explicit reference to May '68 in *Humanism of the Other*, trans. Nidra Poller (Champaign: University of Illinois Press, 2003), 74. Last, one should cite the entire preface to Sade: "Insurrection, the Madness of Writing" (1965), in *The Infinite Conversation*, 217–229.

13. "What founds it is rather an insurrection of thought," Blanchot would say of *Contre-Attaque*, which retrospectively he saw as "prefiguration of what happened in May '68"; *The Unavowable Community*, 13. Robert Antelme would recall that "in that month of May . . . history, as has been said, was thought"; "Sur *L'écriture du désastre* de Maurice Blanchot," *Textes inédits* (Paris: Gallimard, 1997), 68. On this point, the two thinkers express one of the essential truths about the May movement.

14. Maurice Blanchot, "The Most Profound Question" (1960), in *The Infinite Conversation*, 23.

15. Maurice Blanchot, "Insurrection, the Madness of Writing" (1965), ibid., 222, 226.

16. Such was the famous saying by Sade, cited by Blanchot at the end of his preface, just before the main text: "HOWEVER MUCH IT MAY MAKE MANKIND TREMBLE, PHILOSOPHY MUST SAY EVERYTHING," in "Insurrection, the Madness of Writing" (1965), in *The Infinite Conversation*, 229. "Say everything," Blanchot remarked, "one must say everything, freedom is the freedom to say everything" (this was the very truth of the May movement), "this limitless movement that is the temptation of reason, its secret vow, its madness."

17. "We have crossed over to the far side of fear": according to Blanchot, this was one of the statements made by the erection of the barricades. "Exemplary Acts" (October 1968), in *Political Writings*, 99.

18. Blanchot, *Michel Foucault as I Imagine Him*, 63.

19. Ibid., 63–64. See also *The Unavowable Community*, 29–33, and *For Friendship*, 141–142.

20. "Communism: what excludes (and is excluded from) any already constituted community," writes Blanchot in 1968; as well as this, which will also return later: "Communism cannot be an heir. We must be convinced of this: it is not the heir of itself. . . . Between the liberal-capitalist world, our world, and the present of the communist demand (present without presence), there is only the hyphen of a disaster, of a change of star"; "Communism without Heirs" (October 1968), *Political Writings*, 93.

21. Maurice Blanchot, "Atheism and Writing: Humanism and the Cry" (1967), in *The Infinite Conversation*, 262.

22. Ibid., 30.

23. Whence such phrases as: "Everything was accepted. The impossibility of recognizing an enemy, of taking into account a particular form of adversity, all that was vivifying while hastening the resolution, though there was nothing to be resolved, given that the event had taken place." *The Unavowable Community*, 31. This is why in the bulletin of the Committee there is almost no discussion of the actual content of the students' and workers' demands. Nothing concerning the specificities of the possible is essential without the movement of the impossible.

24. Letter from Maurice Blanchot to Jacques Derrida, May 19, 1968. In parallel with this, Blanchot developed several of the terms in this line of thought in "Exemplary Acts."

25. Blanchot, *The Unavowable Community*, 31.

26. Maurice Blanchot, "Tracts, Posters, Bulletins" (October 1968), in *Political Writings*, 95.

27. Ibid.

28. Maurice Blanchot, "The Possible Characteristics" (1968), in *Political Writings*, 85–86.

29. Those cited were: Guevara, Trotsky, Orwell, Flaubert, Baudelaire, Rosa Luxembourg, and Hölderlin, and (twice each) Marx, Lenin, and Mao.

30. Eighteen texts are by Blanchot, seven by Mascolo (but they were longer, and the number of pages provided by each figure is almost equal, with roughly a dozen pages each), four by Bellefroid, one by Schuster, and one by Rochefort.

31. Maurice Blanchot, "Political Death" (October 1968), in *Political Writings*, 89–90. These violent attacks on General De Gaulle have much to do

with the contemporary one by Sartre: "The old man saw red, and said to his supporters: "ENOUGH MESSING AROUND, NOW YOU CAN HIT THEM"" in *Le Nouvel Observateur* (June 19, 1968), 27. Such attacks were not new for Blanchot, nor were they foreign to the caustic humor he always used against De Gaulle. For instance, once when seeing him on television putting on a nuclear protection suit before inspecting a submarine: "no doubt about it, he always finds ways to surprise us," he said to Louis-René des Forêts, with whom he was watching the program.

32. Maurice Blanchot, "For a Long Time, Brutality" (October 1968), in *Political Writings*, 94.

33. Maurice Blanchot, "Clandestine Resistance out in the Open" (October 1968), in *Political Writings*, 103.

34. Maurice Blanchot, "For Comrade Castro" (October 1968), in *Political Writings*, 100. Whence the following peroration or call to reengagement, to vigor: "Comrade Castro, do not dig your own grave, and if you are so tempted, let yourself slip into it from the natural exhaustion of power. Let us write on the walls of Havana, as was magnificently written on the walls of Prague: LENIN WAKE UP!" Ibid., 102.

35. Blanchot, "Exemplary Acts," 99.

36. See the letter on this topic from Maurice Blanchot to Dionys Mascolo, dating from late 1968 and published first anonymously in an issue of *Les Lettres Nouvelles* (June–July 1969): 184–185, then attributed to Blanchot in *À la recherche d'un communisme de pensée* (Paris: Fourbis, 1993), 359–360; also collected in *La condition critique: Articles 1945–1998*, ed. Christophe Bident (Paris: Gallimard, 2010), 315–317.

37. The gap between the positions of Christiane Rochefort and Jean Schuster on Castro's condemnation of the Prague movement, which is clear in the issue of *Committee*, bears witness both to what remained of a relation of nonrelation and to the fact that it probably no longer existed for the other participants.

38. However, in the same period (October–November 1968), against a backdrop of an unquenchable demand, Blanchot was still taking part in some discussions with students about the creation of the "experimental university" of Vincennes.

39. In April 1969, the adolescent nephew of Dionys Mascolo died.

40. Letter from Maurice Blanchot to Jacques Derrida, May 13, 1969.

57. LIFE OUTSIDE: *THE STEP NOT BEYOND*, A JOURNAL WRITTEN IN THE NEUTER (1969–1973)

1. [In French, *pas* can indicate negation, but it can also be a noun referring to a step or pace (or steps or paces). The English title given to Blanchot's

work deals with this ambiguity by translating the term twice: *The Step Not Beyond* could equally (though less polysemically) have been called *The Step Beyond* or *The Not Beyond*. The book itself also contains further play involving *passion*, *passivity*, *patience*, and so on. —Trans.]

2. Maurice Blanchot, "The Absence of the Book" (1969), in *The Infinite Conversation*, trans. Susan Hanson (Minneapolis: University of Minnesota Press, 1993), 435.

3. Ibid., 426, 431. "The Absence of the Book" was the text that he gave to Louis-René des Forêts for *L'Ephémère* in spring 1969, which was included at the last moment in *The Infinite Conversation*. The book appeared in fall 1969.

4. Ibid., 464, 435.

5. Two in 1969, two in 1970, three in 1971, two in 1972, one in 1973. In 1970 he also published a letter to Piera Castoriadis-Aulagnier, in which he apologizes for providing only a few thoughts, instead of a true article, for the special issue that *Topique* was dedicating to Charles Fourier. In doing so he lays down the model for a long series of letters that would bear witness to his weariness with critical writing, to the fact that he would protect his health, to his attempts to sidestep the pressing demands coming at him from all sides, and ultimately to his attentiveness not to let down those demands that seemed to him to have some interest and to which, previously, he would have responded fully.

6. Let us recall the following words from the last lines of the first version of *Death Sentence*: "These pages can end here, and nothing that follows what I have just written will make me add anything to it or take anything away from it. This remains, this will remain until the very end. Whoever would obliterate it from me, in exchange for that end which I am searching for in vain, would himself become the beginning of my own story, and he would be my victim. In the darkness, he would see me: my word would be his silence, and he would think he was holding sway over the world, but that sovereignty would still be mine, his nothingness mine, and he too would know that there is no end for a man who wants to end alone." In *The Station Hill Blanchot Reader*, ed. George Quasha (Barrytown, N.Y.: Station Hill Press, 1998), 187. On the removal of the two final paragraphs of *Death Sentence*, and the shock that it produced, see the book by Pierre Madaule, *Une tâche sérieuse?* (Paris: Gallimard, 1973).

7. Maurice Blanchot, *The Madness of the Day*, trans. Lydia Davis (Barrytown, N.Y.: Station Hill Press, 1981), 18. We should also note the reprinting of *Le ressassement éternel* as *Vicious Circles* in 1970 by Gordon & Breach.

8. Maurice Blanchot, *The Step Not Beyond*, trans. Lycette Nelson (Albany: State University of New York Press, 1992), 33. References in this chapter are henceforth to this translated work, unless stated otherwise.

9. Maurice Blanchot, "The Ease of Dying" (May 1969), in *Friendship*, trans. Elizabeth Rottenberg (Stanford: Stanford University Press, 1997), 149–168.

10. Maurice Blanchot, "A Note on Transgression," in ibid., 187.

11. Blanchot had already given expression to this demand for discontinuity in the second part of an essay of 1960, not included in any book, "Reprises"; in it, the aphorism is distinguished from the maxim in the same way that here, the fragment is distinguished from both these forms; in *NRF* 93 (September 1960): 479–483.

12. Blanchot saw a similar questioning of the "masterful language" of the philosopher, preferring to it the withdrawal of a "pure-impure speech," which he saw in the "philosophical discourse" (the scare quotes are Blanchot's) of Maurice Merleau-Ponty; "Le discours philosophique" (1971), in *La condition critique: Articles 1945–1998*, ed. Christophe Bident (Paris: Gallimard, 2010), 332–337.

13. Maurice Blanchot, *Thomas the Obscure*, trans. Robert Lamberton (Barrytown, N.Y.: Station Hill Press, 1988), 7.

14. "If, coming here, you were to find this little room—which was perhaps not so little, due to the three steps that made it possible to go down toward the part where he waited for him, murmuring in the corner" (18); "He lived there, the house was being reconstructed around him, I saw him behind the window, waiting without hearing me, exhausting the overfullness of our words by waiting" (72); "he must have noticed the room that was suddenly immense, surrounded by books, as if to accentuate the emptiness of the space" (79).

15. [While often the French *banlieue* is a deprived area not translatable by "suburbs," in this case the area Blanchot lived in is in fact suburban in the American sense. —Trans.]

16. In November 1973, on reading *The Step Not Beyond*, Georges Perros wrote coldly to Michel Butor: "Stuck my nose into the latest Blanchot. Death is at hand. It would appear that Gallimard is slipping him a few banknotes so that he can survive"; Michel Butor and Georges Perros, *Correspondance, 1955–1978* (Nantes: Joseph K., 1996), 709.

17. "I am on the side of weakness" (Bram Van Velde, cited by Daniel Dobbels, "Du côté de la faiblesse," text relating to the exhibition "L'oeuvre—le sacré" at Villa du Parc, Annemasse, Atelier Cantoisel, Joigny, 1991.

18. This was also one of the effects of fragmentary writing: "As if the invisible were secretly distributed, without the distribution of points of visibility taking any part, therefore not in the intimacy of a design, but too much outside, in a place beyond Being of which Being bore no trace" (94).

19. The journal of dying is capable of everything, except its initial penchant for self-portraiture (in the reflection in the mirror, dying condemns one to "the

shimmering of an absence of face," 94). For the return of any interest in oneself would only be bearable in the weakening of attentiveness and the powerlessness of speech to which death's imminence condemns one (at such times, it is the most common interest). But such an interest also condemns all words to be erased, and its calmness can cause pain to one's friends (137).

20. This inability of speech was echoed in an article of 1971: "(these dead who are there, and who in their own way speak, speaking, in all of our vain words, against us)," in "Une nouvelle raison?" (1971), in *La condition critique*, 325–332.

21. This response dating from between 1969 and 1971 was not first published in French, but is collected in *Friendship* under the title "War and Literature," 109–110. It contains the first mention of the "holocaust of the Jews" as "an *absolute*." It also evokes the "dark radiance" of the books on the camps, and in closing it mentions the one book among them that was said to be "the simplest, the purest, and the closest to this absolute that it makes us remember: Robert Antelme's *Human Race*."

22. Maurice Blanchot, letter to Emmanuel Levinas (1969), published by the latter in *Nine Talmudic Readings*, trans. Annette Aronowicz (1977; Bloomington: Indiana University Press, 1990), 115–116. The citations in the remainder of this paragraph are taken from this letter; some translations have been modified. Blanchot would express himself in exactly the same terms in 1986, in a text given to Maurice Nadeau; "Do Not Forget!" (1986), trans. Leslie Hill in *Paragraph* 30, no. 3 (November 2007): 34–37. See also Levinas's interviews in *La Vie Protestante* of May 10, 1974, "L'autre est d'abord un visage" (7) and in the *Journal des Communautés* in May 1980: "Quand Sartre découvre l'histoire sainte," collected in *Les imprévus de l'histoire* (Montpellier: Fata Morgana, 1994), 158.

23. Roger Laporte indicates the etymological sense in which Blanchot used the word "absolute": "The Latin *absolvere* means to detach, untie, disengage. An absolute event is one where the chain is broken," in "Tout doit s'effacer. Tout s'effacera," *Lignes* 11 (September 1990): 20; also collected in *Études* (Paris: POL, 1990), 53–62.

24. "A line has been drawn": this was the expression used by Blanchot in a letter of February or March 1969 to Dionys Mascolo.

25. This irritation is clear in his correspondence, but also through many public allusions to it: see the beginning of the article dedicated to Brice Parain, "Une nouvelle raison?" (325), or the end of the homage to Maurice Merleau-Ponty: "this posthumous use of a thinking that is no longer defended, that on the contrary is delivered unto others, to their quarrelling, to the intrigues of the comedy of intellectuals, of vanity, prestige or influence," in "Le discours philosophique" (1971), in ibid. (337). This criticism is

repeated in similar terms in *The Step Not Beyond*: "as if the anonymous, a shadow whose light would be unaware that it shines only in order to project precisely this shadow, arranged the whole comedy of glories, powers, and sanctities in order to move closer to us, signaling to us across signification, and precisely where all signs would be lacking" (37).

26. On this point see *The Step Not Beyond*, 115–116.

27. In the conclusion of the homage to Merleau-Ponty, he put it as follows: "At least when a philosopher or a writer falls silent, we learn from his silence not to appropriate for ourselves what he was in order to serve our own ends, but to disappropriate ourselves from ourselves and to share with him inhuman muteness." *La condition critique*, 337. Mascolo's declaration, "Contre l'exploitation dont sont l'objet les noms d'Antonin Artaud, de Georges Bataille et d'André Breton," was published in *La Quinzaine Littéraire* in March 1971. It was also signed by Robert Antelme and by Michel Leiris.

28. It was a question of taking commentary beyond the illumination of meaning, even polysemic meaning: Blanchot returns to this in *The Step Not Beyond* (50–51). But he had been calling for the "ruination of commentaries, from the coarsest to the subtlest (commentaries that are in fact necessary in order to be refuted)" since *Faux Pas*, trans. Charlotte Mandell (Stanford: Stanford University Press, 2001), 111.

29. Maurice Blanchot, "The Last to Speak" (1972), in *A Voice from Elsewhere*, trans. Charlotte Mandell (Albany: State University of New York Press, 2007), 57.

30. The editorial committee for *L'Ephémère* also included Yves Bonnefoy, Paul Celan, André du Bouchet, Jacques Dupin, and Michel Leiris (Gaëton Picon had been a founding member, but left after May '68). The writers (or poets) that it brought together did not include any not dear to Blanchot. He regretted the closure of this journal, which allowed him to contribute freely with a few texts, now that he was no longer writing regularly for the *NRF*. Over the coming years, *Le Nouveau Commerce* would sometimes occupy this role.

31. The article on Klossowski was published in 1970, and beyond the book that he had just published (*Nietzsche and the Vicious Circle*, 1969), a more general homage to Nietzsche was the subject of the first extract of *The Step Not Beyond* to be published. As for Henri Michaux, beyond the great admiration that Blanchot had for him, he had been particularly receptive to the poet's text published following Celan's death; "Sur le chemin de la vie, Paul Celan . . ." (1970), *L'Ephémère* 17 (Spring–Summer 1971): 116–117. It could be said that this dedication remained secret for a long time: it only appeared on the text's second publication, in 1984, following Michaux's death.

58. FRIENDSHIP IN DISASTER: DISTANCE, DISAPPEARANCE (1974–1978)

1. Letter from Maurice Blanchot to Jacques Derrida, January 7, 1975.
2. Letter from Denise Rollin to Michel Fardoulis-Lagrange, not dated, 1975 or 1976. This letter belongs to a series that bears witness to significant tension between the two correspondents. Fardoulis-Lagrange had asked Denise Rollin to pass to Blanchot his latest manuscript, *L'observance du même*, but he allowed his reader no more than a week before demanding that it be returned (he was in a hurry to find a publisher). Denise Rollin took issue with this wrongheaded haste, which lacked sensitivity and respect. When Fardoulis declared his astonishment that Blanchot had found some passages fascinating, she responded that "if MB writes 'fascinating pages,' it is *true*, *profound*, and *just*, he never says words that do not count, unlike all of those chatterboxes who trade in power." Blanchot had been able to read only part of the manuscript, which he thought very uneven.
3. Letter from Dionys Mascolo to Maurice Blanchot, October 22, 1974, published in *Ralentir Travaux* 7 (Winter 1997): 34.
4. Maurice Blanchot, *The Writing of the Disaster*, trans. Ann Smock (Lincoln: University of Nebraska Press, 1986), 46. He also writes: "Death suddenly powerless, if friendship is the response that one can hear and make heard only by dying ceaselessly," 29.

59. THE LAST BOOK: *THE WRITING OF THE DISASTER* (1974–1980)

1. See *The Writing of the Disaster*, trans. Ann Smock (Lincoln: University of Nebraska Press, 1986), 20. Unless otherwise stated, references in this chapter are to this translated work.
2. On this presumption Blanchot wrote that it is not only the Cartesian "I think therefore I am," but also the affirmations by Nietzsche and Foucault—"God is dead," "mankind is dead"—that resonate. He adds that they were perhaps "only the symptom of a language still too powerful, too sovereign as it were, which thus gives up speaking poorly, in vain and forgetfully, gives up failure, indigence, the extinction of the breath. And these are *the sole marks of poetry*" (92). These words were first published in "La poésie, Mesdames, Messieurs," *Givre* 2–3 (1977): 177.
3. Blanchot selects the word *disaster* for all of these reasons concerning *language*. The disaster allows the "discourse on patience" to come to it: this was the title of the first ensemble of fragments published, in *Le Nouveau Commerce* in 1975, and which would be collected in the first fifty pages of the book. Mascolo underscores that the word "disaster" had appeared for the first time in *Committee*; see *À la recherche d'un communisme de pensée* (Paris: Fourbis,

1993), 408. Indeed, in that context the disaster as a "change of star [*astre*]" underlines what Blanchot had named the departure "from historical space" (*The Infinite Conversation*, trans. Susan Hanson [Minneapolis: University of Minnesota Press, 1993], 269) and the demand made by a communism that he was soon to declare unavowable. We should also recall the "After the Disaster" column that was probably begun by Blanchot at the *Journal des Débats* in July 1940, and that for him had the same sense of a historical rupture. After the war, poetry too would be charged with this sense: "Poetry . . . is the realm of disaster," he wrote in *The Work of Fire*, trans. Charlotte Mandell (Stanford: Stanford University Press, 1995), 263. We can also pick up another occurrence, concerning *A Throw of the Dice*, which speaks to a failure of ontology, the strength for rupture of "the general rule which gives chance the status of law" in *The Book to Come*, trans. Charlotte Mandell (Stanford: Stanford University Press, 2003), 232. And while in *The Step Not Beyond* the "immobile disaster that lets everything remain" (trans. Lycette Nelson [Albany: State University of New York Press, 1992], 120) takes on a more overtly personal turn (it designates the implacable return and something like the law of anguish), we know how much with Blanchot this personal discourse is linked to history.

4. "To write is perhaps to bring to the surface something like absent meaning, to welcome the passive pressure which is not yet what we call thought, for it is already the disastrous ruin of thought. Thought's patience. Between the disaster and the other there would be the contact, the disjunction of absent meaning—friendship" (41).

5. It is not that the disaster *is* the absolute: rather, it faces it: "Unless it be the case that knowledge—because it is not knowledge of the disaster, but knowledge as disaster and knowledge disastrously—carries us, carries us off, deports us (whom it smites and nonetheless leaves untouched), straight to ignorance, and puts us face to face with ignorance of the unknown so that we forget, endlessly" (3).

6. This was the case from the outset, when the book itself had perhaps not yet been formally conceived. The first fragments to appear accompany or extend reflections on other works: the first, in *Change*, fitted into a homage to Jabès; those of "Discours sur la patience" (Discourse on Patience) had the subtitle "(in the margins of the books of Emmanuel Levinas)"; "A Child Is Being Killed" overtly reiterates the title of Serge Leclaire's work *On tue un enfant*, which Blanchot saluted even as he kept his distance from it: "using (perhaps falsifying)," he warned, "the impressive remarks of Serge Leclaire" (67).

7. Mascolo would speak of the Blanchot of *The Writing of the Disaster* in terms of a "revolt against concepts, a struggle with them, which must at all costs be stripped of their unbearable power to exclude" in "Parler de

Blanchot" (1981), in *À la recherche d'un communisme de pensée* (Paris: Fourbis, 1993), 409.

8. Something that Robert Antelme would be the first to recognize: "The most withdrawn life, the thinking the closest to that of others, the least turned toward itself, the self always as the self plus the other," or: "The movement of recognizing the other, the infinite other, the nature of this thought is—its servitude: never abandoning the human race. This thinking is a thinking accompanied, it bears the shadow of the other, it would be the silence, the 'mute speech' of the reader" in "Sur *L'écriture du désastre* de Maurice Blanchot," in *Textes inédits* . . . (Paris: Gallimard, 1997), 67–68.

9. "Since the gift is not the power of any freedom, or the sublime act of a free subject, there would be no gift at all if not the gift of what one does not have, under duress and beyond duress, in answer to the entreaty which strips and flays me and destroys my ability to answer, outside the world, where there is nothing save the attraction and the pressure of the other: the gift of the disaster" (49).

10. [Leclaire's work is named *On tue un enfant: Un essai sur le narcissisme primaire et la pulsion de mort*, and its English translation is *A Child Is Being Killed: On Primary Narcissism and the Death Drive*, trans. Marie-Claude Hays (Stanford: Stanford University Press, 1998). —Trans.]

11. Regarding "A Child Is Being Killed," see *The Writing of the Disaster*, 65–72. The first version of the text reads as follows: "companion, but of no one, whom we seek to particularize [by incarnating it] as an absence." The words in square brackets disappear in the book version: they tend toward not making lack into a fictitious body; the few other modifications also create a similar effect, making the reflections more intensely impersonal, in such a way as to discourage any possibility of the subsequent "scene" being interpreted biographically: an interpretation that Blanchot dismisses as "relatively undemanding," and according to which "a disappointed subject, or one uncertain of his identity, [would] be affirmed in being annulled" (125). See in parallel the rereading of the myth of Narcissus proposed by Blanchot (125–128, 134–135).

12. An echo of this is also present in a citation of Schelling taken from Heidegger: "Only he who one day has abandoned everything and has been abandoned by everything, for whom everything has capsized and who sees himself alone with the infinite, has come to the very bottom of himself and recognized all the profundity of life. This is a great step which Plato compared to death" (99).

13. Here, too, there was an event experienced through the other and kept discreet. In 1997 Jean Rollin would reveal the following episode, which deeply marked his mother after she experienced it as a child: "when she was very small in the countryside, the playmate that she adored had choked to death"; "the atrocious death, the swollen tongue protruding from her friend's

mouth, traumatized Denise for ever." In *Dialogues sans fin* (Trellières: Mirandole, 1998), 30. Blanchot who shared this anguish once wrote to Denise Rollin: "I am thinking about the little girl who was your companion, in life and in death. Each of us lives with a dead infant who is perhaps silence within us. Let me accompany you silently in this silence" (31).

14. Maurice Blanchot, "Our Clandestine Companion" (1980), in *Political Writings, 1953–1993*, trans. Zakir Paul (New York: Fordham University Press, 2010), 152.

15. In 1972, Robert Paxton published *Vichy France: Old Guard and New Order* (New York: Knopf), which was a precursor to further-reaching debates over French anti-Semitism during the Second World War.

16. "Why can we not bear, we do we not desire that which is without end?" Blanchot asks of Christianity, of Hegelianism, of all knowledge, of "political reason" (143).

17. "The unexpected quality of the resurrection of Israel, this promise suddenly extended beyond the realm of the possible, marks how strange the contemporary world is, and how overwhelming it is that we [*on*] have not been able to welcome it as we would welcome a peerless event whose sole witnesses (near or far) we were. What's more, it has troubled our consciousness as temporal men, revealing to us that there is something about life to which we do not match up, which we cannot master, and which delivers us to an infinitely responsible relation which makes demands upon us all the more, given that we are unable to respond to it"; Maurice Blanchot, letter of February 11, 1980, to the editors of *Exercices de la patience*, collected in *La condition critique: Articles 1945–1998*, ed. Christophe Bident (Paris: Gallimard, 2010), 367–368. "Come what may, I am with Israel. I am with Israel when Israel is suffering. I am with Israel when Israel suffers for causing suffering," Blanchot would even write in a short text printed and widely distributed by a monthly magazine on the occasion of the fortieth anniversary of the foundation of the Israeli state; "What is closest to me . . ." (1988), trans. Michael Holland in *Paragraph* 30, no. 3 (2007): 39. Salomon Malka published these lines, stating erroneously that this was "the first time that Blanchot has made a public statement about Israel." But the laconic and brutal nature of the statement in its publication context could lead to misunderstandings. By "Israel," Blanchot of course means an element within the people (the element that was, he wrote, "on the side of Peres," the leader of the Labor Party), or even the element that was its conscience, which is to say Israel strictly speaking or the *name* Israel.

60. FORMING THE MYTH: READINGS AND NONREADINGS (1969–1979)

1. Maurice Nadeau, "A l'écoute de Maurice Blanchot," *La Quinzaine Littéraire* 173 (October 16, 1973): 3.

2. Apart from special issues of *Gramma* in France and of *Sub-stance* in the United States, over the whole decade only one article in *Les Cahiers du Chemin*, one in *Poétique*, and two in *Littérature* appeared.

3. Jeffrey Mehlman, "Orphée scripteur," *Poétique*, 20 (November 1974): 458. The passage is not included in Mehlman's own translation "Orpheus Writing: Blanchot, Rilke, Derrida," *Structuralist Review* 1 (Spring 1978): 42–75. Michel Pierssens, "Cris et chuchotements," *Critique* 367 (December 1977): 1,146.

4. Jean Frémon, "Lire Maurice Blanchot," *La Quinzaine Littéraire* 166 (June 16, 1973): 3.

5. Jude Stéfan in *Dialogue des figures* (Seyssel: Champ Vallon, 1988), 73.

6. Roger Laporte, "Une passion (nouvelle version)," in *A l'extrême pointe* (Montpellier: Fata Morgana, 1994), 34.

7. Maurice Blanchot did not wish to see the film. He asked his brother René, Monique and Robert Antelme, and Louis-René des Forêts to attend the first private projection (spring 1971), which they did. Their judgments were harsh; they made no secret of this to Benoît Jacquot. The film was discreetly shown on television and overall was badly received.

8. Edmond Jabès, "The Unconditional (Maurice Blanchot)." In a later text, "The Unconditional II (Maurice Blanchot)," Jabès would again evoke the "unconditional retreat of the word" into the strangeness of writing: the place where "God dies into God"; *The Book of Margins*, trans. Rosemarie Waldrop (Chicago: University of Chicago Press, 1993), 193. Judaism would clearly be one of the decisive links between Blanchot and Jabès; indeed, it was concerning the latter that Blanchot first made the connection between the errancy and exile of the Jewish people and those of the writer—their shared lack of conditions; "Traces" (May 1964), in *Friendship*, trans. Elizabeth Rottenberg (Stanford: Stanford University Press, 1997), 217–227.

9. Some of them, initially given to the journals *Gramma* (1976), *Glyph* (1980), and *Nuova Corrente* (1981) and to a North American edited volume called *Deconstruction and Criticism* (New York: Seabury, 1979), would be collected in *Parages* (Paris: Galilée, 1986); others are still unpublished.

10. *Maurice Blanchot et la question de l'écriture*. Since then this work has been reprinted by Gallimard in the "Tel" collection (1986). For Levinas's view of it, see *Sur Maurice Blanchot* (Montpellier: Fata Morgana, 1975), 45–46.

11. For criticism of Collin, see Jacques Bersani, "Blanchot l'obscur," in *Le Monde des Livres* (August 20, 1971). He accuses Collin, drawing on comparisons to do so, of "plagiarism, pastiche or paraphrase" and recalls the scruples stated by Blanchot himself at the beginning of a text on Georges Bataille: "The commentator is not being faithful when he faithfully reproduces" in *The Infinite Conversation*, trans. Susan Hanson (Minneapolis: University of Minnesota Press, 1993), 203.

12. Daniel Wilhelm, *Maurice Blanchot: La voix narrative* (Paris: UGE, 1974). See also "Hors de prix," a review of *The Step Not Beyond* published in *Critique* 329 (1974) and reprinted as the first text in *Pierre Klossowski: Le corps impie* (Paris: UGE, 1979), 9–38.

13. Georges Préli, *La force du dehors—extériorité, limite et non-pouvoir à partir de Maurice Blanchot* (Fontenay-sous-Bois: Encres, 1977), published in the "Recherches" series directed by Félix Guattari. Blanchot would refer to Préli's work in *The Unavowable Community*, trans. Pierre Joris (Barrytown, N.Y.: Station Hill Press, 1988), 32. Claude Lévesque, *L'Étrangeté du texte: Essais sur Nietzsche, Freud, Blanchot et Derrida* (Paris : U.G.E., 1978).

14. Henri Meschonnic, "Maurice Blanchot ou l'écriture hors langage," *Les Cahiers du Chemin* 20 (January 15, 1974): 79–117.

15. "Notice" by the editors (Alain Coulange, Christian Limousin, Patrick Rousseau), *Gramma* 3–4 (1976): 4. See also the "Propositions" in the same issue, 11–18.

16. Steven Ungar, "Introduction: Flying White," *Sub-Stance* 14 (1976): 4.

17. Tzvetan Todorov, "La réflexion sur la littérature dans la France contemporaine," *Poétique* 38 (April 1979): 131–148.

61. MAKING THE SECRET UNCOMFORTABLE:
BLANCHOT'S READABILITY AND VISIBILITY (1979–1997)

1. Maurice Blanchot, *The Writing of the Disaster*, trans. Ann Smock (Lincoln: University of Nebraska Press, 1986), 47.

2. He wrote to Christian Limousin in this sense, as the latter was preparing the issue of *Gramma*: "I believe that [the issue] should be conceived in the greatest spirit of freedom in relation to me; this work must not appear to be guaranteed, certified, or prepared in collaboration with an author"; letter of February 13, 1975, in *Gramma* 3–4 (1976): 5. And he wrote again, three months later: "this freedom matters to me above all"; letter of May 4, 1975, ibid., 6. These letters are collected and translated in *Paragraph* 30, no. 3 (November 2007): 16–18.

3. This game of meaning, in its precision, attracted even those closest to him: "How many nuances within white! From the glacial white of mountain peaks to the *warm white* of the paper reserved for his name"; Edmond Jabès in "The Unconditional (Maurice Blanchot)," in *The Book of Margins*, trans. Rosemarie Waldrop (Chicago: University of Chicago Press, 1993), 96.

4. Manuals and dictionaries of literature speak of him with the utmost seriousness in terms of "the granitic heights of his thought," of "reptilian phrases," of an author who has often been turned into "a high priest of the white page"; André Clavel and Michel P. Schmitt, "Blanchot," in *Dictionnaire des littératures de langue française*, ed. Jean-Pierre de Beaumarchais, Daniel Couty, Alain Rey (Paris: Bordas, 1987), 1:284–285.

5. Jude Stéfan relates that a manual of twentieth-century literature released by the Magnard publishing house had even "mistakenly indicated that he died in 1980"; "M.B." in *Limon* 1 (November 1987): 10.

6. See Jean-Paul Curnier, "Esthétique de l'événement," *Lignes* 29 (October 1996): 106–121.

7. Guy Debord, *Comments on the Society of the Spectacle*, trans. Malcolm Imrie (New York: Verso, 1990), 83–84, emphasis added.

8. Let us recall Leiris who, of course with less inflexibility, also detested having his photograph published or his interviews recorded: "One likes to see the author in flesh and blood instead of really being interested in what he has written. . . . One can just about imagine that a day will come when art will only be an irritating mediator, a screen placed between the idol and the audience. Or if art still exists, one can imagine it being reduced to the art of *introducing oneself*"; note of October 27, 1966, in Michel Leiris, *Journal* (Paris: Gallimard, 1992), 617–618.

9. Jean-Louis Ézine, "Peut-on être Blanchot?" *Les Nouvelles Littéraires* (October 16, 1980): 3; Jude Stéfan, *Dialogues avec la soeur* (Seyssel: Champ Vallon, 1987), 18; Georges Perros, *Papiers collés* (Paris: Gallimard, 1978), 3:18–19.

10. Philippe Mesnard, "Une visite," postscript to *Maurice Blanchot, le sujet de l'engagement* (Paris: L'Harmattan, 1996).

11. Maurice Blanchot in *The Infinite Conversation*, 422. The drawing by Ylipe accompanied a text by Maurice Nadeau on *Awaiting Oblivion*; "Un jeu torturant," *L'Express* (May 17, 1962). The white square was surrounded by a text by Jean-Pierre Thibaudat on Juliet, Laporte, and Noël; "Les enfants de Blanchot," *Libération* (August 30, 1979), 9.

12. Maurice Blanchot, "A Letter to Blandine Jeanson," trans. Michael Holland in *Paragraph* 30, no. 3 (2007): 33.

13. Anonymous, "Auteurs cachés," *Lire* 117 (June 1985): 46.

14. Jean-Marc Parisis, "Blanchot et ses voisins," *Le Nouvel Observateur* (March 20, 1987), 103.

15. François Poirié, *Emmanuel Levinas* (1987; Paris: La Manufacture, 1992) (the new edition of 1992 no longer featured the dossier of photographs); Pierre-André Boutang, *Emmanuel Levinas*, an "Océaniques" program produced by La Sept, first broadcast on October 17, 1988.

16. Maurice Blanchot, "From Taine to M. Pesquidoux," in *Desperate Clarity: Chronicles of Intellectual Life, 1942*, trans. Michael Holland (New York: Fordham University Press, 2013), 204.

17. Georges Bataille, *La limite de l'utile*, in *Oeuvres completes* (Paris: Gallimard, 1976), 7:245.

18. "No one is ever anything but the copy of a copy," adds Roland Barthes in a work that owes much to Blanchot's thinking of the image; *Camera Lucida* (1980), trans. Richard Howard (London: Vintage, 2000), 102.

19. Marie-Claire Ropars-Wuilleumier, "Sur le désoeuvrement: L'image dans l'écrire selon Blanchot," *Littérature* 94 (May 1994): 113–124.

20. On what Blanchot himself says about the image, see notably "The Two Version of the Imaginary" (1951), in *The Space of Literature*, trans. Ann Smock (Lincoln: University of Nebraska Press, 1982), 254–263; and "The Laughter of the Gods" (1965), in *Friendship*, trans. Elizabeth Rottenberg (Stanford: Stanford University Press, 1997), 169–182.

21. Robert Antelme, *The Human Race*, trans. Jeffrey Haight and Annie Mahler (Evanston, Ill.: Marlboro/Northwestern, 1998), 3.

22. Dionys Mascolo, *Autour d'un effort de mémoire: Sur une lettre de Robert Antelme* (Paris: M. Nadeau, 1987), 28.

23. Maurice Blanchot, *The Step Not Beyond*, trans. Lycette Nelson (Albany: State University of New York Press, 1992), 76.

24. Jacques Derrida, *Politics of Friendship*, trans. George Collins (London: Verso, 1997), 55, 69.

25. Maurice Blanchot, "Inspiration, Lack of Inspiration" (1953), in *The Space of Literature*, 187; "Friendship" (1962), in *Friendship*, 291.

26. Marguerite Duras, *The War: A Memoir*, trans. Barbara Bray (New York: New Press, 1994), 53.

27. Derrida, *Politics of Friendship*, 69.

28. In terms of Villemaine, having obtained if not consent then at least the absence of any opposition ("I do not wish to be the guardian of "my" works, and even less their owner," Blanchot wrote to him, adding: "What no longer belongs to me does not belong to anyone else, either"—letter of October 19, 1986), he worked with Gisèle Renard to stage *Death Sentence* in 1987, basing himself on the *récit* of that name and on *Thomas the Obscure*. On this production—which led him to think about the possibility of a new mode of communication in the theatre, based on the works of Celan, Jabès, Kafka, Artaud or Giacometti—see "De l'écrit à la parole," a roundtable chaired by Jacques Munier and featuring Maurice Attais, Jacques Derrida, and Philippe Lacoue-Labarthe in *Théâtre/Public* 79 (January–February 1988): 36–41; as well as Pierre-Antoine Villemaine, "Le temps d'une représentation," *Écritures contemporaines et théâtralité* (Paris: Publications de la Sorbonne Nouvelle, 1990), 63–70; and "Un éclair qui se prolonge," *Ralentir Travaux* 7 (Winter 1997): 86–90. In 1995, Micheline Welter also staged *Thomas the Obscure*; see René Solis, "Pari difficile aux Bernardines," *Libération* (February 9, 1995), 32.

29. Daniel Dobbels, "Présentation," *Lignes* 11 (September 1990): 11.

30. [A selection of the proceedings of the London conference appeared in *Maurice Blanchot: The Demand of Writing*, ed. Carolyn Bailey Gill (London: Routledge, 1996). —Trans.]

31. Special issues of reviews have appeared regularly: *Exercices de la Patience* in 1981, *L'Esprit Créateur* in 1984, *Nuova Corrente* in 1985, then *Lignes* and

Ralentir Travaux. Many theses have been written in France and abroad (especially in the United Kingdom, the United States, Belgium, Switzerland, Italy, Germany, Japan, the Netherlands), where they have often addressed Blanchot's relation to other writers (listed at random: Baudelaire, Beckett, Derrida, Gordimer, Heidegger, Lispector, Saussure, Shakespeare). They have been slightly slow in filtering through to publication: none was published in the 1980s, but those by Brian T. Fitch (1992), Anne-Lise Schulte-Nordholt (1995), and Chantal Michel (1997) did appear, and were exclusively dedicated to Blanchot. Last, in 1997, the first accessible work aimed at students was published by Laure Himy.

32. Tzvetan Todorov himself declared that: "I shall therefore take on the thankless task of the boor and try to translate into my own words this speech that says nothing"; this role did in fact seem to fit so nicely with such a "translation" that it can be seen as being as boorish as it had—with ironic intentions—described itself, and is unable to take off this mask; "Les critiques-écrivains," in *Critique de la critique* (Paris: Seuil, 1984), 67.

33. [This is a French translation of a work of the previous year, *Legacies of Anti-Semitism in France* (Minneapolis: University of Minnesota Press, 1983). —Trans.]

34. Zeev Sternhell, *Ni droite ni gauche* (Paris: Seuil, 1983; new ed. Brussels: Complexe, 1988), 257.

35. Philippe Mesnard, *Maurice Blanchot: Le sujet de l'engagement* (Paris: L'Harmattan, 1996). Steven Ungar, *Scandal and Aftereffect* (Minneapolis: University of Minnesota Press, 1996), 83. This is "a test case," he states, relating to what he calls "The Blanchot File," xviii.

36. For instance, it is frightening that Philippe Mesnard is able to state that between a 1936 article for *Combat* and the *Declaration on the Right to Insubordination*, "fundamentally, few elements differ," just as there is something frightening in the repeated judgment in his book regarding Bataille's alleged "superfascism."

62. WITH THIS BREAK IN HISTORY STUCK IN ONE'S THROAT: *THE UNAVOWABLE COMMUNITY* (1982–1983)

1. Maurice Blanchot in *The Unavowable Community*, trans. Pierre Joris (Barrytown, N.Y.: Station Hill Press, 1988), 23. Unless indicated otherwise, references in this chapter are henceforth to this translated work.

2. Maurice Blanchot, "La maladie de la mort (éthique et amour)," *Le Nouveau Commerce* 55 (Spring 1983): 46.

3. This phrase recalls Judith's cry to Claudia in *When the Time Comes*: "*Nescio vos*," translated exactly by Blanchot as "I don't know who you are" (60).

4. This allows us to emphasize once again everything that separates him from Sartre, for instance the priority of the ethical demand (18), or conception of society's relation to community and to communism (7).

5. In this there is an echo of what Duras said about Bataille's narrative: "*Edwarda* will remain sufficiently unintelligible over several centuries that whole theologies will grow up around it"; in "À propos de Georges Bataille" (1958) in *Outside* (Paris: Albin Michel: 1981), 34.

6. Blanchot, "La maladie de la mort," 31.

7. See the collected works *Rejouer le politique* (Paris: Galilée, 1981) and *Le retrait du politique* (Paris: Galilée, 1983); the amalgamated English version is *Retreating the Political*, trans. Simon Sparks (London: Routledge, 1997).

8. See Blanchot, *The Unavowable Community*, 26 n., and Leslie Hill's analysis in *Blanchot: Extreme Contemporary* (London: Routledge, 1997), 197–198.

9. Jean-Luc Nancy, *The Inoperative Community* (Minneapolis: University of Minnesota Press, 1991), 31. Beyond his in-depth meditation on the entirety of Blanchot's work, Nancy was the first to recognize how important the texts published in *Committee* were. It could be said without great risk that his thinking and even the title of his article flows from the rupture in the following phrase, which he cites, from "Communism without Heirs" (1968): "Communism: what excludes (and is excluded from) any already constituted community" in *Political Writings, 1953–1993*, trans. Zakir Paul (New York: Fordham University Press, 2010), 93.

10. He refers to several articles in *The Infinite Conversation* (7), twice cites *The Step Not Beyond* (9, 10), and tacitly borrows from various fragments of *The Writing of the Disaster* (15–16); see *The Writing of the Disaster*, trans. Ann Smock (Lincoln: University of Nebraska Press, 1986), 49–50, 89–90, 108–111.

11. Jean-Luc Nancy, "Compagnie de Blanchot," *Ralentir Travaux* 7 (Winter 1997): 77.

12. Nancy, *The Inoperative Community*, 3. This is taken up in different terms by Blanchot: "the isolated being is the individual, and the individual is only an abstraction, existence as it is represented by the weak-minded concept of everyday liberalism." (18)

13. Ibid., 30.

14. Marguerite Duras in *The Malady of Death*, trans. Barbara Bray (New York: Grove Press, 1986), 55.

15. Sarah Kofman in *Smothered Words*, trans. Madeleine Dobie (Evanston, Ill.: Northwestern University Press, 1998), 70.

16. Duras, *The Malady of Death*, 1. This mistake was noticed by Francis Marmande in "Le mot de passe," *Lignes* 11 (September 1990): 108. Strangely, the citation is correct in the version published in *Le Nouveau Commerce*. Whatever the source of the eventual slippage, the conditional clearly sits uneasily with Blanchot's reading ("there remains this statement (it is true in the conditional)," 37).

17. Maurice Blanchot in "The Narrative Voice (the "It," the Neutral)" (1964), in *The Infinite Conversation*, 462. See also Marguerite Duras, *La vie matérielle* (Paris: POL, 1987), 36.

18. Blanchot, "The Narrative Voice." ["The one"—*celle*—can refer to either a woman or an impersonal feminine noun such as *la pensée*, "thought." The square brackets are Bident's. —Trans.]

19. Ibid.

20. Maurice Blanchot, "Destroy" (1970), in *Friendship*, trans. Elizabeth Rottenberg (Stanford: Stanford University Press, 1997), 113–116.

21. "A reader (but am I?)," he wrote at the beginning of the article in *Le Nouveau Commerce* (31). And in the book: "I am no longer speaking exactly, as I should, of Marguerite Duras's text," (50) recognizing an element of betrayal in what he was writing.

22. Published twenty years after *Awaiting Oblivion*, *The Malady of Death* is strangely close to it and seems to describe the same situation: "She was seated, motionless, at the table; lying next to him on the bed; sometimes standing next to the door and in that case coming from very far away. This is how he had seen her the first time. Standing, having come in without saying a word and not even looking around . . . he ought to have immediately felt like an intruder in this room." *Awaiting Oblivion*, trans. John Gregg (Lincoln: University of Nebraska Press, 1997), 29. The main difference is the man's intimate knowledge of women's bodes ("between him and every feminine figure a long familiarity that made him close to each of them," ibid.). In this *récit*, Blanchot had perhaps written the impossible dialogue that is lacking at the end of *The Malady of Death*: "'You, too, forgot me'—'Perhaps, but in forgetting you, I reached an ability to forget you that far exceeds my understanding and that links me, well beyond me, to what I forget. It is almost too much for one person.'—'You are not alone.'—'Yes, I am not the only one who forgets, if I forget'" (78). But beyond the analogy between the narrative situations, the use of voices whose dialogue punctuates *Awaiting Oblivion* would enter Duras's fiction from the 1960s and especially the 1970s, seeming to guide her practice of effacing genres (and even of the materiality of the signifier: "*text theater film*" would be her subtitle for *India Song*). These voices are placeholders for absence, the place of a third presence in which pleasure is always experienced through loss and death.

23. See Marguerite Duras, "Dans les jardins d'Israël il ne fait jamais nuit" (1985), reprinted in *Les yeux verts*, new ed. (Paris: Cahiers du Cinéma: 1987), 228–248, at 231–233; "Les hommes," in *La vie matérielle*, 38: "People, from Peter Handke to Maurice Blanchot, thought that it was directed against men in their relations with women."

24. See notably *Autour d'un effort de mémoire: sur une lettre de Robert Antelme* (Paris: M. Nadeau, 1987), 39–43, where Mascolo opposes the hypothesis that friendship is an exclusively male construct.

25. Many descriptions or allusions confirm this. Stein is the narrative's discreet authority, the one who utters decisive words, to whom others look,

and who even sees things on behalf of others; *Destroy, She Said*, trans. Barbara Bray (New York: Grove Press, 1970), 28, 31. He walks "with his long indefatigable stride" (11), even at night, when he goes down to the park, an exalted victim of insomnia (13). He is a writer or "in the process of becoming one," and it has "always been like that." This can be seen in "the way [he] keep[s] asking questions. Questions that get [him] nowhere" (10). As if ironically, a character in the narrative mistakenly names him Blum (p. 77). Blum: the missing link in the metonymy leading from Blanchot to Stein. This is a Judaized Blanchot, turning his back on the insults of the past. Duras would even say that Stein is the key element of the book: "First there was no Stein, but then when he arrived then the book also arrived." She added, surprisingly contradicting the narrative itself, that "Stein, for his part, does not make love"; in Marguerite Duras and Xavière Gauthier, *Les parleuses* (Paris: Minuit, 1974), 47.

26. Maurice Blanchot, "Destroy" (Spring 1970), in *Friendship*, 114. Blanchot would therefore see the characters as gods, "new gods, free of all divinity" (115), whom he describes as he did those in *Awaiting Oblivion*.

27. Ibid., 116.

63. EVEN A FEW STEPS TAKE TIME: LITERATURE AND WITNESSING (1983–1997)

1. On October 13, 1992, Blanchot wrote to Dionys Mascolo that "political and social difficulties torment me as passionately as before."

2. Jacques Derrida relates that in 1995 he humorously referred to his health as "his strong nature."

3. Roger Laporte, *Entre deux mondes* (Montpellier: Gris Banal, 1988), 55.

4. Maurice Blanchot, *The Madness of the Day*, trans. Lydia Davis (Barrytown, N.Y.: Station Hill Press, 1981), 9.

5. This nephew is said to have planned to open up the house in Quain to create a museum in honor of his uncle.

6. Maurice Blanchot, *Le dernier à parler* (Montpellier: Fata Morgana, 1984); Maurice Blanchot and Joë Bousquet, *Maurice Blanchot/Joë Bousquet* (Montpellier: Fata Morgana, 1987). Strangely, the latter's table of contents and the copyright information give conflicting information. In fact, although it was included in *Faux pas* in 1943, Blanchot's article had not been published in the *Journal des Débats*.

7. Blanchot had written an article on the art of the book, including sections on the relation of illustration and text: "The Book" (1943), in *A World in Ruins: Chronicles of Intellectual Life, 1943*, trans. Michael Holland (New York: Fordham University Press, 2016), 29–35.

8. *The Blanchot Reader* (Oxford: Blackwell, 1995). It is edited and introduced by Michael Holland and includes translations by Susan Hanson, Michael

Holland, Roland-François Lack, Ian Maclachlan, Ann Smock, Chris Stevens, and Michael Syrotinski.

9. Maurice Blanchot in "After the Fact," in *The Station Hill Blanchot Reader*, ed. George Quasha (Barrytown, N.Y.: Station Hill Press, 1998), 494–495.

10. Maurice Blanchot, "The Great Reducers" (1965), in *Friendship*, trans. Elizabeth Rottenberg (Stanford: Stanford University Press, 1997), 64.

11. Maurice Blanchot in *Intellectuals under Scrutiny* (1984), in *The Blanchot Reader*, 226.

12. Maurice Blanchot in *For Friendship* (1993), in *Political Writings, 1953–1993*, trans. Zakir Paul (New York: Fordham University Press, 2010), 142.

13. "Encounters" (1984), trans. Michael Holland in *Paragraph* 30, no. 3 (November 2007): 27–28.

14. *Maurice Blanchot/Joë Bousquet*, 17.

15. It would recall Blanchot's response to Catherine David's questions about commitment; "Refuse the established order" (1981); trans. Leslie Hill in *Paragraph* 30, no. 3 (November 2007): 20–22.

16. *The Blanchot Reader*, 207.

17. [Blanchot refers to "the air of the time" in a short text accompanying the first appearance of "Intellectuals under Scrutiny" and reproduced in *Les intellectuels en question: Ébauche d'une réflexion* (Tours: Farrago, 2000), 60. The text, which does feature in *The Blanchot Reader*, reads as follows: "These notes were not initially intended for publication. Prompted by the air of the time, by Bredin's book, by the republication of *Social Criticism*, by Glucksmann's recent book—which I most often feel in agreement with, even as I wonder how such an important personal conviction can be imposed on or even proposed to others, or to everybody—; these notes developed beyond what I intended, even without me being able to reach the end of my path. Pierre Nora has persuaded me that they might be able to help the 'permanent debate' which is the journal's raison d'être. I therefore offer them up in their inadequacy, convinced as I am only of the certainty that I must have expressed at the end, under the sign of René Char." —Trans.]

18. *The Blanchot Reader*, 208, 224.

19. Ibid., 225, 207.

20. Ibid., 210.

21. Ibid., 223.

22. Ibid., 213, 225.

23. "The fact that Céline was a writer in the grip of delirium does not make him uncongenial to me, but this delirium found expression in anti-Semitism; delirium here is no excuse; all anti-Semitism is basically a delirium, and even if it is delirious, anti-Semitism remains the *capital offense*": in

a letter of 1966 to Raymond Bellour in *Paragraph* 30, no. 3 (November 2007): 15–16.

24. *The Blanchot Reader*, 223.

25. Ibid., 226.

26. Ibid., 226, 208.

27. Maurice Blanchot in "Our Clandestine Companion" (1980), in *Political Writings*, 145.

28. Ibid., 152.

29. Ibid. Blanchot would ask, in parenthesis, of Emmanuel Levinas: "(what have I not borrowed from him)" in "Writing devoted to silence" (1989), trans. Leslie Hill in *Paragraph* 30, no. 3 (November 2007): 40.

30. Notably Lacoue-Labarthe's *Heidegger, Art and Politics: The Fiction of the Political* (1987), trans. Chris Turner (Oxford: Blackwell, 1990) and his "Transcendence Ends in Politics" (1981), trans. Peter Caws in *Social Research* 49, no. 2 (Summer 1982): 405–440. Blanchot cites the latter in *Intellectuals under Scrutiny* (1984).

31. Maurice Blanchot, "Thinking the Apocalypse" (1988), in *Political Writings*, 123.

32. Maurice Blanchot, *The Writing of the Disaster*, 82; "Do not forget!" (1986), trans. Leslie Hill in *Paragraph* 30, no. 3 (November 2007): 34–37; "Writing devoted to silence" (1989) in ibid., 39–41.

33. Blanchot, "Do not forget" (1988 letter to Salomon Malka), in *Political Writings*, 124–129.

34. Blanchot, *The Writing of the Disaster*, 143.

35. Maurice Blanchot, "Peace, peace to the far and to the near" (1985), trans. Leslie Hill in *Paragraph* 30, no. 3 (November 2007): 28–33. Blanchot had already sketched out in his May 1981 response to Catherine David what can be named as such a "Judaism of thought," something applied to the place left empty by the writer, in which his real sense of engagement would be found. He would return to it in an article dedicated to the figure of Moses as a writer: "Thanks (be given) to Jacques Derrida" (1990), trans. Leslie Hill in *The Blanchot Reader*, 317–323. ["The heaviest blessing" (*Le bienfait le plus lourd*) seems to have been the title given to an extract of this same text published in *Le Nouvel Observateur*. —Trans.]

36. Maurice Blanchot, letter of September 15, 1989, in Bernard-Henri Lévy, *Adventures on the Freedom Road*, trans. Richard Veasey (London: Harvill, 1995), 318. See also the way in which the name of Jabès is used rhythmically, three times, at the end of "Writing devoted to silence" (1989) in *Paragraph* 30, no. 3 (November 2007): 39–41.

37. "Rumor has it that in 1986 Blanchot wrote a seven-page text on the early ('nighttime') texts for inclusion in a forthcoming study by Jean-Luc

Nancy and Philippe Lacoue-Labarthe." Steven Ungar, *Scandal and Aftereffect* (Minneapolis: University of Minnesota Press, 1996), 164.

38. [The letter has since been published, in Jean-Luc Nancy's *Maurice Blanchot: Passion politique, lettre-récit* (Paris: Galilée, 2011), 47–62. —Trans.]

39. Leslie Hill, "Introduction" in *Maurice Blanchot: The Demand of Writing*, ed. Carolyn Bailey Gill (London: Routledge, 1996), 9, 20.

40. Letter of December 24, 1992, from Maurice Blanchot to Roger Laporte, in ibid., 209.

41. Maurice Blanchot, "Our Responsibility" (1986), trans. Michael Holland in *Paragraph* 30, no. 3 (November 2007): 37–38. Dominique Lecoq chairs the association of "The Friends of Georges Bataille," to whose oversight committee Blanchot belonged.

42. Similarly, in a note in *Michel Foucault as I Imagine Him* the same year, he wrote: "disciplines go back to prehistoric times when, for example, a bear was transformed, through successful training, into what would later be a watchdog or courageous policeman." In Michel Foucault and Maurice Blanchot, *Foucault/Blanchot* (New York: Zone Books, 1987), 87.

43. Maurice Blanchot, "I think it is better for a writer . . ." (1991), trans. Michael Holland in *Paragraph* 30, no. 3 (November 2007): 42. Blanchot's regular signing of petitions should also be noted: for instance, for an international Parliament of writers in 1993, for the legal recognition of homosexual couples in 1996, for civil disobedience against the Debré law on immigration in 1997 (this last movement openly echoed the Manifesto of the 121). His presence and intransigence stood firm, even if fitfully, against the banalization of politics that was underway. For instance, at the end of 1996 Blanchot learned that his publisher of nearly thirteen years, Bruno Roy, with whom he had published six books, had recently brought out a work by Alain de Benoist, a theorist of the far right, editor of the review *Krisis*, leader of GRECE (Group for Research and Study of European Civilization), and fellow traveler of the National Front. His reaction was immediate. Blanchot informed those close to him that he was withdrawing his books from Fata Morgana; Jacques Dupin, Louis-René des Forêts, Roger Laporte, and Gerald Macé decided to do the same. On September 2, he wrote a letter to Bruno Roy explaining his departure from the publishing house: "at least for as long as you retain him in your catalogue and on sale." This ultimatum was met by Roy with a threat approaching blackmail: He recalled Blanchot's political texts of the 1930s, a threat that left the latter totally indifferent. Blanchot's letter and an extract from Bruno Roy's were published by Maurice Nadeau in *La Quinzaine Littéraire* of November 1. The dailies, weeklies, and journals took hold of this new "affair," most often with the bad faith and ignorance that might be imagined.

44. Maurice Blanchot, "We work in the dark" (1983), trans. Leslie Hill in *Paragraph* 30, no. 3 (November 2007): 25–27.

45. Maurice Blanchot, "The question is certainly a traditional one" (1985), trans. Michael Holland in ibid., 28.
46. Blanchot, "I think it is better for a writer," 42; "Allow me to reply briefly," 43.
47. Maurice Blanchot, "Who?" in *Who Comes after the Subject?* ed. Eduardo Cadava, Peter Connor, and Jean-Luc Nancy (New York: Routledge, 1991), 58–60.
48. See, for instance, the response to Claire Nouvet for the special issue of *Yale French Studies* on "Literature and the Ethical Question": "Dear Madam, excuse me for responding to you by letter. Reading the one you sent me . . . I became afraid and almost without hope. 'Again, again,' I said to myself. It is not that I claim to have exhausted an inexhaustible subject, but on the contrary that such a subject was returning to me precisely because it is so uncompromising. Even the word 'literature' is suddenly alien to me." "Enigma," *Yale French Studies* 79 (1991): 5. On the frequent use of "again, again" to signal fright in the "literature" of Blanchot, see Leslie Hill, *Blanchot: Extreme Contemporary* (London: Routledge, 1997), 192, 264–265.
49. Maurice Blanchot, "The Inquisition destroyed the Catholic religion . . ." (1993), *Paragraph* 30, no. 3 (November 2007): 43.
50. Blanchot, *Foucault—Blanchot*, 70. He would himself evoke "the insufficiency of commentary" in a text on Louis-René des Forêts; *A Voice from Elsewhere*, 14.
51. Maurice Blanchot, "Oh All to End" (1990), in *The Blanchot Reader*, 635. He thus began this article by signaling his mistrust of words, just as he did with his article on Derrida: "After such a long silence (perhaps hundreds and hundreds of years) I shall begin to write again, not on Derrida (how pretentious!), but with his help, and convinced that I shall betray him immediately" in "Thanks (Be Given) to Jacques Derrida" (1990), trans. Leslie Hill in *The Blanchot Reader*, 317.
52. Blanchot, *A Voice from Elsewhere*, 28.
53. Blanchot, *Foucault—Blanchot*, 108, 81.
54. Maurice Blanchot, "*L'Excès-Usine* ou l'infini morcelé," *Libération* (February 24, 1987), 35.
55. Maurice Blanchot, "The Ascendant Word, or Are We Still Worthy of Poetry?" (1984), in *Political Writings*, 160, 157.
56. Maurice Blanchot in "Thanks (Be Given) to Jacques Derrida" (1990), in *The Blanchot Reader*, 322.
57. Maurice Blanchot, "Oh All to End" (1990), in ibid., 635–637.
58. Maurice Blanchot, "The Ascendant Word" (1984), in *Political Writings*, 154.
59. Blanchot, *A Voice From Elsewhere*, 7.
60. Blanchot, *The Writing of the Disaster*, 72; *A Voice From Elsewhere*, 28.

61. This is what Blanchot says of the "biography" of Roger Laporte, who "supposed (whence the ordeal) that his life only began with writing, meaning that this writing could not be anything anterior or exterior that it would be necessary to write"; Maurice Blanchot, "Ces quelques lignes ne sont qu'une annonce . . . ," in *La condition critique: Articles 1945–1998*, ed. Christophe Bident (Paris: Gallimard, 2010), 426–430.

62. Maurice Blanchot in *A Voice from Elsewhere*, 6, 13. It is easy to understand Blanchot's anger in 1992 when a reprint of *Thomas the Obscure* in the "L'Imaginaire" series included without his agreement two pages of straightforwardly biographical information (some of which was wrong). Such (anonymous) pages *negated* the narrative to follow: they negated nothing less than their essence, their poetry, their *writing*.

63. *Foucault—Blanchot*, 103–104.

64. Daniel Dobbels in Robert Antelme, *Textes inédits* . . . (Paris: Gallimard, 1997), 77.

65. Maurice Blanchot, "Avec Dionys Mascolo," *Lignes* 33 (March 1998). With the sinister affair that set Levinas's two children against one another after his death, Blanchot would also think it necessary to publicly mark his presence by writing a letter supporting Michaël Levinas; see the article by Nicholas Weill in *Le Monde* (June 22–23, 1997), 25.

66. Three years later, on September 22, 1997, for Maurice Blanchot's ninetieth birthday, Didier Cahen and Michel Deguy brought together, in the Maison des Écrivains in Paris, around twenty people who were close either to the man or his work. It is a strange thing to celebrate the birthday of someone who is not there. There were several readings: those from *The Madness of the Day* by Jacques Dupin, and from *Friendship* by Louis-René des Forêts, did bear witness to a presence, a voice, a smile, a trace of happiness.

67. Maurice Blanchot and Jacques Derrida, *The Instant of My Death / Demeure: Fiction and Testimony*, trans. Elizabeth Rottenberg (Stanford: Stanford University Press, 2000), 3.

68. Ibid., 11.

69. Jacques Derrida in *The Instant of My Death / Demeure*, 77. "Fiction and Testimony" is Derrida's subtitle, and he reads Blanchot's narrative as a knot formed by the relation of the two. We are indebted to his analyses, which just like the narrative on which they provide a commentary, mark an epoch. They do so as this narrative and *for* this narrative: published with Fata Morgana in 1994 (two years before the affair that would set Blanchot against Bruno Roy), *The Instant of My Death* was reproduced in its entirety in Derrida's book. Blanchot would also thank his friend for having helped—as it were—"get it across" to Galilée.

70. Blanchot in *The Instant of My Death / Demeure*, 7.

71. In Quain, the family is said to have possessed a saber from the Napoleonic era that had belonged to ancestors who were soldiers of the first Empire.

72. Marguerite was the only other witness of the events, except for his sister-in-law Anna, the wife of René, who was probably also there.

AMOR: BLANCHOT SINCE 2003, BY JOHN MCKEANE

1. Maurice Blanchot in *The Writing of the Disaster*, trans. Ann Smock (1980; Lincoln: University of Nebraska Press, 1995), 71.

2. Maurice Blanchot in "The Madness of the Day," in *The Station Hill Blanchot Reader*, ed. George Quasha (Barrytown, N.Y.: Station Hill, 1998), 191.

3. Daniel Dobbels, "Le grand récit du corps," in the Blanchot dossier in *Magazine Littéraire* 424 (October 2003), 45. My translation, as are those that follow, unless indicated otherwise.

4. Jacques Derrida, "À Maurice Blanchot," in *Chaque fois unique, la fin du monde* (Paris: Galilée, 2003), 323–332. For obvious reasons, the text on Blanchot did not feature in the earlier, English version of this work, *The Work of Mourning* (Chicago: University of Chicago Press, 2001). See also Derrida's more developed text "Maurice Blanchot est mort," in *Parages*, 2nd ed. (1986; Paris: Galilée, 2003), 267–300. Previously, Derrida had published the first edition of *Parages*, a collection of texts on Blanchot (and particularly on *The Madness of the Day*); and, focusing on *The Instant of My Death*, available in Blanchot/Derrida, *The Instant of My Death / Demeure: Fiction and Testimony*, trans. Elizabeth Rottenberg (Stanford: Stanford University Press, 2000).

5. Christophe Bident in *Maurice Blanchot: Récits critiques* (Tours and Paris: Farrago/Scheer, 2003), 61–63. I wish to thank Christophe for his collaboration on the translation as well as his comments on this text.

6. See the anonymously authored obituary in the London *Times* (February 26, 2003). In parallel to this and to Derrida's *Demeure*, a further work functions as bio/thanatography with regards to Blanchot: Philippe Lacoue-Labarthe's *Ending and Unending Agony*, trans. Hannes Opelz (New York: Fordham University Press, 2015). It is constructed around two key Blanchot texts, *The Instant of My Death* and "A Primal Scene?"

7. This point was made by Leslie Hill in "Maurice Blanchot has died . . ." in *Nowhere Without No: in Memory of Maurice Blanchot*, ed. by Kevin Hart (Sydney: Vagabond and Stray Dog, 2003), 20–22.

8. Maurice Blanchot, "Literature and the Right to Death," in *The Work of Fire*, trans. by Charlotte Mandell (Stanford: Stanford University Press, 1995), 320.

9. In the years preceding his death in 2003, Blanchot published nothing. In late 2002, however, he did sign the petition against the Iraq war—this

despite its slogan, "Not in my name," being in direct opposition to his activism of anonymity in the 1960s.

10. The thesis can be consulted in the Blanchot archival holdings at Harvard University (MS Fr 662, box 12).

11. There are localized issues of vocabulary: where there was no clear reason (beyond exoticization, something of which French studies in English is sometimes guilty) to keep a term in French, I have translated it: thus *il y a* has become *there is*. For Blanchot's commonly used term *l'exigence*, I felt that *exigency* added an unnecessary layer of distance, and therefore used *demand*.

12. Maurice Blanchot in "The Essential Solitude" (1953), collected in *The Space of Literature*, trans. Ann Smock (Lincoln: University of Nebraska Press, 1993), 23.

13. Ibid., 258.

14. Exodus 20 and Deuteronomy 5.

15. "Icon" is from Greek *eikein*, to be similar/to be like.

16. Blanchot, *The Space of Literature*, 254, 262.

17. Ibid., 255.

18. See also "The Image" in "The Essential Solitude," in ibid., 32–33. For critical discussions, see Ian Maclachlan, "Blanchot and the Romantic Imagination," in *Blanchot Romantique*, ed. John McKeane and Hannes Opelz (Oxford: Peter Lang, 2010), 155–172; and Sergey Zenkin, "Maurice Blanchot et l'image visuelle," in *Blanchot dans son siècle* (Lyon: Paragon, 2009), 214–227.

19. Blanchot, *The Space of Literature*, 256.

20. Ibid.

21. Ibid., 259.

22. See "Orpheus's Gaze" in ibid., and, for Lazarus, see *The Work of Fire*, 327; "Reading" in *The Space of Literature*; *Thomas the Obscure*, trans. Robert Lamberton (Barrytown, N.Y.: Station Hill, 1988), 38; and Blanchot's response to Jean Cayrol's *Pour un romanesque lazaréen*, "Les justes" in *L'Observateur* 15 (July 20, 1950): 17. Jean-Luc Nancy writes on "Blanchot's Resurrection," in *Dis-Enclosure: The Deconstruction of Christianity*, trans. by Bettina Bergo, Gabriel Malenfant, and Michael B. Smith (2005; New York: Fordham University Press, 2008), 89–97.

23. Full publication details for works cited in this section are available in this volume's bibliography.

24. On the latest acquisition, see http://blogs.harvard.edu/houghton modern/2015/10/01/maurice-blanchot-papers-acquired-by-harvard. On the other, see my "Change in the Archive: Blanchot's *L'entretien infini*," in *Forum for Modern Language Studies* 50, no. 1 (2014): 69–81; and Kevin Hart, "Une réduction infinite," *Cahier de l'Herne: Blanchot* (2014): 323–328.

25. Richard Wolin, *Heidegger's Children: Hannah Arendt, Karl Löwith, Hans Jonas, Herbert Marcuse* (Princeton: Princeton University Press, 2003).

26. Michael Holland, "*État présent*: Maurice Blanchot," *French Studies* 58, no. 4 (October 2004), 533–538.

27. Monique Antelme, Gisèle Berkman, Christophe Bident, et al., eds., *Blanchot dans son siècle* (Lyon: Paragon, 2009); Kevin Hart, *The Dark Gaze: Maurice Blanchot and the Sacred* (Chicago: University of Chicago Press, 2004); McKeane and Opelz, *Blanchot Romantique*; Leslie Hill, *Maurice Blanchot and Fragmentary Writing: A Change of Epoch* (London: Continuum, 2012); Leslie Hill, *Nancy, Blanchot: A Serious Controversy* (Lanham, MD: Rowman and Littlefield, 2018).

28. Kevin Hart, ed., *Clandestine Encounters: Philosophy in the Narratives of Maurice Blanchot* (Notre Dame: University of Notre Dame Press, 2010), and Christopher Langlois (ed.), *Understanding Blanchot, Understanding Modernism* (New York: Bloomsbury, 2018).

29. Éric Hoppenot and Alain Milon, *Maurice Blanchot et la philosophie* (Paris: Presses Universitaires Paris-Ouest, 2010); Éric Hoppenot, ed., *L'oeuvre du féminin dans l'écriture de Maurice Blanchot* (Grignan: Complicités, 2004); Éric Hoppenot and Alain Milon, *Emmanuel Levinas-Maurice Blanchot, penser la différence* (Paris: Presses Universitaires Paris-Ouest, 2007). Links to a further three collective volumes from this period can be found on the website *Maurice Blanchot et ses contemporains*.

30. See *Gramma* 3–4 and 5 (1976); Leslie Hill, *Blanchot: Extreme Contemporary* (London: Routledge, 1997).

31. Maurice Blanchot, letter of December 24, 1992, to Roger Laporte in *Maurice Blanchot: The Demand of Writing*, 209.

32. Edited by David Uhrig (Paris: Gallimard, 2017). This volume appeared after the main body of this afterword was written. Uhrig also writes that "around sixty articles of literary journalism [of the 1930s] are being reserved for publication in a separate volume" (9).

33. Michel Surya, *L'autre Blanchot: L'écriture de jour, l'écriture de nuit* (Paris: Gallimard, 2015); Jean-Luc Nancy, *La communauté désavouée* (Paris: Galilée, 2014), trans. Philip Armstrong as *The Disavowed Community* (New York: Fordham University Press, 2016); Henri de Monvallier and Nicolas Rousseau, *Blanchot l'obscur: ou la déraison littéraire* (Paris: Autrement, 2015).

34. The early Blanchot is attacked for having been "the friend, the collaborator of overt anti-Semites" (20). Surya writes of a "French fascism to which Blanchot was as close as it is possible to be, being close to some of its major representatives" (97). Regarding the later period, the attack focuses on a misjudged statement on Judaism, not directly concerning Blanchot, and made by Dionys Mascolo (122).

35. Philippe Lacoue-Labarthe's *Ending and Unending Agony*, trans. Hannes Opelz (New York: Fordham University Press, 2015), 1. The scare quotes accompanying "break" are Lacoue-Labarthe's.

36. See Michael Holland, "D'un retour au tournant" (2009), in *Avant dire: Essais sur Blanchot* (Paris: Hermann, 2015).

37. Maurice Blanchot, letter to Roger Laporte of December 22, 1984, in *Maurice Blanchot: Passion politique*, 61.

38. Surya's book is divided into three "sequences," the first addressing the 1930s, the second 1958–1968, and the third the period following 1968.

BOOKS BY MAURICE BLANCHOT, WITH TRANSLATIONS INTO ENGLISH

Thomas l'Obscur. (First version.) 1941. Reprint, Paris: Gallimard, 2005.
Comment la littérature est-elle possible? Paris: José Corti, 1942. (See *Faux Pas* and *Chroniques littéraires du Journal des Débats: Avril 1941–août 1944.*)
Aminadab. 1942. Paris: Gallimard, 2004. *Aminadab.* Translated by Jeff Fort. Lincoln: University of Nebraska Press, 2002.
Faux pas. Paris: Gallimard, 1943. *Faux Pas.* Translated by Charlotte Mandell. Stanford: Stanford University Press, 2001.
Le très-haut. 1948. Paris: Gallimard, 1988. *The Most High.* Translated by Allan Stoekl. Lincoln: University of Nebraska Press, 1995.
L'arrêt de mort. 1948. Paris: Gallimard, 1977. *Death Sentence.* Translated by Lydia Davis. Barrytown, N.Y.: Station Hill Press, 1978.
La part du feu. Paris: Gallimard, 1949. *The Work of Fire.* Translated by Charlotte Mandell. Stanford: Stanford University Press, 1995.
Lautréamont et Sade. 1949. Revised edition, Paris: Minuit, 1963. *Lautréamont and Sade.* Translated by Stuart Kendall and Michelle Kendall. Stanford: Stanford University Press, 2004.
Thomas l'obscur, nouvelle version. 1950. Reprint, Paris: Gallimard, 1992. *Thomas the Obscure.* Translated by Robert Lamberton. 1973. Reprint, Barrytown, N.Y.: Station Hill Press, 1988.
Au moment voulu. 1951. Reprint, Paris: Gallimard, 1993. *When the Time Comes.* Translated by Lydia Davis. Barrytown, N.Y.: Station Hill Press, 1985.
Le ressassement éternel. Paris: Minuit, 1951. Reprint, Paris, London, New York: Gordon & Breach, 1970. Later reprinted in *Après coup précédé par Le ressassement éternel.* Paris: Minuit, 1983.
Celui qui ne m'accompagnait pas. 1953. Reprint, Paris: Gallimard, 1993. *The One Who Was Standing Apart From Me.* Translated by Lydia Davis. Barrytown, N.Y.: Station Hill Press, 1992.
L'espace littéraire. 1955. Reprint, 1968. Reprint, Paris: Gallimard, 1988. *The Space of Literature.* Translated by Ann Smock. Lincoln: University of Nebraska Press, 1982.

Le dernier homme. 1957. New edition published 1977. Reprint, Paris: Gallimard, 1992. *The Last Man*. Translated by Lydia Davis. New York: Columbia University Press, 1987.

La bête de Lascaux. Paris: GLM, 1958. Reprint, Montpellier: Fata Morgana, 1982. Reprinted in *Une voix venue d'ailleurs*. Paris: Gallimard, 2002. "The Beast of Lascaux." Translated by Leslie Hill. In *Oxford Literary Review* 22 (2000).

Le livre à venir. 1959. Reprint, 1971. Reprint, Paris: Gallimard, 1986. *The Book to Come*. Translated by Charlotte Mandell. Stanford: Stanford University Press, 2003.

L'attente l'oubli. 1962. Reprint, Paris: Gallimard, 2000. *Awaiting Oblivion*. Translated by John Gregg. Lincoln: University of Nebraska Press, 1997.

L'entretien infini. Paris: Gallimard, 1969. *The Infinite Conversation*. Translated by Susan Hanson. Minneapolis: University of Minnesota Press, 1993.

L'amitié. Paris: Gallimard, 1971. *Friendship*. Translated by Elizabeth Rottenberg. Stanford: Stanford University Press, 1997.

La folie du jour. Montpellier: Fata Morgana, 1973. Reprint, Paris: Gallimard, 2002. *The Madness of the Day*. Translated by Lydia Davis. Barrytown, N.Y.: Station Hill Press, 1981.

Le pas au-delà. Paris: Gallimard, 1973. *The Step Not Beyond*. Translated by Lycette Nelson. Albany: State University of New York Press, 1992.

L'écriture du désastre. Paris: Gallimard, 1980. *The Writing of the Disaster*. Translated by Ann Smock. Lincoln: University of Nebraska Press, 1986.

De Kafka à Kafka. 1981. Reprint, 1982. Reprint, Paris: Gallimard, 1994. (Many of the constituent essays are contained in other volumes; see *The Work of Fire*, *The Space of Literature*, *The Infinite Conversation*, and *Friendship*.)

Après coup, preceded by *Le ressassement éternel*. Paris: Minuit, 1983. *Vicious Circles, followed by "After the Fact."* Translated by Paul Auster. Barrytown, N.Y.: Station Hill Press, 1985.

Le nom de Berlin. Bilingual edition. Berlin: Merve, 1983. Reprinted in *Écrits politiques 1958–1993*, 71–76. Paris: Lignes, éditions Léo Scheer, 2003. Reprinted in *Écrits politiques 1953–1993*, 129–133. Edited and annotated by Eric Hoppenot. Cahiers de la *NRF*. Paris: Gallimard, 2008. See also *Political Writings, 1953–1993*, 73–75. Translated by Zakir Paul. New York: Fordham University Press, 2010.

La communauté inavouable. Paris: Minuit, 1983. *The Unavowable Community*. Translated by Pierre Joris. Barrytown, N.Y.: Station Hill Press, 1988.

Le dernier à parler. 1984. Montpellier: Fata Morgana, 1986. (See *Une voix venue d'ailleurs*, 2002.)

Michel Foucault tel que je l'imagine. Montpellier: Fata Morgana, 1986. *Michel Foucault as I Imagine Him*. Translated by Jeffrey Mehlman. In Michel

Foucault and Maurice Blanchot, *Foucault/Blanchot*. New York: Zone Books, 1987.
Sade et Restif de la Bretonne. Brussels: Complexe, 1986. Partially reprinted in *La condition critique: Articles 1945–1998*, 133–163. Edited by Christophe Bident. Cahiers de la *NRF*. Paris: Gallimard, 2010.
Sur Lautréamont. Brussels: Complexe, 1987. Includes texts by Maurice Blanchot, Julien Gracq and J.-M.G. Le Clézio. *Lautréamont and Sade*. Translated by Stuart Kendall and Michelle Kendall. Stanford: Stanford University Press, 2004.
Joë Bousquet. Montpellier: Fata Morgana, 1987. Includes texts by Maurice Blanchot and Joë Bousquet.
Une voix venue d'ailleurs: Sur les poèmes de Louis-René des Forêts. Plombières-les-Dijon: Ulysse Fin de Siècle, 1992. (See *Une voix venue d'ailleurs*, 2002.)
L'instant de ma mort. Montpellier: Fata Morgana, 1994. Reprint, Paris: Gallimard, 2002. "The Instant of My Death." In Maurice Blanchot and Jacques Derrida, *The Instant of My Death/Demeure: Fiction and Testimony*. Translated by Elizabeth Rottenberg. Stanford: Stanford University Press, 2000.
Les intellectuels en question. Paris: Fourbis, 1996. Reprint, Tours: Farrago, 2000. "Intellectuals under Scrutiny." Translated by Michael Holland. In *The Blanchot Reader*, 206–227. Edited by Michael Holland. Oxford: Blackwell, 1995.
Pour l'amitié. Paris: Fourbis, 1996. Reprint, Tours: Farrago, 2000. "For Friendship." In *Political Writings, 1953–1993*, 134–143.
Henri Michaux ou le refus de l'enfermement. Tours: Farrago, 1999.
Une voix venue d'ailleurs. Paris: Gallimard, 2002. Includes "Une voix venue d'ailleurs: Sur les poèmes de Louis-René des Forêts," "La bête de Lascaux," "Le dernier à parler," and "Michel Foucault tel que je l'imagine." *A Voice from Elsewhere*. Translated by Charlotte Mandell. Albany: State University of New York Press, 2007.
Écrits politiques 1958–1993. Paris: Lignes, éditions Léo Scheer, 2003. *Political Writings, 1953–1993*. Translated with an introduction by Zakir Paul. New York: Fordham University Press, 2010.
Chroniques littéraires du Journal des Débats: Avril 1941–août 1944. Edited by Christophe Bident. Cahiers de la *NRF*. Paris: Gallimard, 2007. (Includes all articles published in the *Journal des Débats* during this period that are not collected in *Faux pas*.) *Into Disaster: Chronicles of Intellectual Life, 1941*. Translated by Michael Holland. New York: Fordham University Press, 2013. *Desperate Clarity: Chronicles of Intellectual Life, 1942*. Translated by Michael Holland. New York: Fordham University Press, 2013. *A World in Ruins: Chronicles of Intellectual Life, 1943*. Translated by Michael Holland. New York: Fordham University Press, 2016. *Death Now: Chronicles of*

Intellectual Life, 1944. Translated by Michael Holland. New York: Fordham University Press, 2018.

Écrits politiques 1953–1993. Edited and annotated by Eric Hoppenot. Cahiers de la NRF. Paris: Gallimard, 2008. (See *Écrits politiques 1958–1993*, 2003.)

Lettres à Vadim Kozovoï. Followed by "La parole ascendante." Edited and annotated by Denis Aucouturier. Houilles: Manucius, 2009.

La condition critique: Articles 1945–1998. Edited by Christophe Bident. Cahiers de la NRF. Paris: Gallimard, 2010. (Includes all critical articles published by Blanchot during the indicated period that are not collected in any other volume.) See "Responses and Interventions (1946–98)." Translated by Leslie Hill and Michael Holland. In *Paragraph*, 30, no. 3 (November 2007). See also *Political Writings, 1953–1993*.

Jean-Luc Nancy. *Maurice Blanchot: Passion politique, lettre-récit de 1984 suivie d'une lettre de Dionys Mascolo.* Paris: Galilée, 2011.

Correspondance 1953–2002. Edited by Pierre Madaule. Contains letters by Maurice Blanchot and Pierre Madaule. Paris: Gallimard, 2012.

Entretien avec le traducteur: Correspondance 1963–1973. Edited by Éric Hoppenot and Philippe Mesnard. Contains letters by Maurice Blanchot and Johannes Hübner. Paris: Kimé, 2014.

Chroniques politiques des années trente: 1931–1940. Edited by David Uhrig. Paris: Gallimard, 2017.

COLLECTIONS OF TEXTS IN TRANSLATION

The Gaze of Orpheus and Other Literary Essays. Translated by Lydia Davis. Edited with an afterword by P. Adams Sitney. Barrytown, N.Y.: Station Hill Press, 1981.

The Sirens' Song. Edited by Gabriel Josipovici. Translated by Sacha Rabinovitch. Brighton: Harvester, 1982.

The Blanchot Reader. Edited with commentary by Michael Holland. Oxford: Blackwell, 1995.

The Station Hill Blanchot Reader. Edited by George Quasha. Translated by Lydia Davis, Paul Auster, and Robert Lamberton, with a preface by George Quasha, a foreword by Christopher Fynsk, and an afterword by George Quasha and Charles Stein. Barrytown, N.Y.: Station Hill Press, 1998. Includes a selection of critical essays plus shorter fiction: *Vicious Circles, Thomas the Obscure, Death Sentence, The Madness of the Day, When the Time Comes,* and *The One Who Was Standing Apart From Me*.

"Three Texts." Translated by Leslie Hill. In *Oxford Literary Review* 22 (2000), edited by Timothy Clark, Leslie Hill and Nicholas Royle.

"Responses and Interventions (1946–98)." Translated by Leslie Hill and Michael Holland. *Paragraph* 30, no. 3 (November 2007).

Political Writings, 1953–1993. Translated with an introduction by Zakir Paul. New York: Fordham University Press, 2010.

TRANSLATIONS OF SHORTER TEXTS

A full bibliography of Blanchot's many shorter texts in French can be found at www. blanchot.fr.

"Our Clandestine Companion." Translated by David B. Allison. In *Face to Face with Levinas*, 41–50. Edited by Ralph A. Cohen. Albany: State University of New York Press, 1986.

"Our Responsibility." In *Texts for Nelson Mandela*. Edited by Jacques Derrida and Mustapha Tilli. New York: Seaver, 1987.

"Who?" In *Who Comes after the Subject?* 58–60. Edited by Eduardo Cadava, Peter Connor, and Jean-Luc Nancy. New York: Routledge, 1991.

"Extract from a Letter to Roger Laporte (9 December 1984)." Translated by Leslie Hill. In *Blanchot and the Demand of Writing*. Edited by Carolyn Bailey Gill. London: Routledge, 1996.

"A Letter (to Roger Laporte, 24 December 1992)." Translated by Leslie Hill. In ibid.

"Mahatma Gandhi." July 1931. Translated by Franson Manjali in consultation with Michael Holland. *Journal for Cultural Research* 16, no. 4 (2012): 366–370.

CRITICAL WORKS

The number of books, book chapters, articles, and other texts addressing Maurice Blanchot has grown exponentially in recent years. Readers are invited to consult the website www.blanchot.info/bc, where these texts can be searched electronically by author, date, popularity, and so on.

INDEX

Adamov, Arthur, 182, 267, 555n12
Added, Serge, 504n1
Adorno, Theodor, 188, 293, 452
Alain, 94, 146
Alain-Fournier, 92
Alphant, Marianne, 570n8
Amar, David, 479
Amrouche, Jean, 190
Andreu, Pierre, 64, 321, 497n9, 520n14
Anglès, Auguste, 522n14
Anouilh, Jean, 93
Antelme, Monique, 377, 479, 597n27
Antelme, Robert, xii, 16, 179, 185, 187, 214, 215, 223, 230, 237, 270, 287, 291, 297–300, 303, 304, 305, 306, 307, 310, 317, 318, 319, 321, 322, 325, 326, 332, 334, 338, 347, 348, 354, 355, 356, 360, 375, 377, 378, 384, 398, 429, 430, 431, 433, 437, 442, 443, 446, 458, 461, 462, 500n10, 547n32, 550nn2–3, 10, 550–551n11, 553n10, 571nn11,13, 576n21, 577n27, 580n8, 582n7
Arafat, Yasser, 398
Aragon, Louis, 188
Ariès, Philippe, 35
Aristotle, 22, 140, 560n13
Arland, Marcel, 36, 91, 92, 94, 161, 173, 179, 193, 271, 524n9, 525n10
Armel, Aliette, 479
Arnem, Bettina von, 156
Arnold, Edwin, 43
Arnoult, Pierre, 514n37
Aron, Robert, 45, 46, 524n9
Artaud, Antonin, 170, 196, 273, 284, 287, 291, 294, 363, 368, 399, 549n7, 577n27, 585n28
Assouline, Pierre, 521n3
Audry, Colette, 319
Augier, Fabien, 553nn1,2
Auriol, Vincent, 73

Aury, Dominique, 16, 64
Axelos, Kostas, 370
Aymé, Marcel, 92

Bachmann, Ingeborg, 325
Badré, Frédéric, 541n3
Bainville, Jacques, 36, 92
Balibar, Etienne, 553n10
Balzac, Honoré de, 146
Barbey, D'Aurevilly, Jules-Amédée, 111
Bardèche, Maurice, 42, 45, 52, 130
Barjavel, René, 128
Barrat, Robert, 322
Barrelet, Marie-Thérèse, 121
Barrès, Maurice, 22, 35, 36, 37, 38, 45, 50, 89, 92, 93, 487n7,8
Barthes, Roland, 273, 281–282, 288, 318, 325, 329, 332, 364, 367, 419, 422, 446, 469, 564n19, 566n8, 568n10, 584n18
Bastier, Marcel, 52
Bataille, Georges, 14, 17, 18, 26, 31, 32, 35, 46, 98, 99, 100, 112, 124, 135–144, 146, 148, 151, 152, 154, 156, 164, 165, 167, 177, 178, 180, 182, 184, 187, 188, 189, 193, 194, 195, 196, 198, 219, 220, 221, 222, 227, 235–237, 239–240, 246, 249, 271, 273, 282, 285, 286, 291, 293, 294, 297, 302, 304, 325, 326, 328, 331, 332, 334, 336, 337–338, 340, 345, 347, 348, 354, 355, 360, 362, 363, 364, 367, 368, 369, 399, 408, 421, 422, 426, 428, 429, 431, 436–440, 449, 450, 460, 467, 478, 483n3, 484n21, 496n7, 498n22, 499n2, 505nn1,4–5, 506nn8,11, 506–507n12, 508nn22,25–26,28, 509n31, 510n10, 511n23, 512n25, 515–517n4, 518n7, 523n9, 524nn5,9, 525nn12,1 527n8, 528nn15–16, 529n24, 532–533n11, 534n1, 535n3, 537n1, 538n2, 539n7, 541nn10,6, 547n24, 550–551n11, 551n5,

605

Bataille, Georges *(continued)*
554n4, 557n14, 559n1, 561n15, 563n7, 566n7, 567n16, 587n5
Bataille, Julie, 252
Bataille, Laurence, 531n3
Baudelaire, Charles, 36, 92, 97, 146, 148, 156, 158, 481n11, 527n8, 572n29, 585–586n31
Baudry, Jean-Louis, 571n11
Baum, Vicky, 535–536n5, 539n4
Bazaine, Jean, 128–130, 134, 149, 174, 479, 504n1
Beauchamp, Georges, 430
Beaufret, Jean, 52, 370–374, 376, 384, 569nn1–2
Beaumarchais, Jean-Pierre de, 583n4
Beauvoir, Simone de, 182
Beckett, Samuel, 15, 168, 273, 279, 291, 347, 446, 458, 459, 460, 524n9, 561n15, 585–586n31
Bellefroid, Jacques, 378, 572n30
Bellessort, André, 52, 91
Bellour, Raymond, 364, 479, 496n4, 590–591n23
Bénézet, Mathieu, 432
Benoist, Alain de, 15, 483n9, 592n43
Benoist-Méchin, Jacques, 146
Bérardan, Georges, 479
Berdjaev, Nicolas, 23
Berg, Alban, 459
Bergson, Henri, 23, 146, 486n5
Bernanos, Georges, 35–36, 42, 64, 98, 111, 147, 188, 193, 515–517n4
Bernus, Pierre, 54
Bersani, Jacques, 582n11
Blake, William, 146
Blanc, Philippe, 479
Blanchot, Françoise Léon (Edmond), 4–5, 10
Blanchot, George, 481–482n7
Blanchot, Joseph, 4
Blanchot, Joseph Isidore Léon, 4–5, 6, 8, 66
Blanchot, Léon, 4
Blanchot, Marguerite, 5, 6, 10–12, 446–447
Blanchot, Marthe, 481n4
Blanchot, René, 5, 6, 12, 21, 87, 239, 302, 375, 395, 405, 547n27, 582n7, 595n72
Blanzat, Roger, 522n14, 561n15
Blin, Roger, 377, 555n12
Blond, Georges, 64
Blondel, Charles, 22, 30

Bloy, Léon, 111, 161
Blum, Léon, 27, 37, 67–68, 72–75, 77, 451, 493n6, 589n25
Bonnefoy, Yves, 577n30
Borch-Jacobsen, Mikkel, 527n9
Boschetti, Anna, 516n4
Bosco, Henri, 513n35, 535n2
Boulez, Pierre, 12, 555n12
Bourget, Paul, 54, 92
Bousquet, Joë, 164, 167, 179, 450
Boutang, Pierre, 35, 193, 321, 414–415, 487n12
Boutang, Pierre-André, 584n15
Boyer, Jean-Pierre, 479
Brasillach, Robert, 16, 35, 39, 45, 52, 63, 79, 89, 91, 92, 94, 188, 492nn1,3, 494n10, 499n35, 514n2
Breton, André, 139, 147, 188, 196, 240, 304, 307, 308, 316, 337, 399, 508n22, 546n15, 577n27
Briand, Aristide, 27, 485n8, 489n2
Brisac, Geneviève, 457
Broch, Hermann, 273
Brontë, Emily, 45
Brousse, Jacques, 492n3
Brunschvicg, Léon, 23
Buber, Martin, 454
Buchet, Edmond, 121, 504n2, 524n9
Burgelin, Claude, 479
Butor, Michel, 15, 325, 378, 483n8, 548n39, 575n16

Cahen, Didier, 431, 479, 594n66
Caillois, Roger, 160, 170, 193, 364, 514n3, 542n4, 545n2
Calvino, Italo, 558n23
Camus, Albert, 124, 146, 155, 161, 164, 179, 182, 188–190, 272, 280, 282, 337, 362, 524n9, 546n20
Canque, Marie, 10
Carcopino, Jérôme, 133
Carrouges, Michel, 548n39
Carteron, Henri, 22, 485n3
Cassirer, Ernest, 29
Cassou, Jean, 189
Castoriadis-Aulagnier, Piera, 574n5
Castro, Fidel, 383, 573n34
Catalogne, Gérard de, 49
Cayrol, Jean, 267
Celan, Paul, 337, 400–402, 447, 577n30, 585n28

Index

Céline, Louis-Ferdinand, 35–36, 64, 73, 432, 590n23
Chabrol, Véronique, 131, 504n1
Chamberlain, Neville, 87
Chapsal, Madeleine, 16, 317, 553n1
Char, René, 125, 144, 167, 193, 199, 246–247, 276–277, 288, 311, 319–320, 329, 335, 346, 350, 352, 364, 370, 372, 374, 428, 446, 447, 451, 524n9, 526n4, 528n15, 537n4, 557n14, 590n17
Chardonne, Jacques, 92, 146, 147, 193
Chateaubriand, François-René de, 51
Chatelion, Hubert, 497n13
Châtelet, François, 556n22
Chautemps, Camille, 71
Chesterton, Gilbert Keith, 42, 43
Chestov, Léon, 23
Chouchani, 547n27
Cioran, E. M., 549n11
Clair, René, 45
Claudel, Paul, 92, 146, 148, 173, 282, 498n26, 510n10, 545n7
Clavel, André, 583n4
Clemenceau, Georges, 55
Cocteau, Jean, 38, 49, 94
Cohen-Solal, Annie, 499n35
Cohn-Bendit, Daniel, 383
Colette, 92
Collin, Françoise, 365, 366, 419, 421, 422, 582n11
Constant, Benjamin, 51, 221, 532n11
Corneille, Pierre, 93, 513
Corti, José, 151, 172
Coulange, Alain, 422,
Couty, Daniel, 583n4
Creton, Maurice, 72
Curnier, Jean-Paul, 584n6
Cyrano de Bergerac, Savinien, 147, 193

Daladier, Édouard, 56, 65
Dalmas, André, 416, 419, 458, 548n39
Damisch, Hubert, 555n12, 564n19
Dandieu, Arnaud, 48
Daniélou, Jean, 182
Daniel-Rops, 42, 45, 46, 49, 488n1, 490n4, 497n16, 499n31
Dante, 146
Darlan, François, 143
Daudet, Léon, 36, 92–93, 497n8
Daumier, Honoré, 306
David, Alain, 486n5

David, Catherine, 453, 590n15, 591n35
Debord, Guy, 426, 556n22
Decaunes, Luc, 240
Decour, Jacques, 170
Deguy, Michel, 370, 371, 479, 566n8, 594n66
Deleuze, Gilles, 15, 144, 273, 368, 419, 431, 446, 458, 561n15, 564n19, 565n25, 568n26
Deloncle, Eugène, 72, 493n2
Delorme, Danièle, 556n22
Derrida, Jacques, 1, 17, 23, 24, 114, 140, 273, 368–369, 371–374, 378–379, 385, 395, 404, 414, 415, 418, 419, 420, 421, 430, 431, 438, 439, 456, 558, 460, 463, 466, 478, 479, 518–519n10, 522–523n5, 523n11, 529n18, 534n5, 542n9, 546n17, 564n19, 569nn2,3, 571n11, 585n28, 586n31, 589n1, 591n35, 593n51, 594n69, 595nn4,6
Des Forêts, Louis-René, 12, 16, 146, 164, 262, 297, 302, 304, 305, 325, 328–330, 334, 337, 338, 357, 376, 377, 401, 408, 443, 458, 459, 460–461, 479, 551n3, 564n20, 573n30, 574n3, 582n7, 592n43, 593n49, 594n66
Descartes, René, 33, 142
Desportes, Bernard, 479
Déssolin, Hubert, 479
Dhôtel, André, 172, 524n9, 525n10
Didi-Huberman, Georges, 509n30
Dobbels, Daniel, 299, 431, 461, 479
Domenach, Jean-Marie, 319, 555n19
Doriot, Jacques, 39, 72
Dormoy, Marx, 73
Dort, Bernard, 555n12, 564n19
Dorval, Marie, 156
Dostoevsky, Fyodor, 30, 94, 95, 111, 136, 138, 148, 221–224, 532n10, 536n7
Doubrovsky, Serge, 564n19
Dreyfus, Alfred, 35, 323, 450–451
Drieu la Rochelle, Pierre, 176, 497n9
Drot, Geneviève, 480
Drot, Guislain, 479
Drot, Marie-Christine, 480
Drumont, Édouard, 35, 63, 71
Du Bellay, Joachim, 190
Du Bos, Charles, 525n10
Du Bouchet, André, 284, 577n30
Du Marais (Baron), 4, 479
Dubuffet, Jean, 193

Dufrenne, Mikel, 648
Dufresne, Gérard, 479
Duhamel, Georges, 64
Dumas, Roland, 321
Dumay, Raymond, 134, 510n4
Dumesnil, Suzanne, 561n15
Dumézil, Georges, 146
Dupin, Jacques, 284, 319, 320, 479, 577n30, 592n43, 594n66
Dupré, Marcel, 6, 11, 481n6
Duras, Marguerite, 17, 146, 179, 249, 284, 300, 302, 303, 304, 317, 321, 325, 332, 366, 376, 377, 378, 402, 408, 426, 431, 436–438, 440–443, 446, 467, 483n3, 484n23, 521n5, 550n3, 554n5, 564n20, 587n5, 588nn21,22, 589n25
Duvignaud, Jean, 304, 318

Eckermann, Johann Peter, 157–158
Eckhart, Johannes, 142, 155
El Greco, 519n13
Eliot, T. S., 42
Elly, Claude, 479
Éluard, Paul, 179
Enzensberger, Hans-Magnus, 325, 328, 329, 330
Ernoult, Claude, 548
Ertel, Rachel, 433
Étiemble, René, 319
Ewbank, Ed, 548n39
Ézine, Jean-Louis, 427

Fabrègues, Jean de, 42, 45, 48, 49, 60, 62–64, 78, 89, 492n2
Fardoulis-Lagrange, Francine, 479, 531n2
Fardoulis-Lagrange, Michel, 141, 146, 219, 220, 404, 530n5, 531n2, 578n2
Fargue, Léon-Paul, 173
Farias, Victor, 453
Faulkner, William, 148
Faurisson, Robert, 569n2
Fautrier, Jean, 193
Favreau, Bertrand, 491n15
Faye, Jean-Pierre, 273, 378, 399, 564n19
Fedida, Pierre, 226, 540n6
Fédier, François, 370, 371–372, 374, 376, 569n3
Fénelon, François, 147
Fernandez, Ramon, 64, 535n5
Fink, Eugen, 486n7
Fitch, Brian T., 586n31
Flamand, Paul, 128, 131, 133, 174, 504n1

Flandin, Pierre-Étienne, 71
Flaubert, Gustave, 92, 147, 572n29
Flesch, William, 455
Fogel, Jean-François, 457
Foldes, Jolan, 497n13
Foligno, Angèle de, 142
Follain, Jean, 179
Forest, Philippe, 568n20
Förster-Nietzsche, Elizabeth, 60
Foucault, Michel, 144, 273, 354, 363–369, 378, 379, 408, 419, 446, 450, 458–459, 534n4, 542n9, 564n19, 566nn3,6–8, 567n9, 570n7
Fouché, Pascal, 520n16
Fouchet, Max-Pol, 189, 227, 524n9
Fourier, Charles, 574n5
Fraigneau, André, 121
Francis, Robert, 41, 45, 59, 147
Franco, Francisco, 69, 76, 77
Frank, Bernard, 556n22
Frémon, Jean, 417
Frénaud, André, 321
Freud, Sigmund, 31, 147, 280, 420, 568n26
Fuentes, Carlos, 556n6
Fumaroli, Marc, 504n1
Fustel de Coulanges, Numa Denis, 38

Galletti, Marina, 479
Gallimard, Gaston, 179, 240, 272, 473
Gallimard, Michel, 179
Gallimard, Robert, 391
Gandhi, Mahatma, 41–43, 95
Gandillac, Maurice de, 182
García Lorca, Federico, 189
Gaulle, Charles de, 28, 80, 122, 285, 303, 307, 308, 309–310, 315, 322, 352, 383, 385, 509n2, 548n37, 552n14, 553n19, 563n9, 570n2, 572–573n31
Gauthey, Pierre (Mrs.), 479
Gauthier, Michel, 549n6
Gauthier, Xavière, 589n25
Gaxotte, Pierre, 64, 492n2
Genet, Jean, 329, 332
Genette, Gérard, 367, 419, 431, 565n25
Giacometti, Alberto, 429, 585n28
Gide, André, 36, 38, 92, 94, 124, 138, 146, 147, 155, 173, 188, 190, 193
Giono, Jean, 54, 173
Giraudoux, Jean, 91, 93, 111, 112, 121, 122, 124, 134, 148, 161, 177, 510n9, 511n10, 514n2, 525n10
Girodias, Maurice, 194

Index

Giron, Roger, 525
Godard, Jean-Luc, 366, 567n16
Goering, Hermann, 55
Goethe, Johann Wolfgang von, 93, 146, 156, 157, 174, 267, 530n1
Gordimer, Nadine, 456, 586n31
Gorz, André, 283
Gouhier, Henri, 33
Goux, Jean-Joseph, 571
Goytisolo, Juan, 456
Gracq, Julien, 428, 447, 501n1
Grass, Gunther, 325
Grenier, Roger, 179, 189
Grover, Frédéric, 497n9
Guattari, Félix, 419, 565n26, 583n13
Guérin, Daniel, 378
Guéry, Madeleine, 29
Guesde, Jules, 451
Guevara, Ernesto Che, 572n29
Guirec, Jean, 497n13
Gurvitch, Georges, 23

Haedens, Kléber, 64, 73, 91, 94, 121, 122, 146, 147, 499n2
Halbwachs, Maurice, 22
Halévy, Daniel, 49, 55
Handke, Peter, 588n23
Hansel-Levinas, Simone, 503n9
Hawthorne, Nathaniel, 518n5
Hegel, Georg Wilhelm Friedrich, 23, 28, 32, 47, 113, 142, 198, 199, 214, 249, 272, 306, 308, 354, 364, 410, 421, 463, 467, 527n9, 533n3
Heidegger, Martin, 23, 27, 28, 29, 31–32, 99, 138, 199–200, 250, 272, 275, 277–278, 281, 354, 369, 370–371, 437, 452–454, 476, 486n5, 495n3, 507n12, 516n4, 529n1, 544nn23–24, 547n26, 558n26, 569n3, 580n12, 586n31
Hemingway, Ernest, 189
Heraclitus, 32, 113, 226, 354, 560n7, 565n28
Herbinet, Jean, 302, 479
Hervieu, Louise, 497n13
Hesse, Hermann, 251, 282, 291, 545n2, 548n5
Hill, Leslie, 433, 455, 475, 479, 595n7
Himy, Laure, 586n31
Hitler Adolf, 39, 51, 53–61, 63, 66, 67, 69, 70, 76–77, 87, 88, 105, 122, 147, 353, 451–452, 455, 492n2, 495n3, 503n3, 509n2

Hölderlin, Friedrich, 7, 118, 148, 199, 204, 266, 267, 269, 304, 305, 364, 365, 368, 528n15, 541n8, 542n9, 566n6, 572n29
Holland, Michaël, 421, 448, 479
Hollier, Denis, 505n5
Hugo, Victor, 147
Huizinga, Johan, 545n2
Humphrey, Doris, 539n9
Husserl, Edmund, 23, 29–31, 486n5
Huxley, Aldous, 95
Huysmans, Joris-Karl, 146

Israel, Henri, 491n18

Jabès, Edmond, 402, 419, 446, 454, 455, 524n9, 564n21, 579n6, 582n8, 586n28, 591n36
Jabès-Crasson, Viviane, 479
Jacob, Max, 42
Jacquemont, Maurice, 128
Jacquin, Louise, 4
Jacquin, Marie, 4
Jacquot, Benoît, 418, 582n7
Jaloux, Edmond, 92
James, Henry, 13, 226, 251, 252, 264, 461
Jarach, Andrès, 479
Jaspers, Karl, 267, 273, 563n11
Jaurès, Jean, 37, 451
Jeandet, Yette, 128
Jean-Paul, 93, 122, 148, 153
Jeanson, Blandine, 427
Jeanson, Francis, 315, 316, 320–323
Jenny, Laurent, 511n23
Johnson, Uwe, 325, 328–330, 334
Jouhandeau, Élise, 182
Jouhandeau, Marcel, 94, 98, 146, 171, 301
Jouvenel, Bertrand de, 64
Joyce, James, 95, 119, 146, 148, 153
Judrin, Roger, 289
Juliet, Charles, 479

Kafka, Franz, 8–9, 86, 92, 103, 106, 111, 148, 154, 155, 158, 160, 165, 181, 193, 197, 220, 236, 249
Kant, Immanuel, 29, 198
Kaplan, Leslie, 458, 459, 479
Kéchichian, Patrick, 479
Kertész, André, 35
Khomeini, Ruhollah, 225, 458, 537n2
Kierkegaard, Sören, 23, 137, 146, 160, 193, 221
Kipling, Rudyard, 93

Klossowski, Pierre, 182, 240, 354, 363, 364, 367, 368, 377, 401, 422, 565n23, 566n7, 577n31
Kofman, Sarah, 431, 433, 439, 440, 534n3
Kojève, Alexandre, 527n9
Kolakowski, Leszek, 556n6
Koyré, Alexandre, 33
Kozovoï, Vadim, 458, 460, 473, 479
Kristeva, Julia, 273

La Fayette, Marie-Madeleine de, 146
La Fontaine, Jean de, 156
La Rocque, François de, 72, 78
La Tour du Pin, Patrice de, 35, 93, 128
Lacan, Jacques, 34, 273, 377, 421, 446, 502n10, 527n9, 564n19
Laclos, Pierre Choderlos de, 147
Lacoue-Labarthe, Philippe, 431, 432, 438, 453, 455, 477
Lagrange, Henri, 38
Lamartine, Alphonse de, 146
Lampin, Georges, 531n8
Lanzmann, Claude, 321, 454
Laporte, Roger, 12, 17, 21, 145, 164, 183, 246, 363, 364, 366, 368, 370, 371–372, 374, 391, 395, 403, 417–419, 431, 446, 455, 458, 463, 473, 479, 484n20, 564n20, 566n3, 568n28, 569nn1,7, 576n23, 592n43, 594n61
Lassaigne, Jacques, 190
Lautréamont, 79, 98, 111, 112, 122, 138, 147, 148, 153, 154, 160, 161, 167, 180, 193, 197, 198, 200, 201, 205–207, 256, 284, 447, 511n23, 528n15
Laval, Pierre, 65, 123, 134, 174, 509n2
Le Clézio, J. M. G., 447
Léautaud, Paul, 173, 520n13
Leclaire, Serge, 411, 579n6
Lecoq, Dominique, 456, 592n41
Leenhardt, Roger, 128
Lefebvre, Maurice-Jean, 519n6
Lefebvre, Henri, 353, 377, 555n12
Lefort, Claude, 304, 319
Leiris, Michel, 35, 111, 124, 138, 141, 146, 148, 170, 182, 194, 197, 198, 318, 325, 376, 377, 422, 446, 516n4, 518n7, 526n2, 557n21, 570n5, 577nn27,30, 584n8
Lemaigre-Dubreuil, Jacques, 71–72, 78
Lenin, Vladimir Ilitch, 572n29
Leonetti, Francesco, 329, 332
Lermontov, Mikhaïl Iourévitch, 95
Lescourret, Marie-Anne, 16

Lesur, Daniel, 127, 128
Levesque, Claude, 420
Levinas, Emmanuel, xi, 15, 16, 22, 23, 24–33, 34, 37, 60, 76, 88, 99, 102, 109, 122, 125, 138, 143, 154, 165, 175, 187, 188, 200, 227, 237, 246, 272, 277, 285, 291, 298, 305, 336, 343, 347, 354, 355, 356, 360, 363, 364, 368, 371, 372, 373, 374, 376, 395, 398, 403, 413, 418, 419, 428, 429, 431, 437, 446, 452, 453, 454, 455, 478, 485nn2,7, 486n5, 489n2, 495n1, 506–507n12, 527n8, 530–531n9, 542n6, 547n27, 552n7, 558n26, 564n21, 567nn9,12, 569nn2,6,8, 579n6, 591n29, 594n65
Levinas, Michaël, 479, 484n20, 594n65
Lévis Mano, Guy, 277, 288, 436, 447
Lévy, Bernard-Henri, 433, 455, 456, 487n12
Lévy, Paul, 55, 59, 60, 76, 82, 88, 89, 123, 125, 454, 491nn15,18,19, 514n2, 555n12
Lignac, Xavier de, 15, 17, 124, 125, 128–134, 141, 149, 172, 174, 178, 182, 246, 479, 487n3, 503n7, 504n1
Limbour, Georges, 141, 556n22
Limousin, Christian, 320, 422, 583n2
Lindon, Jérôme, 508n25, 555n12
Lispector, Clarisse, 586n31
Loiseau, Jean-Claude, 483n8
Londyn, Evelyne, 419
Lonsdale, Michaël, 418
Loranquin, Albert, 548n39
Losfeld, Éric, 555n12
Loubet del Bayle, Jean-Louis, 422
Lowry, Malcolm, 267, 541n8
Luria, Isaac, 285–286, 308
Luther, Martin, 457
Luxembourg, Rosa, 572n29

Macé, Gérard, 592n43
Machiavelli, 146, 177
Madaule, Pierre, 366, 417, 418, 431, 473, 479
Maeterlinck, Maurice, 94
Magnane, Georges, 179
Malka, Salomon, 26, 433, 453, 454, 581n17
Mallarmé, Stéphane, 17, 92, 95, 96, 146–148, 152–155, 157, 158, 200, 201, 250, 272, 273, 274, 277, 284, 285, 286, 287, 294, 364, 420, 449, 486n5, 498n18, 510n9, 511n23, 512nn25,30, 517n4, 566n6

Index 611

Malraux, André, 36, 111, 148, 179, 184, 188, 189, 266, 267–269, 272, 273, 462, 525nn10,12, 546n20, 555n12
Malraux, Clara, 556n22
Man, Paul de, 364, 476, 567n9
Mandel, Georges, 55, 71, 76, 491n15
Mandela, Nelson, 456
Manessier, Alfred, 130
Mann, Thomas, 86, 95, 97, 98, 99, 111, 113, 148, 251, 266, 267, 291, 497n13, 541n8
Mao Zedong, 572n29
Marc, Alexandre, 508n26
Marcel, Gabriel, 23, 42, 63, 182, 188
Marchon, Manuel, 72
Marin, Robert, 270
Marion, Paul, 131
Maritain, Jacques, 36–37, 42, 48
Marmande, Francis, 310, 431, 479, 587n16
Martin du Gard, Roger, 49, 95
Marx, Karl, 38, 305, 572n29
Mascolo, Dionys, 15, 16, 142, 179, 183, 184, 187, 203, 275, 297, 302–311, 315–323, 324–334, 337, 339, 340, 348, 362, 364, 375–378, 380, 383, 384, 399, 400, 404, 405, 408, 413, 415, 429, 430, 431, 437, 439, 440, 442, 443, 446, 449, 458, 461, 479, 483n3, 551n5, 551–552n7, 570n10, 571nn11,30, 573n39, 578n3, 579n7, 588n24, 597n34
Mascolo, Jean, 430
Maspero, François, 555n12
Massis, Henri, 36, 42, 43, 46, 55, 89, 94, 321, 486n5
Masson, André, 138, 555n12
Maulnier, Thierry, 16, 36–39, 45–46, 52, 55, 59, 60, 62–64, 71–73, 78, 79, 88, 89, 91, 92, 94, 121, 122, 124, 129, 146, 147, 161, 164, 180, 188, 321, 431, 491n19, 492nn1,2, 493n2, 494nn7,9,10, 496n1, 515n1, 524nn4,9
Maupassant, Guy de, 146, 156
Mauriac, Claude, 416
Mauriac, François, 45, 49, 94, 95, 96, 98, 99, 124, 147, 173, 188, 310, 499n35, 524n4
Maurois, André, 36, 49, 55
Maurras, Charles, 35–39, 42, 44, 48, 58, 63, 64, 72, 74, 77–79, 89, 91–94, 138, 188, 455, 487n8 497n7
Maxence, Jean-Luc, 484n18
Maxence, Jean-Pierre, 16, 39, 41, 42, 45, 46, 54, 55, 59, 60, 64, 71, 73, 79, 89, 92, 94, 491nn15,19, 493n2, 499n35

Mazeline, Guy, 497n13
Mehlman, Jeffrey, 173, 174, 432, 434, 582n3
Melville, Herman, 146, 148, 152, 525n10
Mendès-France, Pierre, 377
Mercey, Alexandre, 3
Mercey, Elise, 4
Mercey, Marie, 3, 4
Merleau-Ponty, Maurice, 182, 272, 319, 402, 449, 526n1, 575n12, 576n25, 577n27
Merley, Philippe, 11
Meschonnic, Henri, 420–422
Mesnard, Philippe, 432, 586n36
Messiaen, Olivier, 127
Michaux, Henri, 15, 144, 146, 147, 148, 154, 170, 180, 193, 197, 291, 401, 446, 577n31
Michel, Chantal, 586n31
Milleret, Bernard, 130
Mitchell, Margaret, 93
Mitterrand, François, 438
Molière, 146, 158
Mondor, Henri, 92, 157, 158
Monnier, Pierre, 16, 92, 493, 499n2
Monnier, Thyde, 497n13
Monod, Théodore, 555n12
Montaigne, Michel de, 512n34, 521n28
Montety, Etienne de, 38, 428
Montherlant, Henry de, 49, 55, 124, 146, 147, 173–177, 188
Morand, Paul, 38, 49, 92
Moré, Marcel, 182
Moreau, Marie, 3
Morin, Edgar, 303, 304, 318, 323
Mounier, Emmanuel, 47, 131, 504n1
Mounin, Georges, 555n12
Mousset, Jean, 161
Munier, Jacques, 585n28
Munier, Roger, 370
Murdoch, Iris, 556n6
Musil, Robert, 211, 546n15
Musset, Alfred de, 147
Mussolini, Benito, 39, 49, 69, 70, 93

Nadeau, Maurice, 16, 183, 240, 299, 300, 303, 304, 316, 318, 321, 322, 323, 324, 325, 328, 363, 377, 378, 401, 416, 417, 431, 463, 479, 515n4, 524–525n9, 552n7, 561n15, 571n11, 592n43
Nalèche, Etienne de, 52
Nancy, Jean-Luc, 139, 369, 379, 408, 431, 432, 435, 436, 438, 439, 440, 455, 457, 473, 476, 478, 479, 558n31, 587n9

Naud, Albert, 491n18
Nef, Frédéric, 502n10
Nerval, Gérard de, 79, 93, 95, 124, 148, 153, 161, 498n22
Nietzsche, Friedrich, xii, 31, 36, 37, 111, 125, 138, 142, 148, 193, 203, 226, 260, 280, 282, 284, 287, 291, 305, 330, 354, 363, 404, 409, 420, 421, 490n6, 528n16, 530n1, 532n9, 539n4, 547n26, 558n26, 577n31, 578n2
Nizan, Paul, 35, 499n35
Noël, Bernard, 366, 417, 418, 479, 535n3
Nora, Pierre, 450, 590n17
Nouvet, Claire, 593n48
Novalis, Friedrich, 148

Ollier, Claude, 332
Ollivier, Albert, 128, 129, 141, 178, 246
Ollivier, Louis, 479, 504n1
Orwell, George, 572n29
Oswald, Marianne, 538n2

Pachet, Pierre, 479
Parain, Brice, 146, 148, 267, 304, 402, 512n25, 576n25
Parisis, Jean-Marc, 428
Pascal, Blaise, 38, 137, 138, 198, 280, 284, 503n7, 532n8
Pasolini, Pier-Paolo, 325
Patron, Sylvie, 479
Paulhan, Claire, 479
Paulhan, Jean, 36, 101, 146, 147, 151–152, 154, 156, 160, 164, 170–174, 179, 182, 188, 193, 203, 246, 271, 272, 310, 321, 337, 352, 392, 402, 448, 462, 473, 512n25, 519n6, 520n8, 524n9, 528n15
Paxton, Robert, 581n15
Péguy, Charles, 35, 42, 92, 148, 451, 510n10
Peiffer, Gabrielle, 33
Peignot, Colette (Laure), 136
Péju, Marcel, 318, 321
Pelletier, Virginie, 479
Pelorson, Georges, 45, 92, 129, 499n1, 505n5
Pentillas, Suzanne, 29
Péret, Benjamin, 304
Perlini, Tito, 568n24
Perros, Georges, 427, 575n16
Pétain, Philippe, 38, 122–124, 127, 134, 145, 503n6, 509n2

Petitot, Romain, 128, 129, 131, 132, 134, 141, 174, 178, 246
Pfeiffer, Jean, 548n39, 568n23
Pfister, Christian, 22
Phan, Liliane, 479–480
Philipe, Gérard, 531–532n8
Philippenko, Georges, 532n8
Picard, Raymond, 367
Picon, Gaëtan, 545–546n12, 577n30
Piel, Jean, 364, 479, 557n21, 566n8
Pierre-Quint, Léon, 267
Pierssens, Michel, 582n3
Pingaud, Bernard, 525n9, 548n39
Pirandello, Luigi, 92
Pivot, Bernard, 427
Plato, 354, 364, 580n12
Pleynet, Marcelin, 433
Plisnier, Charles, 497n13
Poe, Edgar, 95, 153, 240
Poirié, François, 428, 479
Ponge, Francis, 148, 170, 172, 520n8
Pontalis, J.-B., 555n12
Pouillon, Jean, 194, 304, 318, 321, 555n19
Poulet, Georges, 364, 548n39, 564n19, 567n9
Pourrat, Henri, 519n7
Pradines, Maurice, 22, 33
Préli, Georges, 419, 583n13
Prévert, Jacques, 319, 524n9
Prévost, Jean, 172
Prévost, Pierre, 16, 26, 129, 136, 141, 174, 178, 182, 183, 187, 189, 191, 194, 225, 246, 431, 479, 493n4, 499n1, 522n5, 524n5, 542n10
Proudhon, Pierre Joseph, 36, 38, 63, 71
Proust, Marcel, 11, 25, 30, 86, 92, 111, 142, 148, 161, 180, 221, 427
Pucheu, Pierre, 131
Puech, Jean-Benoît, 479

Queneau, Raymond, 141, 148, 170, 179, 188, 272, 505n5, 509n31, 524n9, 558n27
Quero-Morales, Juan, 189

Rabant, Claude, 237
Rabaté, Dominique, 480
Rabaté, Jean-Michel, 495n3
Racine, Jean, 38, 96, 146, 177, 561n16
Rahmani, Sabah, 480
Ramnoux, Clémence, 370

Index 613

Ramuz, Charles Ferdinand, 497n18
Rebatet, Lucien , 37, 39, 89, 514n2
Rebérioux, Madeleine, 556n21
Réda, Jacques, 364
Rédier, Antoine, 45
Régnier, Monique. *See* Antelme, Monique
Renard, Gisèle, 585n28
Renoir, Jean, 35
Resnais, Alain, 322, 555n12
Restif de la Bretonne, Nicolas, 193, 447
Reverdy, Pierre, 42
Rey, Alain, 583n4
Rey, Henri-François, 505n1
Reyer, Georges, 497n13
Reynaud, Paul, 71, 122
Richelet, Guy, 73, 499n2
Rilke, Rainer Maria, 7, 45, 94, 95, 103, 146, 156, 160, 170, 180, 249, 273, 274, 514n2, 539–540n4
Rimbaud, Arthur, 32, 36, 92, 146–148, 176, 200, 249, 514n37, 529n21
Rivet, Auguste, 161
Robbe-Grillet, Alain, 317, 555n12
Robert, Marthe, 564n19
Robespierre, Maximilien, 69, 204, 491n16
Rochefort, Christiane, 378, 572n30, 573n37
Rolland, Romain, 42
Rollin, Denise, 125, 136, 141, 178, 219–224, 237, 246, 255, 404, 405, 487n8, 531nn1,8, 532n11, 538n2, 578n2, 581n13
Rollin, Jean, 479, 487n8, 531n1, 580n13
Romains, Jules, 525n10
Rondeau, Daniel, 457
Rontchewski, Rémi, 29
Ropars-Wuilleumier, Marie-Claire, 429
Roubaud, Jacques, 378
Rougemont, Denis de, 497n7
Rousseau, Patrick, 421
Rousseaux, André, 36, 49, 91, 94, 188, 498n22
Roussel, Raymond, 395
Roy, Bruno, 15, 391, 436, 447, 592n43, 594n69
Roy, Claude, 16, 35, 64, 91, 92, 93, 125, 128, 146, 160, 171, 303, 317, 378, 446, 479, 504n11
Roy, Pierre, 504n2
Rushdie, Salman, 225, 458
Ruskin, John, 43
Ryga, Pierre-Paul, 480

Sabato, Ernesto, 556n6
Sade, Donatien-Alphonse-François de, 98, 111, 112, 147, 148, 150, 193, 204, 205, 207, 221, 240, 256, 284, 354, 365, 379, 413, 440, 447, 508nn22,25, 511n23, 517n4, 529n24, 571n16
Sadoul, Georges, 505n5
Sagan, Françoise, 524n9, 556n22
Saint-Hélier, Monique, 160, 171, 172, 173
Saint-Just, Louis Antoine de, 204
Santiago, Hugo, 479
Sarraut, Maurice, 64–66, 68
Sarraute, Nathalie, 377–378, 555n12
Sartre, Jean-Paul, 35, 65, 79, 98, 99, 103, 124, 146, 164, 179, 182, 183, 188, 193, 271–273, 316, 321–325, 353, 362, 377, 398, 426, 446, 450, 499n35, 515–517n4, 525n10, 526nn2,5, 527n8, 547n24, 548n37, 556n4, 563n7, 573n31, 586n4
Satomi, Tatsuo, 480
Saussure, Ferdinand de, 586n31
Schaeffer, Pierre, 127–128, 131–133, 174, 504n1
Schefer, Jean-Louis, 332
Schelling, Friedrich von, 580n12
Scherer, Jacques, 286
Schmidt, Albert-Marie, 130, 134
Schmitt, Michel, 583n4
Schoenberg, Arnold, 12
Schulte-Nordholt, Anne-Lise, 586n31
Schumann, Robert, 12, 459
Schuster, Jean, 303, 304, 307, 308, 310, 316, 318, 321, 376, 377, 378, 384, 570n5, 572n30, 573n37
Schuwer, Camille, 246
Seaver, Richard, 556n6
Séché, Alphonse, 490n6
Serreau, Geneviève, 321
Settanni, Ettore, 98, 180
Severac, Claude, 82–83
Shakespeare, William, 32, 586n31
Signoret, Simone, 317, 322, 555n12
Simon, Claude, 555n12
Simonin, Anne, 536n1
Siné, 556n22
Socrates, 354, 518n7
Solis, René, 585n28
Sollers, Philippe, 273, 367, 399, 571n11
Sorel, Georges, 36, 38, 63
Soupault, Ralp, 72, 73
Souvarine, Boris, 449

Starobinski, Jean, 364, 534n1, 564n19
Stavisky, Serge Alexandre, 36, 64
Stéfan, Jude, 427, 584n5
Stendhal, 36, 146, 147
Stéphane, Roger, 266
Sternhell, Zeev, 432
Strindberg, August, 267
Supervielle, Jules, 42, 93
Suquet, Jean, 479, 481n7
Surya, Michel, 300, 431, 439,476–478, 479, 508n28, 597n34

Taine, Hippolyte, 428
Tal Coat, Pierre, 130, 447
Tappy, José-Flore, 519n3
Terzieff, Laurent, 556n22
Thévenin, Paule, 322
Thévenot, Anne-Marie, 6
Thévenot, Jules, 481n4
Thibaudat, Jean-Pierre, 584n11
Thibaudet, Albert, 36, 146
Thomas, Henri, 146, 525n10
Thorez, Maurice, 72, 73, 77
Tibloux, Emmanuel, 480, 533–534n3
Tixier-Vignancourt, Jean-Louis, 73
Tocqueville, Alexis de, 500n12
Todorov, Tzvetan, 364, 422, 432, 567n9, 586n32
Tolstoy, Leo, 43, 185
Trotsky, Leon, 546n15, 572n29
Truffaut, François, 322, 556n22
Tzara, Tristan, 556n22

Ungar, Steven, 422, 433, 455

Valéry, Paul, 25, 30, 93, 103, 124, 146, 147, 148, 151, 173, 198, 249, 451, 496n5, 510n9, 512n25
Vallès, Jules, 36, 71

Valois, Georges, 80
Van Gogh, Vincent, 267
Van Velde, Bram, 391, 409, 447
Vercors, 555n12
Verdès-Leroux, Jeannine, 492n1
Verlaine, Paul, 147
Vernant, Jean-Pierre, 555n12
Vienot, Pierre, 75, 493n5
Vigny, Alfred de, 156
Vilar, Jean, 128,
Vilar, Pierre, 466, 480
Vildrac, Charles, 556n22
Villemaine, Pierre-Antoine, 431, 479, 585n28
Vincent, René, 64
Vittorini, Elio, 304, 324, 325, 329–330, 332–334, 337, 340, 375, 558n23, 563n7
Vittorini, Ginetta, 303
Voltaire, 147, 288, 322, 548n37

Wahl, Jean, 23, 371, 556n22
Walser, Martin, 325
Watanabe, M., 566n7
Weber, Eugen, 422
Weil, Éric, 194
Weil, Simone, 280, 285, 287, 550n13
Weill, Nicolas, 594n65
Welter, Micheline, 585n28
Wendel, François de, 52
Wilhem, Daniel, 114
Wismann, Heinz, 414
Wolf, Anna, 87, 465
Woolf, Virginia, 95, 97, 98, 99, 148, 180, 497n13
Wybrands, Francis, 486n5

Yacine, Kateb, 332
Ylipe, 584n11

www.ingramcontent.com/pod-product-compliance
Lightning Source LLC
Chambersburg PA
CBHW022101290426
44112CB00008B/511